CONTENTS

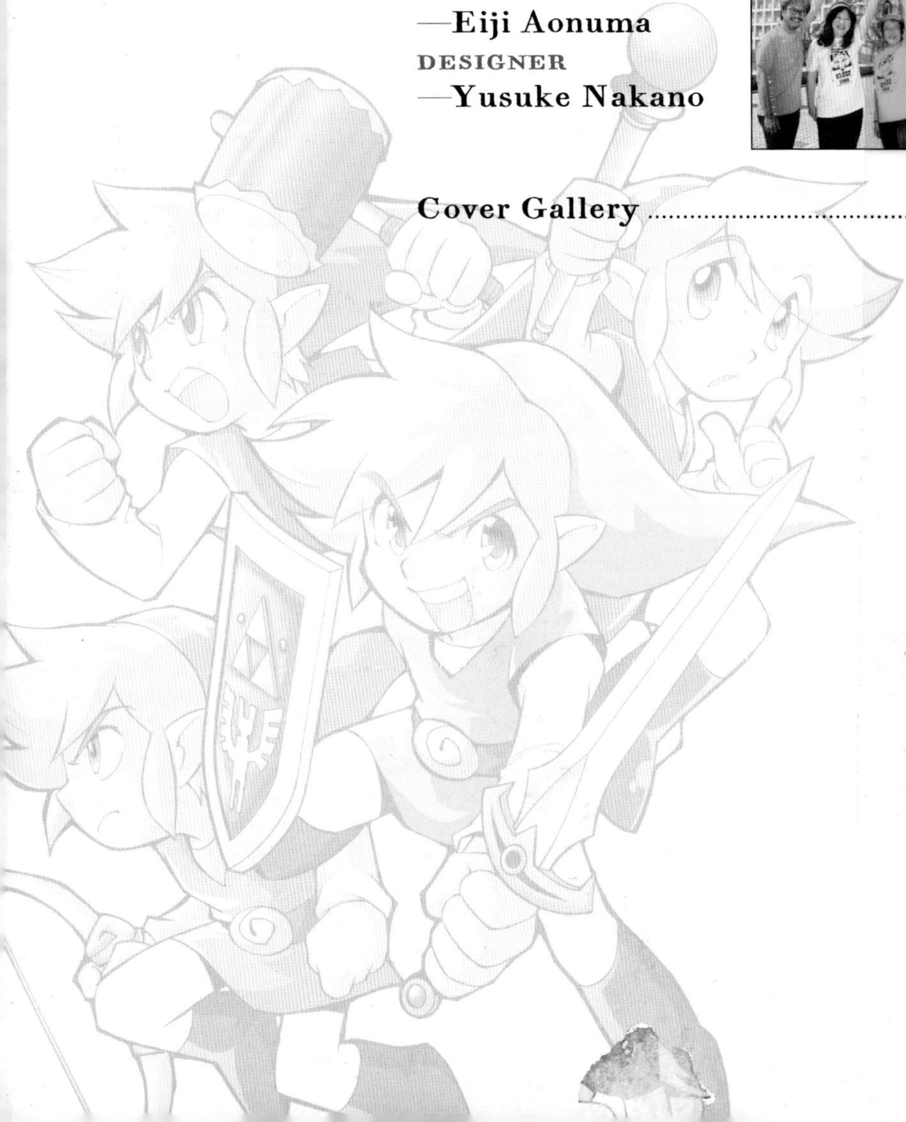

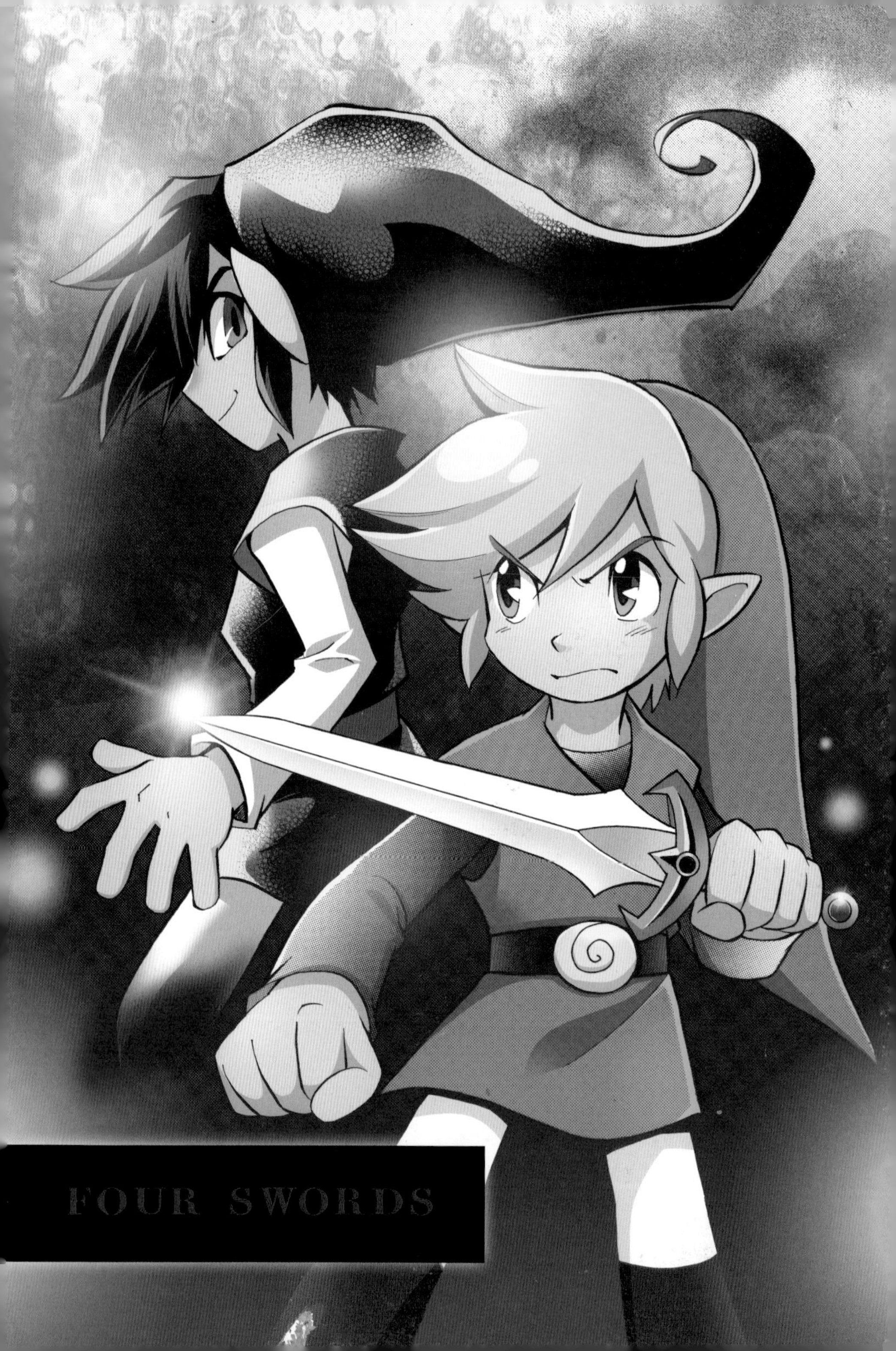
FOUR SWORDS

CHAPTER 1 Four Links

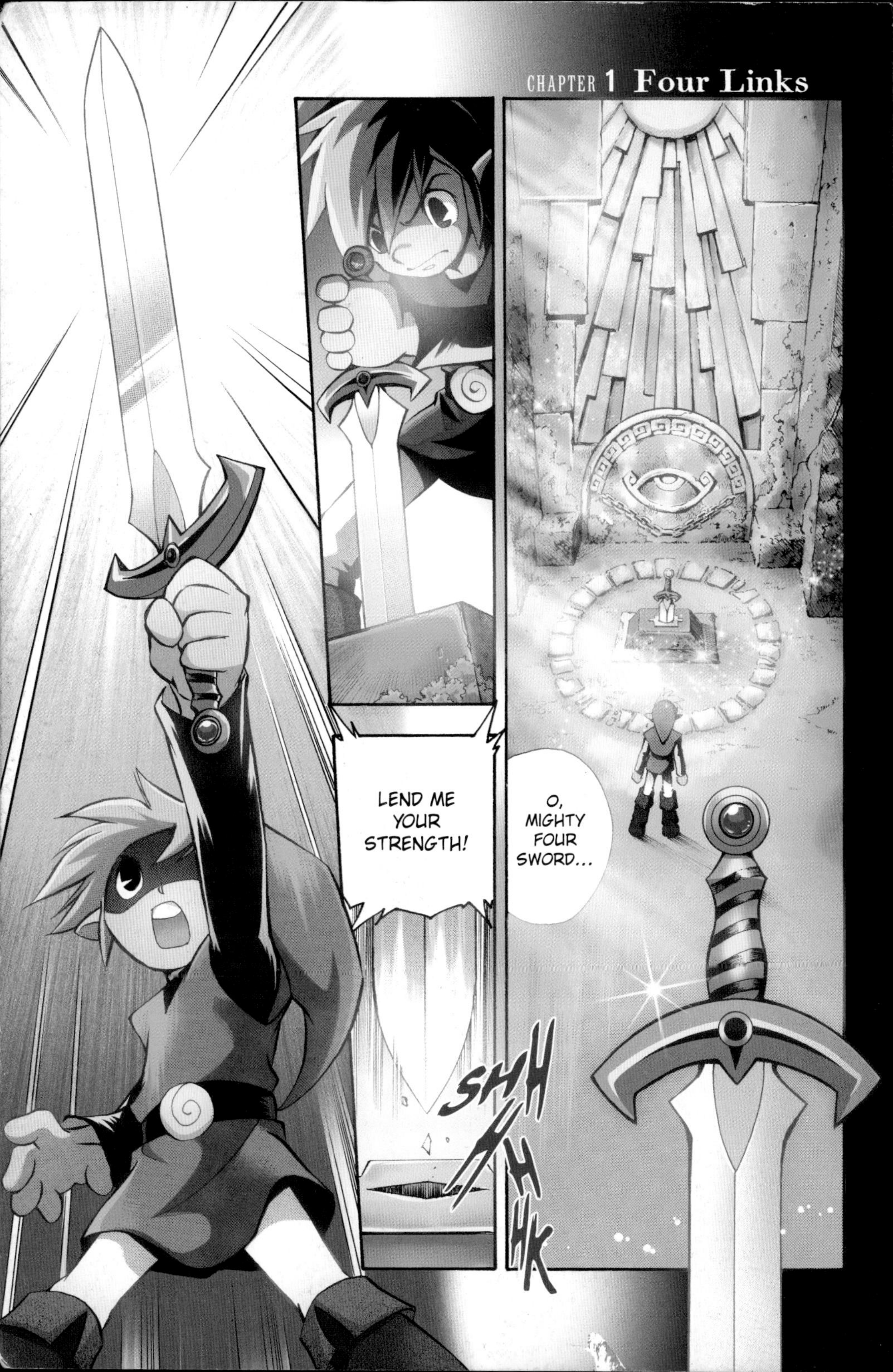
O, MIGHTY FOUR SWORD...
LEND ME YOUR STRENGTH!
SHHHHHHK

CHAPTER 1 Four Links

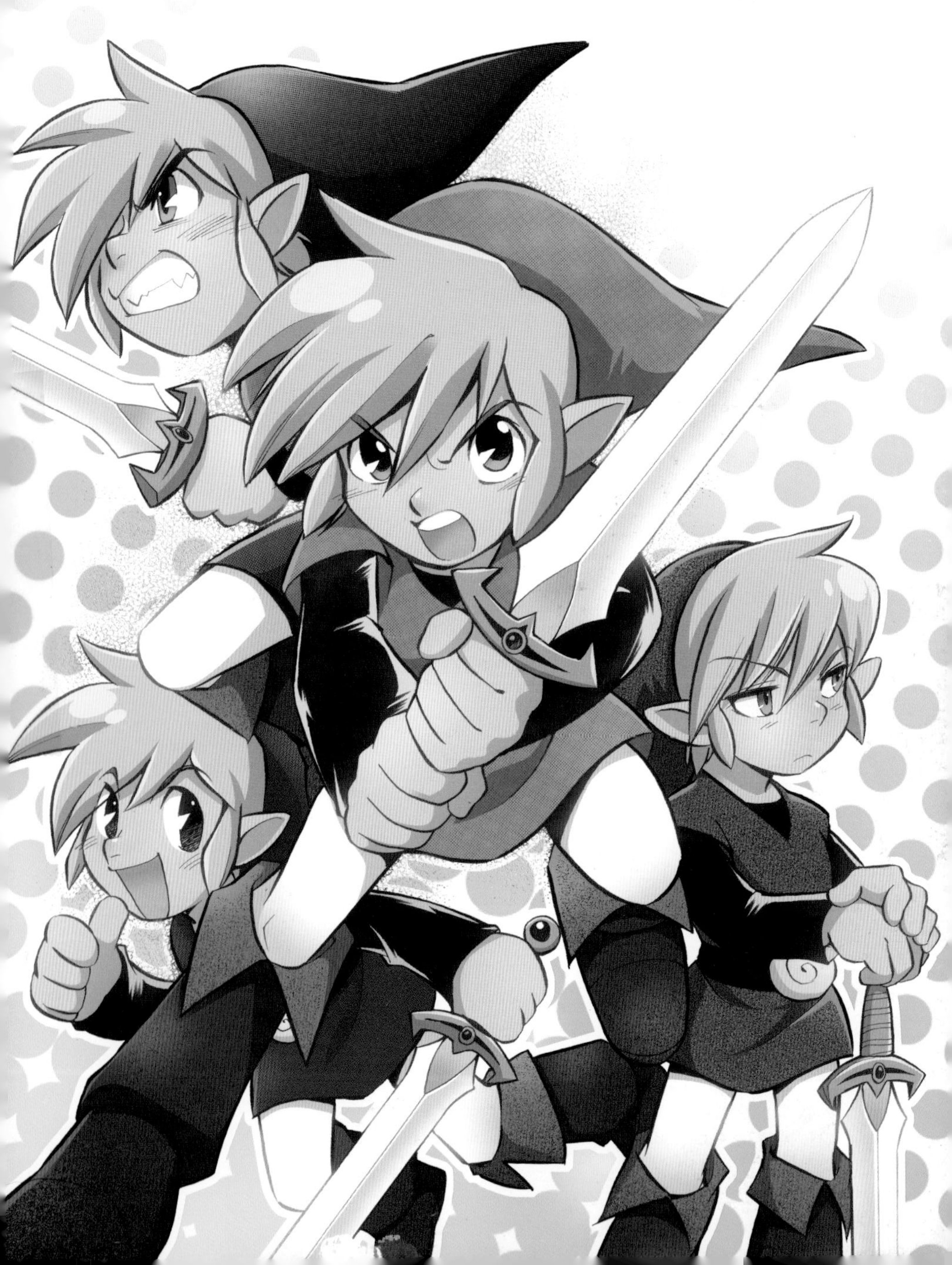

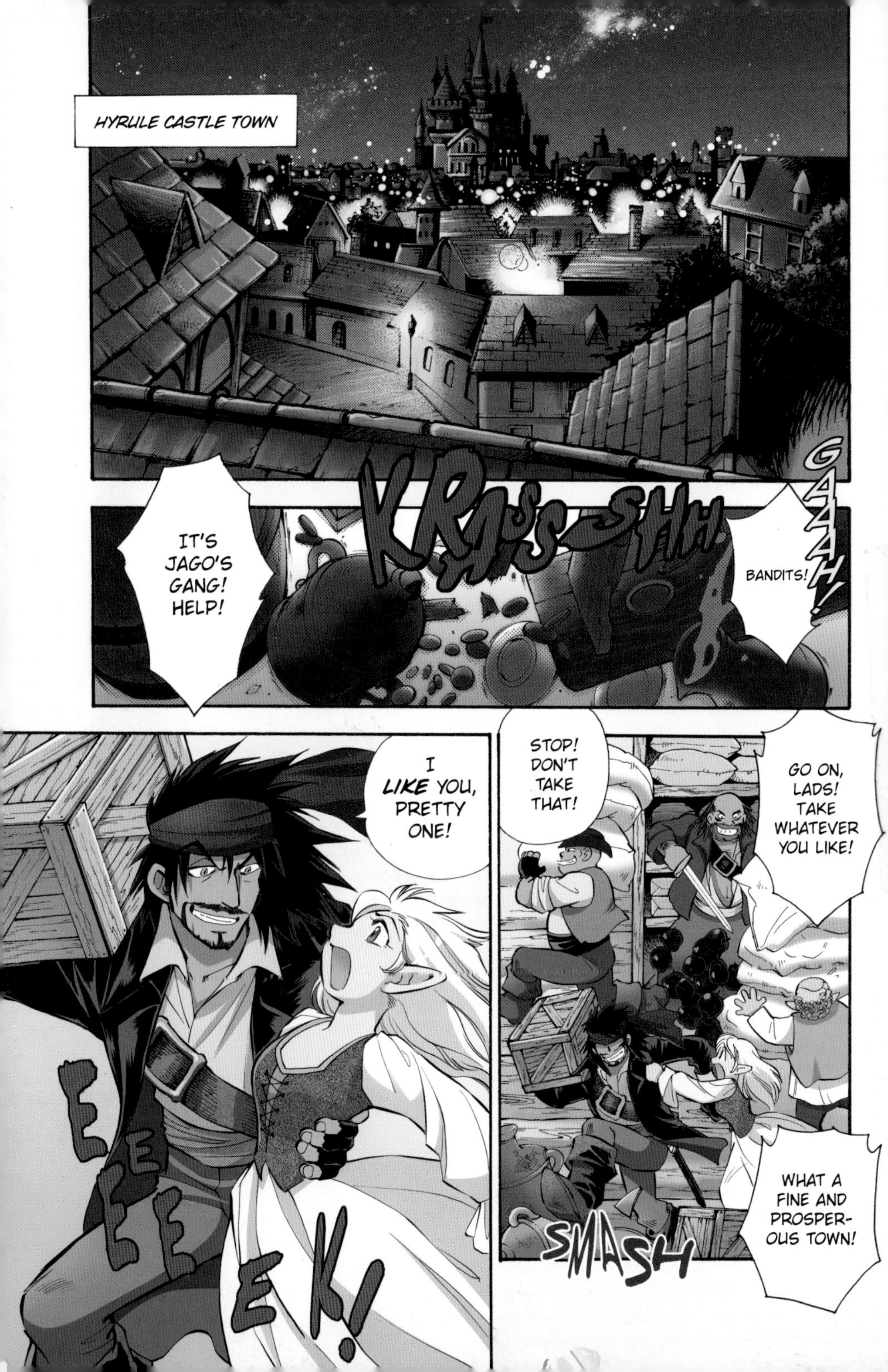
HYRULE CASTLE TOWN
GAAAH!
BANDITS!
KRASSS-SHH
IT'S JAGO'S GANG! HELP!
GO ON, LADS! TAKE WHATEVER YOU LIKE!
STOP! DON'T TAKE THAT!
WHAT A FINE AND PROSPER-OUS TOWN!
SMASH
I **LIKE** YOU, PRETTY ONE!
EEEEEK!

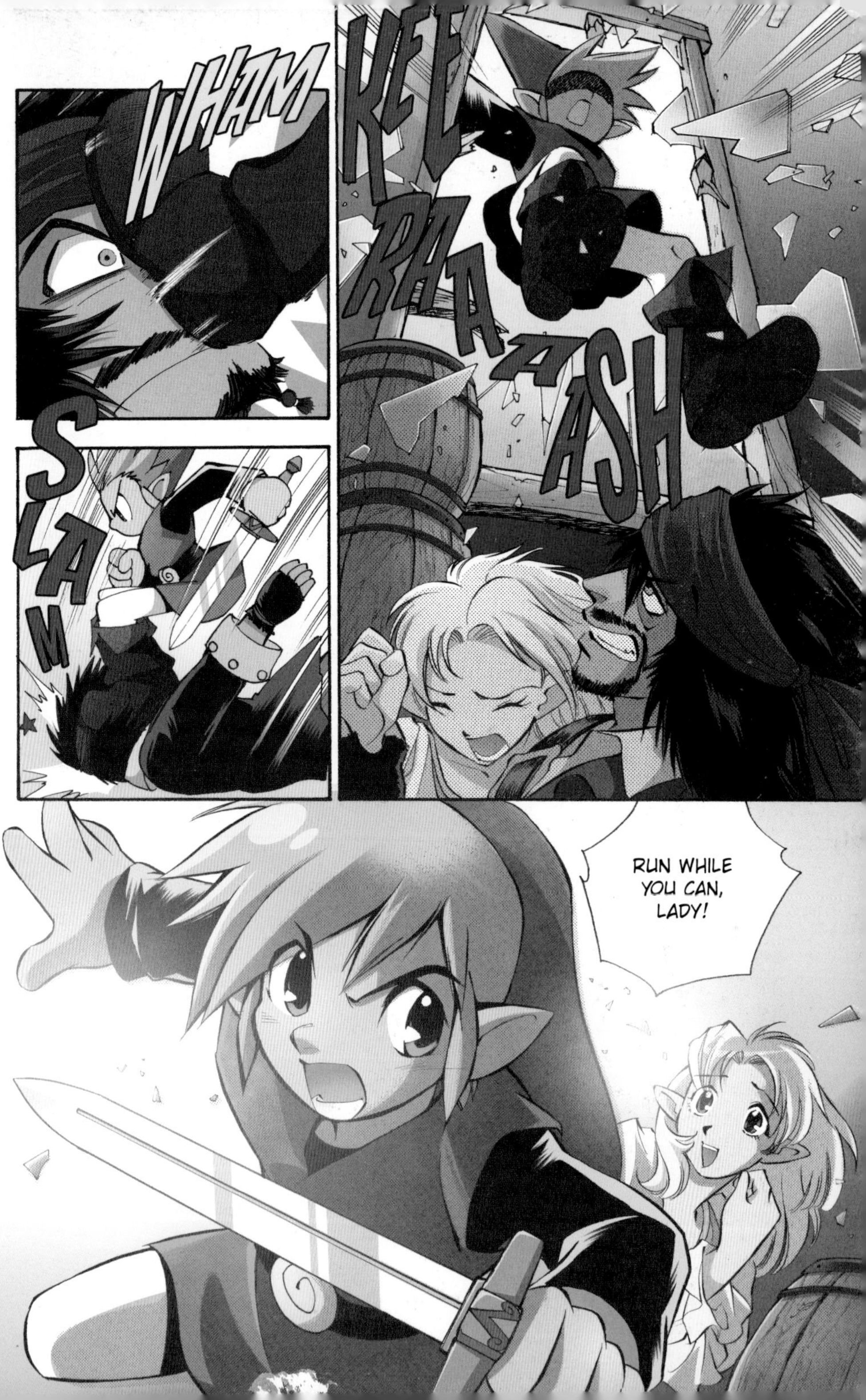
KEE
RAAAASH
WHAM
SLAM
RUN WHILE YOU CAN, LADY!

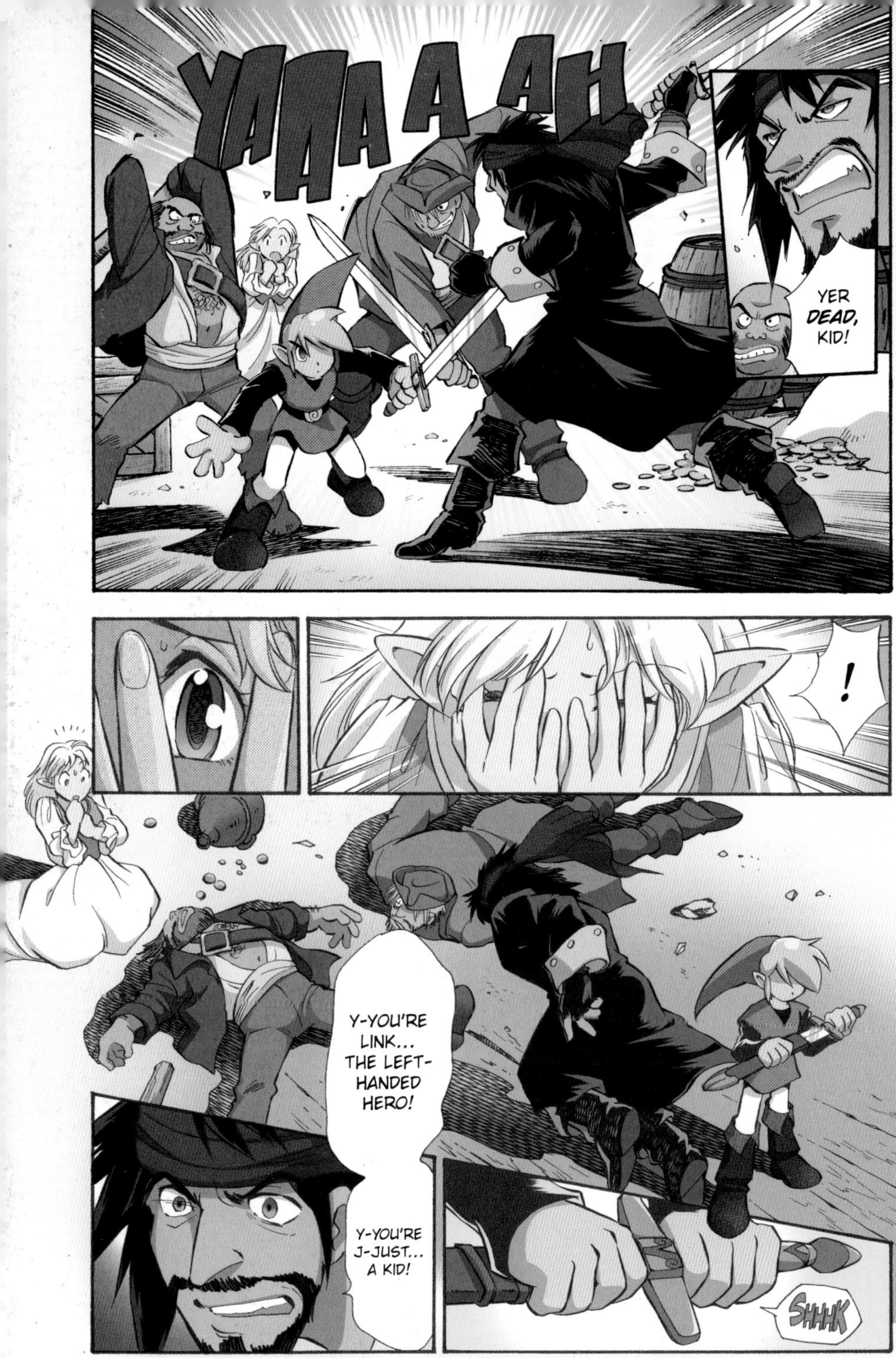
YER DEAD, KID!
YAAAA A AH
!
Y-YOU'RE LINK… THE LEFT-HANDED HERO!
SHHHK
Y-YOU'RE J-JUST… A KID!

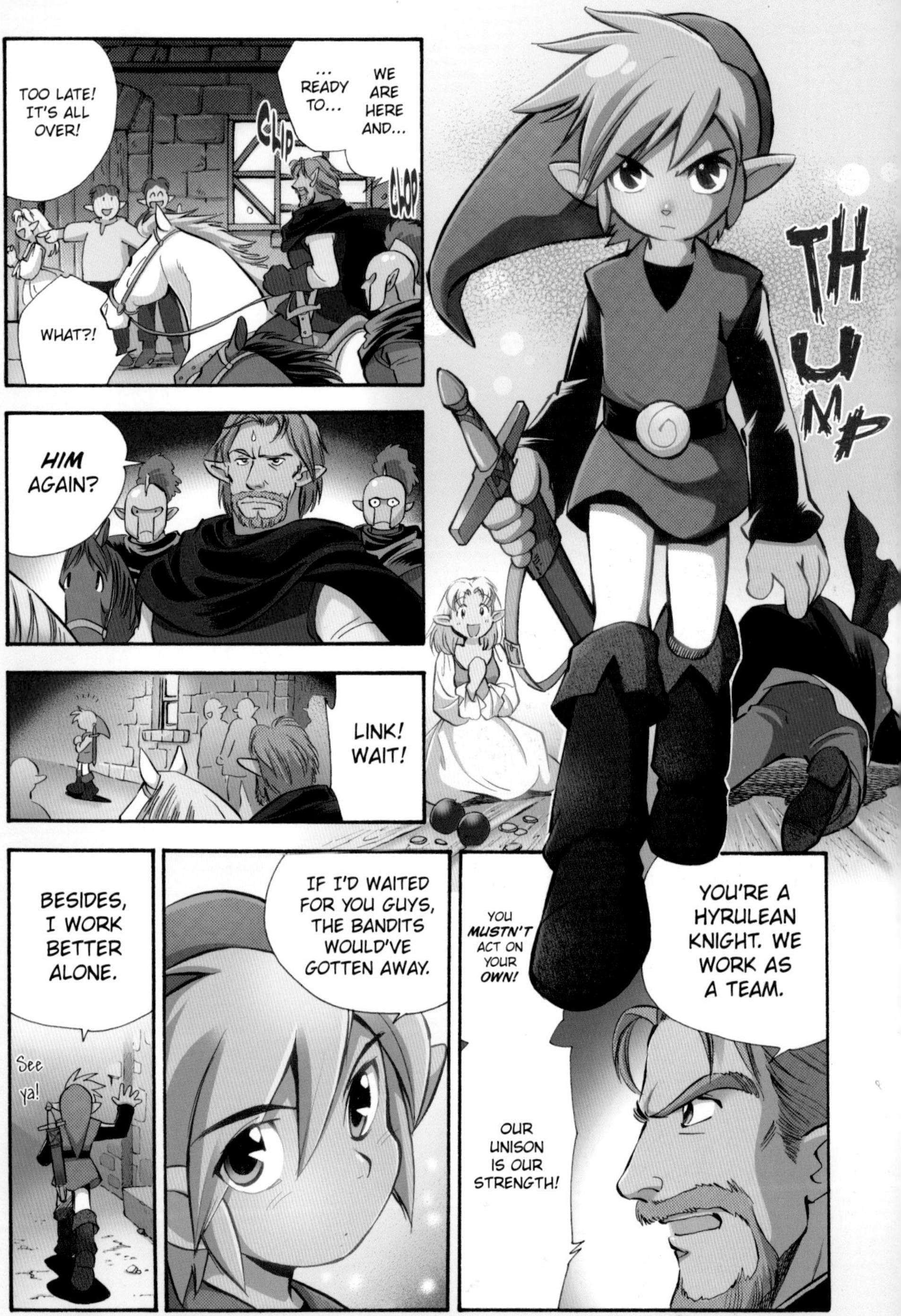
THUMP
WE ARE HERE AND...
... READY TO...
CLIP
CLOP
TOO LATE! IT'S ALL OVER!
WHAT?!
HIM AGAIN?
LINK! WAIT!
YOU'RE A HYRULEAN KNIGHT. WE WORK AS A TEAM.
YOU *MUSTN'T* ACT ON YOUR *OWN!*
OUR UNISON IS OUR STRENGTH!
IF I'D WAITED FOR YOU GUYS, THE BANDITS WOULD'VE GOTTEN AWAY.
BESIDES, I WORK BETTER ALONE.
See ya!

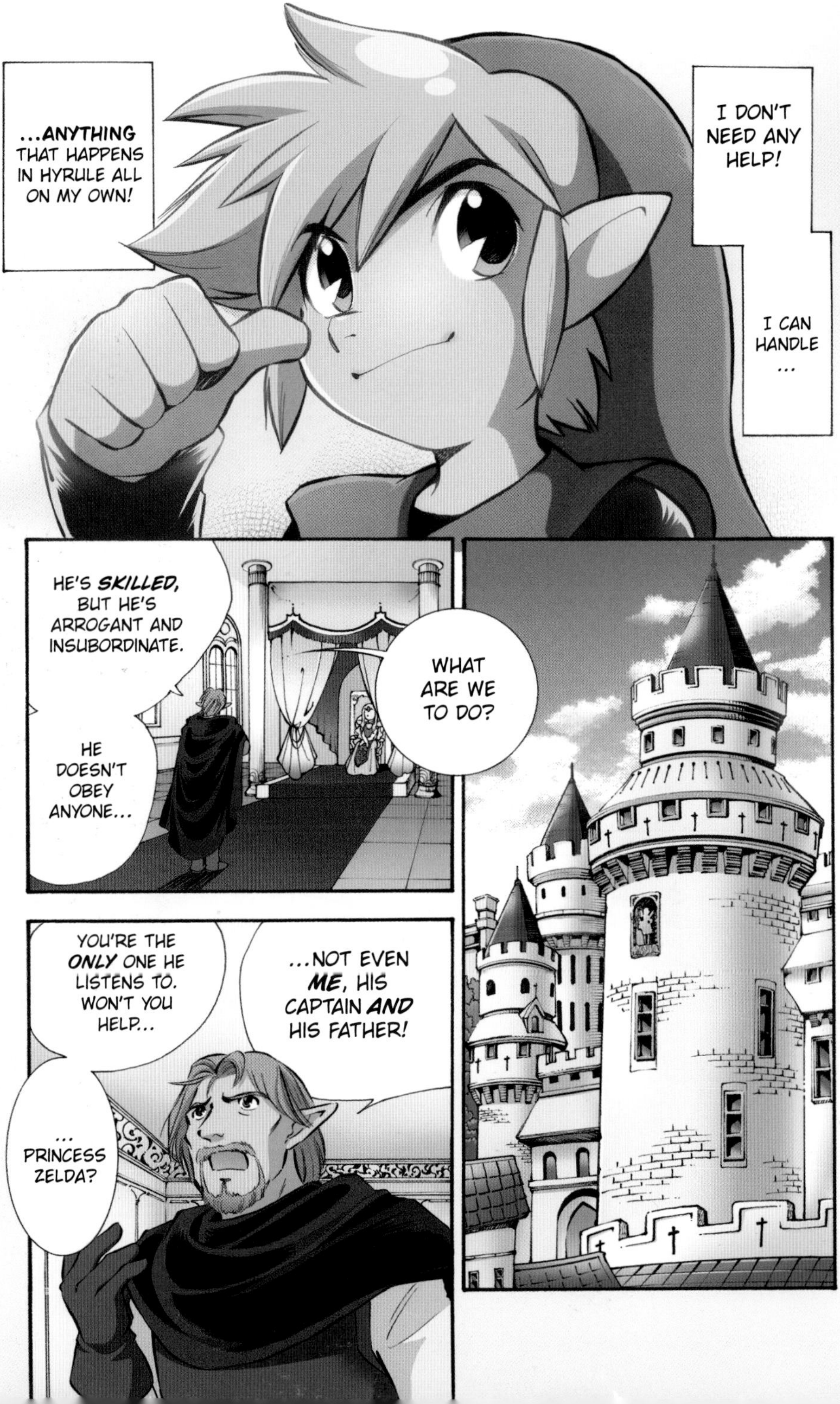
I DON'T NEED ANY HELP!
I CAN HANDLE ...
...ANYTHING THAT HAPPENS IN HYRULE ALL ON MY OWN!
WHAT ARE WE TO DO?
HE'S *SKILLED*, BUT HE'S ARROGANT AND INSUBORDINATE.
HE DOESN'T OBEY ANYONE...
...NOT EVEN *ME*, HIS CAPTAIN *AND* HIS FATHER!
YOU'RE THE *ONLY* ONE HE LISTENS TO. WON'T YOU HELP...
... PRINCESS ZELDA?

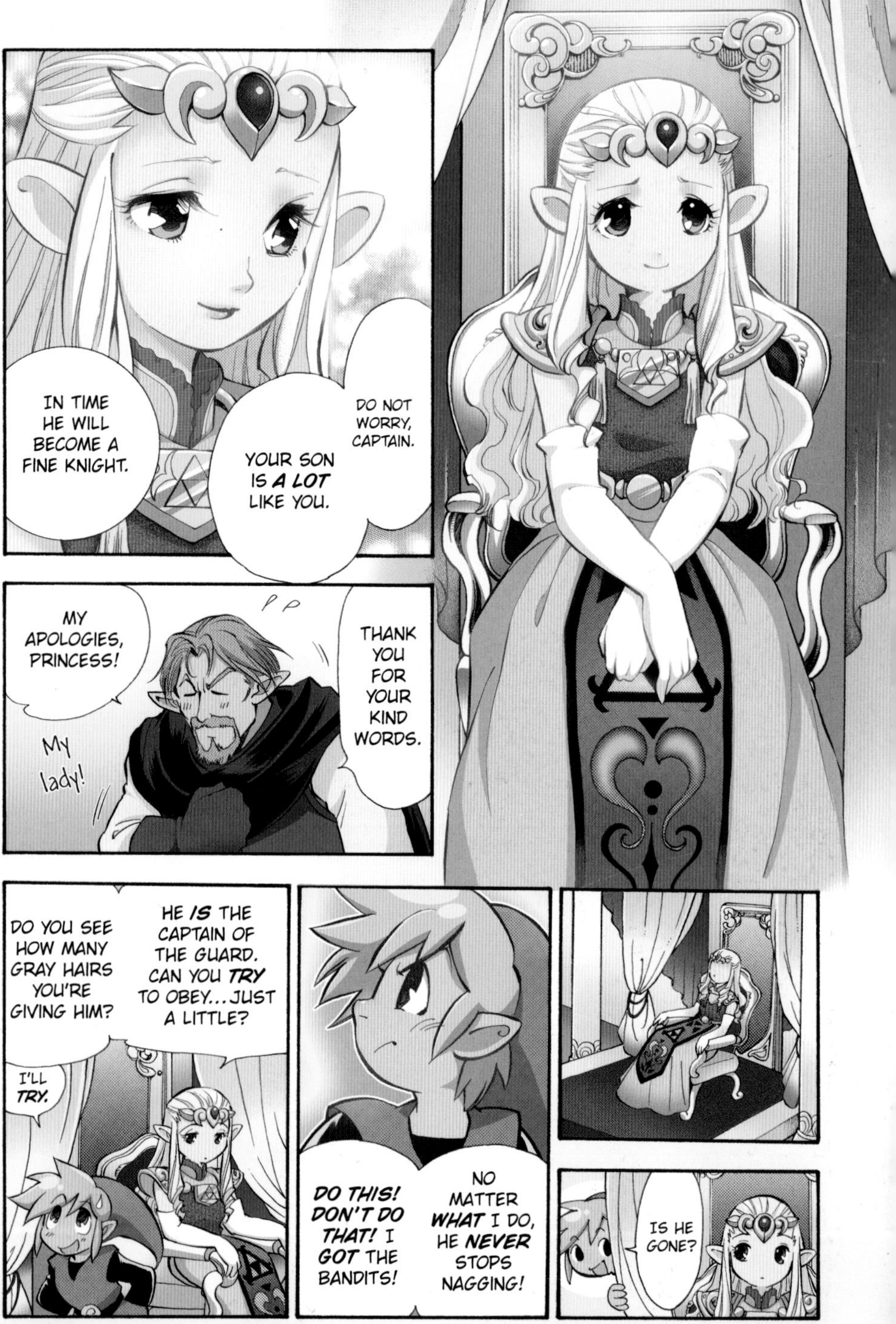
DO NOT WORRY, CAPTAIN.
YOUR SON IS A LOT LIKE YOU.
IN TIME HE WILL BECOME A FINE KNIGHT.
THANK YOU FOR YOUR KIND WORDS.
MY APOLOGIES, PRINCESS!
My lady!
IS HE GONE?
NO MATTER WHAT I DO, HE NEVER STOPS NAGGING!
DO THIS! DON'T DO THAT! I GOT THE BANDITS!
HE IS THE CAPTAIN OF THE GUARD. CAN YOU TRY TO OBEY... JUST A LITTLE?
DO YOU SEE HOW MANY GRAY HAIRS YOU'RE GIVING HIM?
I'LL TRY.

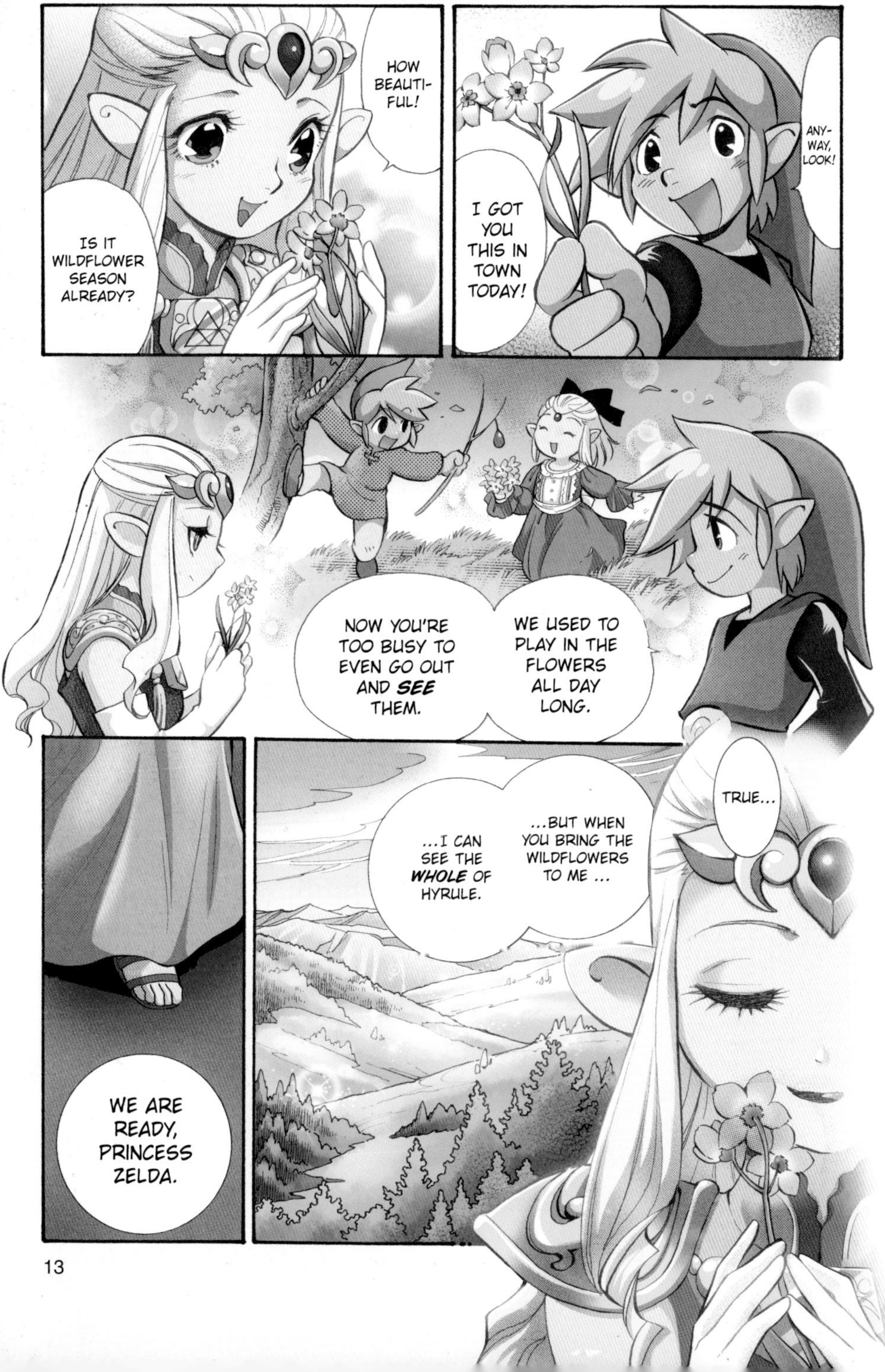
ANY-WAY, LOOK!
I GOT YOU THIS IN TOWN TODAY!
HOW BEAUTIFUL!
IS IT WILDFLOWER SEASON ALREADY?
WE USED TO PLAY IN THE FLOWERS ALL DAY LONG.
NOW YOU'RE TOO BUSY TO EVEN GO OUT AND **SEE** THEM.
TRUE...
...BUT WHEN YOU BRING THE WILDFLOWERS TO ME ...
...I CAN SEE THE ***WHOLE*** OF HYRULE.
WE ARE READY, PRINCESS ZELDA.

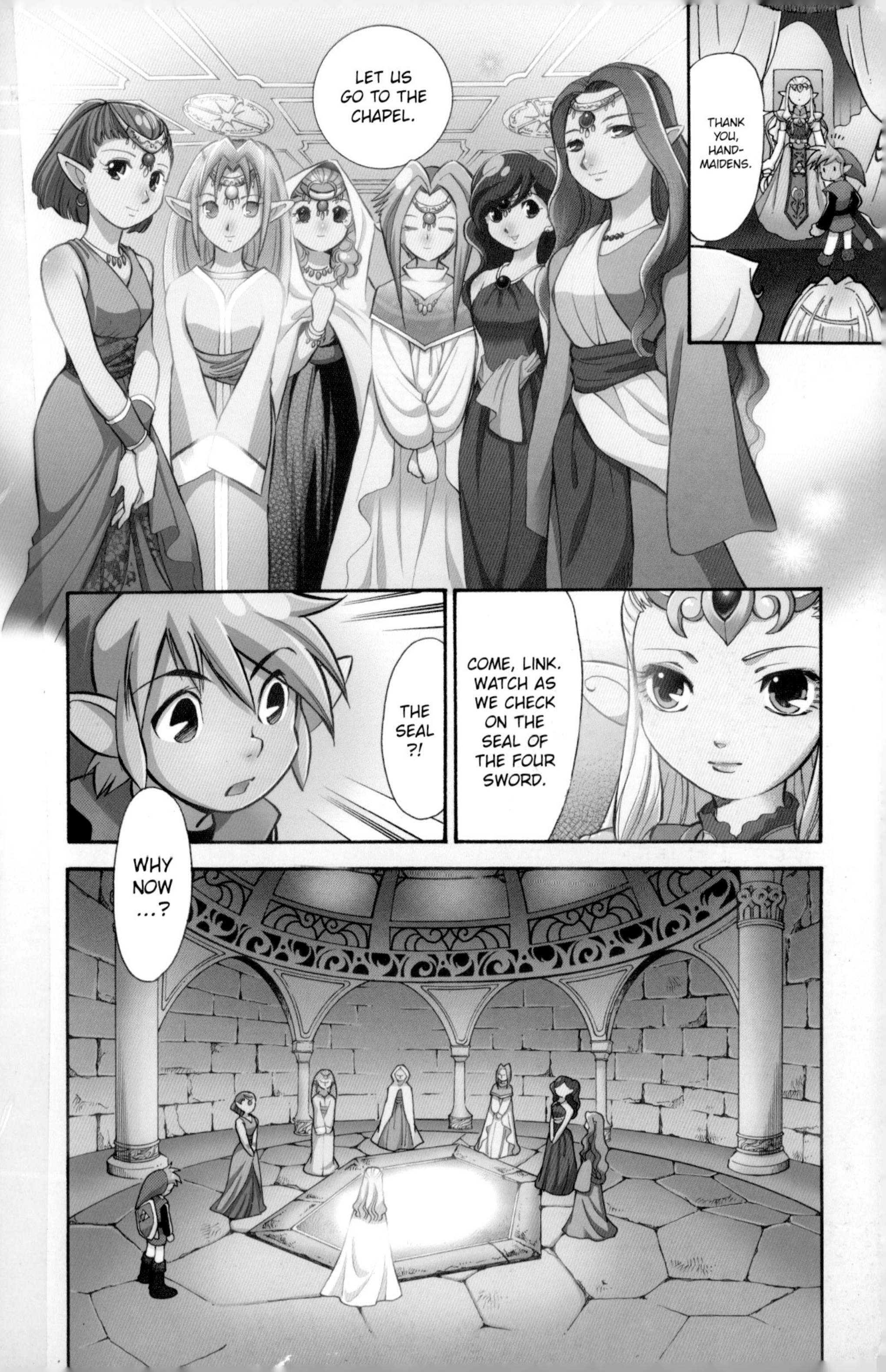
THANK YOU, HAND-MAIDENS.
LET US GO TO THE CHAPEL.
COME, LINK. WATCH AS WE CHECK ON THE SEAL OF THE FOUR SWORD.
THE SEAL ?!
WHY NOW ...?

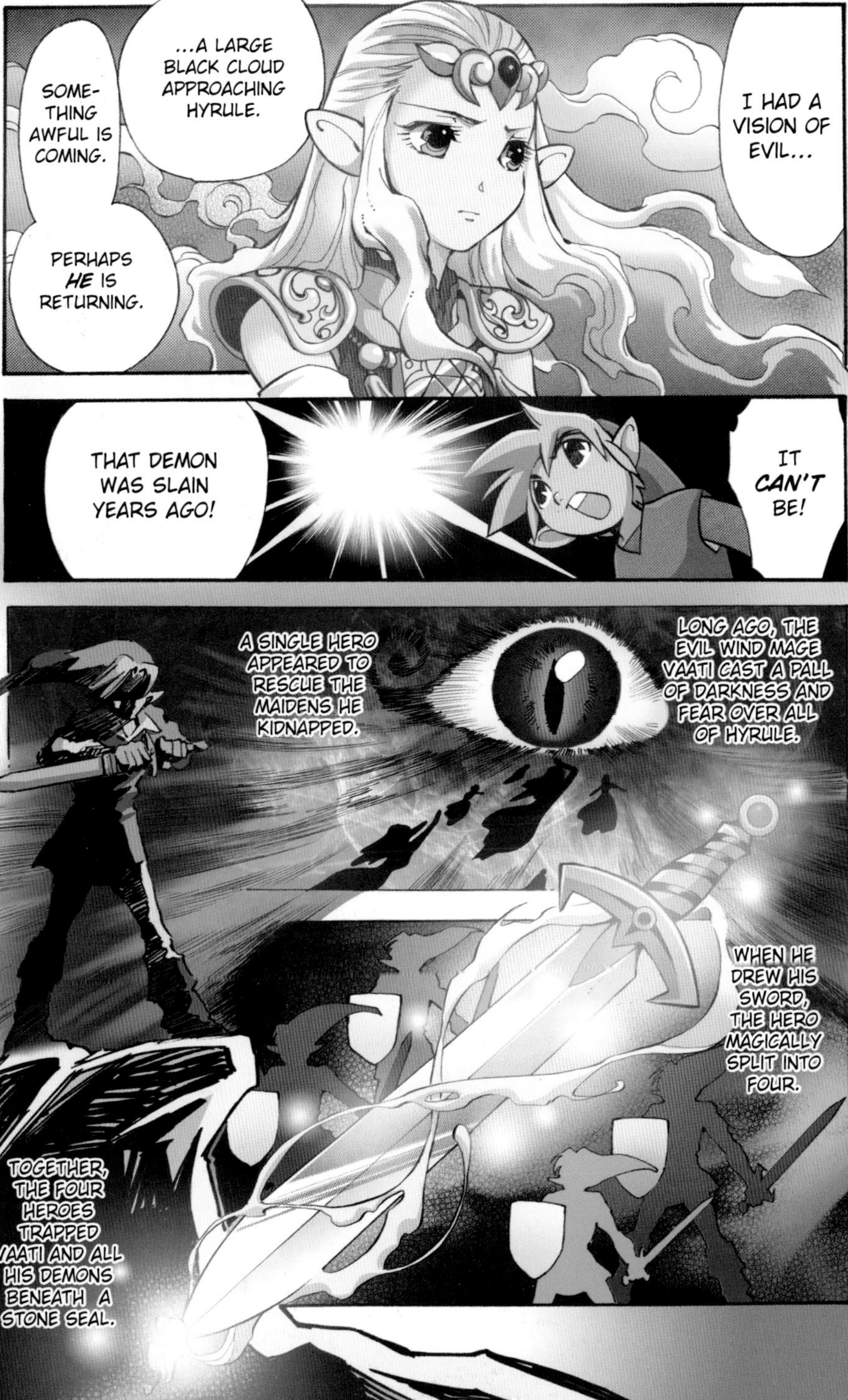
I HAD A VISION OF EVIL...
...A LARGE BLACK CLOUD APPROACHING HYRULE.
SOME-THING AWFUL IS COMING.
PERHAPS *HE* IS RETURNING.
IT *CAN'T* BE!
THAT DEMON WAS SLAIN YEARS AGO!
LONG AGO, THE EVIL WIND MAGE VAATI CAST A PALL OF DARKNESS AND FEAR OVER ALL OF HYRULE.
A SINGLE HERO APPEARED TO RESCUE THE MAIDENS HE KIDNAPPED.
WHEN HE DREW HIS SWORD, THE HERO MAGICALLY SPLIT INTO FOUR.
TOGETHER, THE FOUR HEROES TRAPPED VAATI AND ALL HIS DEMONS BENEATH A STONE SEAL.

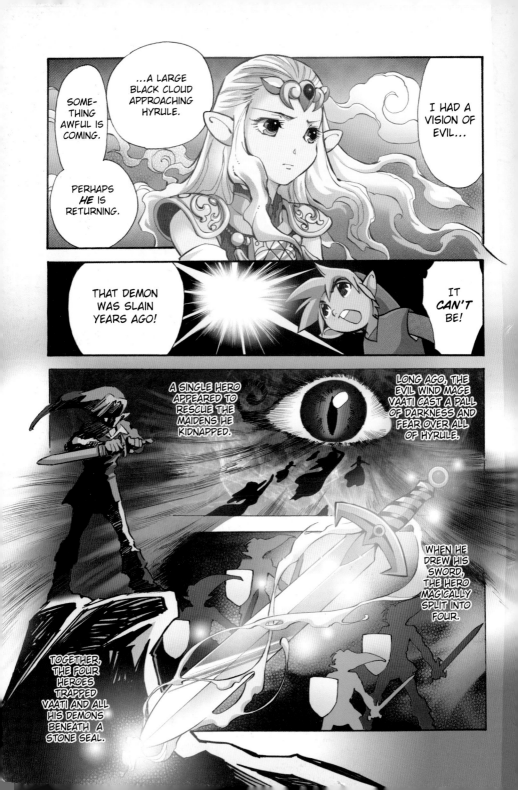

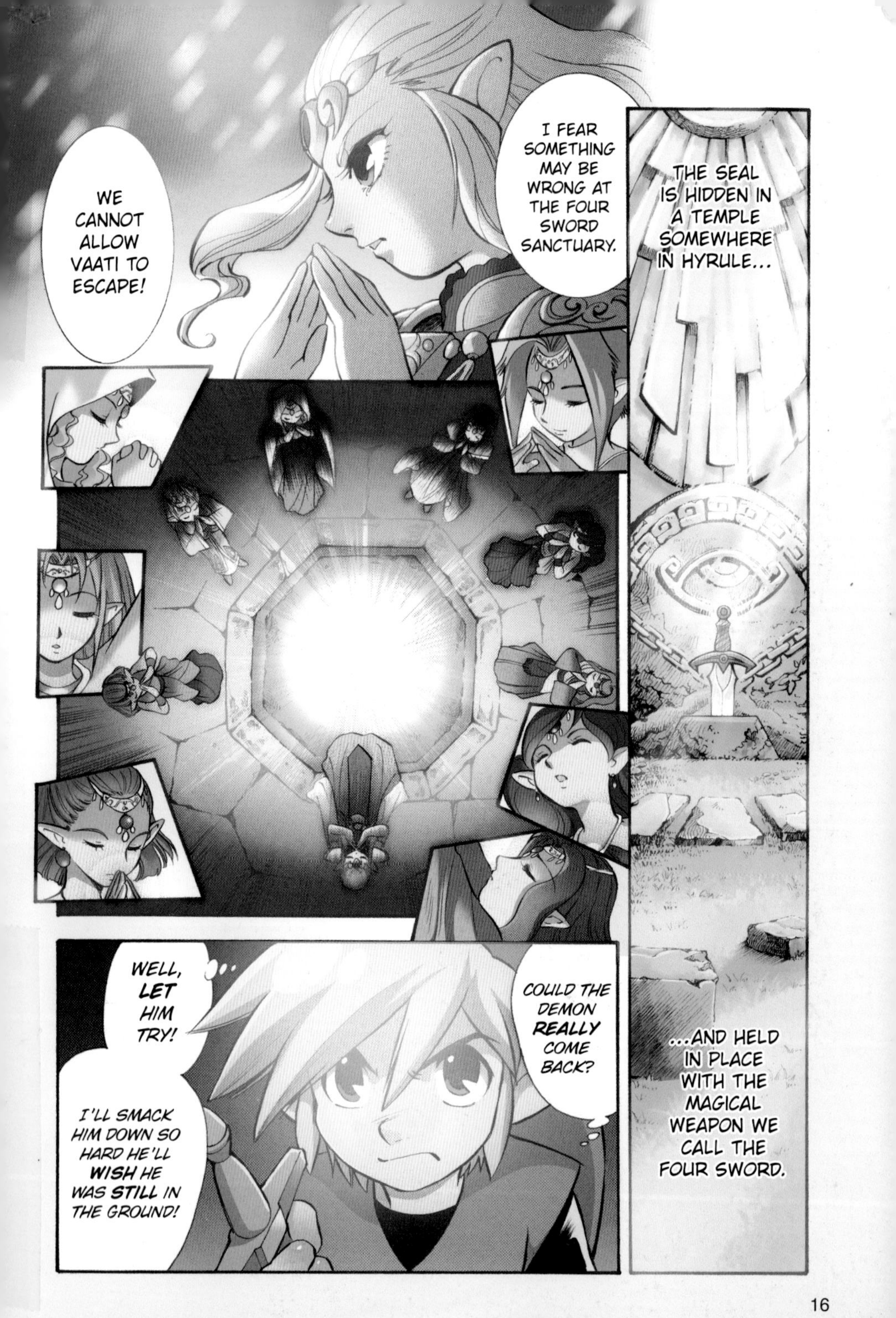
THE SEAL IS HIDDEN IN A TEMPLE SOMEWHERE IN HYRULE...
...AND HELD IN PLACE WITH THE MAGICAL WEAPON WE CALL THE FOUR SWORD.
I FEAR SOMETHING MAY BE WRONG AT THE FOUR SWORD SANCTUARY.
WE CANNOT ALLOW VAATI TO ESCAPE!
COULD THE DEMON **REALLY** COME BACK?
WELL, **LET** HIM TRY!
I'LL SMACK HIM DOWN SO HARD HE'LL **WISH** HE WAS **STILL** IN THE GROUND!

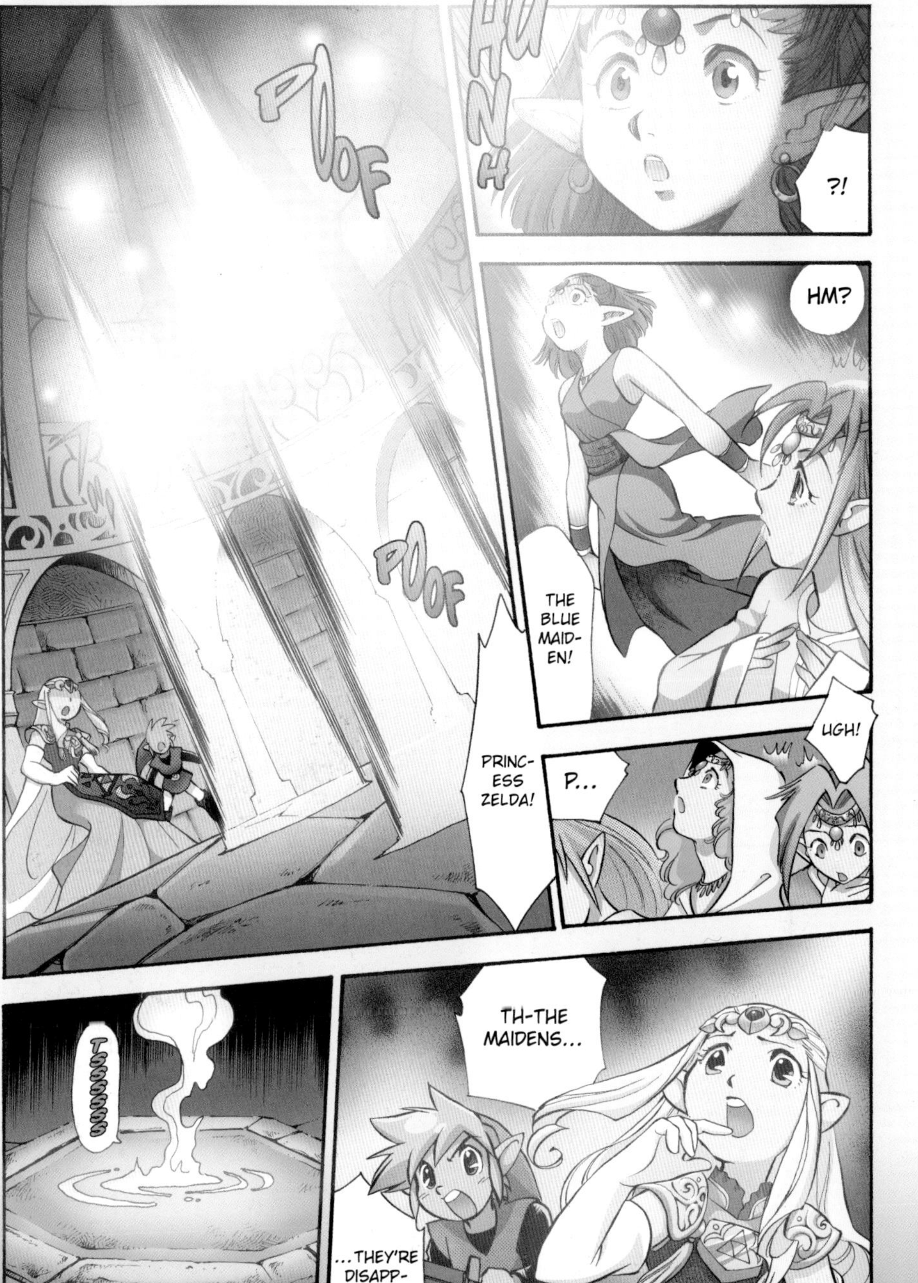
HUNH
?!
HM?
UGH!
P...
POOF
POOF
THE BLUE MAIDEN!
PRINCESS ZELDA!
TH-THE MAIDENS...
...THEY'RE DISAPPEARING!
TSSSSSS

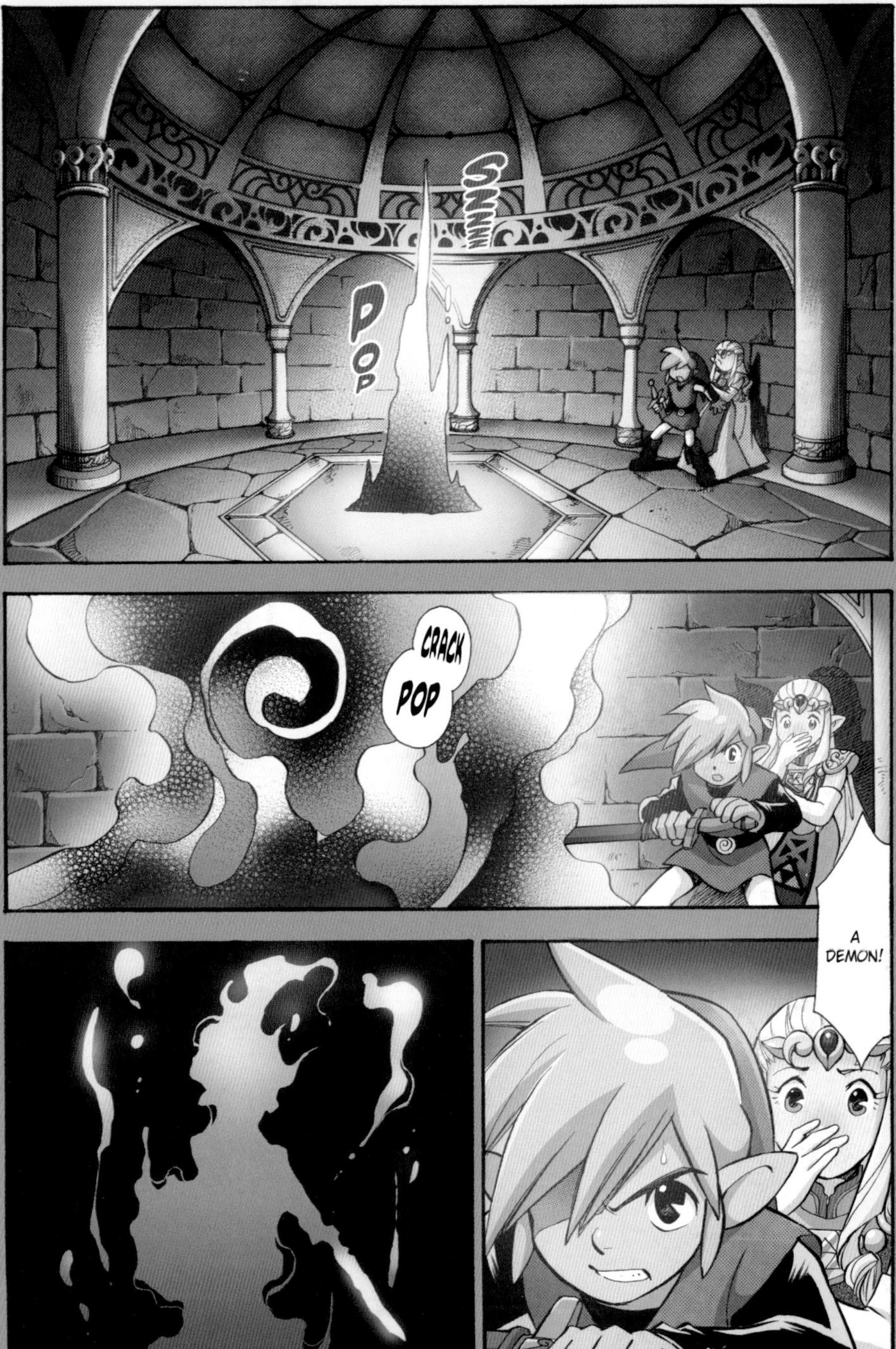
SZNNN
POP
POP
CRACK
POP
A DEMON!

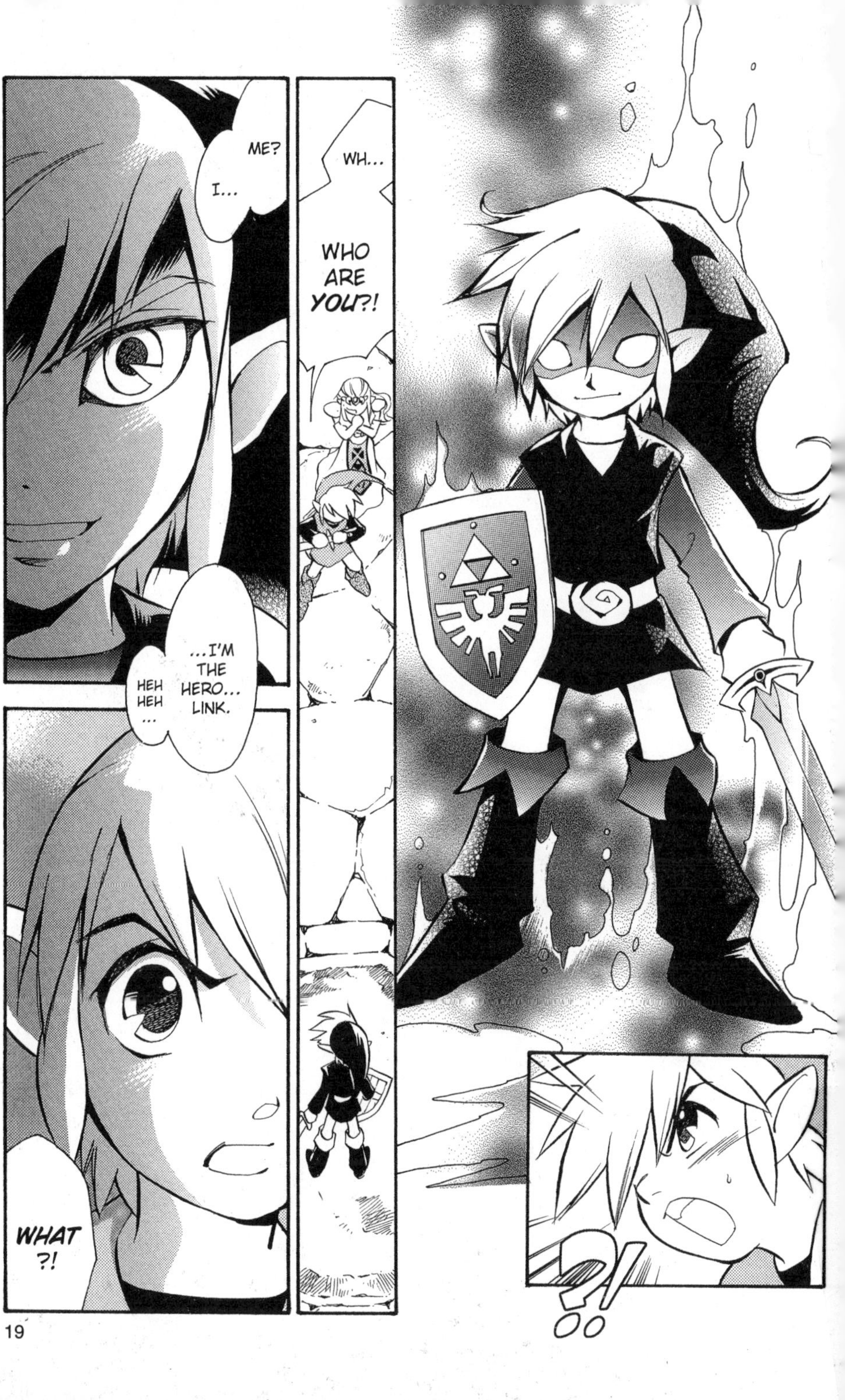
WH...
WHO ARE YOU?!
ME? I...
...I'M THE HERO... LINK.
HEH HEH ...
WHAT ?!
?!

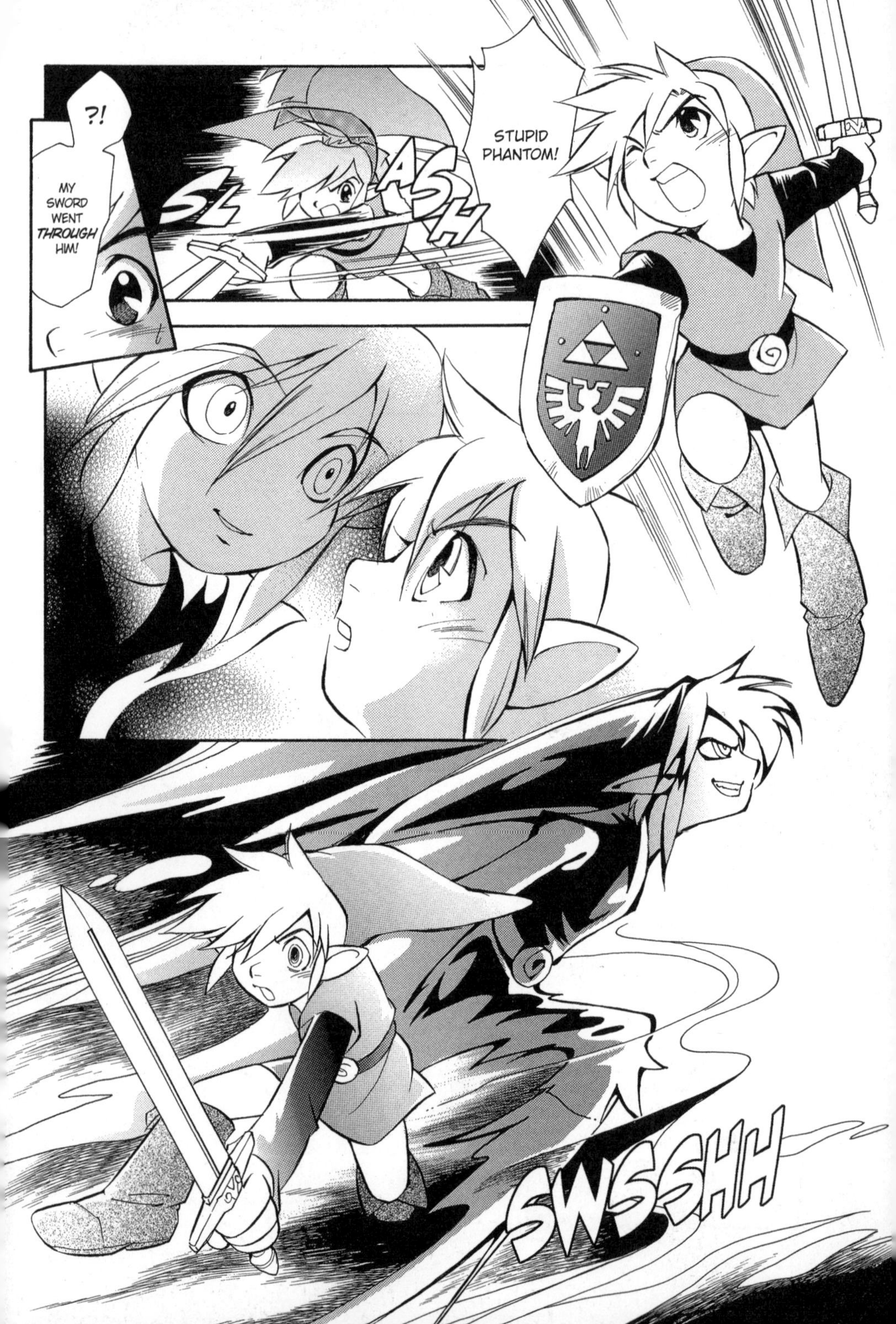

STUPID PHANTOM!
SLASH
?!
MY SWORD WENT THROUGH HIM!
SWSSHH

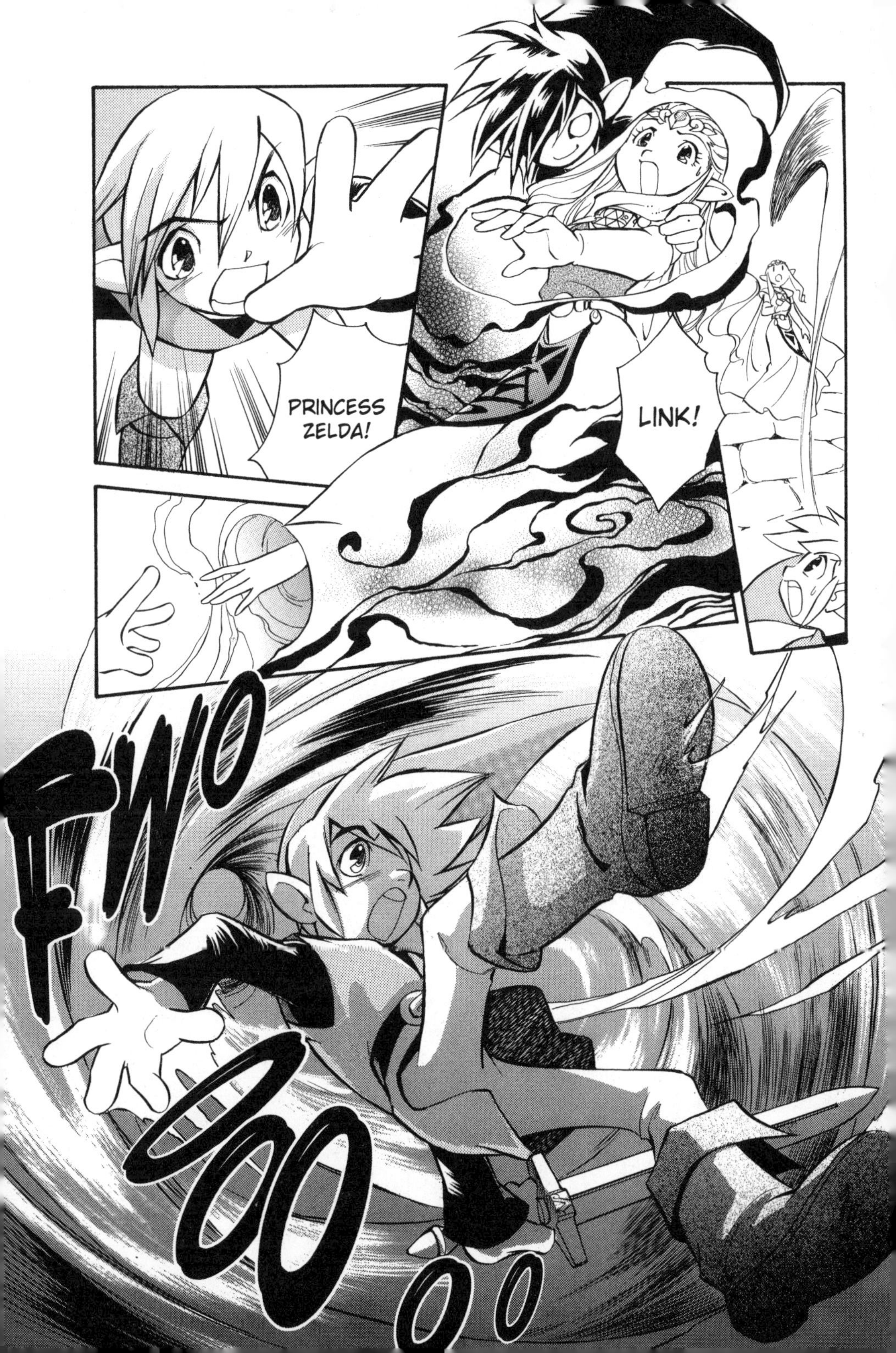
LINK!
PRINCESS ZELDA!
FWOOOO

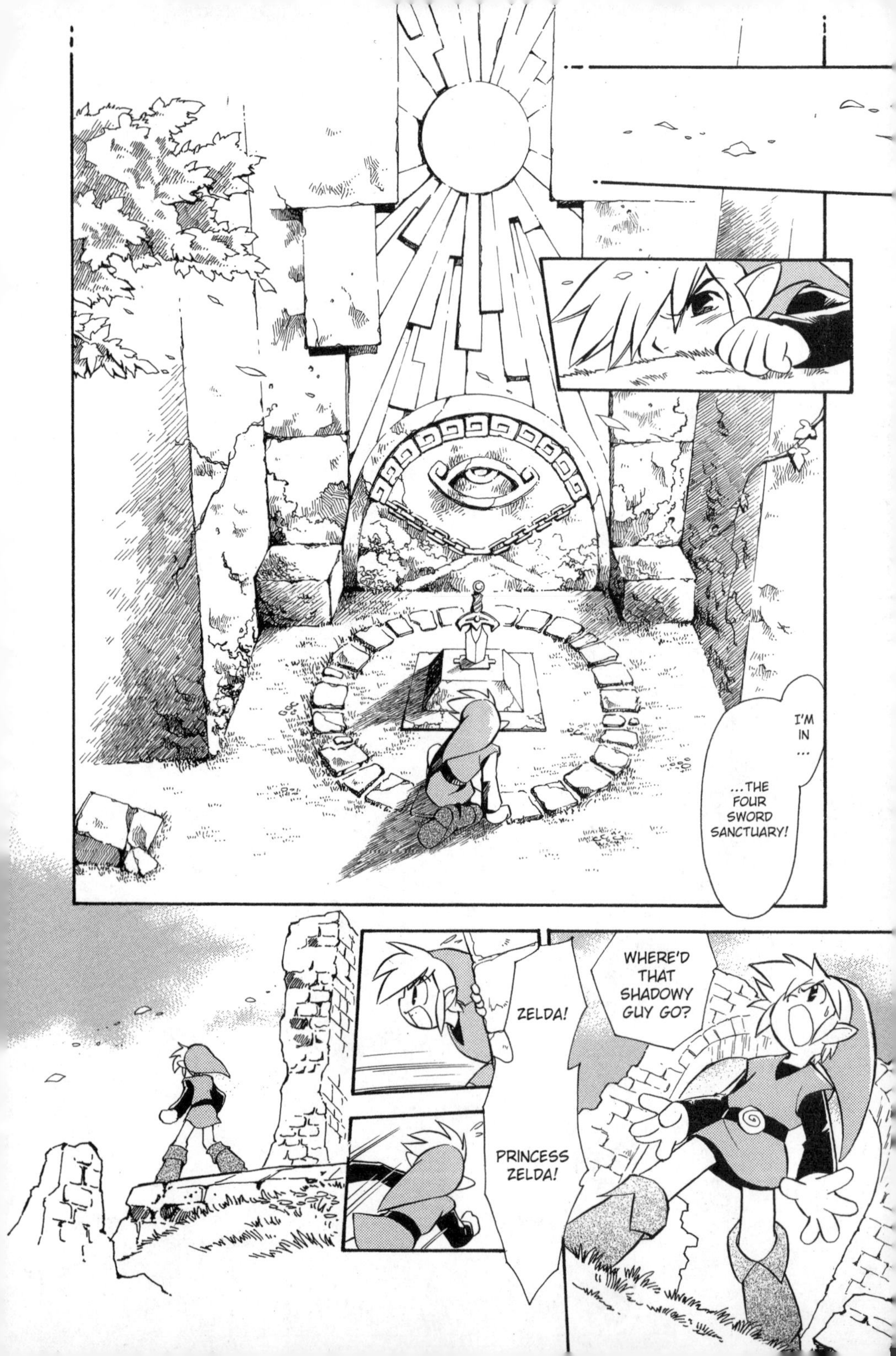
I'M IN...
...THE FOUR SWORD SANCTUARY!
WHERE'D THAT SHADOWY GUY GO?
ZELDA!
PRINCESS ZELDA!

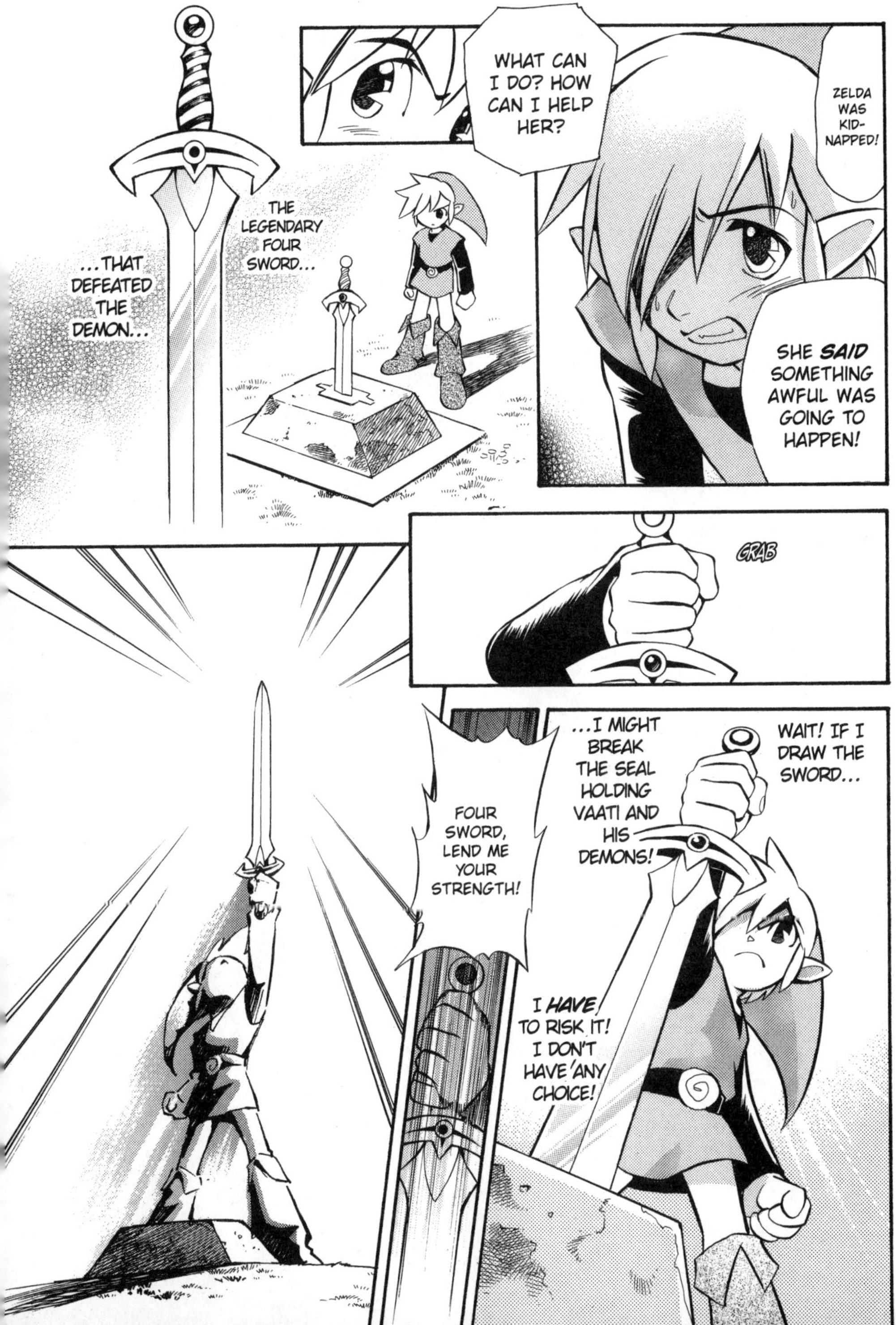
ZELDA WAS KID-NAPPED!
WHAT CAN I DO? HOW CAN I HELP HER?
SHE **SAID** SOMETHING AWFUL WAS GOING TO HAPPEN!
THE LEGENDARY FOUR SWORD...
...THAT DEFEATED THE DEMON...
GRAB
WAIT! IF I DRAW THE SWORD...
...I MIGHT BREAK THE SEAL HOLDING VAATI AND HIS DEMONS!
I **HAVE** TO RISK IT! I DON'T HAVE ANY CHOICE!
FOUR SWORD, LEND ME YOUR STRENGTH!

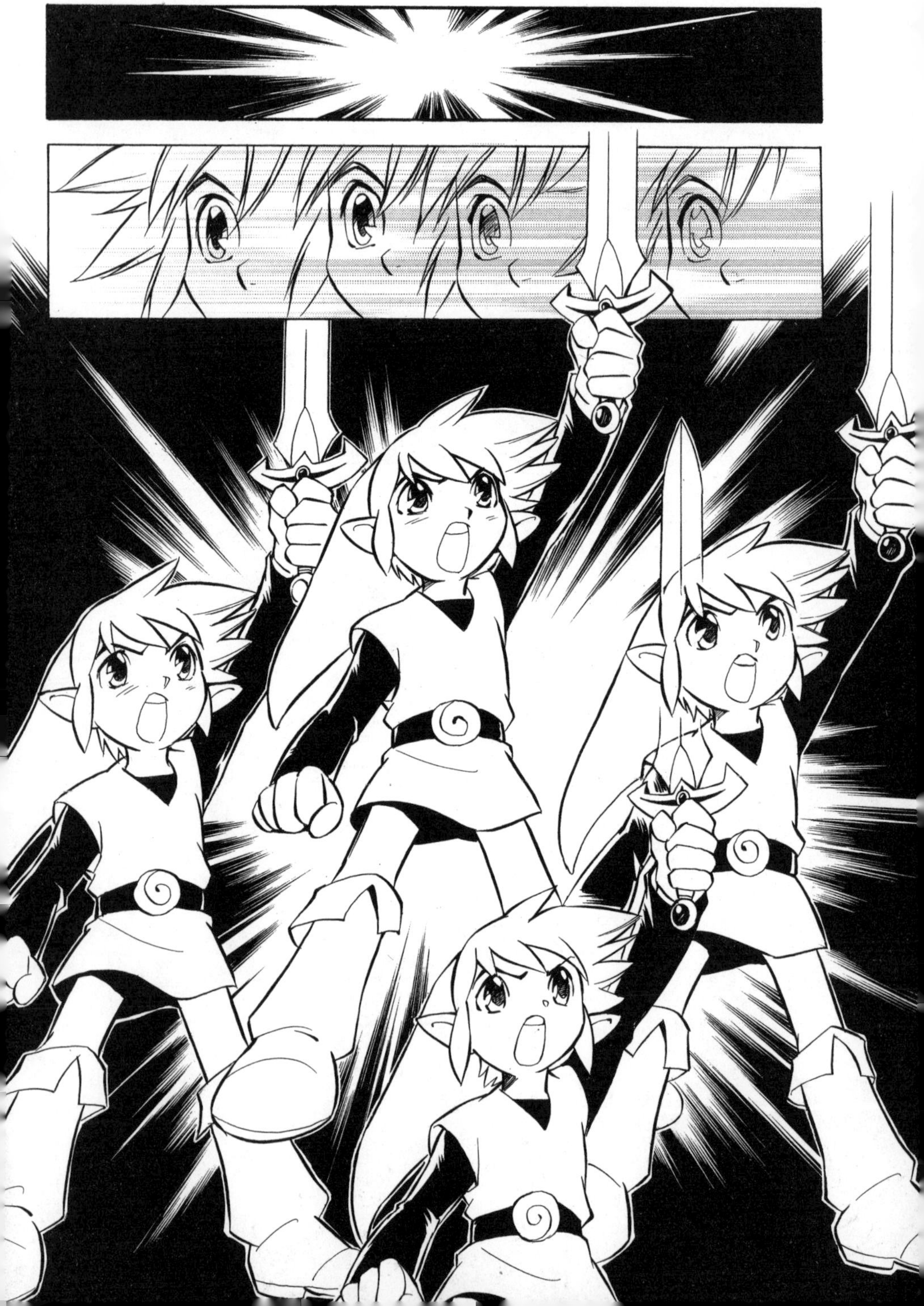

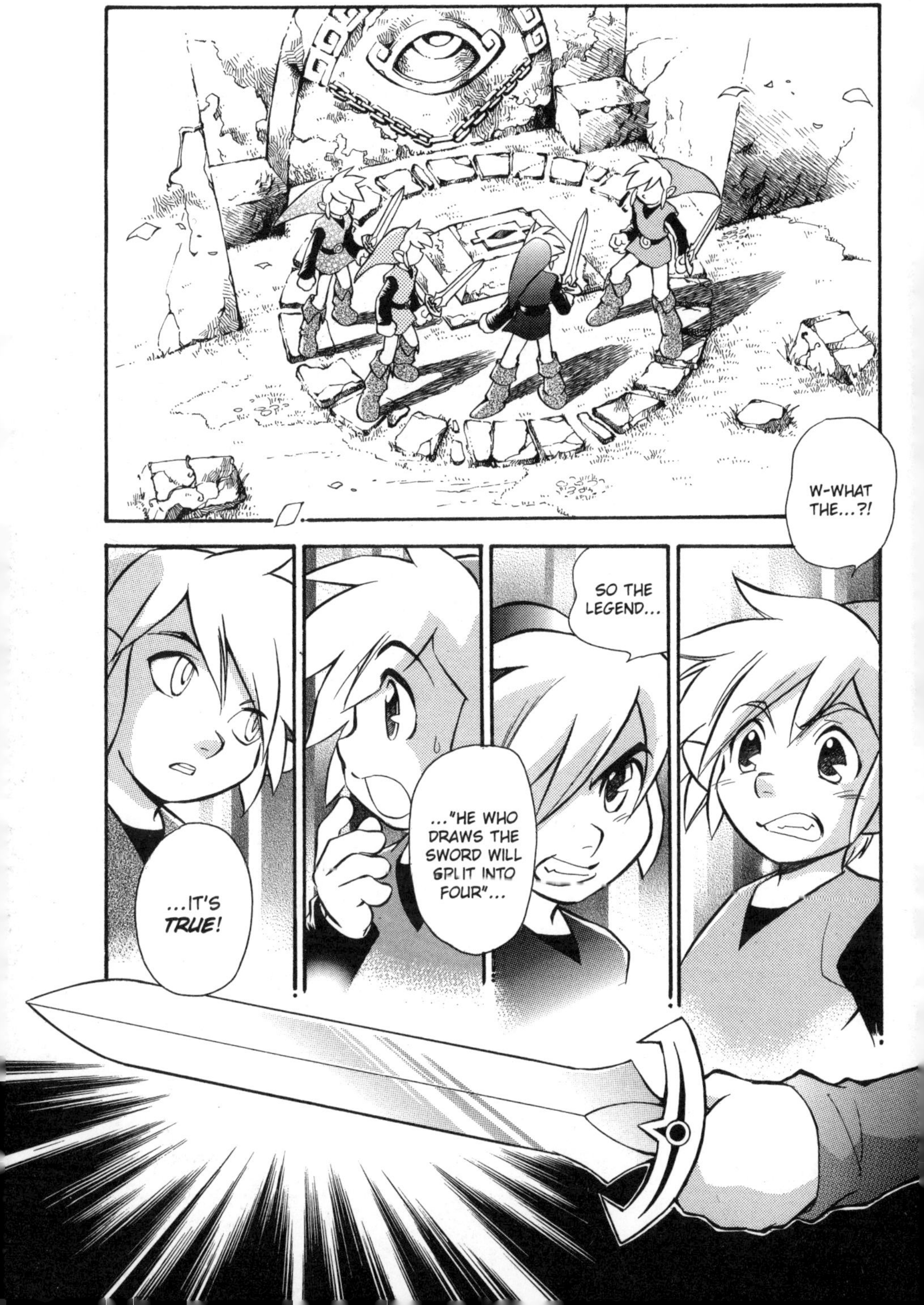
W-WHAT THE...?!
SO THE LEGEND...
..."HE WHO DRAWS THE SWORD WILL SPLIT INTO FOUR"...
...IT'S *TRUE!*

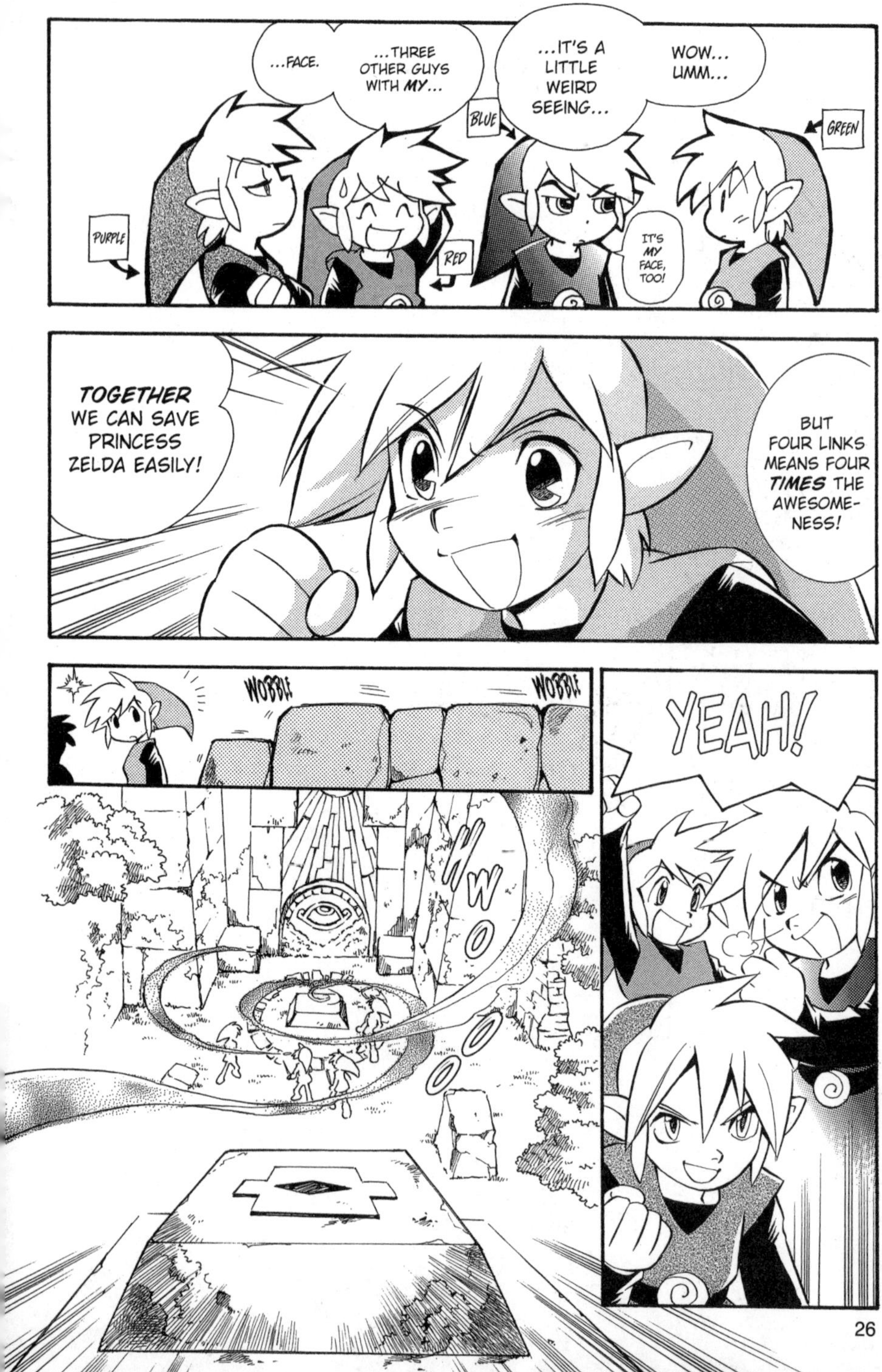

WOW... UMM...
...IT'S A LITTLE WEIRD SEEING...
...THREE OTHER GUYS WITH *MY*...
...FACE.
GREEN
BLUE
IT'S *MY* FACE, TOO!
RED
PURPLE
BUT FOUR LINKS MEANS FOUR *TIMES* THE AWESOMENESS!
TOGETHER WE CAN SAVE PRINCESS ZELDA EASILY!
YEAH!
WOBBLE
WOBBLE

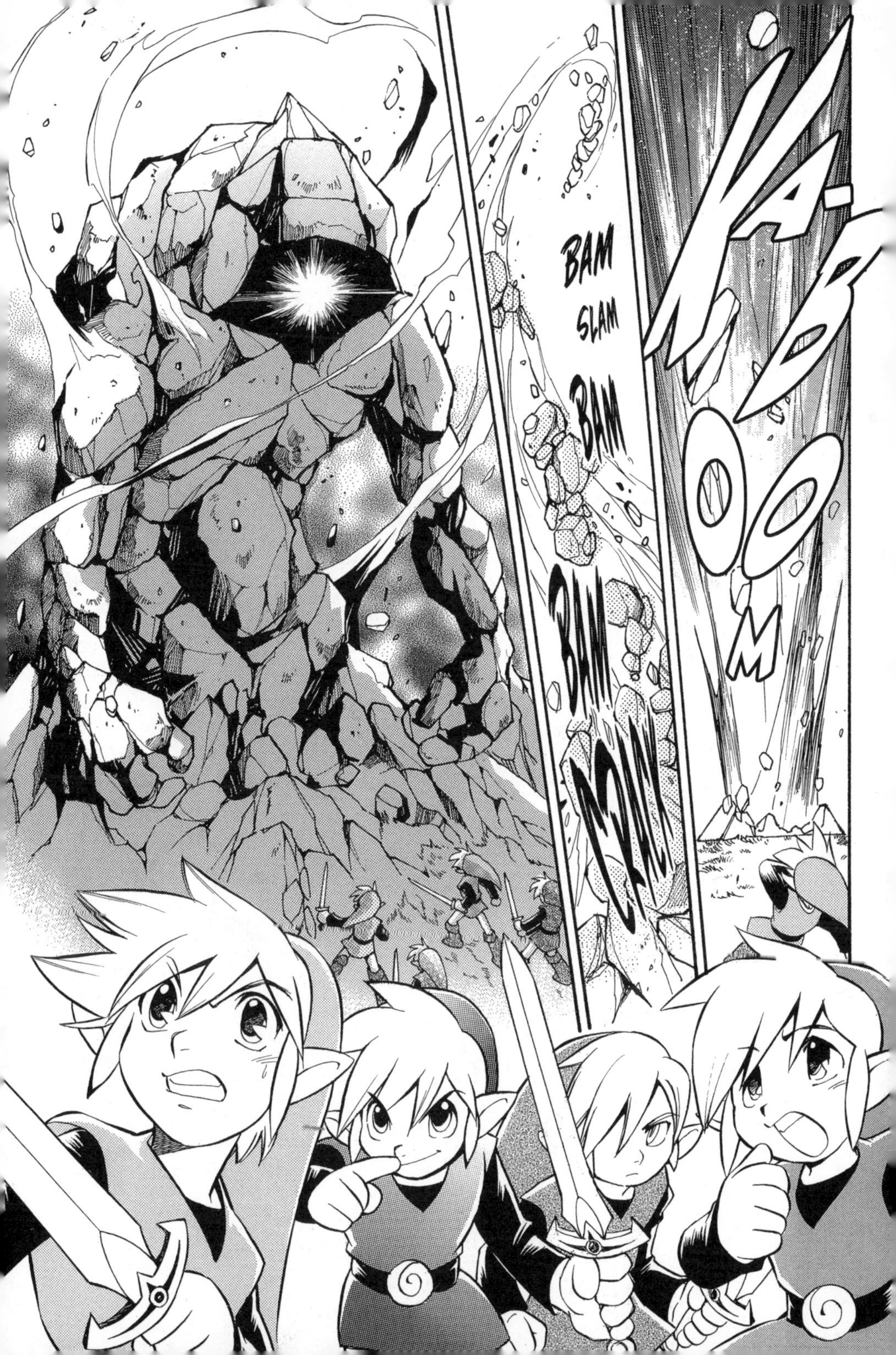
KA-BOOM
BAM
SLAM
BAM
BAM
CRACK

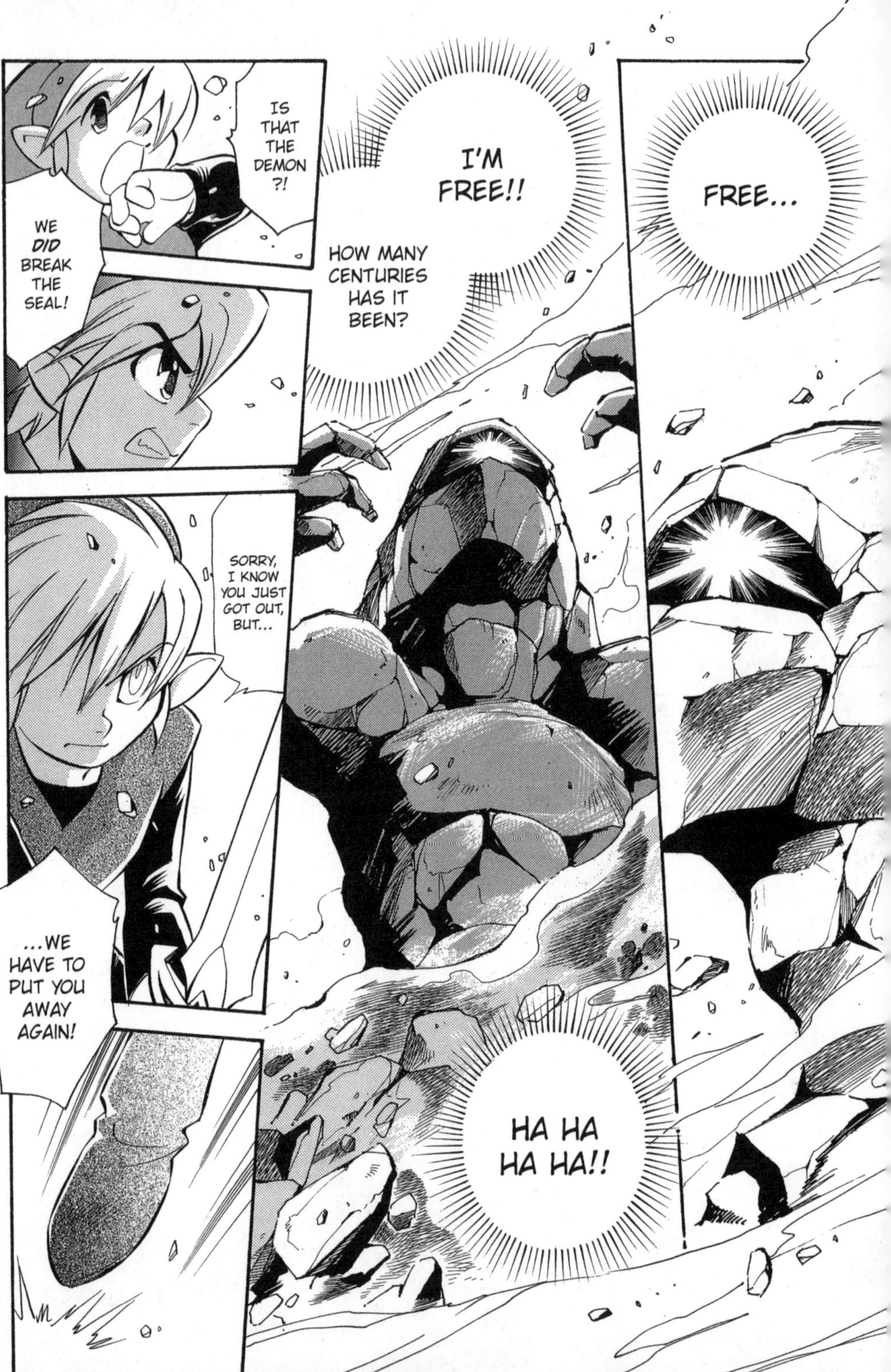
FREE...
I'M FREE!!
HOW MANY CENTURIES HAS IT BEEN?
HA HA HA HA!!
IS THAT THE DEMON?!
WE *DID* BREAK THE SEAL!
SORRY, I KNOW YOU JUST GOT OUT, BUT...
...WE HAVE TO PUT YOU AWAY AGAIN!

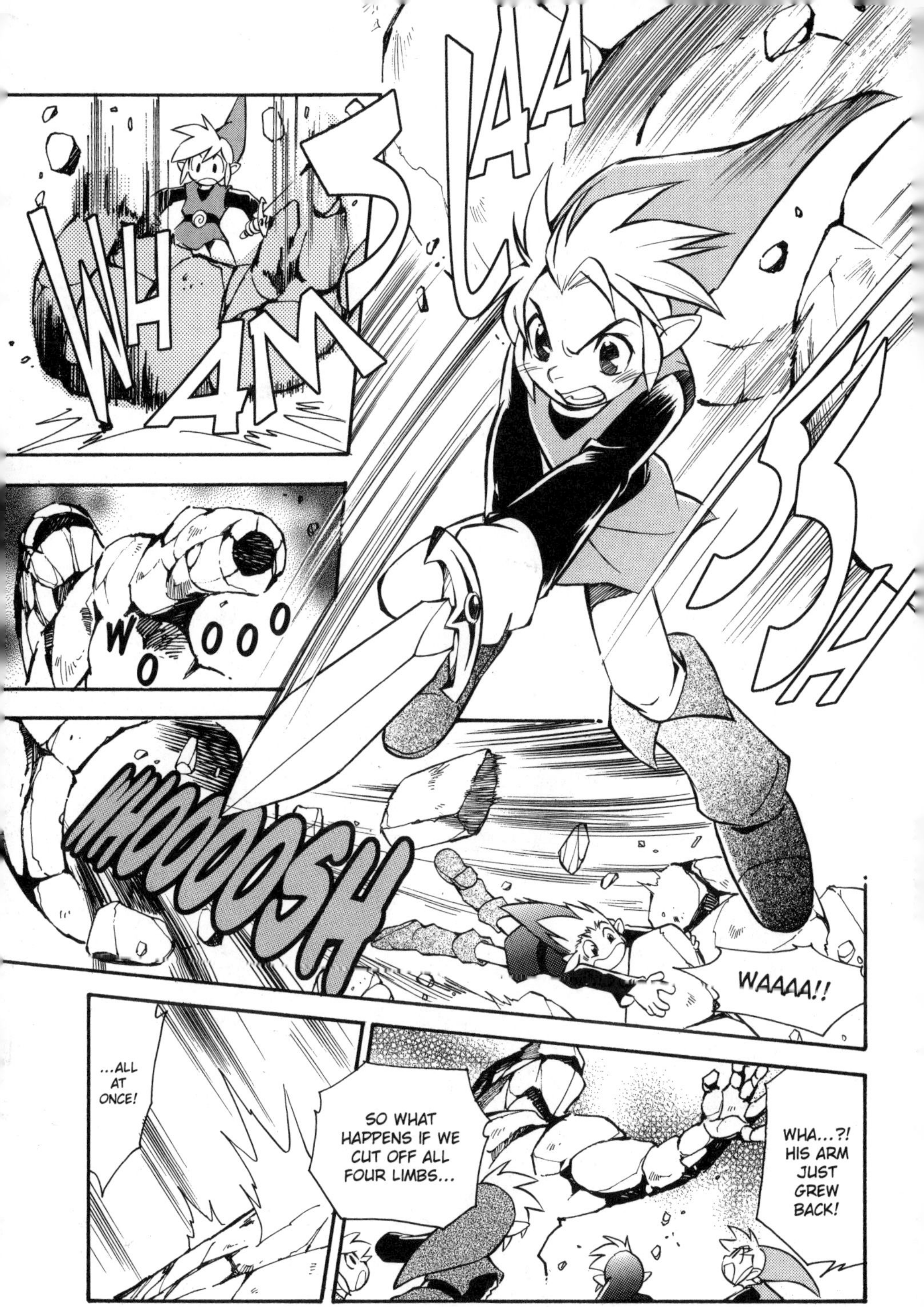
SLAASH
WHAM
WOOOO
WHOOOSH
WAAAA!!
WHA...?! HIS ARM JUST GREW BACK!
SO WHAT HAPPENS IF WE CUT OFF ALL FOUR LIMBS...
...ALL AT ONCE!

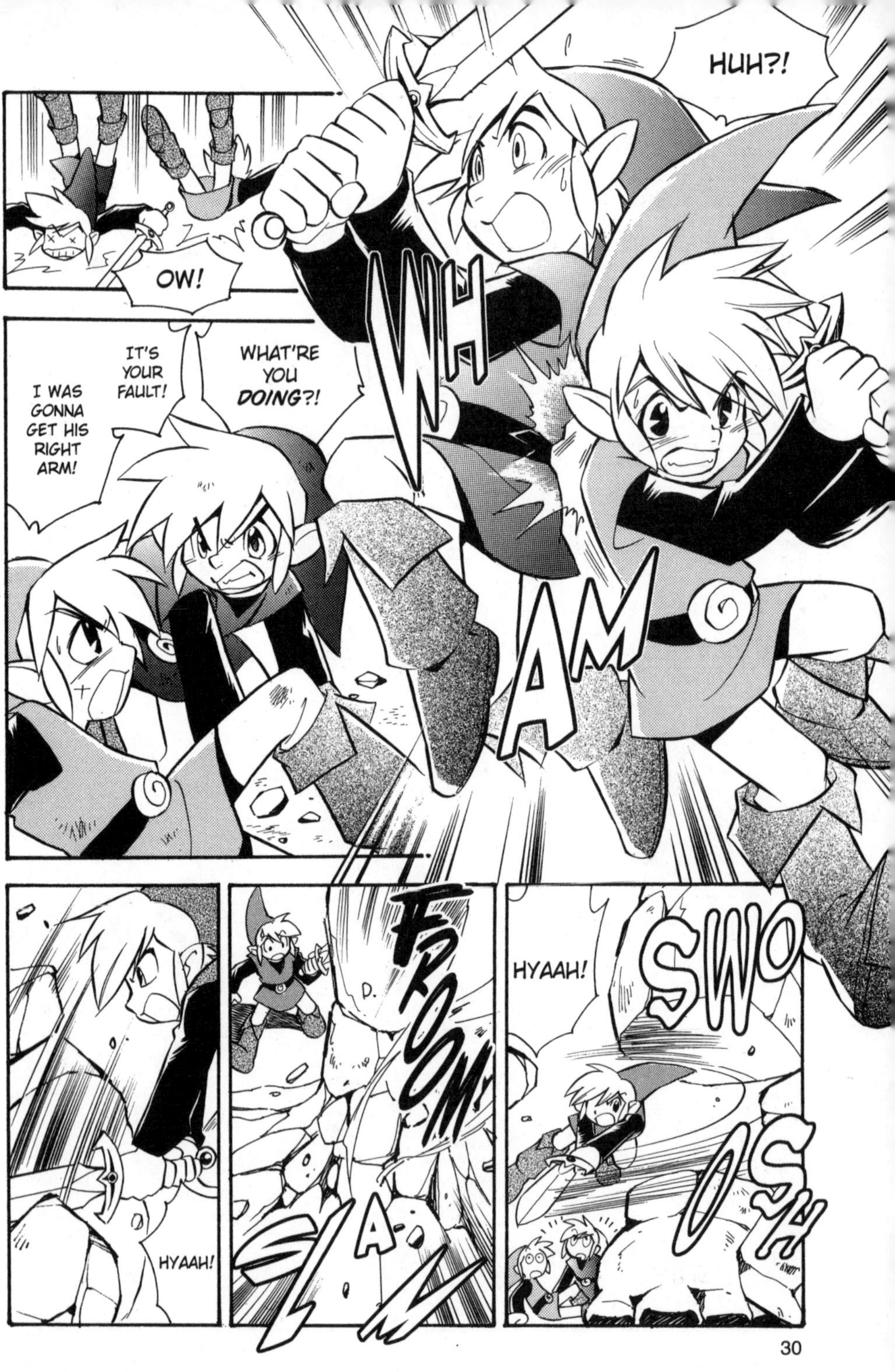

HUH?!
WHAM
OW!
WHAT'RE YOU DOING?!
IT'S YOUR FAULT!
I WAS GONNA GET HIS RIGHT ARM!
HYAAH!
SWOOSH
FROOM!
SLAM
HYAAH!

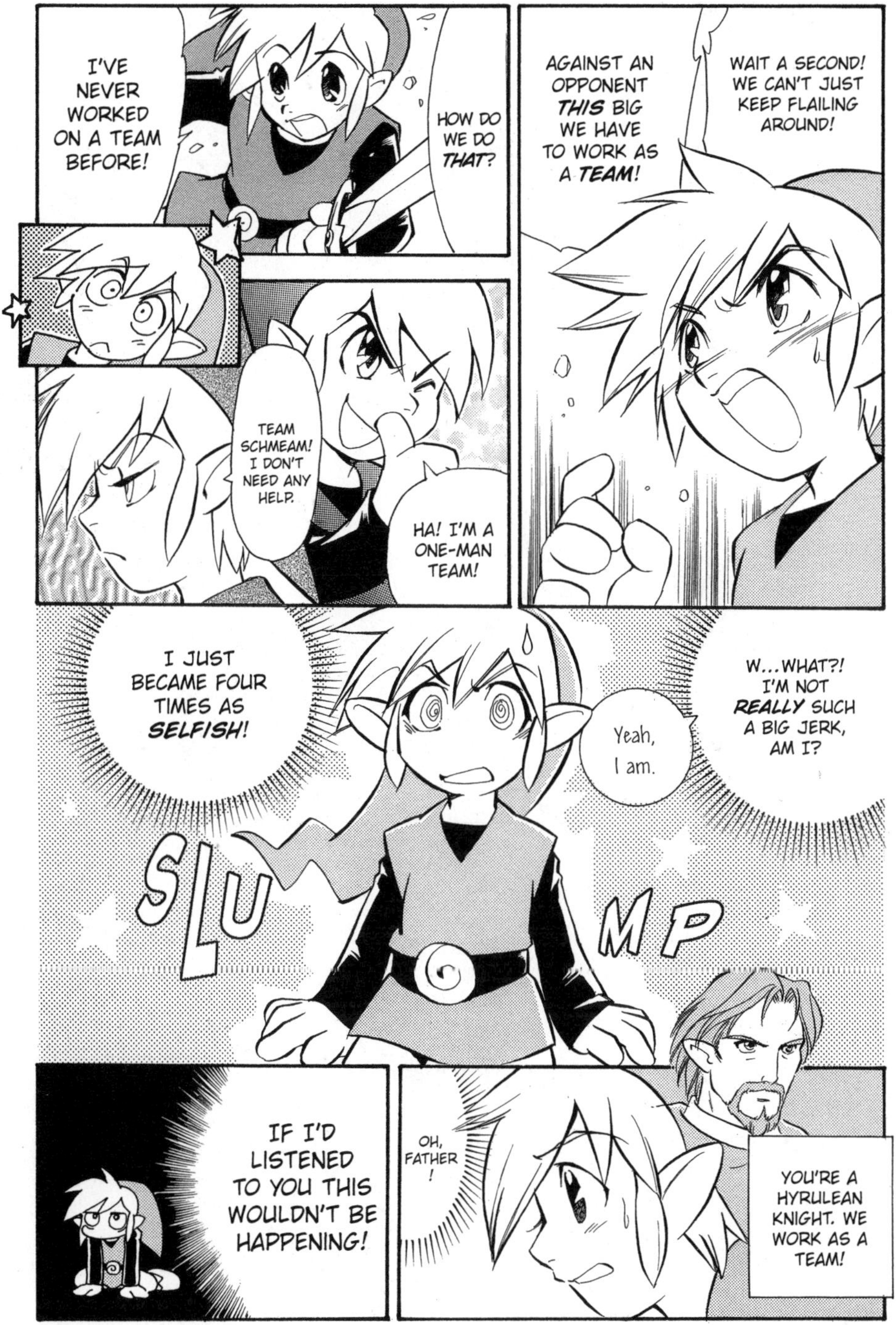

WAIT A SECOND! WE CAN'T JUST KEEP FLAILING AROUND!
AGAINST AN OPPONENT **THIS** BIG WE HAVE TO WORK AS A **TEAM**!
HOW DO WE DO **THAT**?
I'VE NEVER WORKED ON A TEAM BEFORE!
HA! I'M A ONE-MAN TEAM!
TEAM SCHMEAM! I DON'T NEED ANY HELP.
W...WHAT?! I'M NOT **REALLY** SUCH A BIG JERK, AM I?
Yeah, I am.
I JUST BECAME FOUR TIMES AS **SELFISH**!
SLUMP
YOU'RE A HYRULEAN KNIGHT. WE WORK AS A TEAM!
OH, FATHER!
IF I'D LISTENED TO YOU THIS WOULDN'T BE HAPPENING!

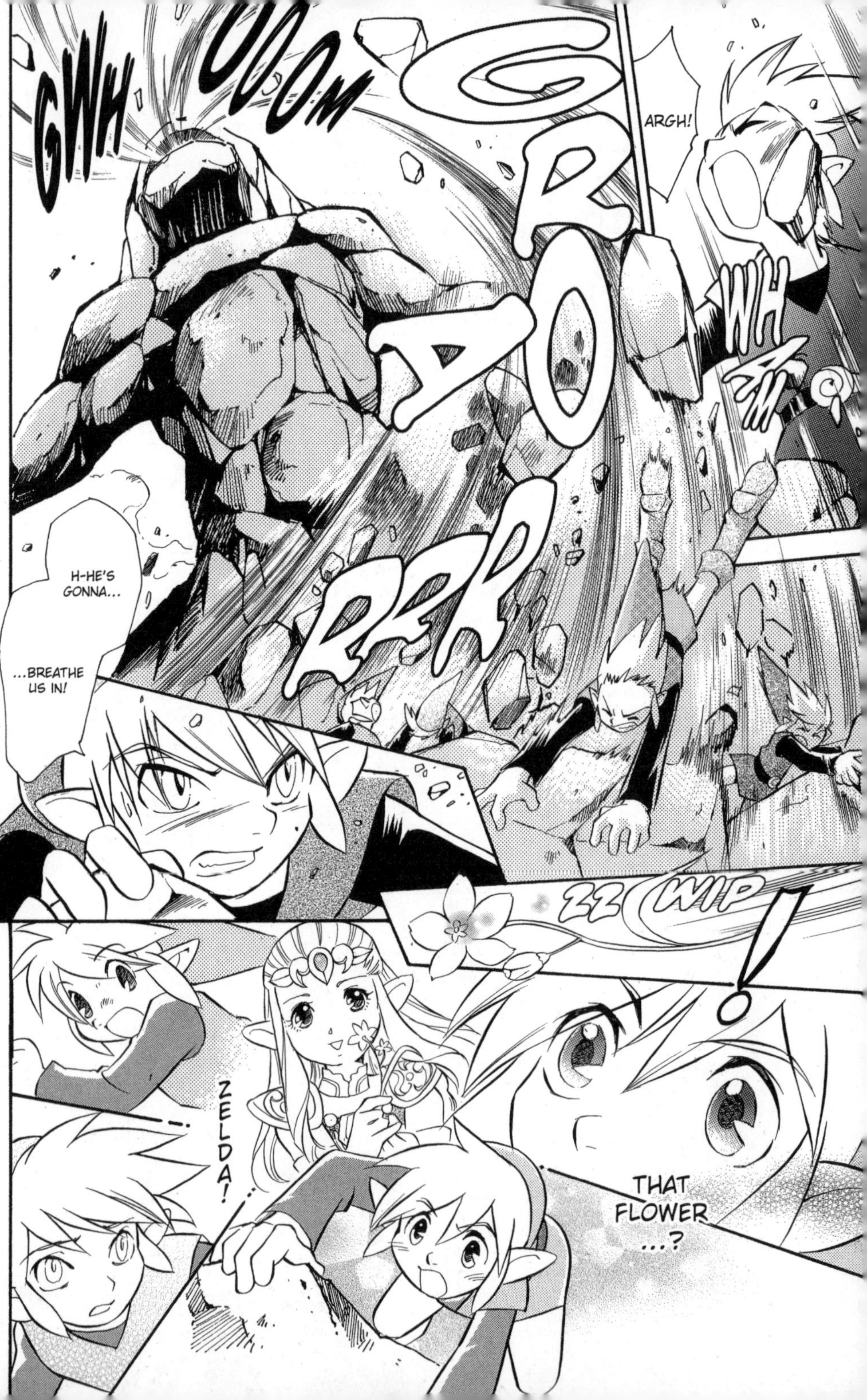
ARGH!
WHAA
GWHUUOOM
GROARR
H-HE'S GONNA...
...BREATHE US IN!
ZZWIP
!
THAT FLOWER ...?
ZELDA!

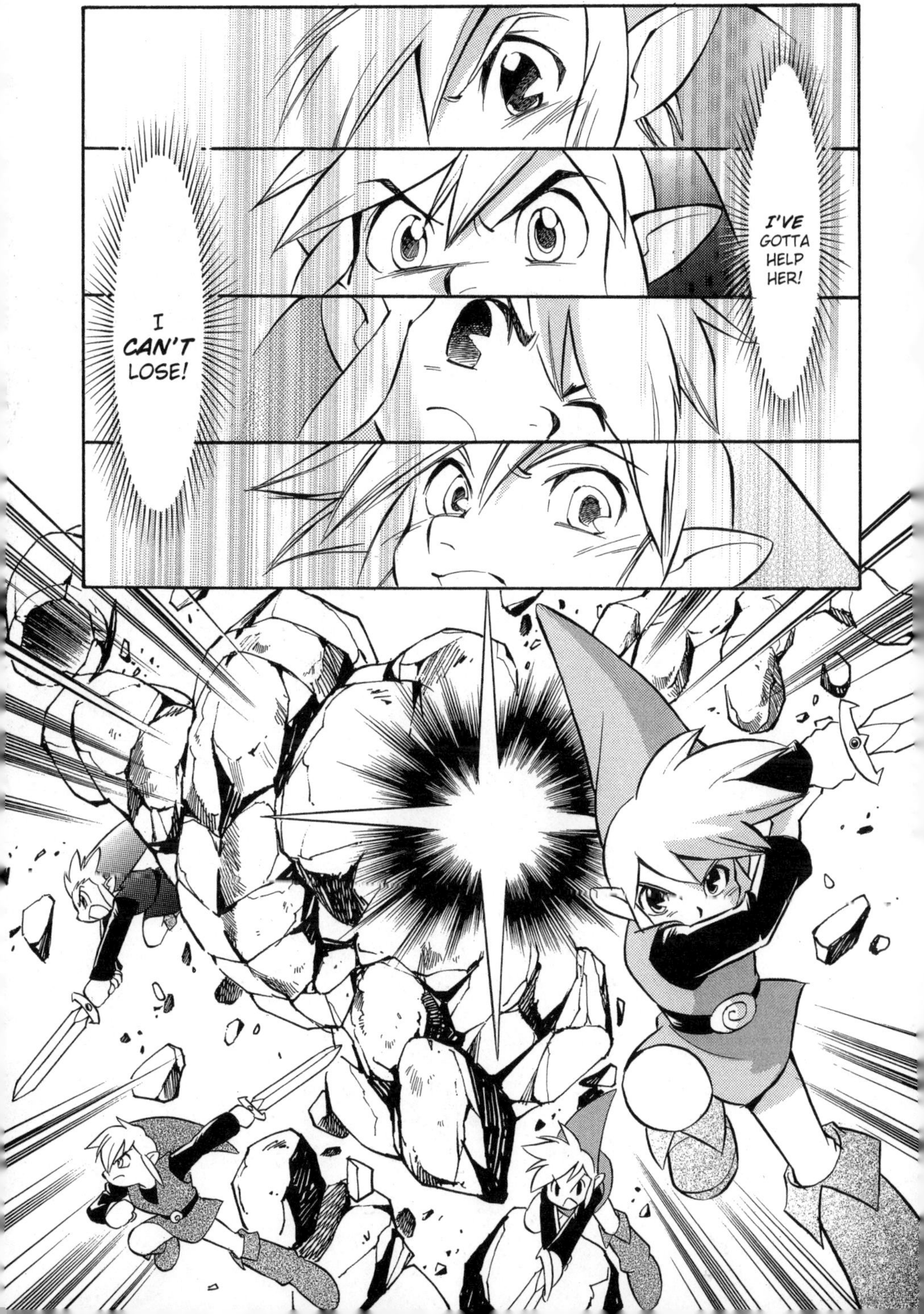
I'VE GOTTA HELP HER!
I CAN'T LOSE!

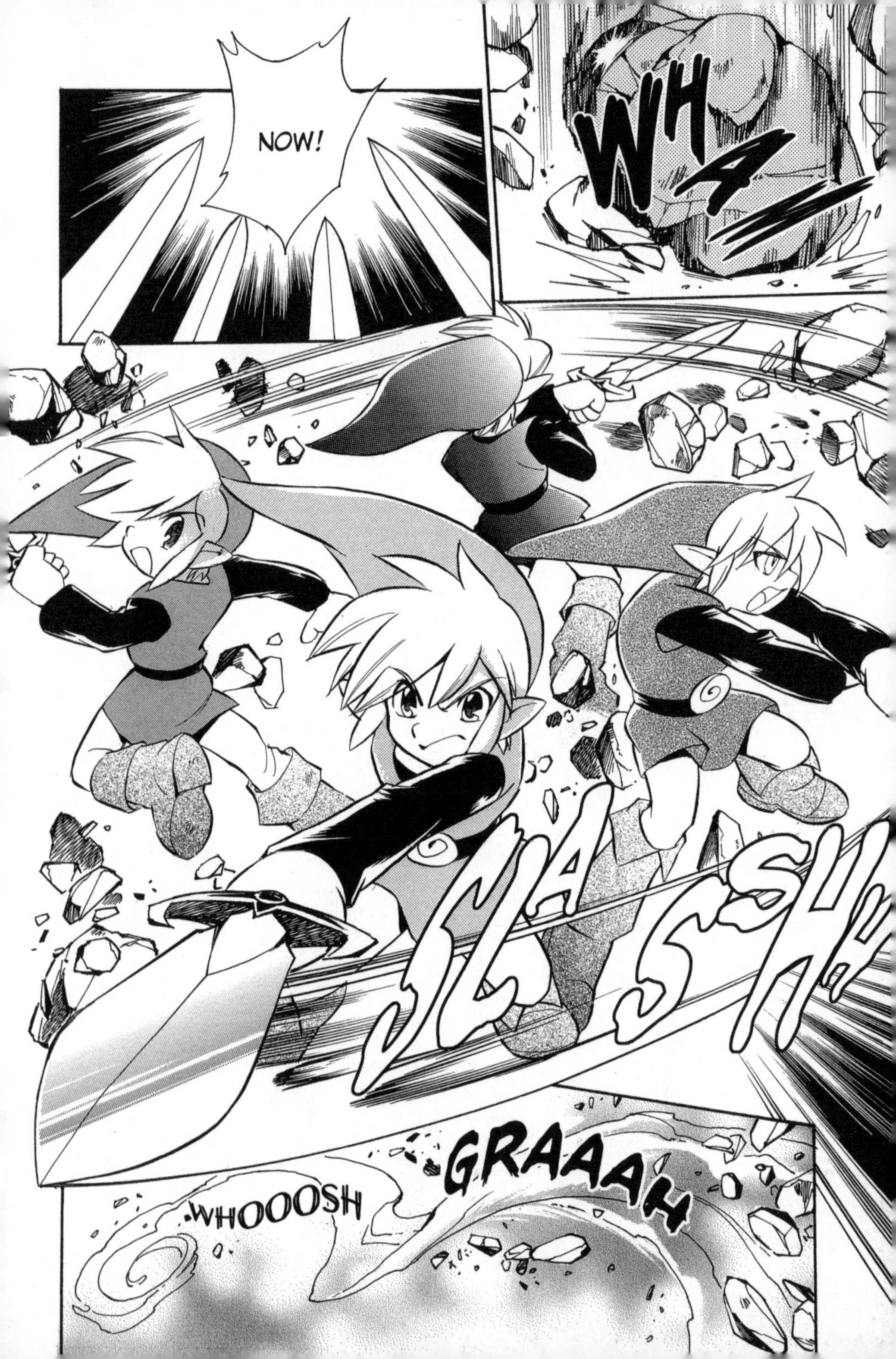
WHA
NOW!
SLASH
GRAAAH
WHOOOSH

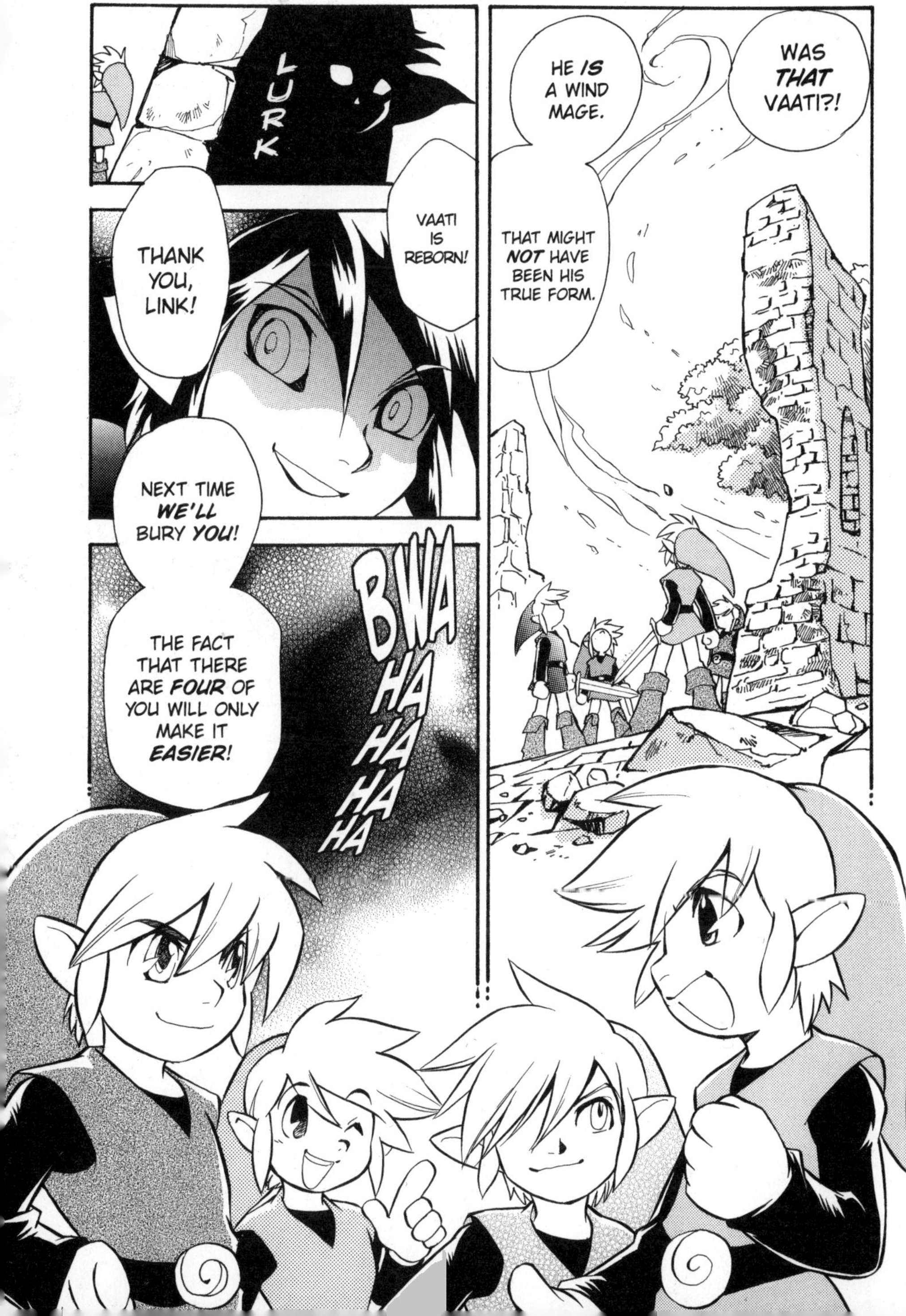
WAS THAT VAATI?!
HE IS A WIND MAGE.
THAT MIGHT NOT HAVE BEEN HIS TRUE FORM.
LURK
VAATI IS REBORN!
THANK YOU, LINK!
NEXT TIME WE'LL BURY YOU!
THE FACT THAT THERE ARE FOUR OF YOU WILL ONLY MAKE IT EASIER!
BWA HA HA HA HA HA

[Link] We had in mind a design somewhere between the ones in the Oracle books and The Wind Waker.

[Green]
Leader.
The classic
Link.

**FOUR SWORDS
ROUGH CHARACTER
ILLUSTRATION 1**

CHAPTER 2

The Fall of Hyrule Castle

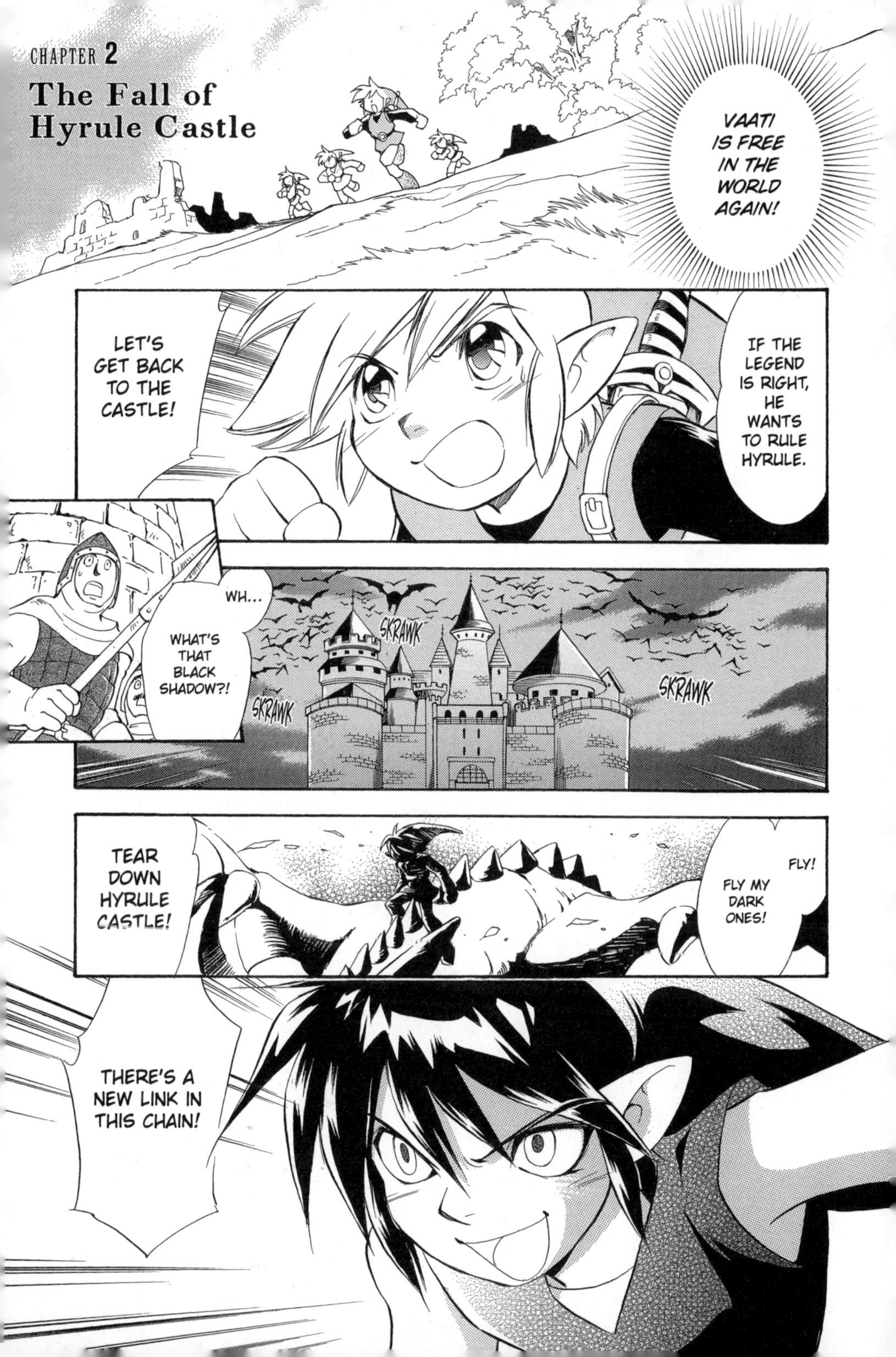
VAATI IS FREE IN THE WORLD AGAIN!
IF THE LEGEND IS RIGHT, HE WANTS TO RULE HYRULE.
LET'S GET BACK TO THE CASTLE!
SKRAWK
SKRAWK
SKRAWK
WH...
WHAT'S THAT BLACK SHADOW?!
FLY!
FLY MY DARK ONES!
TEAR DOWN HYRULE CASTLE!
THERE'S A NEW LINK IN THIS CHAIN!

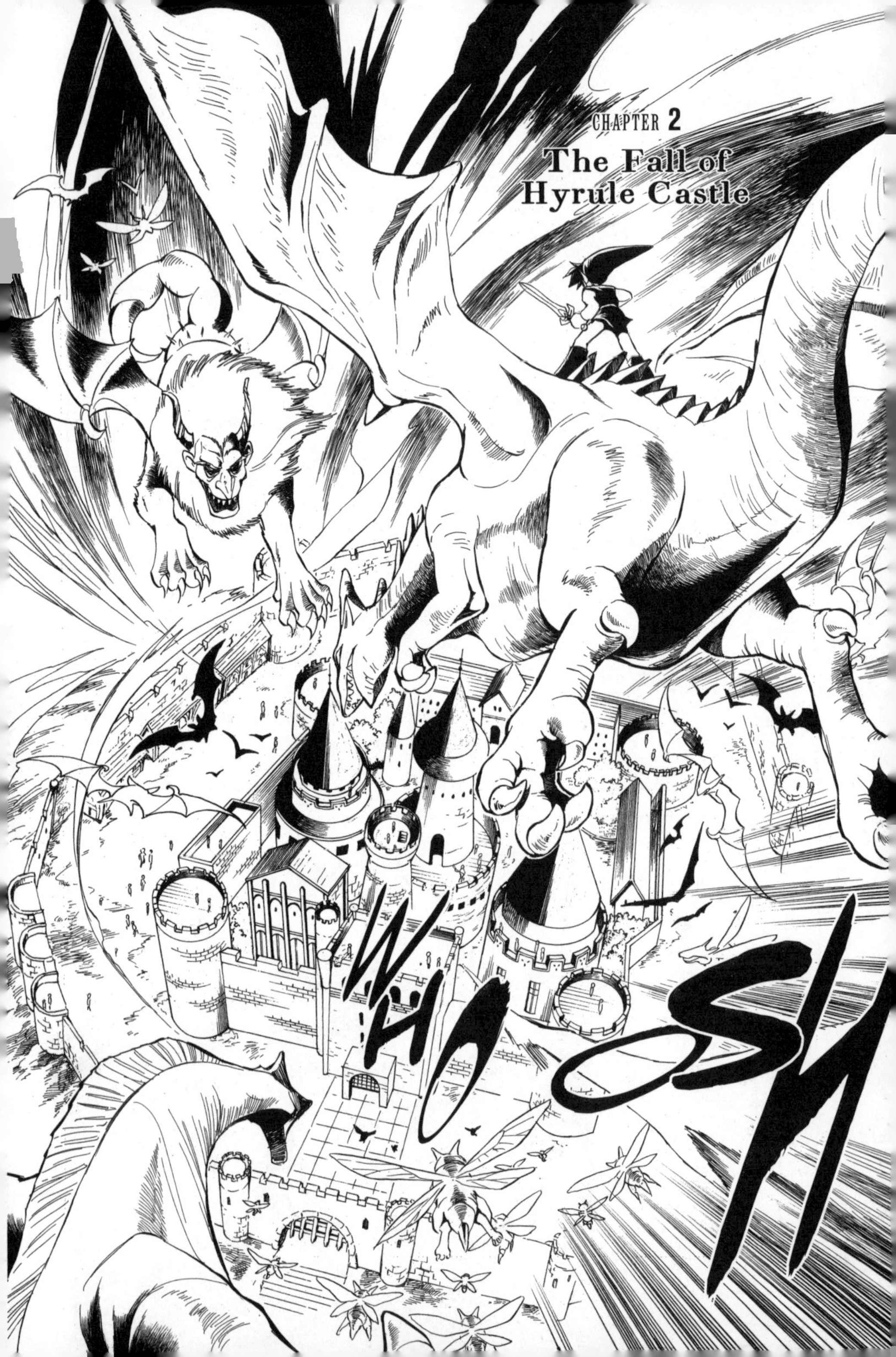
CHAPTER 2
The Fall of Hyrule Castle
WHOOSH

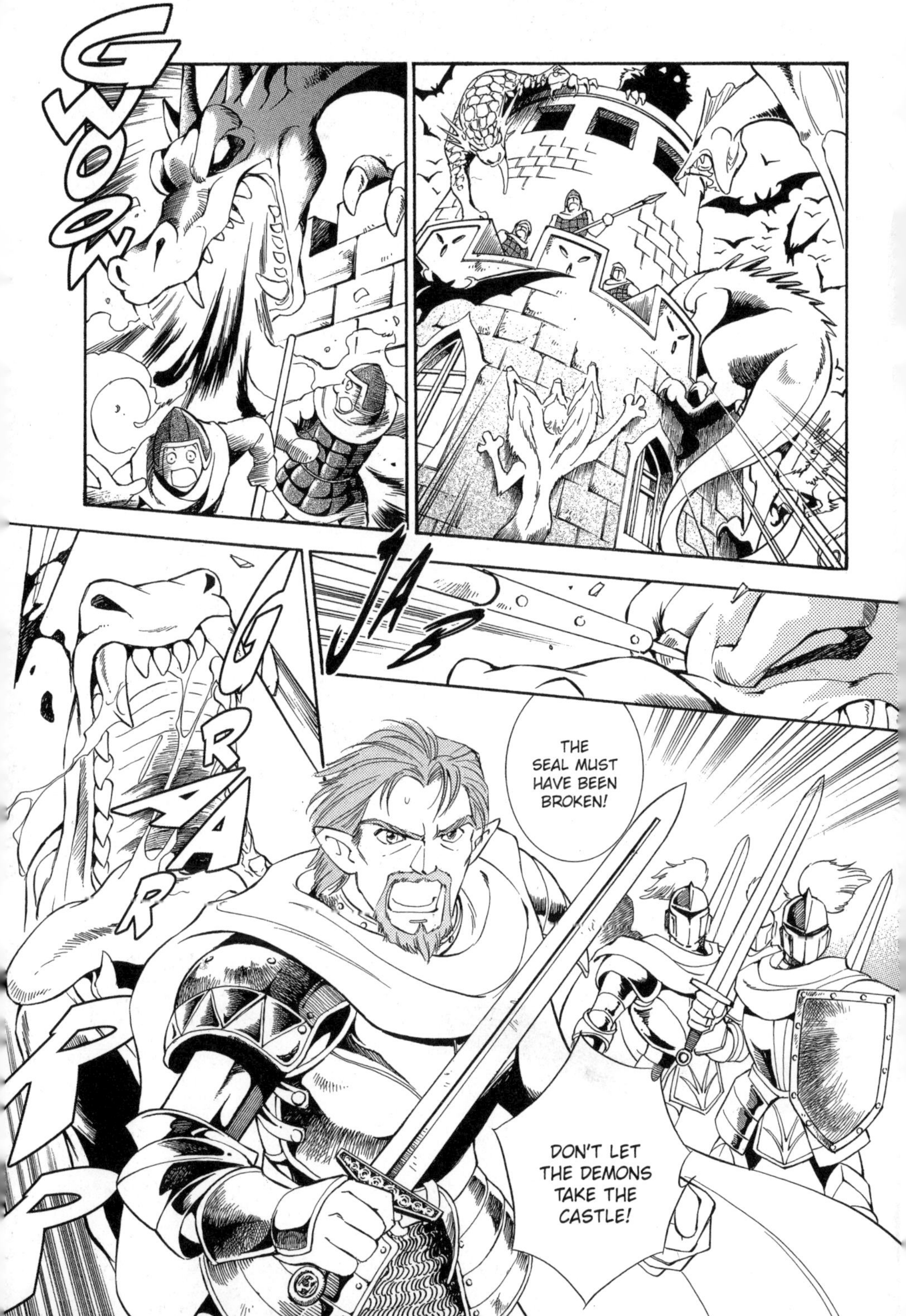
GWOOW
JAB
THE SEAL MUST HAVE BEEN BROKEN!
GRAARRR
DON'T LET THE DEMONS TAKE THE CASTLE!

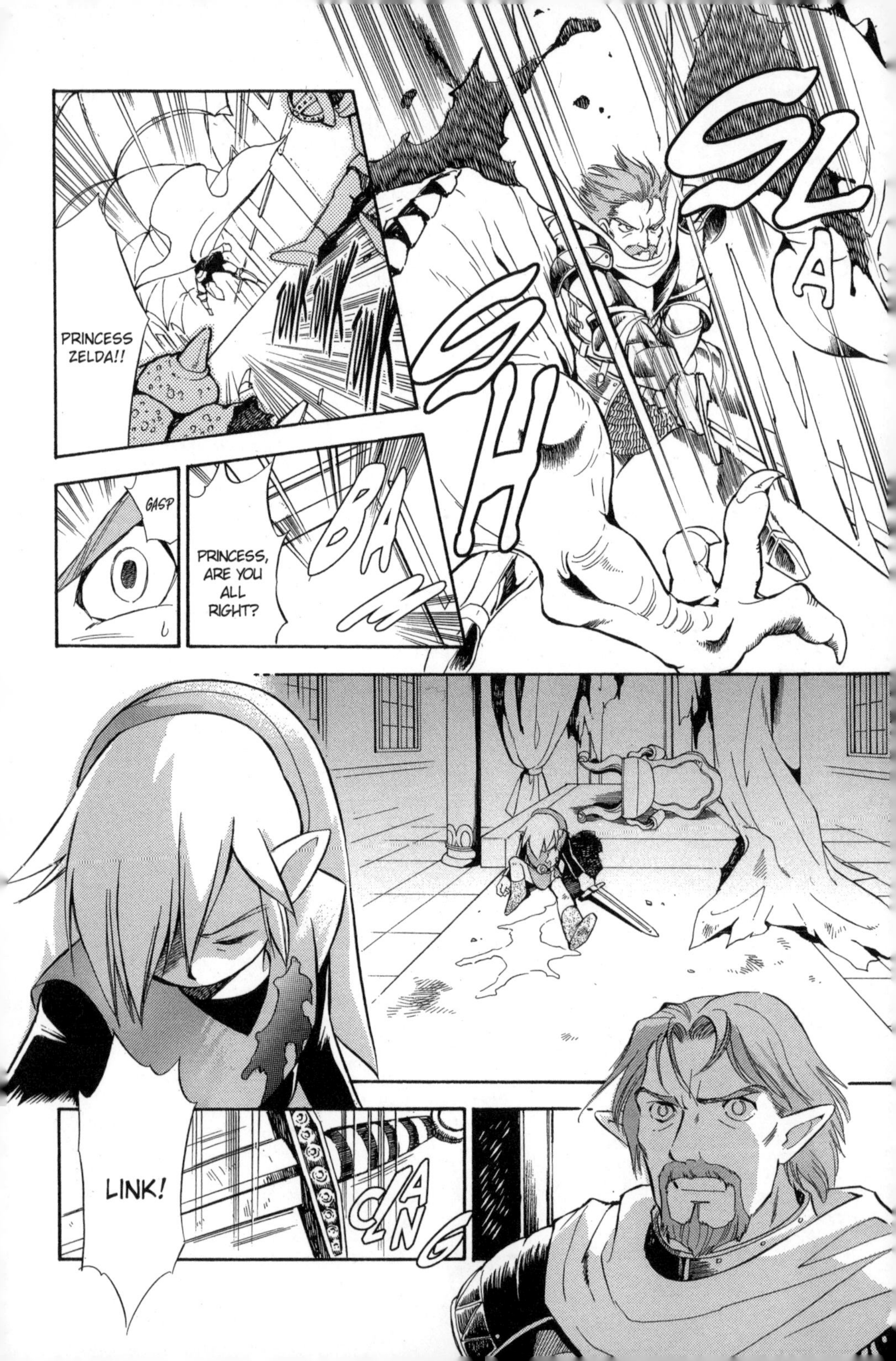
SLASH
PRINCESS ZELDA!!
BAM
PRINCESS, ARE YOU ALL RIGHT?
GASP
CLANG
LINK!

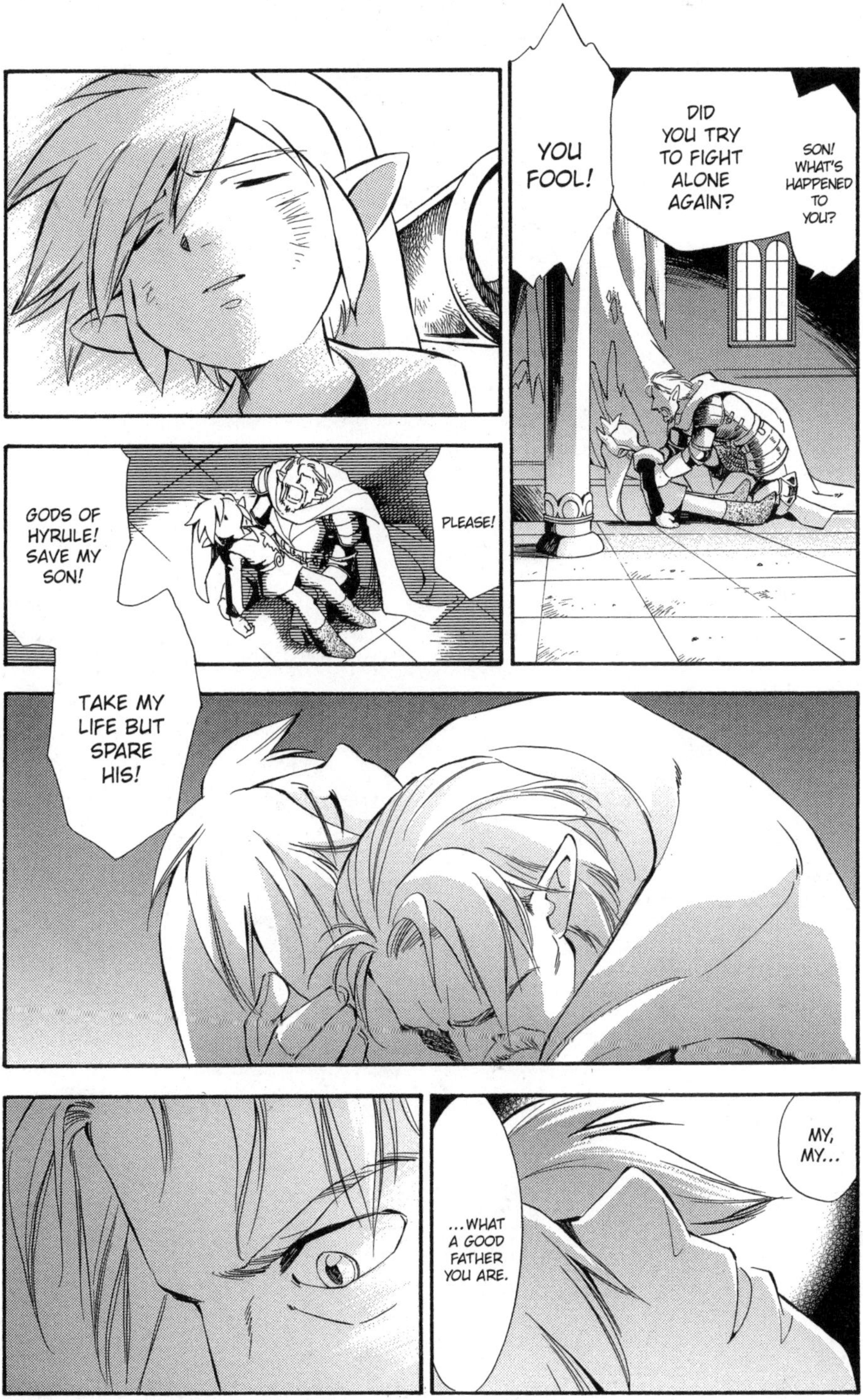
SON! WHAT'S HAPPENED TO YOU?
DID YOU TRY TO FIGHT ALONE AGAIN?
YOU FOOL!
PLEASE!
GODS OF HYRULE! SAVE MY SON!
TAKE MY LIFE BUT SPARE HIS!
MY, MY...
...WHAT A GOOD FATHER YOU ARE.

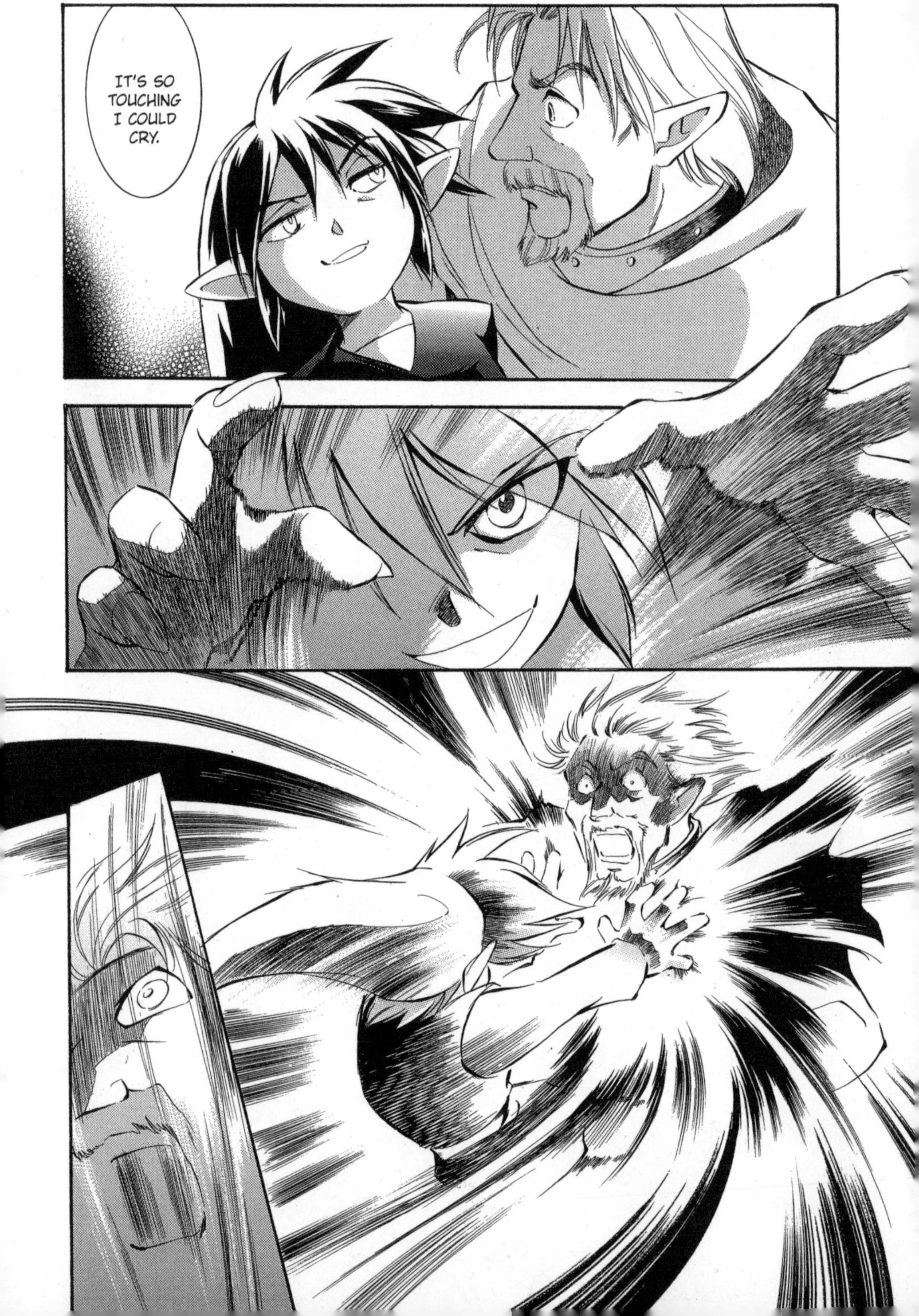
IT'S SO TOUCHING I COULD CRY.

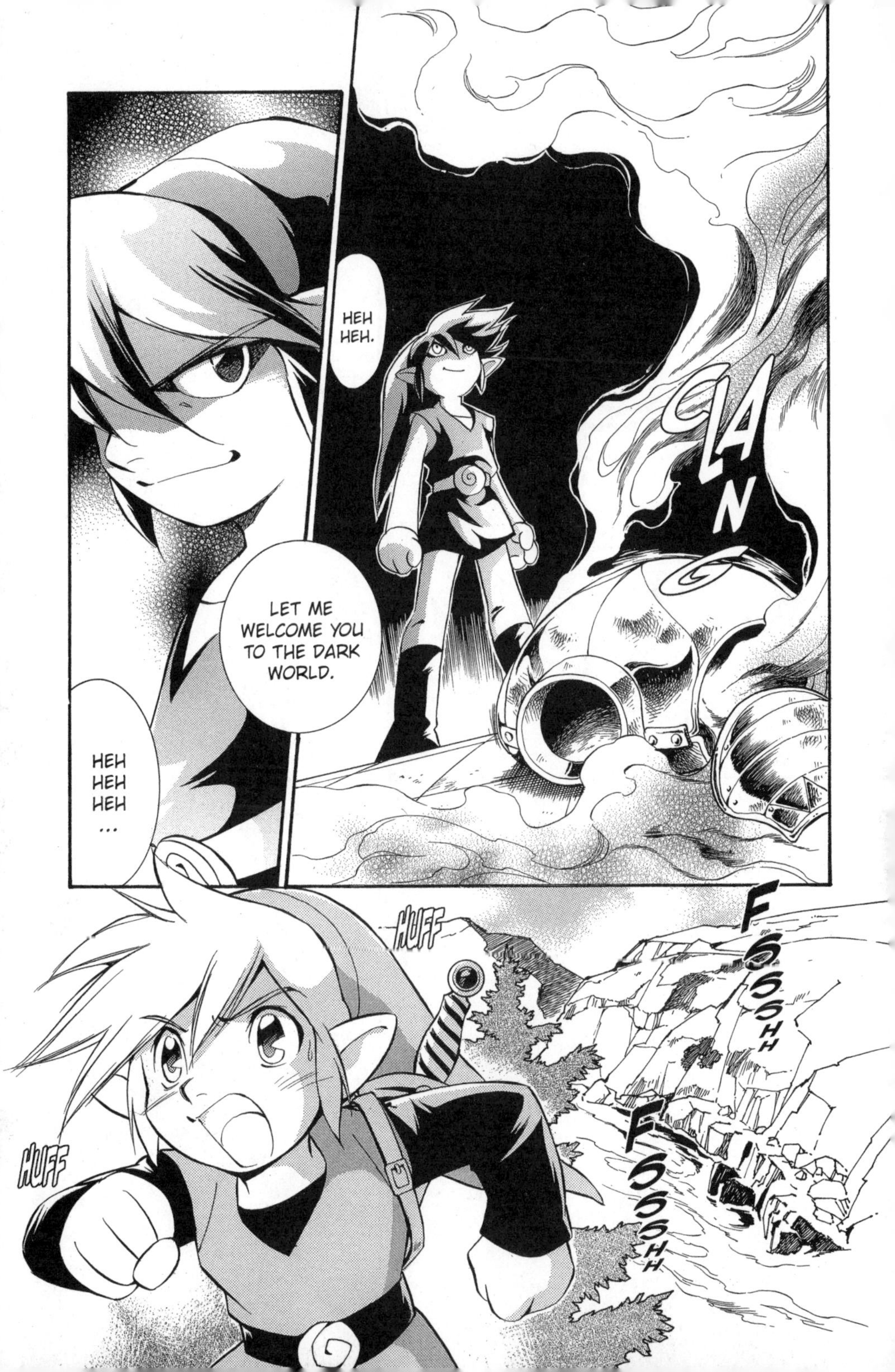
CLANG
HEH HEH.
LET ME WELCOME YOU TO THE DARK WORLD.
HEH HEH HEH ...
FSSSHH
FSSSHH
HUFF
HUFF

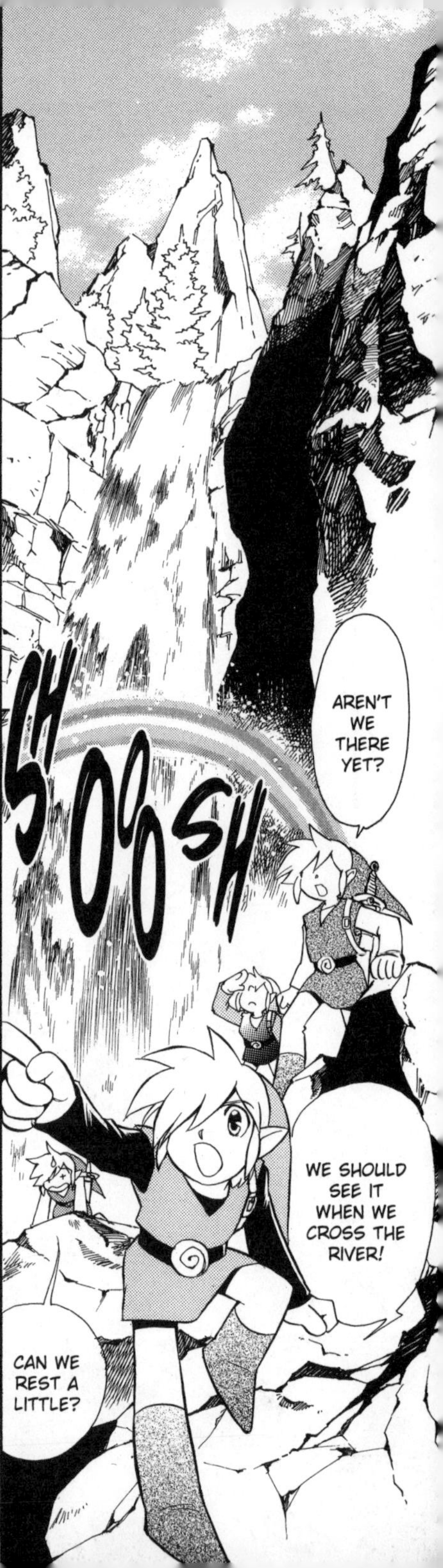
SCHOOOOSH
AREN'T WE THERE YET?
WE SHOULD SEE IT WHEN WE CROSS THE RIVER!
CAN WE REST A LITTLE?

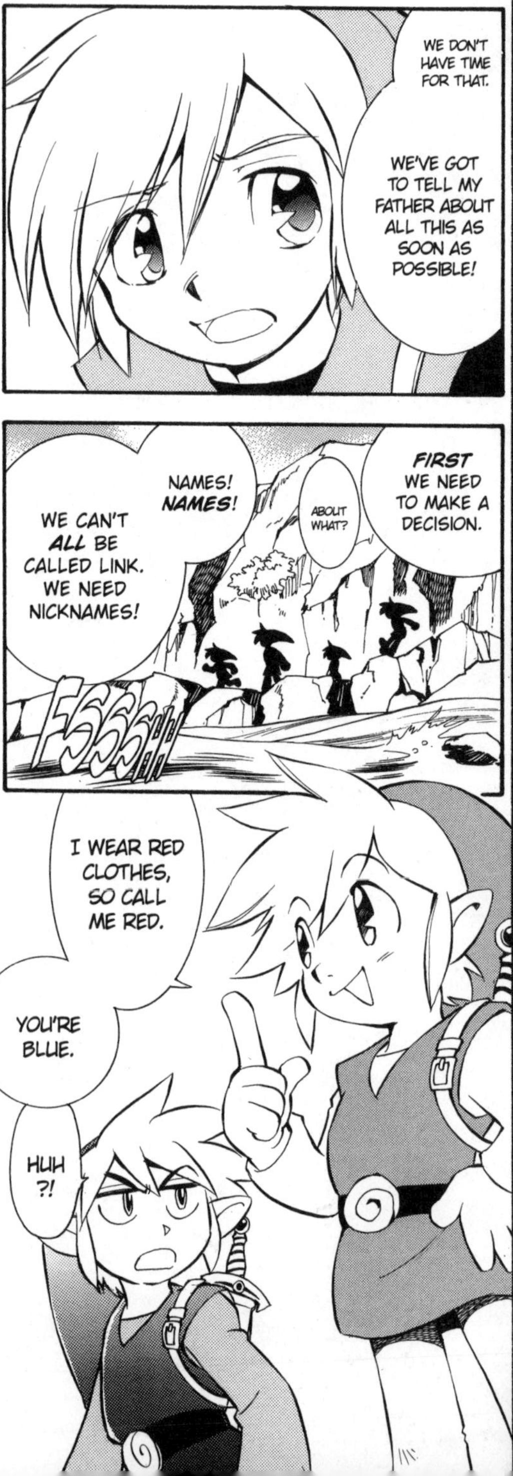
WE DON'T HAVE TIME FOR THAT.
WE'VE GOT TO TELL MY FATHER ABOUT ALL THIS AS SOON AS POSSIBLE!
FIRST WE NEED TO MAKE A DECISION.
ABOUT WHAT?
NAMES! *NAMES*!
WE CAN'T *ALL* BE CALLED LINK. WE NEED NICKNAMES!
FSSSSHHH
I WEAR RED CLOTHES, SO CALL ME RED.
YOU'RE BLUE.
HUH?!

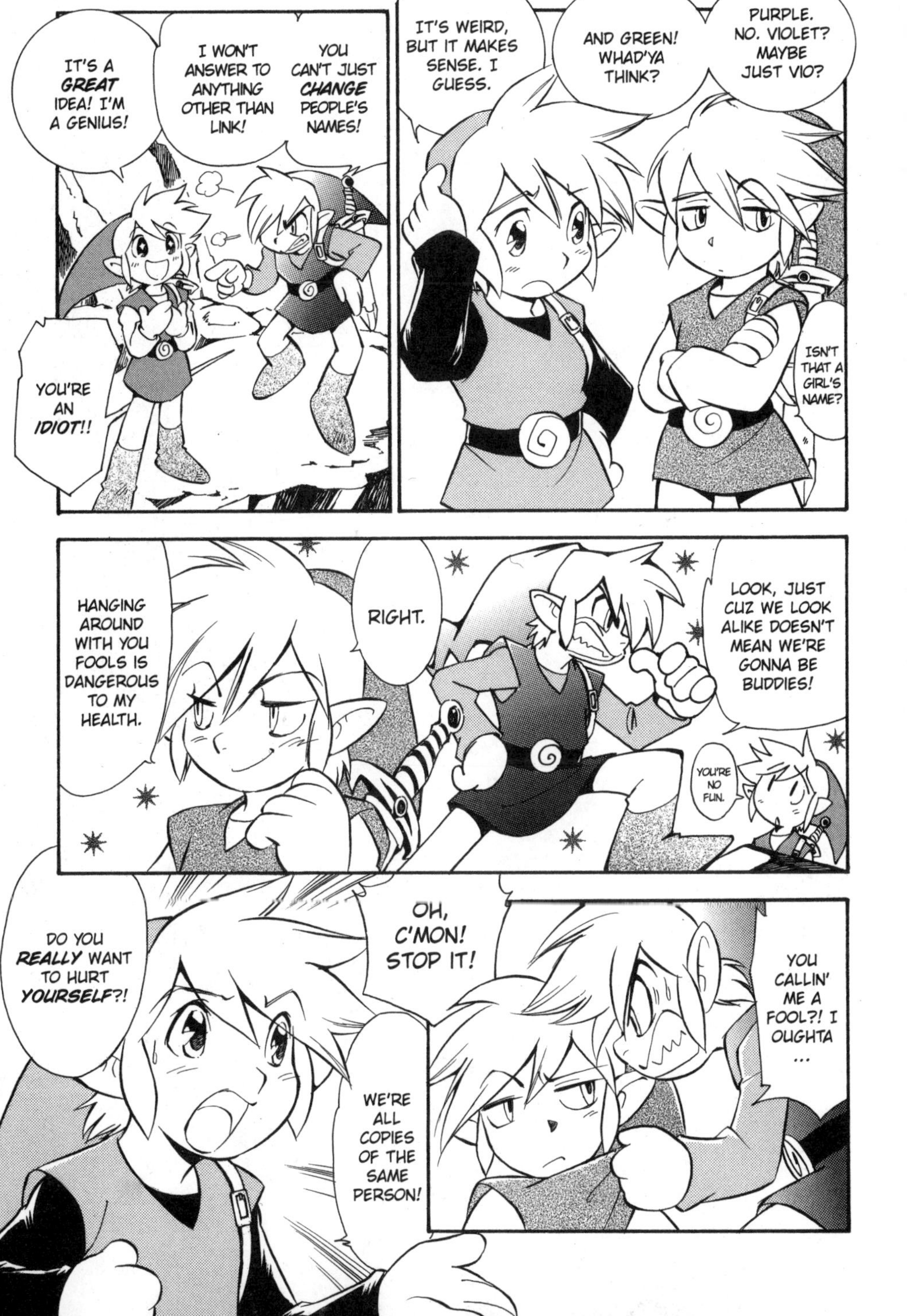
PURPLE. NO. VIOLET? MAYBE JUST VIO?
AND GREEN! WHAD'YA THINK?
IT'S WEIRD, BUT IT MAKES SENSE. I GUESS.
ISN'T THAT A GIRL'S NAME?
YOU CAN'T JUST CHANGE PEOPLE'S NAMES!
I WON'T ANSWER TO ANYTHING OTHER THAN LINK!
IT'S A GREAT IDEA! I'M A GENIUS!
YOU'RE AN IDIOT!!
LOOK, JUST CUZ WE LOOK ALIKE DOESN'T MEAN WE'RE GONNA BE BUDDIES!
YOU'RE NO FUN.
RIGHT.
HANGING AROUND WITH YOU FOOLS IS DANGEROUS TO MY HEALTH.
YOU CALLIN' ME A FOOL?! I OUGHTA ...
OH, C'MON! STOP IT!
WE'RE ALL COPIES OF THE SAME PERSON!
DO YOU REALLY WANT TO HURT YOURSELF?!

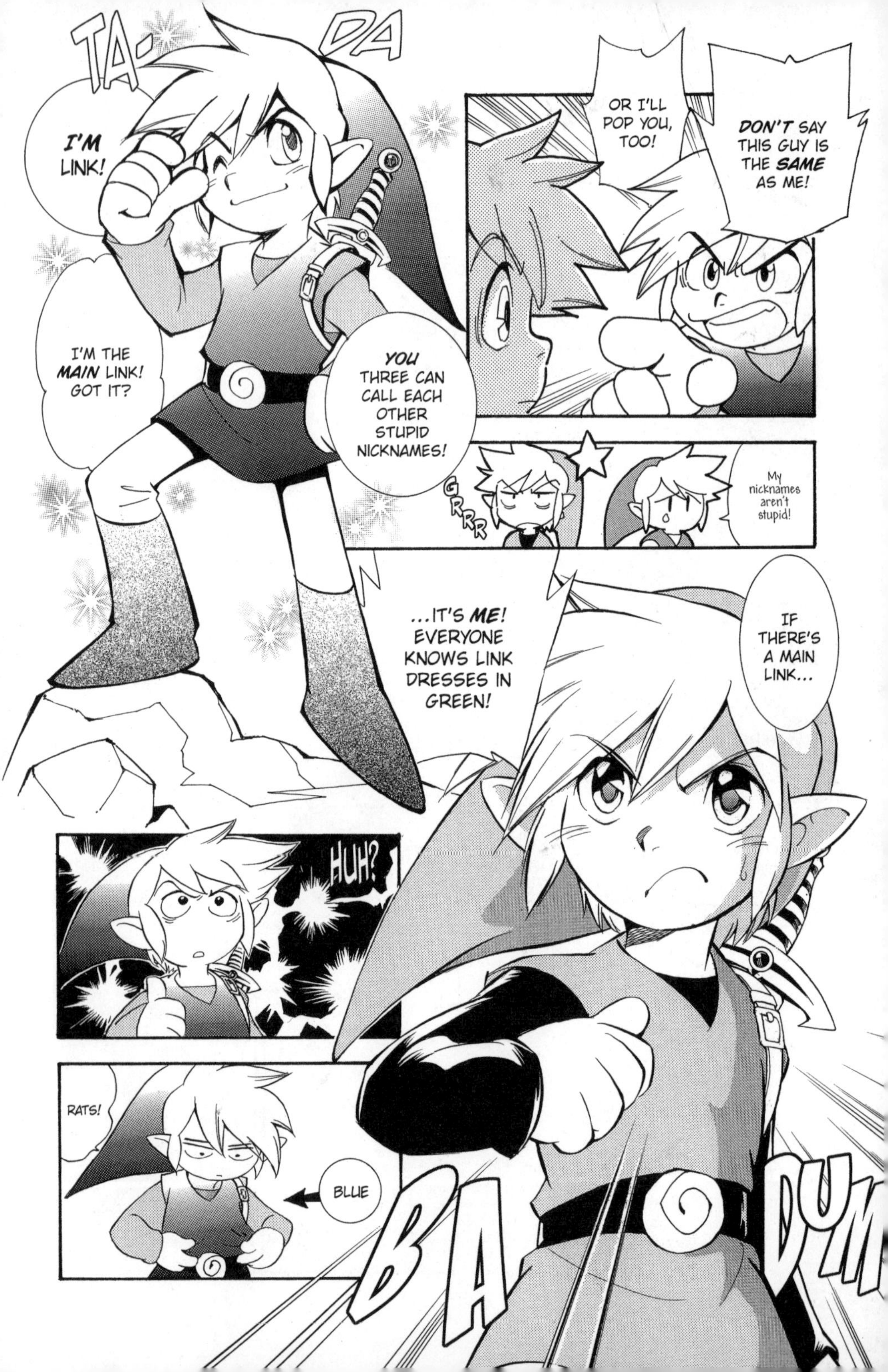
DON'T SAY THIS GUY IS THE SAME AS ME!
OR I'LL POP YOU, TOO!
My nicknames aren't stupid!
GRRR
TA-DA
I'M LINK!
I'M THE MAIN LINK! GOT IT?
YOU THREE CAN CALL EACH OTHER STUPID NICKNAMES!
IF THERE'S A MAIN LINK...
...IT'S ME! EVERYONE KNOWS LINK DRESSES IN GREEN!
BA-DUM
HUH?
RATS!
BLUE

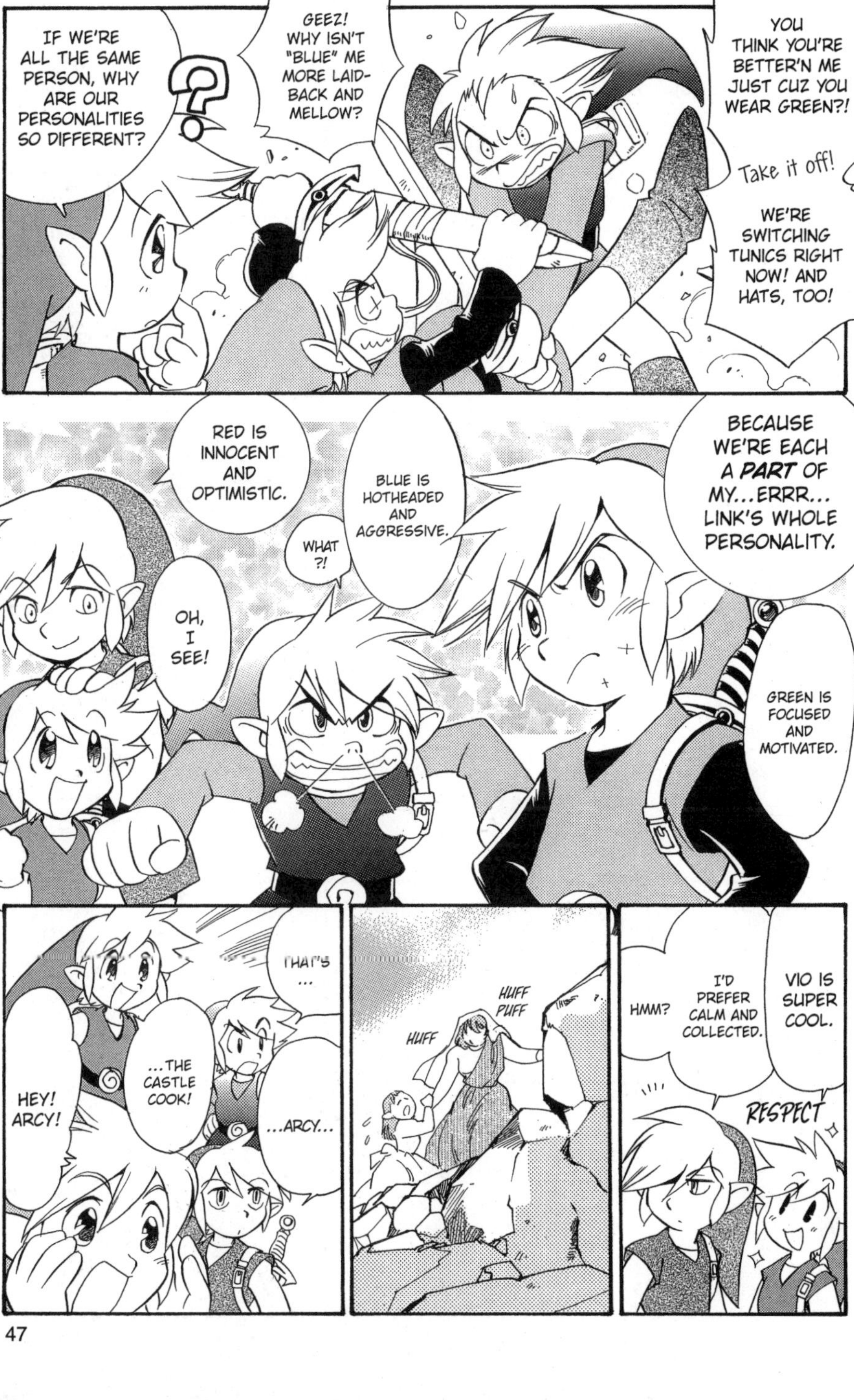
YOU THINK YOU'RE BETTER'N ME JUST CUZ YOU WEAR GREEN?!
Take it off!
WE'RE SWITCHING TUNICS RIGHT NOW! AND HATS, TOO!
GEEZ! WHY ISN'T "BLUE" ME MORE LAID-BACK AND MELLOW?
IF WE'RE ALL THE SAME PERSON, WHY ARE OUR PERSONALITIES SO DIFFERENT?
BECAUSE WE'RE EACH A **PART** OF MY...ERRR... LINK'S WHOLE PERSONALITY.
GREEN IS FOCUSED AND MOTIVATED.
BLUE IS HOTHEADED AND AGGRESSIVE.
WHAT?!
RED IS INNOCENT AND OPTIMISTIC.
OH, I SEE!
VIO IS SUPER COOL.
I'D PREFER CALM AND COLLECTED.
HMM?
RESPECT
HUFF PUFF
HUFF
THAT'S ...
...ARCY...
...THE CASTLE COOK!
HEY! ARCY!

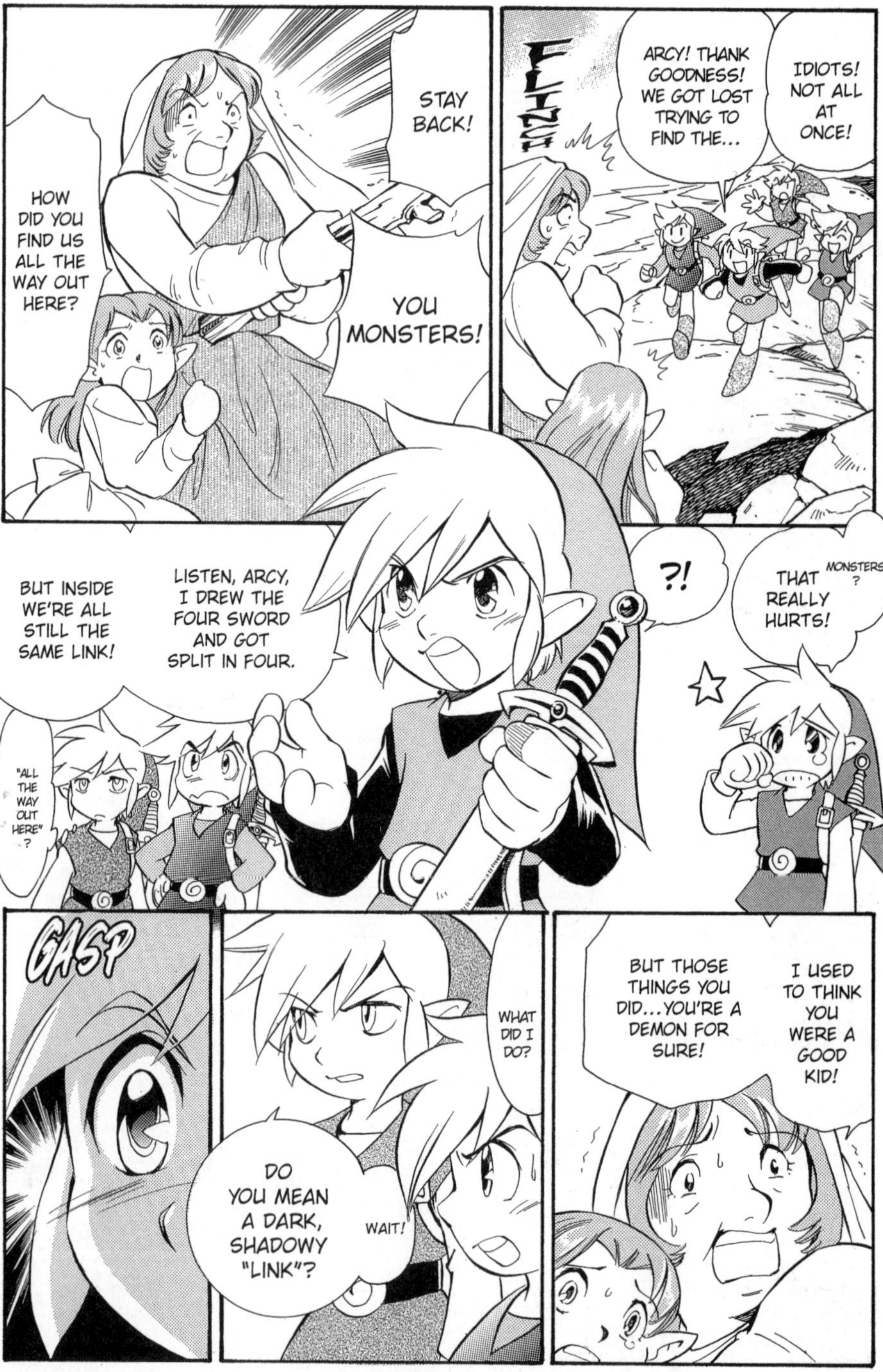

FLINCH
IDIOTS! NOT ALL AT ONCE!
ARCY! THANK GOODNESS! WE GOT LOST TRYING TO FIND THE...
STAY BACK!
YOU MONSTERS!
HOW DID YOU FIND US ALL THE WAY OUT HERE?
?!
MONSTERS?
THAT REALLY HURTS!
LISTEN, ARCY, I DREW THE FOUR SWORD AND GOT SPLIT IN FOUR.
BUT INSIDE WE'RE ALL STILL THE SAME LINK!
"ALL THE WAY OUT HERE"?
I USED TO THINK YOU WERE A GOOD KID!
BUT THOSE THINGS YOU DID...YOU'RE A DEMON FOR SURE!
WHAT DID I DO?
WAIT!
DO YOU MEAN A DARK, SHADOWY "LINK"?
GASP

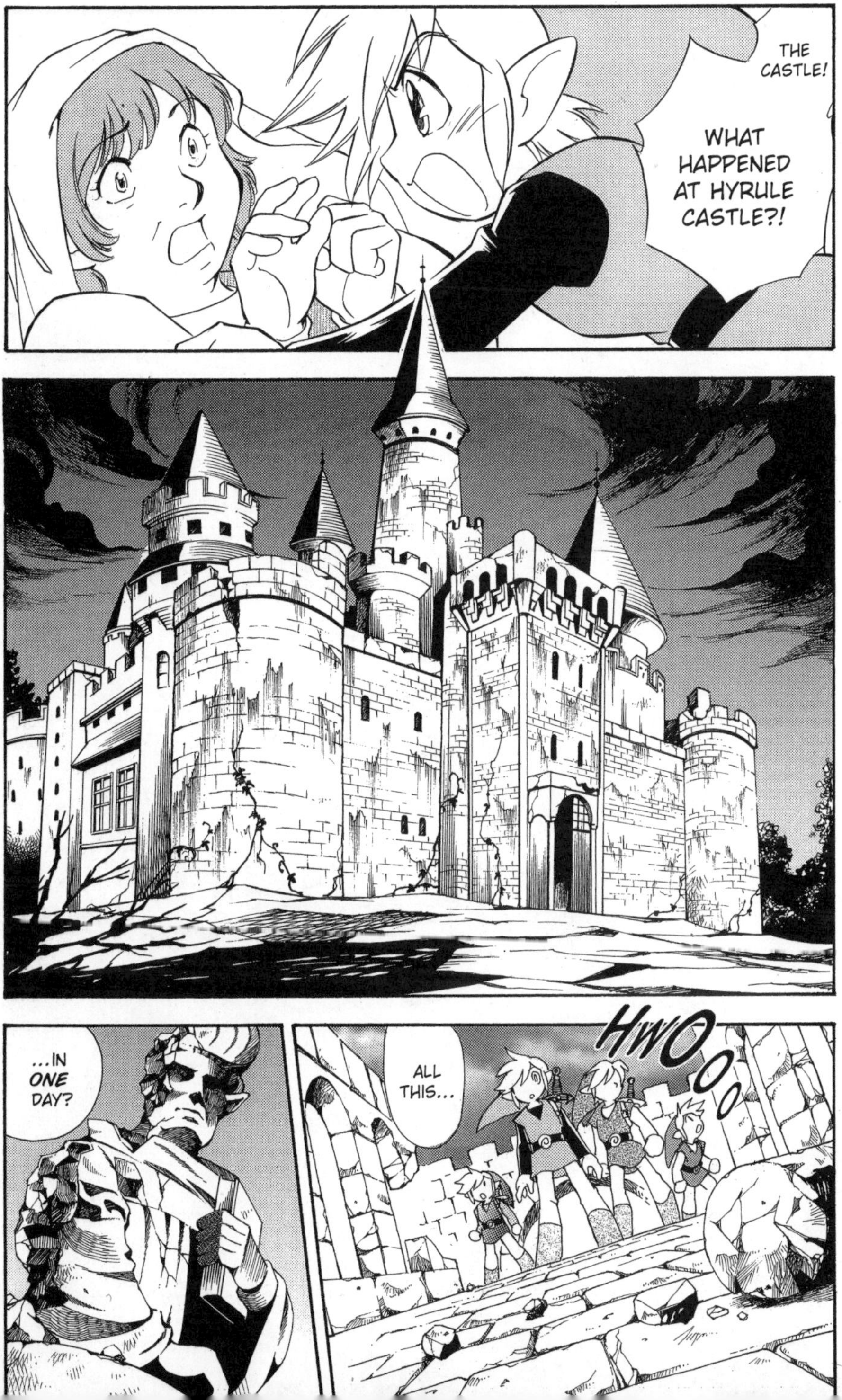
THE CASTLE!
WHAT HAPPENED AT HYRULE CASTLE?!
HWOOOO
ALL THIS...
...IN ONE DAY?

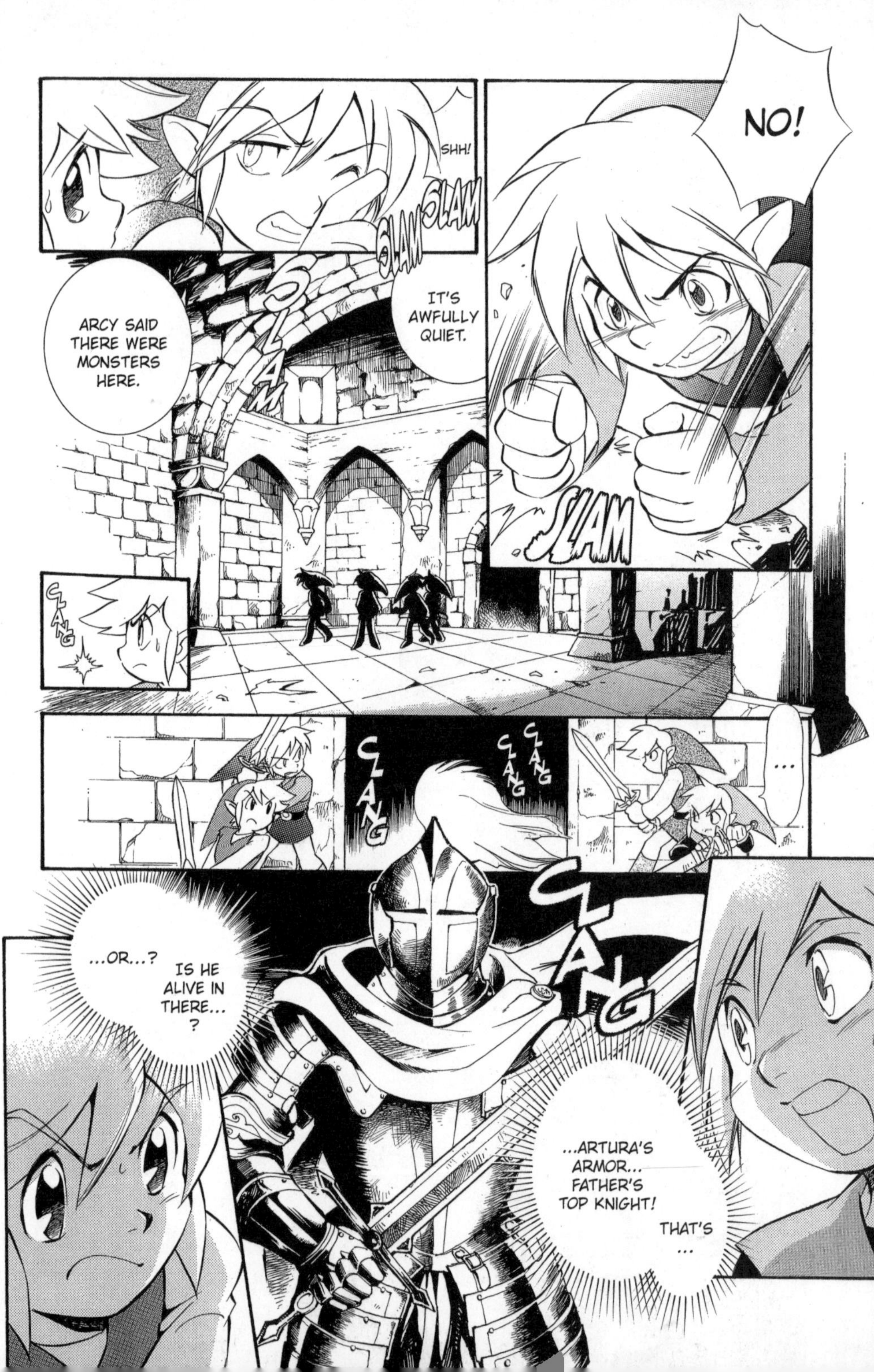
NO!
SLAM
SHH!
SLAM SLAM
SLAM
IT'S AWFULLY QUIET.
ARCY SAID THERE WERE MONSTERS HERE.
CLANG
...
CLANG CLANG CLANG
CLANG
THAT'S ...
...ARTURA'S ARMOR... FATHER'S TOP KNIGHT!
IS HE ALIVE IN THERE... ?
...OR...?

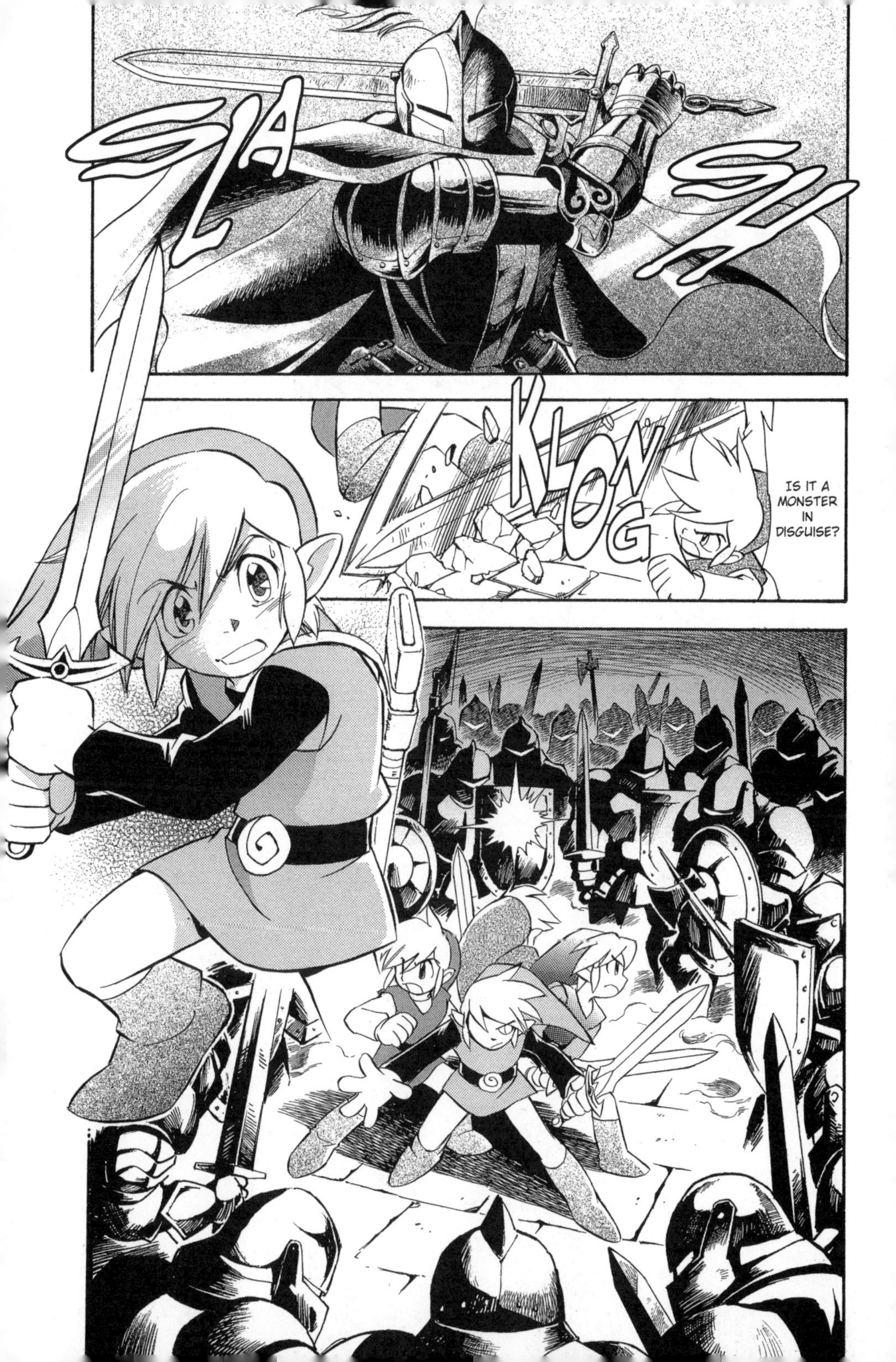
SLASH
IS IT A MONSTER IN DISGUISE?
KLONG

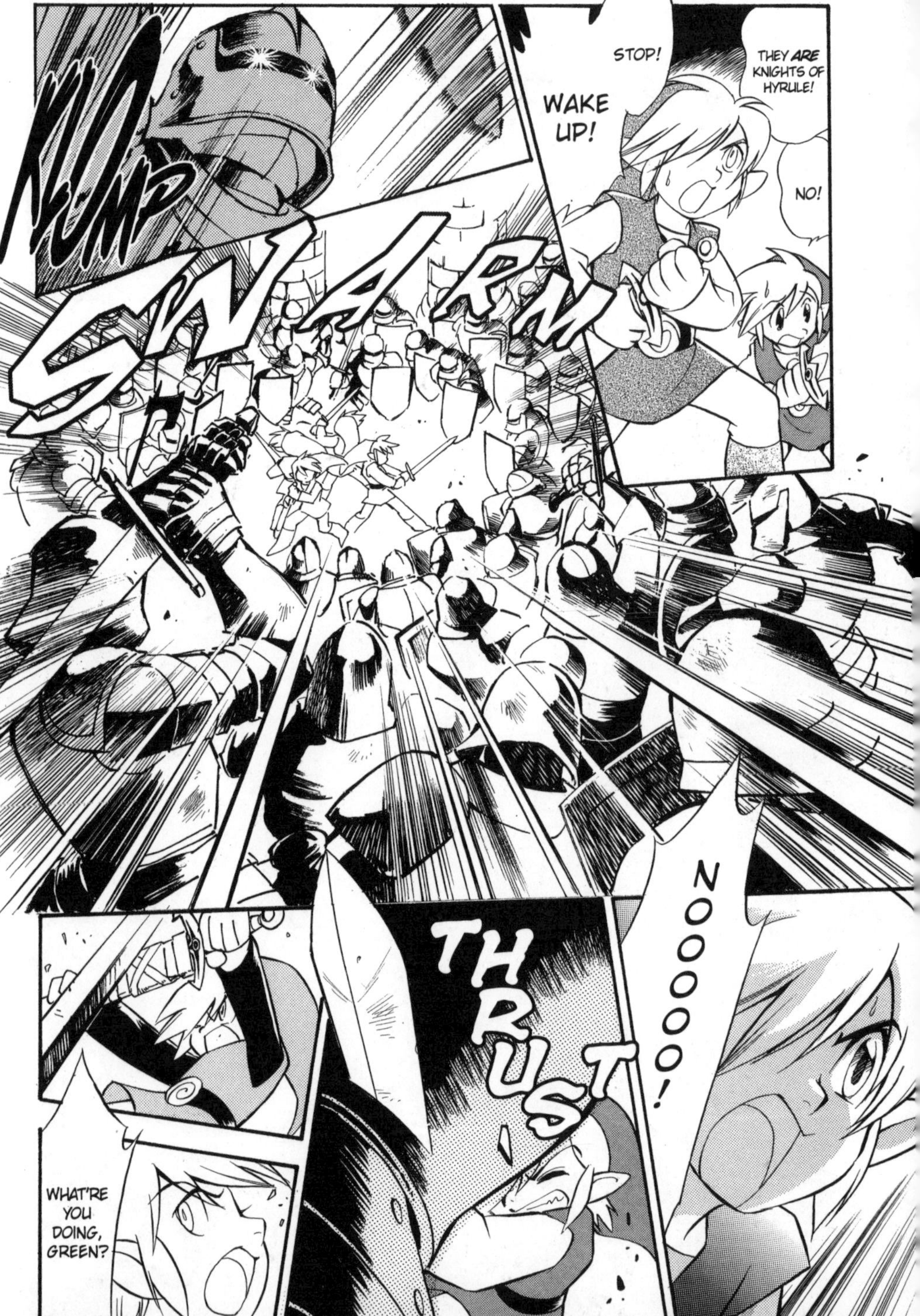

THEY *ARE* KNIGHTS OF HYRULE!
STOP!
WAKE UP!
NO!
KLUMP
SWARM
NOOOOOO!
THRUST
WHAT'RE YOU DOING, GREEN?

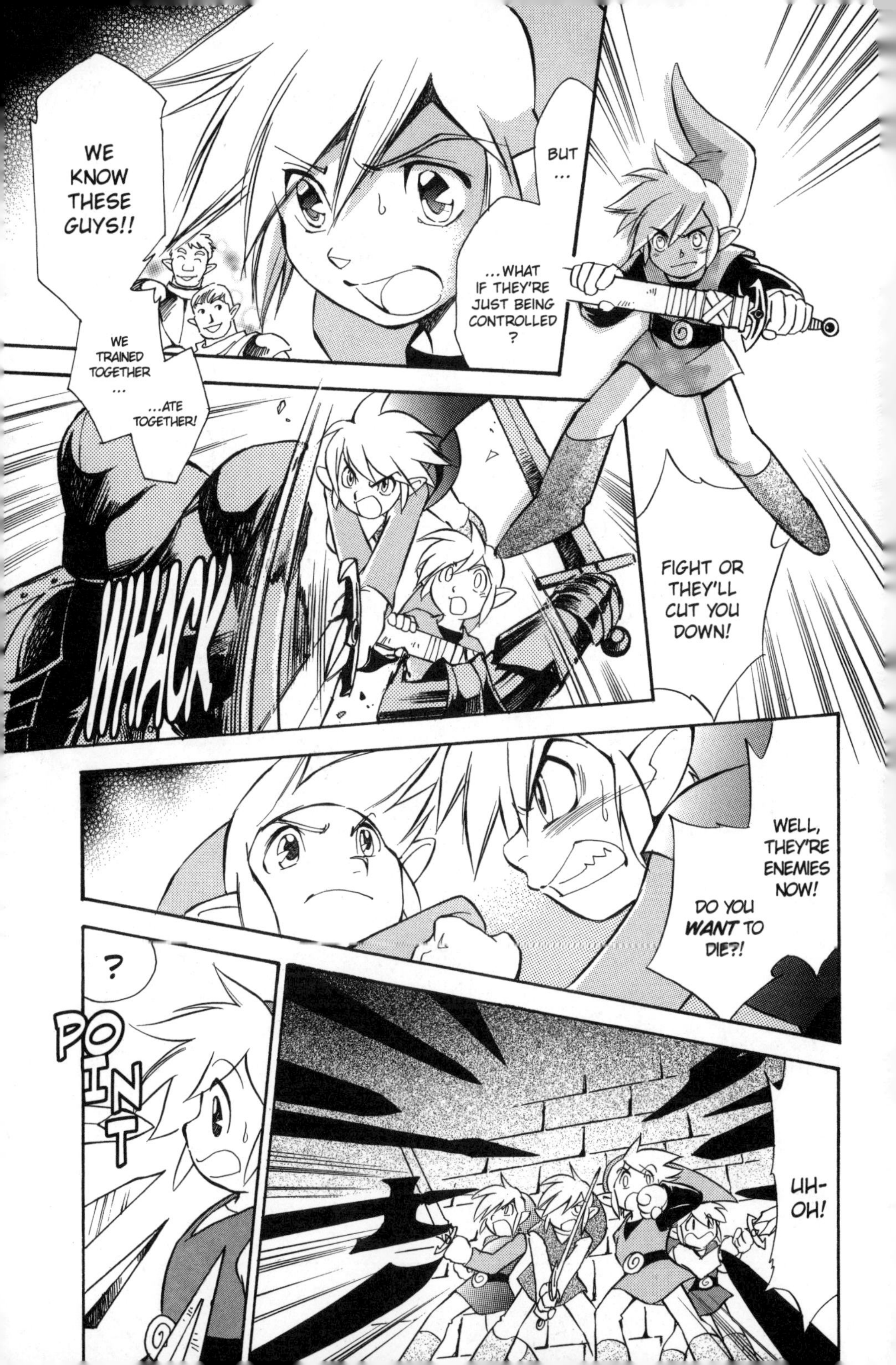
BUT ...
...WHAT IF THEY'RE JUST BEING CONTROLLED?
WE KNOW THESE GUYS!!
WE TRAINED TOGETHER ...
...ATE TOGETHER!
FIGHT OR THEY'LL CUT YOU DOWN!
WHACK
WELL, THEY'RE ENEMIES NOW!
DO YOU *WANT* TO DIE?!
UH-OH!
?
POINT

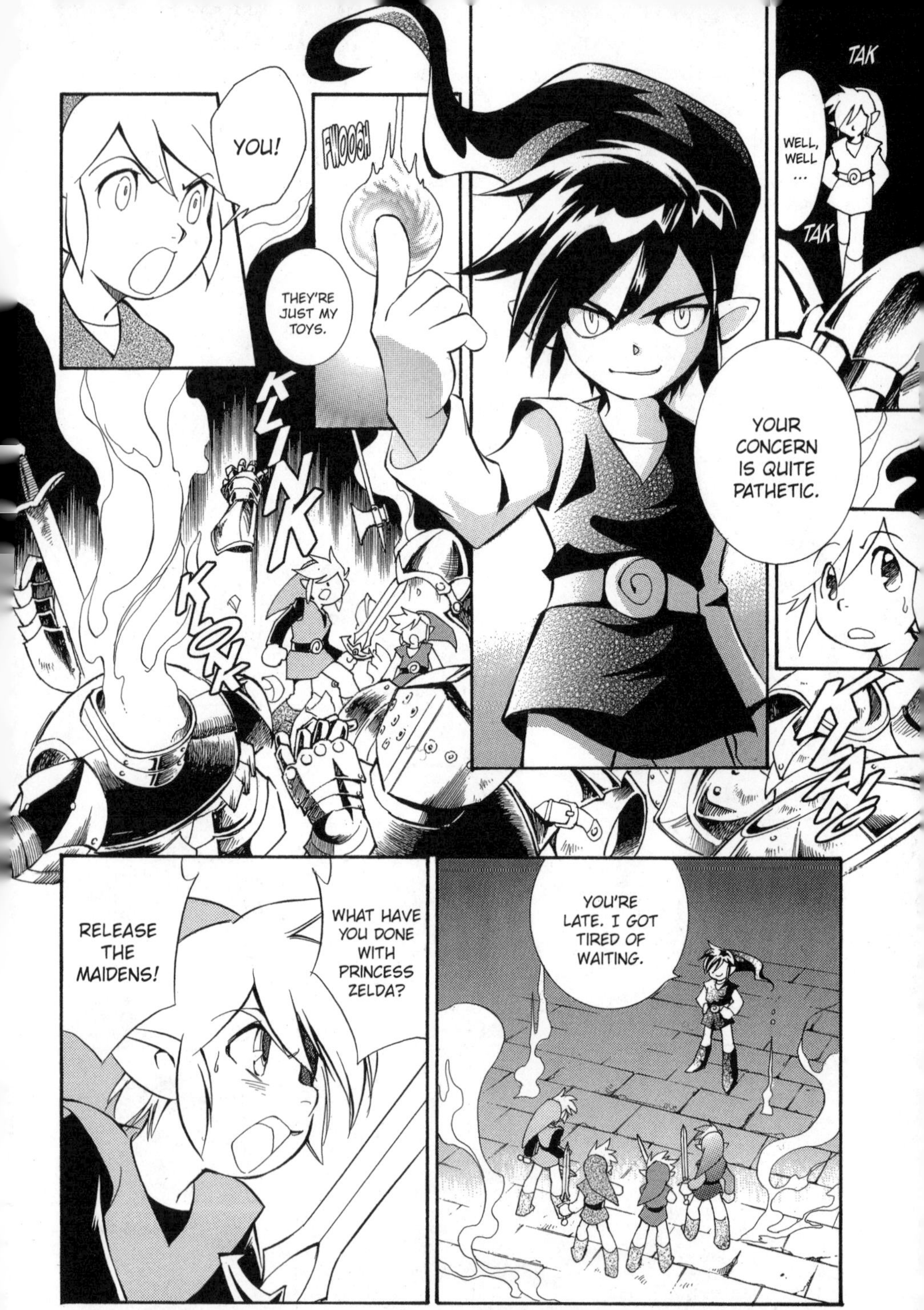
TAK
WELL, WELL ...
TAK
YOUR CONCERN IS QUITE PATHETIC.
FWOOSH
THEY'RE JUST MY TOYS.
YOU!
KLINK
KLOK
KLANG
YOU'RE LATE. I GOT TIRED OF WAITING.
WHAT HAVE YOU DONE WITH PRINCESS ZELDA?
RELEASE THE MAIDENS!

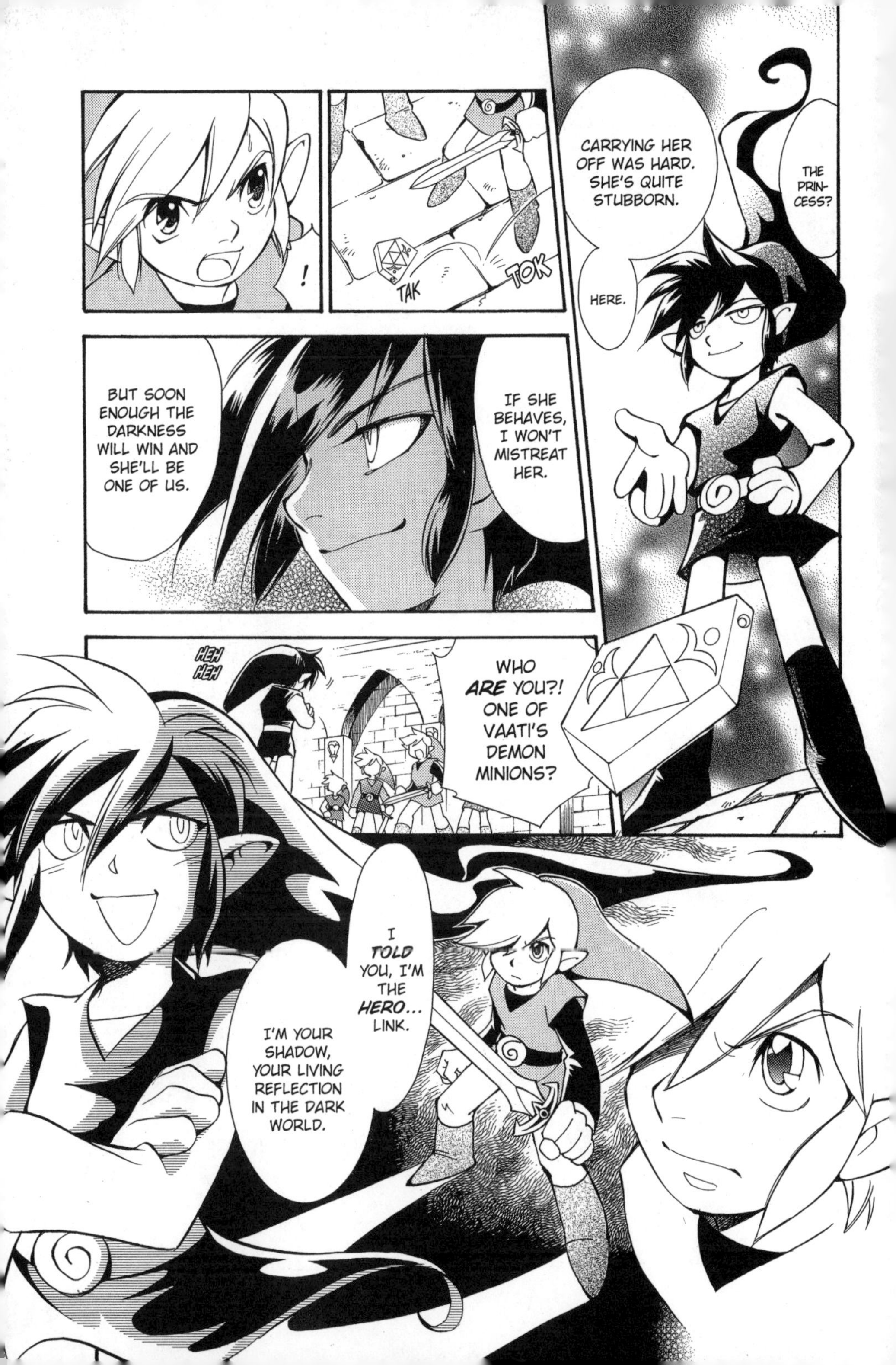
THE PRIN-CESS?
CARRYING HER OFF WAS HARD. SHE'S QUITE STUBBORN.
HERE.
TOK
TAK
!
IF SHE BEHAVES, I WON'T MISTREAT HER.
BUT SOON ENOUGH THE DARKNESS WILL WIN AND SHE'LL BE ONE OF US.
WHO **ARE** YOU?! ONE OF VAATI'S DEMON MINIONS?
HEH HEH
I **TOLD** YOU, I'M THE **HERO**... LINK.
I'M YOUR SHADOW, YOUR LIVING REFLECTION IN THE DARK WORLD.

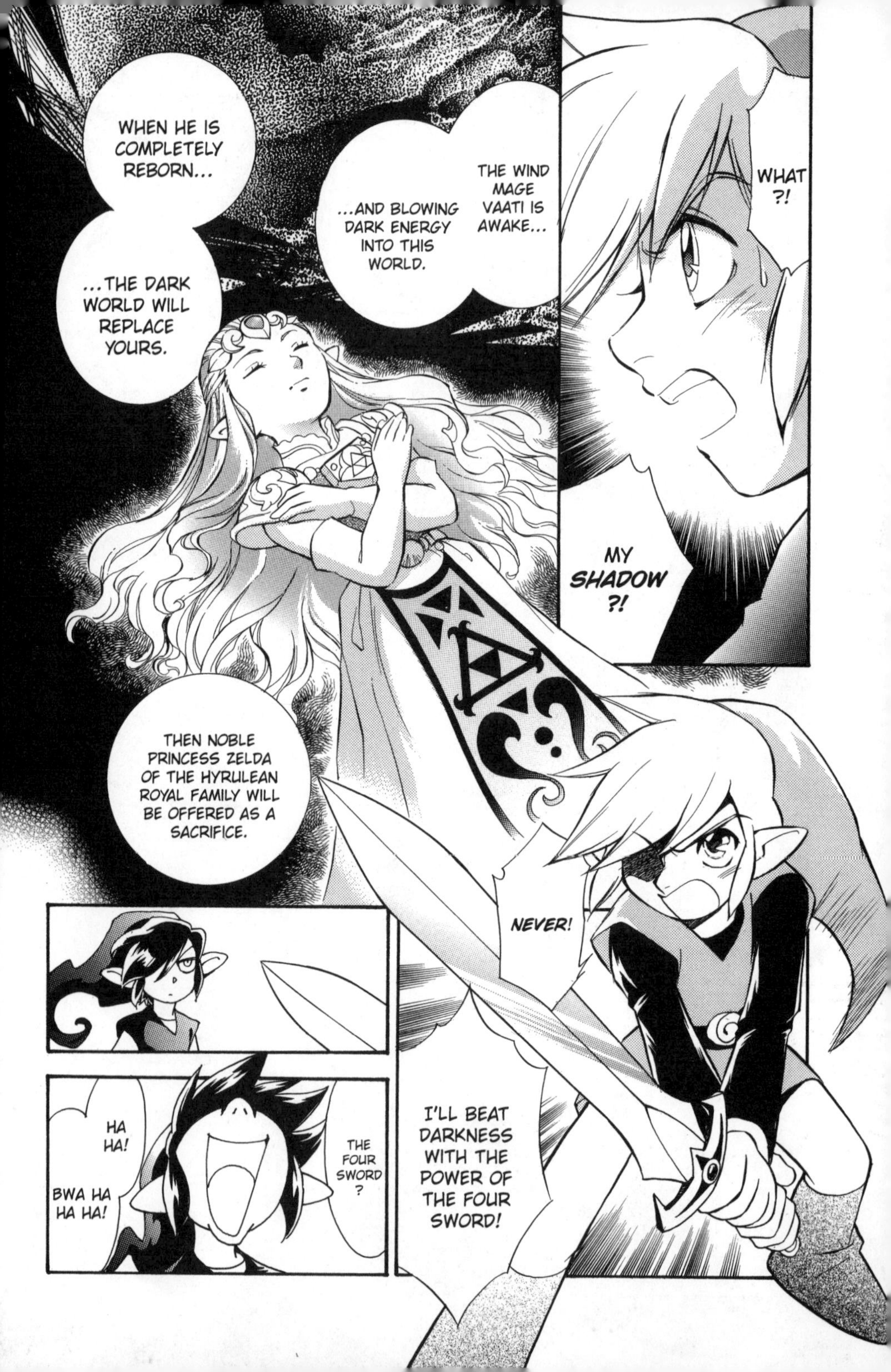
WHAT ?!
MY SHADOW ?!
THE WIND MAGE VAATI IS AWAKE...
...AND BLOWING DARK ENERGY INTO THIS WORLD.
WHEN HE IS COMPLETELY REBORN...
...THE DARK WORLD WILL REPLACE YOURS.
THEN NOBLE PRINCESS ZELDA OF THE HYRULEAN ROYAL FAMILY WILL BE OFFERED AS A SACRIFICE.
NEVER!
I'LL BEAT DARKNESS WITH THE POWER OF THE FOUR SWORD!
THE FOUR SWORD ?
HA HA!
BWA HA HA HA!

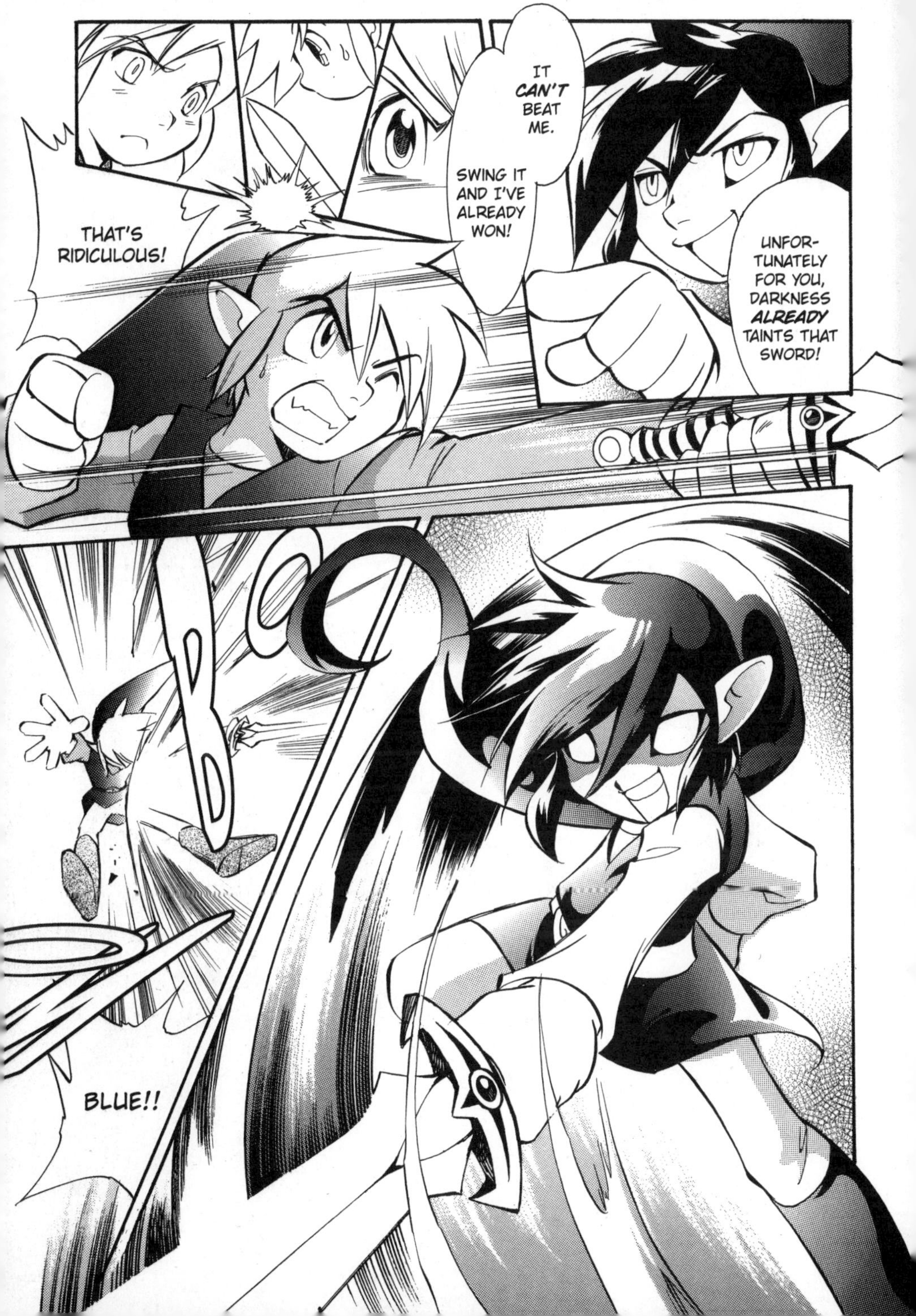
UNFOR-TUNATELY FOR YOU, DARKNESS ALREADY TAINTS THAT SWORD!
IT CAN'T BEAT ME.
SWING IT AND I'VE ALREADY WON!
THAT'S RIDICULOUS!
BLUE!!

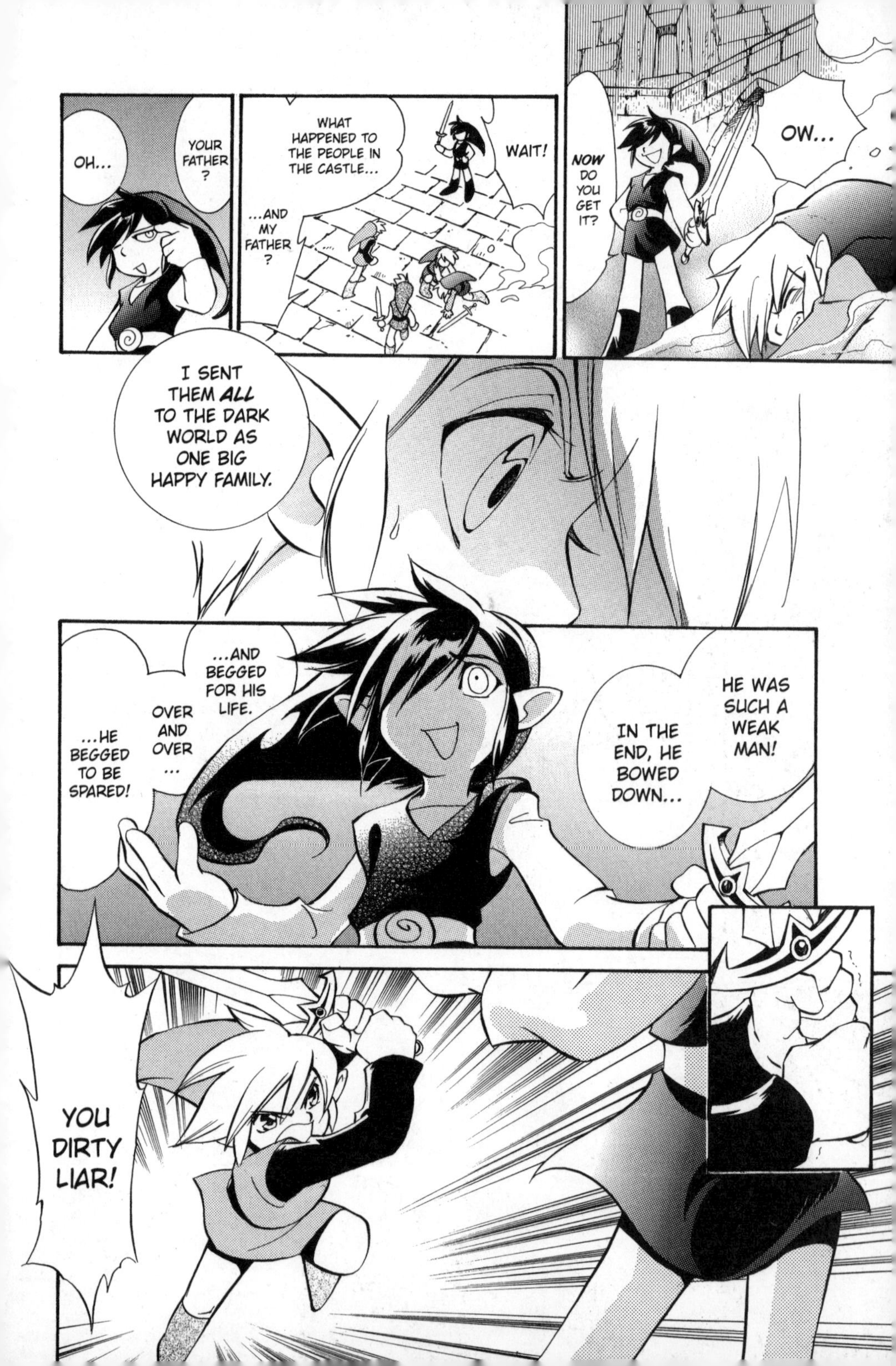
OW...
NOW DO YOU GET IT?
WAIT!
WHAT HAPPENED TO THE PEOPLE IN THE CASTLE...
...AND MY FATHER?
YOUR FATHER?
OH...
I SENT THEM ALL TO THE DARK WORLD AS ONE BIG HAPPY FAMILY.
HE WAS SUCH A WEAK MAN!
IN THE END, HE BOWED DOWN...
...AND BEGGED FOR HIS LIFE.
OVER AND OVER...
...HE BEGGED TO BE SPARED!
YOU DIRTY LIAR!

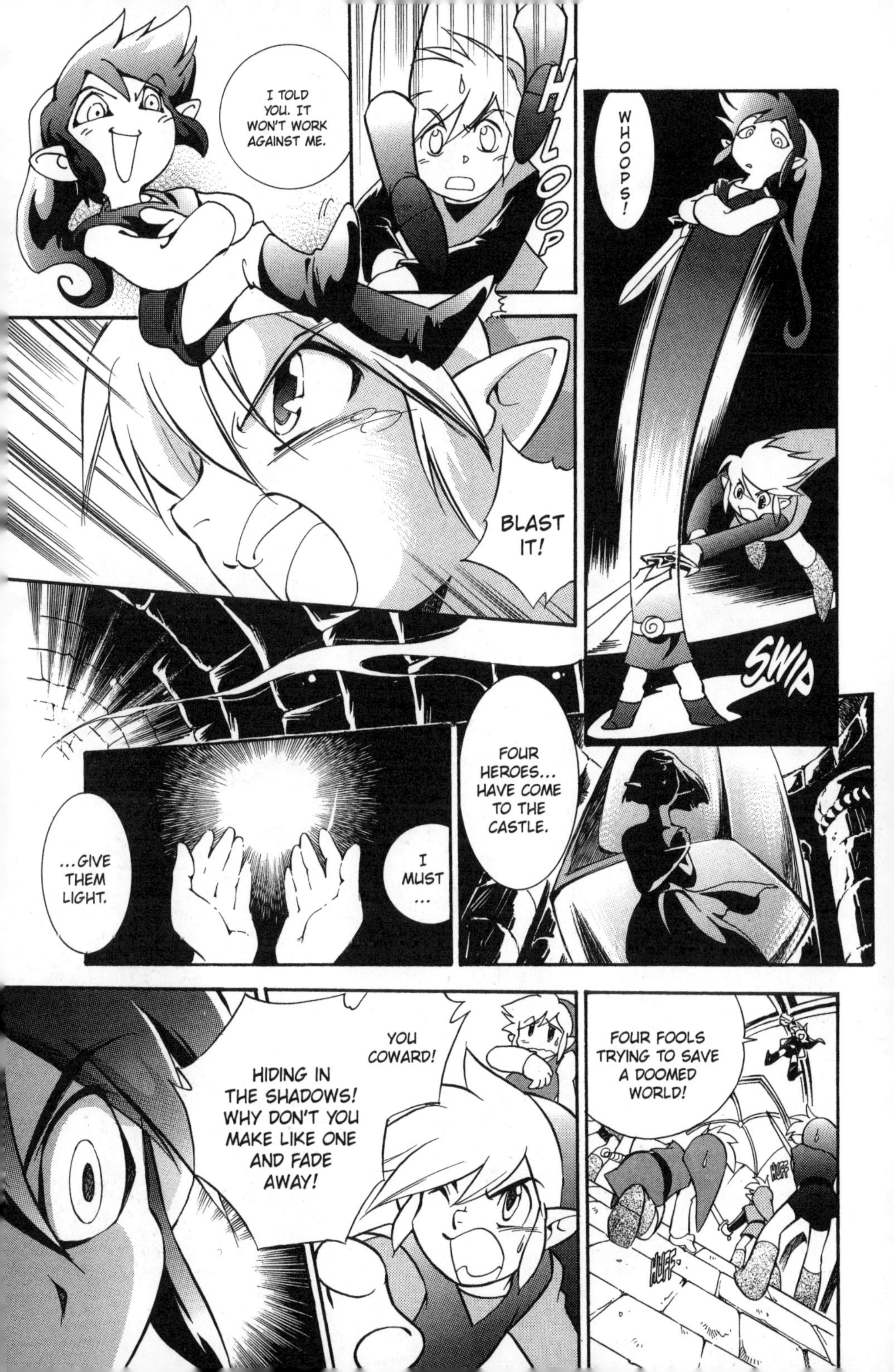
WHOOPS!
SWIP
HLOOOP
I TOLD YOU. IT WON'T WORK AGAINST ME.
BLAST IT!
FOUR HEROES... HAVE COME TO THE CASTLE.
I MUST ...
...GIVE THEM LIGHT.
FOUR FOOLS TRYING TO SAVE A DOOMED WORLD!
HUFF
HUFF
YOU COWARD!
HIDING IN THE SHADOWS! WHY DON'T YOU MAKE LIKE ONE AND FADE AWAY!

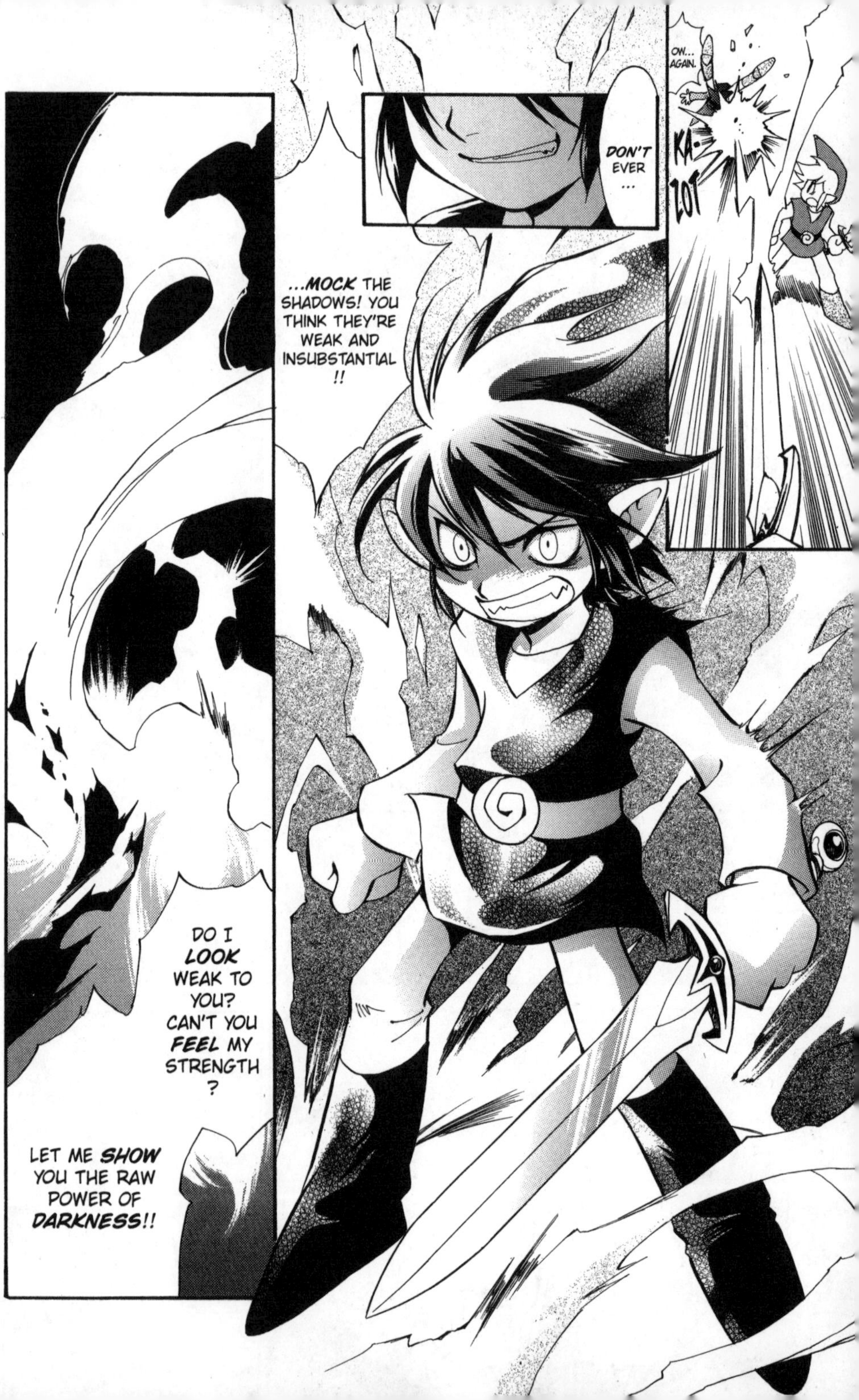
OW... AGAIN.
KA-ZOT
DON'T EVER ...
...MOCK THE SHADOWS! YOU THINK THEY'RE WEAK AND INSUBSTANTIAL !!
DO I LOOK WEAK TO YOU? CAN'T YOU FEEL MY STRENGTH ?
LET ME SHOW YOU THE RAW POWER OF DARKNESS!!

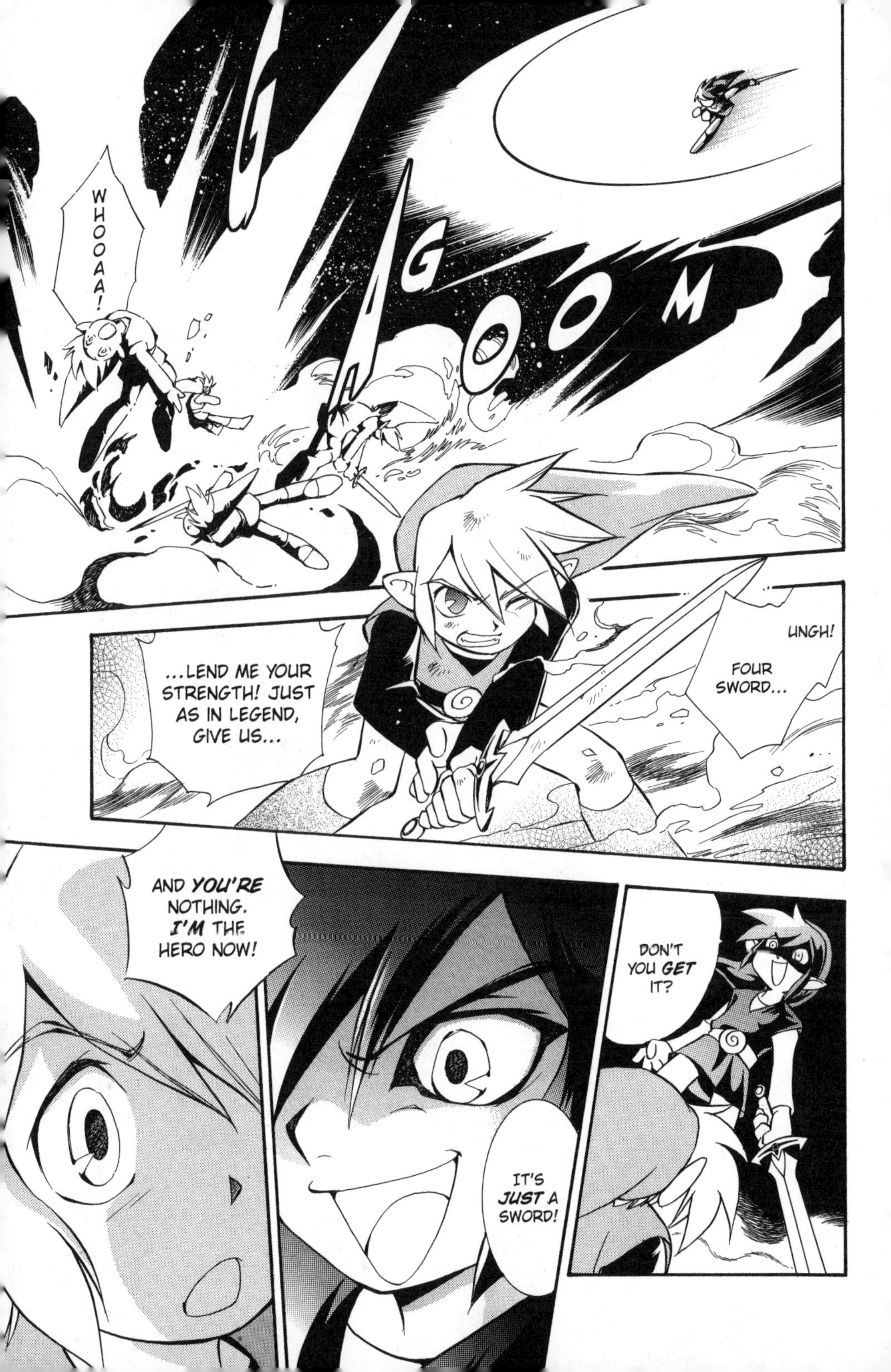
GAGOOM
WHOOAAA!
UNGH!
FOUR SWORD...
...LEND ME YOUR STRENGTH! JUST AS IN LEGEND, GIVE US...
DON'T YOU **GET** IT?
IT'S ***JUST*** A SWORD!
AND ***YOU'RE*** NOTHING. ***I'M*** THE HERO NOW!

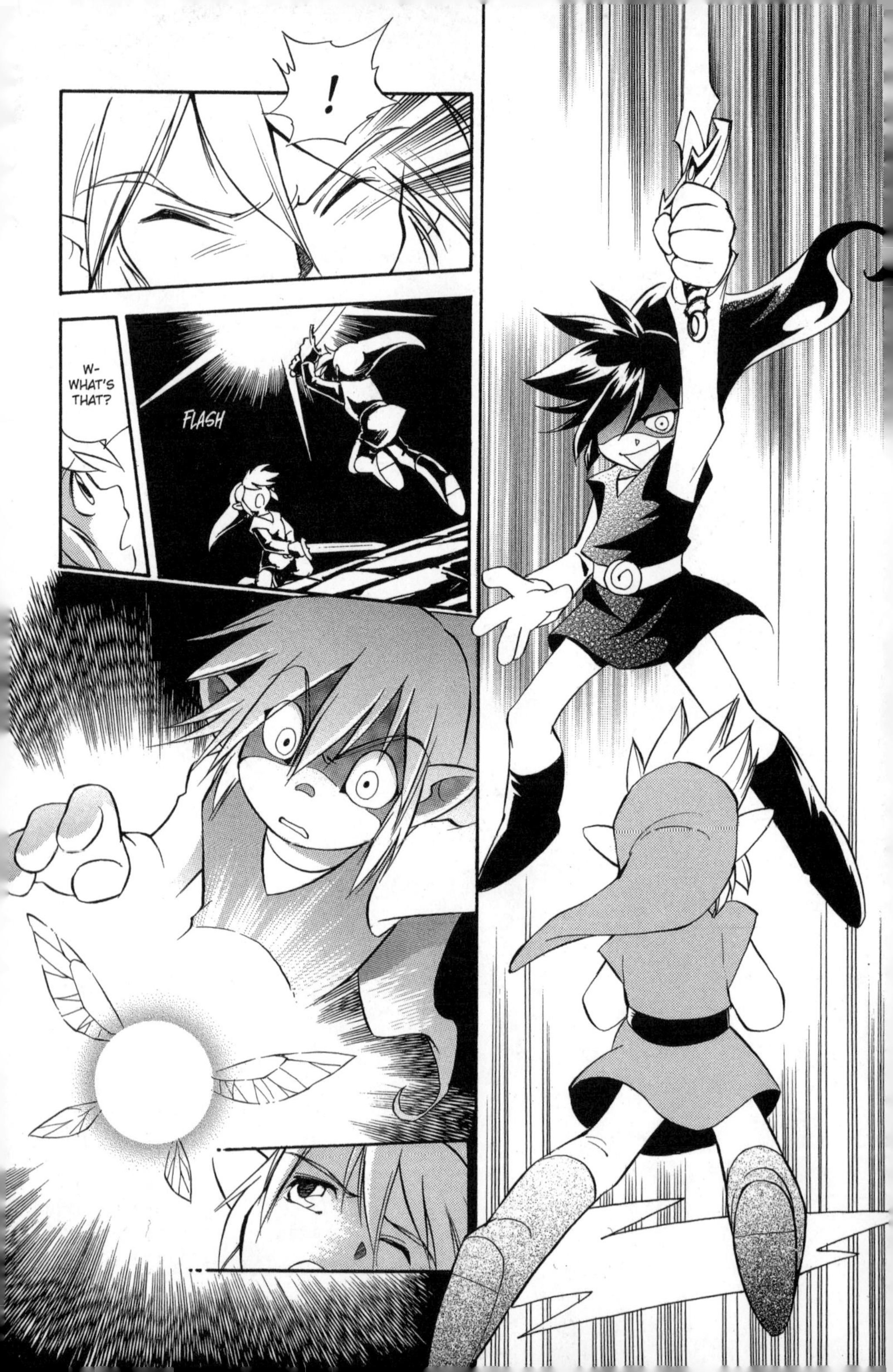
!
W- WHAT'S THAT?
FLASH

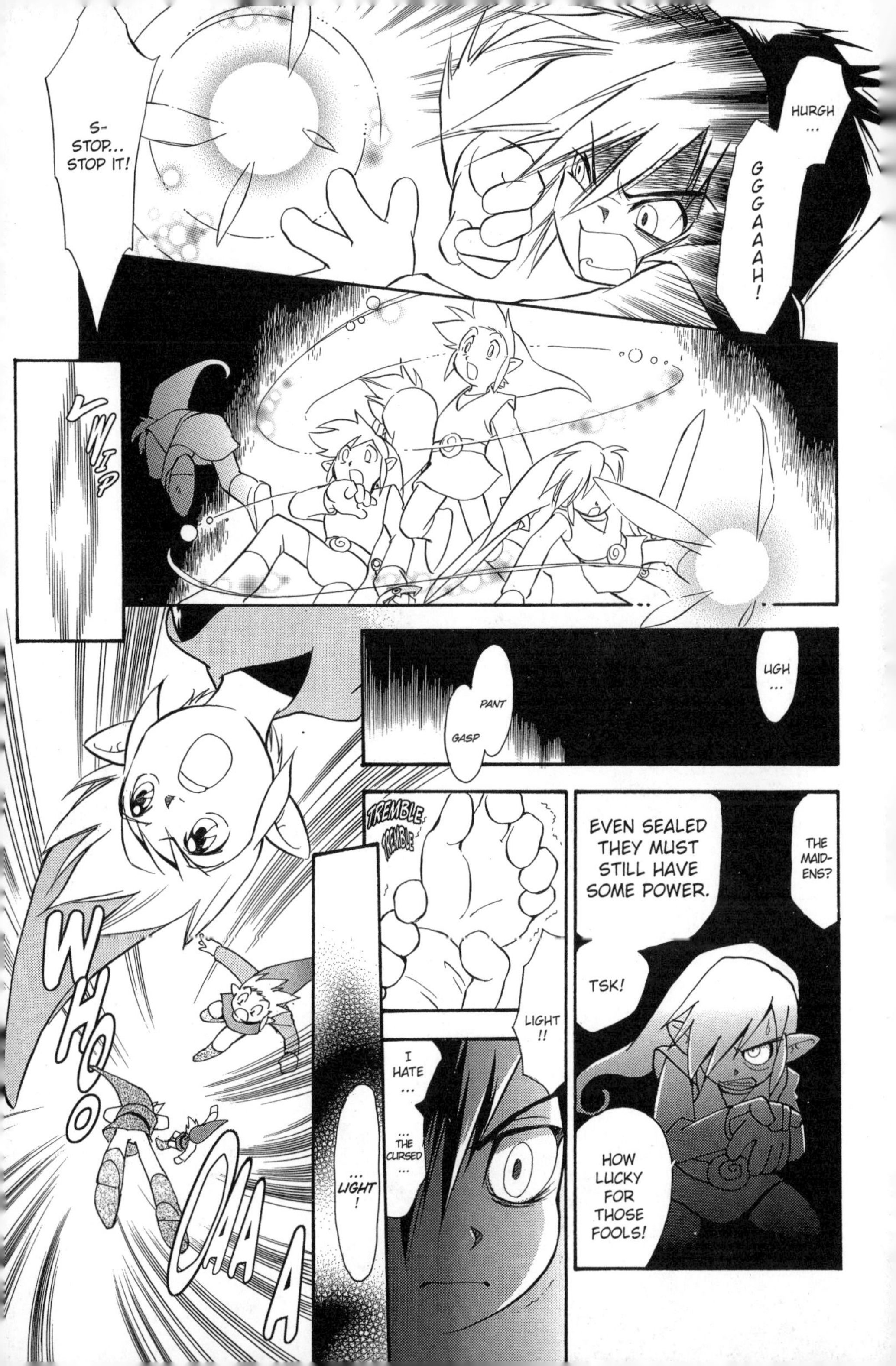
HURGH...
GGGAAAH!
S-STOP... STOP IT!
WHIP
UGH...
PANT
GASP
THE MAIDENS?
EVEN SEALED THEY MUST STILL HAVE SOME POWER.
TREMBLE TREMBLE
TSK!
HOW LUCKY FOR THOSE FOOLS!
LIGHT!!
I HATE...
...THE CURSED...
...LIGHT!
WHOOOAAAA

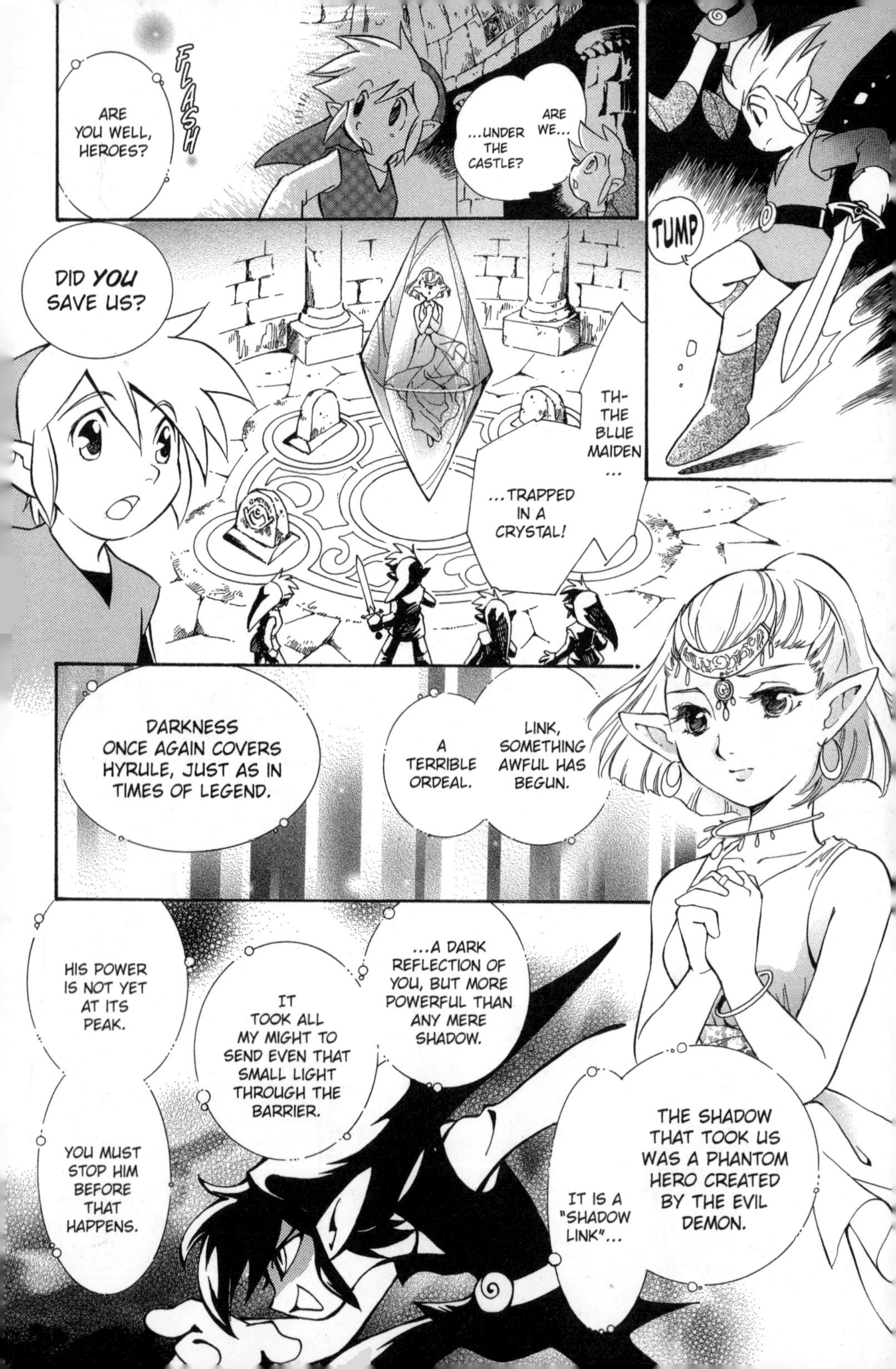
TUMP
ARE WE...
...UNDER THE CASTLE?
FLASH
ARE YOU WELL, HEROES?
TH-THE BLUE MAIDEN...
...TRAPPED IN A CRYSTAL!
DID *YOU* SAVE US?
LINK, SOMETHING AWFUL HAS BEGUN.
A TERRIBLE ORDEAL.
DARKNESS ONCE AGAIN COVERS HYRULE, JUST AS IN TIMES OF LEGEND.
THE SHADOW THAT TOOK US WAS A PHANTOM HERO CREATED BY THE EVIL DEMON.
IT IS A "SHADOW LINK"...
...A DARK REFLECTION OF YOU, BUT MORE POWERFUL THAN ANY MERE SHADOW.
IT TOOK ALL MY MIGHT TO SEND EVEN THAT SMALL LIGHT THROUGH THE BARRIER.
HIS POWER IS NOT YET AT ITS PEAK.
YOU MUST STOP HIM BEFORE THAT HAPPENS.

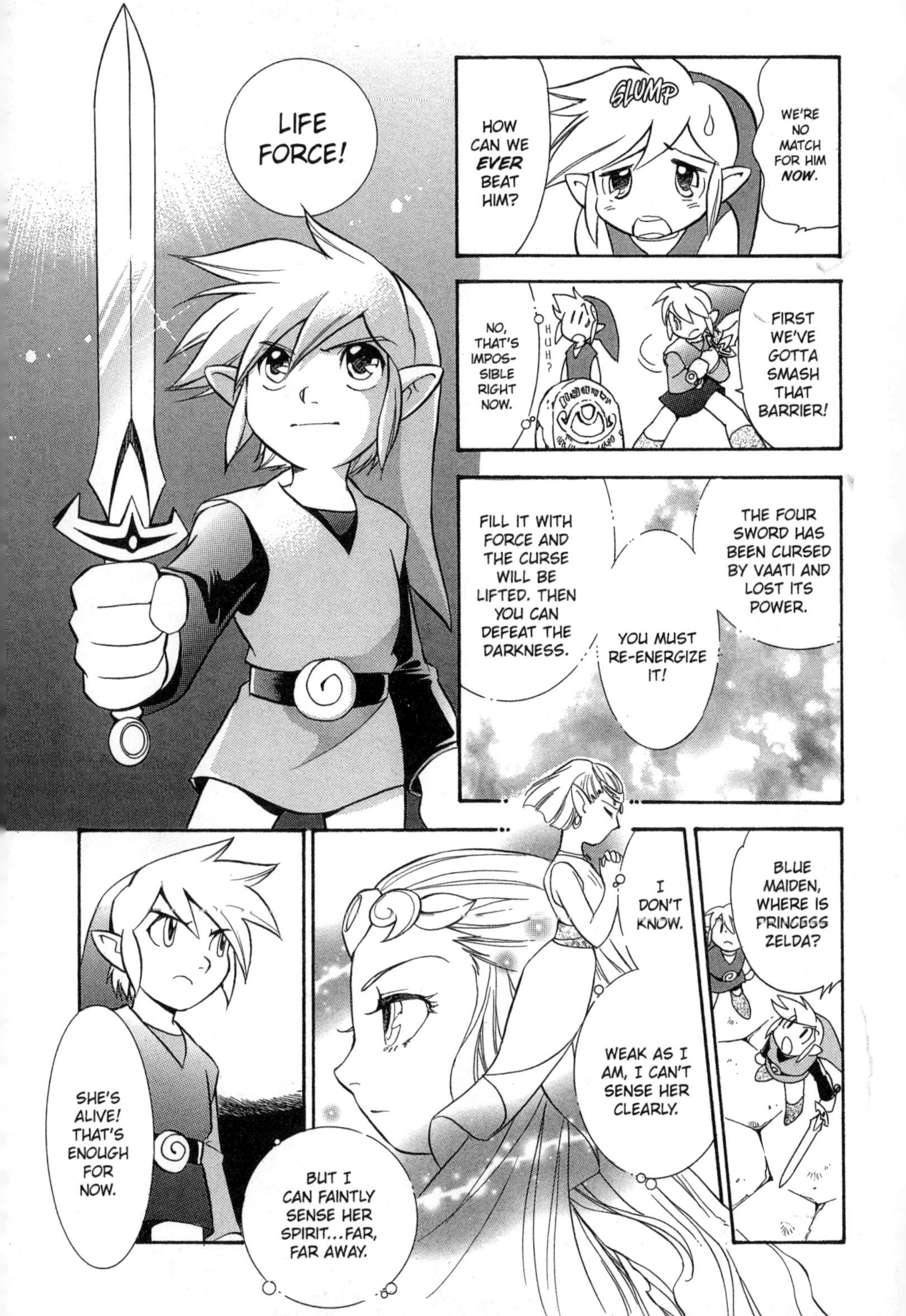

SLUMP
WE'RE NO MATCH FOR HIM NOW.
HOW CAN WE EVER BEAT HIM?
FIRST WE'VE GOTTA SMASH THAT BARRIER!
HUH?
NO, THAT'S IMPOS-SIBLE RIGHT NOW.
THE FOUR SWORD HAS BEEN CURSED BY VAATI AND LOST ITS POWER.
YOU MUST RE-ENERGIZE IT!
FILL IT WITH FORCE AND THE CURSE WILL BE LIFTED. THEN YOU CAN DEFEAT THE DARKNESS.
LIFE FORCE!
BLUE MAIDEN, WHERE IS PRINCESS ZELDA?
I DON'T KNOW.
WEAK AS I AM, I CAN'T SENSE HER CLEARLY.
BUT I CAN FAINTLY SENSE HER SPIRIT...FAR, FAR AWAY.
SHE'S ALIVE! THAT'S ENOUGH FOR NOW.

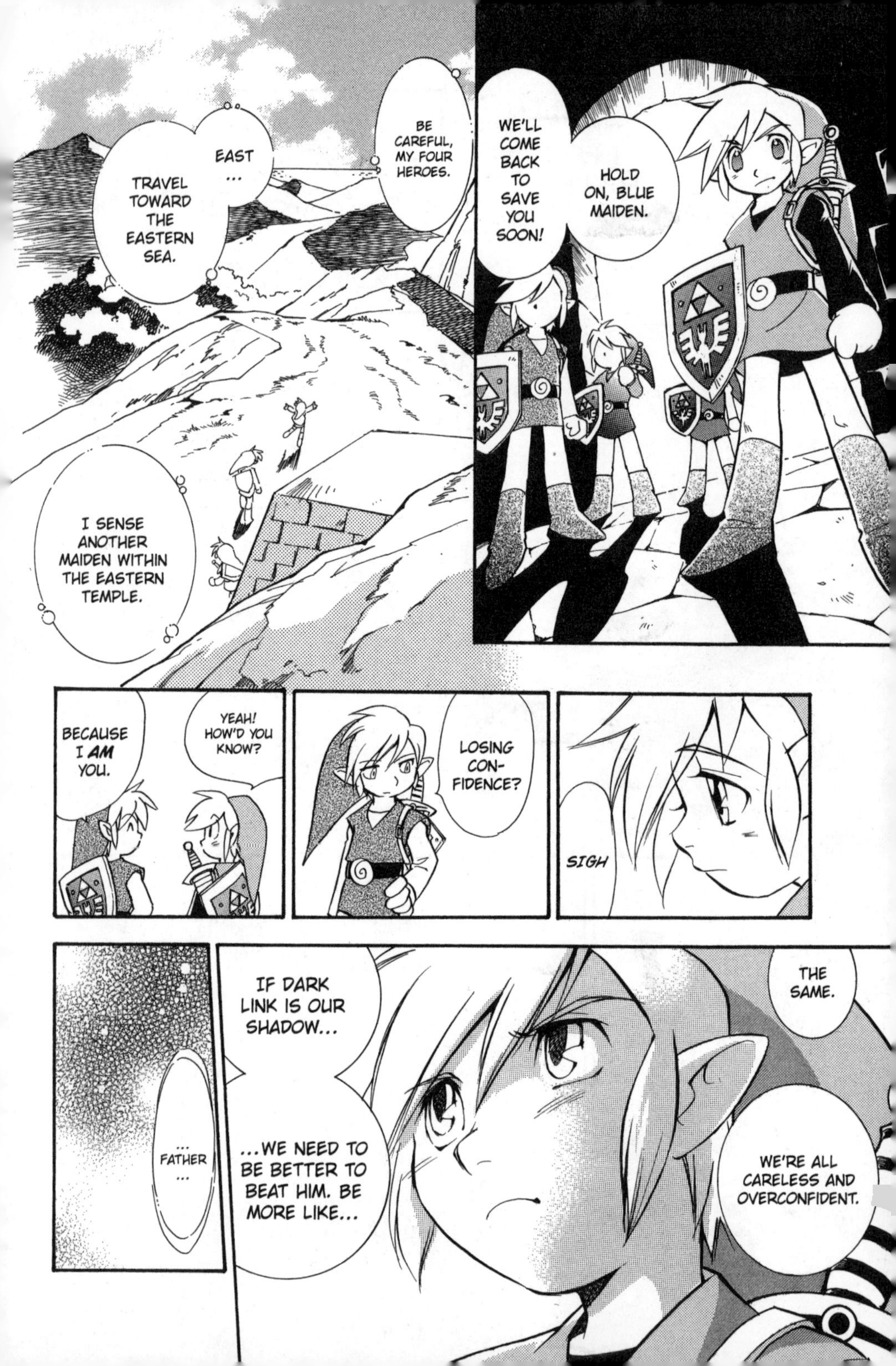

HOLD ON, BLUE MAIDEN.
WE'LL COME BACK TO SAVE YOU SOON!
BE CAREFUL, MY FOUR HEROES.
EAST ...
TRAVEL TOWARD THE EASTERN SEA.
I SENSE ANOTHER MAIDEN WITHIN THE EASTERN TEMPLE.
SIGH
LOSING CON-FIDENCE?
YEAH! HOW'D YOU KNOW?
BECAUSE I *AM* YOU.
THE SAME.
WE'RE ALL CARELESS AND OVERCONFIDENT.
IF DARK LINK IS OUR SHADOW...
...WE NEED TO BE BETTER TO BEAT HIM. BE MORE LIKE...
... FATHER ...

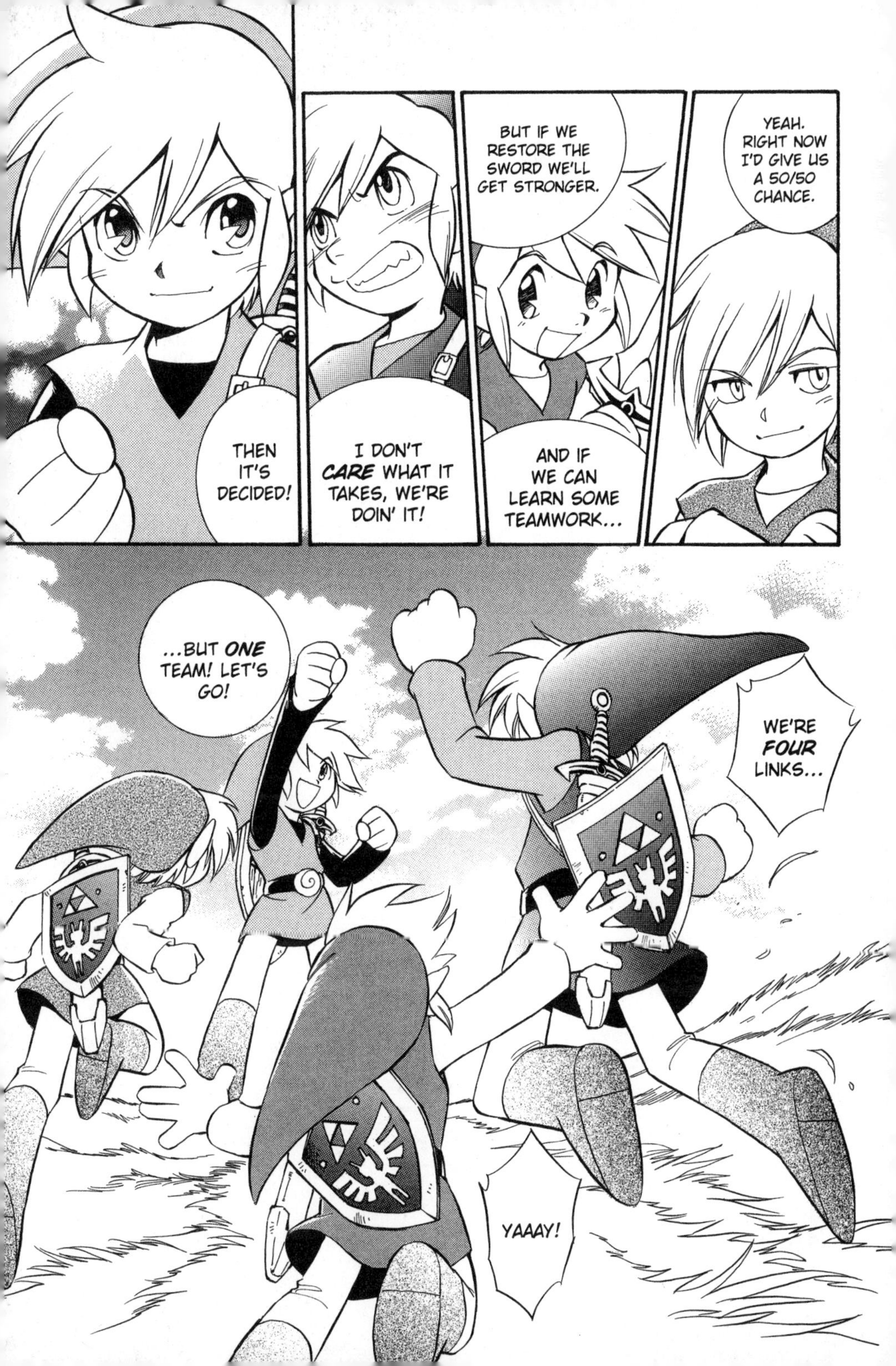
YEAH. RIGHT NOW I'D GIVE US A 50/50 CHANCE.
BUT IF WE RESTORE THE SWORD WE'LL GET STRONGER.
AND IF WE CAN LEARN SOME TEAMWORK...
I DON'T CARE WHAT IT TAKES, WE'RE DOIN' IT!
THEN IT'S DECIDED!
WE'RE FOUR LINKS...
...BUT ONE TEAM! LET'S GO!
YAAAY!

Purple

Cool, contrary,
brainy, sarcastic.

**FOUR SWORDS
ROUGH CHARACTER
ILLUSTRATION 2**

CHAPTER 3 Erune and Rosie

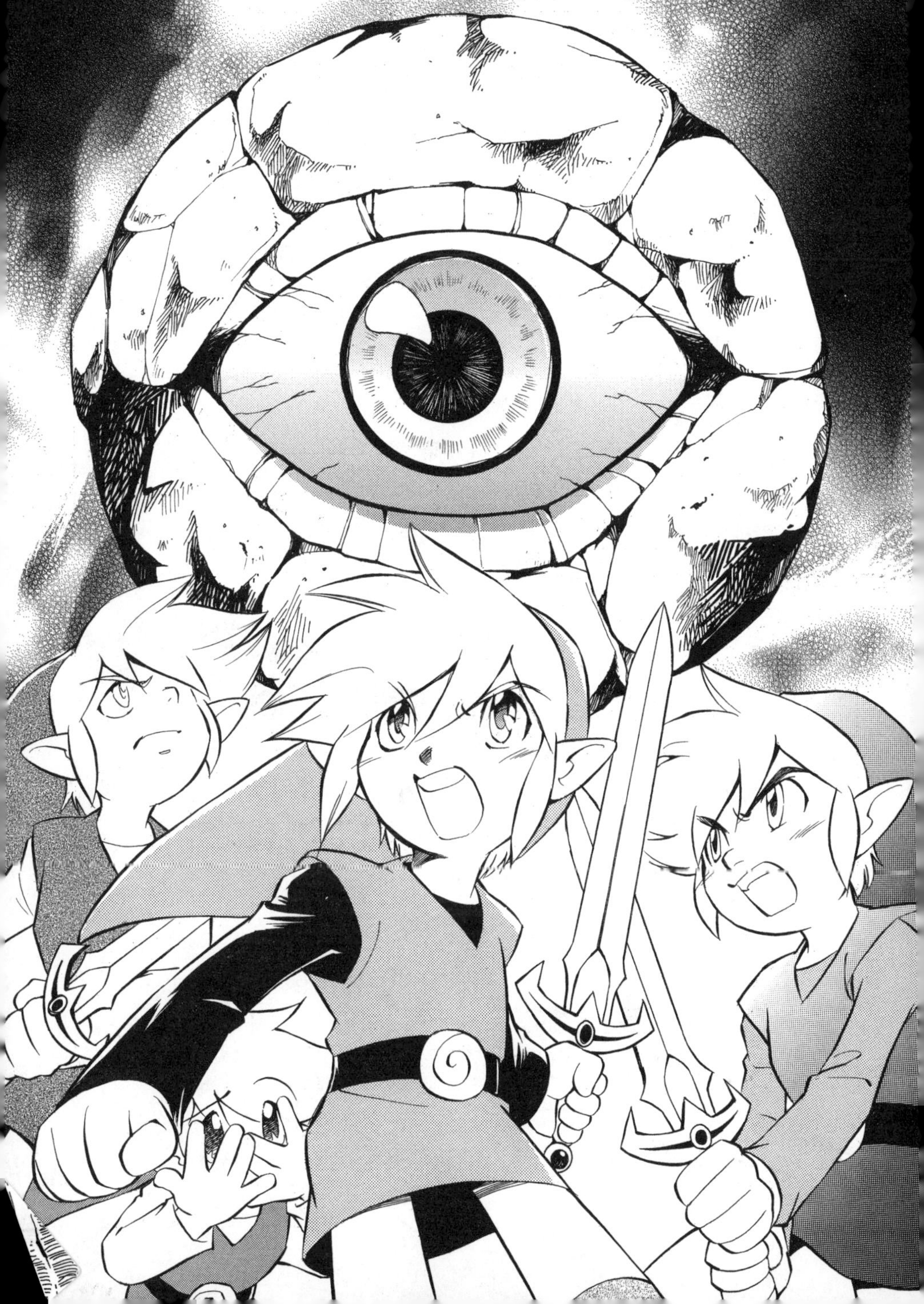

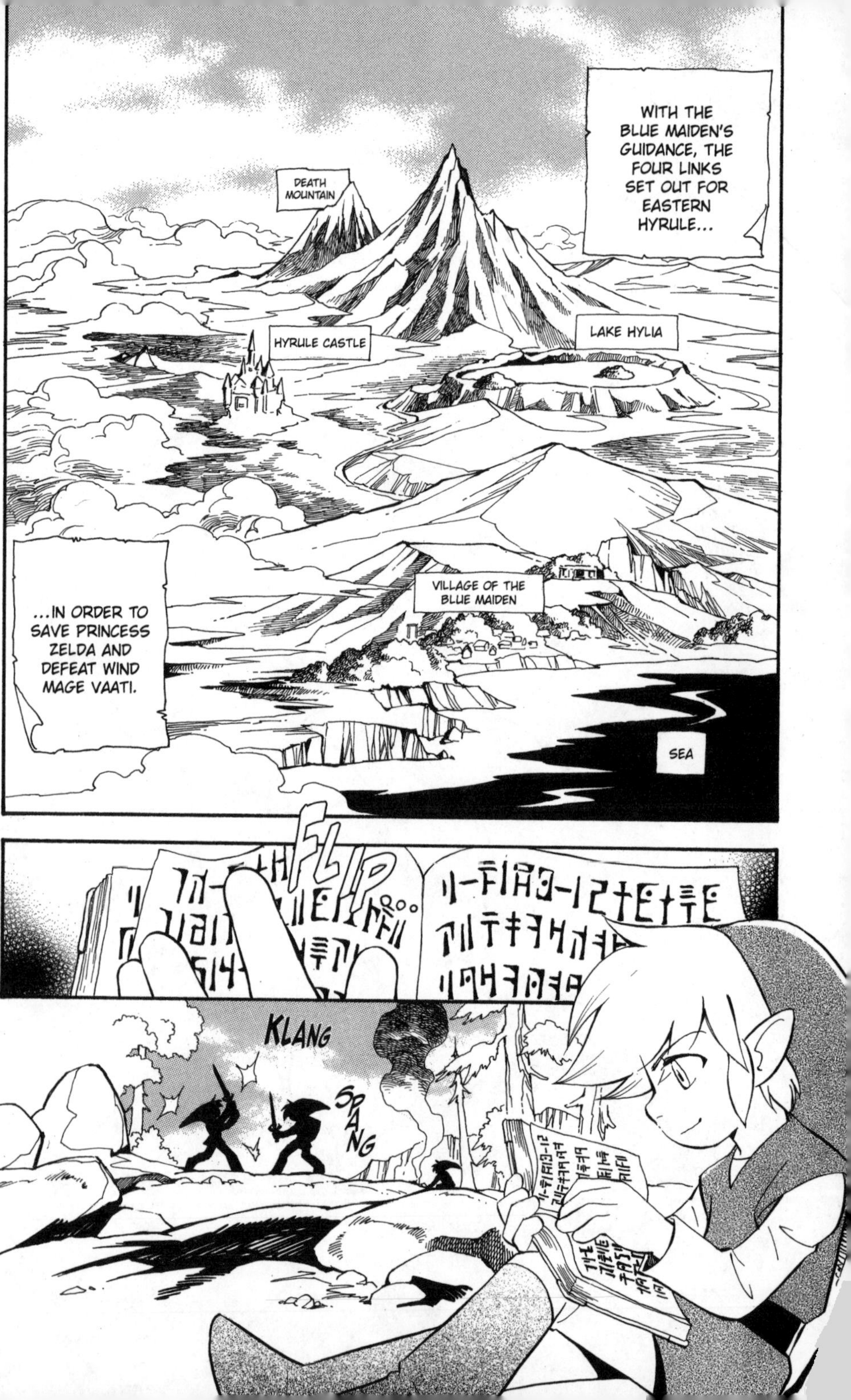
WITH THE BLUE MAIDEN'S GUIDANCE, THE FOUR LINKS SET OUT FOR EASTERN HYRULE...
DEATH MOUNTAIN
LAKE HYLIA
HYRULE CASTLE
VILLAGE OF THE BLUE MAIDEN
SEA
...IN ORDER TO SAVE PRINCESS ZELDA AND DEFEAT WIND MAGE VAATI.
FLIP
KLANG
SPANG

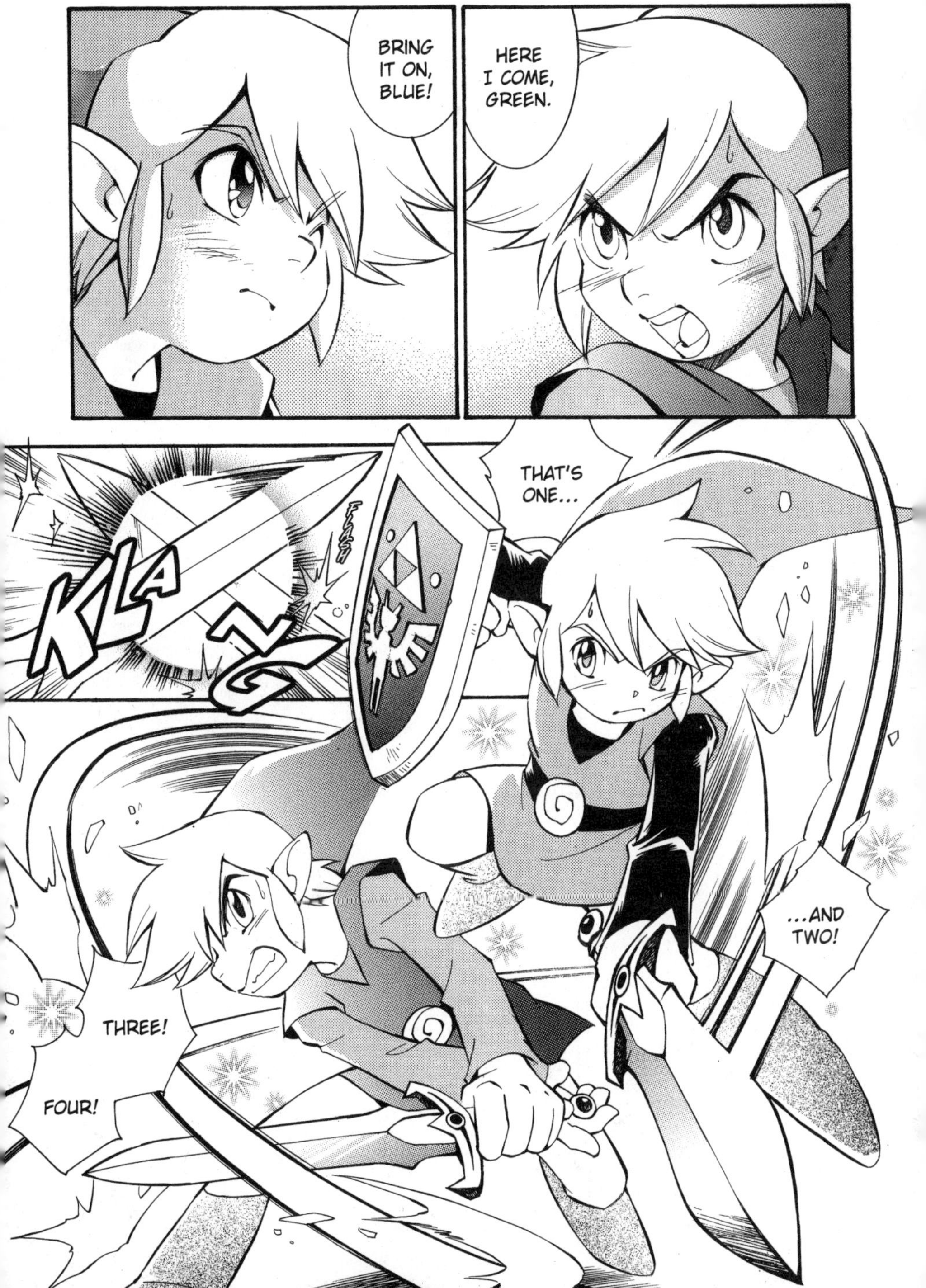
HERE I COME, GREEN.
BRING IT ON, BLUE!
THAT'S ONE...
FLASH
KLANG
...AND TWO!
THREE!
FOUR!

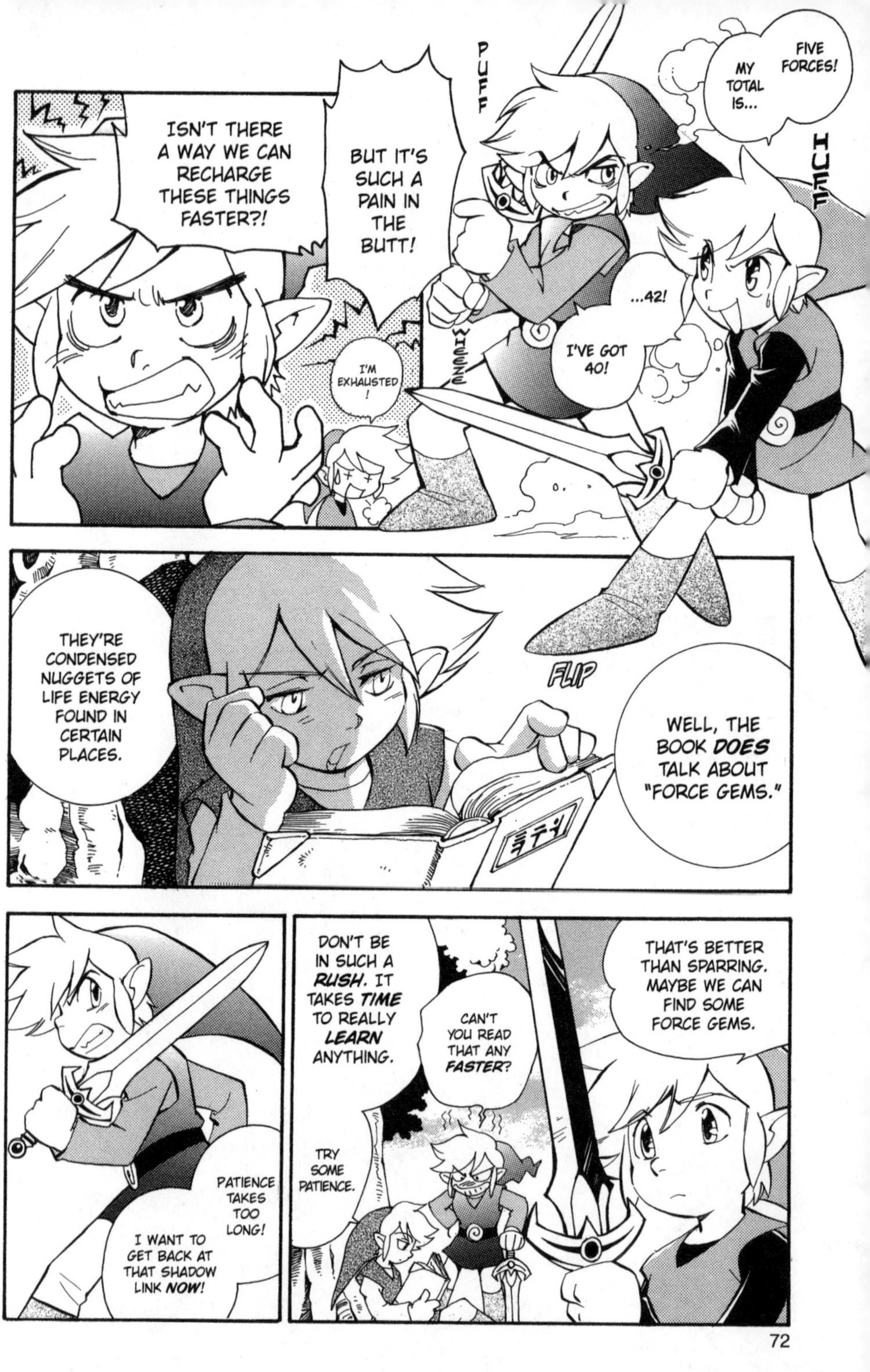
MY TOTAL IS... FIVE FORCES!
HUFF
PUFF
BUT IT'S SUCH A PAIN IN THE BUTT!
ISN'T THERE A WAY WE CAN RECHARGE THESE THINGS FASTER?!
...42!
I'VE GOT 40!
WHEEZE
I'M EXHAUSTED!
FLIP
WELL, THE BOOK **DOES** TALK ABOUT "FORCE GEMS."
THEY'RE CONDENSED NUGGETS OF LIFE ENERGY FOUND IN CERTAIN PLACES.
THAT'S BETTER THAN SPARRING. MAYBE WE CAN FIND SOME FORCE GEMS.
DON'T BE IN SUCH A **RUSH**. IT TAKES **TIME** TO REALLY **LEARN** ANYTHING.
CAN'T YOU READ THAT ANY **FASTER**?
TRY SOME PATIENCE.
PATIENCE TAKES TOO LONG!
I WANT TO GET BACK AT THAT SHADOW LINK **NOW**!

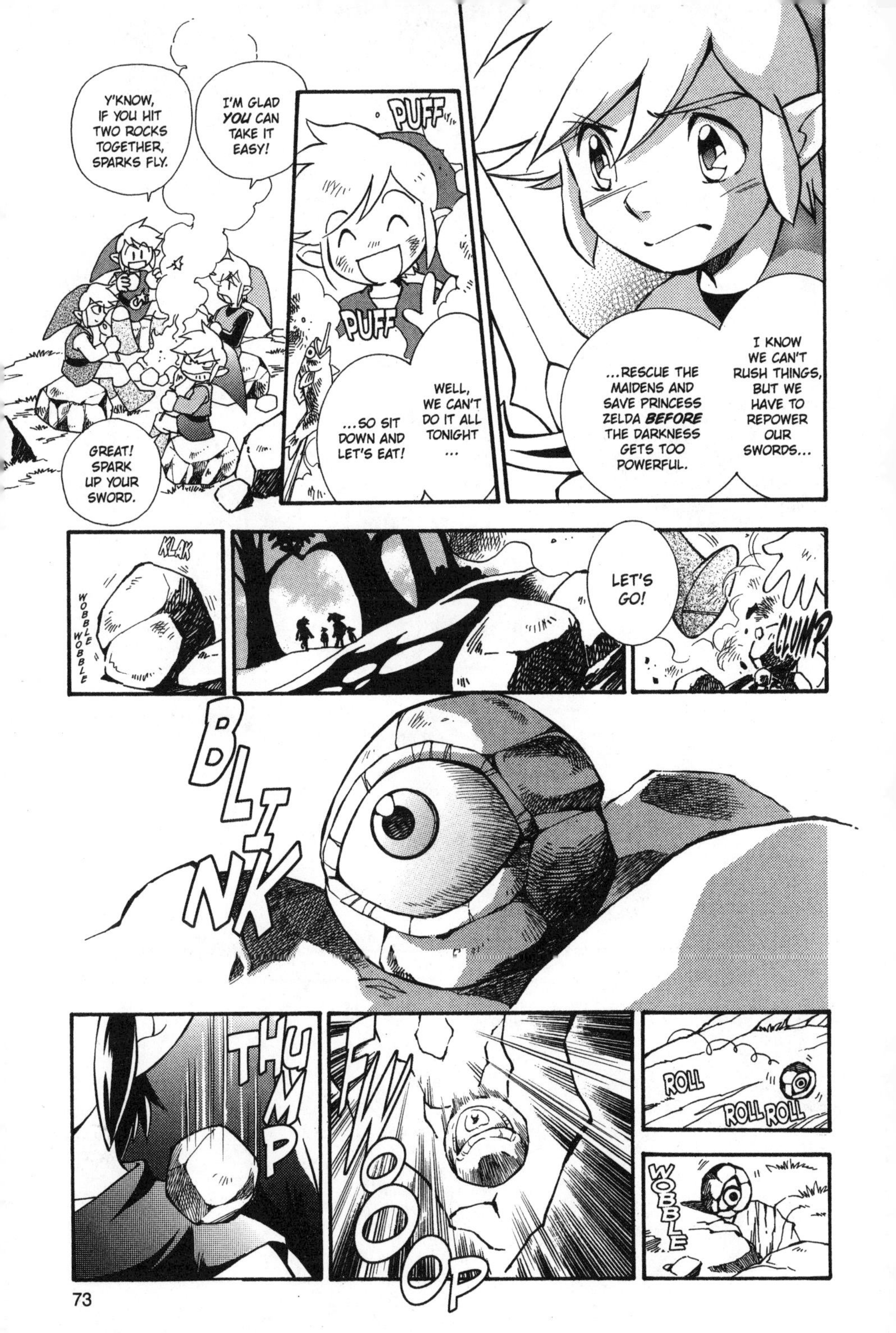
I KNOW WE CAN'T RUSH THINGS, BUT WE HAVE TO REPOWER OUR SWORDS...
...RESCUE THE MAIDENS AND SAVE PRINCESS ZELDA **BEFORE** THE DARKNESS GETS TOO POWERFUL.
PUFF
WELL, WE CAN'T DO IT ALL TONIGHT ...
PUFF
...SO SIT DOWN AND LET'S EAT!
I'M GLAD ***YOU*** CAN TAKE IT EASY!
Y'KNOW, IF YOU HIT TWO ROCKS TOGETHER, SPARKS FLY.
GREAT! SPARK UP YOUR SWORD.
LET'S GO!
CLUMP
KLAK
WOBBLE WOBBLE
BLINK
ROLL
ROLL ROLL
WOBBLE
FWOOOP
THUMP

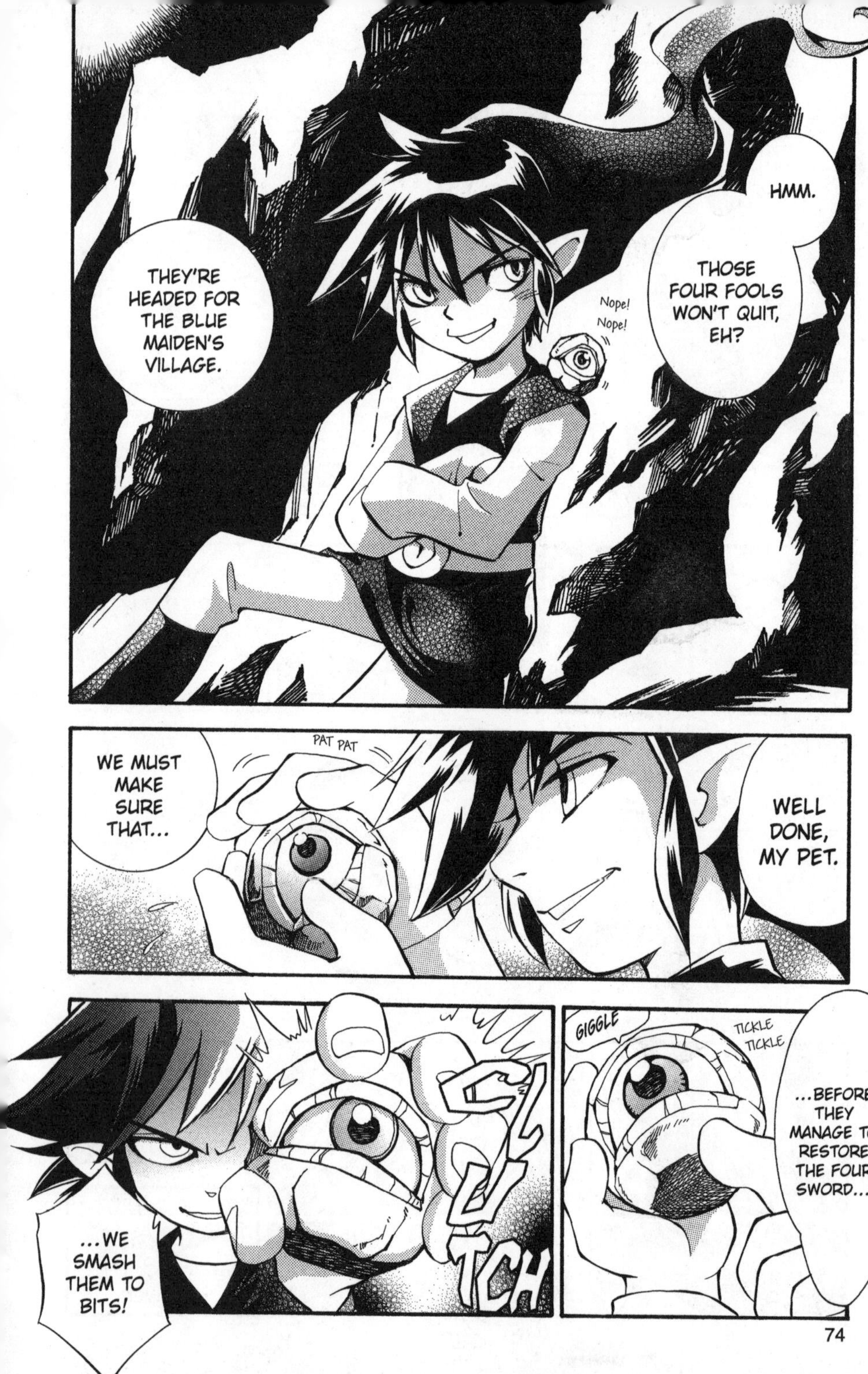
HMM.
THOSE FOUR FOOLS WON'T QUIT, EH?
Nope! Nope!
THEY'RE HEADED FOR THE BLUE MAIDEN'S VILLAGE.
WELL DONE, MY PET.
PAT PAT
WE MUST MAKE SURE THAT...
...BEFORE THEY MANAGE TO RESTORE THE FOUR SWORD...
TICKLE TICKLE
GIGGLE
CLUTCH
...WE SMASH THEM TO BITS!

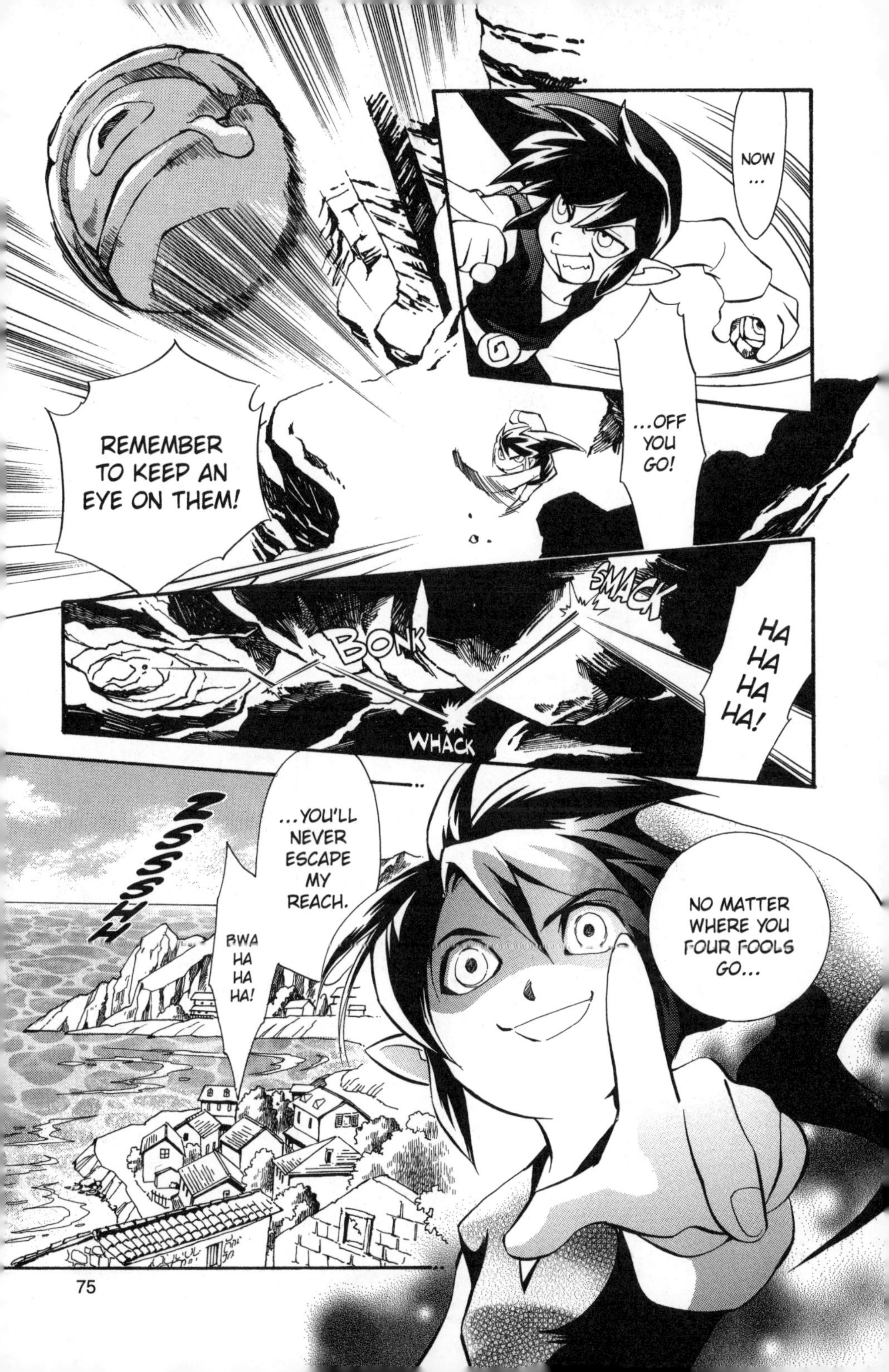
NOW ...
...OFF YOU GO!
REMEMBER TO KEEP AN EYE ON THEM!
HA HA HA HA!
SMACK
BONK
WHACK
NO MATTER WHERE YOU FOUR FOOLS GO...
...YOU'LL NEVER ESCAPE MY REACH.
BWA HA HA HA!
ZSSSHH

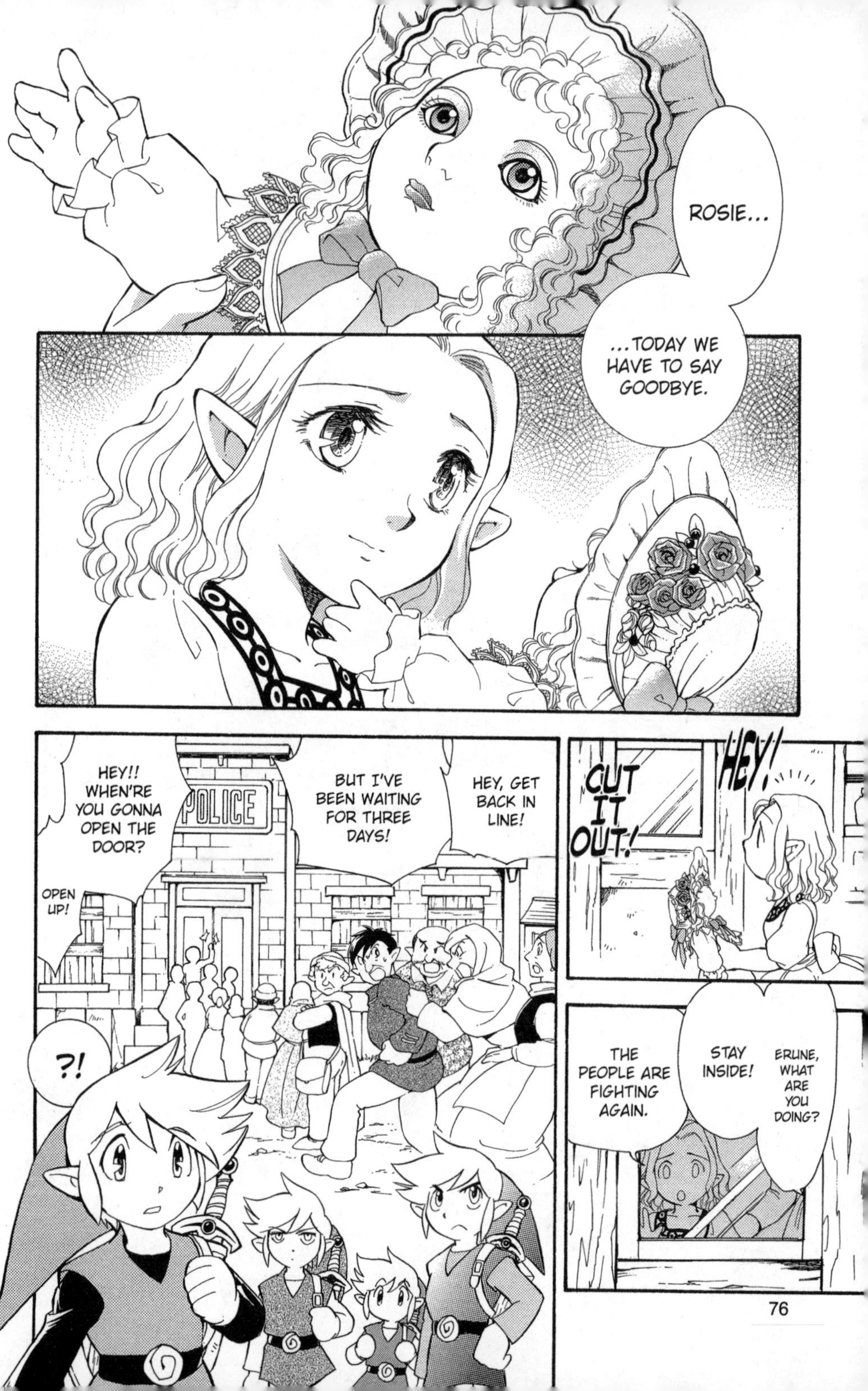
ROSIE...
...TODAY WE HAVE TO SAY GOODBYE.
HEY!
CUT IT OUT!
ERUNE, WHAT ARE YOU DOING?
STAY INSIDE!
THE PEOPLE ARE FIGHTING AGAIN.
HEY, GET BACK IN LINE!
BUT I'VE BEEN WAITING FOR THREE DAYS!
HEY!! WHEN'RE YOU GONNA OPEN THE DOOR?
POLICE
OPEN UP!
?!

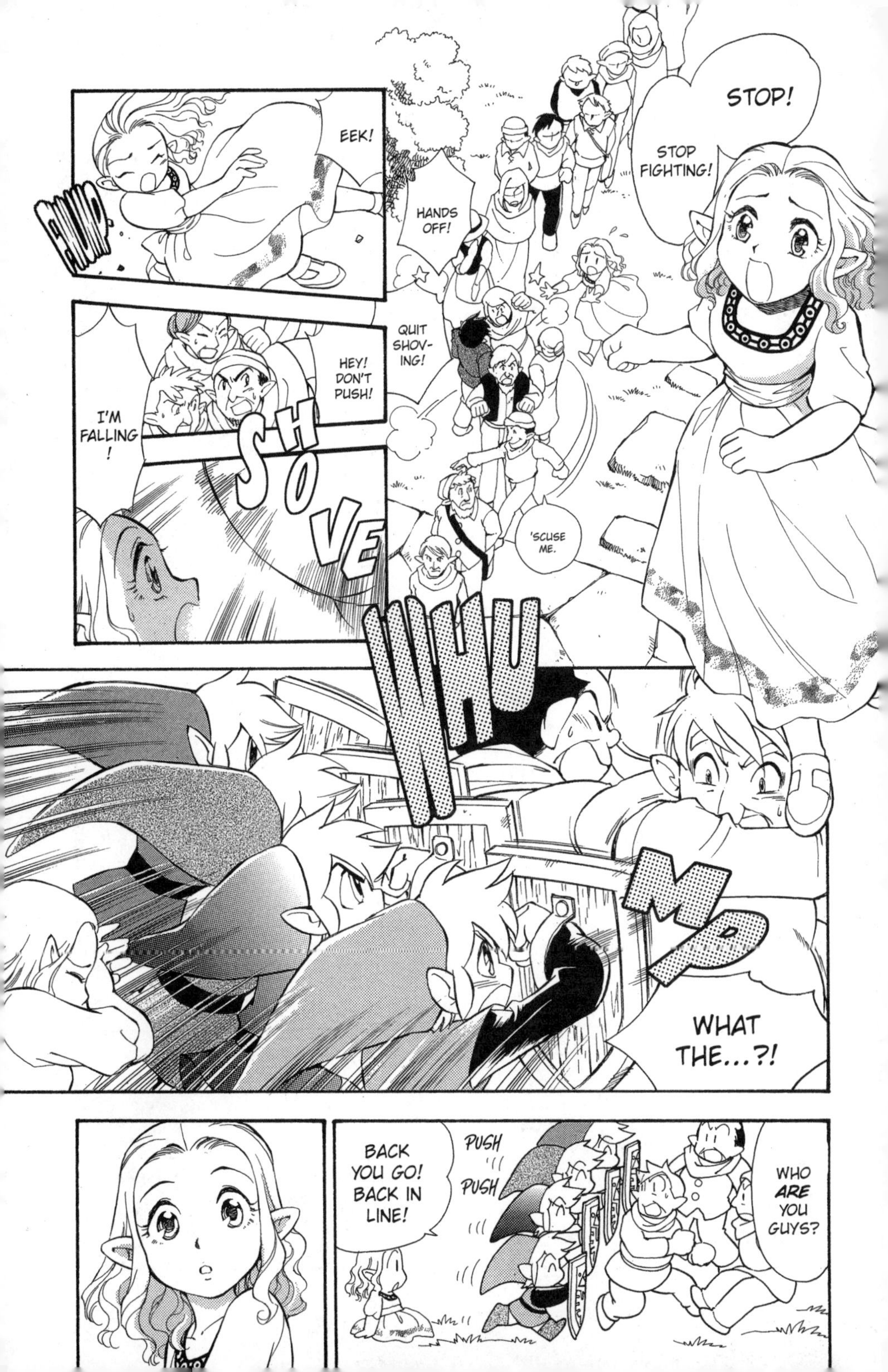
STOP!
STOP FIGHTING!
HANDS OFF!
QUIT SHOV-ING!
'SCUSE ME.
EEK!
HEY! DON'T PUSH!
I'M FALLING!
SHOVE
WHUMP
WHAT THE...?!
WHO ARE YOU GUYS?
PUSH PUSH
BACK YOU GO! BACK IN LINE!

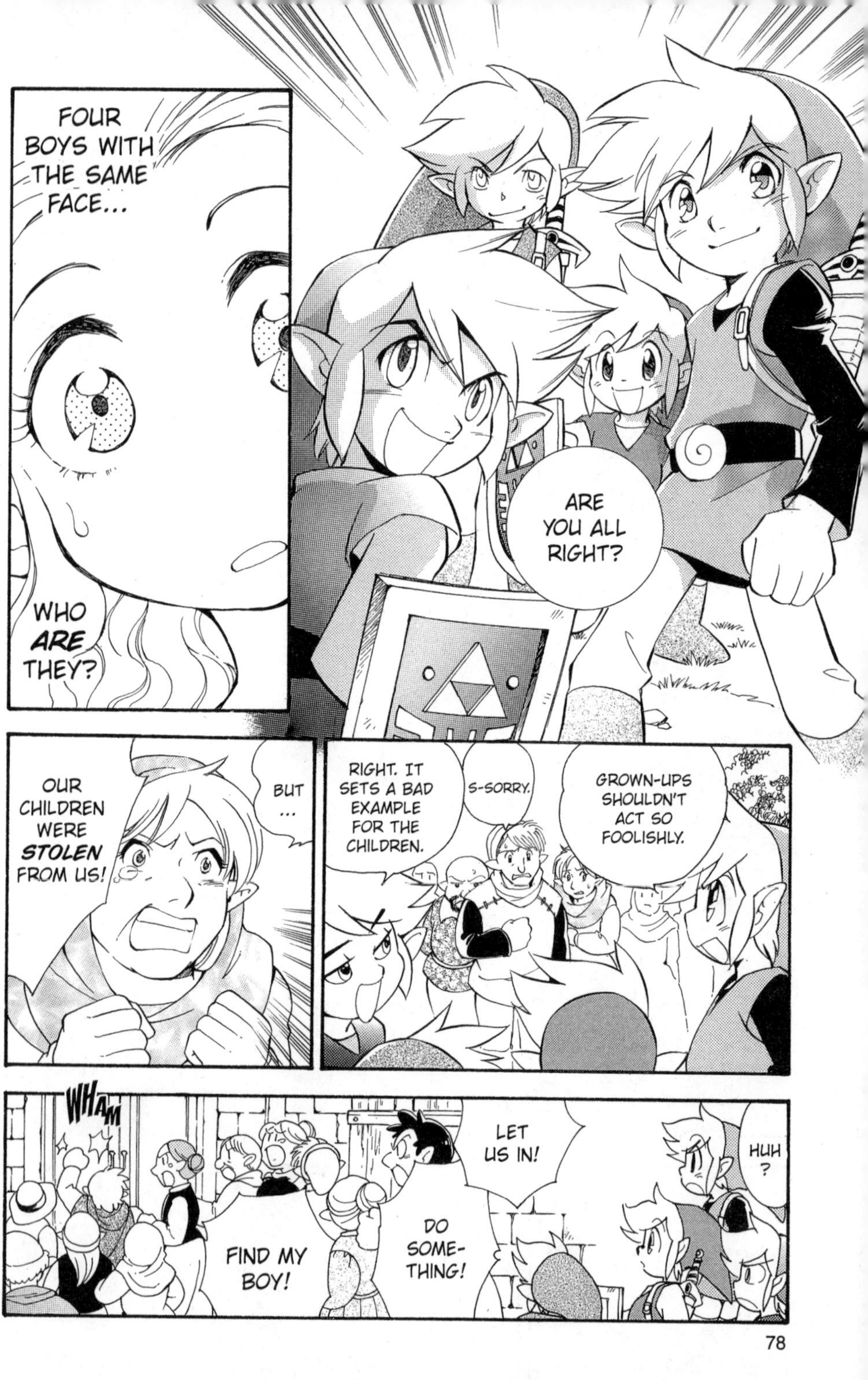
ARE YOU ALL RIGHT?
FOUR BOYS WITH THE SAME FACE...
WHO *ARE* THEY?
GROWN-UPS SHOULDN'T ACT SO FOOLISHLY.
S-SORRY.
RIGHT. IT SETS A BAD EXAMPLE FOR THE CHILDREN.
BUT ...
OUR CHILDREN WERE *STOLEN* FROM US!
HUH ?
LET US IN!
DO SOME-THING!
FIND MY BOY!
WHAM

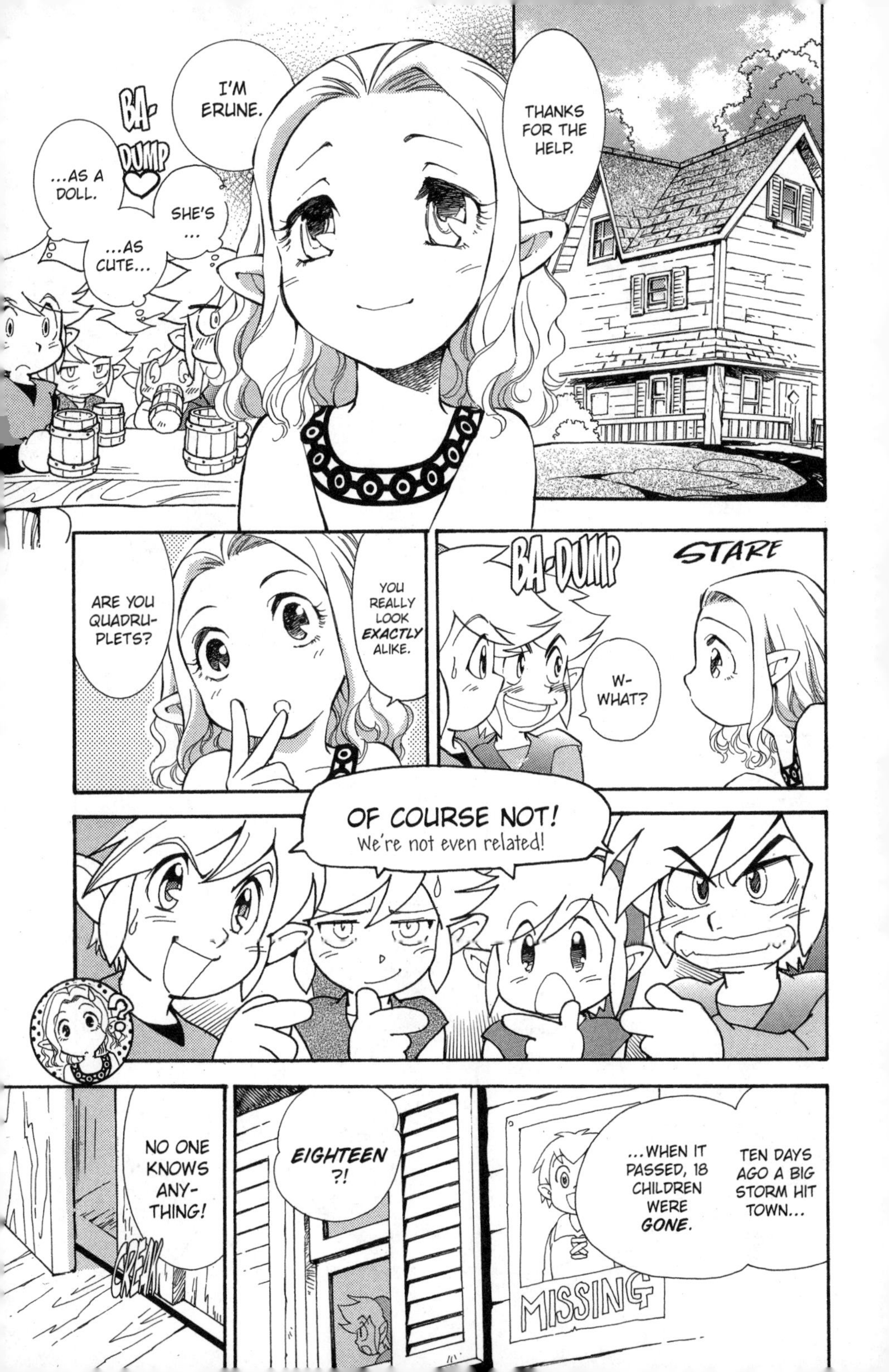
THANKS FOR THE HELP.
I'M ERUNE.
BA-DUMP
SHE'S ...
...AS CUTE...
...AS A DOLL.
BA-DUMP
STARE
W-WHAT?
YOU REALLY LOOK *EXACTLY* ALIKE.
ARE YOU QUADRUPLETS?
OF COURSE NOT! We're not even related!
TEN DAYS AGO A BIG STORM HIT TOWN...
...WHEN IT PASSED, 18 CHILDREN WERE **GONE**.
MISSING
EIGHTEEN ?!
NO ONE KNOWS ANY-THING!
CREEAK

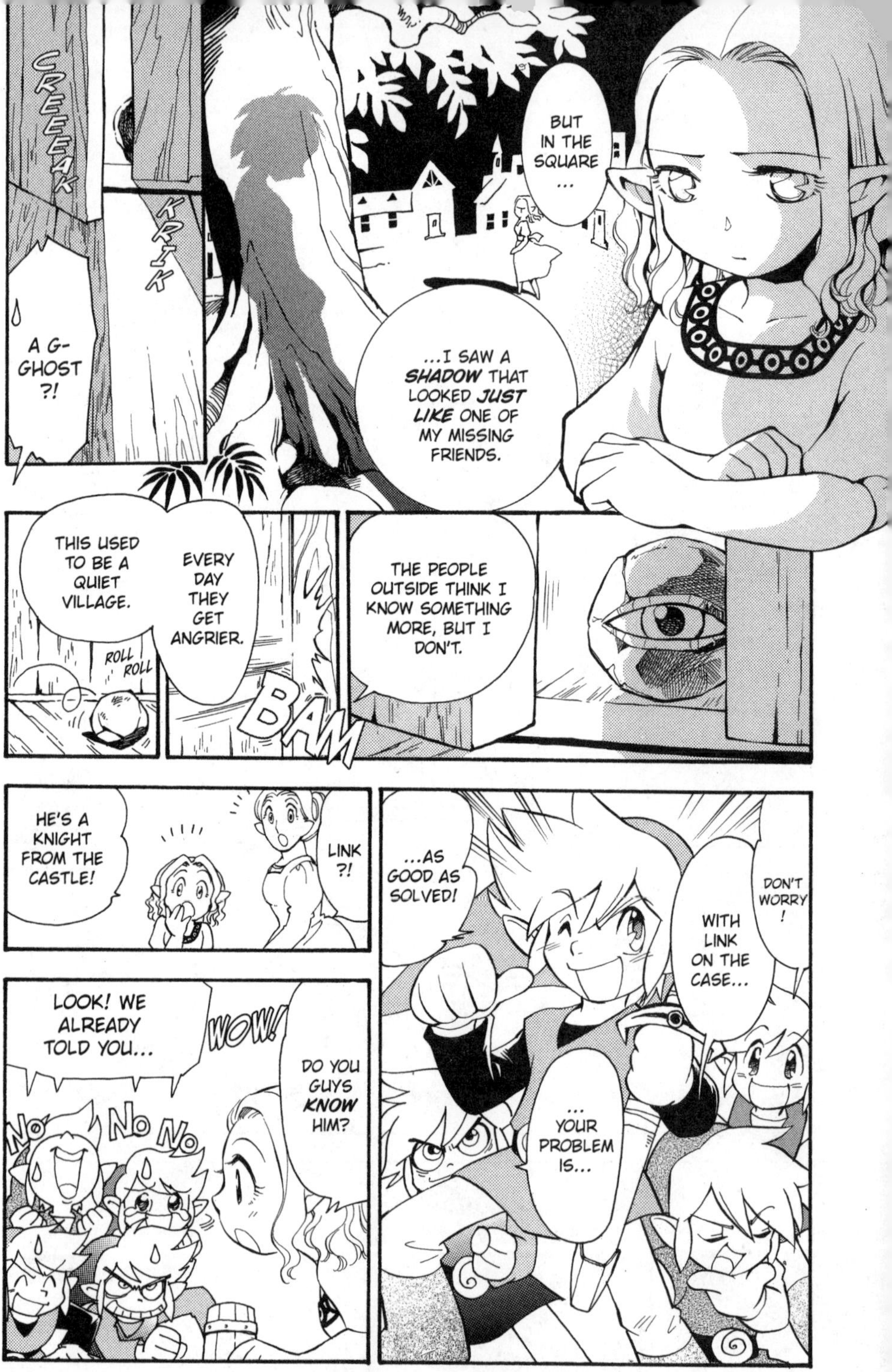

BUT IN THE SQUARE...
...I SAW A SHADOW THAT LOOKED JUST LIKE ONE OF MY MISSING FRIENDS.
CREEEAK
KRIK
A G-GHOST?!
THE PEOPLE OUTSIDE THINK I KNOW SOMETHING MORE, BUT I DON'T.
BAM
EVERY DAY THEY GET ANGRIER.
THIS USED TO BE A QUIET VILLAGE.
ROLL ROLL
DON'T WORRY!
WITH LINK ON THE CASE...
...YOUR PROBLEM IS...
...AS GOOD AS SOLVED!
LINK?!
HE'S A KNIGHT FROM THE CASTLE!
DO YOU GUYS KNOW HIM?
WOW!
LOOK! WE ALREADY TOLD YOU...
No No No

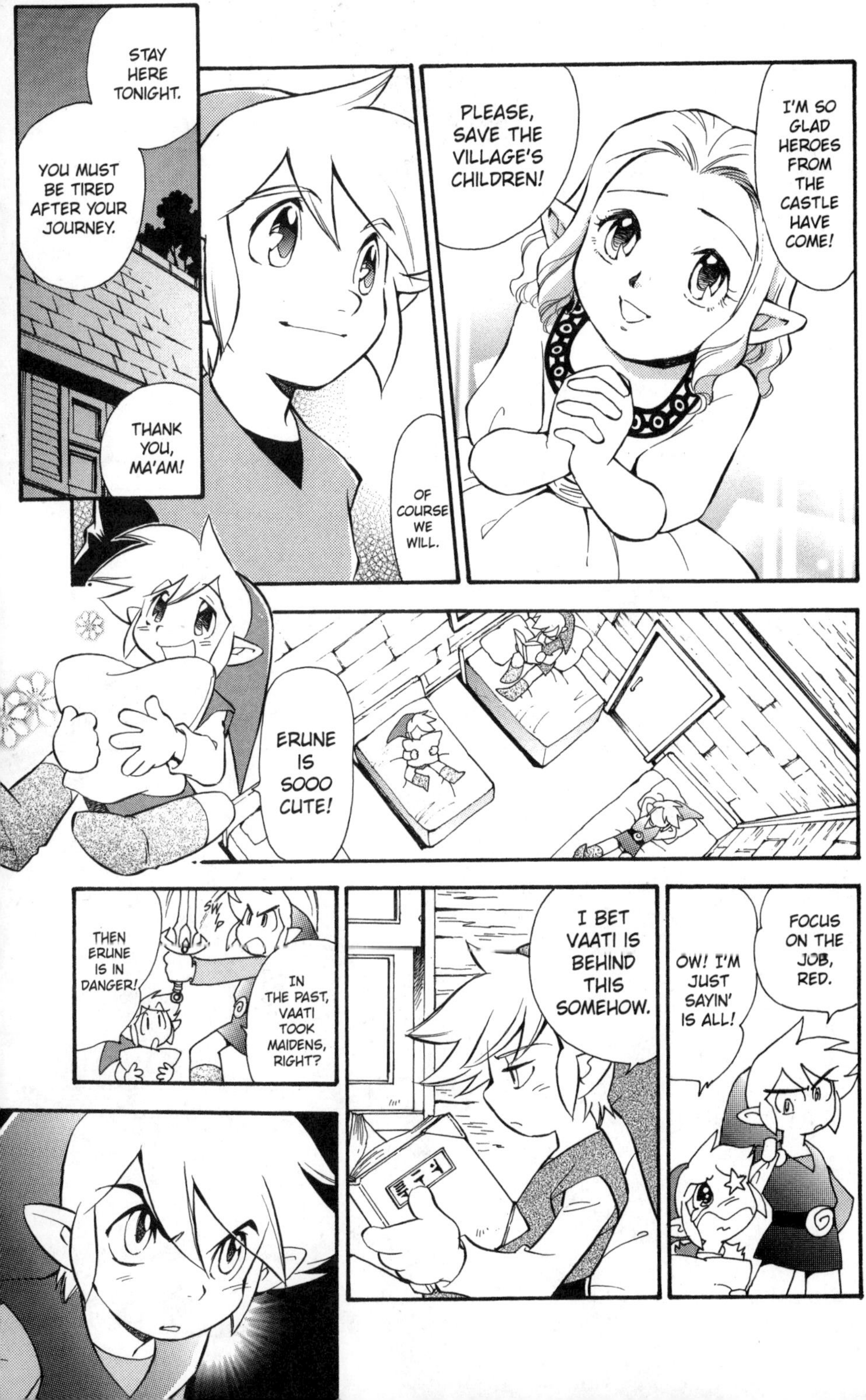
I'M SO GLAD HEROES FROM THE CASTLE HAVE COME!
PLEASE, SAVE THE VILLAGE'S CHILDREN!
OF COURSE WE WILL.
STAY HERE TONIGHT.
YOU MUST BE TIRED AFTER YOUR JOURNEY.
THANK YOU, MA'AM!
ERUNE IS SOOO CUTE!
FOCUS ON THE JOB, RED.
OW! I'M JUST SAYIN' IS ALL!
I BET VAATI IS BEHIND THIS SOMEHOW.
IN THE PAST, VAATI TOOK MAIDENS, RIGHT?
THEN ERUNE IS IN DANGER!

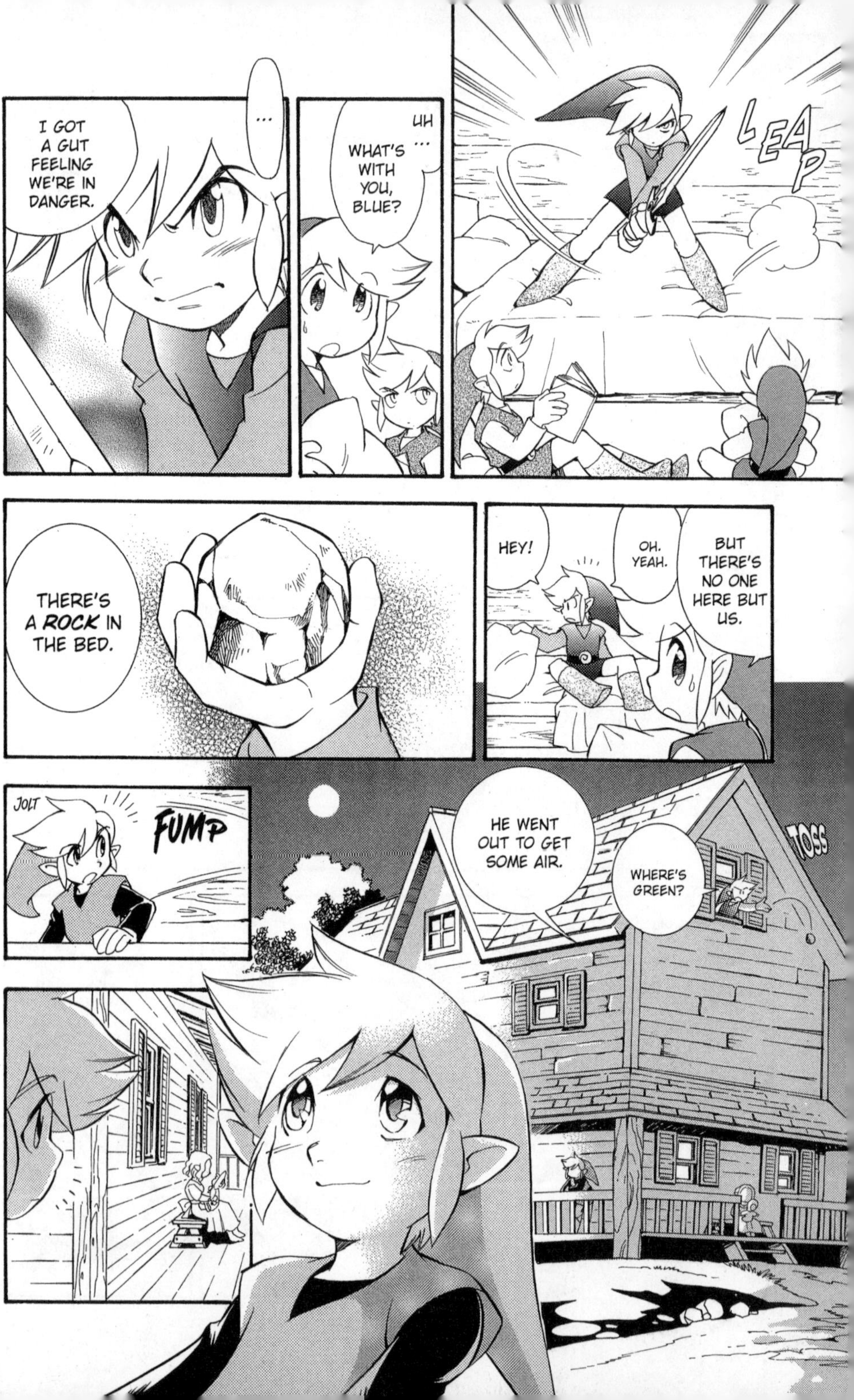
LEAP
UH ...
WHAT'S WITH YOU, BLUE?
...
I GOT A GUT FEELING WE'RE IN DANGER.
BUT THERE'S NO ONE HERE BUT US.
OH. YEAH.
HEY!
THERE'S A ROCK IN THE BED.
TOSS
WHERE'S GREEN?
HE WENT OUT TO GET SOME AIR.
FUMP
JOLT

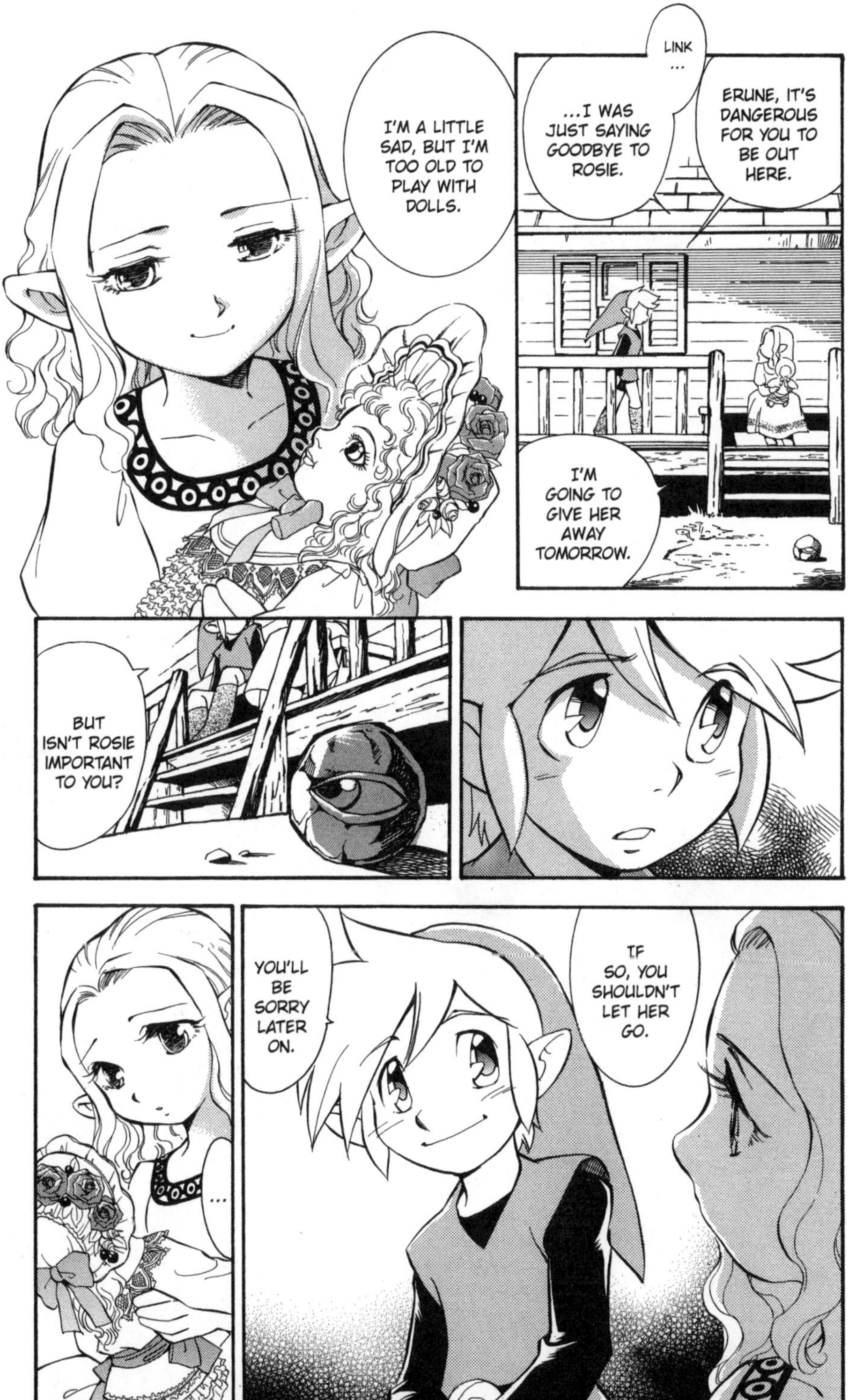
ERUNE, IT'S DANGEROUS FOR YOU TO BE OUT HERE.
LINK ...
...I WAS JUST SAYING GOODBYE TO ROSIE.
I'M GOING TO GIVE HER AWAY TOMORROW.
I'M A LITTLE SAD, BUT I'M TOO OLD TO PLAY WITH DOLLS.
BUT ISN'T ROSIE IMPORTANT TO YOU?
IF SO, YOU SHOULDN'T LET HER GO.
YOU'LL BE SORRY LATER ON.
...

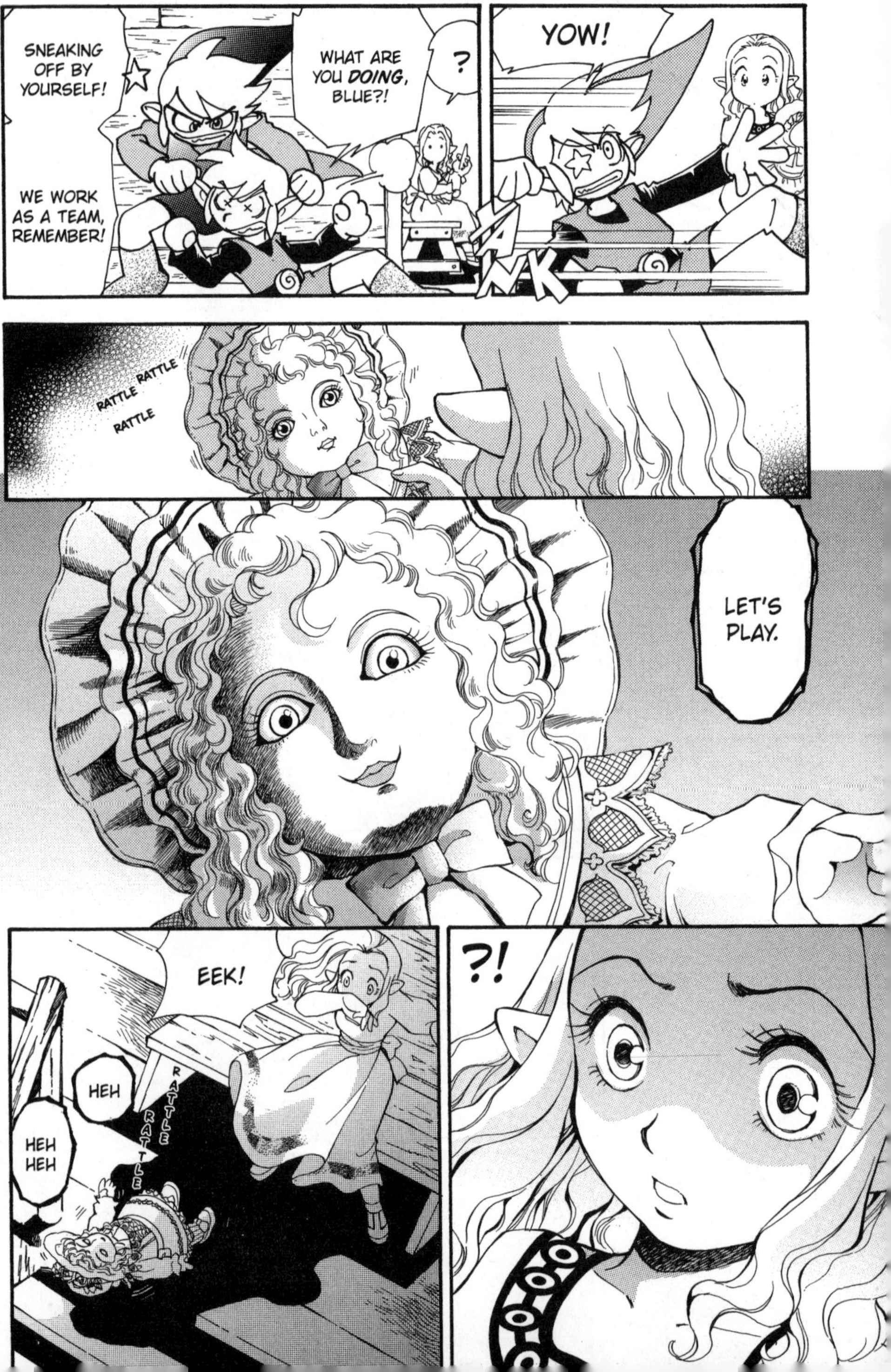
YOW!
YANK
?
WHAT ARE YOU DOING, BLUE?!
SNEAKING OFF BY YOURSELF!
WE WORK AS A TEAM, REMEMBER!
RATTLE RATTLE
RATTLE
LET'S PLAY.
?!
EEK!
RATTLE
RATTLE
HEH
HEH HEH

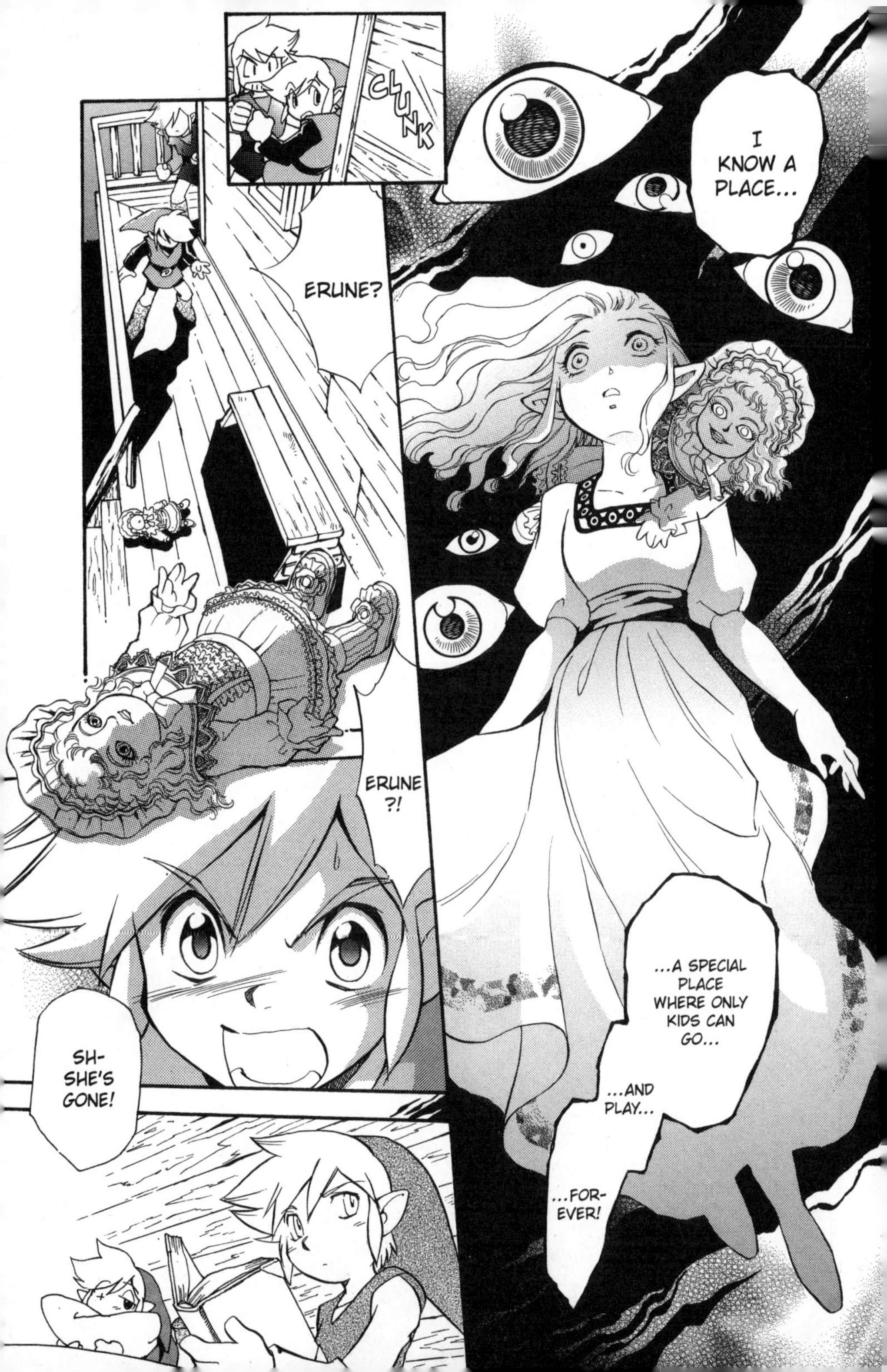
I KNOW A PLACE...
...A SPECIAL PLACE WHERE ONLY KIDS CAN GO...
...AND PLAY...
...FOR-EVER!
CLUNK
ERUNE?
ERUNE?!
SH-SHE'S GONE!

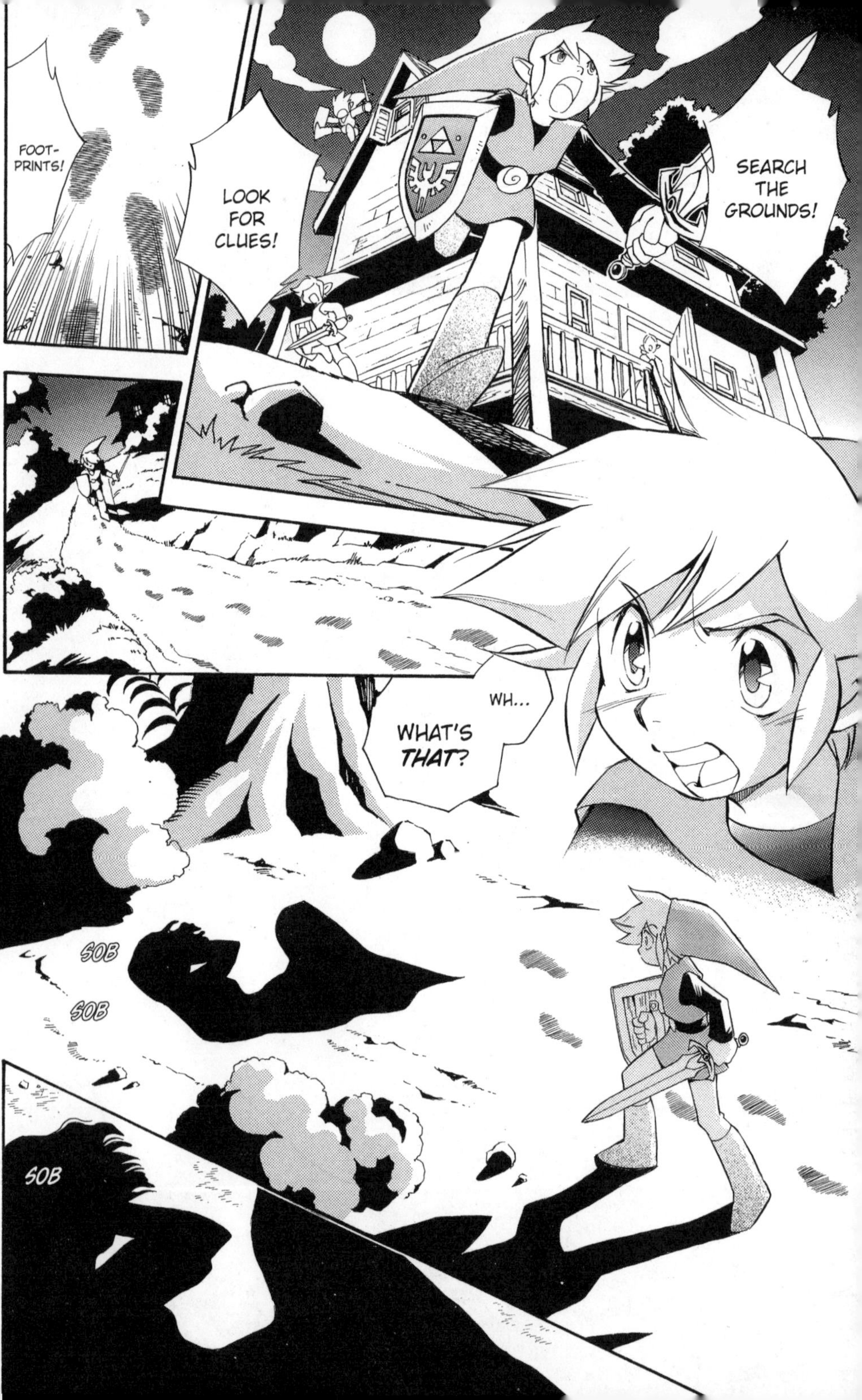
SEARCH THE GROUNDS!
LOOK FOR CLUES!
FOOT-PRINTS!
WH...
WHAT'S *THAT*?
SOB
SOB
SOB

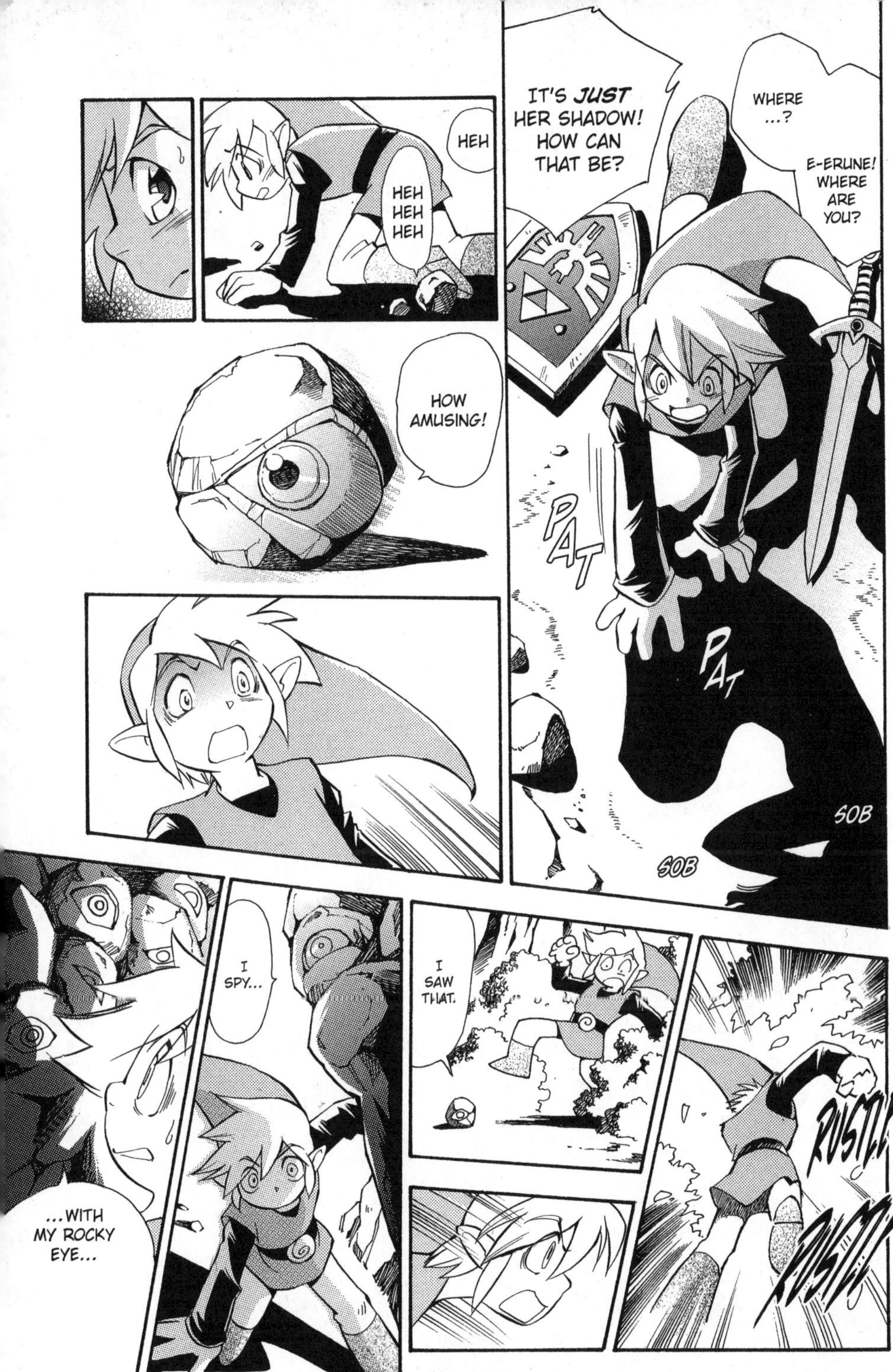
WHERE ...?
E-ERUNE! WHERE ARE YOU?
IT'S JUST HER SHADOW! HOW CAN THAT BE?
PAT
PAT
SOB
SOB
HEH
HEH HEH HEH
HOW AMUSING!
RUSTLE
RUSTLE
I SAW THAT.
I SPY...
...WITH MY ROCKY EYE...

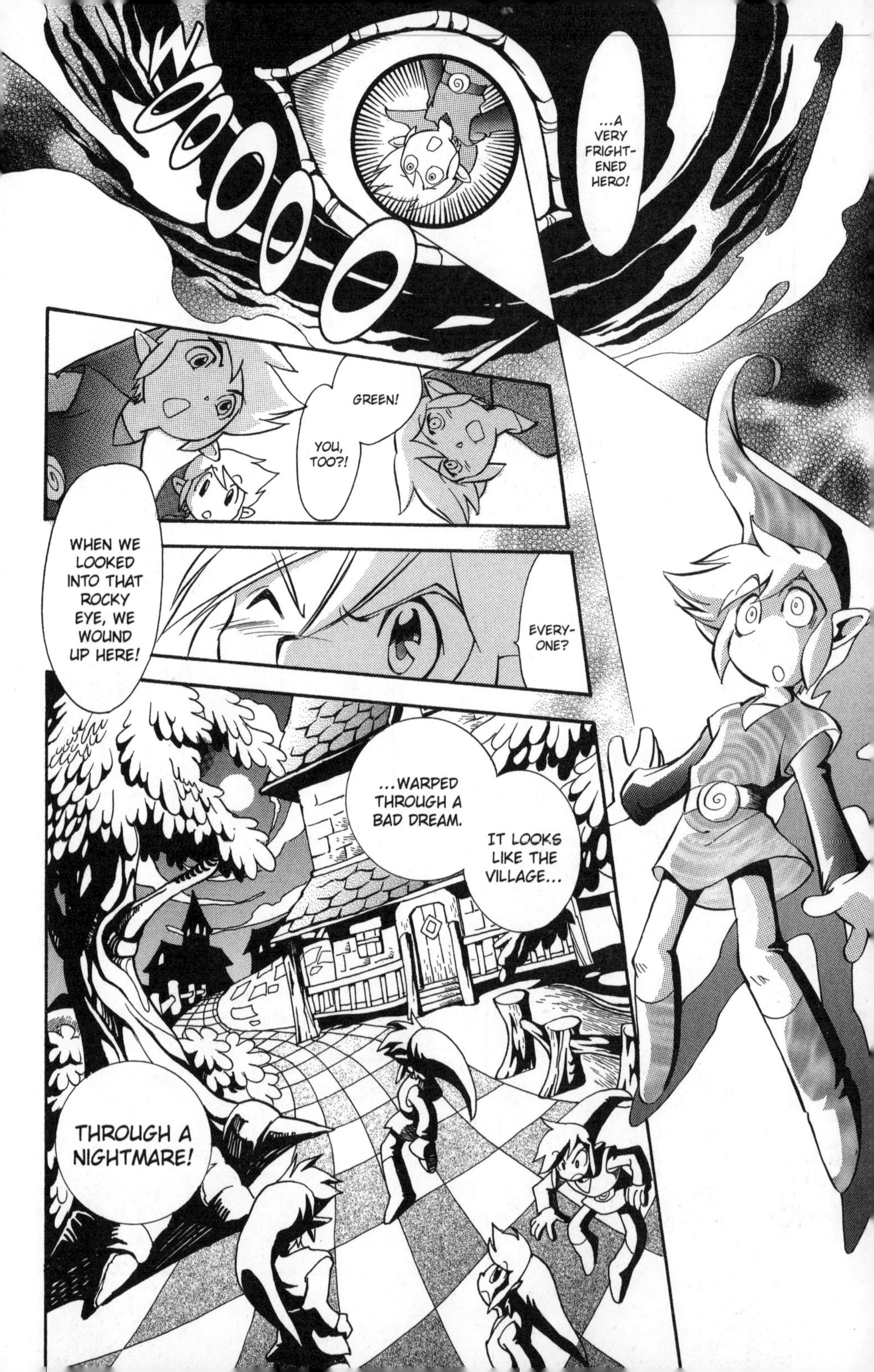
...A VERY FRIGHT-ENED HERO!
WOOOOO
EVERY-ONE?
GREEN!
YOU, TOO?!
WHEN WE LOOKED INTO THAT ROCKY EYE, WE WOUND UP HERE!
IT LOOKS LIKE THE VILLAGE...
...WARPED THROUGH A BAD DREAM.
THROUGH A NIGHTMARE!

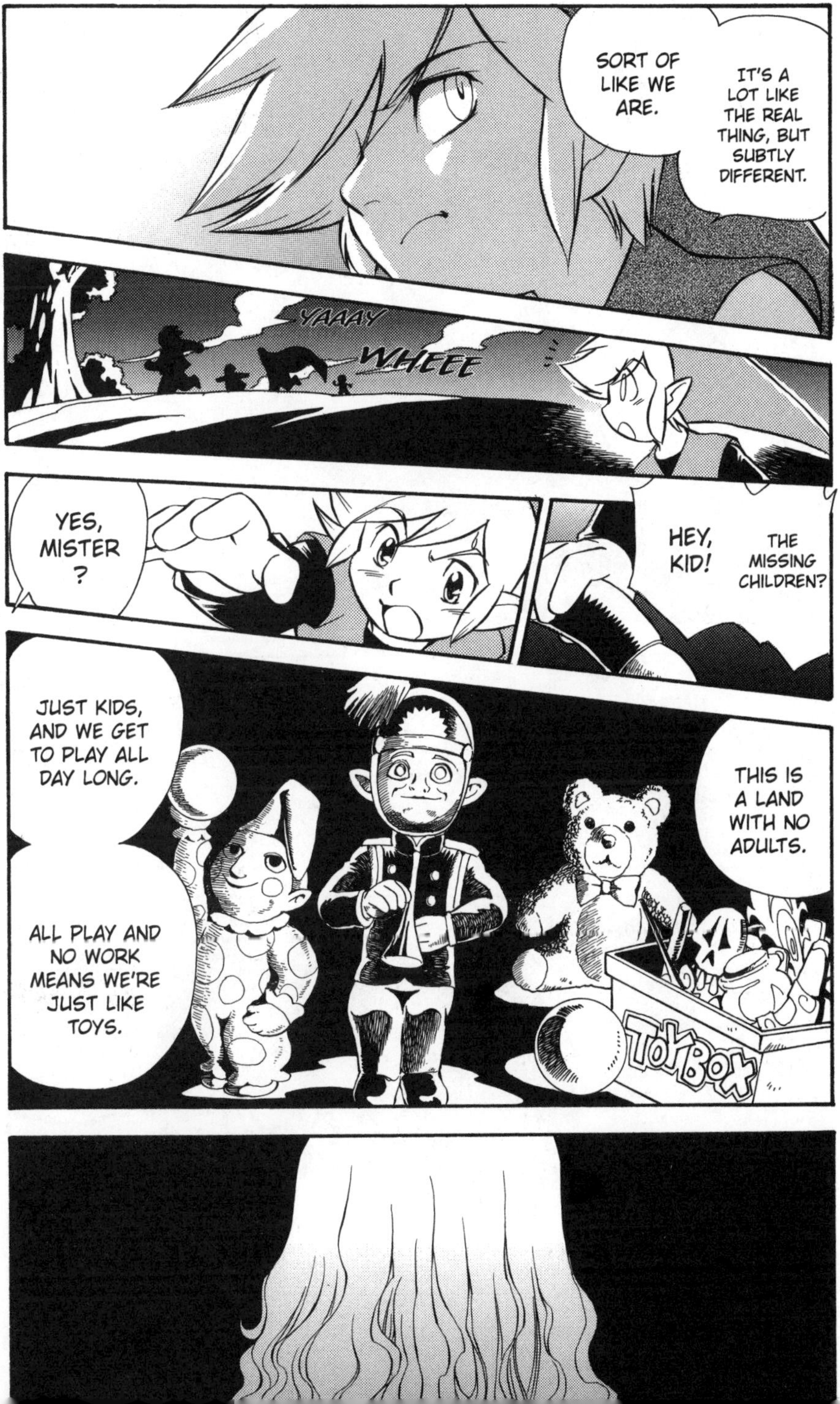
IT'S A LOT LIKE THE REAL THING, BUT SUBTLY DIFFERENT.
SORT OF LIKE WE ARE.
YAAAY
WHEEE
THE MISSING CHILDREN?
HEY, KID!
YES, MISTER?
THIS IS A LAND WITH NO ADULTS.
JUST KIDS, AND WE GET TO PLAY ALL DAY LONG.
ALL PLAY AND NO WORK MEANS WE'RE JUST LIKE TOYS.
TOYBOX

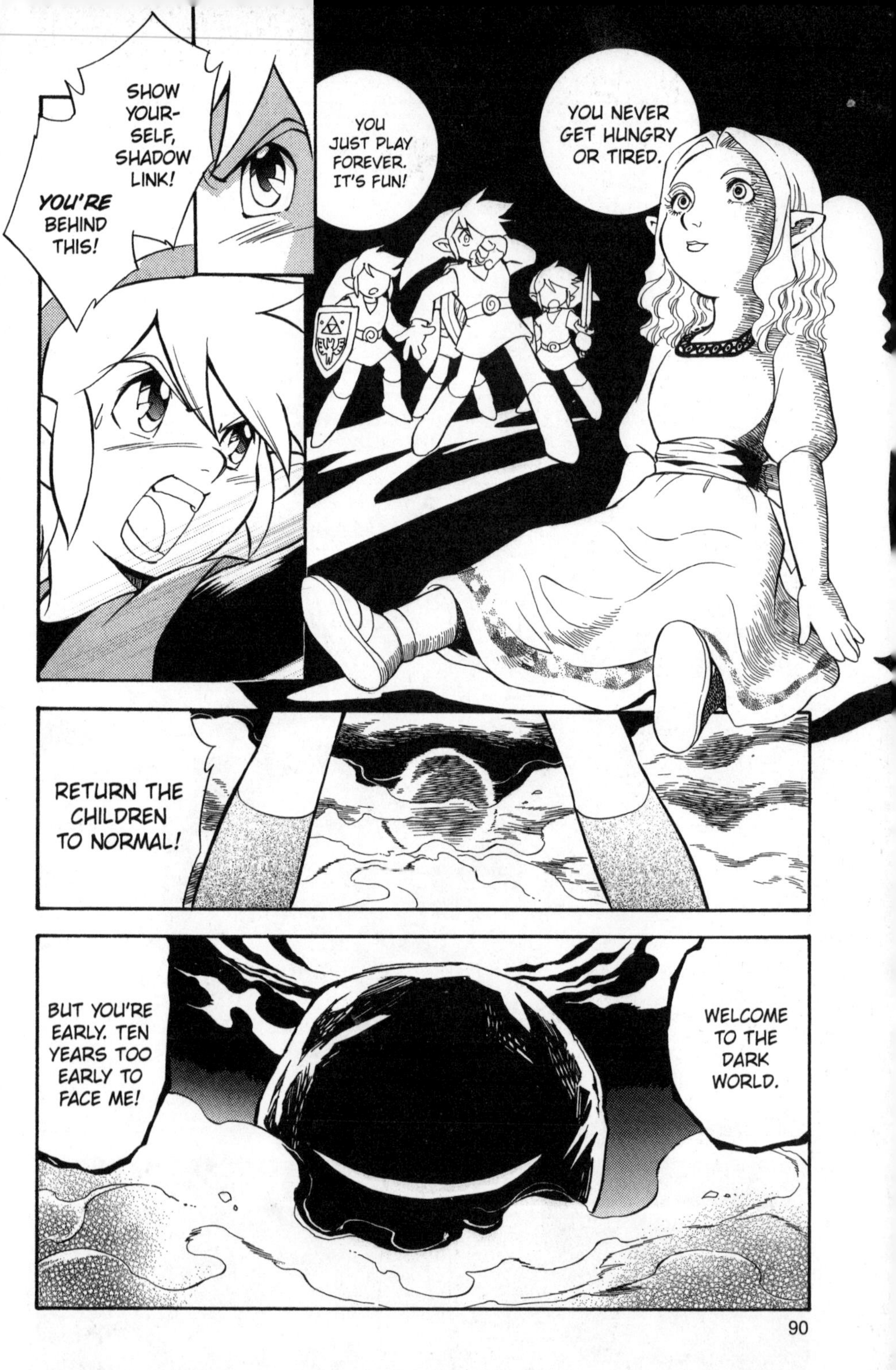
YOU NEVER GET HUNGRY OR TIRED.
YOU JUST PLAY FOREVER. IT'S FUN!
SHOW YOUR-SELF, SHADOW LINK!
YOU'RE BEHIND THIS!
RETURN THE CHILDREN TO NORMAL!
WELCOME TO THE DARK WORLD.
BUT YOU'RE EARLY. TEN YEARS TOO EARLY TO FACE ME!

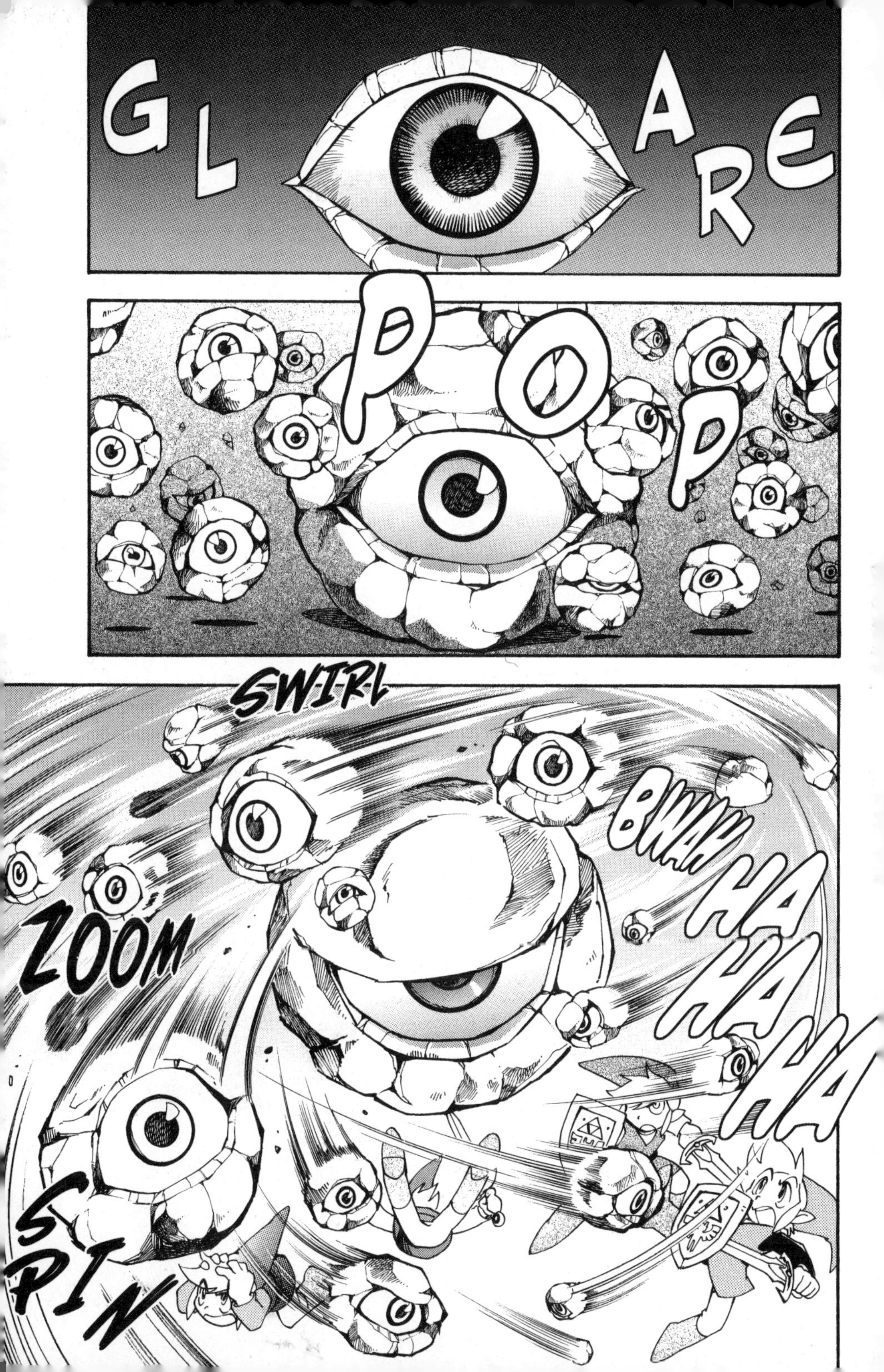
GLARE
POP
POP
BWAH HA HA HA HA
SWIRL
ZOOM
SPIN

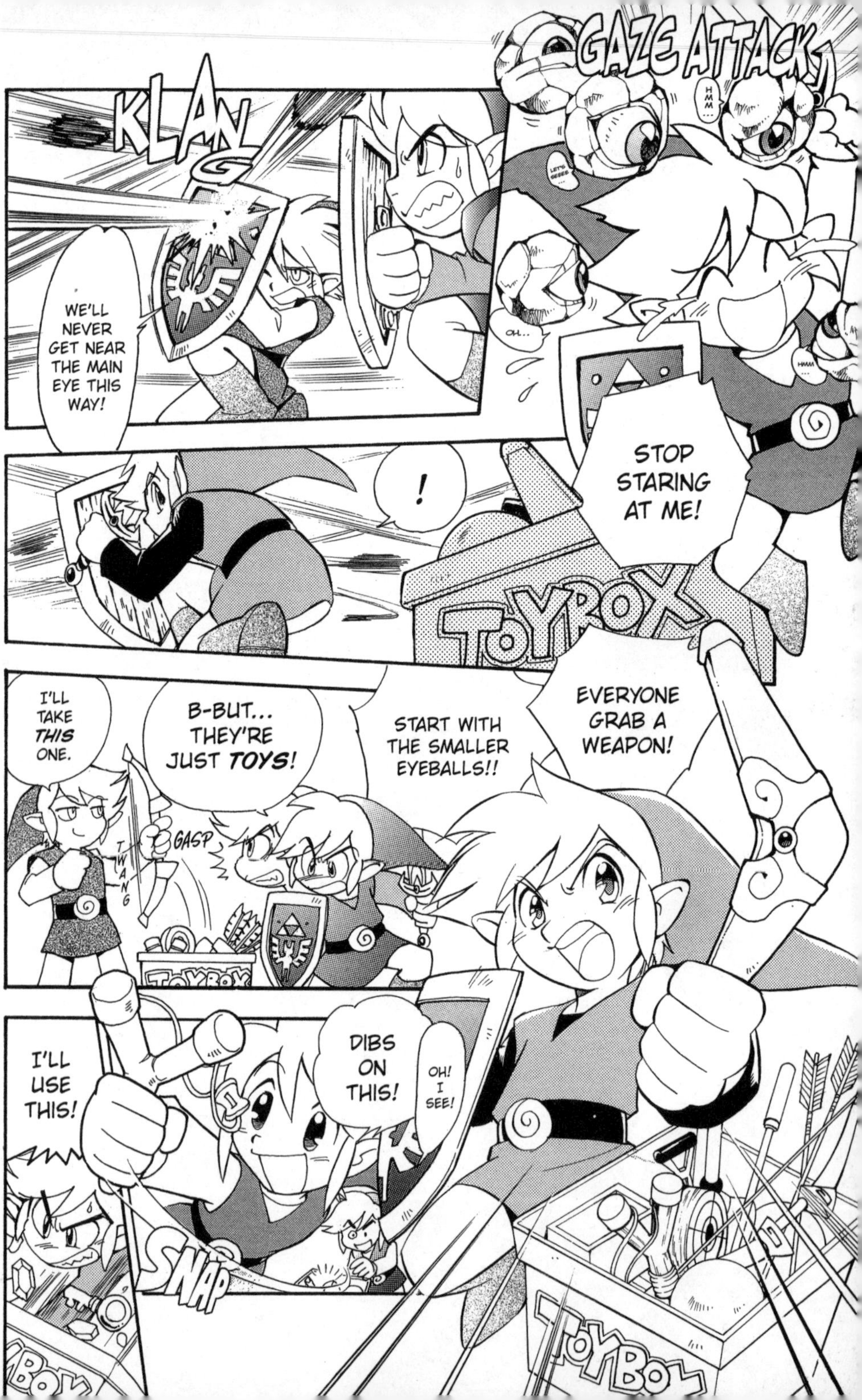
GAZE ATTACK
HMM...
OH...
HMM
KLANG
WE'LL NEVER GET NEAR THE MAIN EYE THIS WAY!
STOP STARING AT ME!
TOYBOX
!
EVERYONE GRAB A WEAPON!
START WITH THE SMALLER EYEBALLS!!
B-BUT... THEY'RE JUST *TOYS*!
GASP
TWANG
I'LL TAKE *THIS* ONE.
OH! I SEE!
DIBS ON THIS!
I'LL USE THIS!
SNAP
TOYBOX
TOYBOX

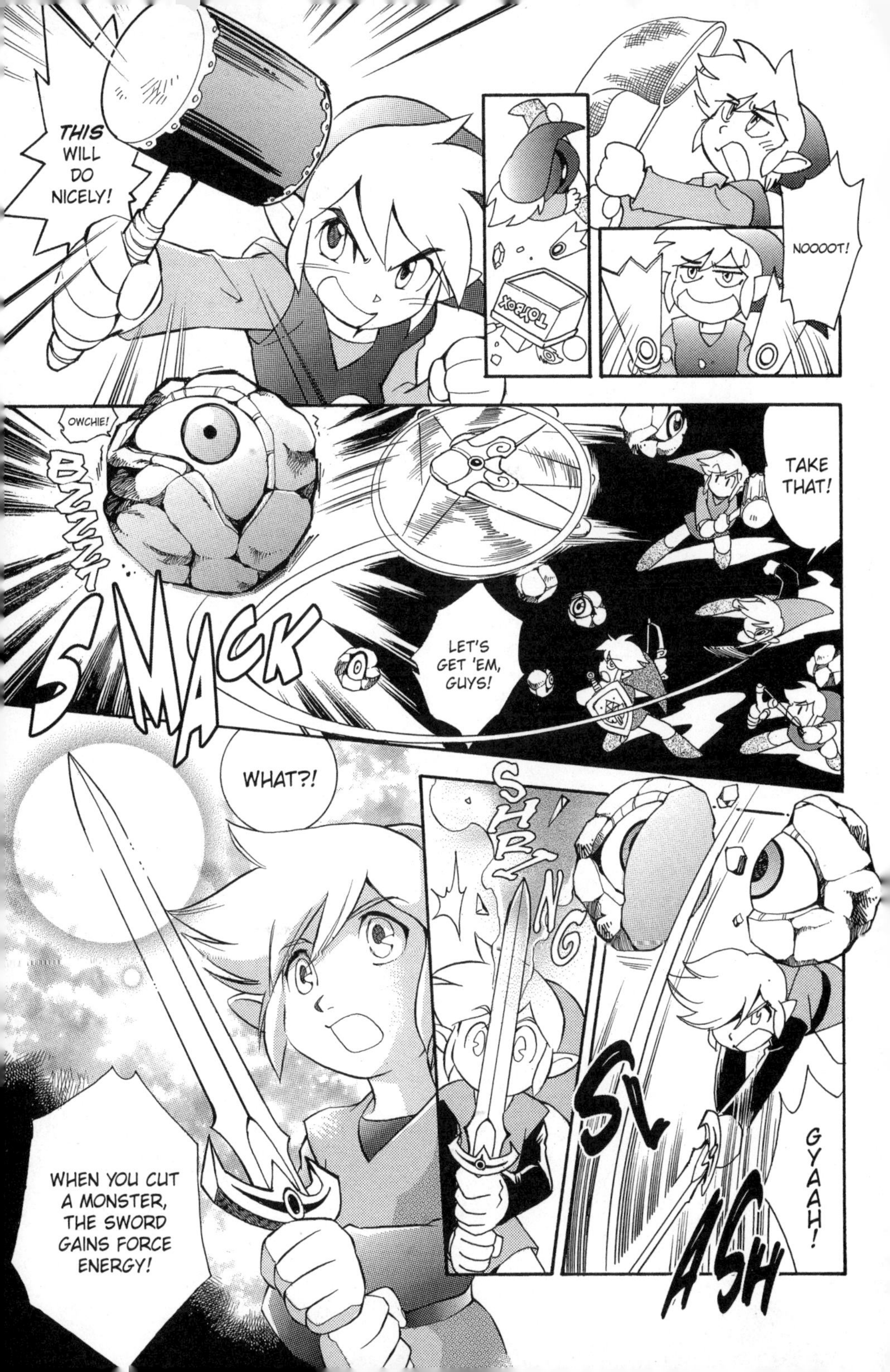

NOOOOT!
TOYBOX
THIS WILL DO NICELY!
TAKE THAT!
OWCHIE!
BZZZT
LET'S GET 'EM, GUYS!
SMACK
GYAAH!
SLASH
SHRING
WHAT?!
WHEN YOU CUT A MONSTER, THE SWORD GAINS FORCE ENERGY!

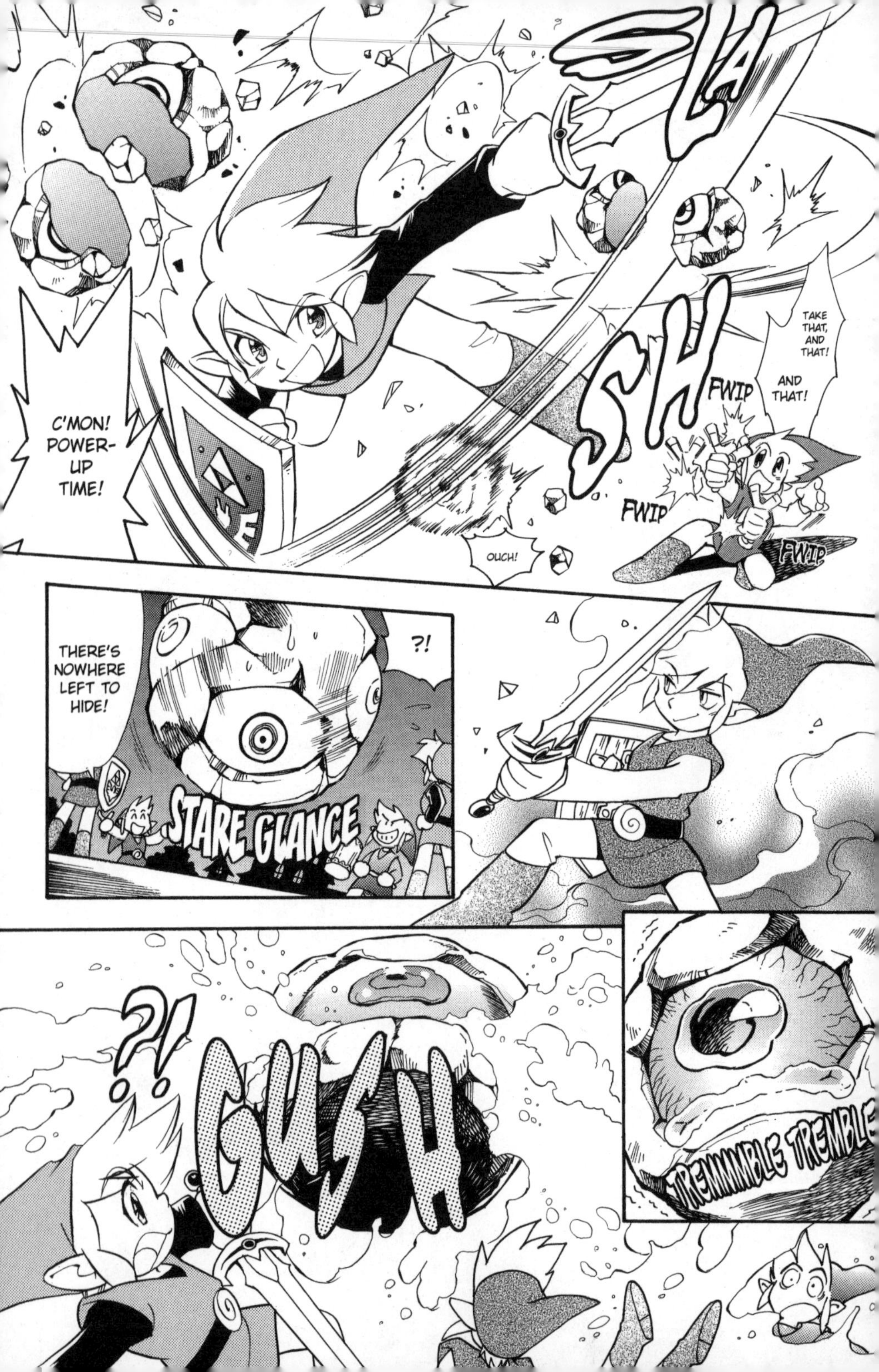
SLA
TAKE THAT, AND THAT!
AND THAT!
SH
FWIP
FWIP
FWIP
OUCH!
C'MON! POWER-UP TIME!
?!
THERE'S NOWHERE LEFT TO HIDE!
STARE GLANCE
TREMMMBLE TREMBLE
GUSH
?!

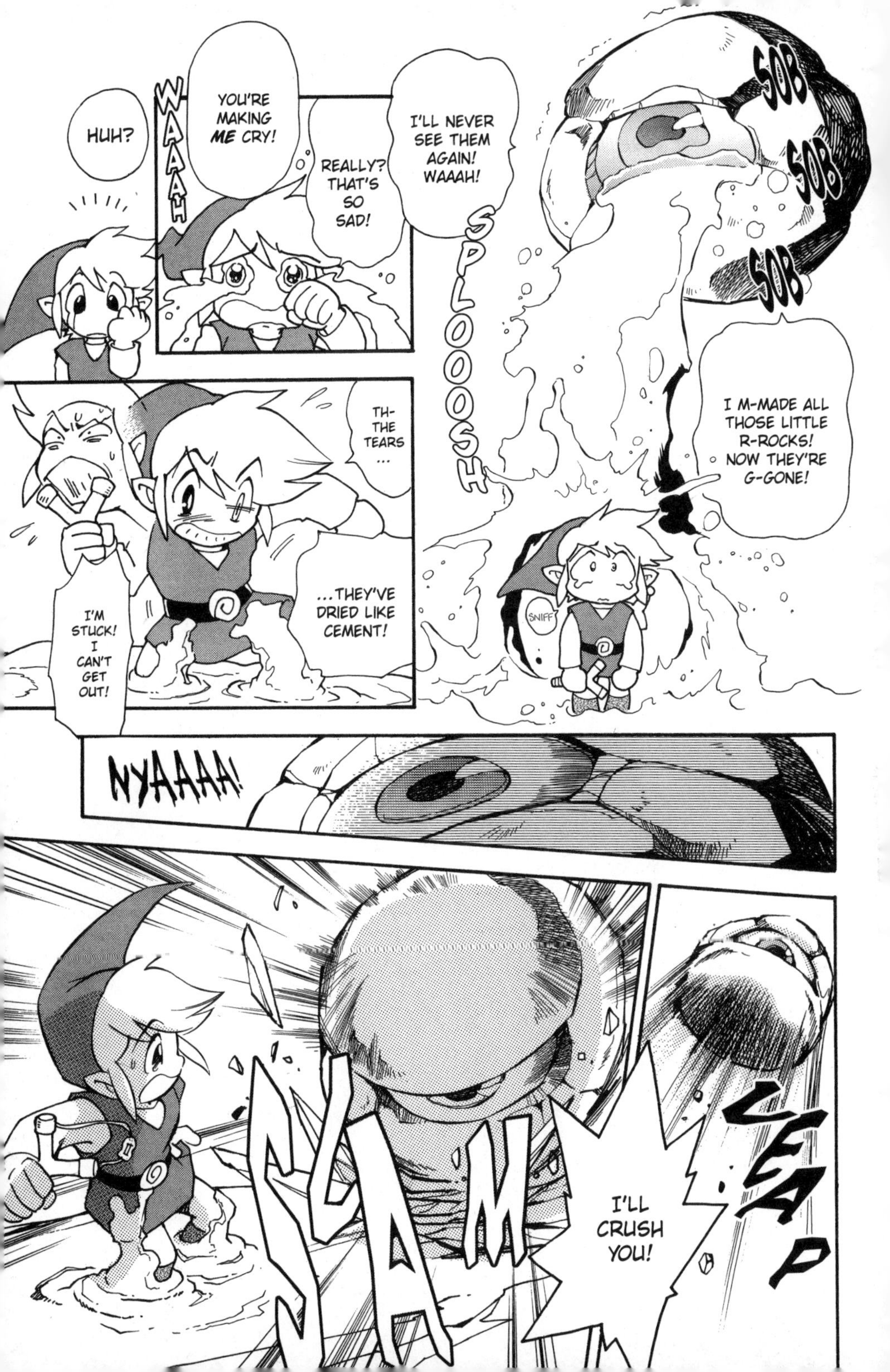
SOB SOB SOB
I'LL NEVER SEE THEM AGAIN! WAAAH!
SPLOOOOSH
I M-MADE ALL THOSE LITTLE R-ROCKS! NOW THEY'RE G-GONE!
SNIFF
REALLY? THAT'S SO SAD!
YOU'RE MAKING *ME* CRY!
WAAAAH
HUH?
TH- THE TEARS ...
...THEY'VE DRIED LIKE CEMENT!
I'M STUCK! I CAN'T GET OUT!
NYAAAA!
LEAP
I'LL CRUSH YOU!
SLAM

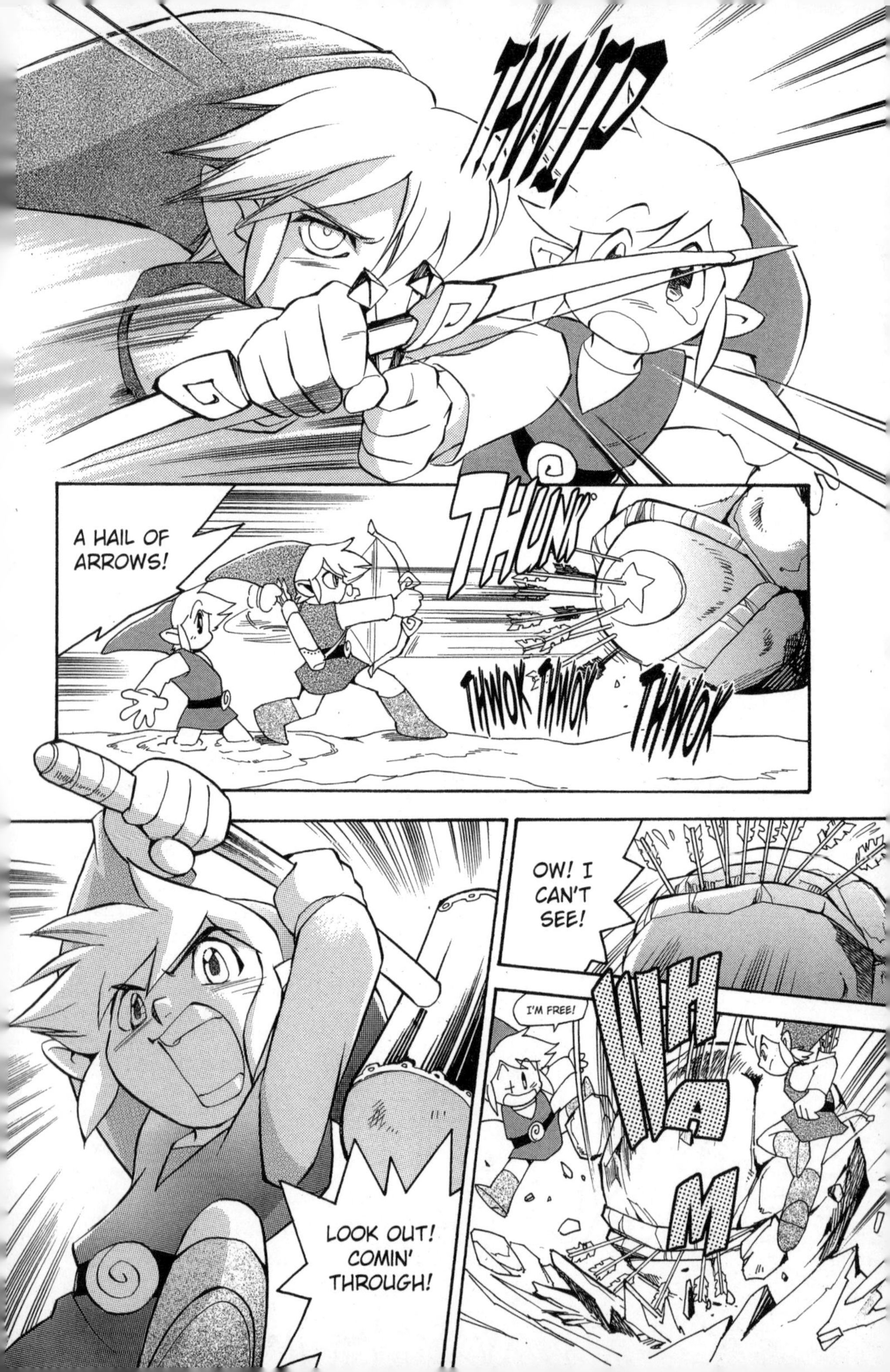

THWIP
THUNK
A HAIL OF ARROWS!
THWOK THWOK
THWOK
OW! I CAN'T SEE!
I'M FREE!
WHAM
LOOK OUT! COMIN' THROUGH!

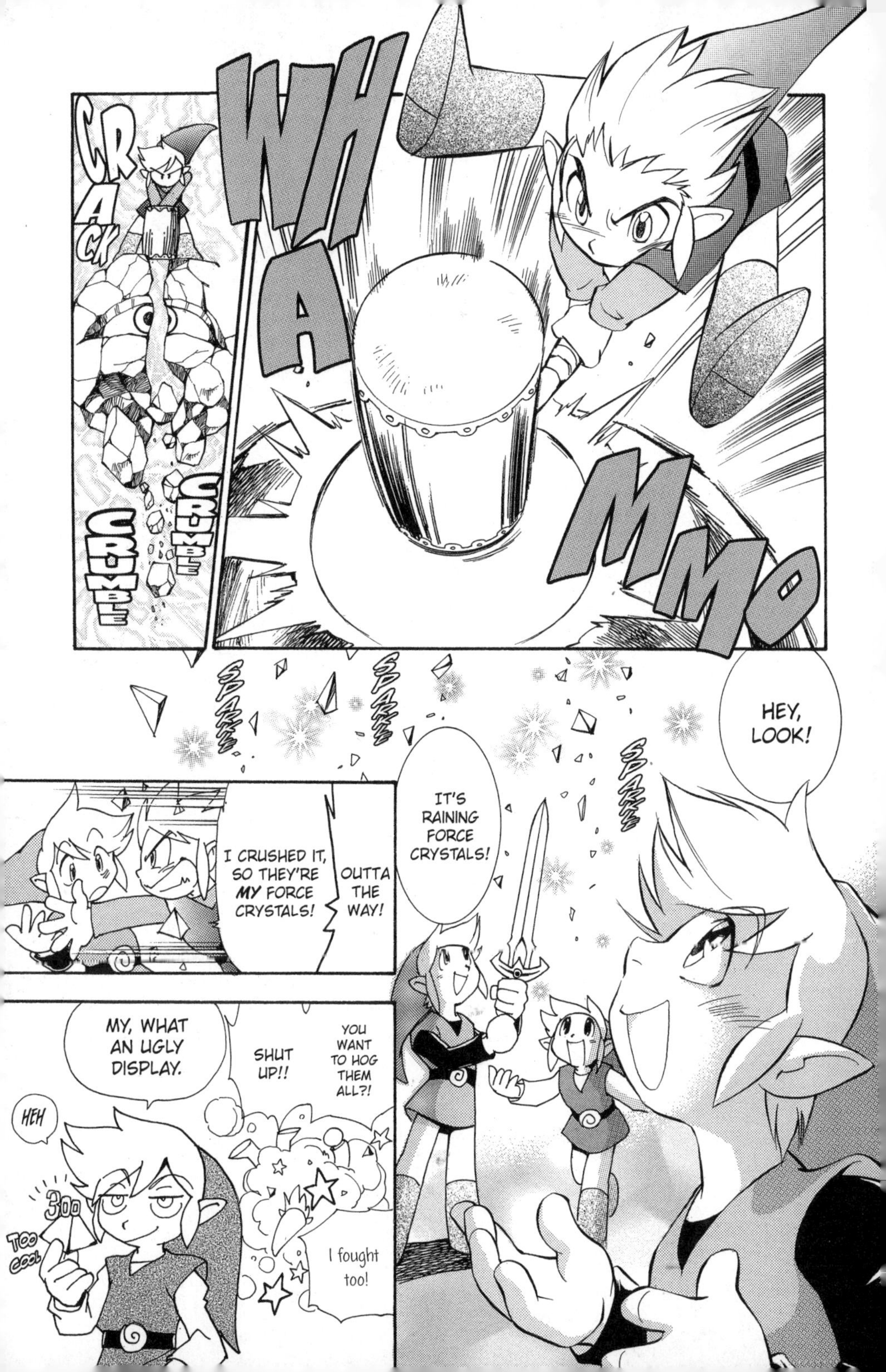
WHAMMO
CRACK
CRUMBLE
CRUMBLE
SPARKLE
SPARKLE
SPARKLE
HEY, LOOK!
IT'S RAINING FORCE CRYSTALS!
OUTTA THE WAY!
I CRUSHED IT, SO THEY'RE *MY* FORCE CRYSTALS!
YOU WANT TO HOG THEM ALL?!
SHUT UP!!
MY, WHAT AN UGLY DISPLAY.
HEH
I fought too!
300
TOO COOL

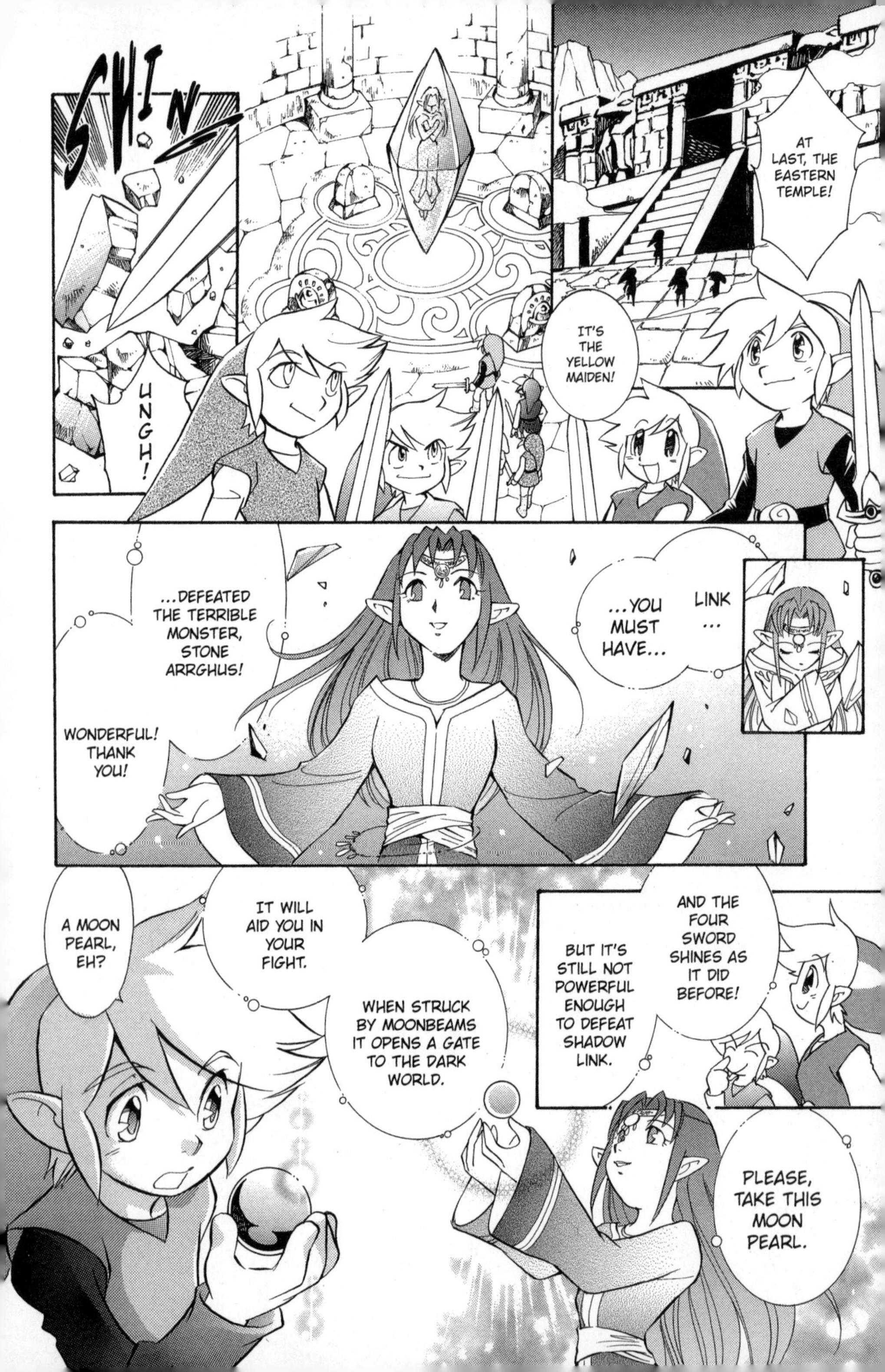
AT LAST, THE EASTERN TEMPLE!
IT'S THE YELLOW MAIDEN!
SHIN
UNGH!
LINK...
...YOU MUST HAVE...
...DEFEATED THE TERRIBLE MONSTER, STONE ARRGHUS!
WONDERFUL! THANK YOU!
AND THE FOUR SWORD SHINES AS IT DID BEFORE!
BUT IT'S STILL NOT POWERFUL ENOUGH TO DEFEAT SHADOW LINK.
PLEASE, TAKE THIS MOON PEARL.
WHEN STRUCK BY MOONBEAMS IT OPENS A GATE TO THE DARK WORLD.
IT WILL AID YOU IN YOUR FIGHT.
A MOON PEARL, EH?

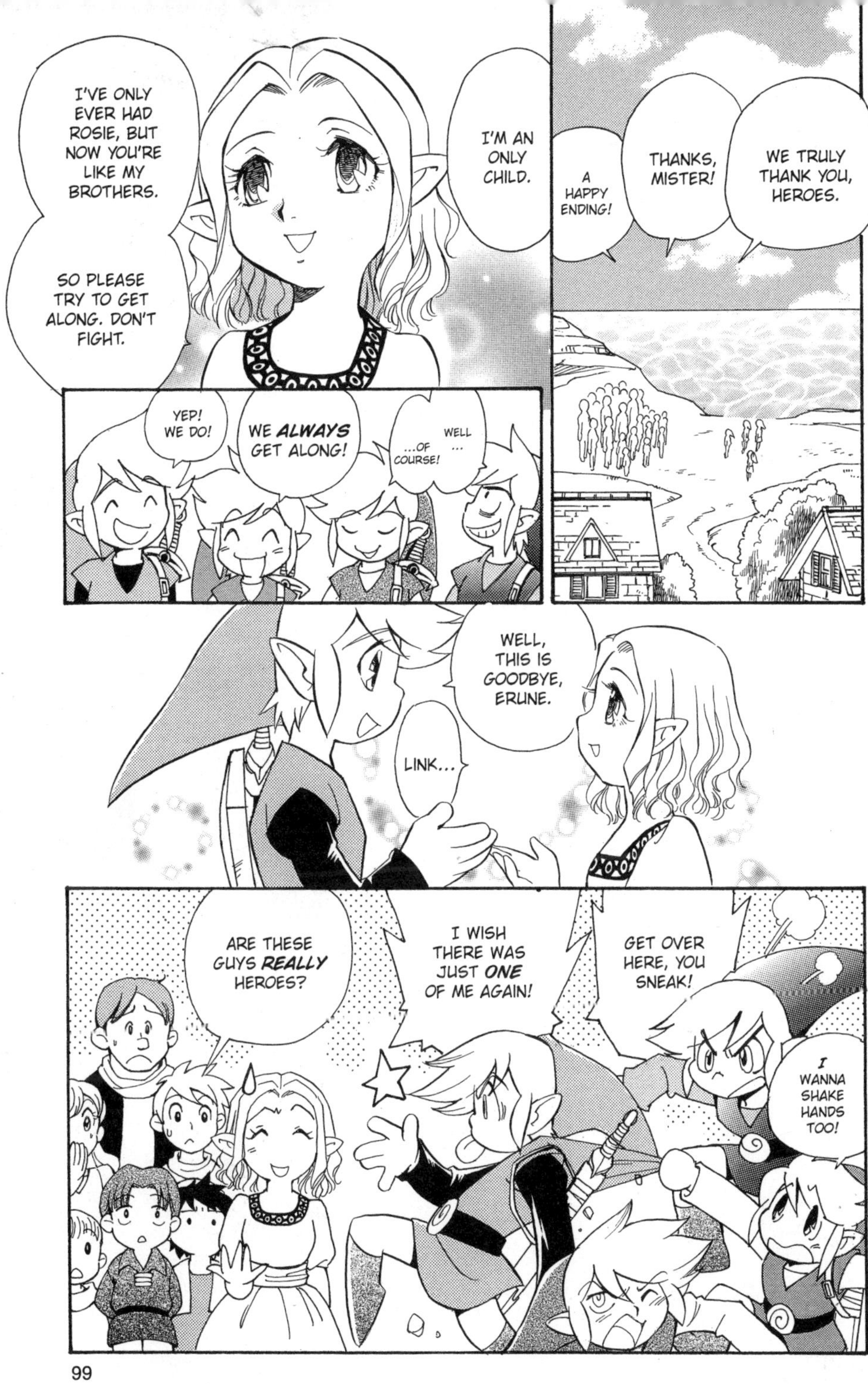
WE TRULY THANK YOU, HEROES.
THANKS, MISTER!
A HAPPY ENDING!
I'M AN ONLY CHILD.
I'VE ONLY EVER HAD ROSIE, BUT NOW YOU'RE LIKE MY BROTHERS.
SO PLEASE TRY TO GET ALONG. DON'T FIGHT.
WELL...
...OF COURSE!
WE ALWAYS GET ALONG!
YEP! WE DO!
WELL, THIS IS GOODBYE, ERUNE.
LINK...
I WANNA SHAKE HANDS TOO!
GET OVER HERE, YOU SNEAK!
I WISH THERE WAS JUST ONE OF ME AGAIN!
ARE THESE GUYS REALLY HEROES?

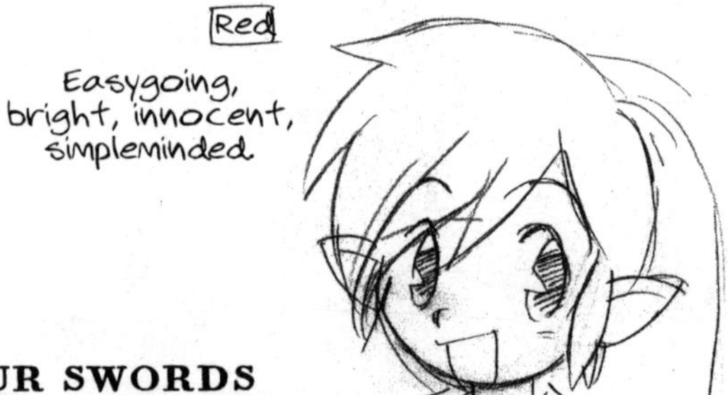
Red
Easygoing, bright, innocent, simpleminded

FOUR SWORDS ROUGH CHARACTER ILLUSTRATION 3

CHAPTER 4 Links Torn Apart

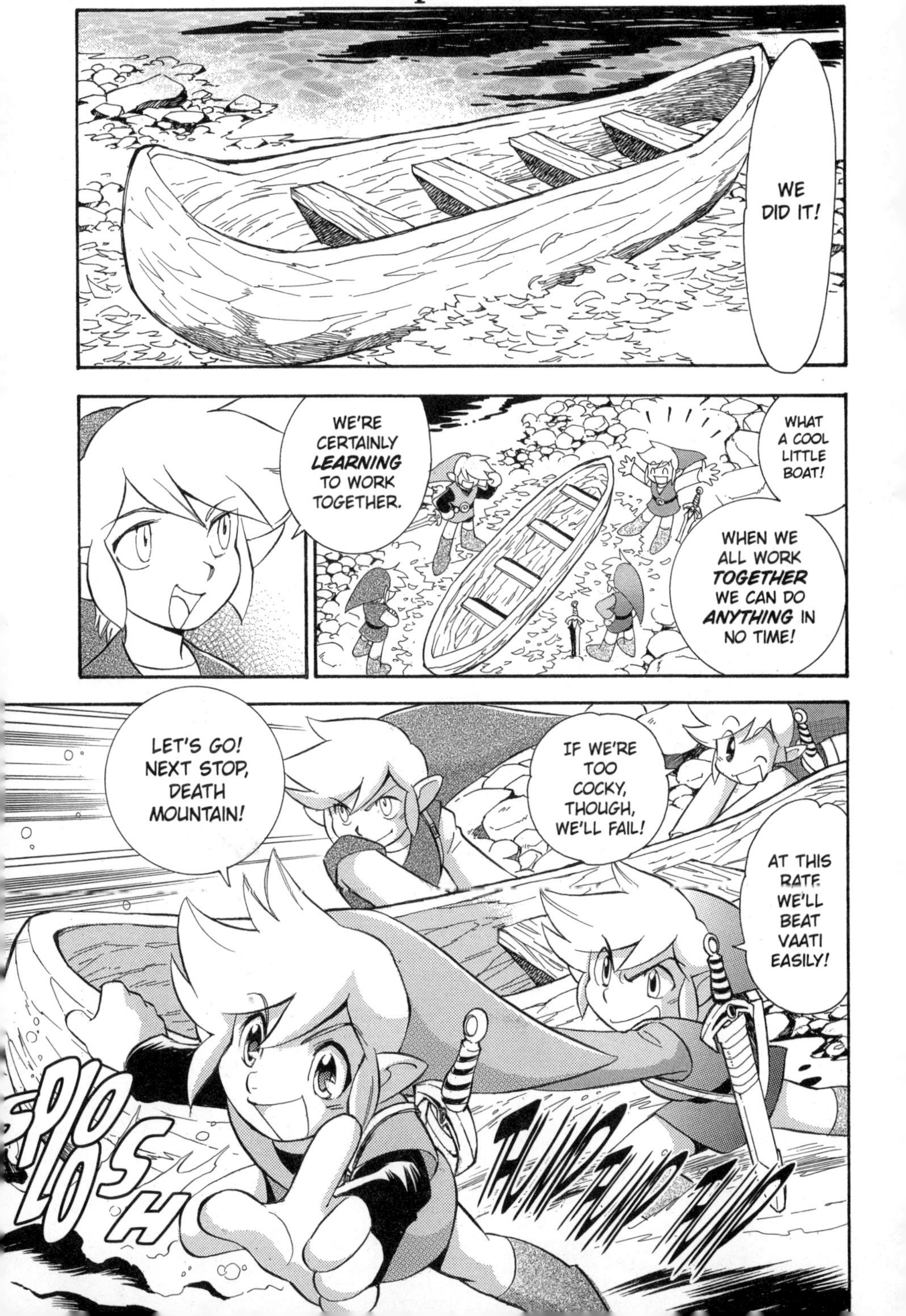
WE DID IT!
WHAT A COOL LITTLE BOAT!
WHEN WE ALL WORK TOGETHER WE CAN DO ANYTHING IN NO TIME!
WE'RE CERTAINLY LEARNING TO WORK TOGETHER.
AT THIS RATE WE'LL BEAT VAATI EASILY!
IF WE'RE TOO COCKY, THOUGH, WE'LL FAIL!
LET'S GO! NEXT STOP, DEATH MOUNTAIN!

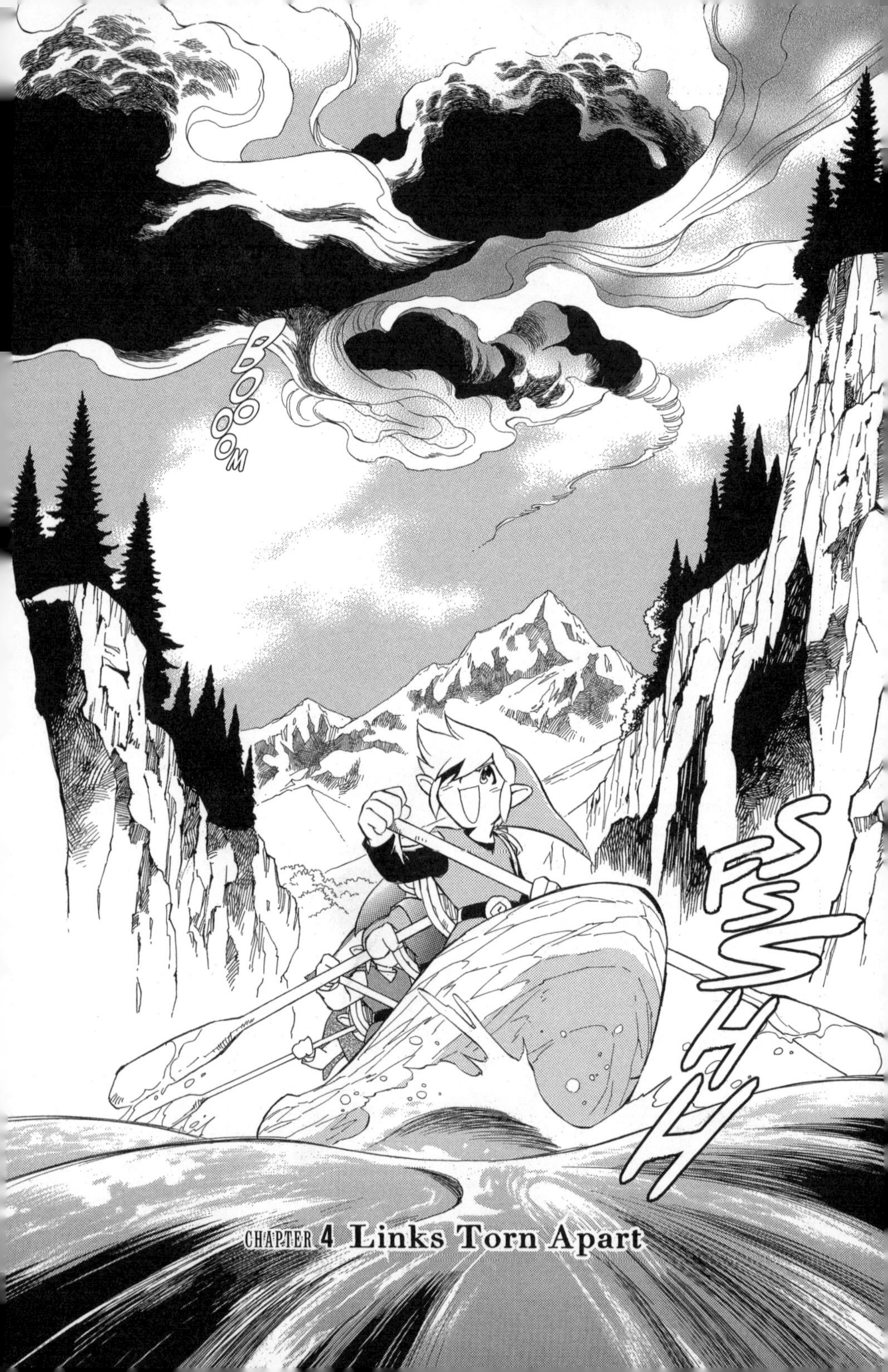
BOOOOM
SFSSHHH
CHAPTER 4 Links Torn Apart

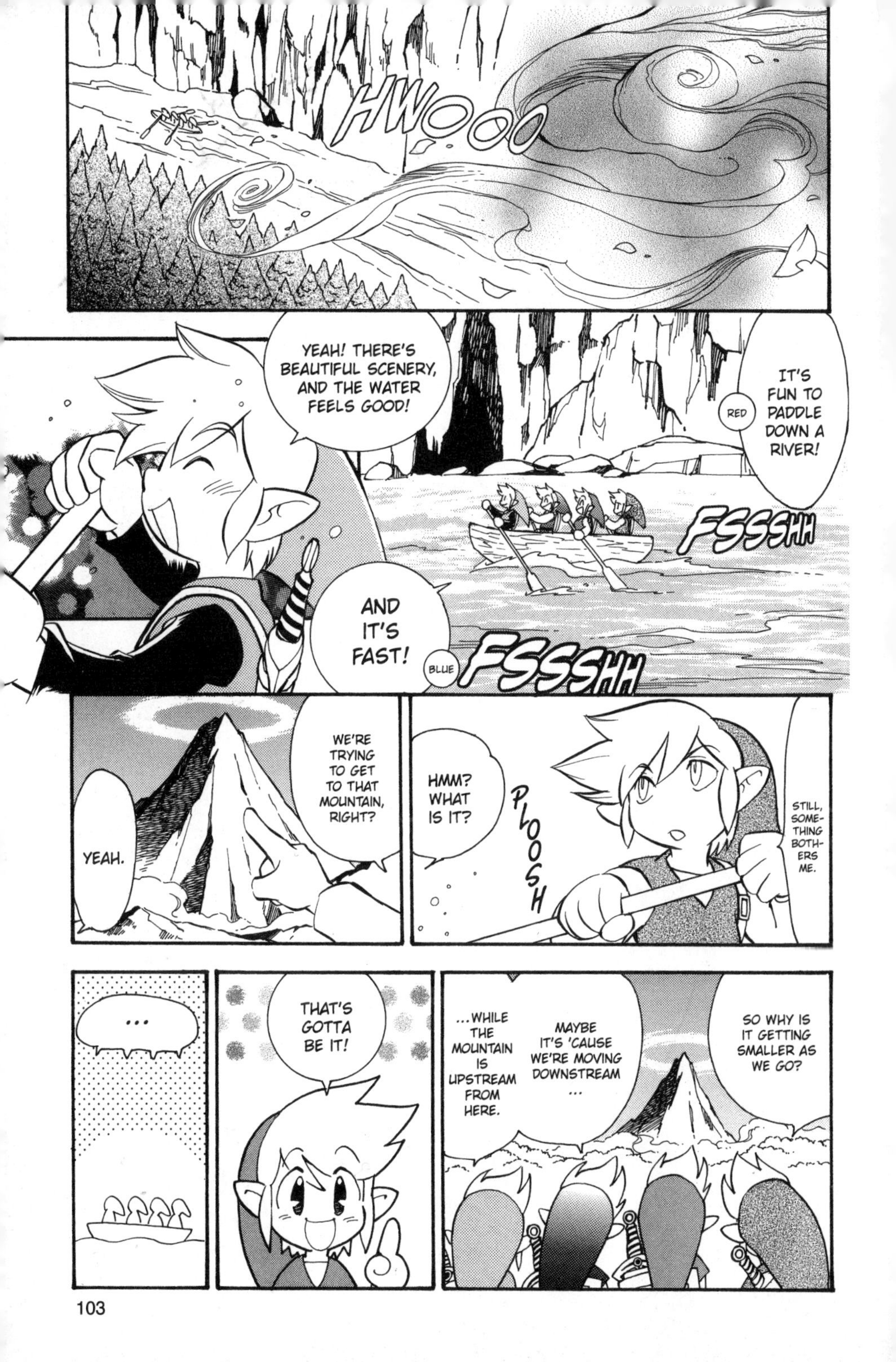
HWOOO
RED
IT'S FUN TO PADDLE DOWN A RIVER!
YEAH! THERE'S BEAUTIFUL SCENERY, AND THE WATER FEELS GOOD!
FSSSHH
BLUE
AND IT'S FAST!
FSSSHH
STILL, SOMETHING BOTHERS ME.
PLOOSH
HMM? WHAT IS IT?
WE'RE TRYING TO GET TO THAT MOUNTAIN, RIGHT?
YEAH.
SO WHY IS IT GETTING SMALLER AS WE GO?
MAYBE IT'S 'CAUSE WE'RE MOVING DOWNSTREAM ...
...WHILE THE MOUNTAIN IS UPSTREAM FROM HERE.
THAT'S GOTTA BE IT!
...

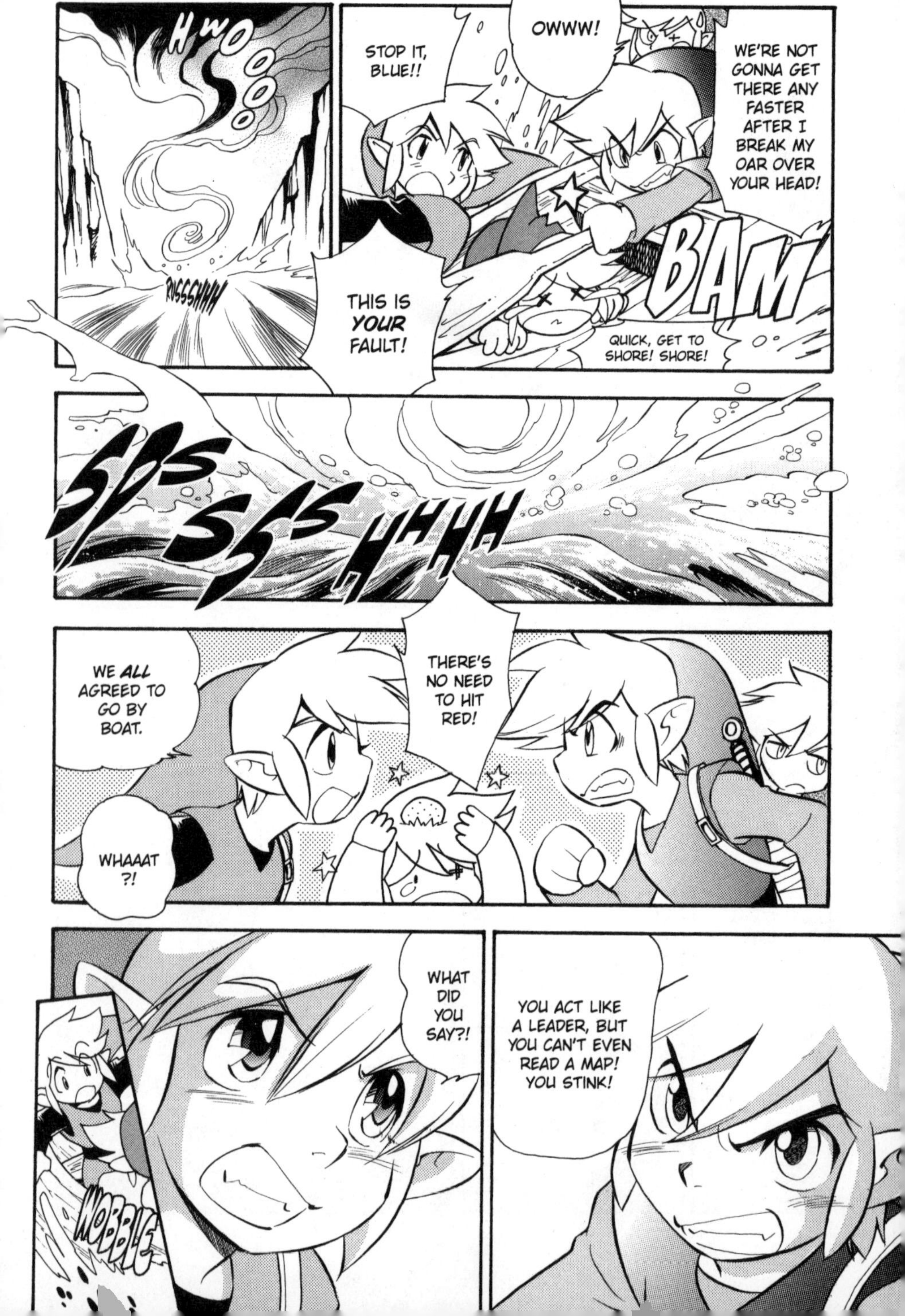
WE'RE NOT GONNA GET THERE ANY FASTER AFTER I BREAK MY OAR OVER YOUR HEAD!
OWWW!
STOP IT, BLUE!!
BAM
QUICK, GET TO SHORE! SHORE!
THIS IS *YOUR* FAULT!
HWOOOOOO
RUSSSHHH
THERE'S NO NEED TO HIT RED!
WE *ALL* AGREED TO GO BY BOAT.
WHAAAT?!
YOU ACT LIKE A LEADER, BUT YOU CAN'T EVEN READ A MAP! YOU STINK!
WHAT DID YOU SAY?!
WOBBLE

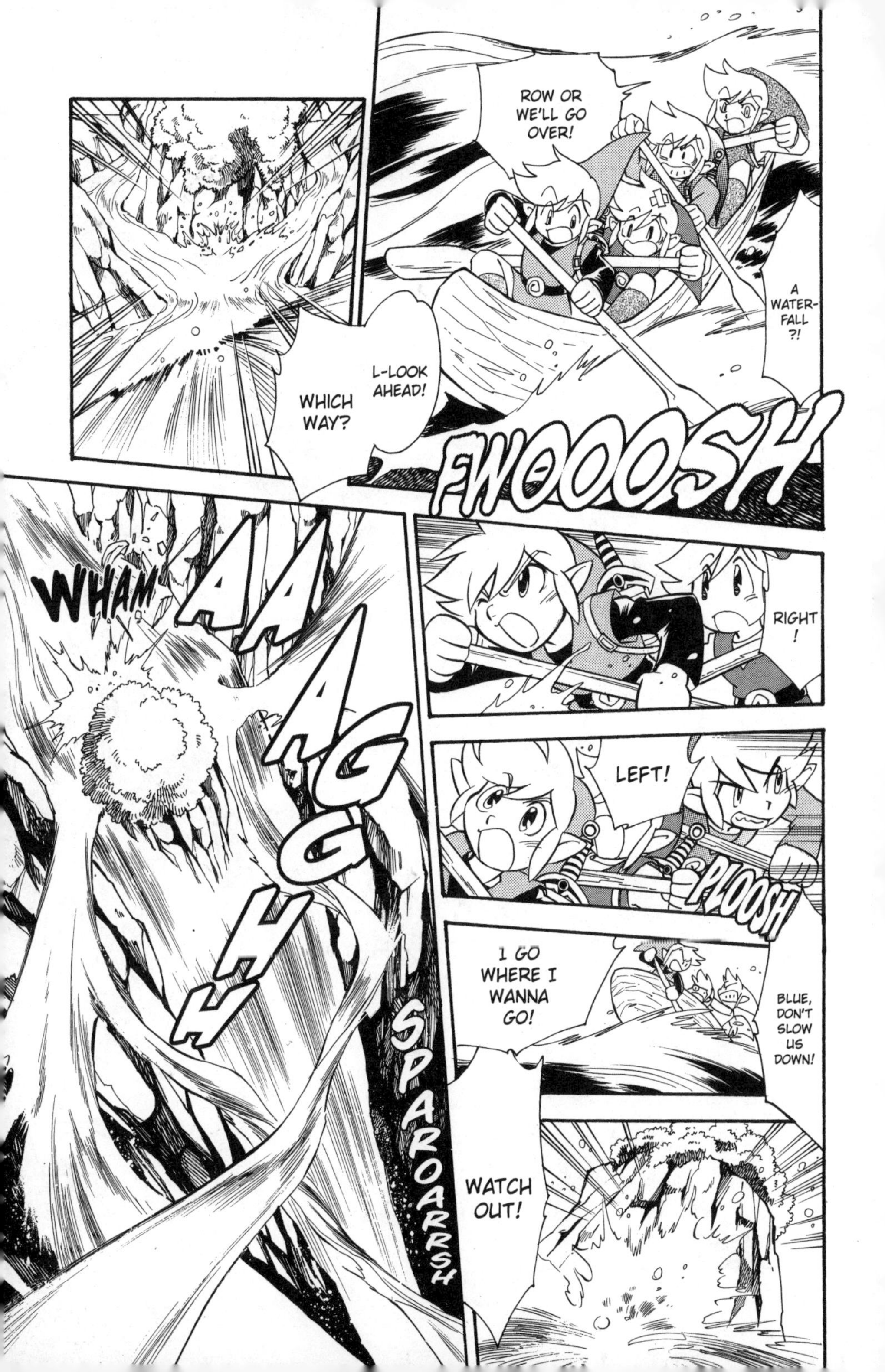
ROW OR WE'LL GO OVER!
A WATERFALL?!
L-LOOK AHEAD!
WHICH WAY?
FWOOOSH
RIGHT!
LEFT!
PLOOSH
BLUE, DON'T SLOW US DOWN!
I GO WHERE I WANNA GO!
WATCH OUT!
WHAM
AAAGGHHH
SPAROARRSH

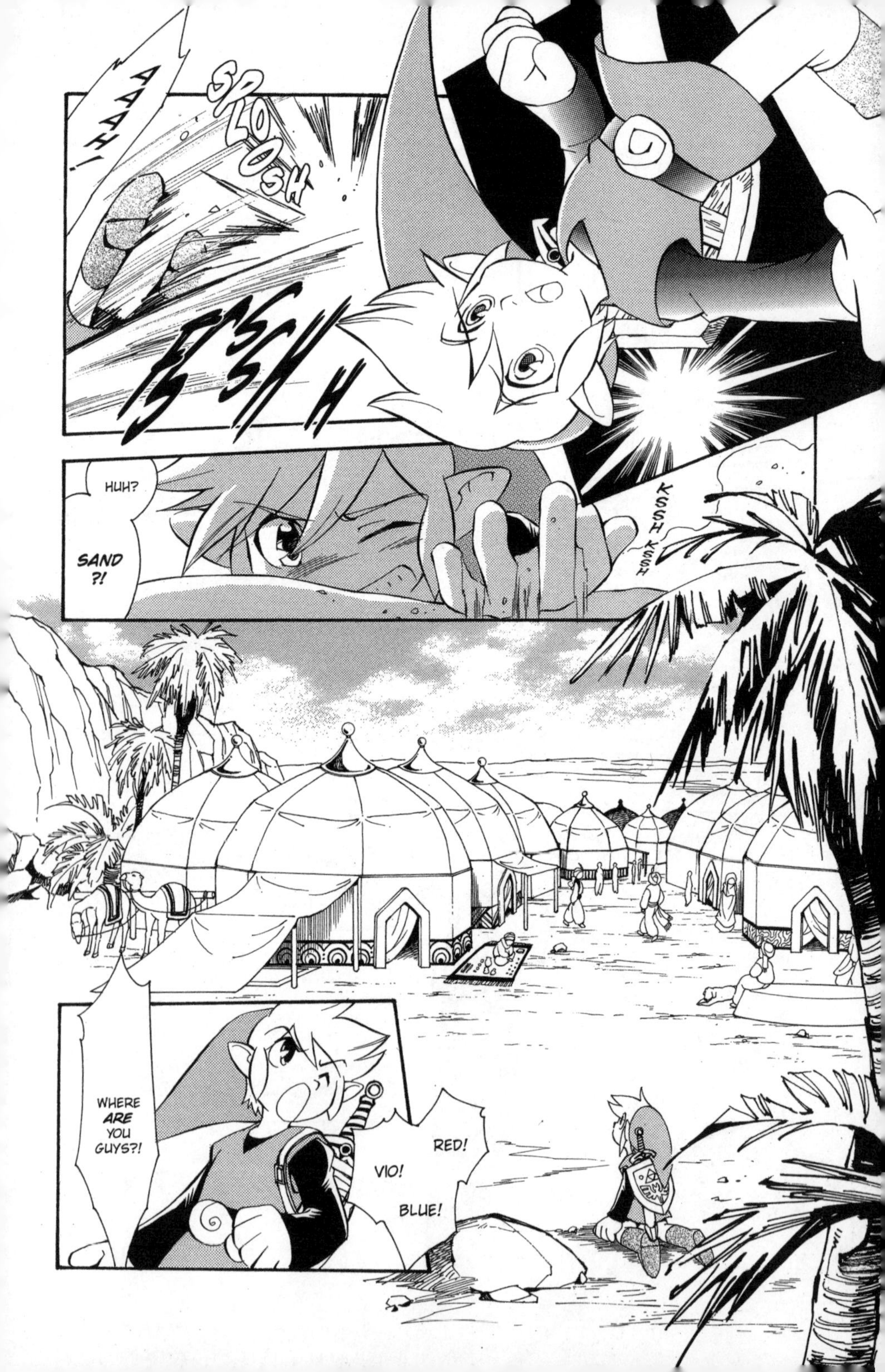
AAAAH!
SPLOSH
FSSHH
KSSH KSSH
HUH?
SAND?!
WHERE ARE YOU GUYS?!
RED!
VIO!
BLUE!

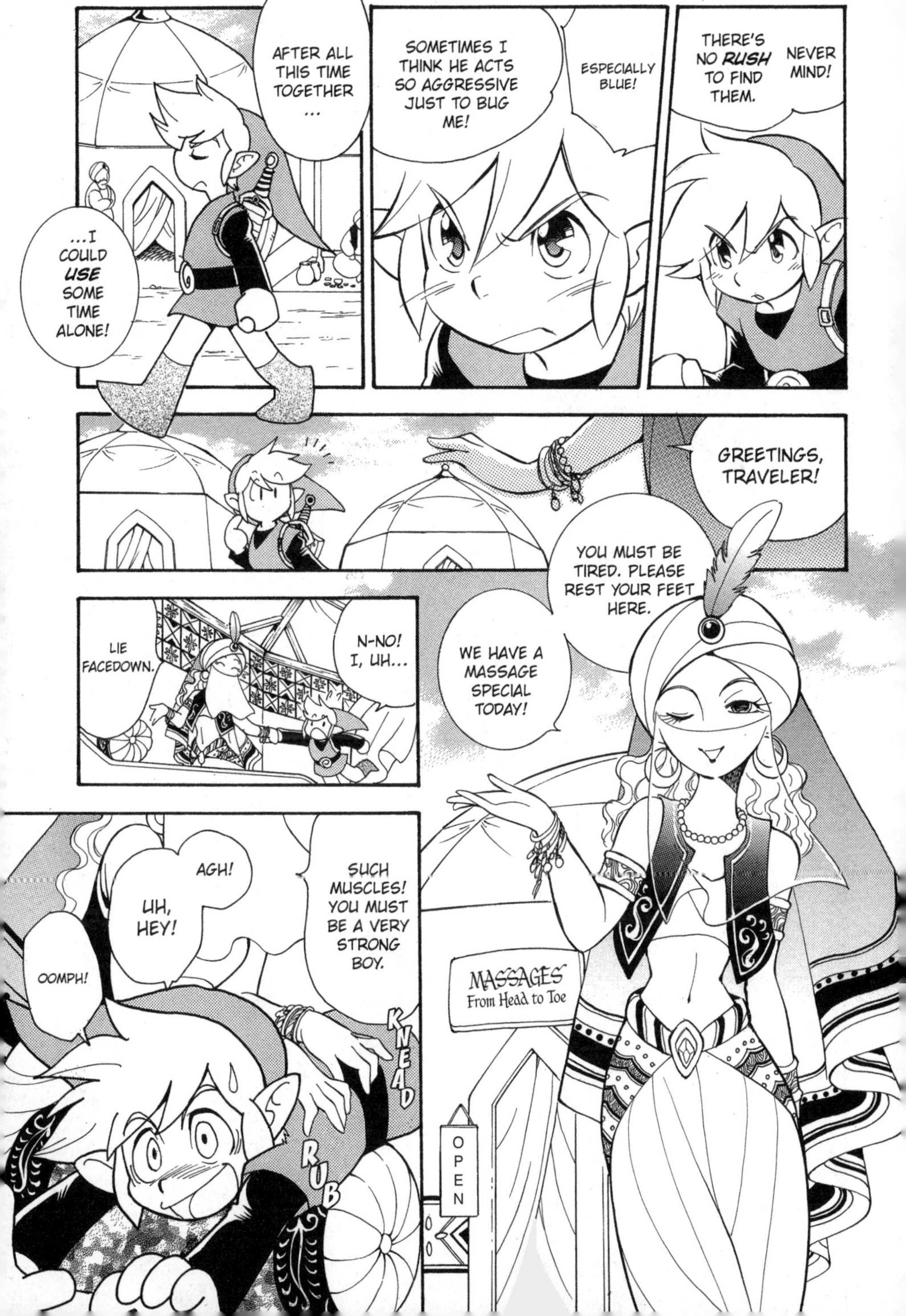
NEVER MIND!
THERE'S NO RUSH TO FIND THEM.
SOMETIMES I THINK HE ACTS SO AGGRESSIVE JUST TO BUG ME!
ESPECIALLY BLUE!
AFTER ALL THIS TIME TOGETHER...
...I COULD USE SOME TIME ALONE!
GREETINGS, TRAVELER!
YOU MUST BE TIRED. PLEASE REST YOUR FEET HERE.
WE HAVE A MASSAGE SPECIAL TODAY!
MASSAGES
From Head to Toe
OPEN
N-NO! I, UH...
LIE FACEDOWN.
SUCH MUSCLES! YOU MUST BE A VERY STRONG BOY.
AGH!
UH, HEY!
OOMPH!
KNEAD
RUB

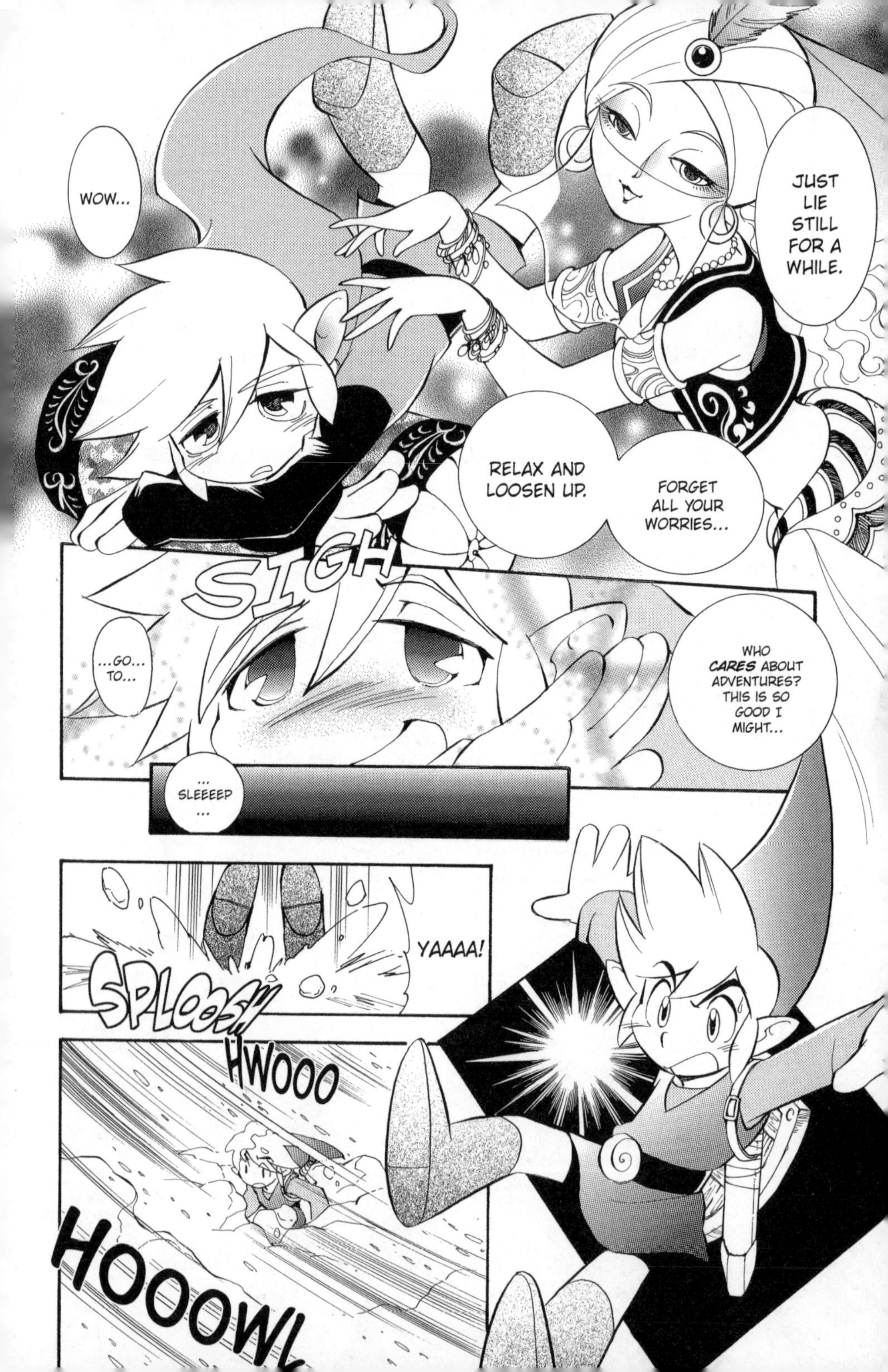
JUST LIE STILL FOR A WHILE.
FORGET ALL YOUR WORRIES...
RELAX AND LOOSEN UP.
WOW...
SIGH
WHO *CARES* ABOUT ADVENTURES? THIS IS SO GOOD I MIGHT...
...GO... TO...
... SLEEEEP ...
YAAAA!
SPLOOSH
HWOOO
HOOOWL

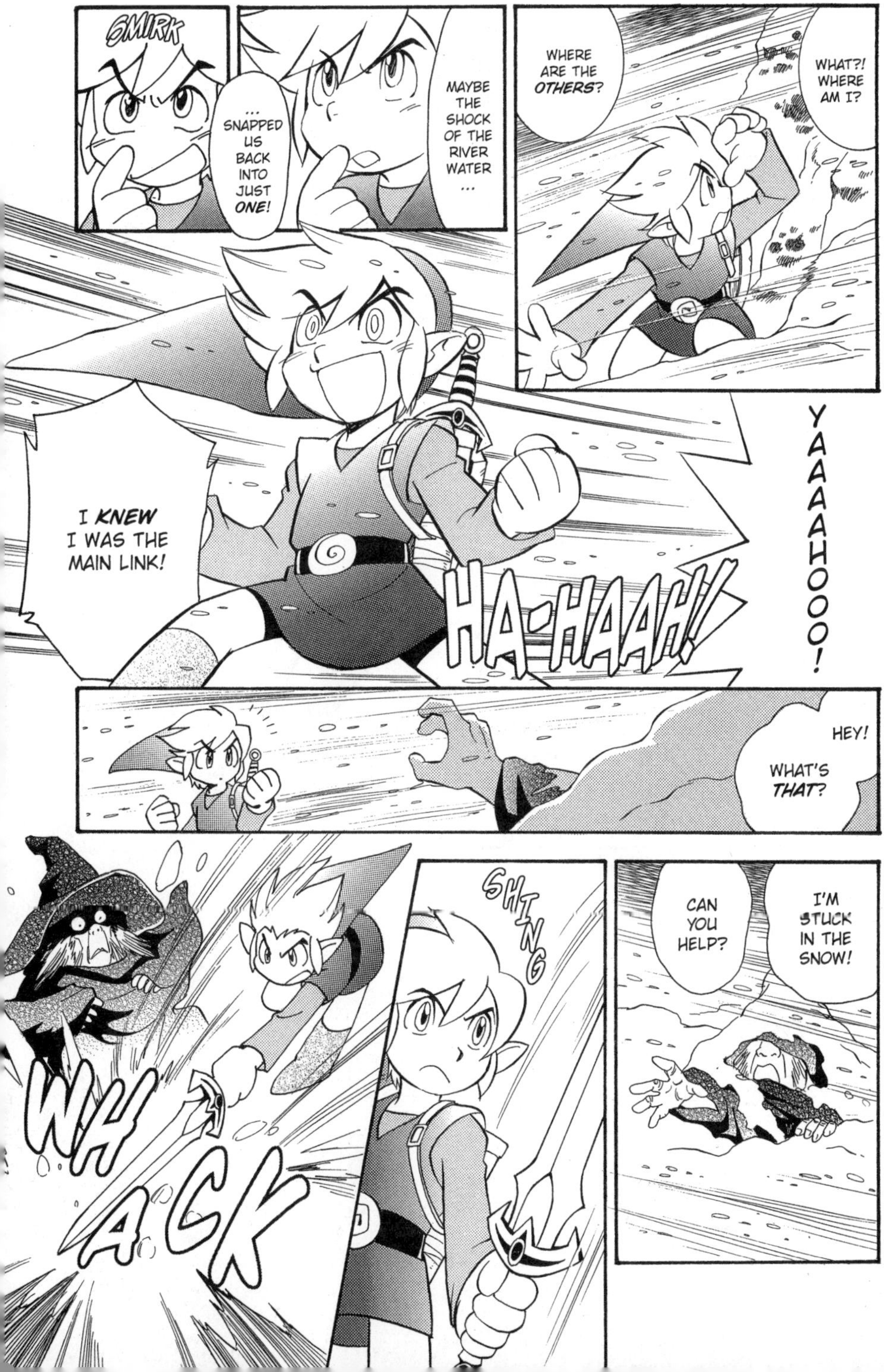
WHAT?! WHERE AM I?
WHERE ARE THE OTHERS?
MAYBE THE SHOCK OF THE RIVER WATER...
...SNAPPED US BACK INTO JUST ONE!
SMIRK
YAAAAAHOOOO!
HA-HAAAH!!
I KNEW I WAS THE MAIN LINK!
HEY!
WHAT'S THAT?
I'M STUCK IN THE SNOW!
CAN YOU HELP?
SHING
WHACK

THANK YOU, HERO... HERO... ERRR....
WHAT'S YOUR NAME, KID?
DON'T YOU KNOW?
I AM THE ONE AND ONLY LINK!
WOW!
IT FEELS GREAT TO BE THE ONLY ONE AGAIN!
OLD WOMAN, WHAT'S GOING ON HERE?
IT'S TOO EARLY IN THE YEAR FOR SNOW LIKE THIS.
WELL, WHEN THE WIND MAGE VAATI RETURNED, AN EVIL, FREEZING WIND BEGAN TO BLOW.
THIS BLIZZARD HAS BEEN RAGING EVER SINCE.
ALL THE PLANTS AND ANIMALS ARE DYING.
IS THAT ALL?
I CAN TAKE CARE OF THAT.
WHAT A GREAT HERO!
THE WIND MAGE LURKS IN THAT CAVE...
...THE ONE THE WIND COMES FROM.
I'M GOING IN!
FWUMP
FWUMP

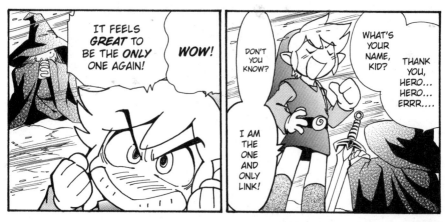

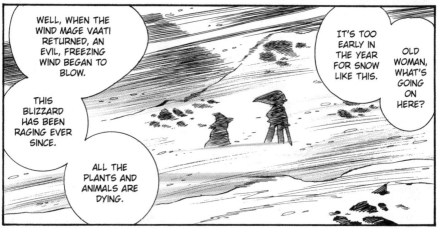

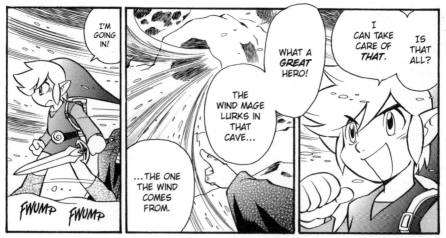

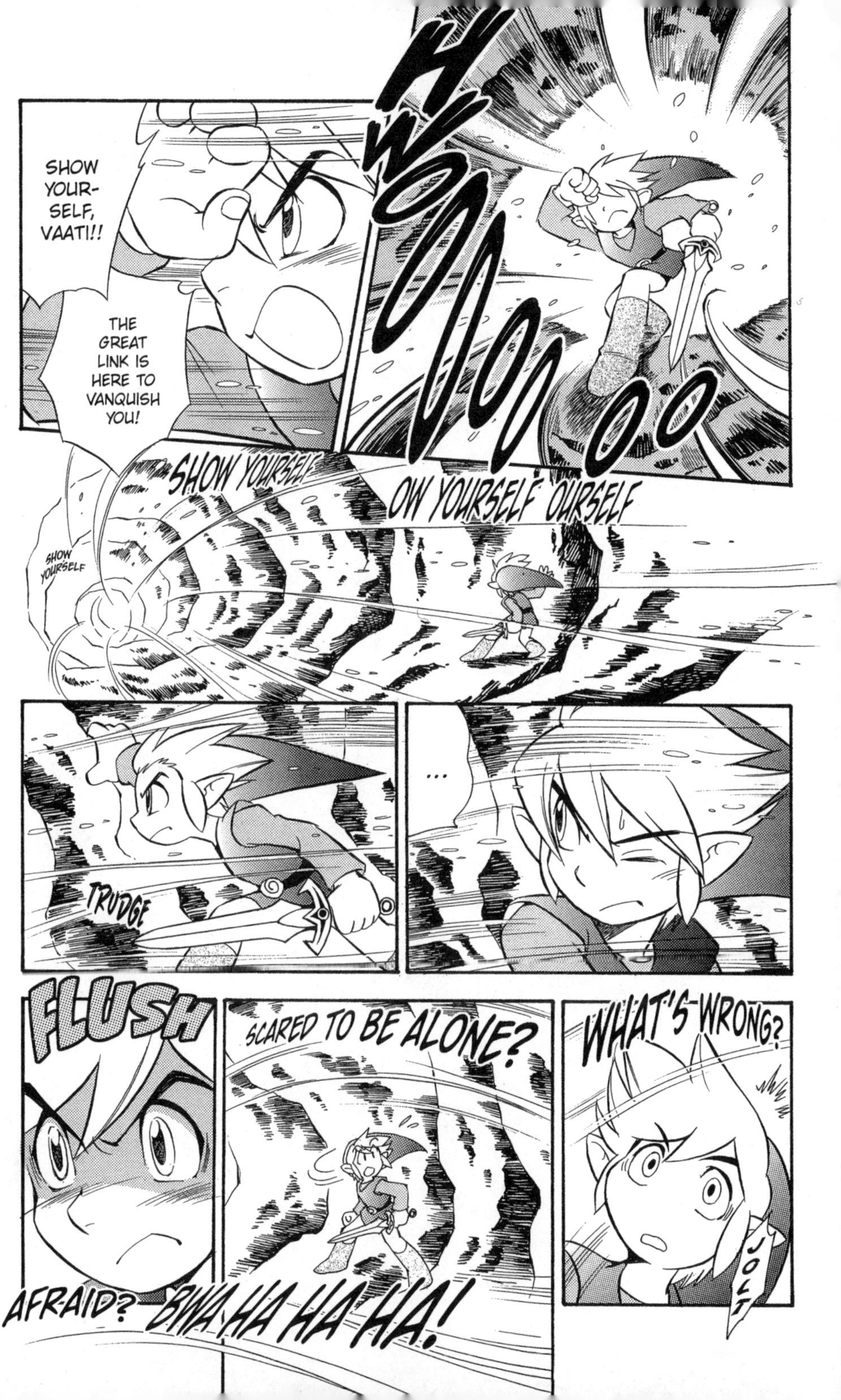
WHOOOOOOOOO
SHOW YOUR-SELF, VAATI!!
THE GREAT LINK IS HERE TO VANQUISH YOU!
SHOW YOURSELF
OW YOURSELF
OURSELF
SHOW YOURSELF
...
TRUDGE
WHAT'S WRONG?
JOLT
SCARED TO BE ALONE?
FLUSH
AFRAID?
BWA-HA HA HA HA!

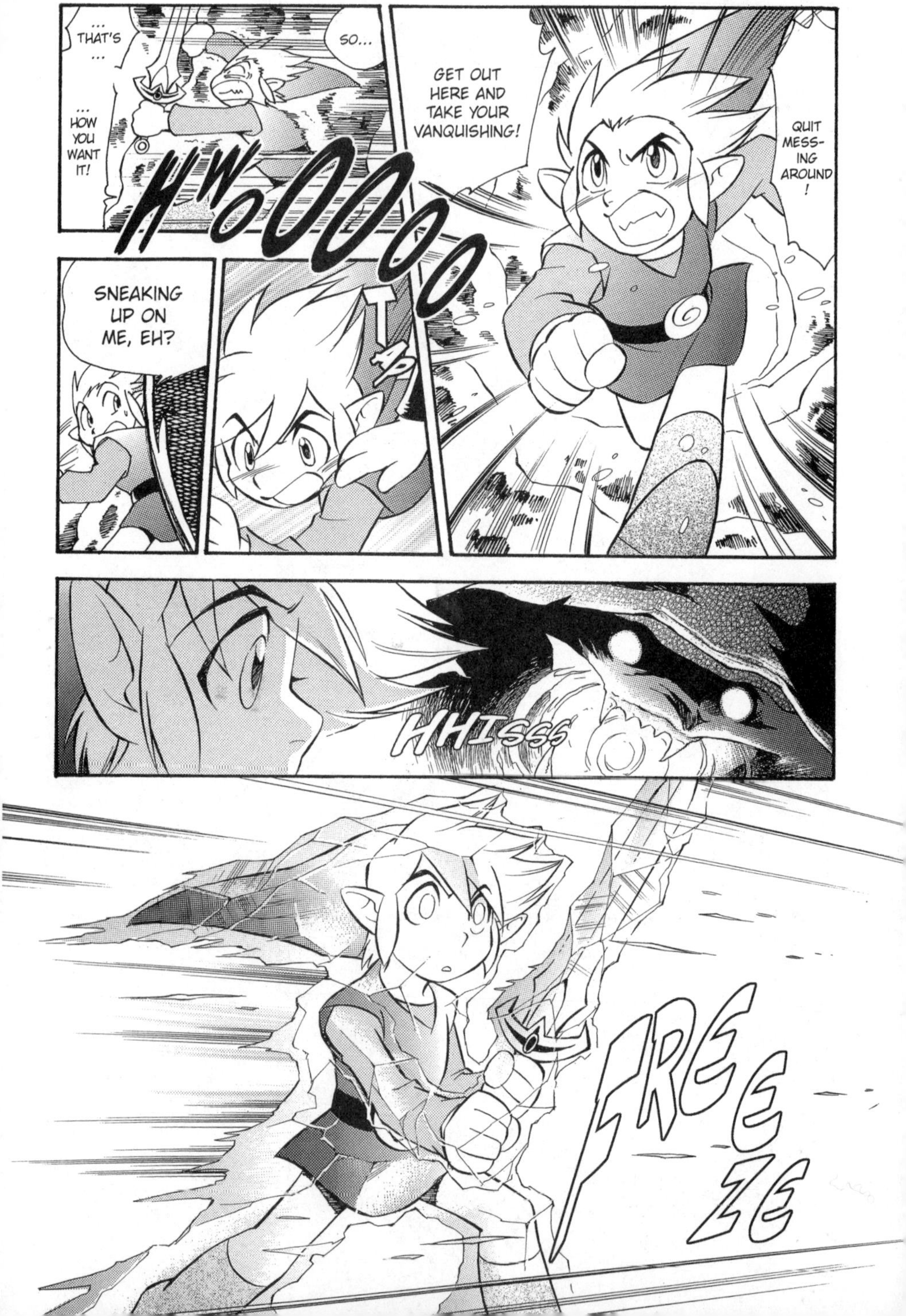
QUIT MESSING AROUND!
GET OUT HERE AND TAKE YOUR VANQUISHING!
SO...
...THAT'S...
...HOW YOU WANT IT!
HWOOOOOO
TAP
SNEAKING UP ON ME, EH?
HHISSS
FREEZE

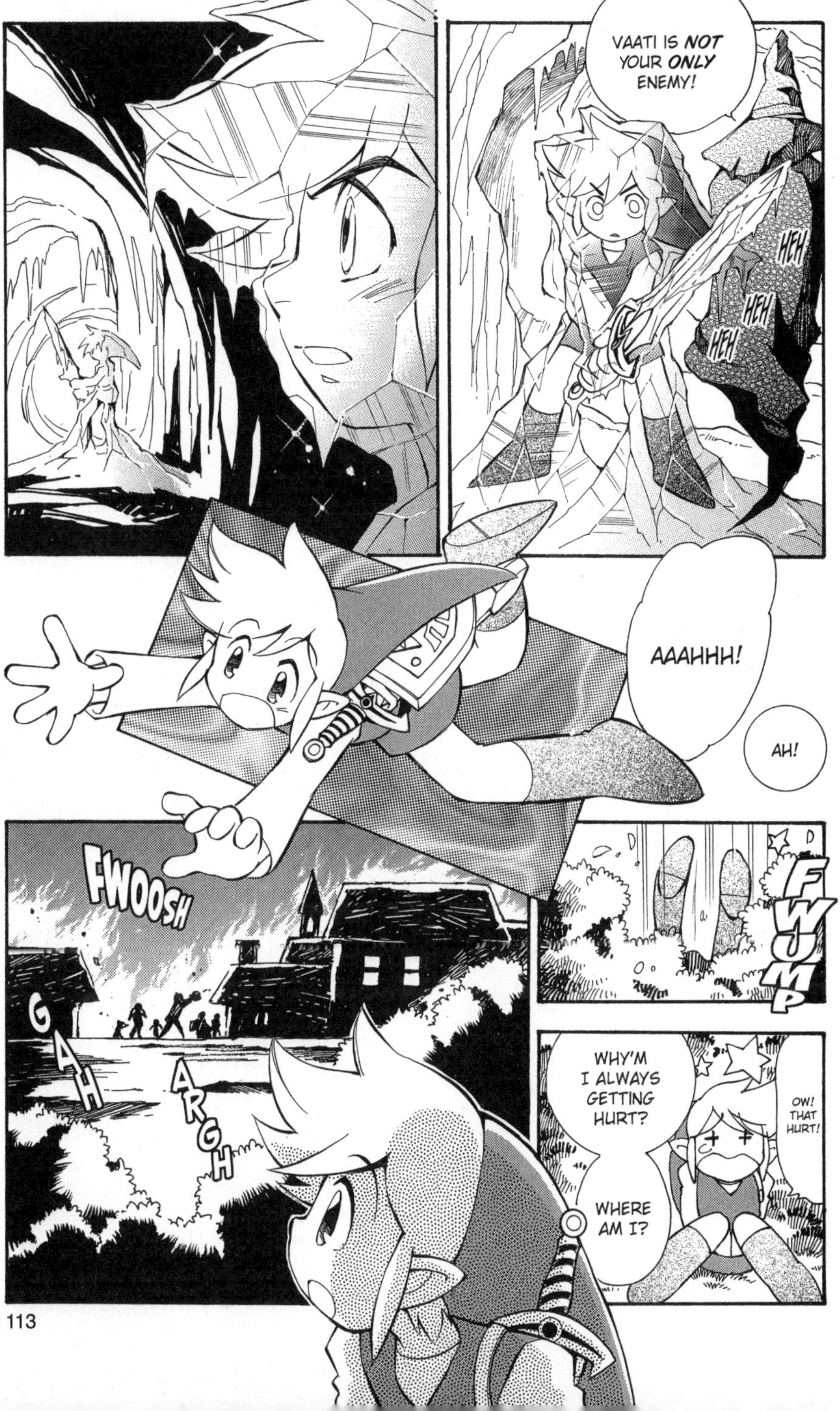
VAATI IS **NOT** YOUR **ONLY** ENEMY!
HEH
HEH
HEH
AAAHHH!
AH!
FWUMP
OW! THAT HURT!
WHY'M I ALWAYS GETTING HURT?
WHERE AM I?
FWOOSH
GAAH
ARGH

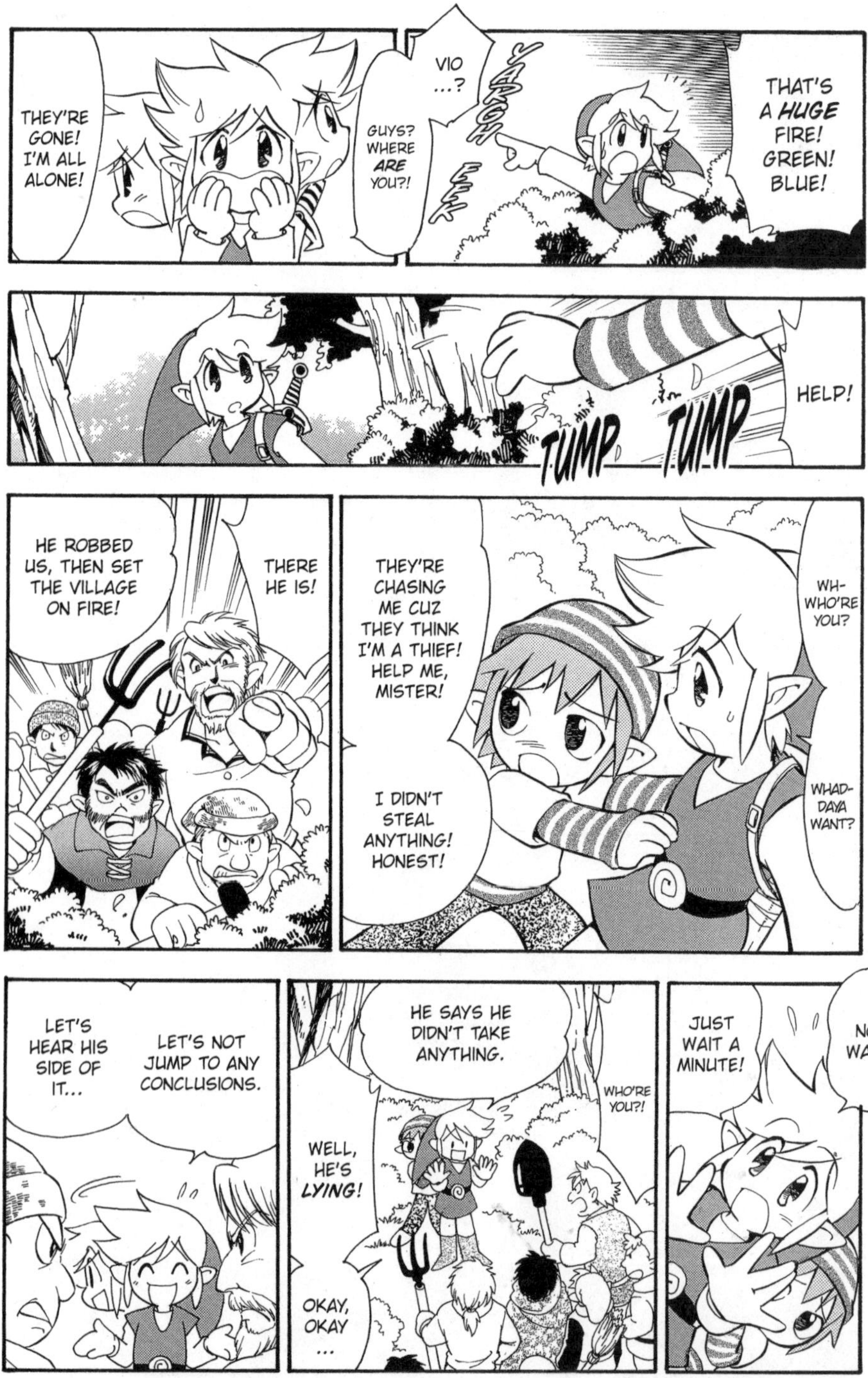
THAT'S A *HUGE* FIRE! GREEN! BLUE!
YAARGH
EEEK
VIO ...?
GUYS? WHERE *ARE* YOU?!
THEY'RE GONE! I'M ALL ALONE!
HELP!
TUMP TUMP
WH-WHO'RE YOU?
WHADDAYA WANT?
THEY'RE CHASING ME CUZ THEY THINK I'M A THIEF! HELP ME, MISTER!
I DIDN'T STEAL ANYTHING! HONEST!
THERE HE IS!
HE ROBBED US, THEN SET THE VILLAGE ON FIRE!
NO, WAIT!
JUST WAIT A MINUTE!
HE SAYS HE DIDN'T TAKE ANYTHING.
WHO'RE YOU?!
WELL, HE'S *LYING*!
OKAY, OKAY ...
LET'S NOT JUMP TO ANY CONCLUSIONS.
LET'S HEAR HIS SIDE OF IT...

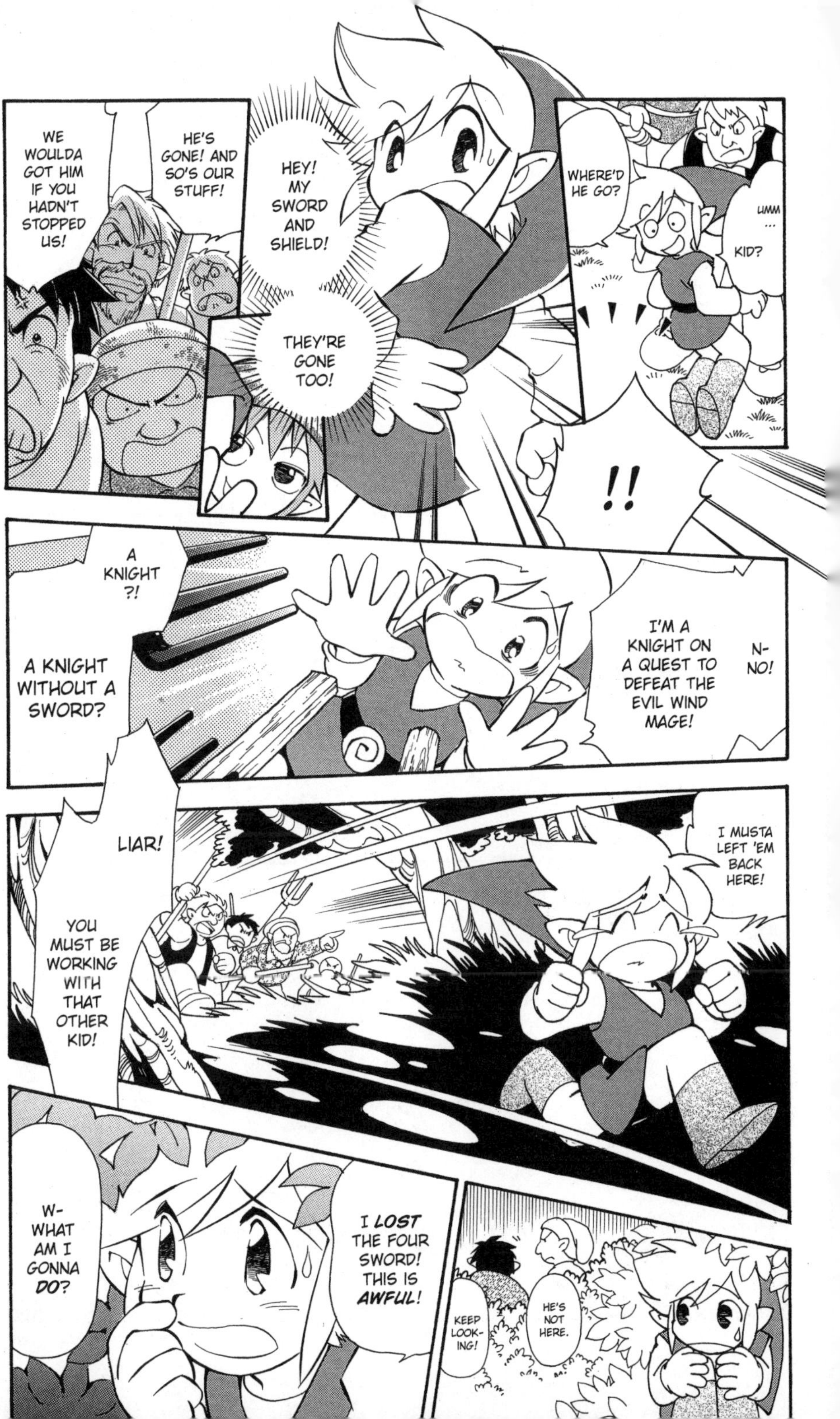
WHERE'D HE GO?
UMM... KID?
HEY! MY SWORD AND SHIELD!
THEY'RE GONE TOO!
HE'S GONE! AND SO'S OUR STUFF!
WE WOULDA GOT HIM IF YOU HADN'T STOPPED US!
!!
N-NO!
I'M A KNIGHT ON A QUEST TO DEFEAT THE EVIL WIND MAGE!
A KNIGHT ?!
A KNIGHT WITHOUT A SWORD?
I MUSTA LEFT 'EM BACK HERE!
LIAR!
YOU MUST BE WORKING WITH THAT OTHER KID!
HE'S NOT HERE.
KEEP LOOKING!
I *LOST* THE FOUR SWORD! THIS IS *AWFUL*!
W-WHAT AM I GONNA *DO*?

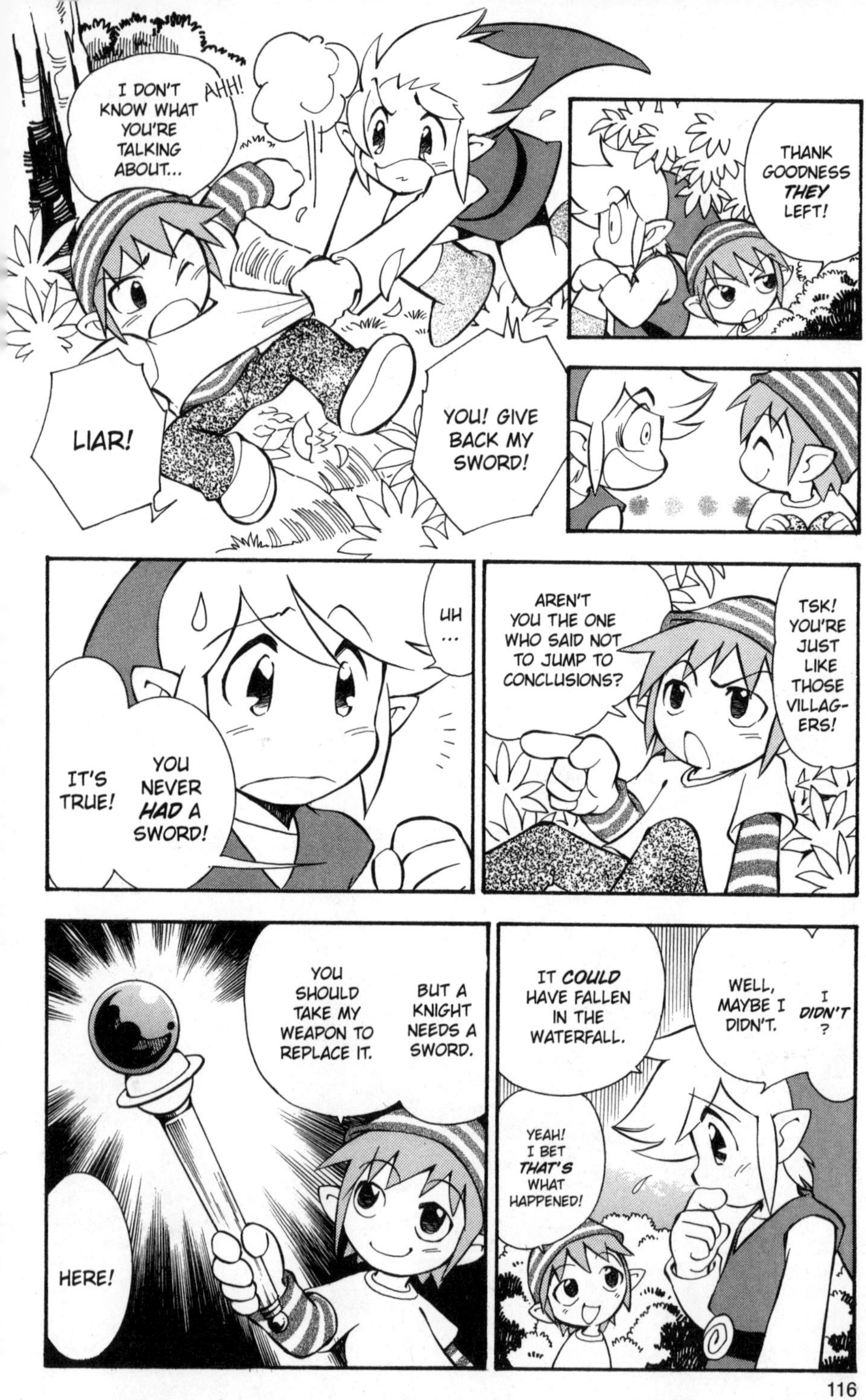
THANK GOODNESS **THEY** LEFT!
YOU! GIVE BACK MY SWORD!
I DON'T KNOW WHAT YOU'RE TALKING ABOUT...
AHH!
LIAR!
TSK! YOU'RE JUST LIKE THOSE VILLAGERS!
AREN'T YOU THE ONE WHO SAID NOT TO JUMP TO CONCLUSIONS?
UH ...
YOU NEVER **HAD** A SWORD!
IT'S TRUE!
I **DIDN'T**?
WELL, MAYBE I DIDN'T.
IT **COULD** HAVE FALLEN IN THE WATERFALL.
YEAH! I BET **THAT'S** WHAT HAPPENED!
BUT A KNIGHT NEEDS A SWORD.
YOU SHOULD TAKE MY WEAPON TO REPLACE IT.
HERE!

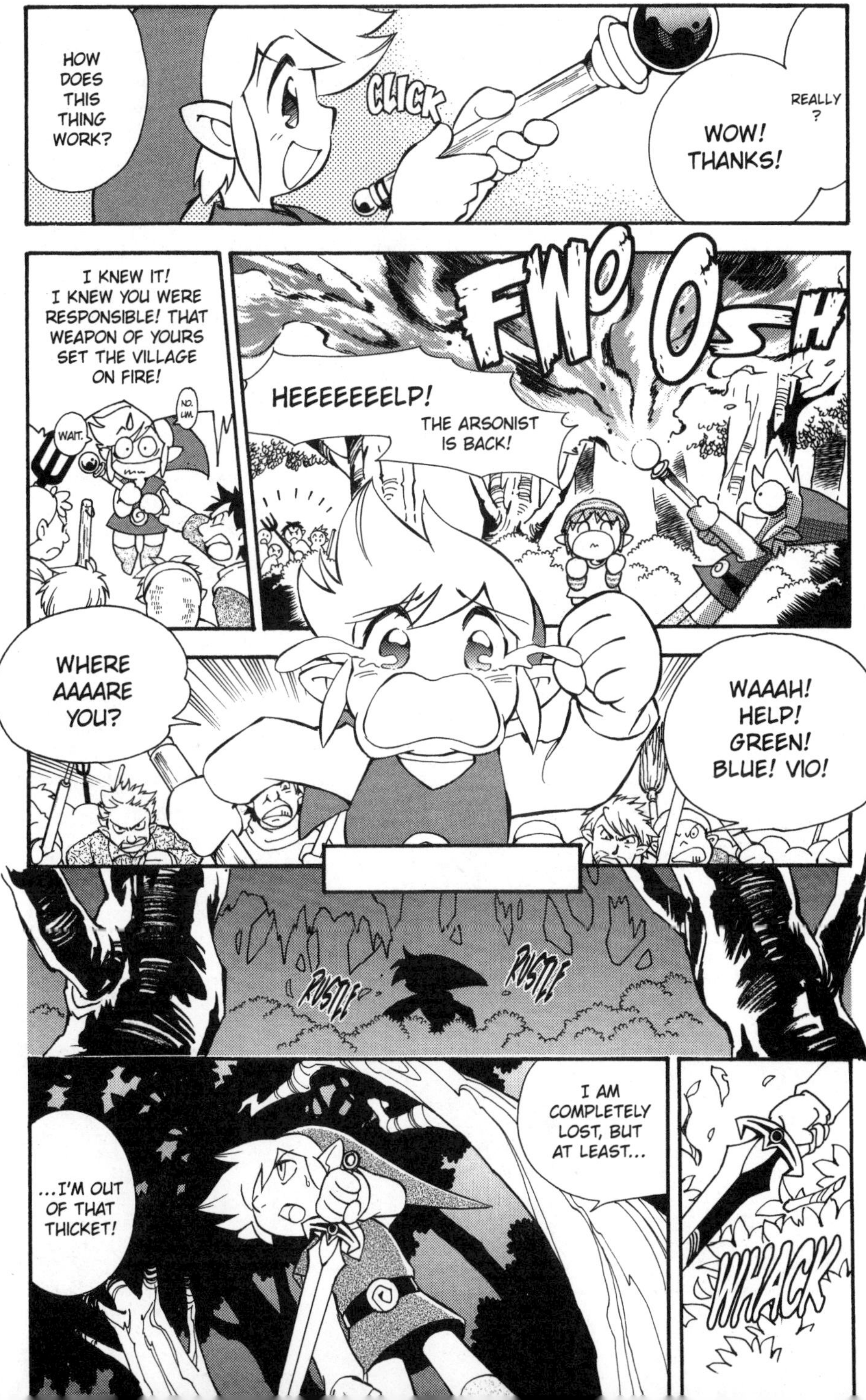
REALLY ?
WOW! THANKS!
CLICK
HOW DOES THIS THING WORK?
FWOOSH
HEEEEEEELP!
THE ARSONIST IS BACK!
I KNEW IT! I KNEW YOU WERE RESPONSIBLE! THAT WEAPON OF YOURS SET THE VILLAGE ON FIRE!
NO. UM.
WAIT.
WAAAH! HELP! GREEN! BLUE! VIO!
WHERE AAAARE YOU?
RUSTLE
RUSTLE
WHACK
I AM COMPLETELY LOST, BUT AT LEAST...
...I'M OUT OF THAT THICKET!

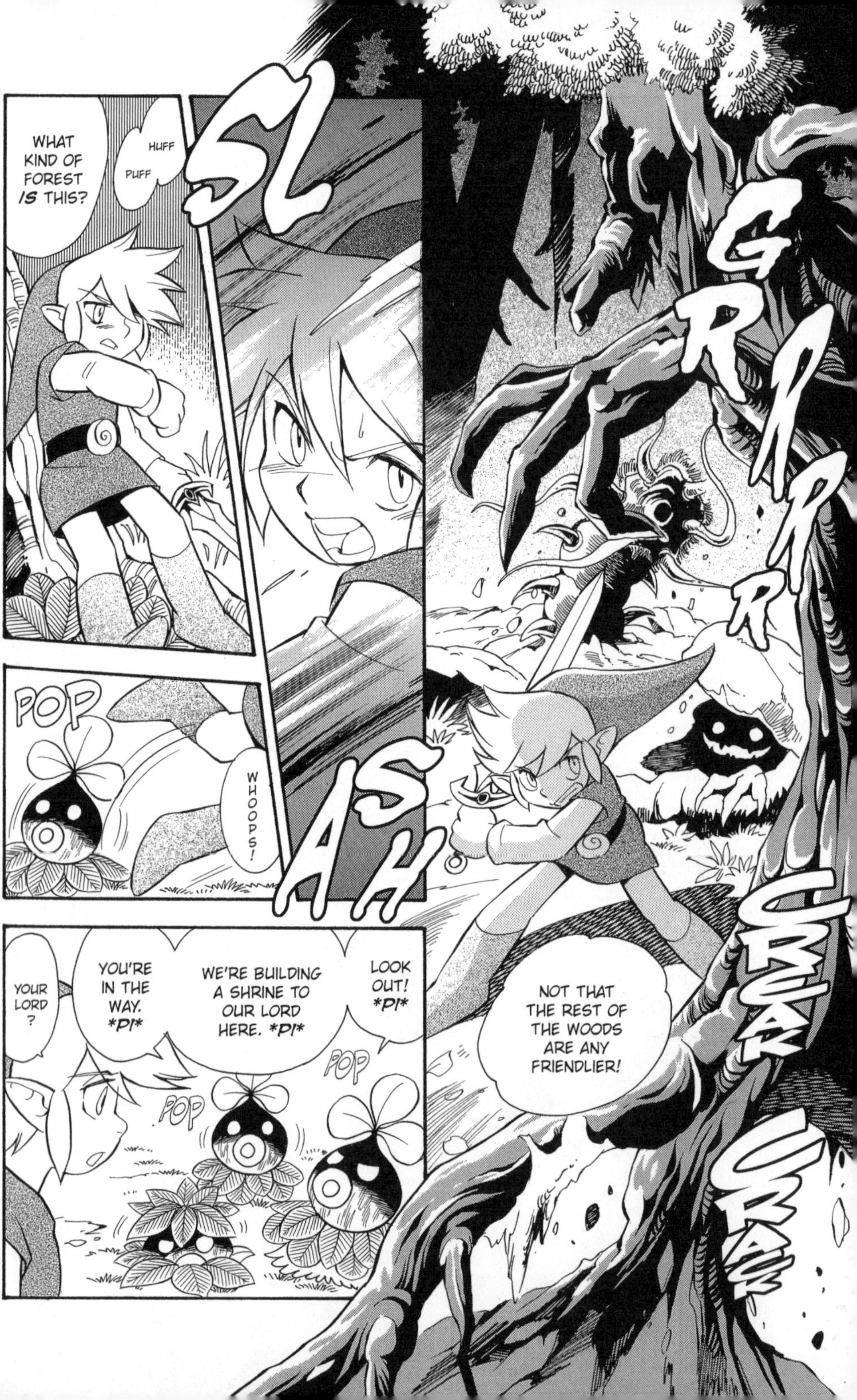
GRRRR
NOT THAT THE REST OF THE WOODS ARE ANY FRIENDLIER!
SLASH
WHAT KIND OF FOREST *IS* THIS?
HUFF
PUFF
WHOOPS!
POP
LOOK OUT! *PI*
WE'RE BUILDING A SHRINE TO OUR LORD HERE. *PI*
YOU'RE IN THE WAY. *PI*
YOUR LORD ?
POP
POP

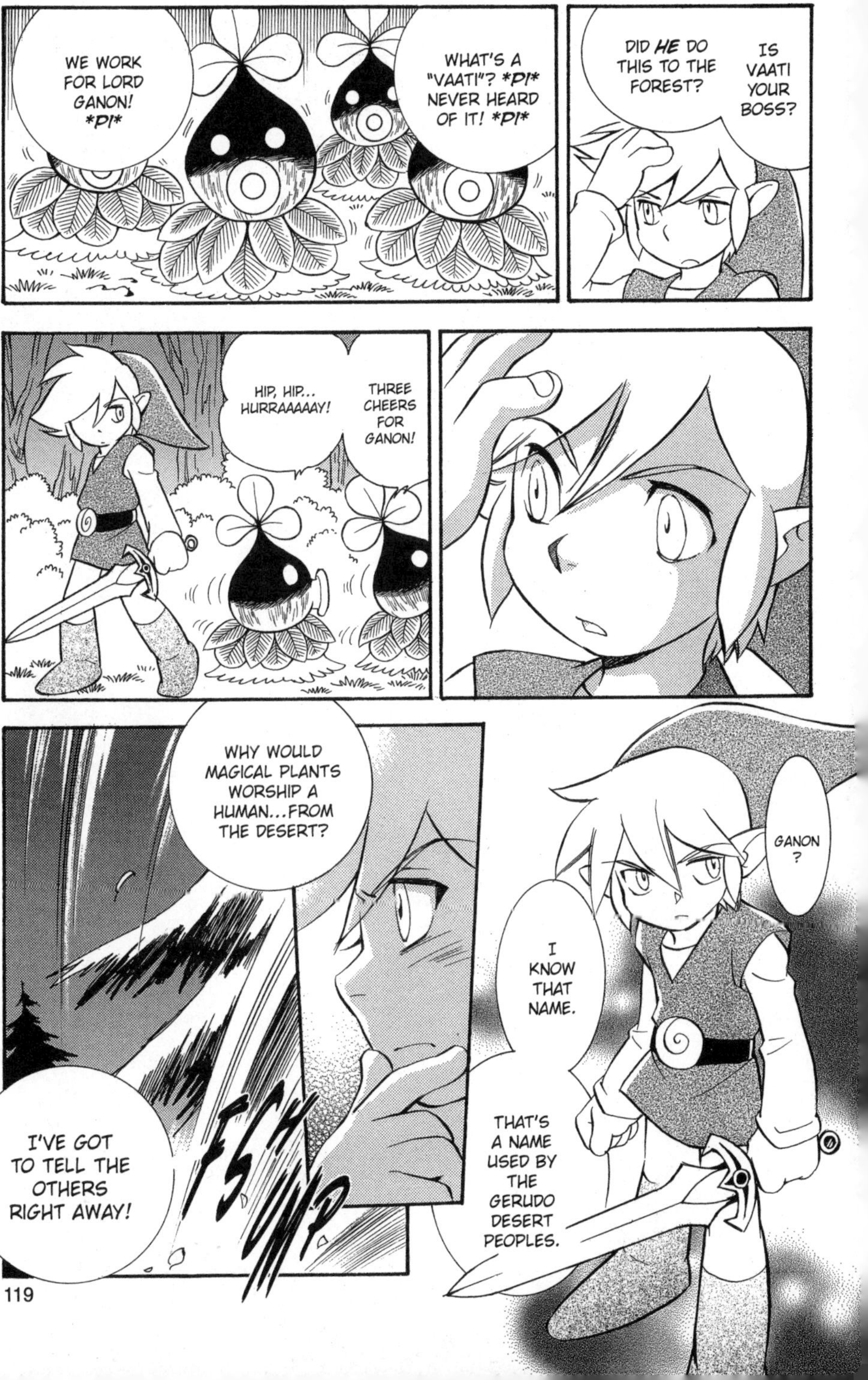
IS VAATI YOUR BOSS?
DID *HE* DO THIS TO THE FOREST?
WHAT'S A "VAATI"? *PI* NEVER HEARD OF IT! *PI*
WE WORK FOR LORD GANON! *PI*
THREE CHEERS FOR GANON!
HIP, HIP... HURRAAAAAY!
GANON?
I KNOW THAT NAME.
THAT'S A NAME USED BY THE GERUDO DESERT PEOPLES.
WHY WOULD MAGICAL PLANTS WORSHIP A HUMAN...FROM THE DESERT?
I'VE GOT TO TELL THE OTHERS RIGHT AWAY!

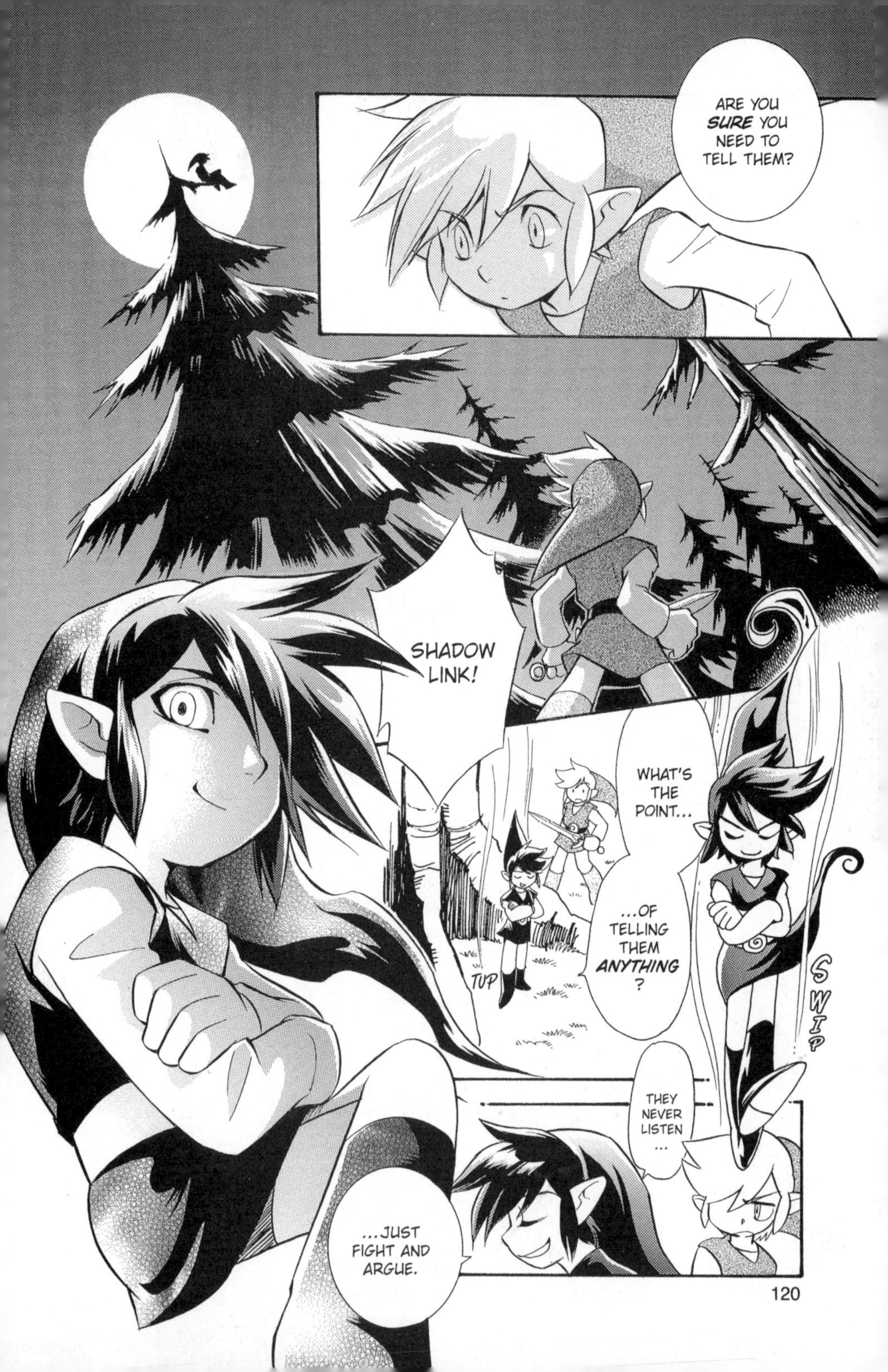
ARE YOU **SURE** YOU NEED TO TELL THEM?
SHADOW LINK!
WHAT'S THE POINT...
...OF TELLING THEM **ANYTHING**?
SWIP
TUP
THEY NEVER LISTEN...
...JUST FIGHT AND ARGUE.

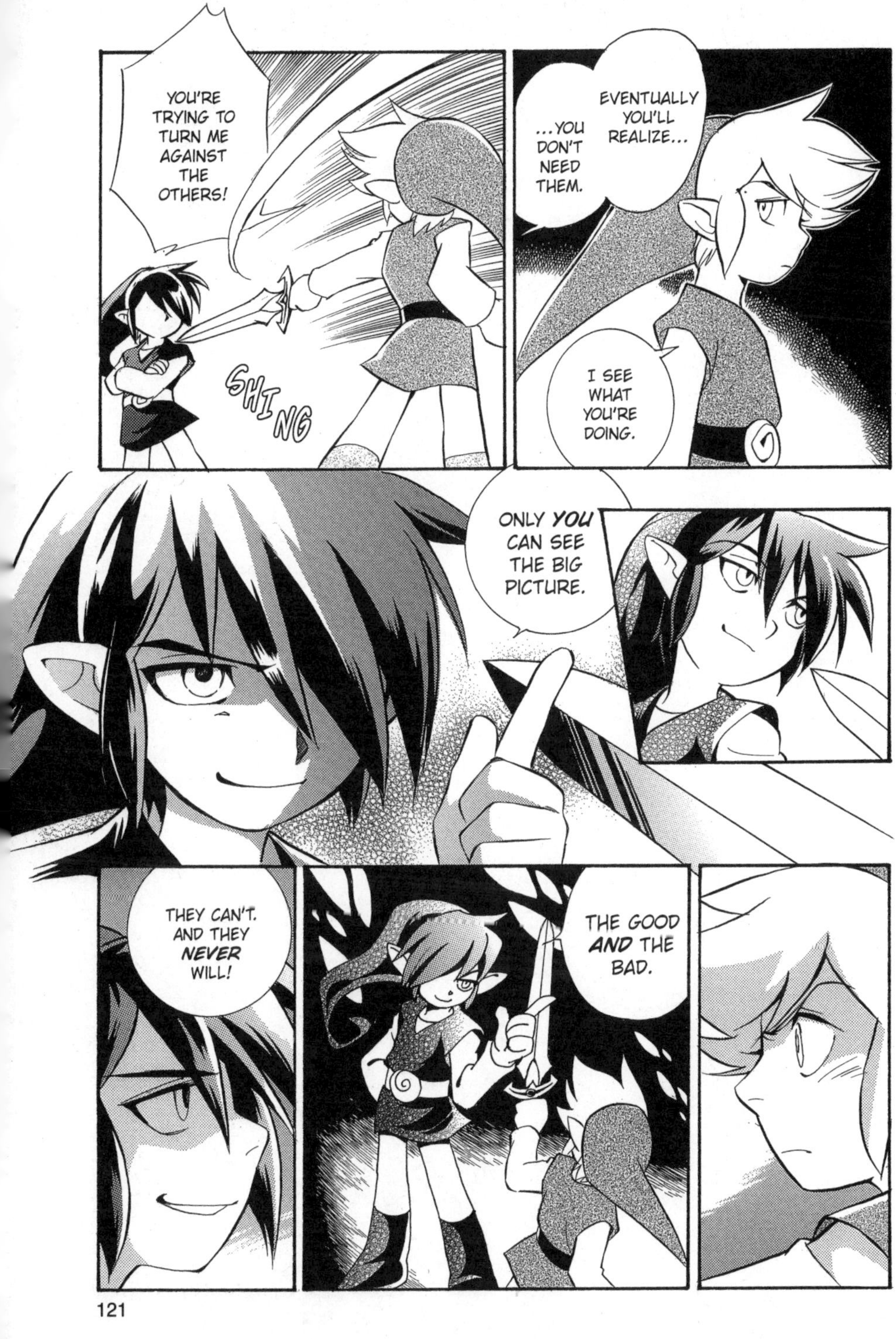
EVENTUALLY YOU'LL REALIZE...
...YOU DON'T NEED THEM.
I SEE WHAT YOU'RE DOING.
YOU'RE TRYING TO TURN ME AGAINST THE OTHERS!
SHING
ONLY **YOU** CAN SEE THE BIG PICTURE.
THE GOOD **AND** THE BAD.
THEY CAN'T. AND THEY ***NEVER*** WILL!

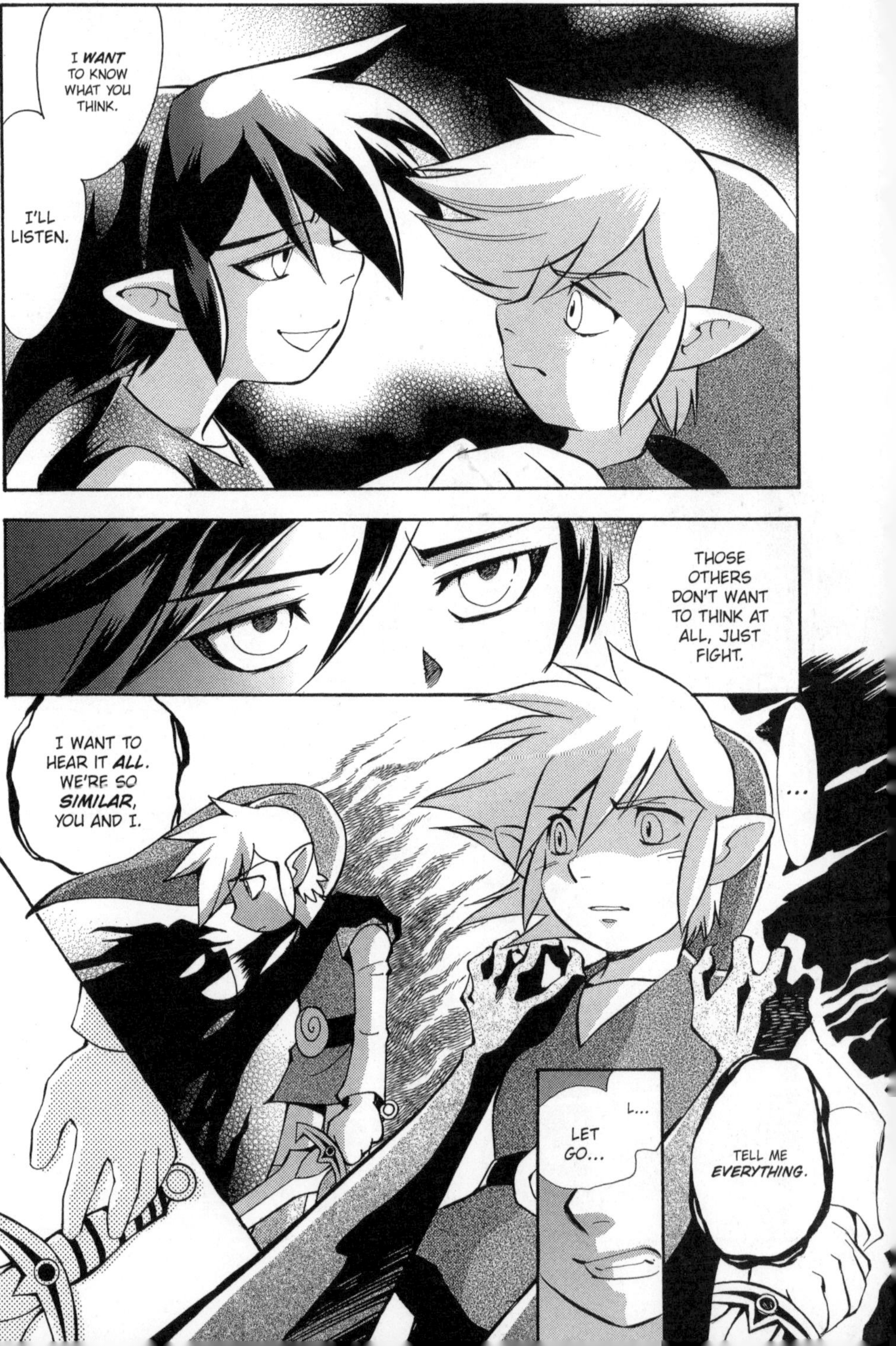

I *WANT* TO KNOW WHAT YOU THINK.
I'LL LISTEN.
THOSE OTHERS DON'T WANT TO THINK AT ALL, JUST FIGHT.
...
I WANT TO HEAR IT *ALL*. WE'RE SO *SIMILAR*, YOU AND I.
TELL ME *EVERYTHING*.
L...
LET GO...

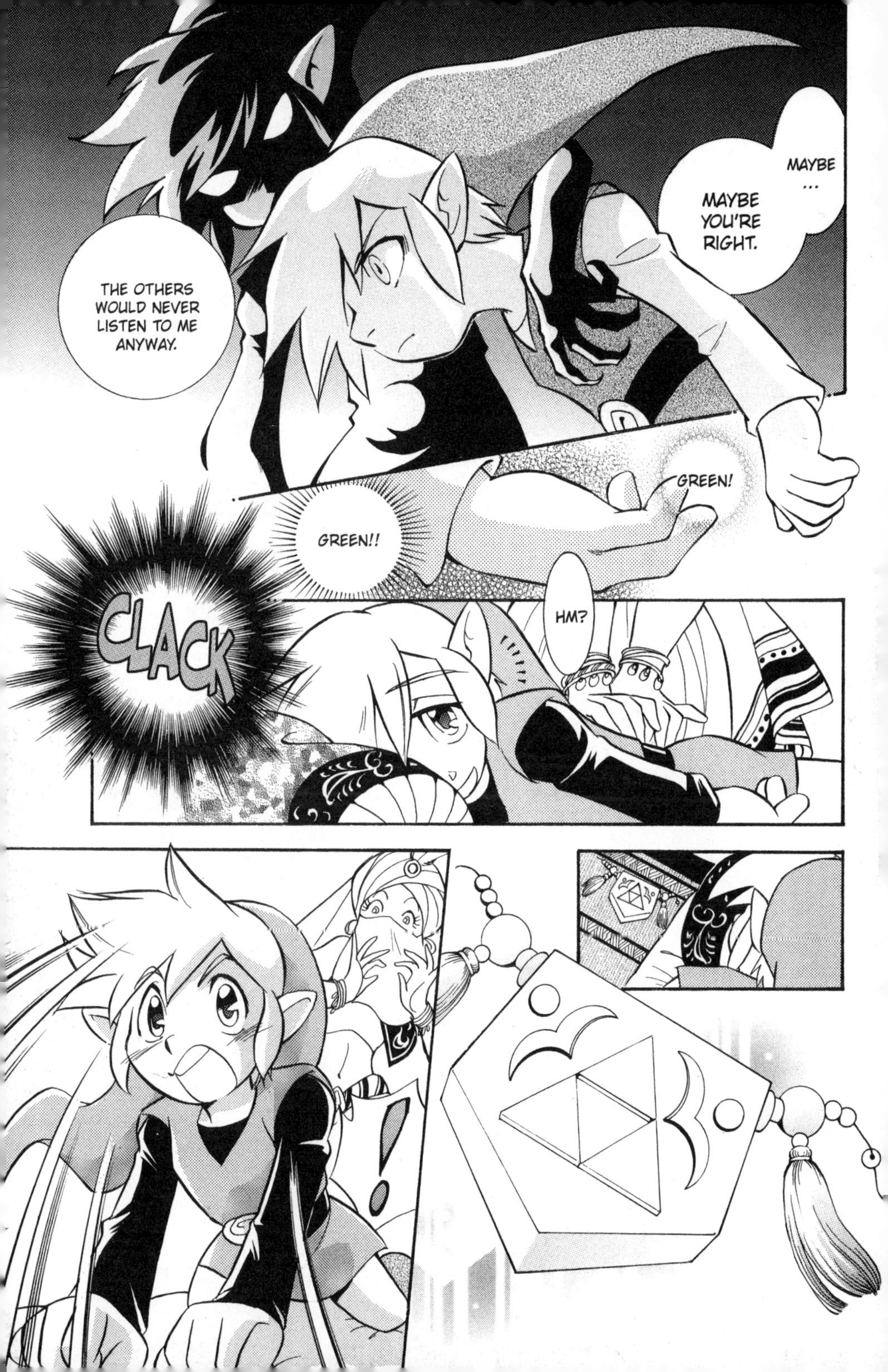
MAYBE ...
MAYBE YOU'RE RIGHT.
THE OTHERS WOULD NEVER LISTEN TO ME ANYWAY.
GREEN!
GREEN!!
CLACK
HM?

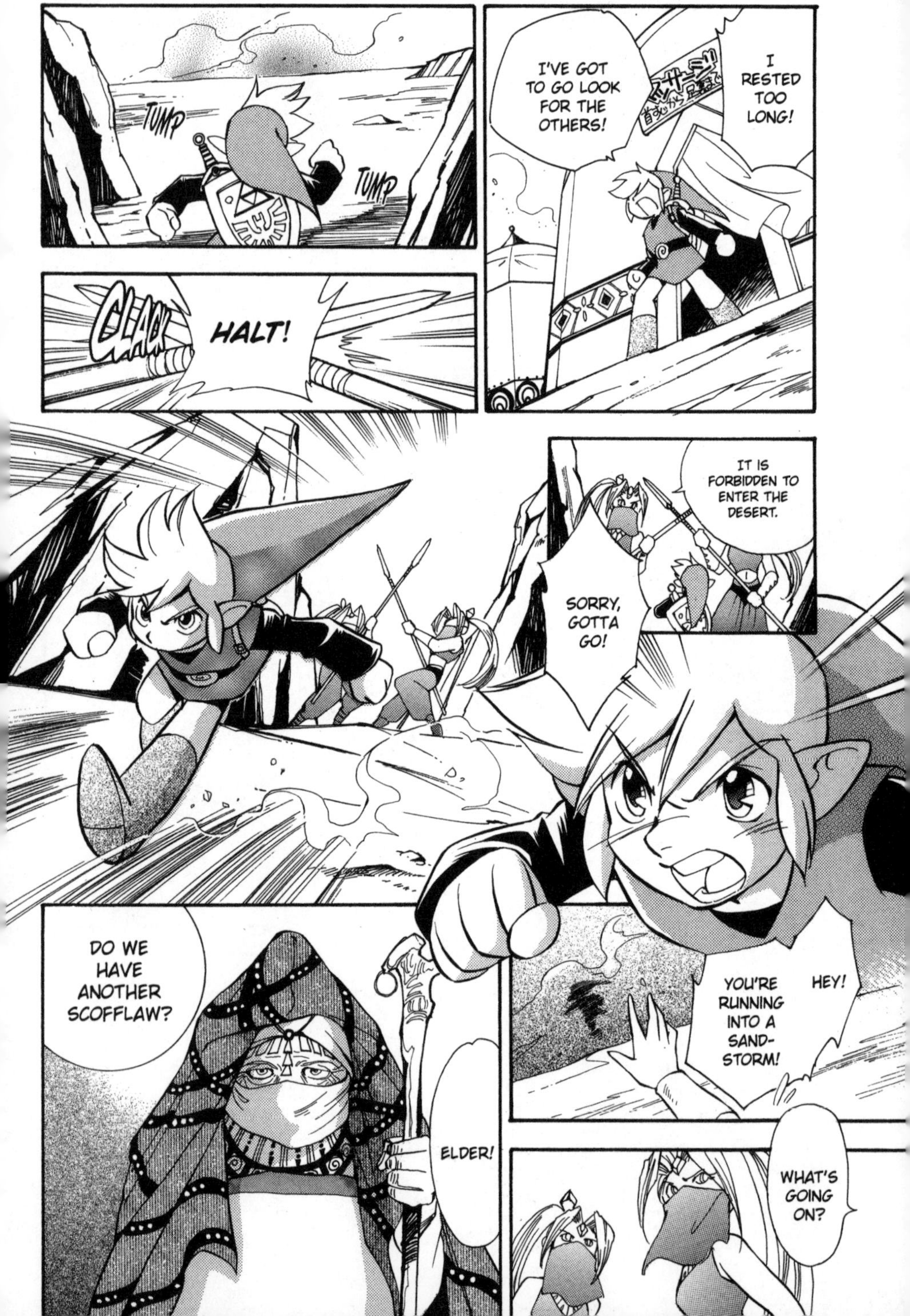
I RESTED TOO LONG!
I'VE GOT TO GO LOOK FOR THE OTHERS!
TUMP
TUMP
CLACK
HALT!
IT IS FORBIDDEN TO ENTER THE DESERT.
SORRY, GOTTA GO!
HEY!
YOU'RE RUNNING INTO A SAND-STORM!
WHAT'S GOING ON?
ELDER!
DO WE HAVE ANOTHER SCOFFLAW?

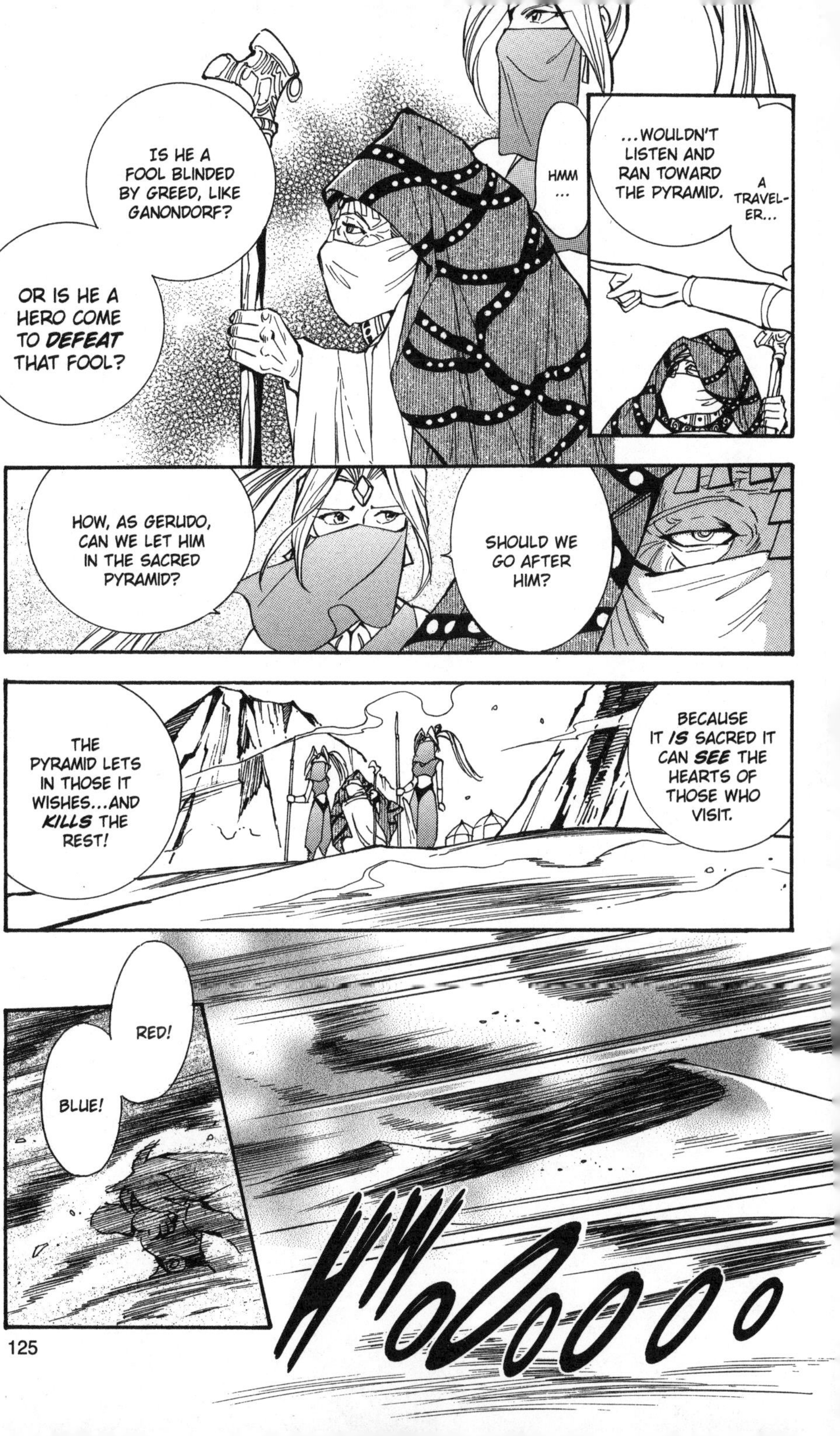
A TRAVELER...
...WOULDN'T LISTEN AND RAN TOWARD THE PYRAMID.
HMM...
IS HE A FOOL BLINDED BY GREED, LIKE GANONDORF?
OR IS HE A HERO COME TO **DEFEAT** THAT FOOL?
SHOULD WE GO AFTER HIM?
HOW, AS GERUDO, CAN WE LET HIM IN THE SACRED PYRAMID?
BECAUSE IT ***IS*** SACRED IT CAN ***SEE*** THE HEARTS OF THOSE WHO VISIT.
THE PYRAMID LETS IN THOSE IT WISHES...AND ***KILLS*** THE REST!
HWOOOOOO
RED!
BLUE!

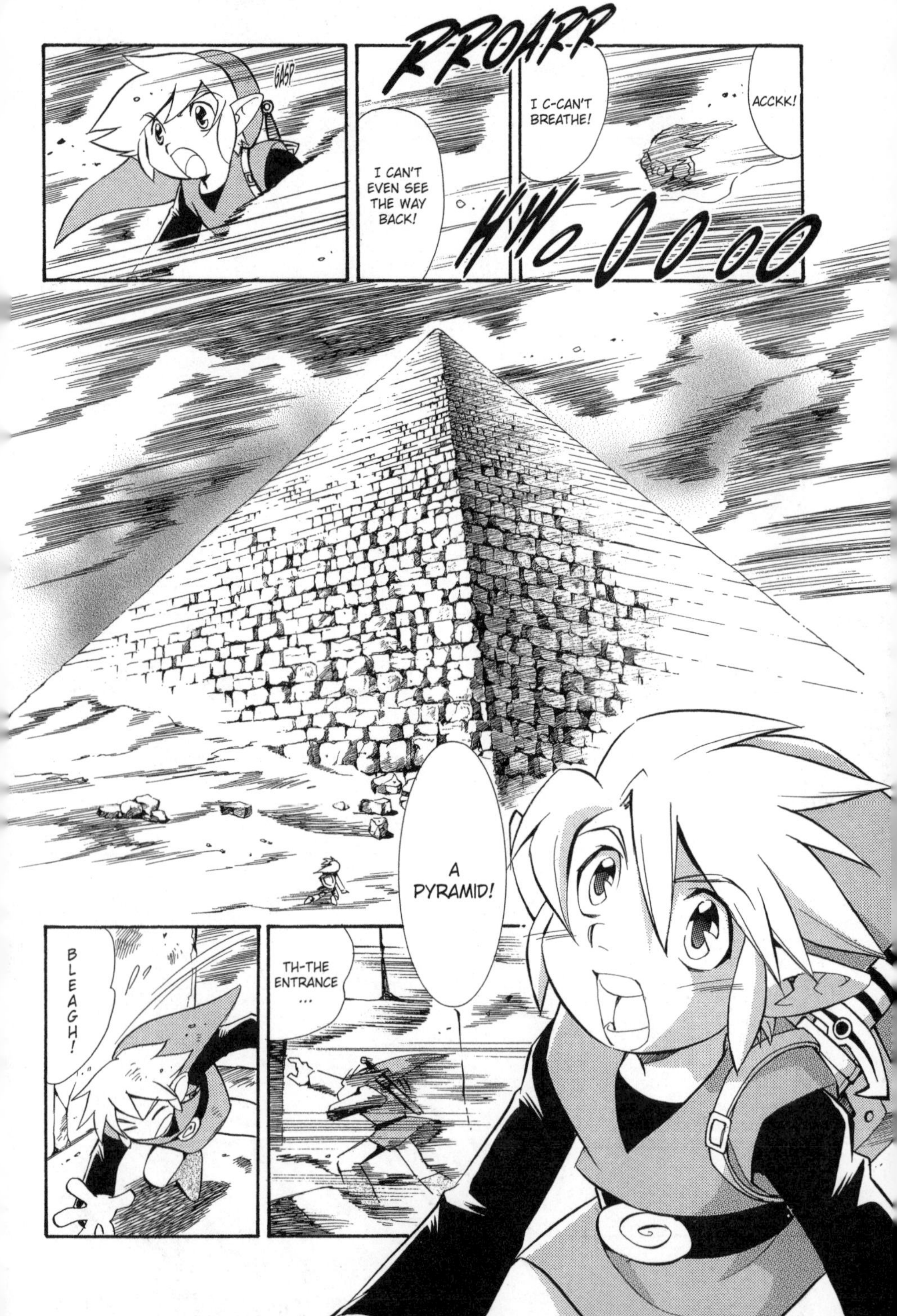

ACCKK!
I C-CAN'T BREATHE!
HWOOOOO
RROARR
I CAN'T EVEN SEE THE WAY BACK!
GASP
A PYRAMID!
TH-THE ENTRANCE ...
BLEAGH!

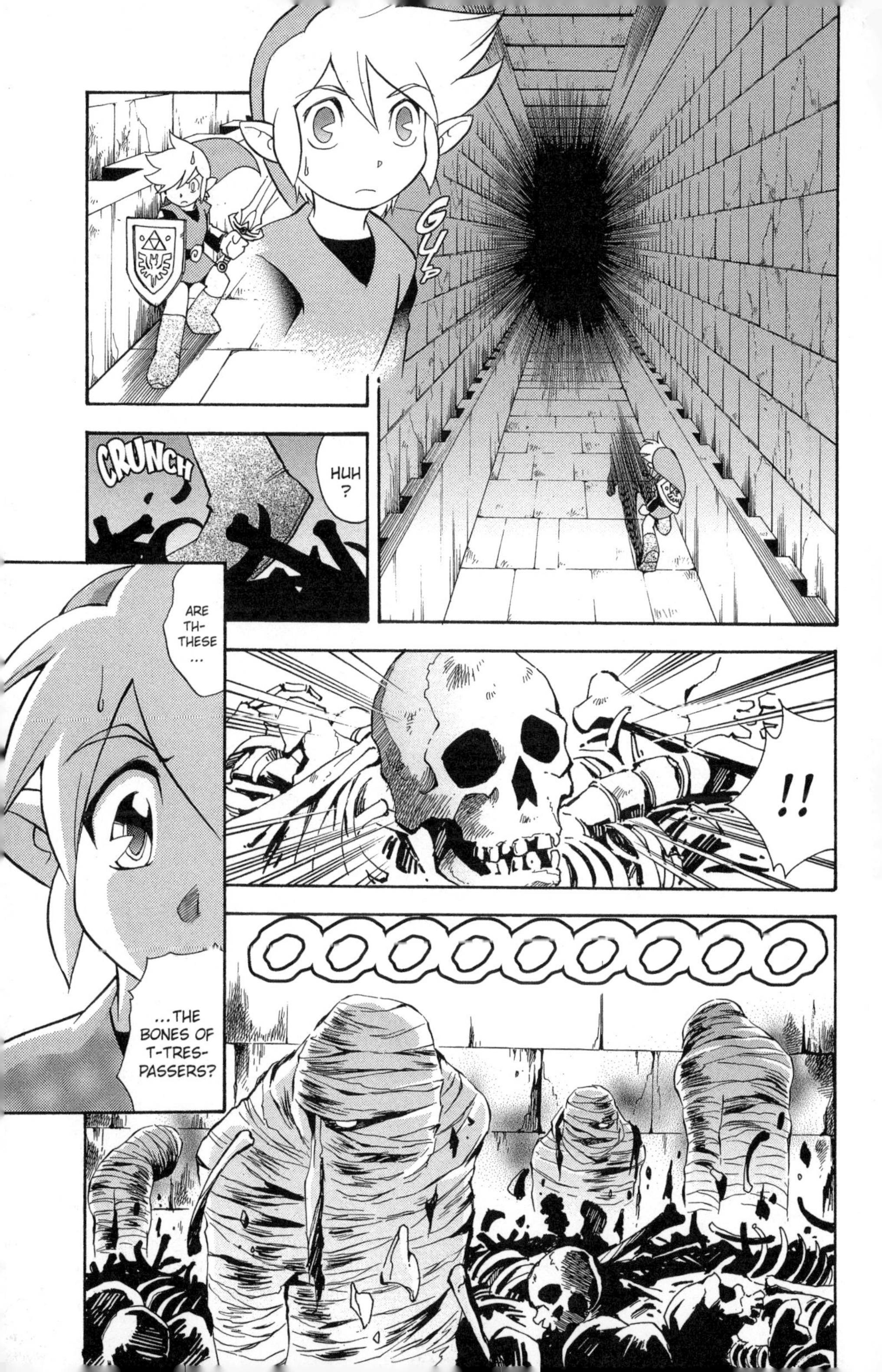
GULP
CRUNCH
HUH?
!!
OOOOOOOOOO
ARE TH-THESE...
...THE BONES OF T-TRES-PASSERS?

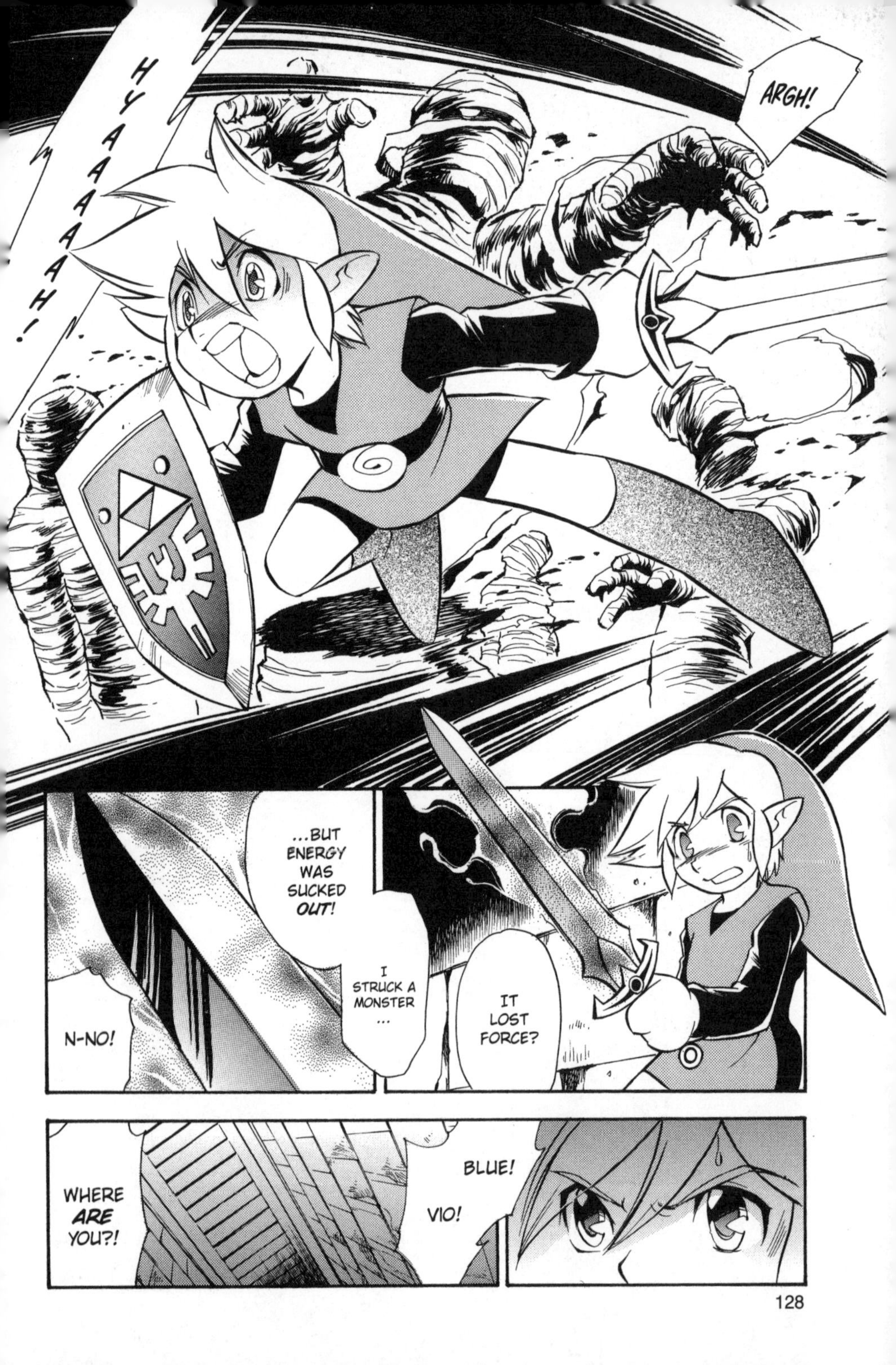
ARGH!
HYAAAAAH!
IT LOST FORCE?
I STRUCK A MONSTER ...
...BUT ENERGY WAS SUCKED **OUT**!
N-NO!
BLUE!
VIO!
WHERE **ARE** YOU?!

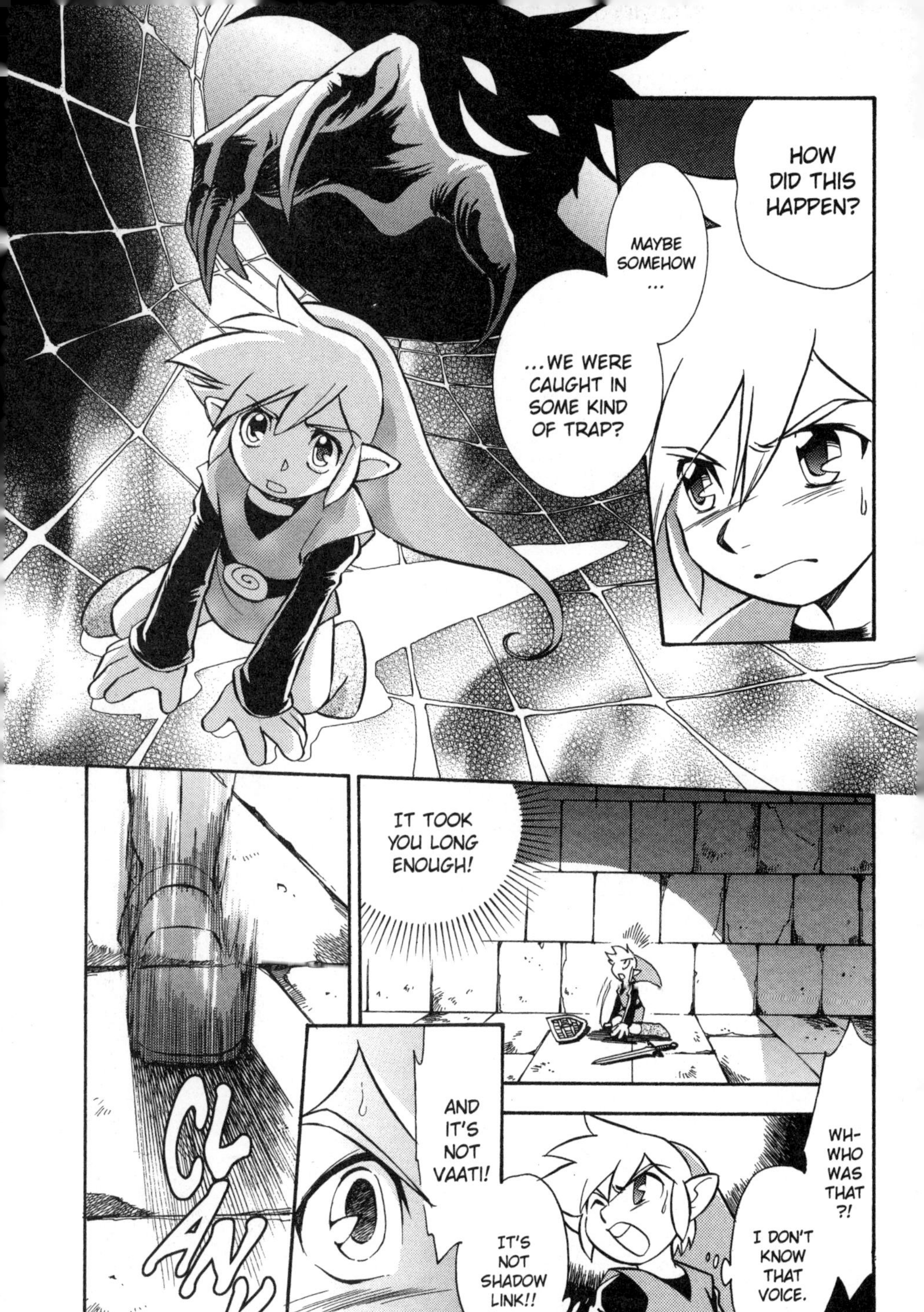
HOW DID THIS HAPPEN?
MAYBE SOMEHOW ...
...WE WERE CAUGHT IN SOME KIND OF TRAP?
IT TOOK YOU LONG ENOUGH!
WH-WHO WAS THAT?!
I DON'T KNOW THAT VOICE.
AND IT'S NOT VAATI!
IT'S NOT SHADOW LINK!!
CLANK

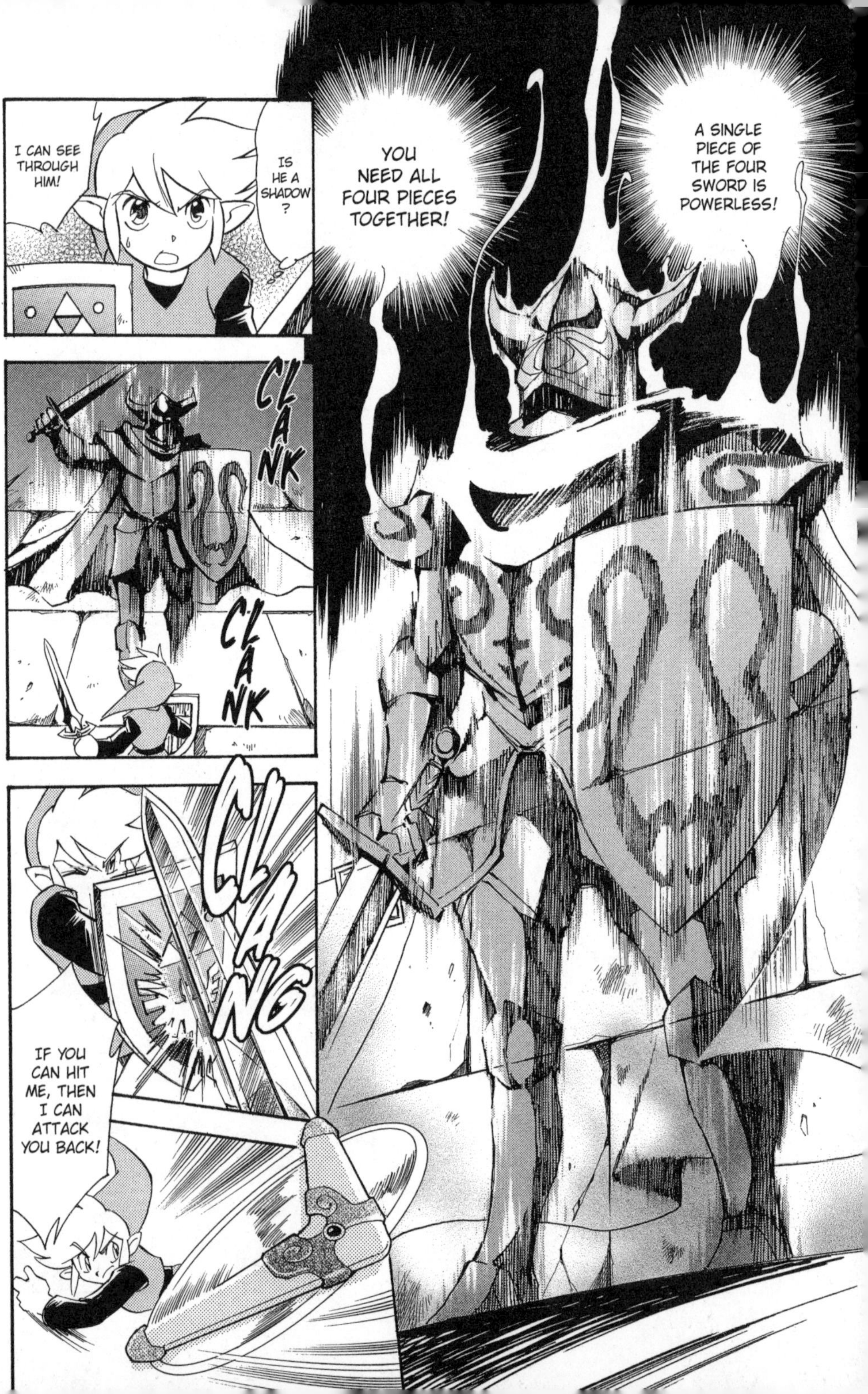
A SINGLE PIECE OF THE FOUR SWORD IS POWERLESS!
YOU NEED ALL FOUR PIECES TOGETHER!
IS HE A SHADOW?
I CAN SEE THROUGH HIM!
CLANK
CLANK
CLANG
IF YOU CAN HIT ME, THEN I CAN ATTACK YOU BACK!

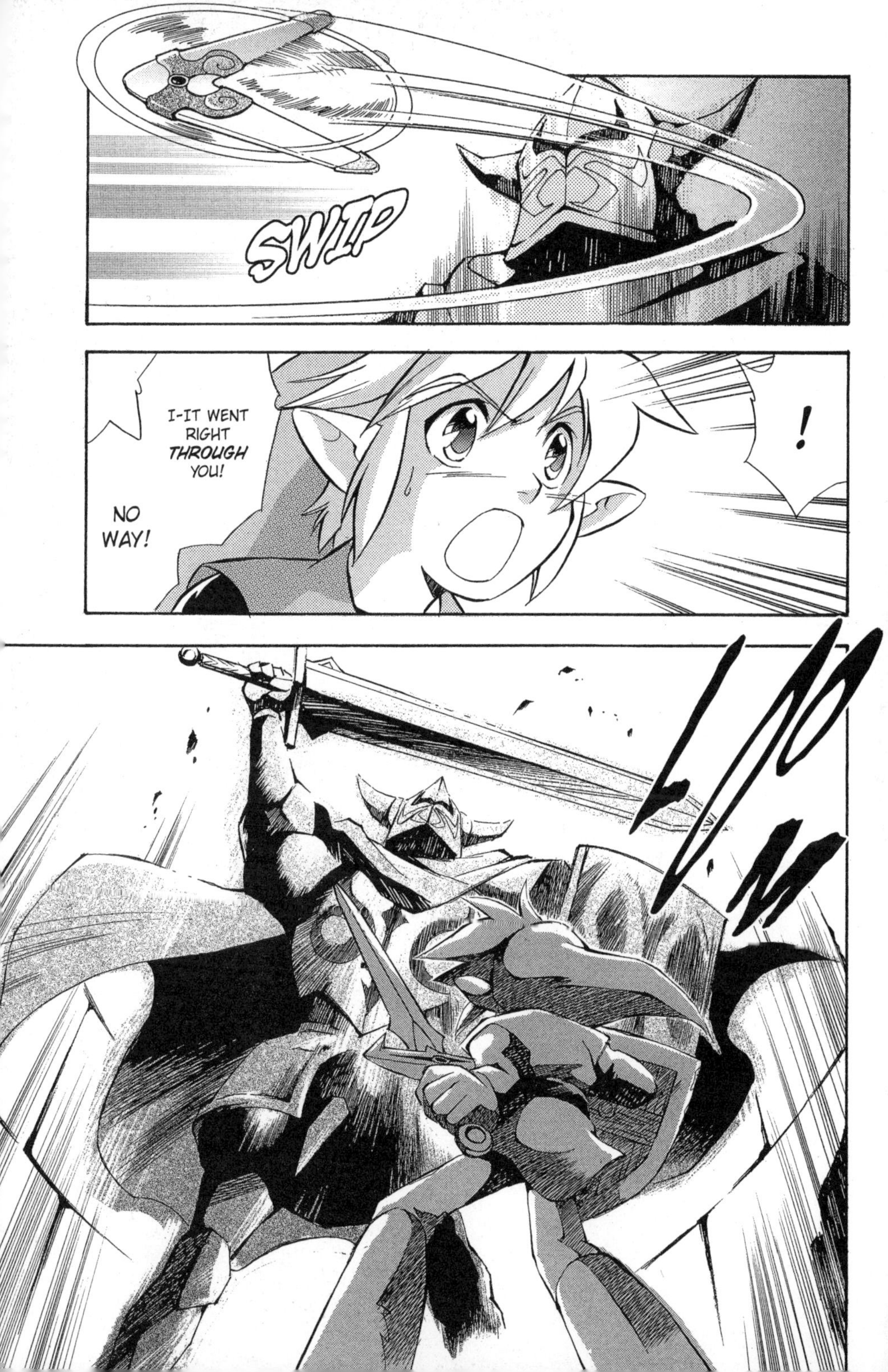
SWIP
!
I-IT WENT RIGHT THROUGH YOU!
NO WAY!

FOUR SWORDS
ROUGH CHARACTER
ILLUSTRATION 4

Blue

Hotheaded,
stubborn, takes
action, good
at fighting.

CHAPTER 5 Deadly Battle at the Pyramid

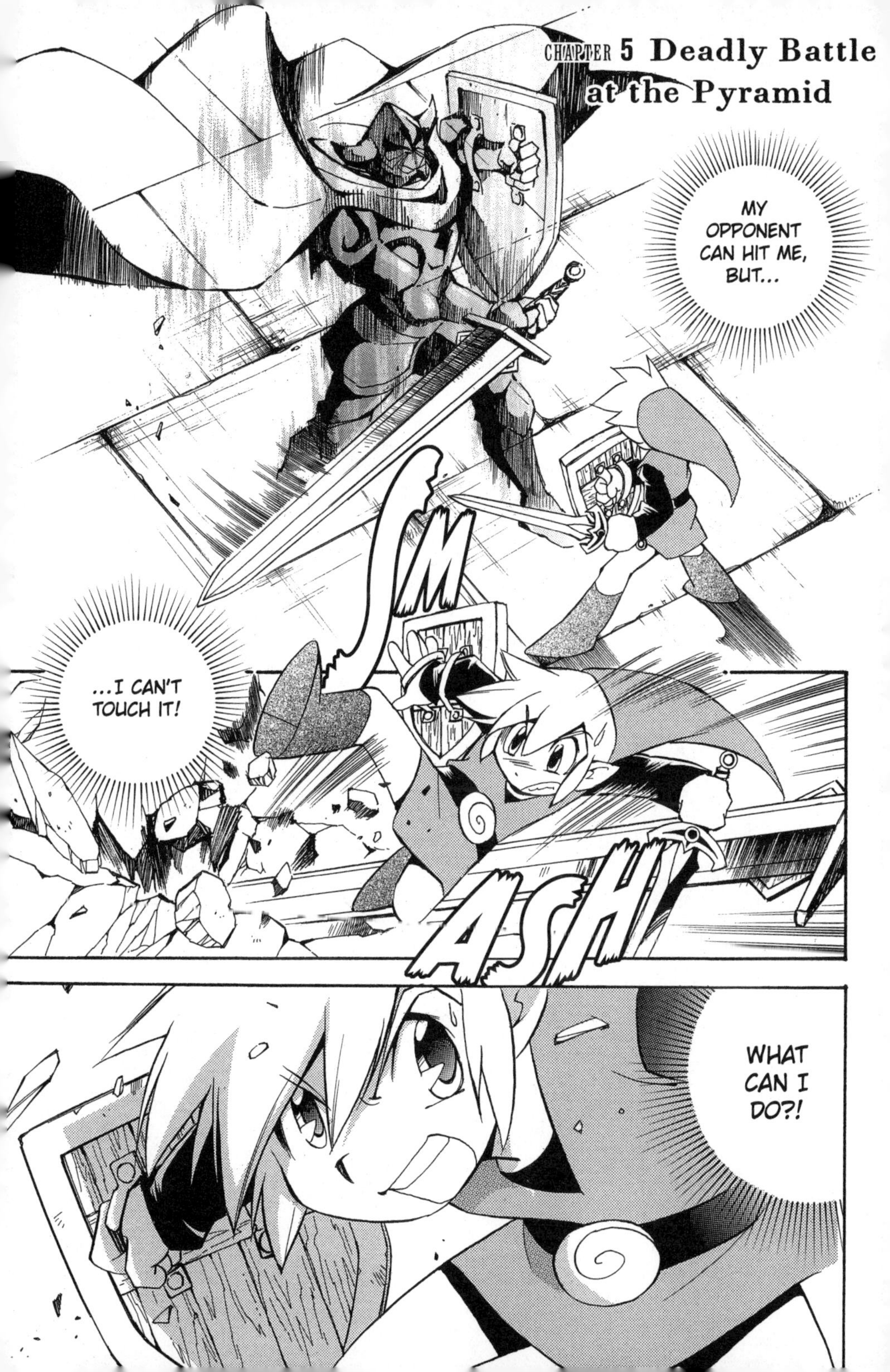
MY OPPONENT CAN HIT ME, BUT...
...I CAN'T TOUCH IT!
SMASH!
WHAT CAN I DO?!

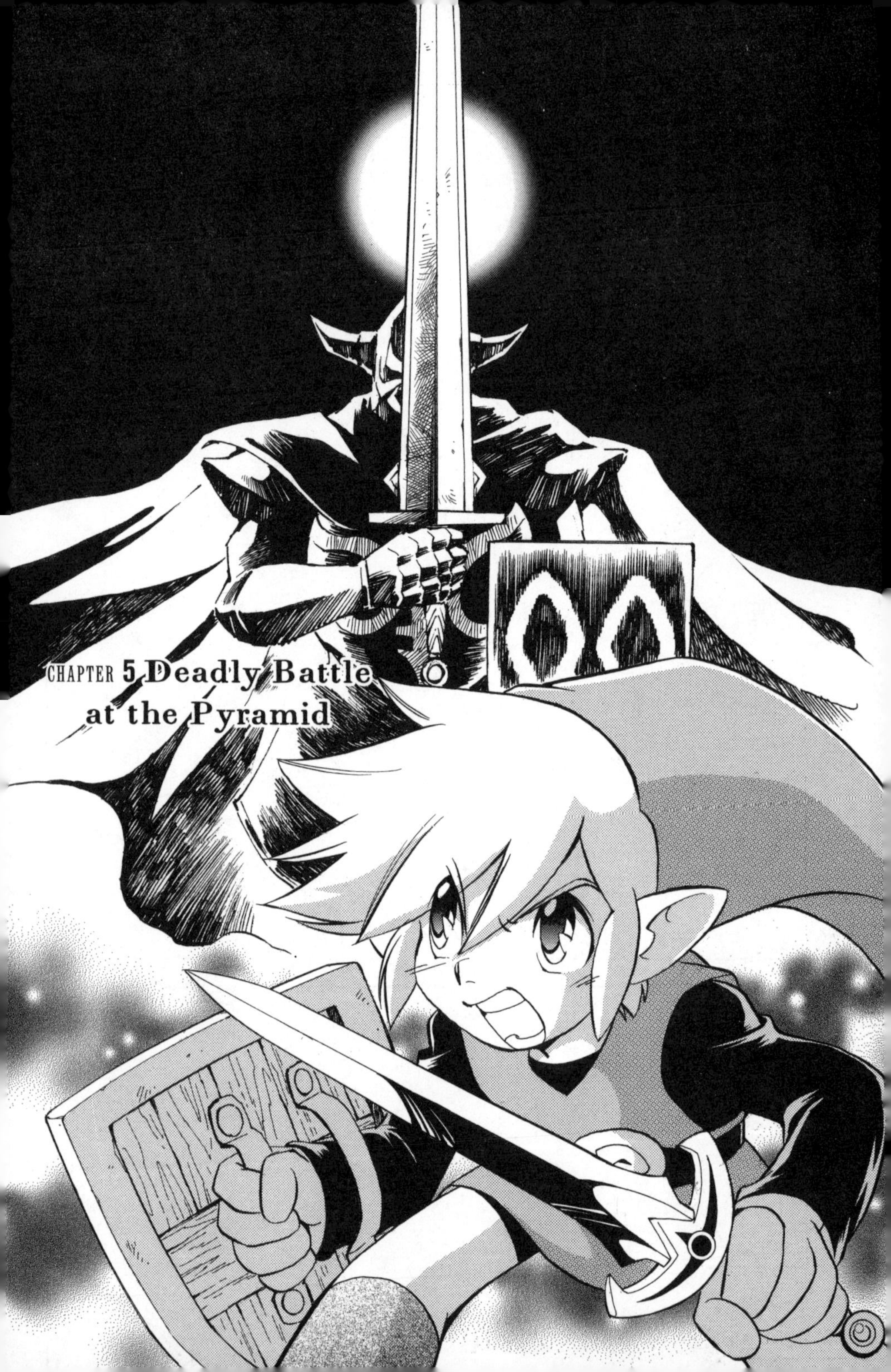
CHAPTER 5 Deadly Battle at the Pyramid

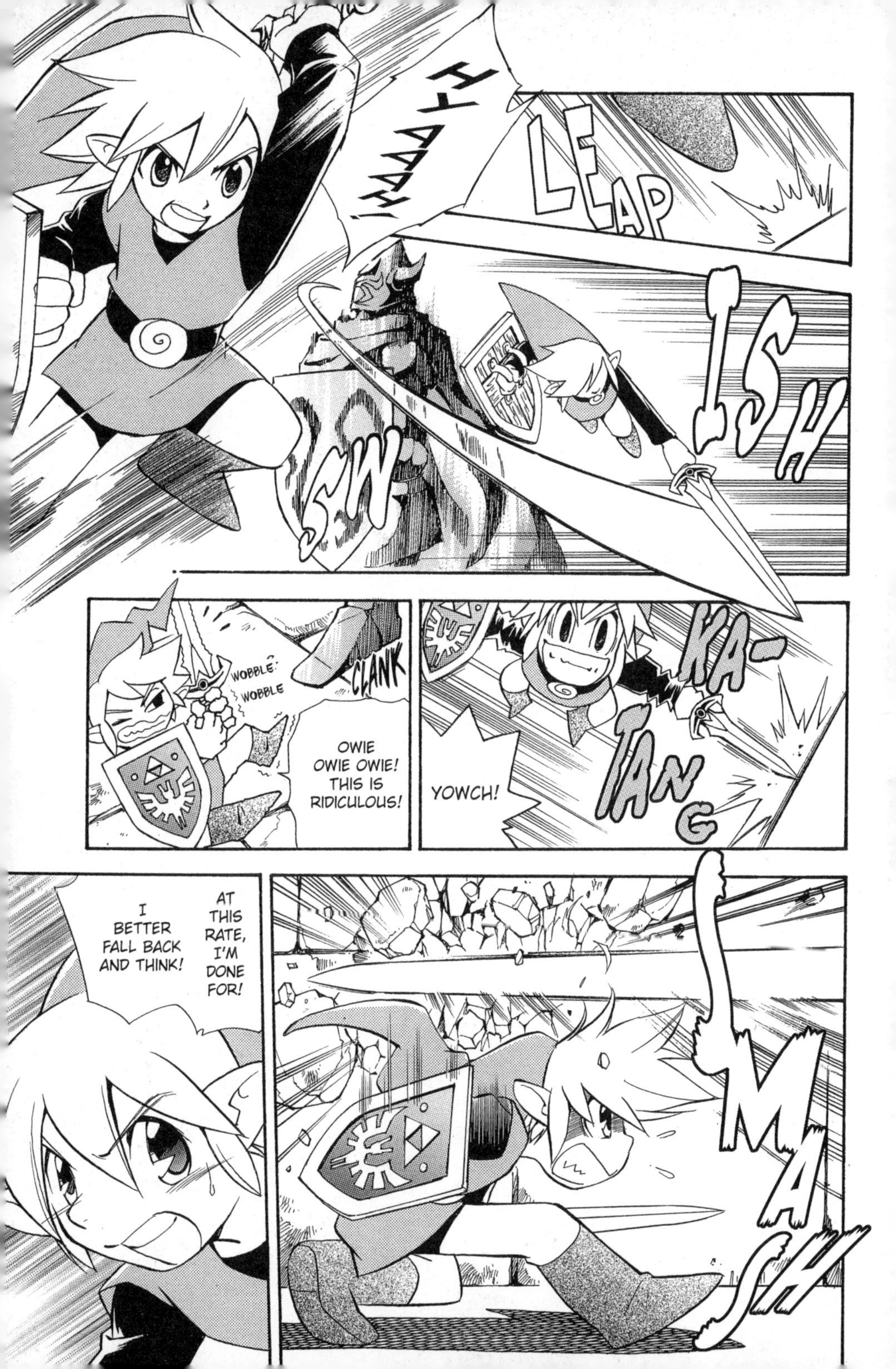
LEAP
SWISH
HYAAAH!
KA-TANG
YOWCH!
CLANK
WOBBLE WOBBLE
OWIE OWIE OWIE! THIS IS RIDICULOUS!
SMASH
AT THIS RATE, I'M DONE FOR!
I BETTER FALL BACK AND THINK!

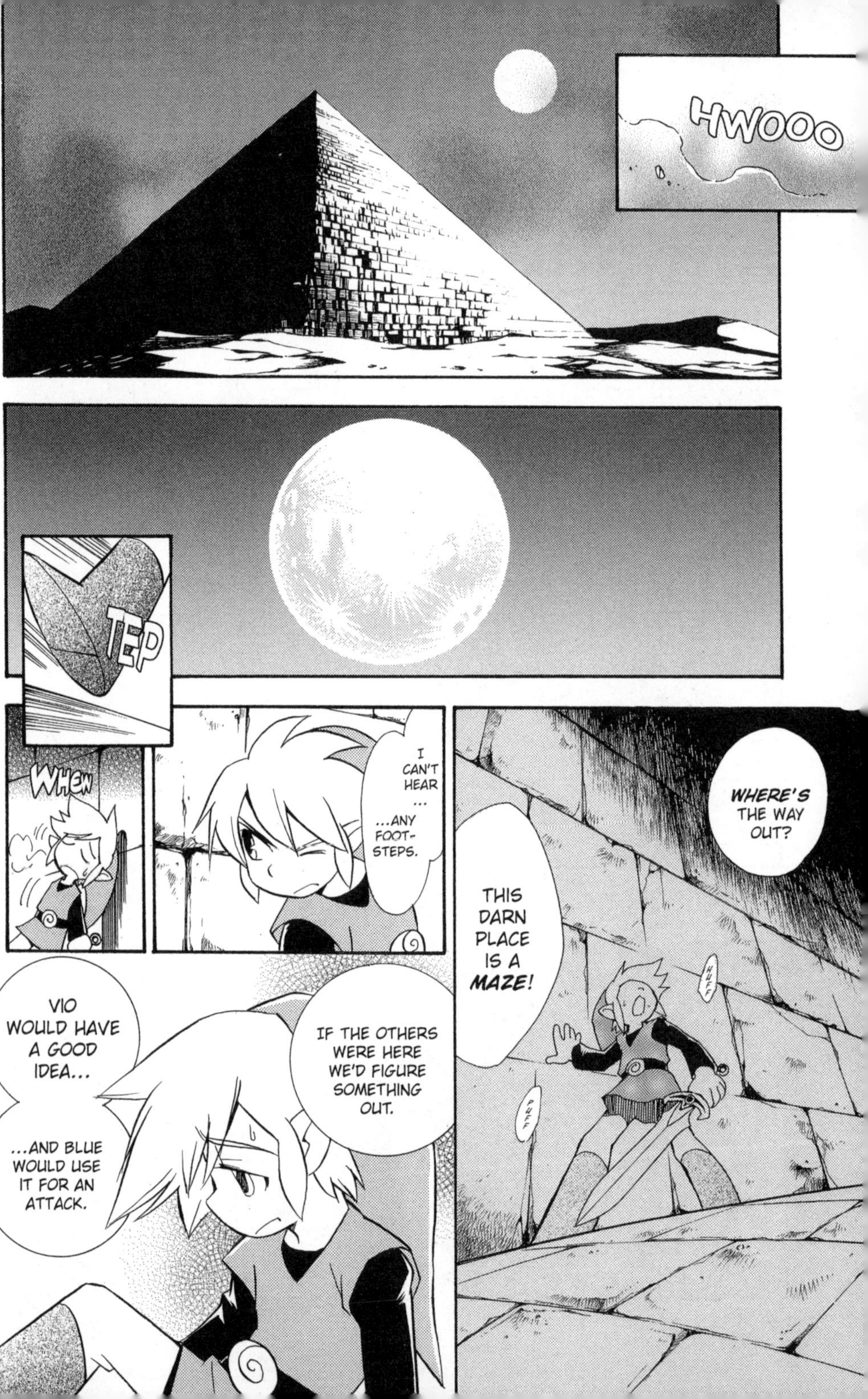
HWOOO
TEP
WHERE'S THE WAY OUT?
THIS DARN PLACE IS A MAZE!
HUFF
PUFF
I CAN'T HEAR...
...ANY FOOTSTEPS.
WHEW
IF THE OTHERS WERE HERE WE'D FIGURE SOMETHING OUT.
VIO WOULD HAVE A GOOD IDEA...
...AND BLUE WOULD USE IT FOR AN ATTACK.

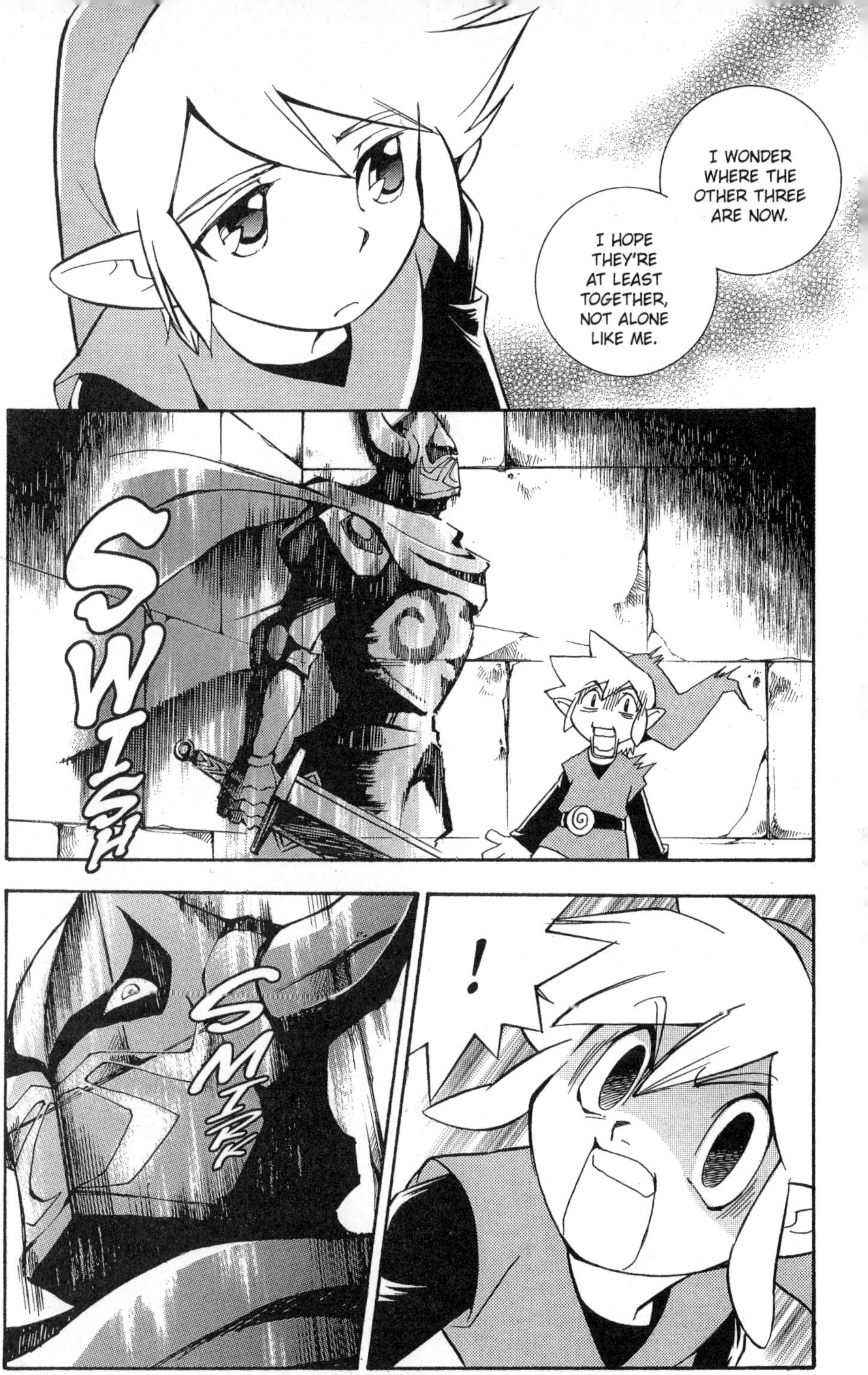
I WONDER WHERE THE OTHER THREE ARE NOW.
I HOPE THEY'RE AT LEAST TOGETHER, NOT ALONE LIKE ME.
SWISH
!
SMIRK

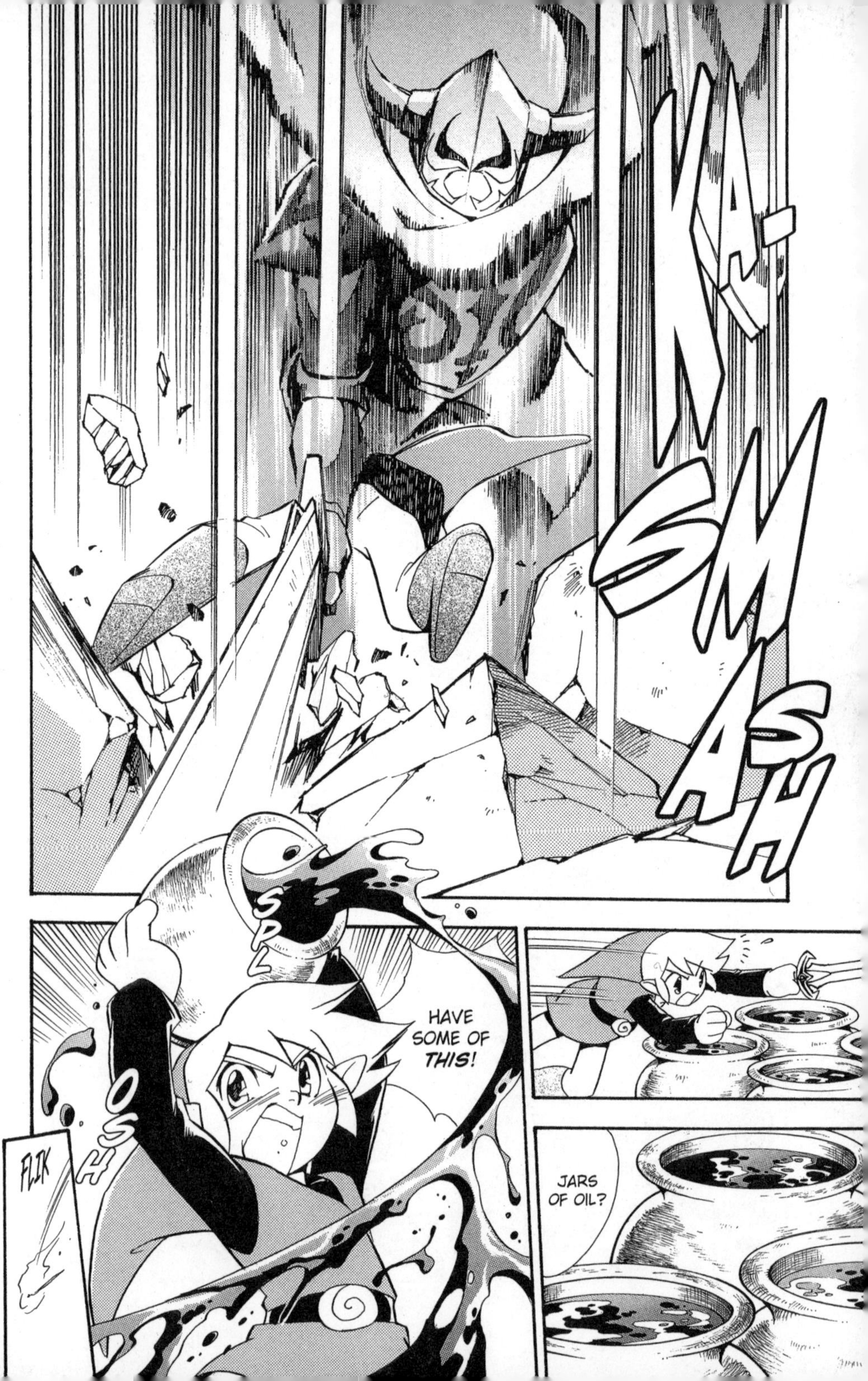
KA-SMASH
JARS OF OIL?
SPL
HAVE SOME OF *THIS!*
OSH
FLIK

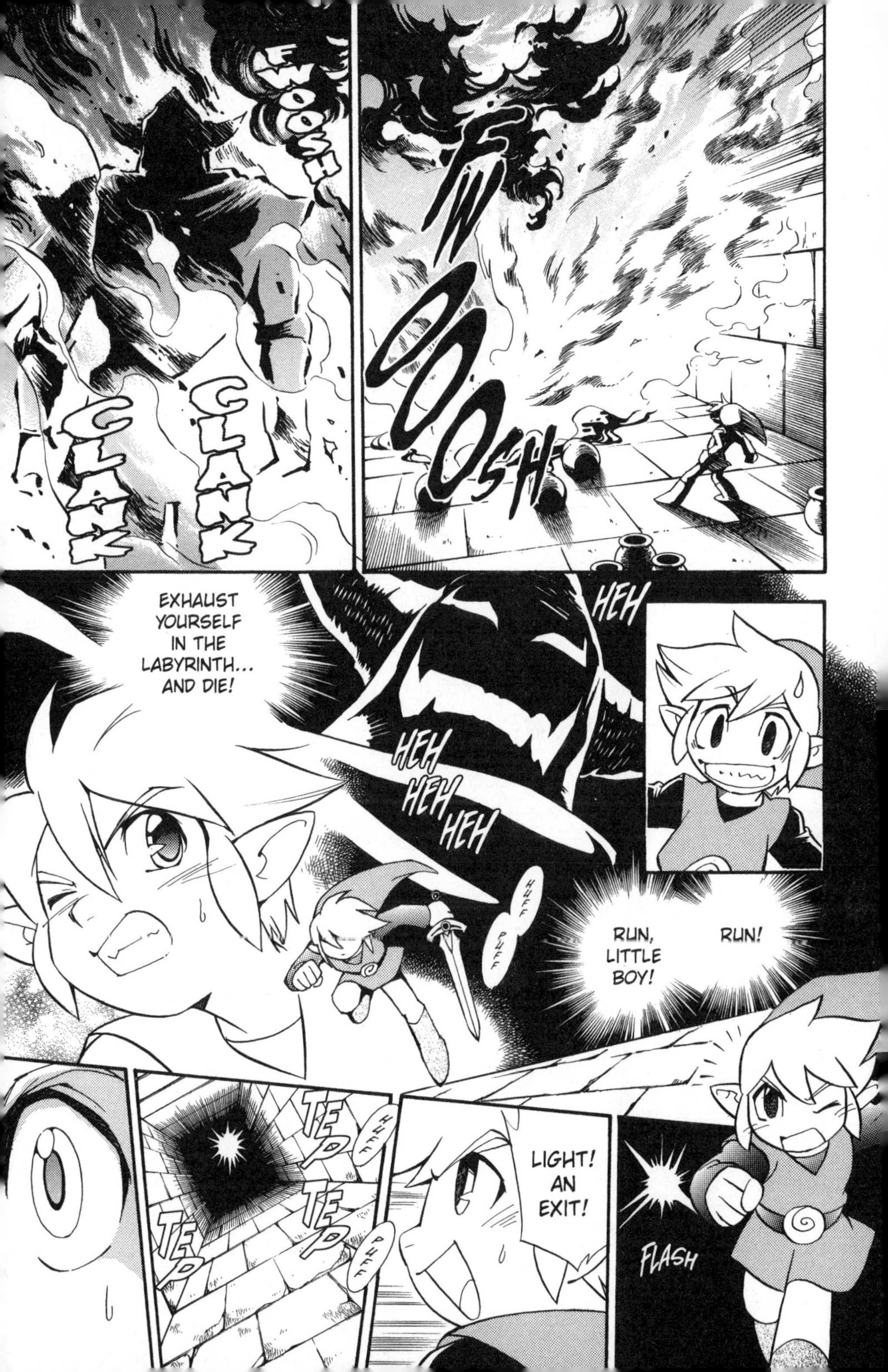
FWOOOOSH
FWOOSH
CLANK
CLANK
HEH
EXHAUST YOURSELF IN THE LABYRINTH... AND DIE!
HEH HEH HEH
HUFF
PUFF
RUN, LITTLE BOY! RUN!
FLASH
LIGHT! AN EXIT!
PUFF
TEP
TEP
TEP
HUFF

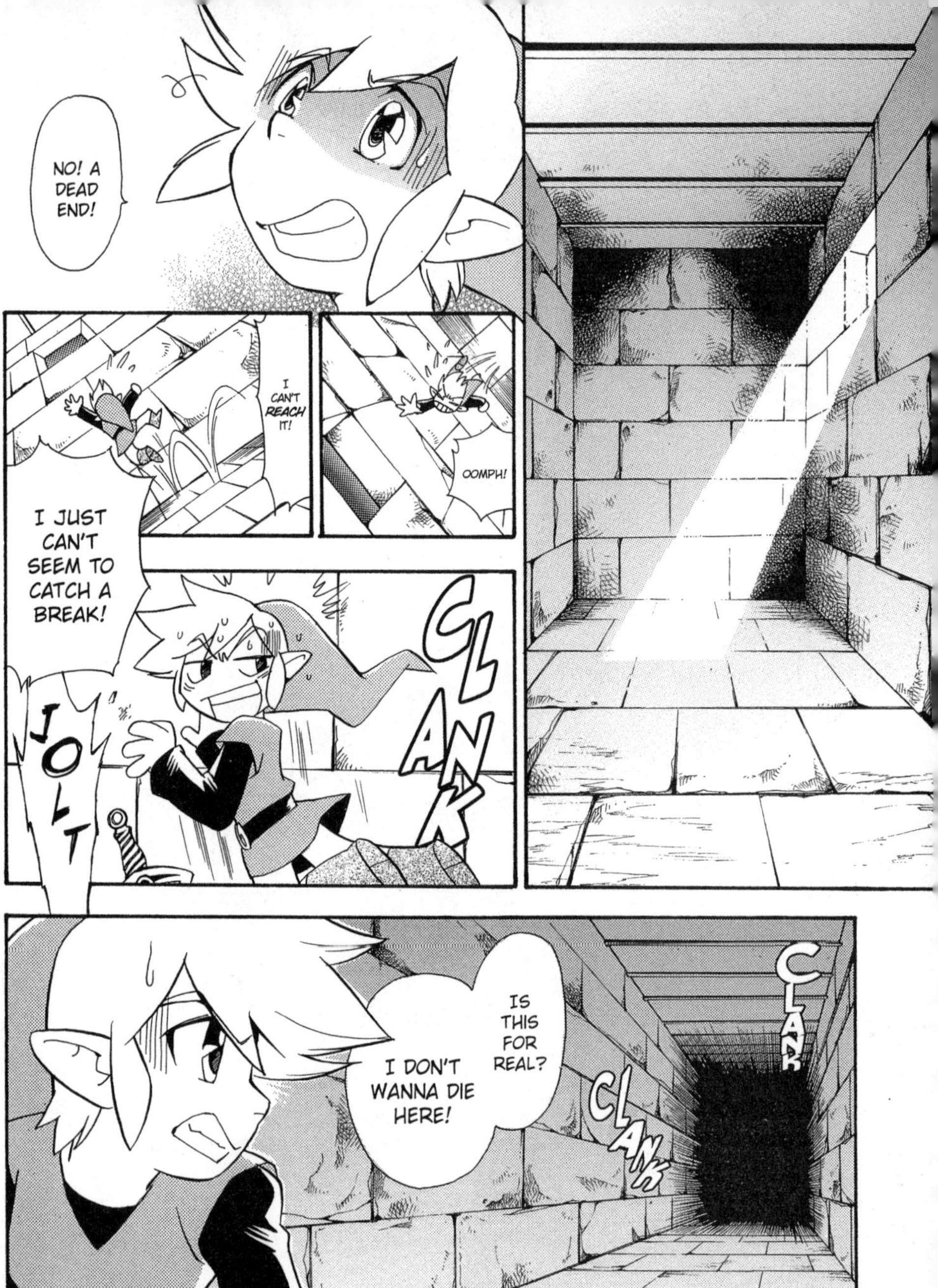
NO! A DEAD END!
OOMPH!
I CAN'T REACH IT!
I JUST CAN'T SEEM TO CATCH A BREAK!
CLANK
JOLT
IS THIS FOR REAL?
I DON'T WANNA DIE HERE!
CLANK
CLANK

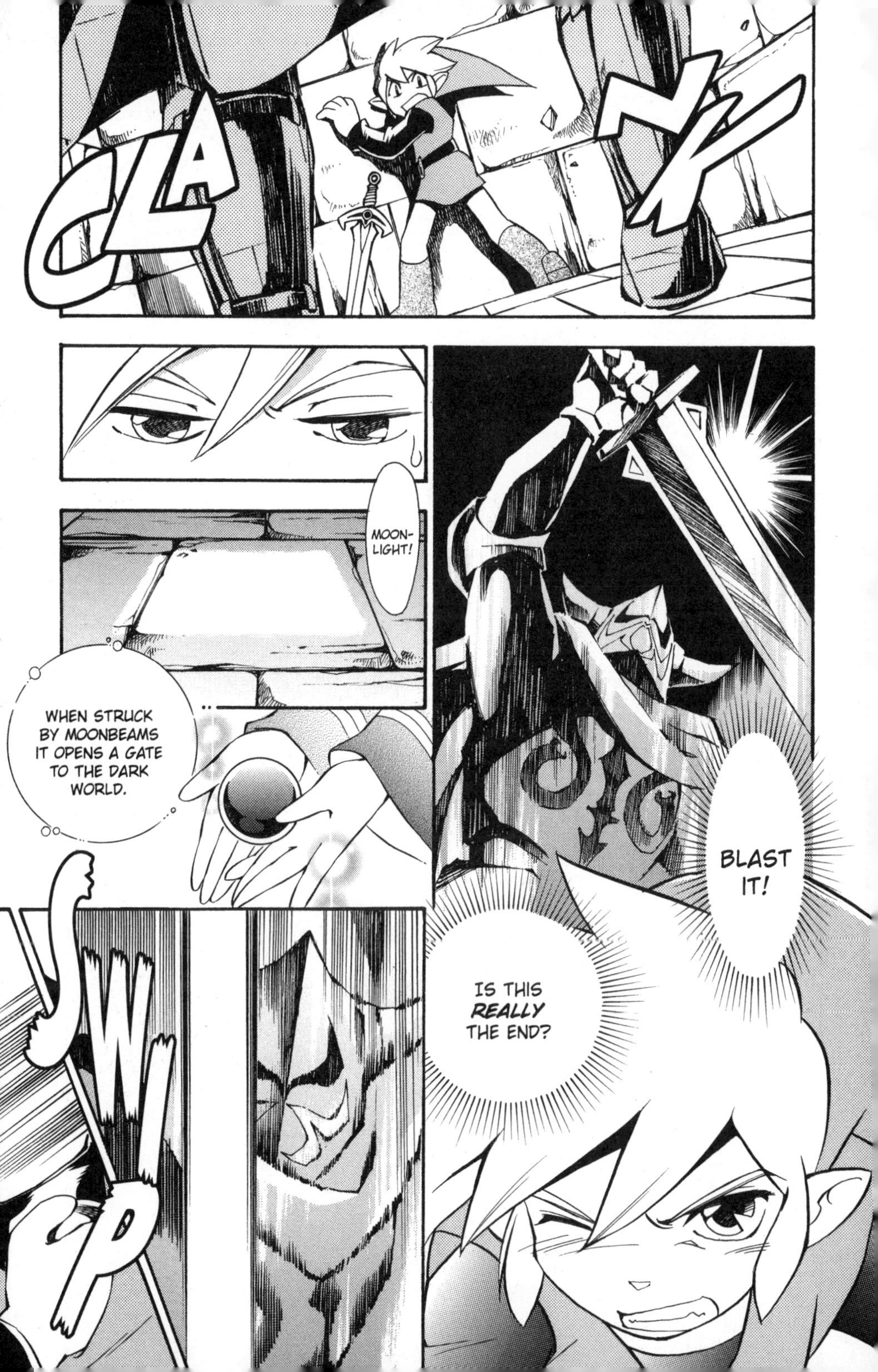
CLANK
BLAST IT!
IS THIS *REALLY* THE END?
MOON-LIGHT!
WHEN STRUCK BY MOONBEAMS IT OPENS A GATE TO THE DARK WORLD.
SWIP

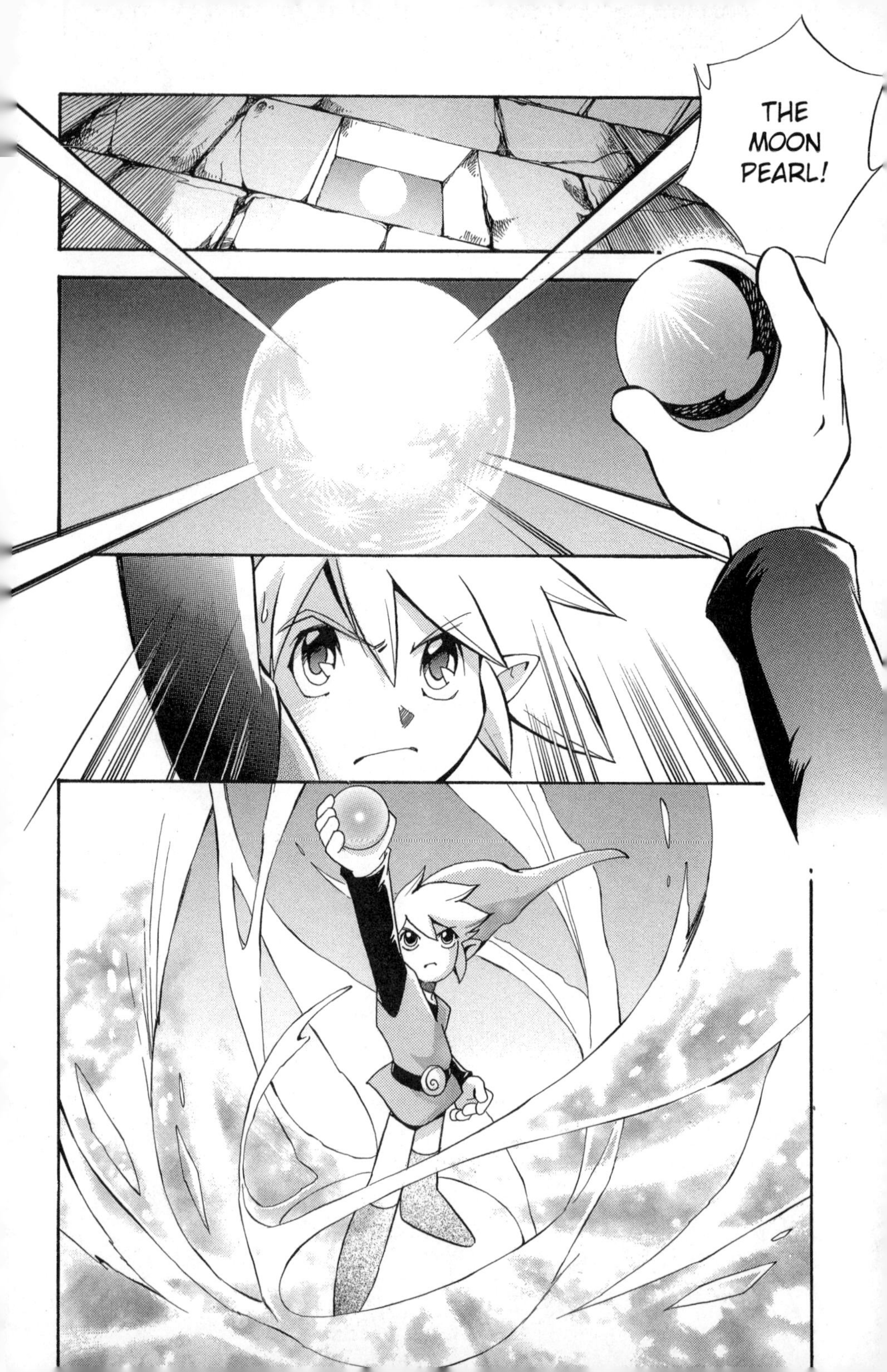
THE MOON PEARL!

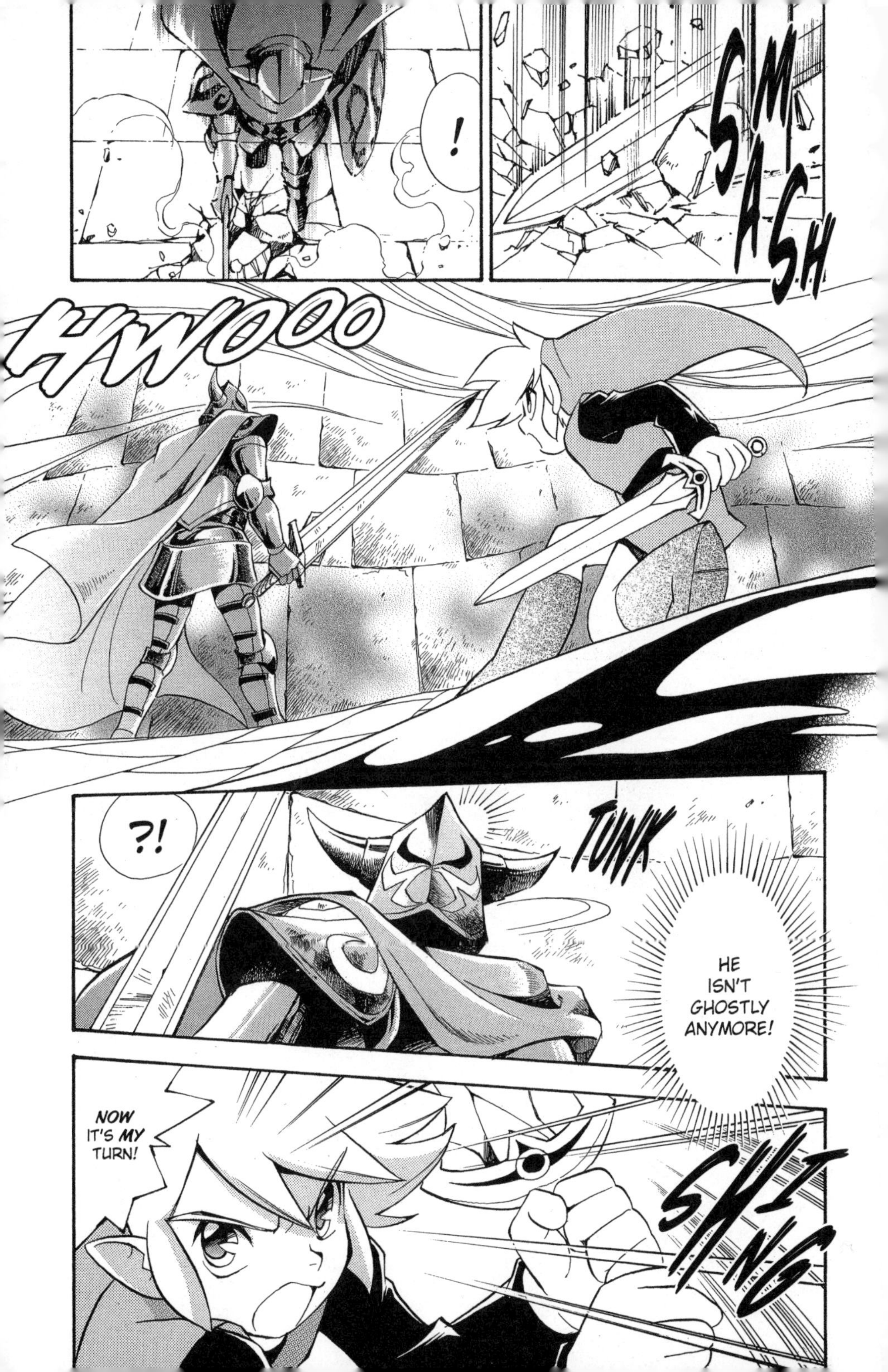
SMASH
!
HWOOO
?!
TUNK
HE ISN'T GHOSTLY ANYMORE!
NOW IT'S *MY* TURN!
SHING

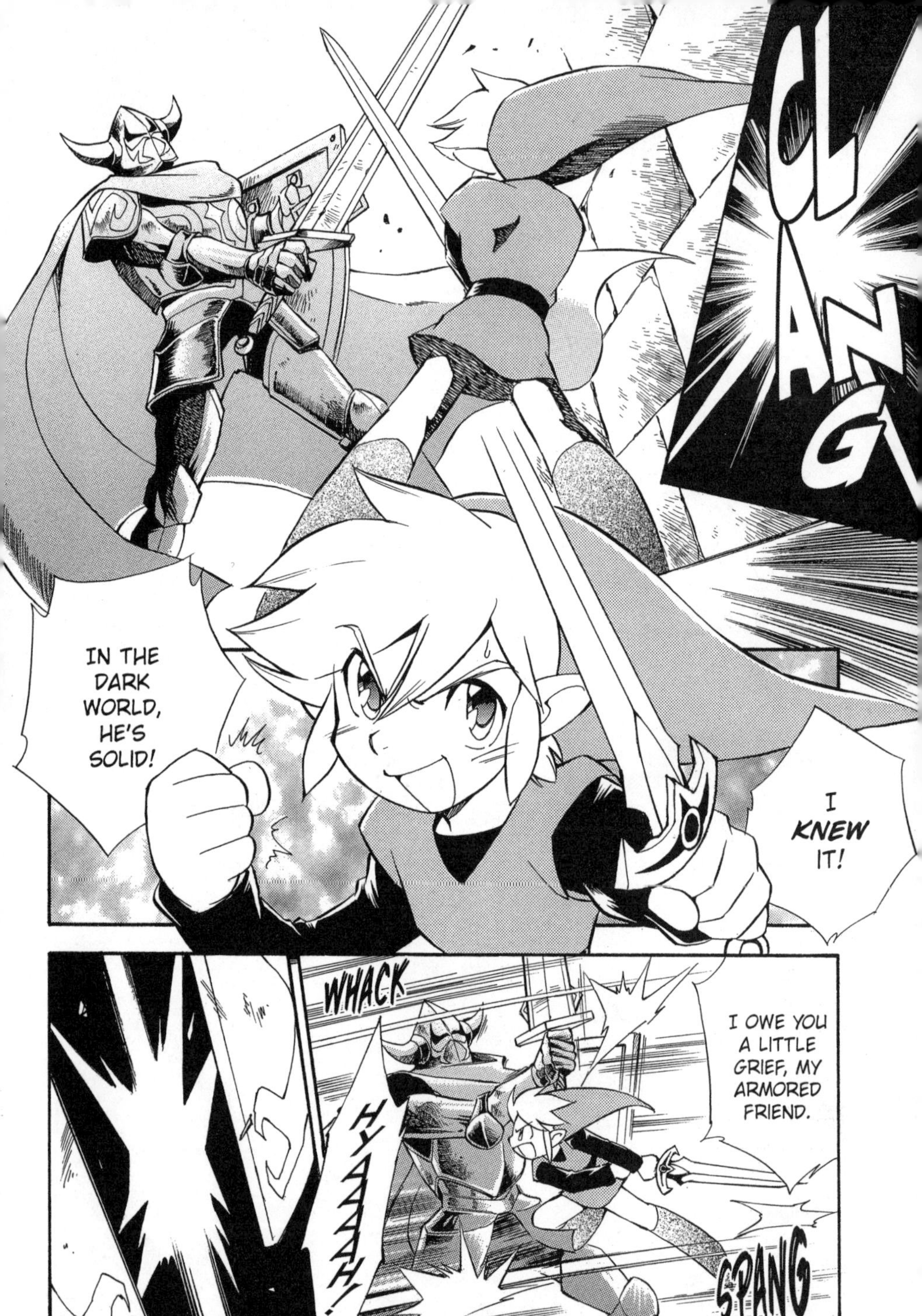
CLANG
I KNEW IT!
IN THE DARK WORLD, HE'S SOLID!
I OWE YOU A LITTLE GRIEF, MY ARMORED FRIEND.
WHACK
HYAAAAH!
SPANG

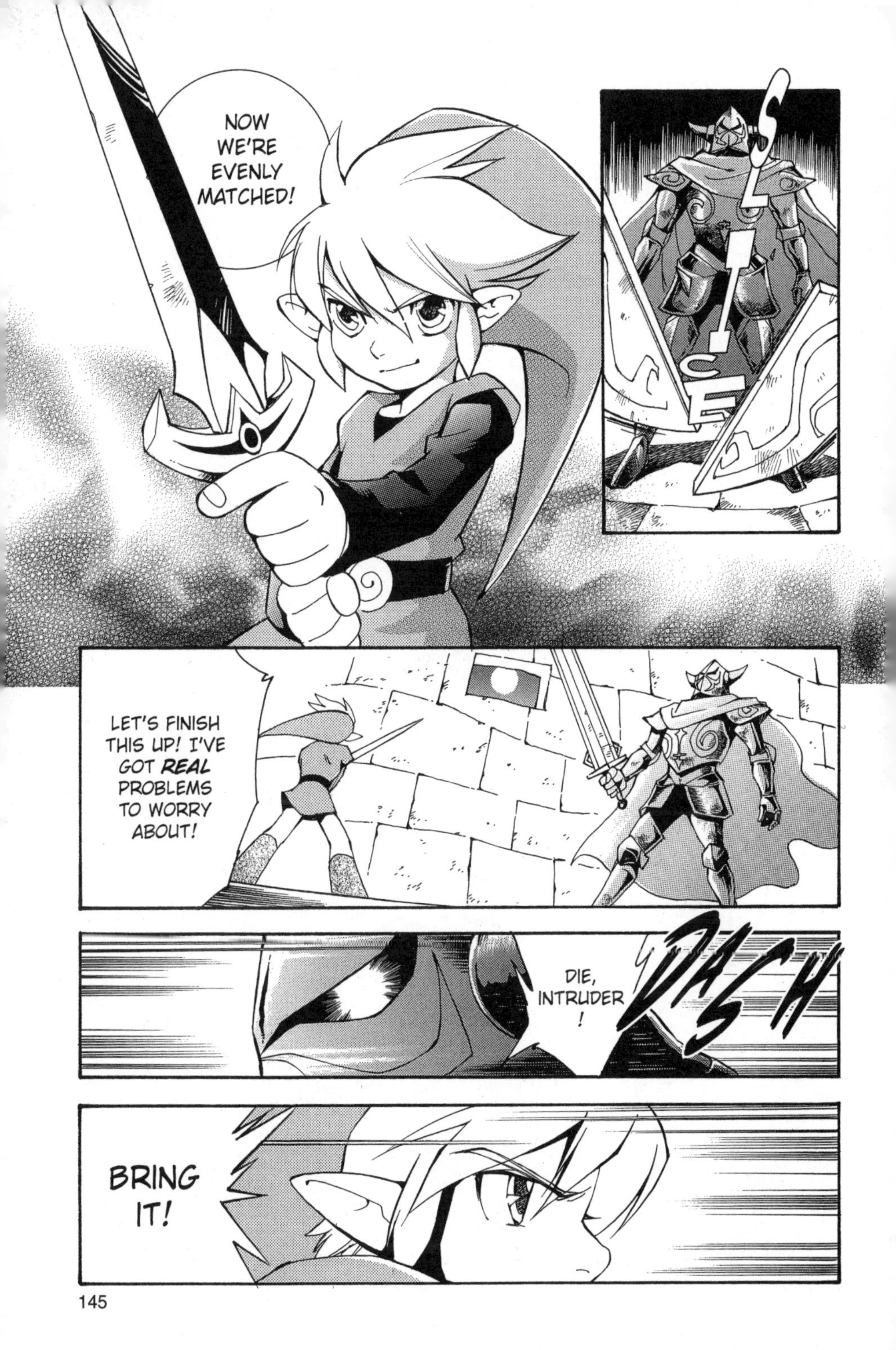
SLICE
NOW WE'RE EVENLY MATCHED!
LET'S FINISH THIS UP! I'VE GOT **REAL** PROBLEMS TO WORRY ABOUT!
DASH
DIE, INTRUDER!
BRING IT!

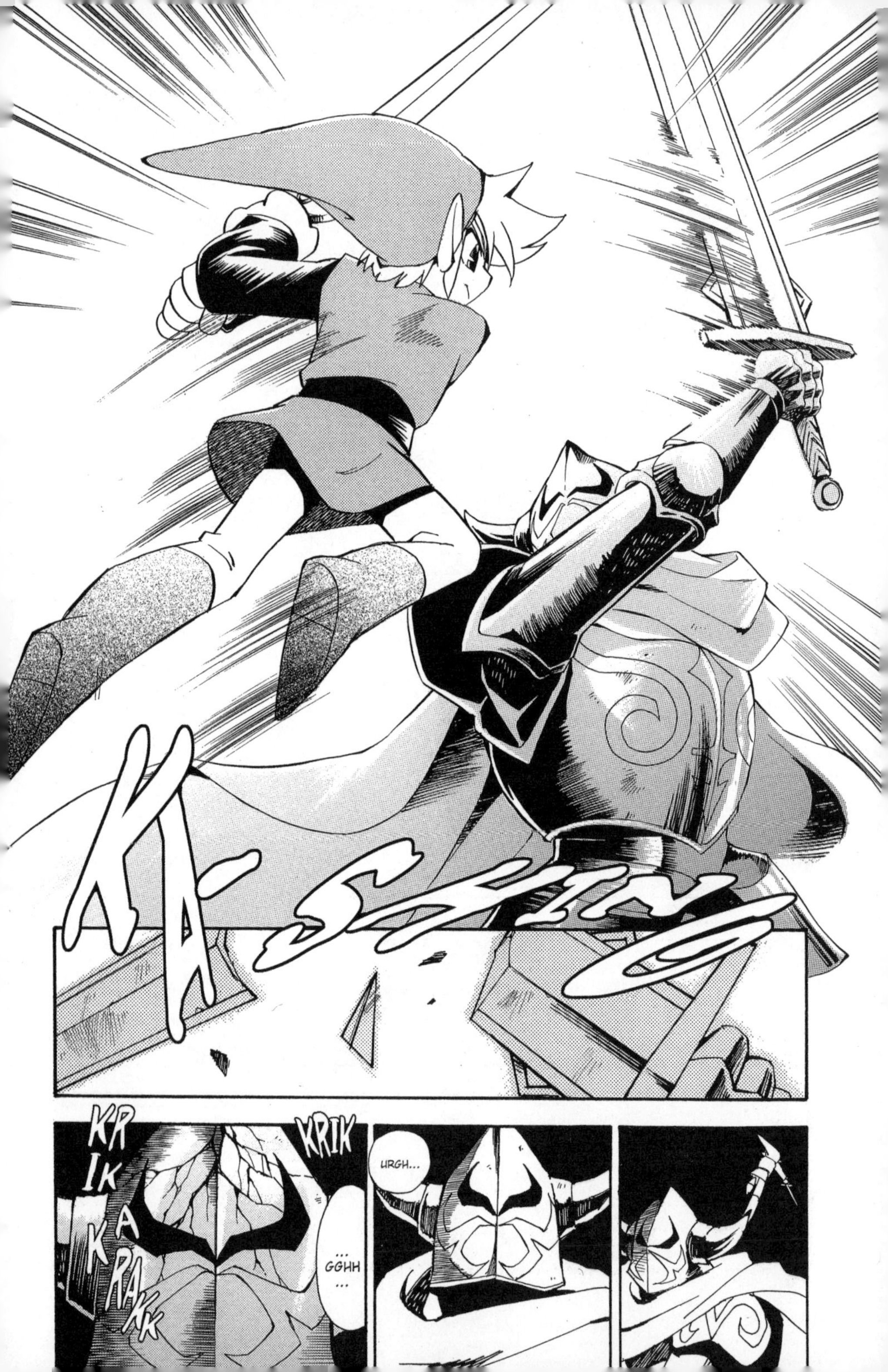
KA-SHING
URGH...
KRIK
KRIKAKRAKK
... GGHH ...

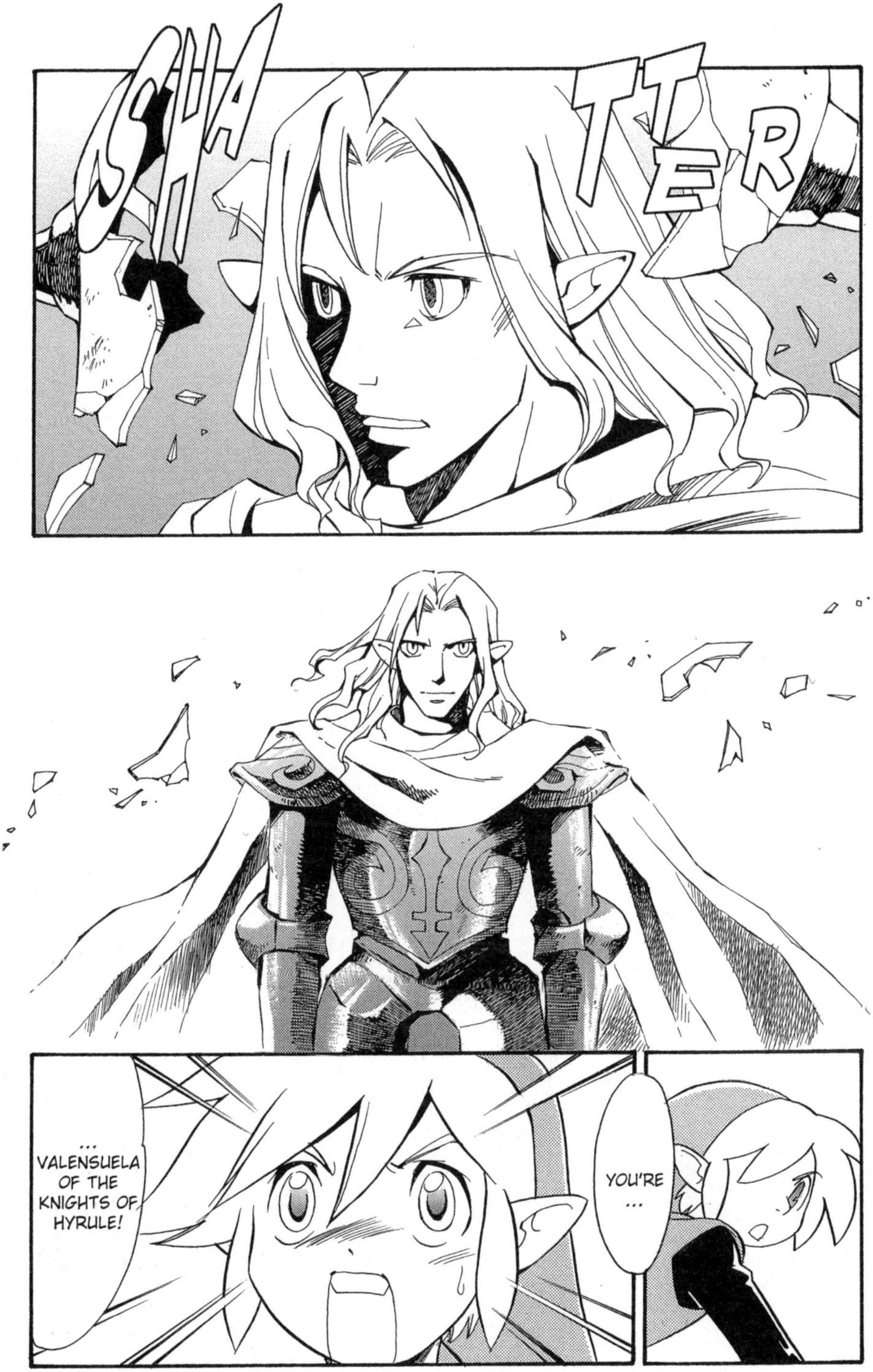
SHATTER
YOU'RE ...
... VALENSUELA OF THE KNIGHTS OF HYRULE!

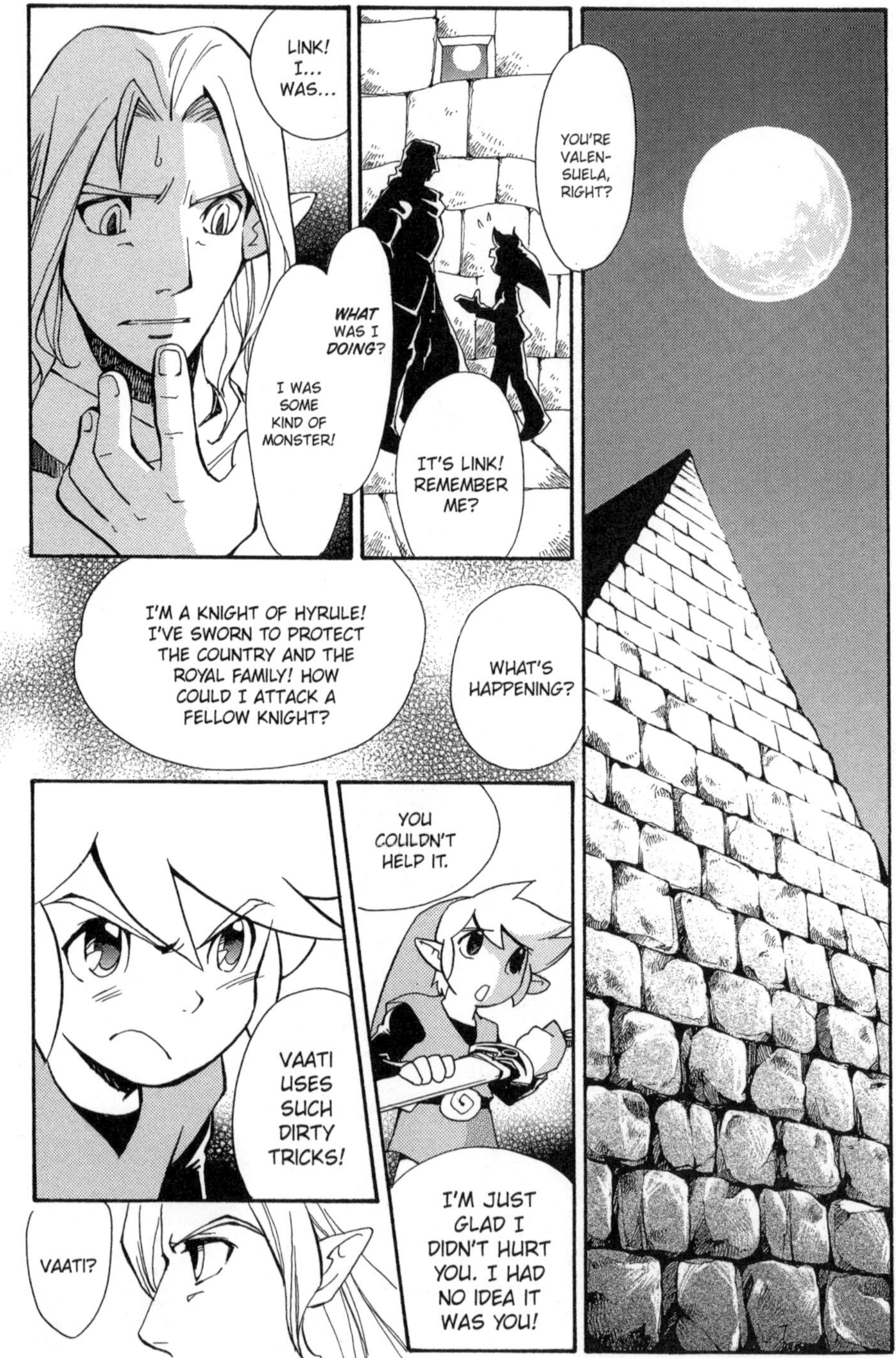
YOU'RE VALEN-SUELA, RIGHT?
IT'S LINK! REMEMBER ME?
LINK! I... WAS...
WHAT WAS I *DOING*?
I WAS SOME KIND OF MONSTER!
I'M A KNIGHT OF HYRULE! I'VE SWORN TO PROTECT THE COUNTRY AND THE ROYAL FAMILY! HOW COULD I ATTACK A FELLOW KNIGHT?
WHAT'S HAPPENING?
YOU COULDN'T HELP IT.
I'M JUST GLAD I DIDN'T HURT YOU. I HAD NO IDEA IT WAS YOU!
VAATI USES SUCH DIRTY TRICKS!
VAATI?

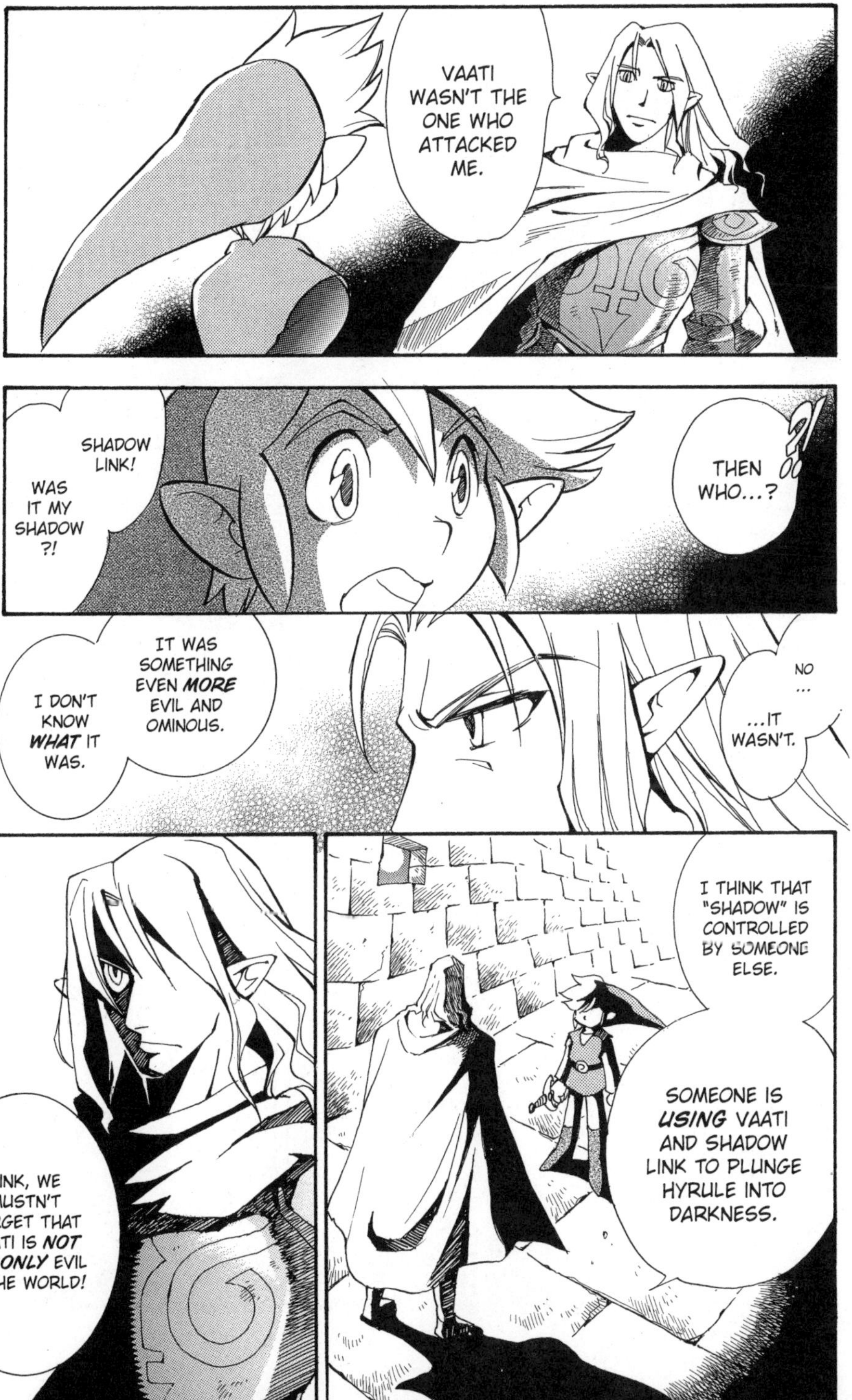
VAATI WASN'T THE ONE WHO ATTACKED ME.
THEN WHO...?
SHADOW LINK!
WAS IT MY SHADOW ?!
NO ...
...IT WASN'T.
IT WAS SOMETHING EVEN **MORE** EVIL AND OMINOUS.
I DON'T KNOW **WHAT** IT WAS.
I THINK THAT "SHADOW" IS CONTROLLED BY SOMEONE ELSE.
SOMEONE IS **USING** VAATI AND SHADOW LINK TO PLUNGE HYRULE INTO DARKNESS.
LINK, WE MUSTN'T FORGET THAT VAATI IS **NOT** THE **ONLY** EVIL IN THE WORLD!

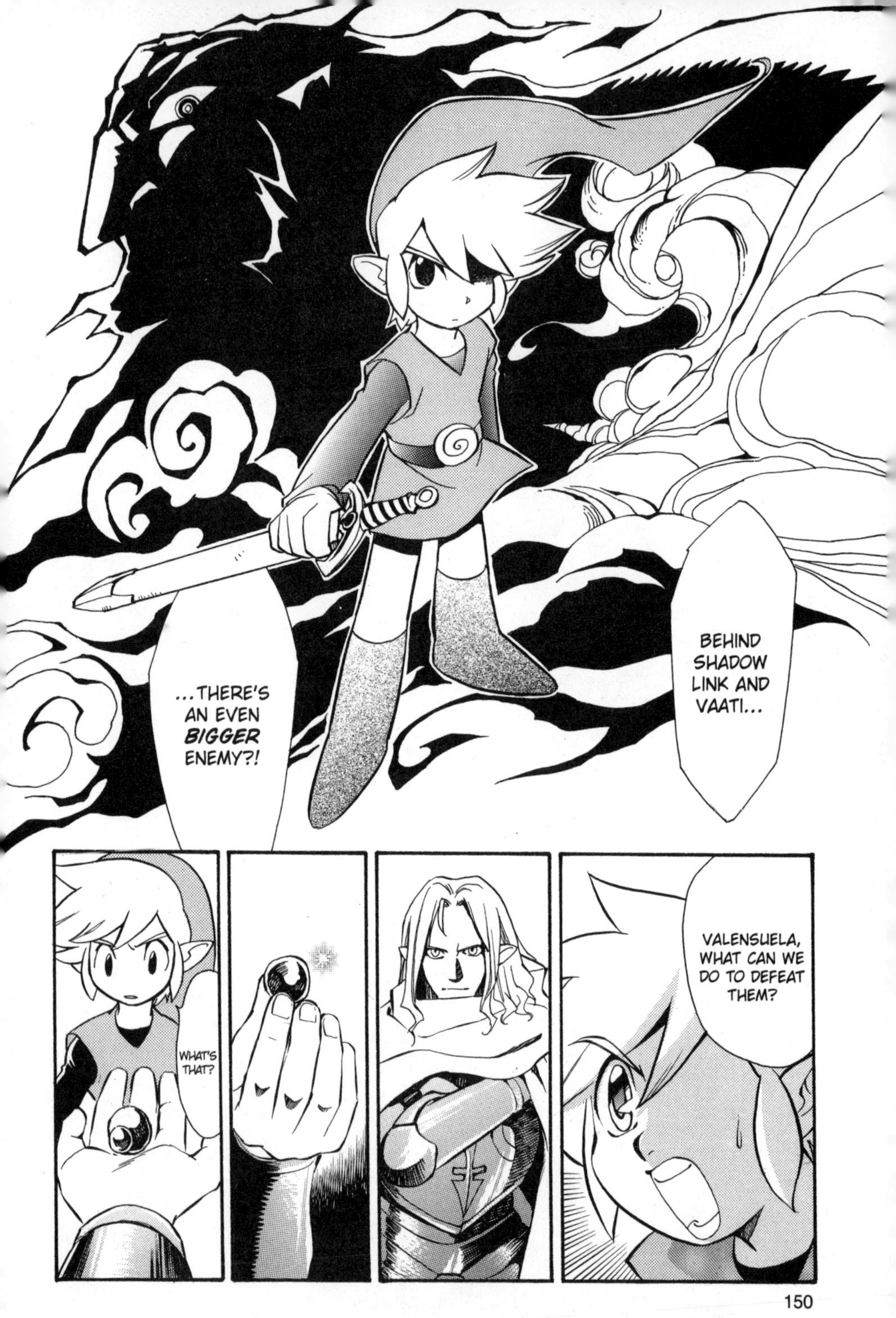
BEHIND SHADOW LINK AND VAATI...
...THERE'S AN EVEN BIGGER ENEMY?!
VALENSUELA, WHAT CAN WE DO TO DEFEAT THEM?
WHAT'S THAT?

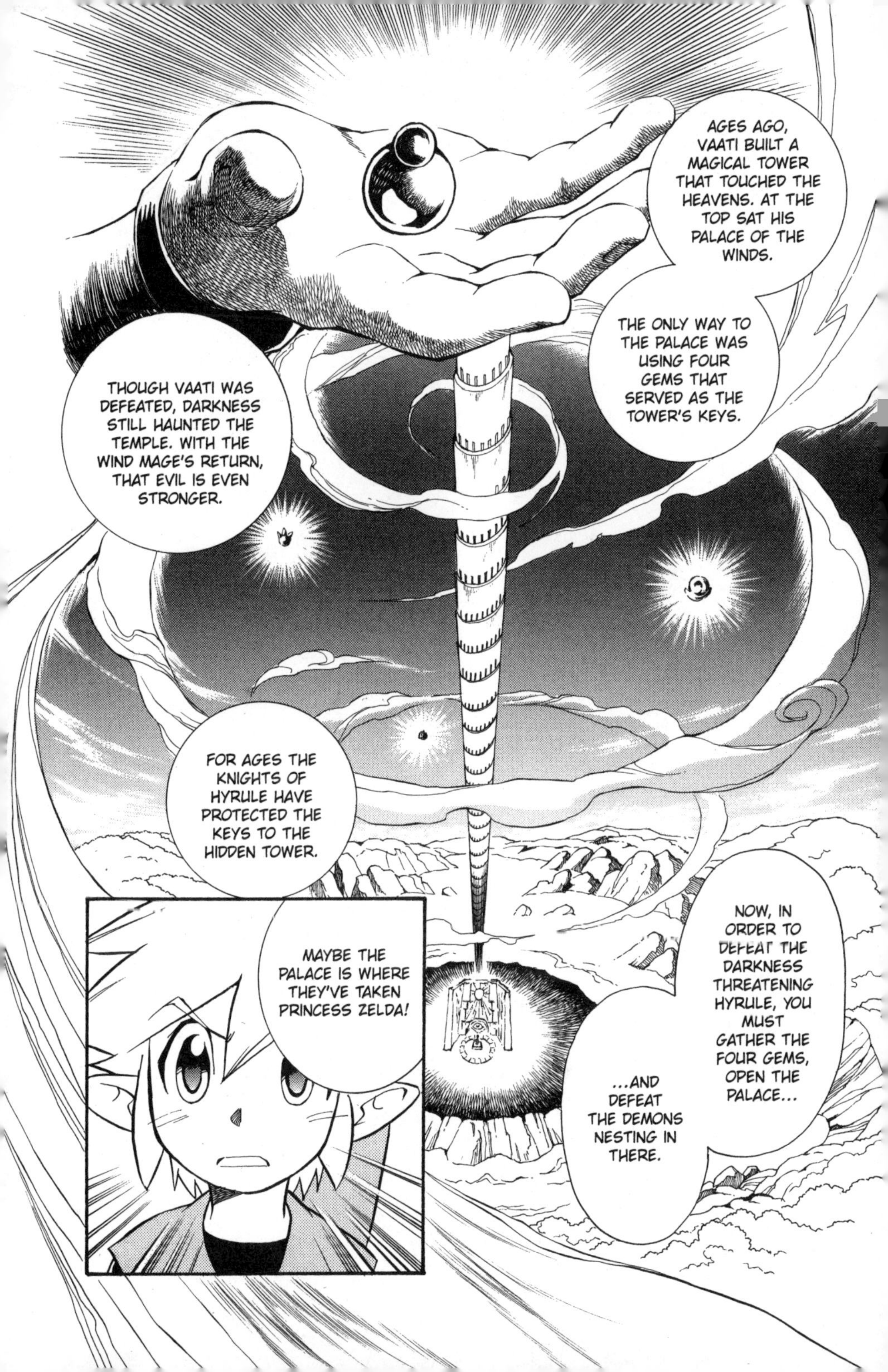
AGES AGO, VAATI BUILT A MAGICAL TOWER THAT TOUCHED THE HEAVENS. AT THE TOP SAT HIS PALACE OF THE WINDS.
THE ONLY WAY TO THE PALACE WAS USING FOUR GEMS THAT SERVED AS THE TOWER'S KEYS.
THOUGH VAATI WAS DEFEATED, DARKNESS STILL HAUNTED THE TEMPLE. WITH THE WIND MAGE'S RETURN, THAT EVIL IS EVEN STRONGER.
FOR AGES THE KNIGHTS OF HYRULE HAVE PROTECTED THE KEYS TO THE HIDDEN TOWER.
NOW, IN ORDER TO DEFEAT THE DARKNESS THREATENING HYRULE, YOU MUST GATHER THE FOUR GEMS, OPEN THE PALACE...
...AND DEFEAT THE DEMONS NESTING IN THERE.
MAYBE THE PALACE IS WHERE THEY'VE TAKEN PRINCESS ZELDA!

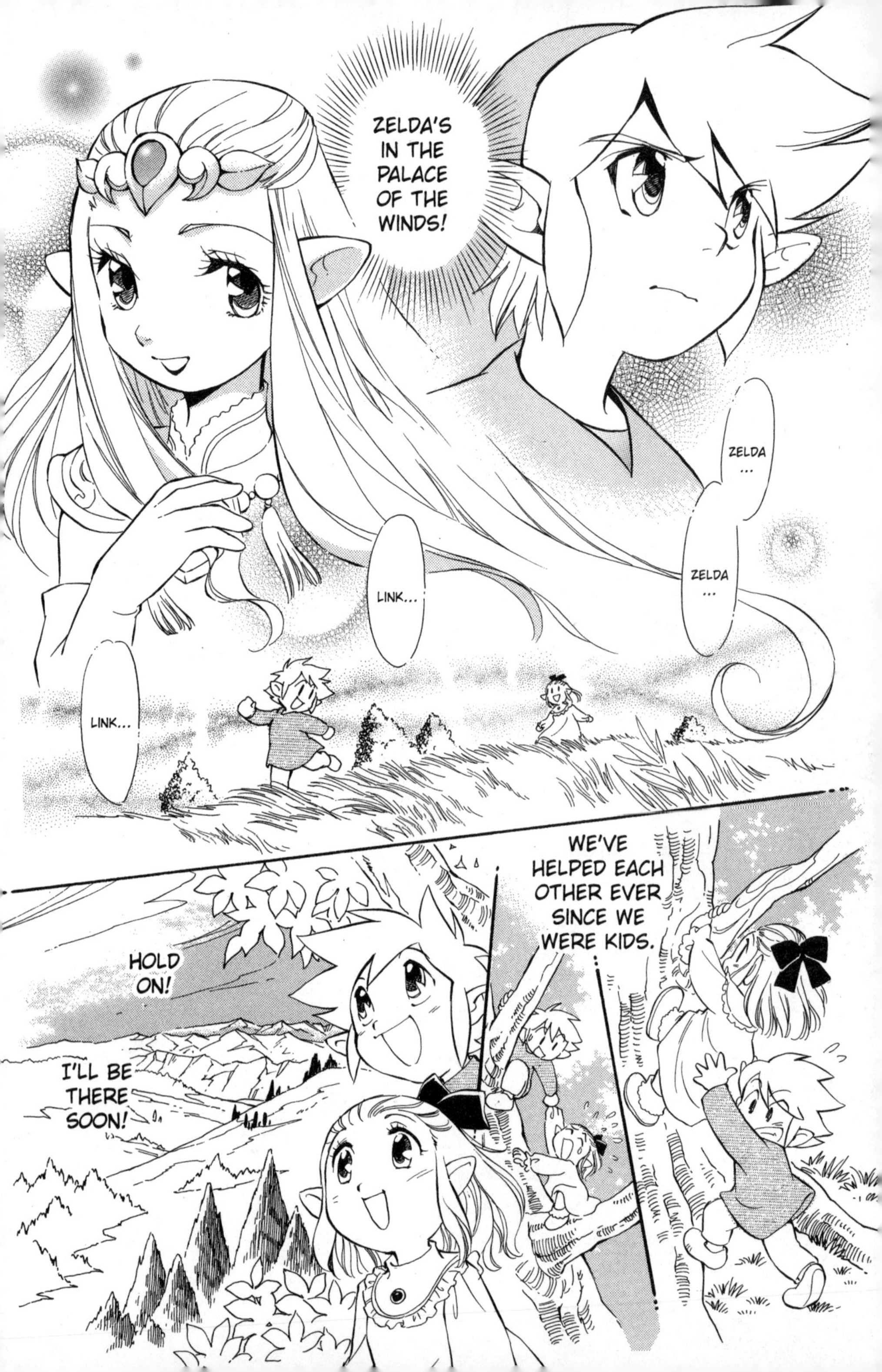
ZELDA'S IN THE PALACE OF THE WINDS!
ZELDA...
ZELDA...
LINK...
LINK...
WE'VE HELPED EACH OTHER EVER SINCE WE WERE KIDS.
HOLD ON!
I'LL BE THERE SOON!

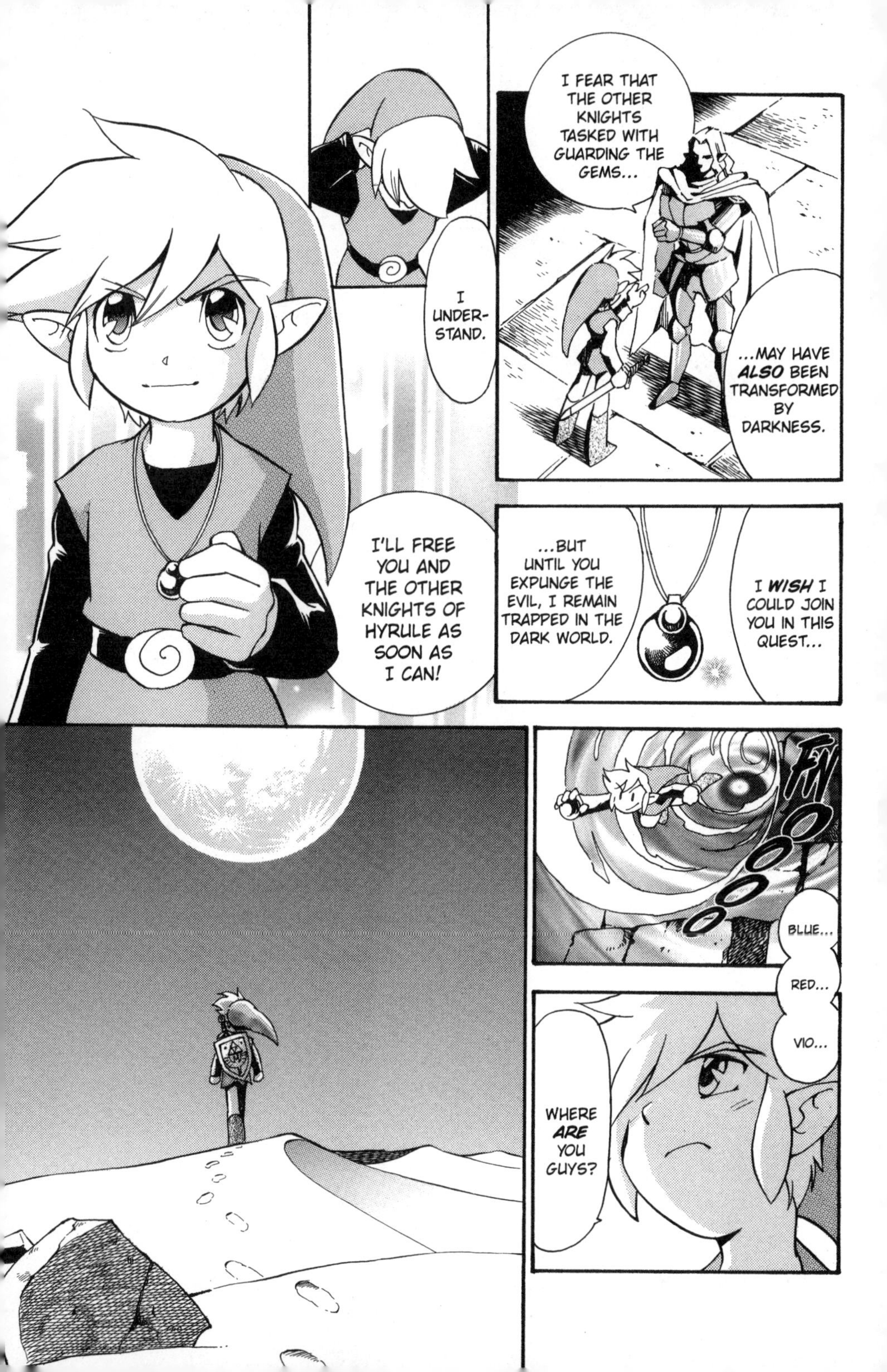
I FEAR THAT THE OTHER KNIGHTS TASKED WITH GUARDING THE GEMS...
...MAY HAVE ALSO BEEN TRANSFORMED BY DARKNESS.
I UNDER-STAND.
I WISH I COULD JOIN YOU IN THIS QUEST...
...BUT UNTIL YOU EXPUNGE THE EVIL, I REMAIN TRAPPED IN THE DARK WORLD.
I'LL FREE YOU AND THE OTHER KNIGHTS OF HYRULE AS SOON AS I CAN!
FWOOOOOOO
BLUE...
RED...
VIO...
WHERE ARE YOU GUYS?

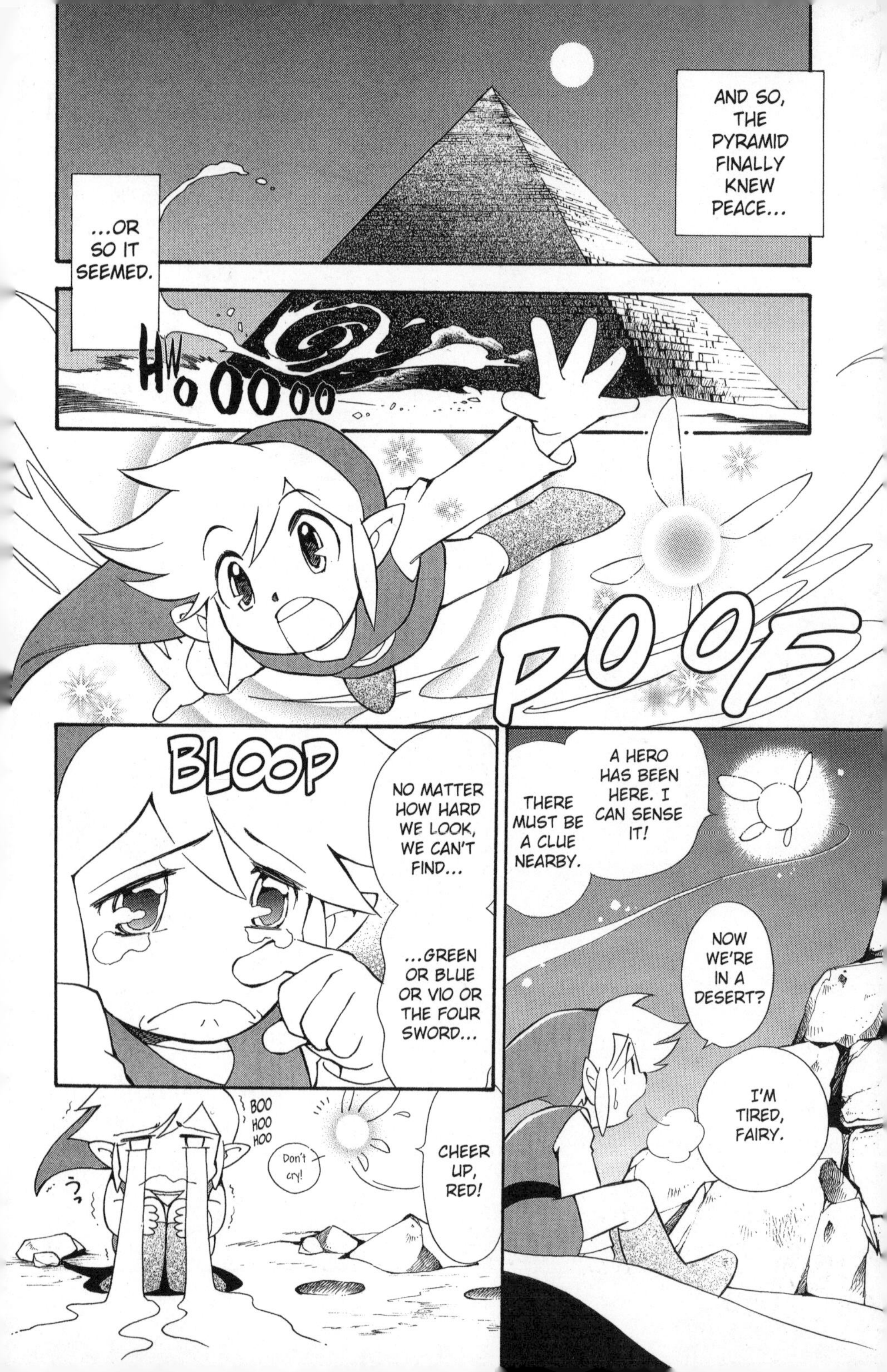
AND SO, THE PYRAMID FINALLY KNEW PEACE...
...OR SO IT SEEMED.
HWOOOOO
POOF
A HERO HAS BEEN HERE. I CAN SENSE IT!
THERE MUST BE A CLUE NEARBY.
NOW WE'RE IN A DESERT?
I'M TIRED, FAIRY.
BLOOP
NO MATTER HOW HARD WE LOOK, WE CAN'T FIND...
...GREEN OR BLUE OR VIO OR THE FOUR SWORD...
CHEER UP, RED!
Don't cry!
BOO HOO HOO

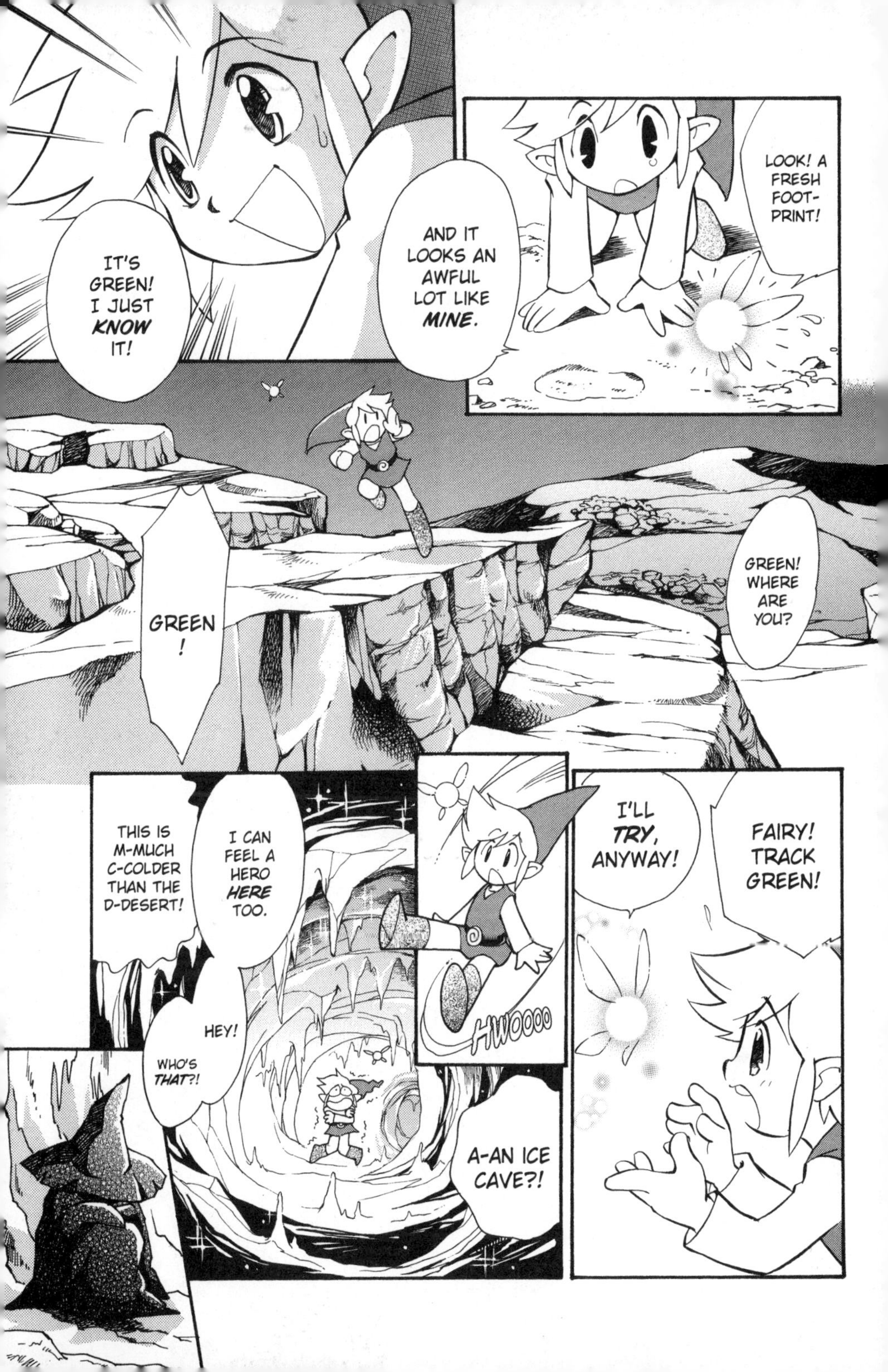
LOOK! A FRESH FOOT-PRINT!
AND IT LOOKS AN AWFUL LOT LIKE **MINE**.
IT'S GREEN! I JUST **KNOW** IT!
GREEN! WHERE ARE YOU?
GREEN!
FAIRY! TRACK GREEN!
I'LL **TRY**, ANYWAY!
HWOOOO
A-AN ICE CAVE?!
THIS IS M-MUCH C-COLDER THAN THE D-DESERT!
I CAN FEEL A HERO **HERE** TOO.
HEY!
WHO'S **THAT**?!

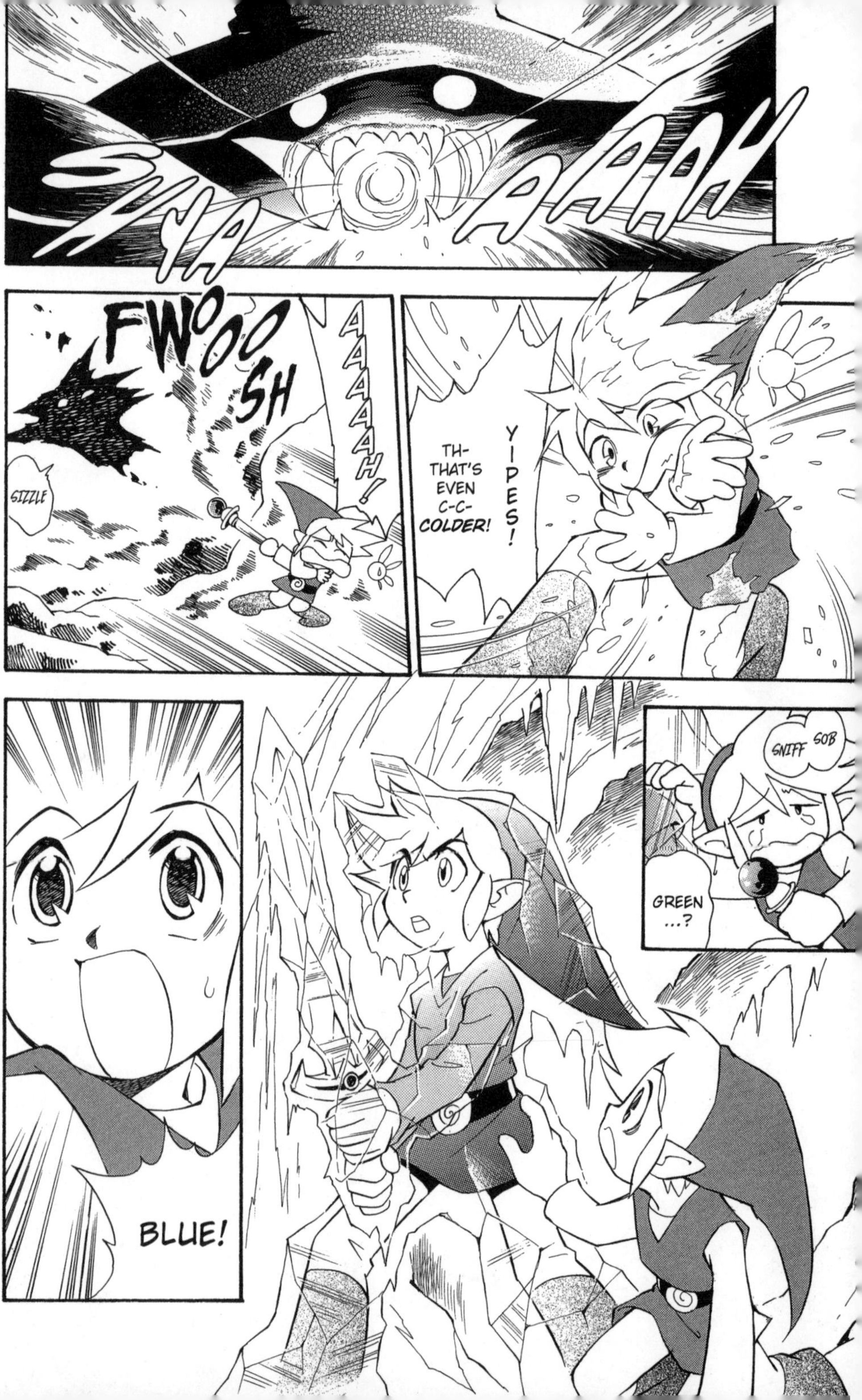
SHYAAAAAH
YIPES!
TH- THAT'S EVEN C-C-COLDER!
FWOOOSH
AAAAAAH!
SIZZLE
SNIFF SOB
GREEN ...?
BLUE!

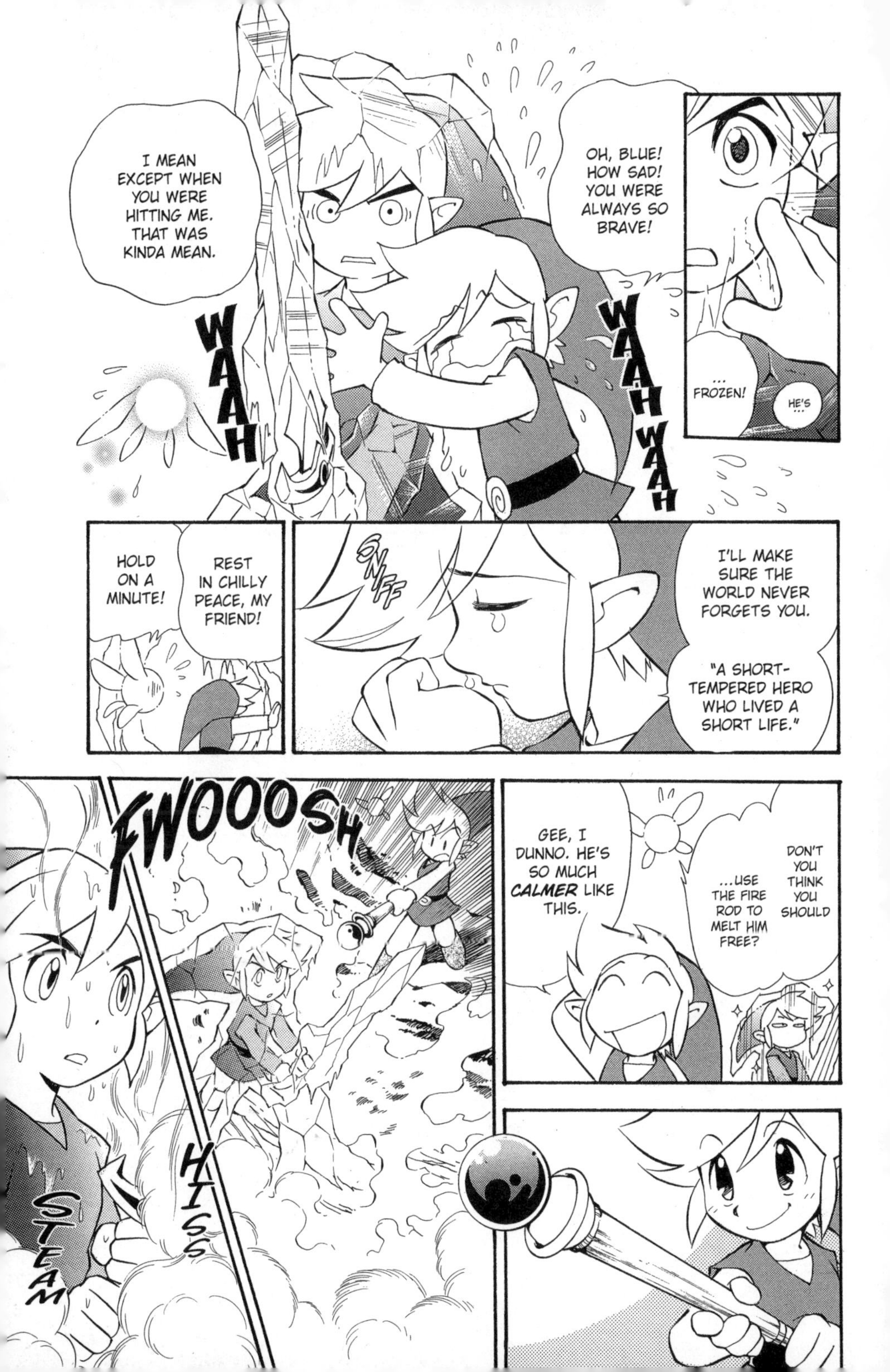
HE'S ...
... FROZEN!
OH, BLUE! HOW SAD! YOU WERE ALWAYS SO BRAVE!
WAAH WAAH
I MEAN EXCEPT WHEN YOU WERE HITTING ME. THAT WAS KINDA MEAN.
WAAH
SNIFF
I'LL MAKE SURE THE WORLD NEVER FORGETS YOU.
"A SHORT-TEMPERED HERO WHO LIVED A SHORT LIFE."
REST IN CHILLY PEACE, MY FRIEND!
HOLD ON A MINUTE!
DON'T YOU THINK YOU SHOULD
...USE THE FIRE ROD TO MELT HIM FREE?
GEE, I DUNNO. HE'S SO MUCH **CALMER** LIKE THIS.
FWOOOSH
HISS
STEAM

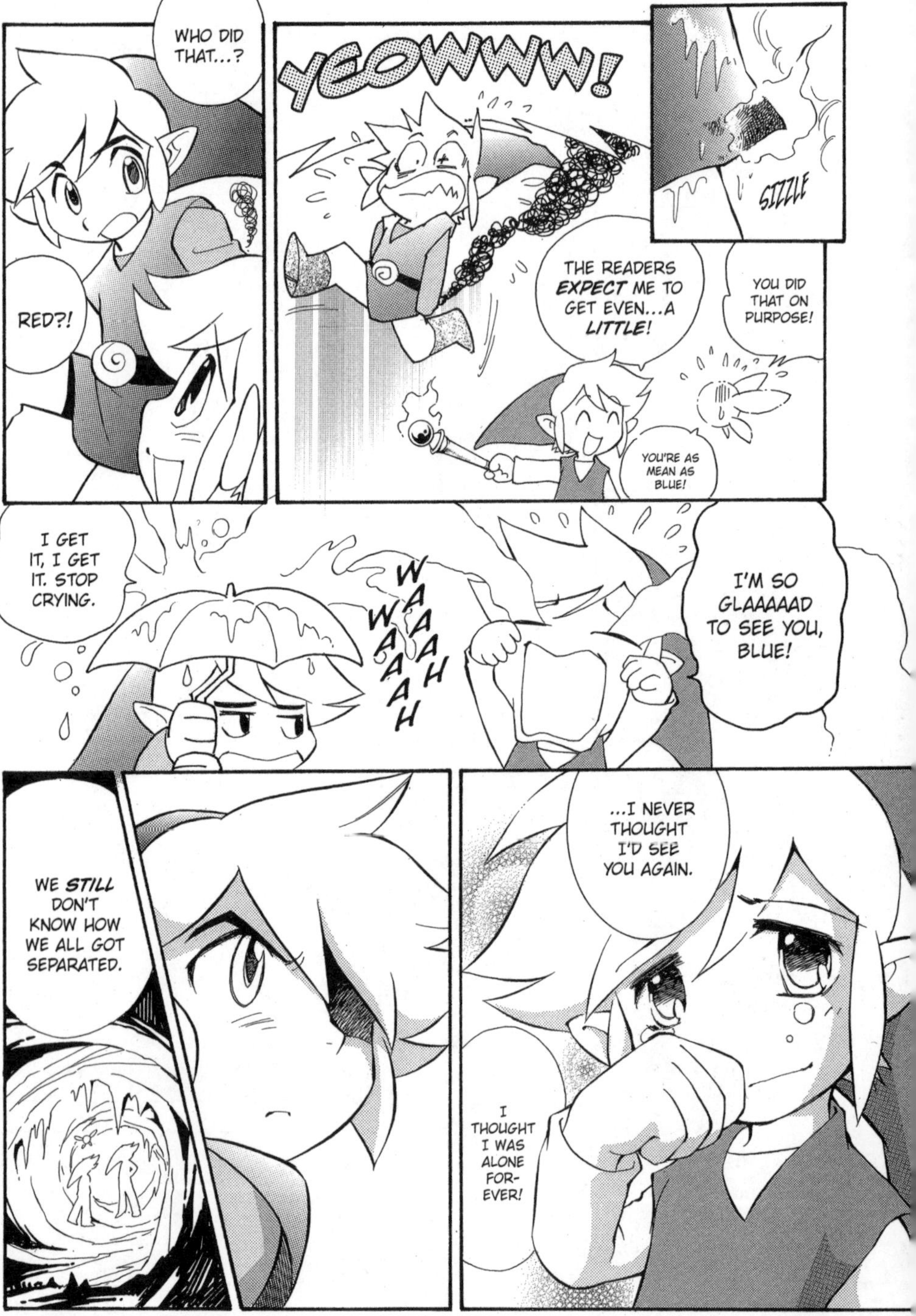
SIZZLE
YEOWWW!
YOU DID THAT ON PURPOSE!
THE READERS *EXPECT* ME TO GET EVEN...A *LITTLE*!
YOU'RE AS MEAN AS BLUE!
WHO DID THAT...?
RED?!
I'M SO GLAAAAAD TO SEE YOU, BLUE!
WAAAH
WAAAAH
I GET IT, I GET IT. STOP CRYING.
...I NEVER THOUGHT I'D SEE YOU AGAIN.
I THOUGHT I WAS ALONE FOR-EVER!
WE *STILL* DON'T KNOW HOW WE ALL GOT SEPARATED.

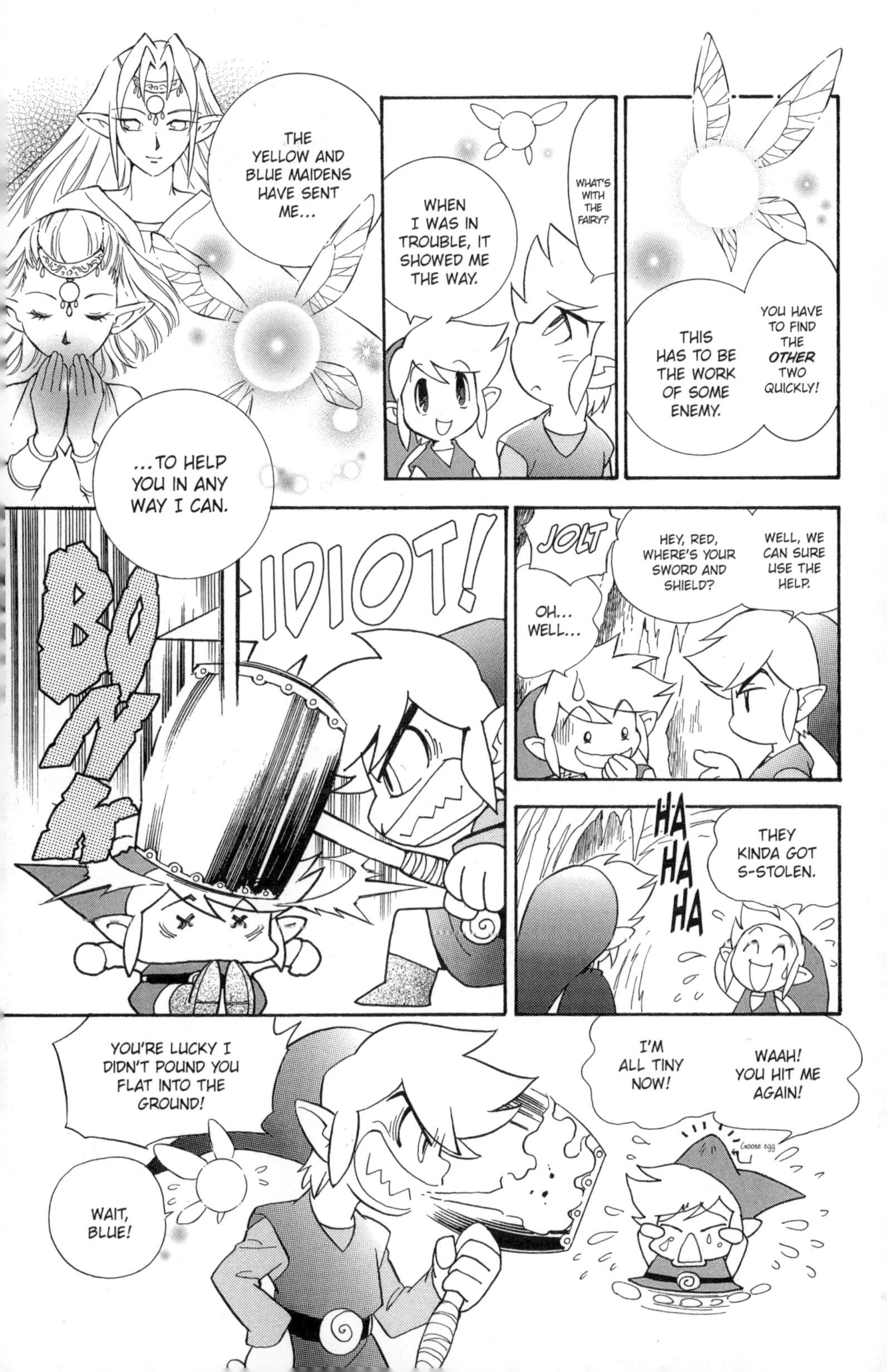
THIS HAS TO BE THE WORK OF SOME ENEMY.
YOU HAVE TO FIND THE *OTHER* TWO QUICKLY!
WHAT'S WITH THE FAIRY?
WHEN I WAS IN TROUBLE, IT SHOWED ME THE WAY.
THE YELLOW AND BLUE MAIDENS HAVE SENT ME...
...TO HELP YOU IN ANY WAY I CAN.
WELL, WE CAN SURE USE THE HELP.
HEY, RED, WHERE'S YOUR SWORD AND SHIELD?
JOLT
OH... WELL...
THEY KINDA GOT S-STOLEN.
HA HA HA HA
IDIOT!
BONK
WAAH! YOU HIT ME AGAIN!
I'M ALL TINY NOW!
Goose egg
YOU'RE LUCKY I DIDN'T POUND YOU FLAT INTO THE GROUND!
WAIT, BLUE!

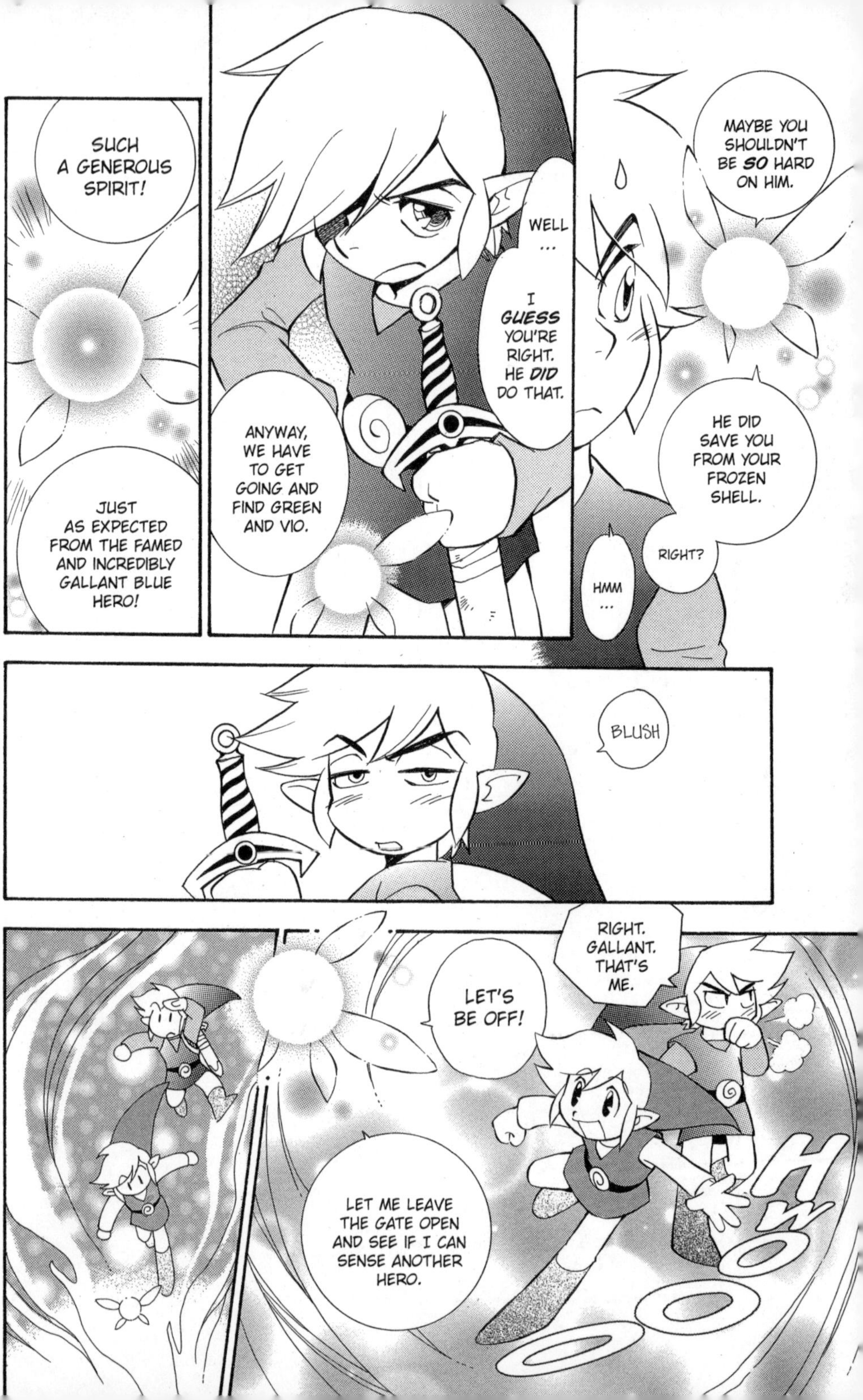
MAYBE YOU SHOULDN'T BE **SO** HARD ON HIM.
HE DID SAVE YOU FROM YOUR FROZEN SHELL.
RIGHT?
HMM ...
WELL ...
I ***GUESS*** YOU'RE RIGHT. HE ***DID*** DO THAT.
ANYWAY, WE HAVE TO GET GOING AND FIND GREEN AND VIO.
SUCH A GENEROUS SPIRIT!
JUST AS EXPECTED FROM THE FAMED AND INCREDIBLY GALLANT BLUE HERO!
BLUSH
RIGHT. GALLANT. THAT'S ME.
LET'S BE OFF!
LET ME LEAVE THE GATE OPEN AND SEE IF I CAN SENSE ANOTHER HERO.

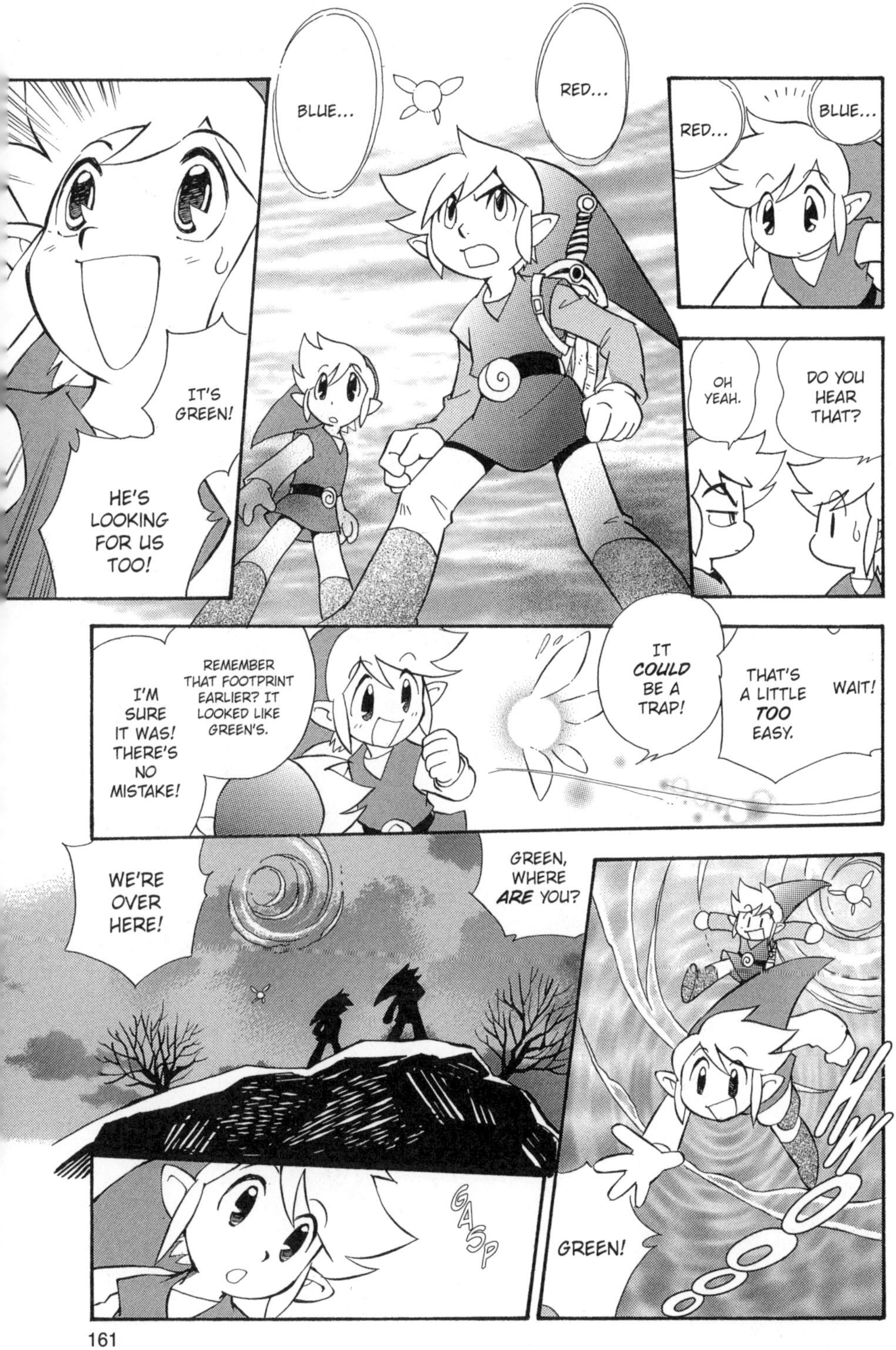
BLUE...
RED...
DO YOU HEAR THAT?
OH YEAH.
RED...
BLUE...
IT'S GREEN!
HE'S LOOKING FOR US TOO!
WAIT!
THAT'S A LITTLE TOO EASY.
IT COULD BE A TRAP!
REMEMBER THAT FOOTPRINT EARLIER? IT LOOKED LIKE GREEN'S.
I'M SURE IT WAS! THERE'S NO MISTAKE!
GREEN!
HWOOOOO
GREEN, WHERE ARE YOU?
WE'RE OVER HERE!
GASP

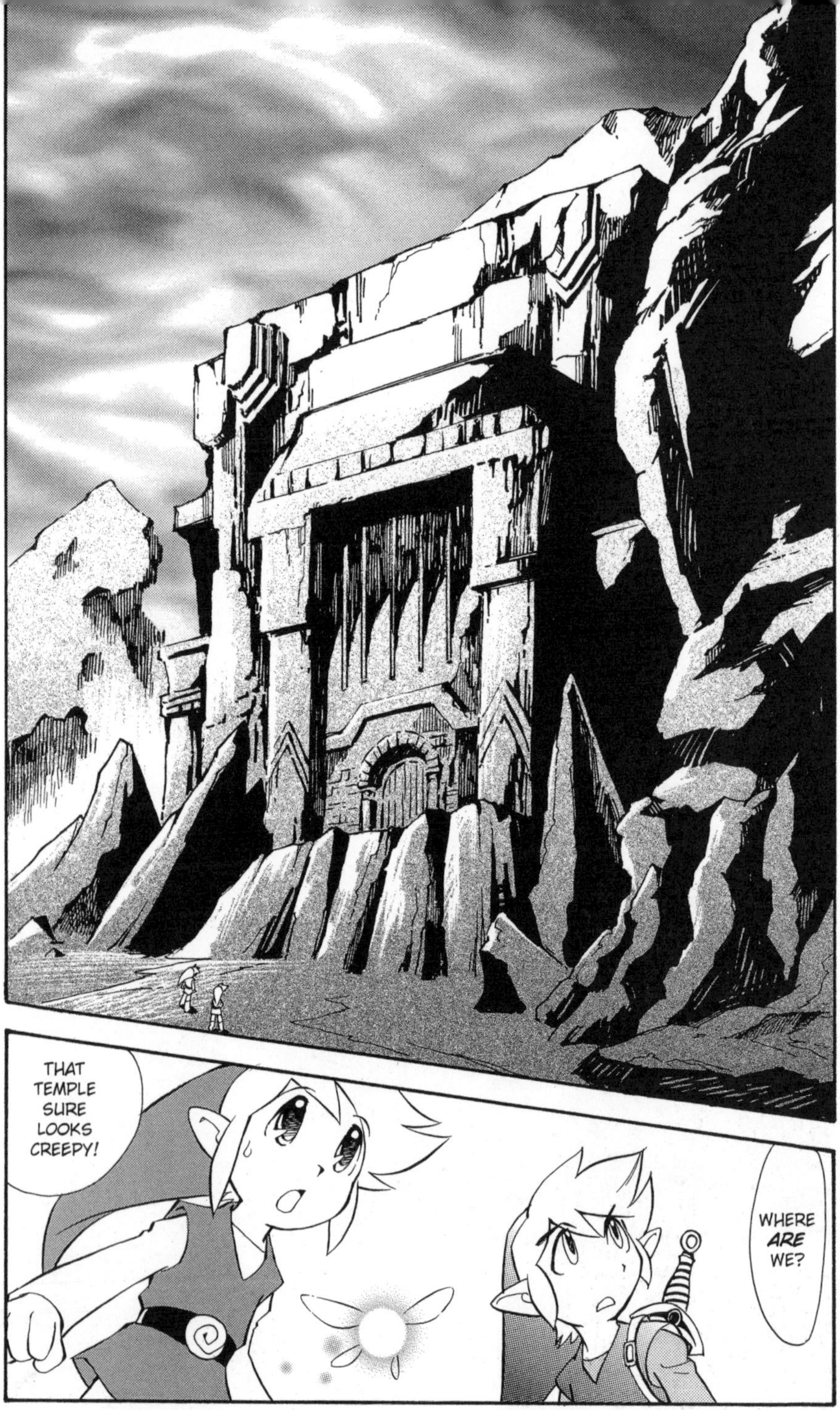
WHERE *ARE* WE?
THAT TEMPLE SURE LOOKS CREEPY!

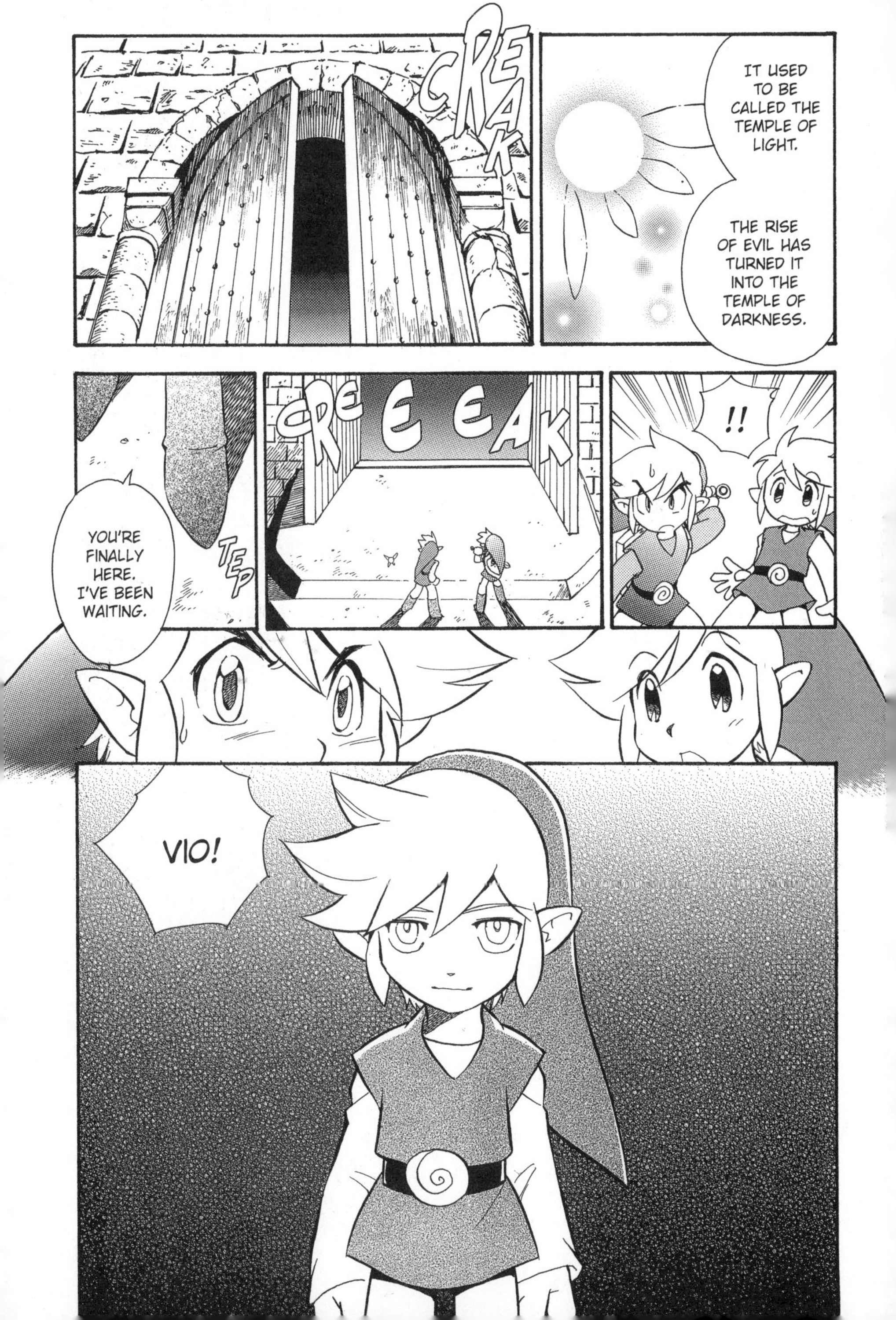

IT USED TO BE CALLED THE TEMPLE OF LIGHT.
THE RISE OF EVIL HAS TURNED IT INTO THE TEMPLE OF DARKNESS.
CREAK
!!
CREEEAK
YOU'RE FINALLY HERE. I'VE BEEN WAITING.
TEP
VIO!

FOUR SWORDS ROUGH CHARACTER ILLUSTRATION 5

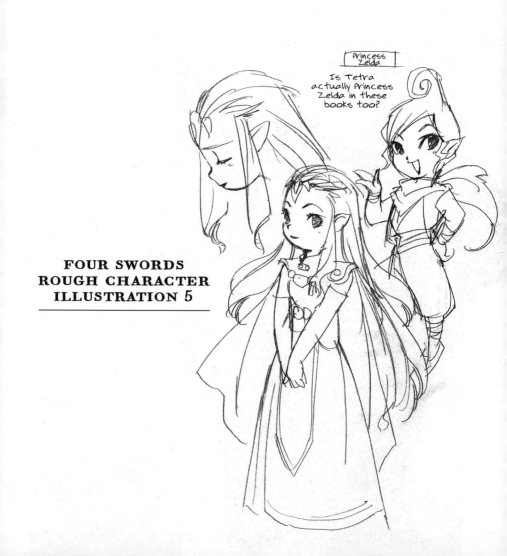

Princess Zelda
Is Tetra actually Princess Zelda in these books too?

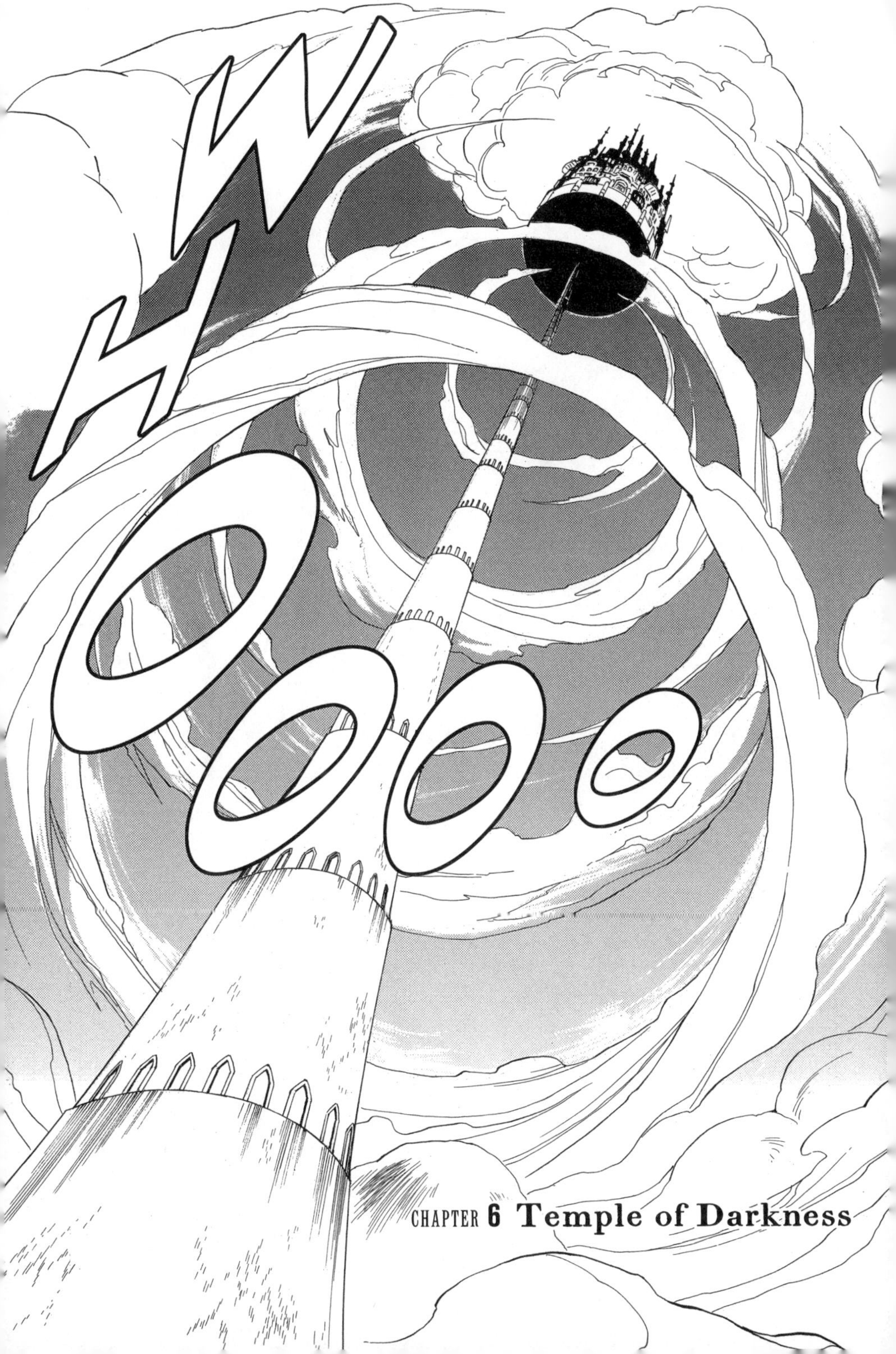
WHOOOO

CHAPTER 6 Temple of Darkness

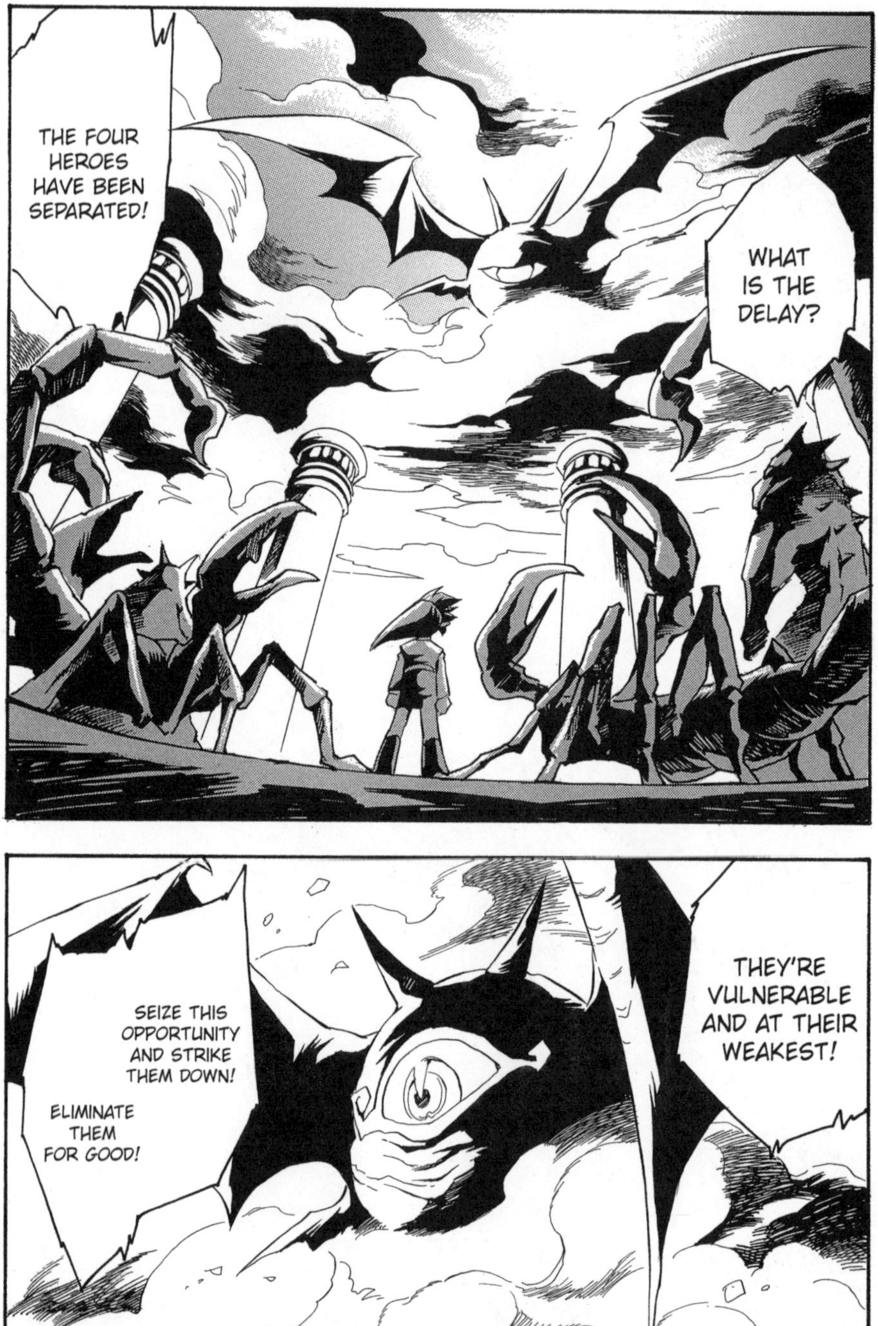
WHAT IS THE DELAY?
THE FOUR HEROES HAVE BEEN SEPARATED!
THEY'RE VULNERABLE AND AT THEIR WEAKEST!
SEIZE THIS OPPORTUNITY AND STRIKE THEM DOWN!
ELIMINATE THEM FOR GOOD!

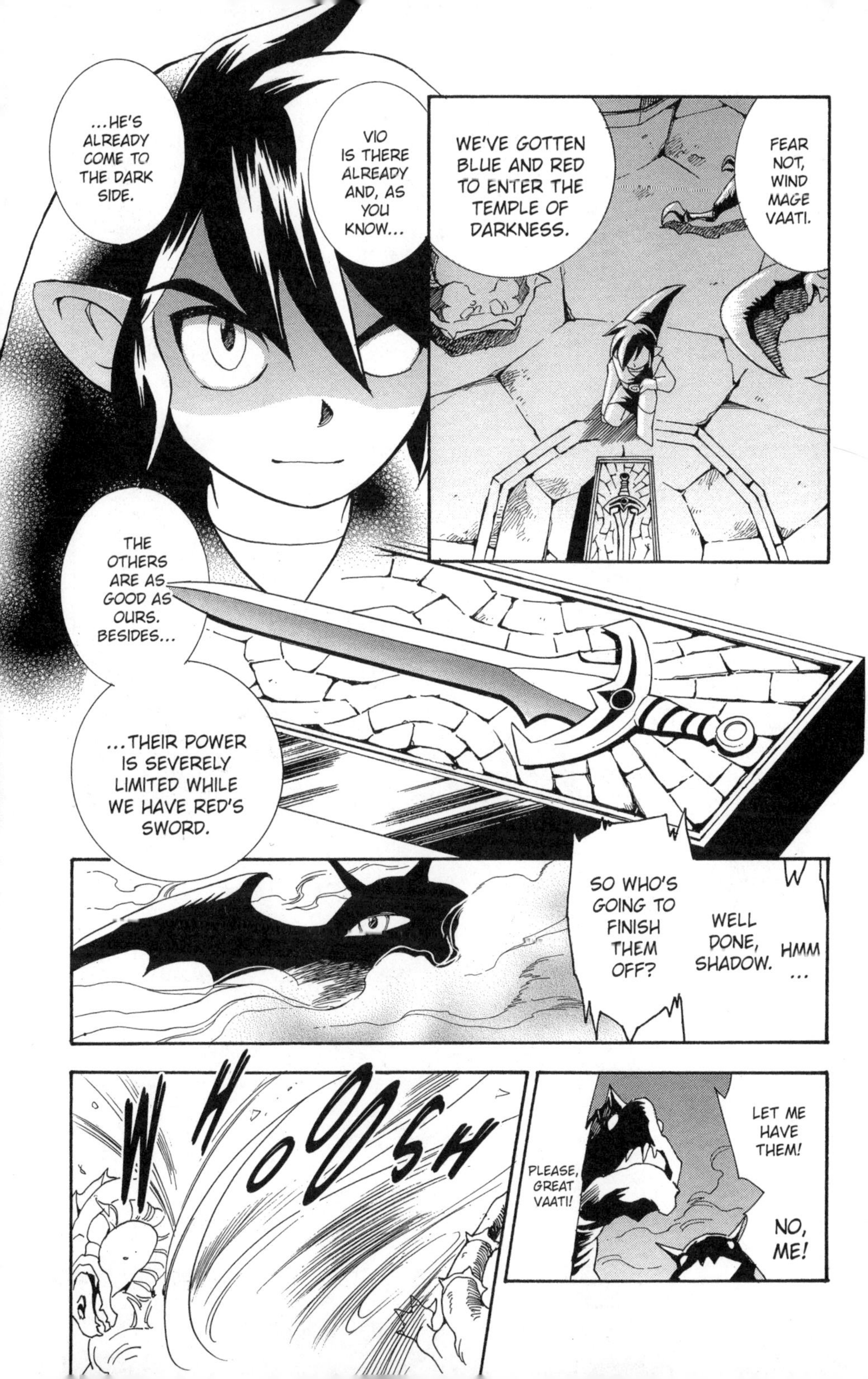
FEAR NOT, WIND MAGE VAATI.
WE'VE GOTTEN BLUE AND RED TO ENTER THE TEMPLE OF DARKNESS.
VIO IS THERE ALREADY AND, AS YOU KNOW...
...HE'S ALREADY COME TO THE DARK SIDE.
THE OTHERS ARE AS GOOD AS OURS. BESIDES...
...THEIR POWER IS SEVERELY LIMITED WHILE WE HAVE RED'S SWORD.
HMM...
WELL DONE, SHADOW.
SO WHO'S GOING TO FINISH THEM OFF?
LET ME HAVE THEM!
NO, ME!
PLEASE, GREAT VAATI!
WHOOSH

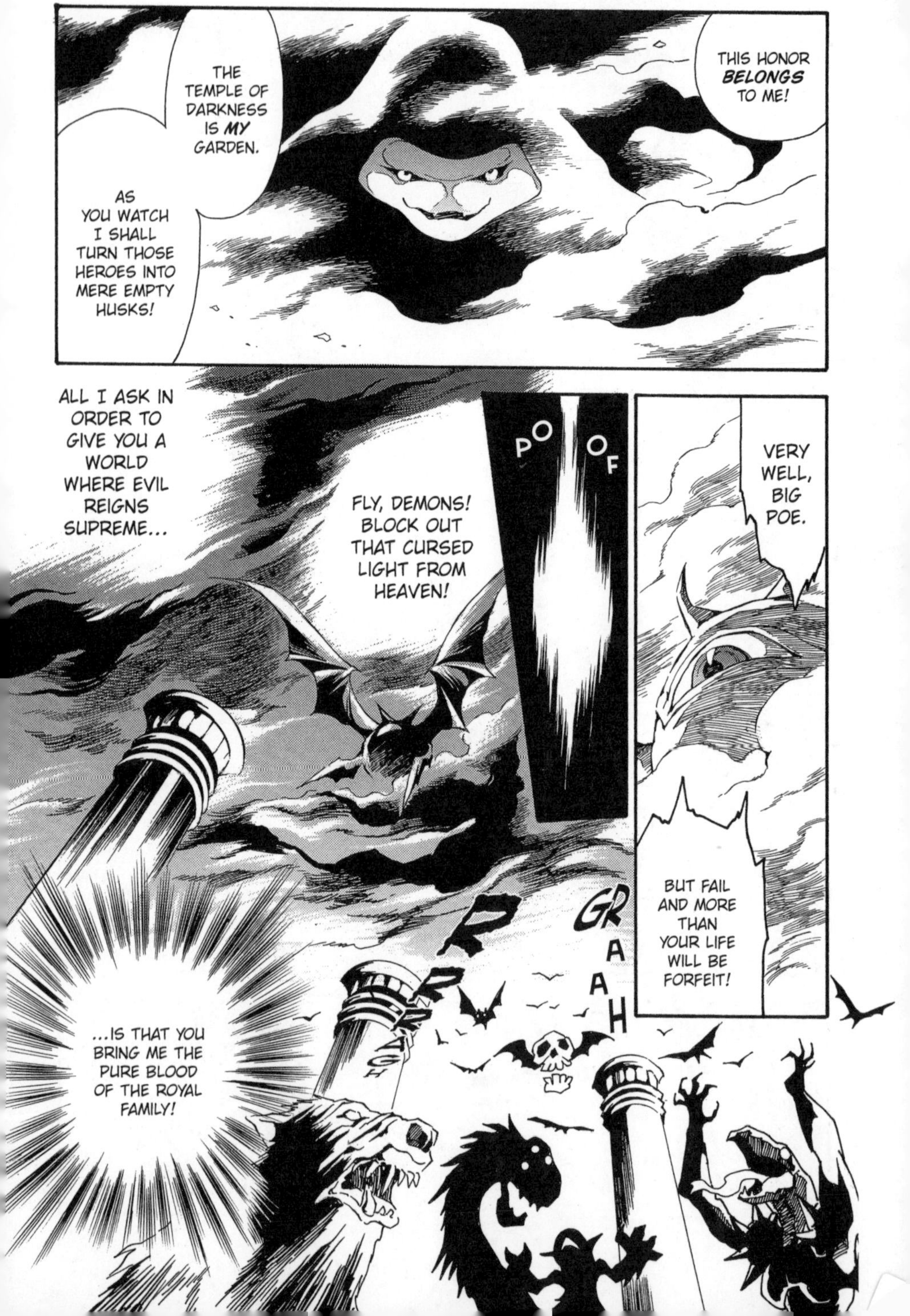
THIS HONOR *BELONGS* TO ME!
THE TEMPLE OF DARKNESS IS *MY* GARDEN.
AS YOU WATCH I SHALL TURN THOSE HEROES INTO MERE EMPTY HUSKS!
VERY WELL, BIG POE.
BUT FAIL AND MORE THAN YOUR LIFE WILL BE FORFEIT!
POOF
FLY, DEMONS! BLOCK OUT THAT CURSED LIGHT FROM HEAVEN!
ALL I ASK IN ORDER TO GIVE YOU A WORLD WHERE EVIL REIGNS SUPREME...
GRAAH
...IS THAT YOU BRING ME THE PURE BLOOD OF THE ROYAL FAMILY!

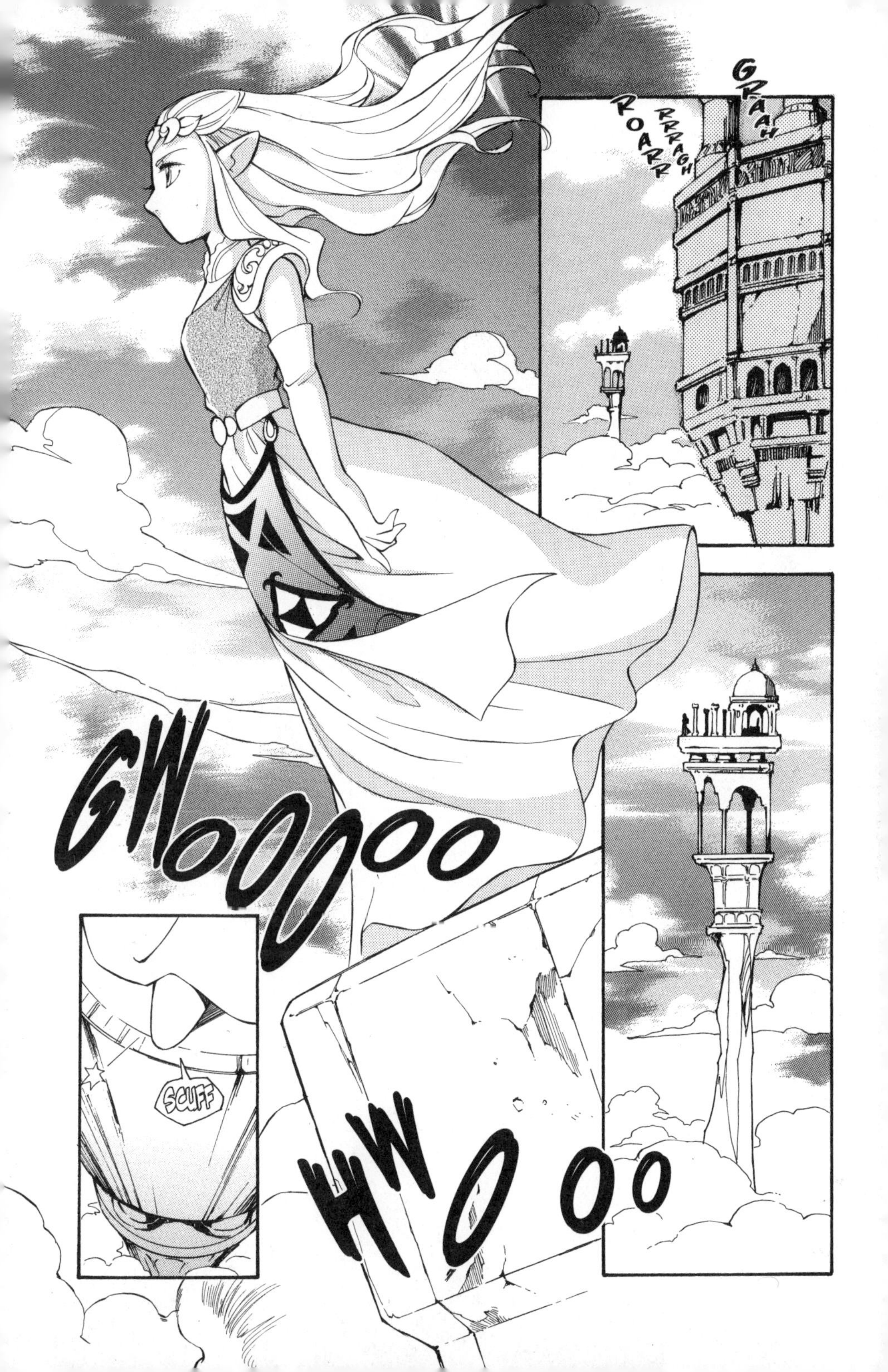
GRAAH
RRRAGH
ROARR
GWOOOOOO
HWOOO
SCUFF

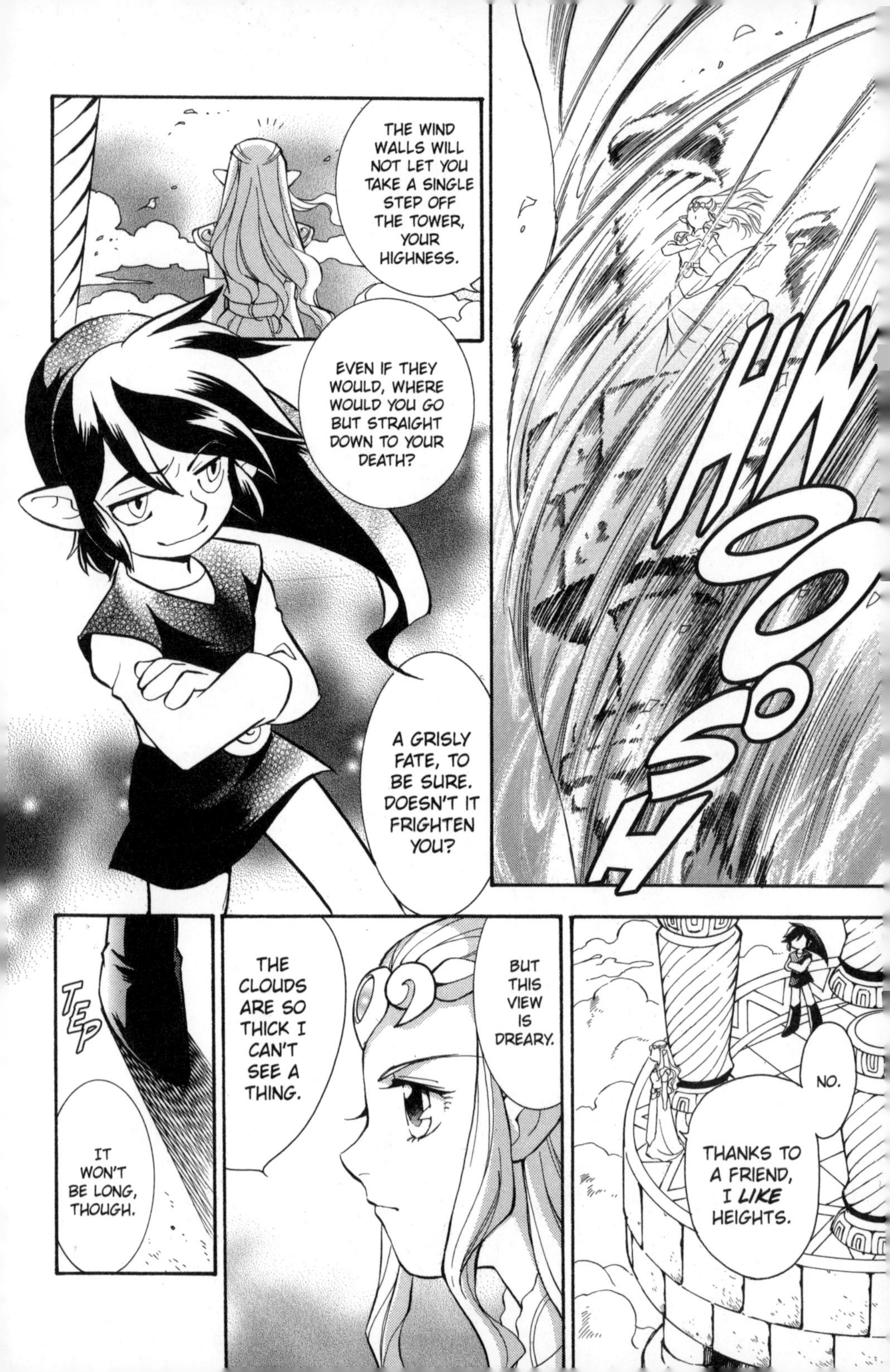
HWOOOSH
THE WIND WALLS WILL NOT LET YOU TAKE A SINGLE STEP OFF THE TOWER, YOUR HIGHNESS.
EVEN IF THEY WOULD, WHERE WOULD YOU GO BUT STRAIGHT DOWN TO YOUR DEATH?
A GRISLY FATE, TO BE SURE. DOESN'T IT FRIGHTEN YOU?
NO.
THANKS TO A FRIEND, I *LIKE* HEIGHTS.
BUT THIS VIEW IS DREARY.
THE CLOUDS ARE SO THICK I CAN'T SEE A THING.
TEP
IT WON'T BE LONG, THOUGH.

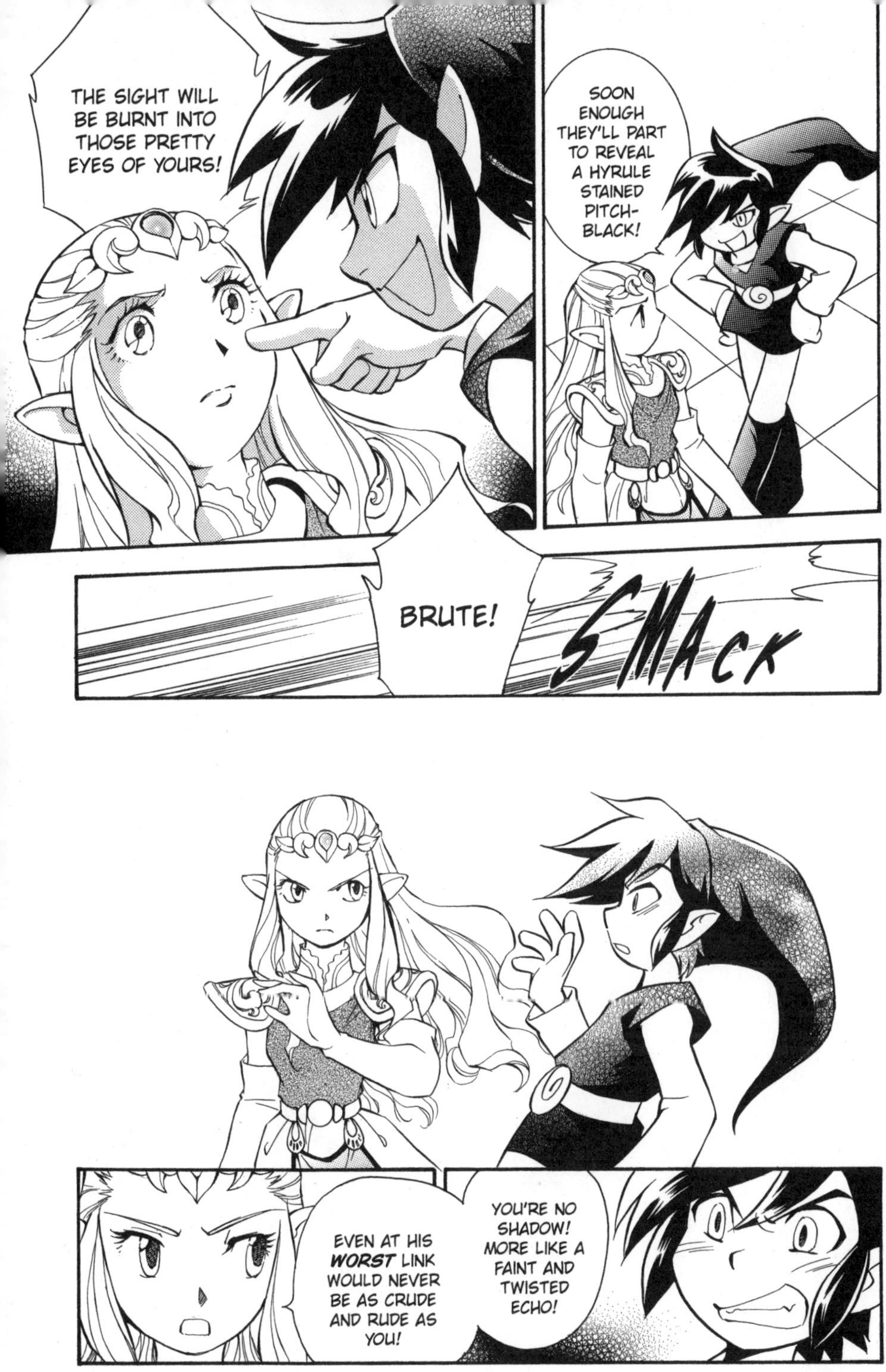
SOON ENOUGH THEY'LL PART TO REVEAL A HYRULE STAINED PITCH-BLACK!
THE SIGHT WILL BE BURNT INTO THOSE PRETTY EYES OF YOURS!
SMACK
BRUTE!
YOU'RE NO SHADOW! MORE LIKE A FAINT AND TWISTED ECHO!
EVEN AT HIS WORST LINK WOULD NEVER BE AS CRUDE AND RUDE AS YOU!

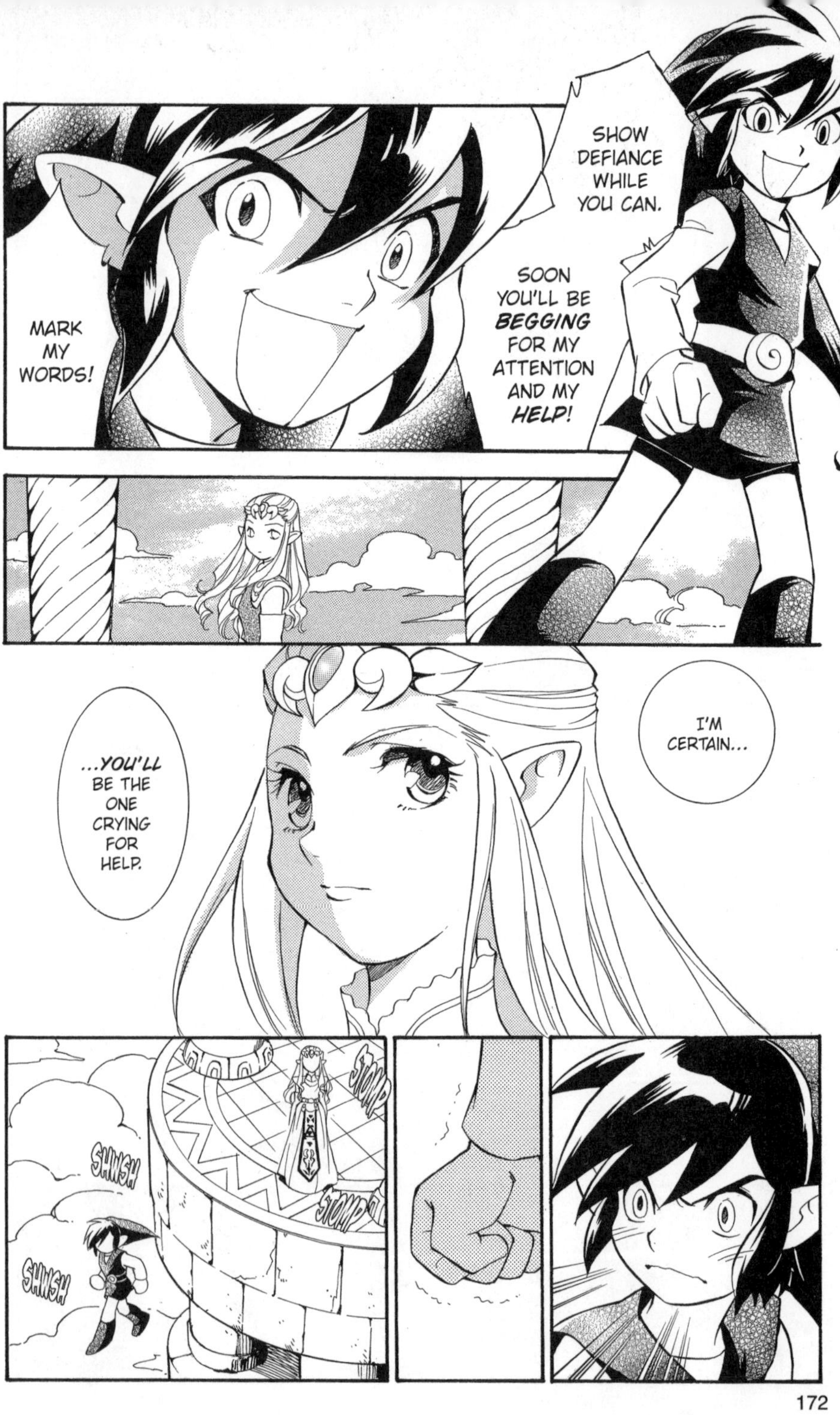
SHOW DEFIANCE WHILE YOU CAN.
SOON YOU'LL BE **BEGGING** FOR MY ATTENTION AND MY **HELP!**
MARK MY WORDS!
I'M CERTAIN...
...**YOU'LL** BE THE ONE CRYING FOR HELP.
STOMP
STOMP
SHWSH
SHWSH

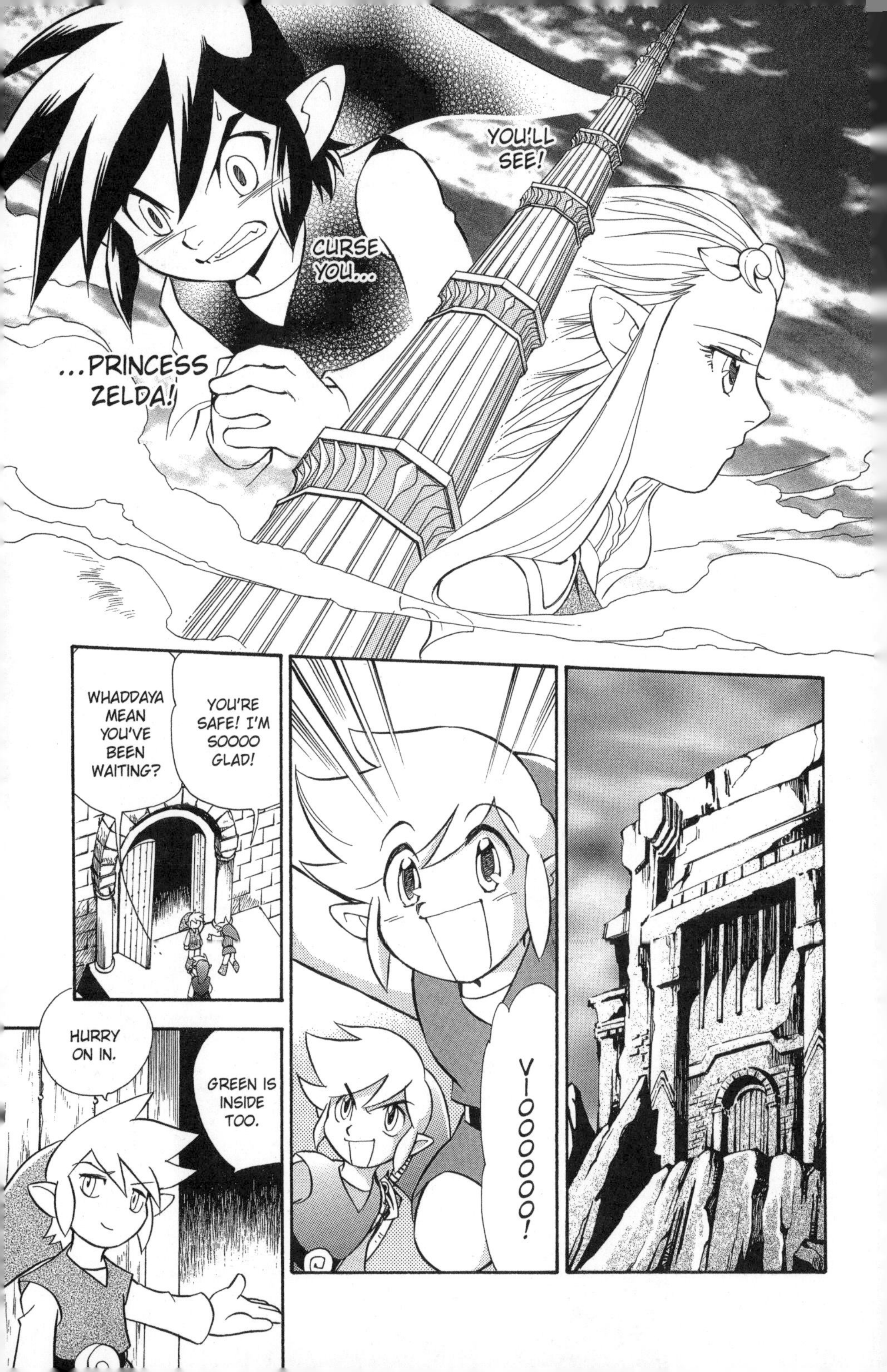
YOU'LL SEE!
CURSE YOU...
...PRINCESS ZELDA!
VIOOOOOOO!
YOU'RE SAFE! I'M SOOOO GLAD!
WHADDAYA MEAN YOU'VE BEEN WAITING?
HURRY ON IN.
GREEN IS INSIDE TOO.

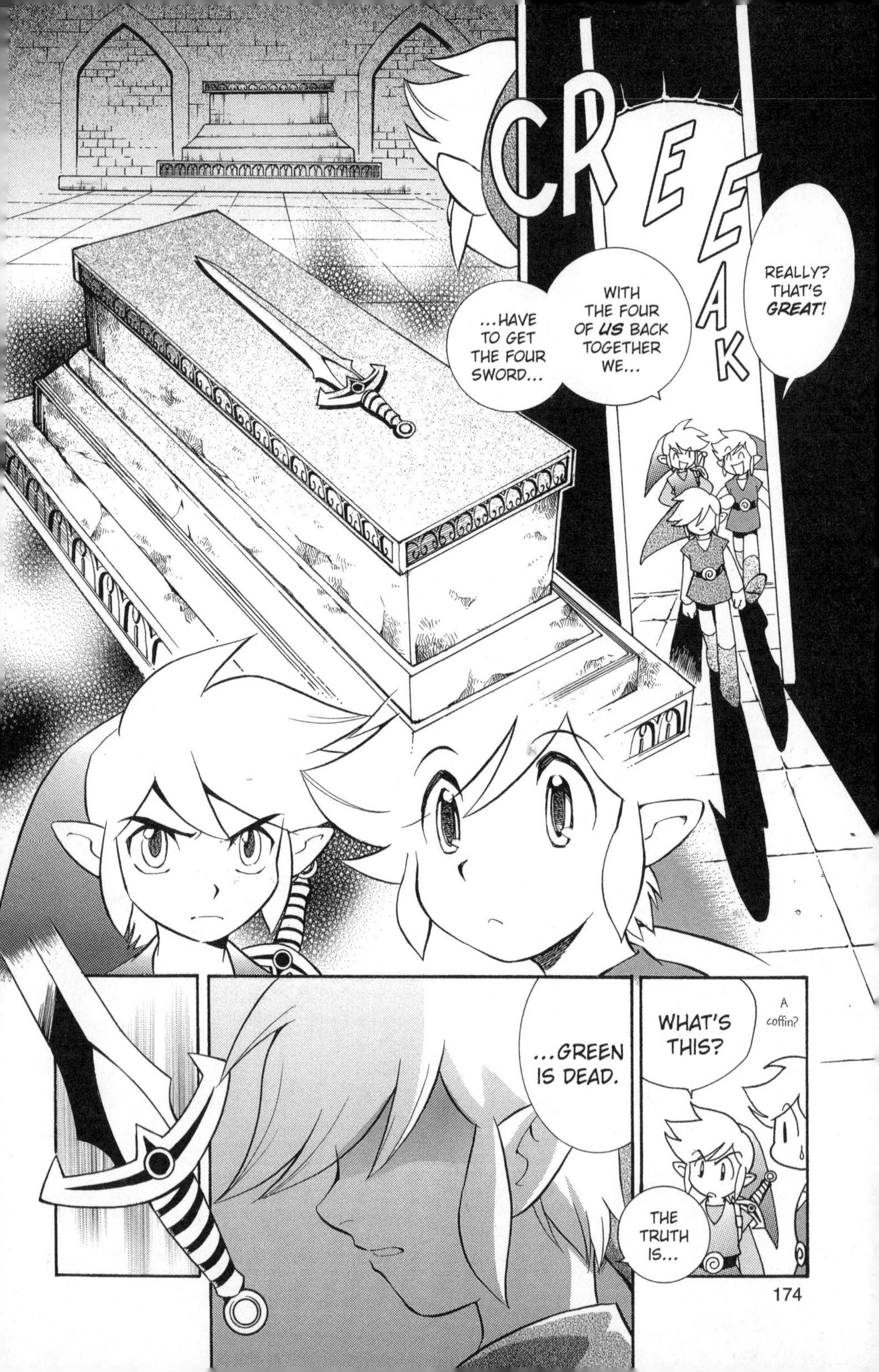
CREEAK
REALLY? THAT'S *GREAT*!
WITH THE FOUR OF *US* BACK TOGETHER WE...
...HAVE TO GET THE FOUR SWORD...
A coffin?
WHAT'S THIS?
THE TRUTH IS...
...GREEN IS DEAD.

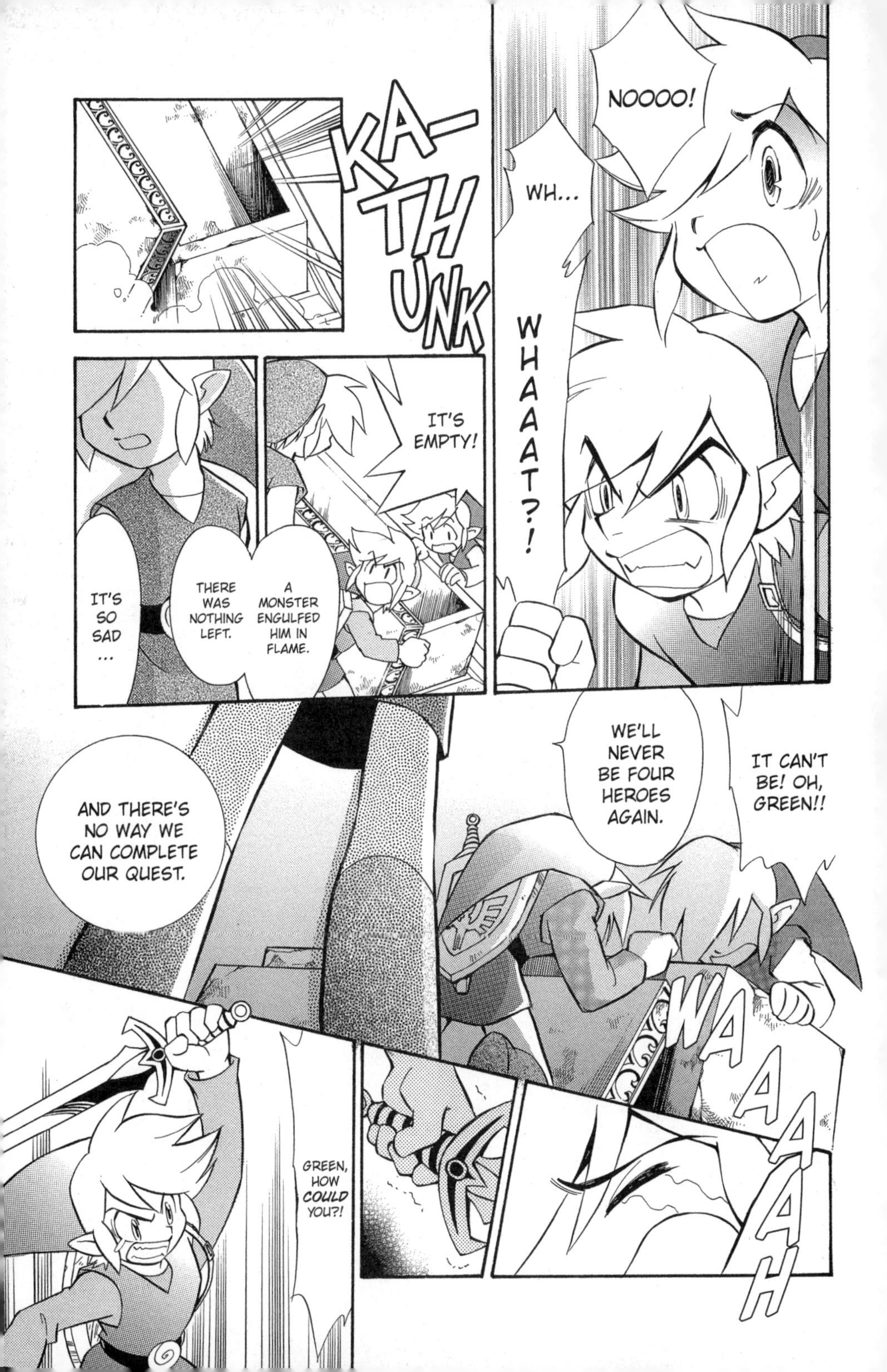
NOOOO!
WH...
WHAAAAT?!
KA-THUNK
IT'S EMPTY!
A MONSTER ENGULFED HIM IN FLAME.
THERE WAS NOTHING LEFT.
IT'S SO SAD...
IT CAN'T BE! OH, GREEN!!
WE'LL NEVER BE FOUR HEROES AGAIN.
AND THERE'S NO WAY WE CAN COMPLETE OUR QUEST.
WAAAAAH
GREEN, HOW *COULD* YOU?!

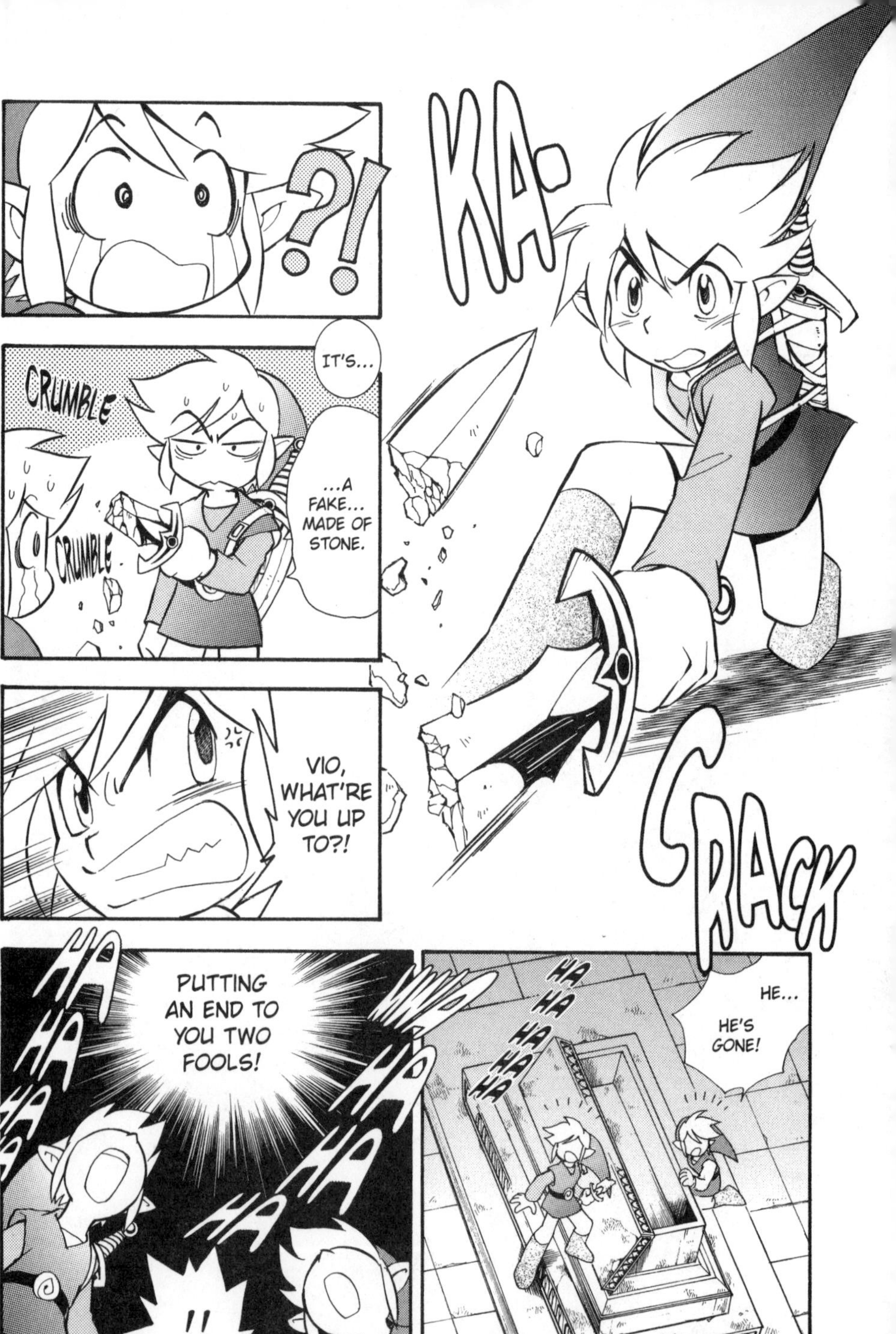
KA-
CRACK
?!
IT'S...
...A FAKE... MADE OF STONE.
CRUMBLE
CRUMBLE
VIO, WHAT'RE YOU UP TO?!
HA HA HA HA HA HA
HE...
HE'S GONE!
PUTTING AN END TO YOU TWO FOOLS!
HA HA HA HA HA
!!

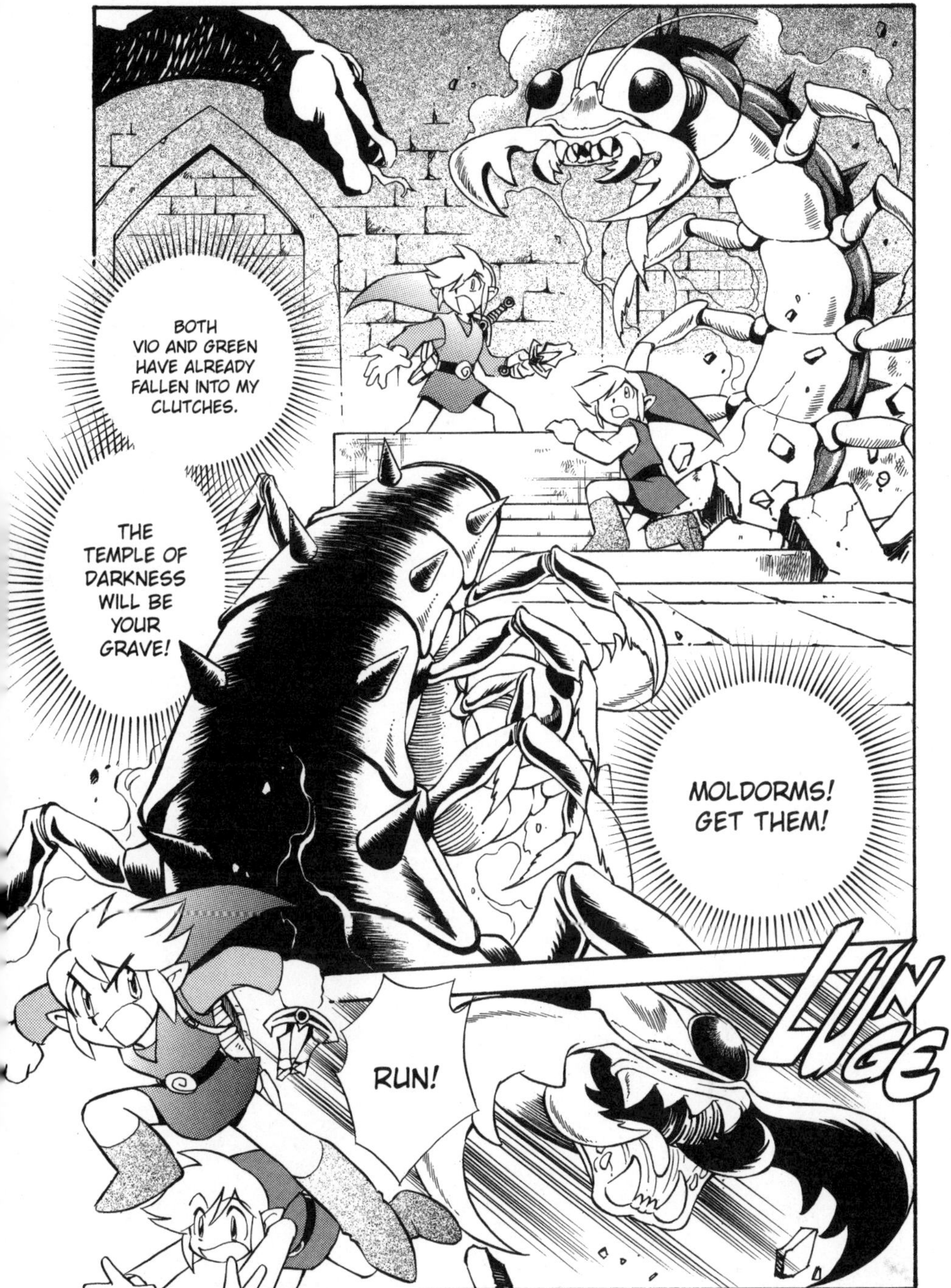
BOTH VIO AND GREEN HAVE ALREADY FALLEN INTO MY CLUTCHES.
THE TEMPLE OF DARKNESS WILL BE YOUR GRAVE!
MOLDORMS! GET THEM!
LUNGE
RUN!

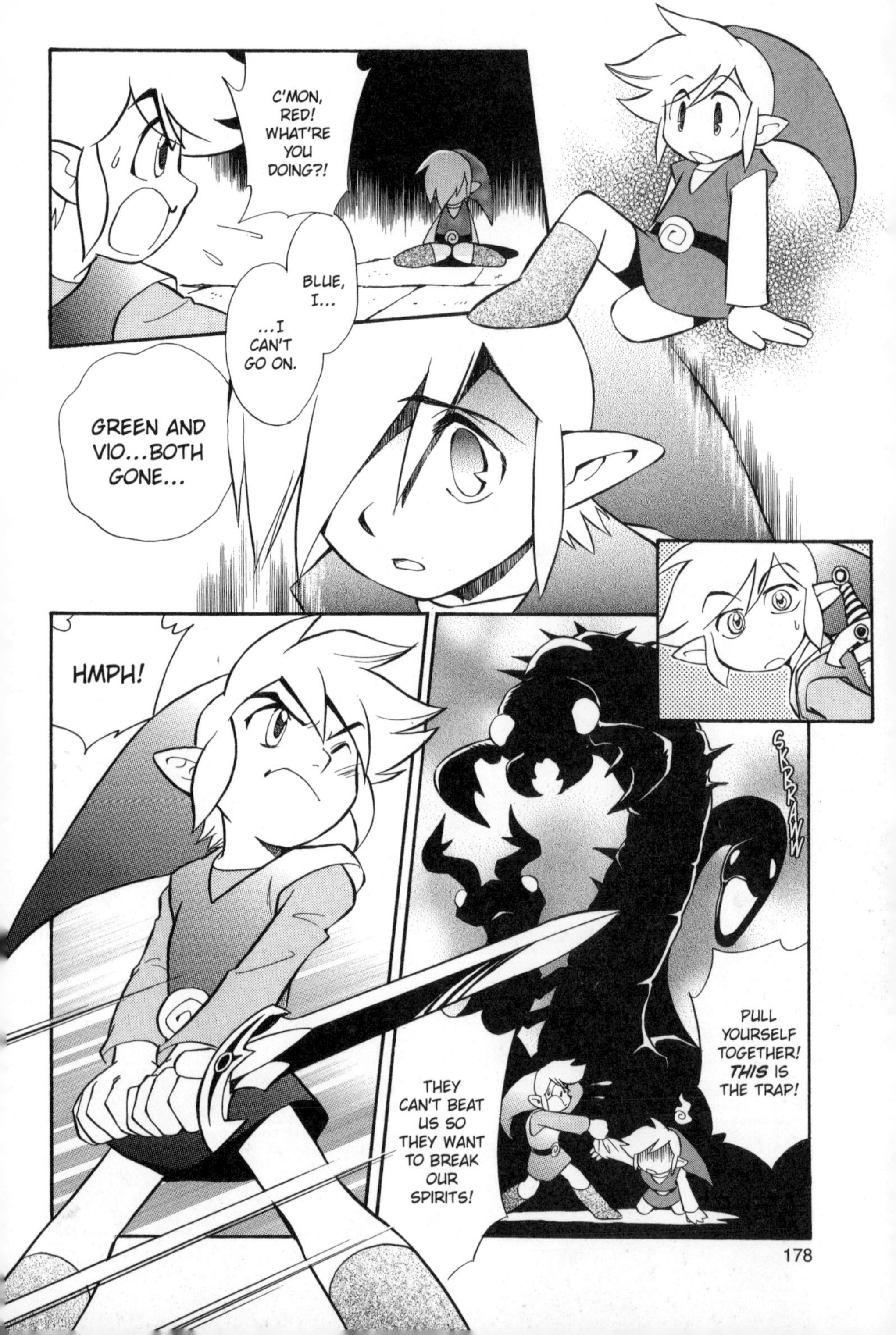
C'MON, RED! WHAT'RE YOU DOING?!
BLUE, I...
...I CAN'T GO ON.
GREEN AND VIO...BOTH GONE...
SKRAW
PULL YOURSELF TOGETHER! *THIS* IS THE TRAP!
THEY CAN'T BEAT US SO THEY WANT TO BREAK OUR SPIRITS!
HMPH!

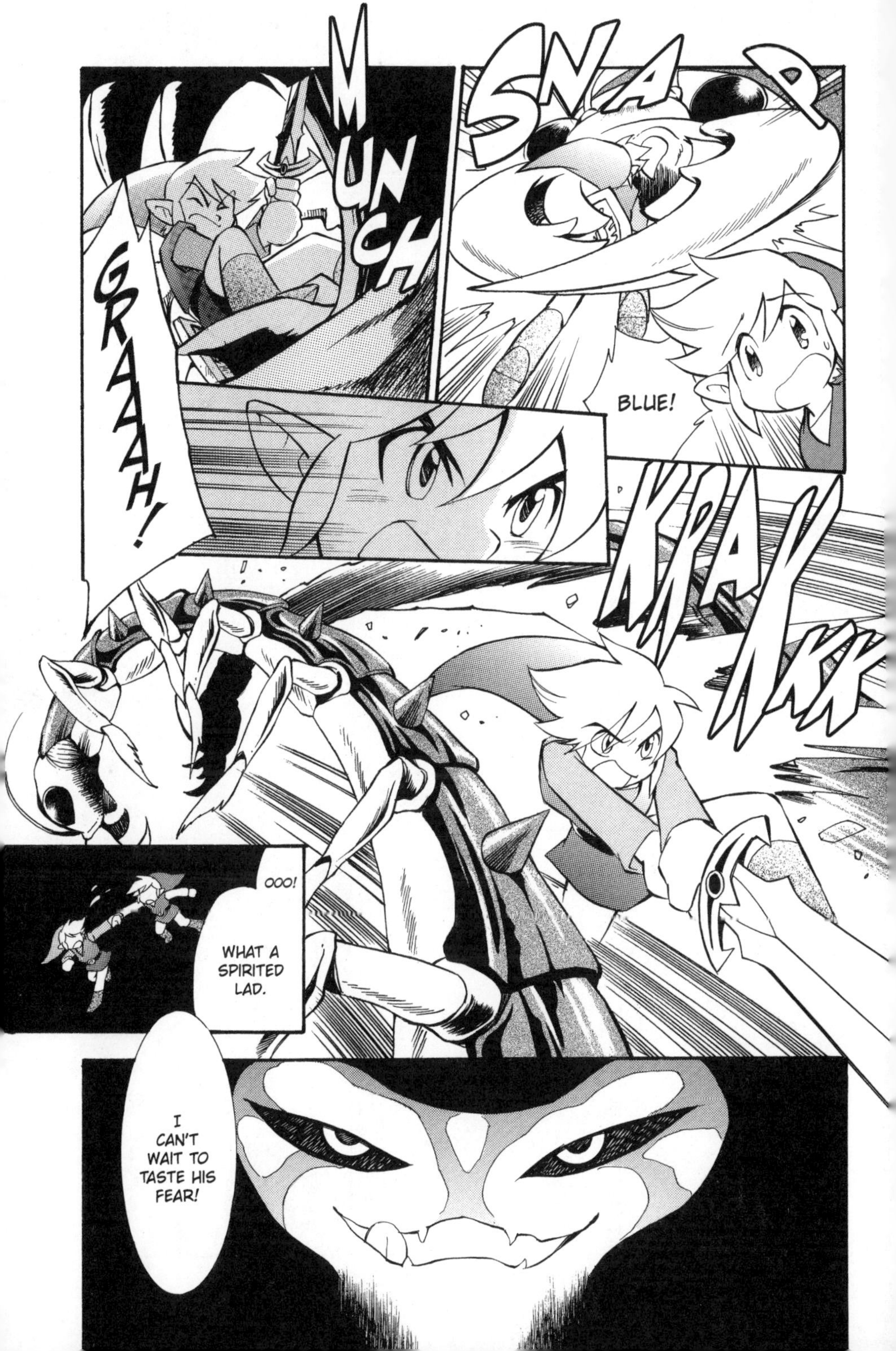
SNAP
BLUE!
MUNCH
GRAAAAH!
KRAKKK
OOO!
WHAT A SPIRITED LAD.
I CAN'T WAIT TO TASTE HIS FEAR!

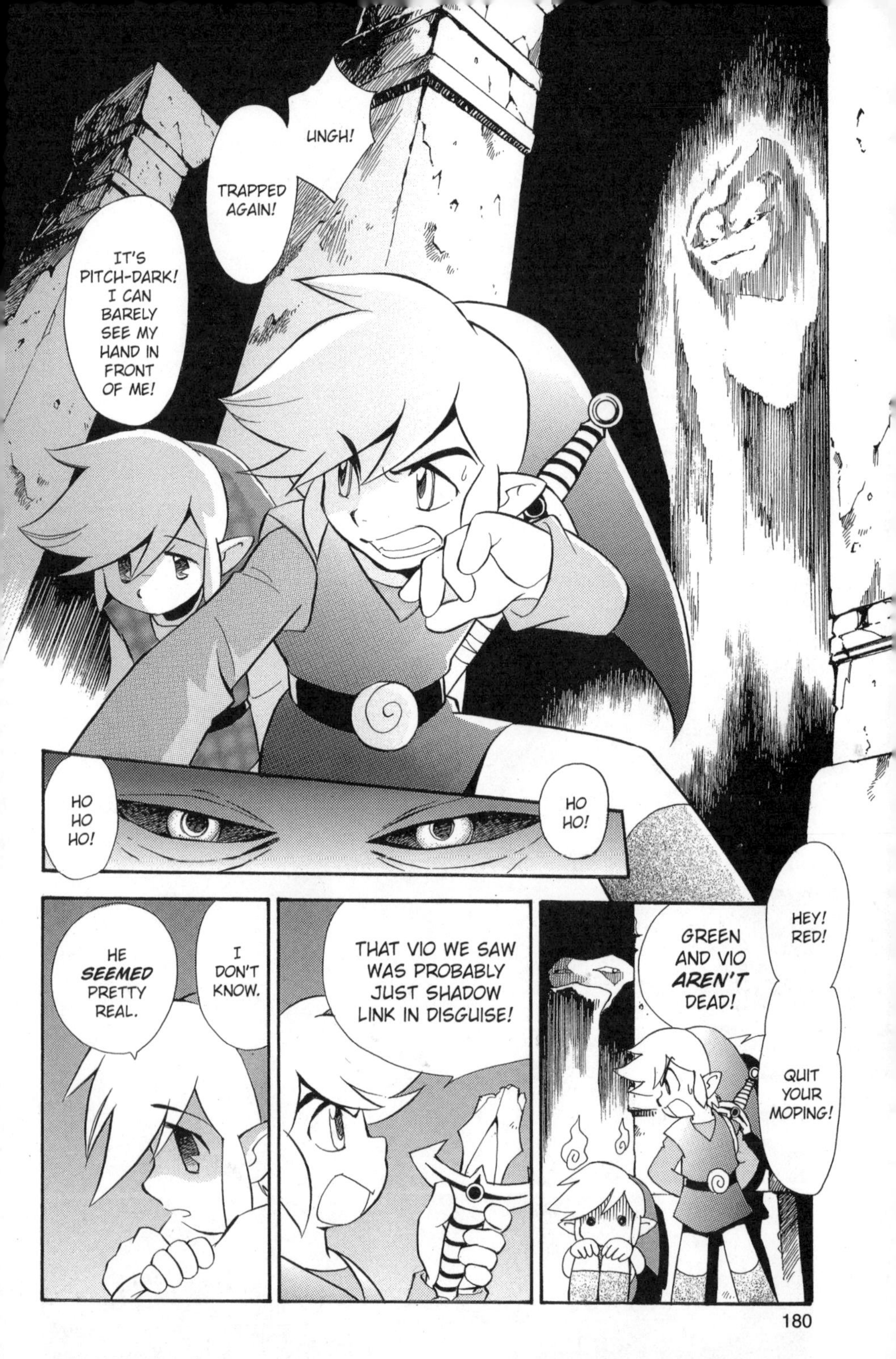
UNGH!
TRAPPED AGAIN!
IT'S PITCH-DARK! I CAN BARELY SEE MY HAND IN FRONT OF ME!
HO HO!
HO HO HO!
HEY! RED!
GREEN AND VIO ***AREN'T*** DEAD!
QUIT YOUR MOPING!
THAT VIO WE SAW WAS PROBABLY JUST SHADOW LINK IN DISGUISE!
I DON'T KNOW.
HE ***SEEMED*** PRETTY REAL.

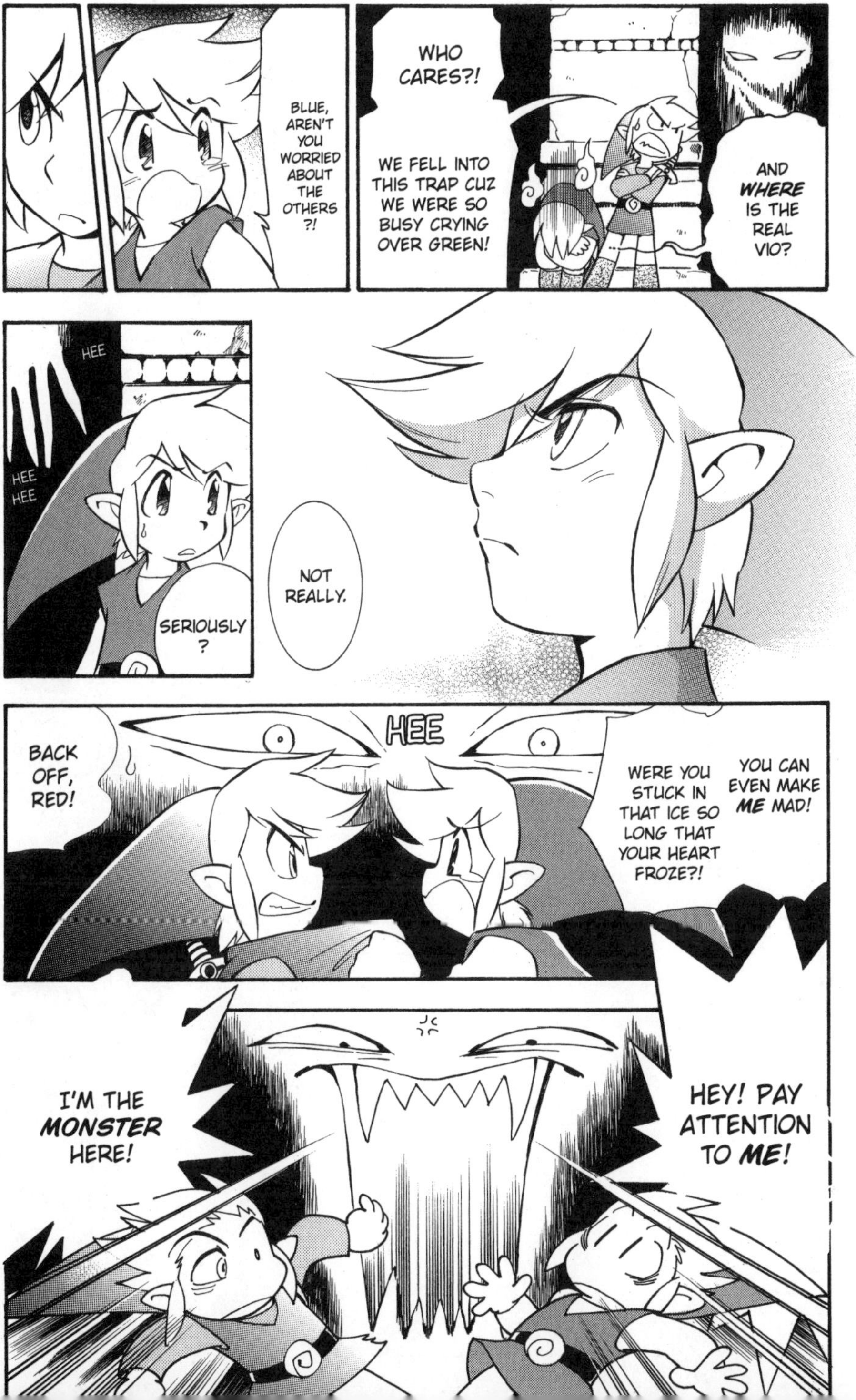
BLUE, AREN'T YOU WORRIED ABOUT THE OTHERS ?!
WHO CARES?!
WE FELL INTO THIS TRAP CUZ WE WERE SO BUSY CRYING OVER GREEN!
AND *WHERE* IS THE REAL VIO?
HEE
HEE HEE
SERIOUSLY ?
NOT REALLY.
BACK OFF, RED!
HEE
WERE YOU STUCK IN THAT ICE SO LONG THAT YOUR HEART FROZE?!
YOU CAN EVEN MAKE *ME* MAD!
I'M THE *MONSTER* HERE!
HEY! PAY ATTENTION TO *ME*!

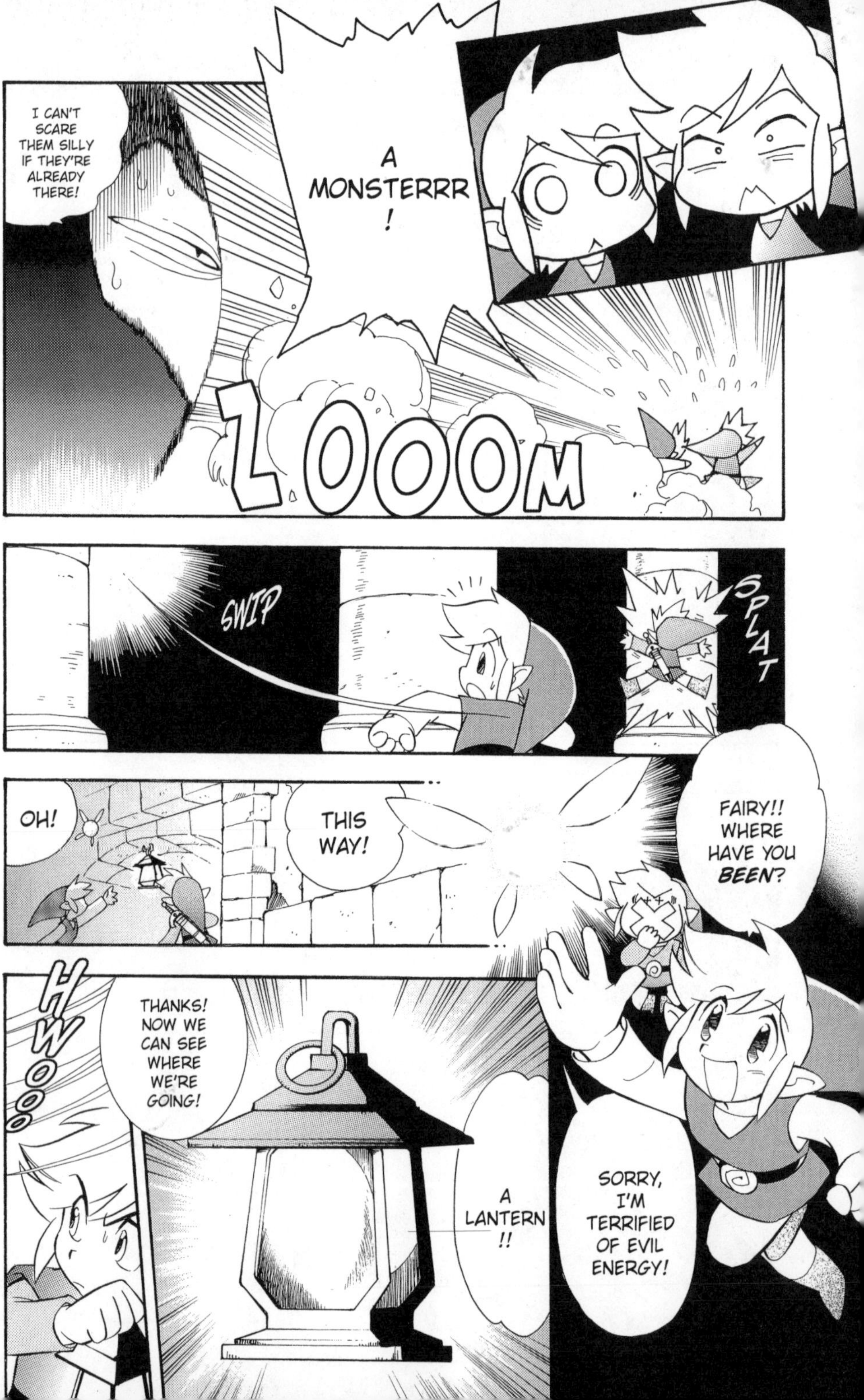
A MONSTERRR!
I CAN'T SCARE THEM SILLY IF THEY'RE ALREADY THERE!
ZOOOM
SPLAT
SWIP
FAIRY!! WHERE HAVE YOU *BEEN*?
THIS WAY!
OH!
SORRY, I'M TERRIFIED OF EVIL ENERGY!
A LANTERN!!
THANKS! NOW WE CAN SEE WHERE WE'RE GOING!
HWOOOO

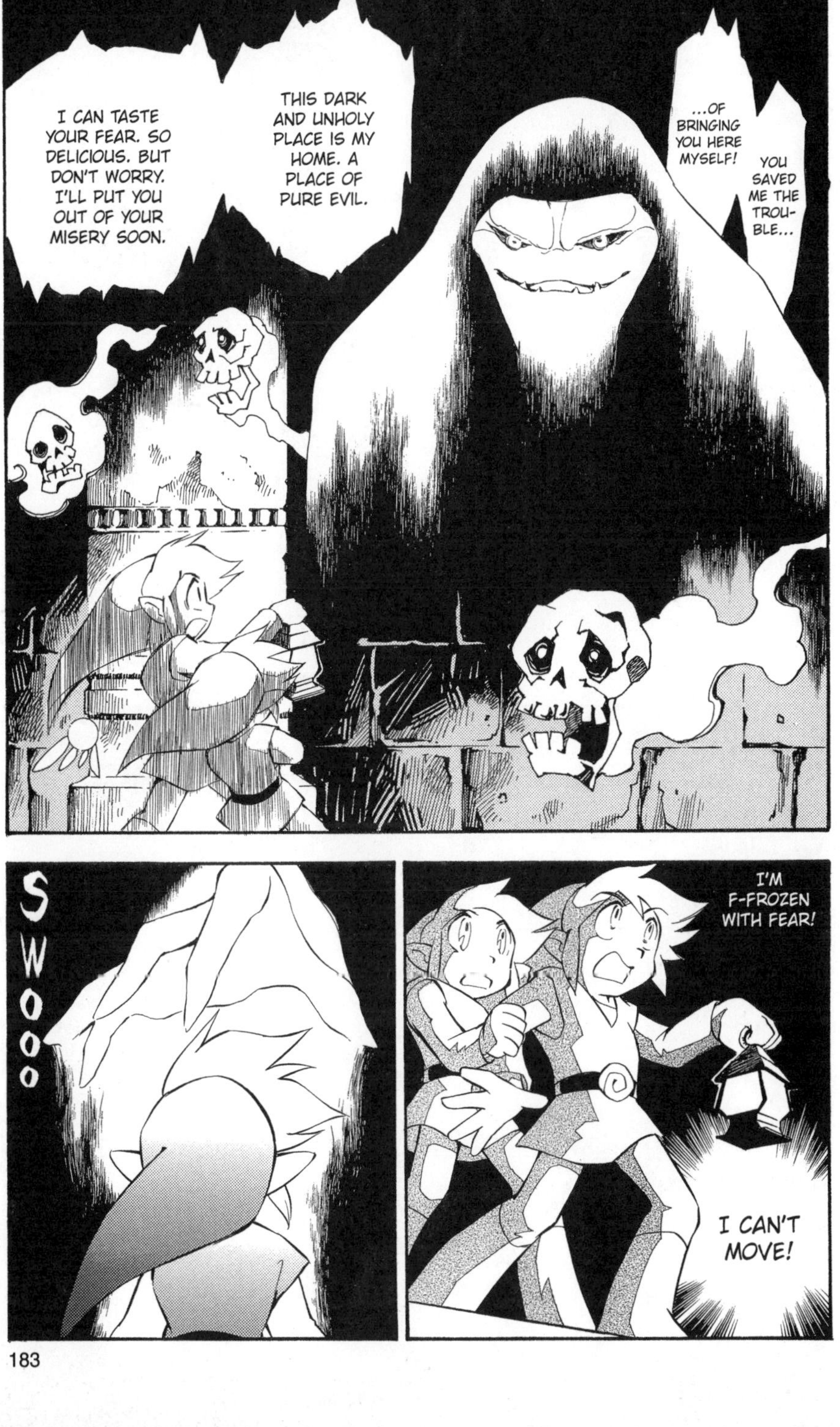
YOU SAVED ME THE TROUBLE...
...OF BRINGING YOU HERE MYSELF!
THIS DARK AND UNHOLY PLACE IS MY HOME. A PLACE OF PURE EVIL.
I CAN TASTE YOUR FEAR. SO DELICIOUS. BUT DON'T WORRY. I'LL PUT YOU OUT OF YOUR MISERY SOON.
I'M F-FROZEN WITH FEAR!
I CAN'T MOVE!
SWOOO

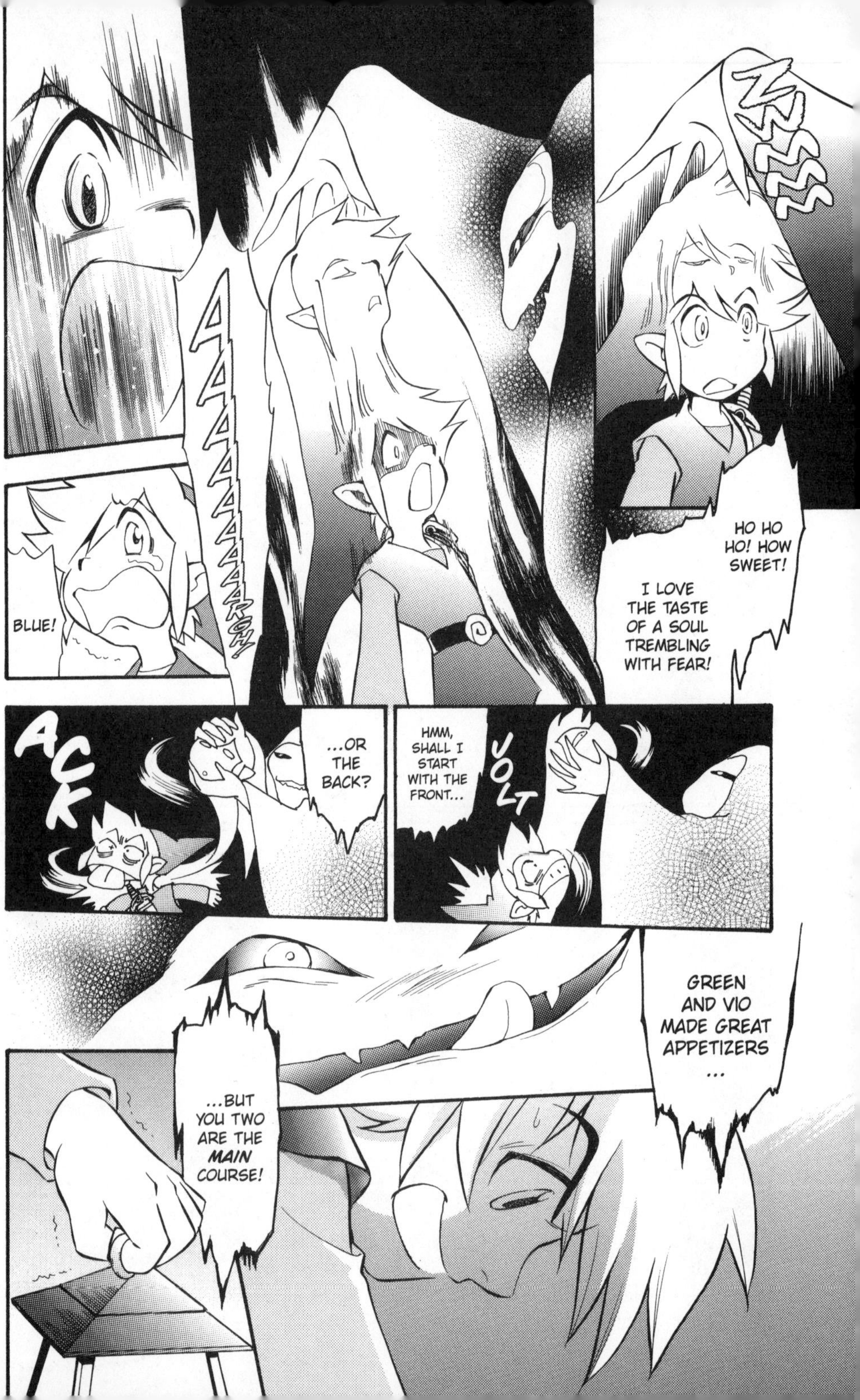
HO HO HO! HOW SWEET!
I LOVE THE TASTE OF A SOUL TREMBLING WITH FEAR!
AAAAAAAAAARGH!
BLUE!
HMM, SHALL I START WITH THE FRONT...
JOLT
...OR THE BACK?
ACK
GREEN AND VIO MADE GREAT APPETIZERS...
...BUT YOU TWO ARE THE MAIN COURSE!

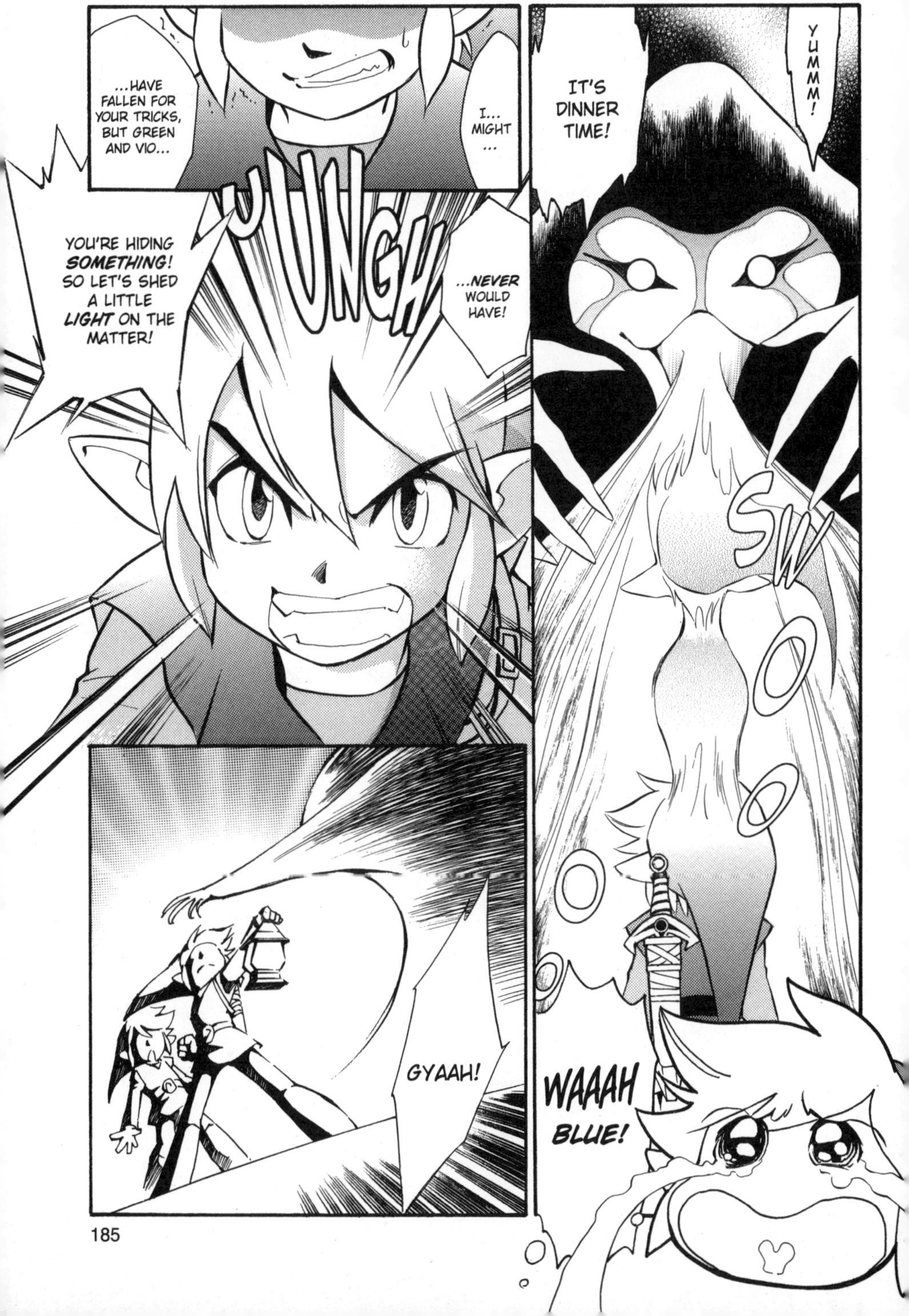
YUMMM!
IT'S DINNER TIME!
SWOOOO
WAAAH
BLUE!
I... MIGHT ...
...HAVE FALLEN FOR YOUR TRICKS, BUT GREEN AND VIO...
UUNGH
...**NEVER** WOULD HAVE!
YOU'RE HIDING **SOMETHING**! SO LET'S SHED A LITTLE **LIGHT** ON THE MATTER!
GYAAH!

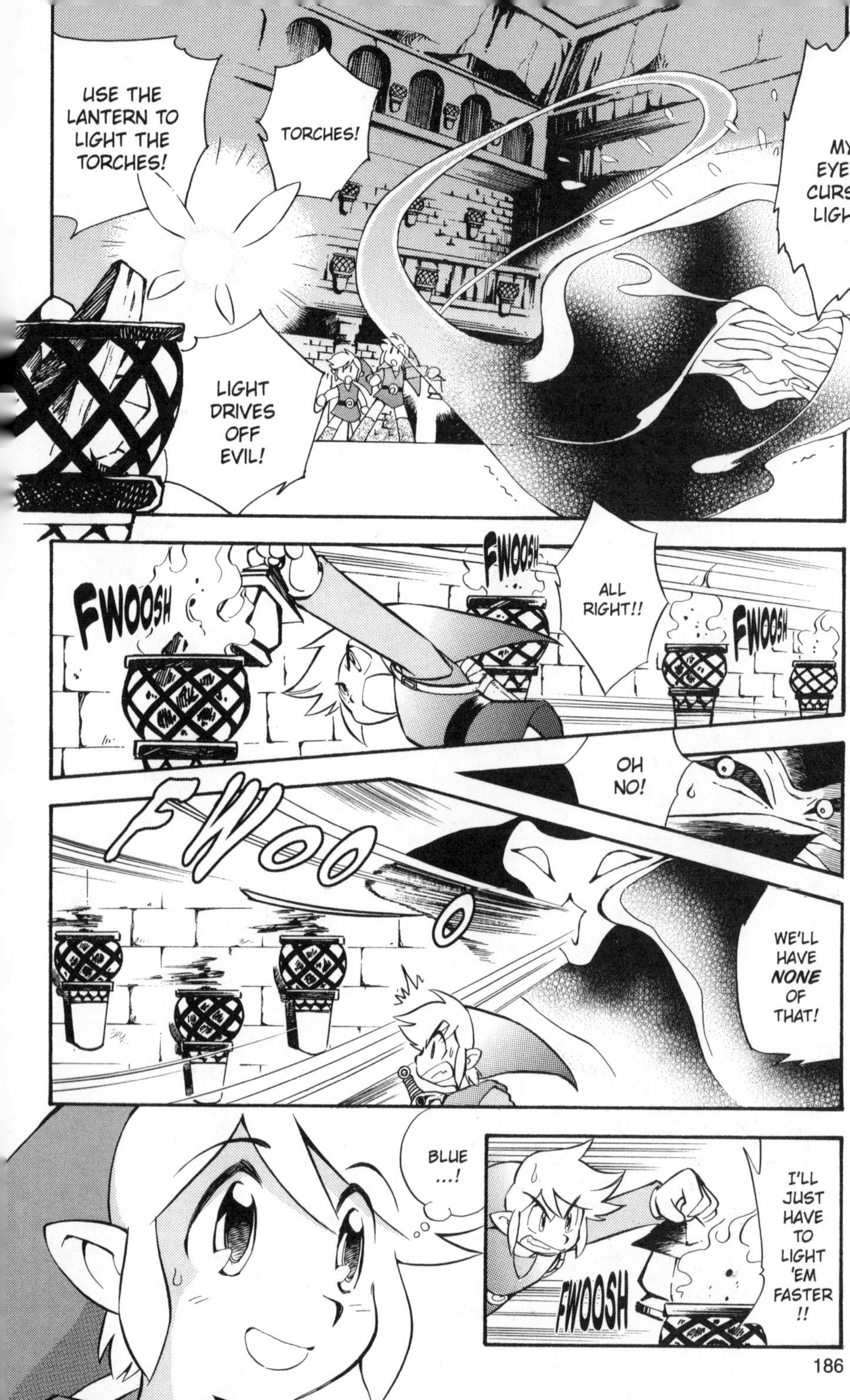
MY EYES! CURSED LIGHT!
TORCHES!
USE THE LANTERN TO LIGHT THE TORCHES!
LIGHT DRIVES OFF EVIL!
FWOOSH
ALL RIGHT!!
FWOOSH
FWOOSH
OH NO!
WE'LL HAVE *NONE* OF THAT!
FWOOO
I'LL JUST HAVE TO LIGHT 'EM FASTER!!
FWOOSH
BLUE ...!

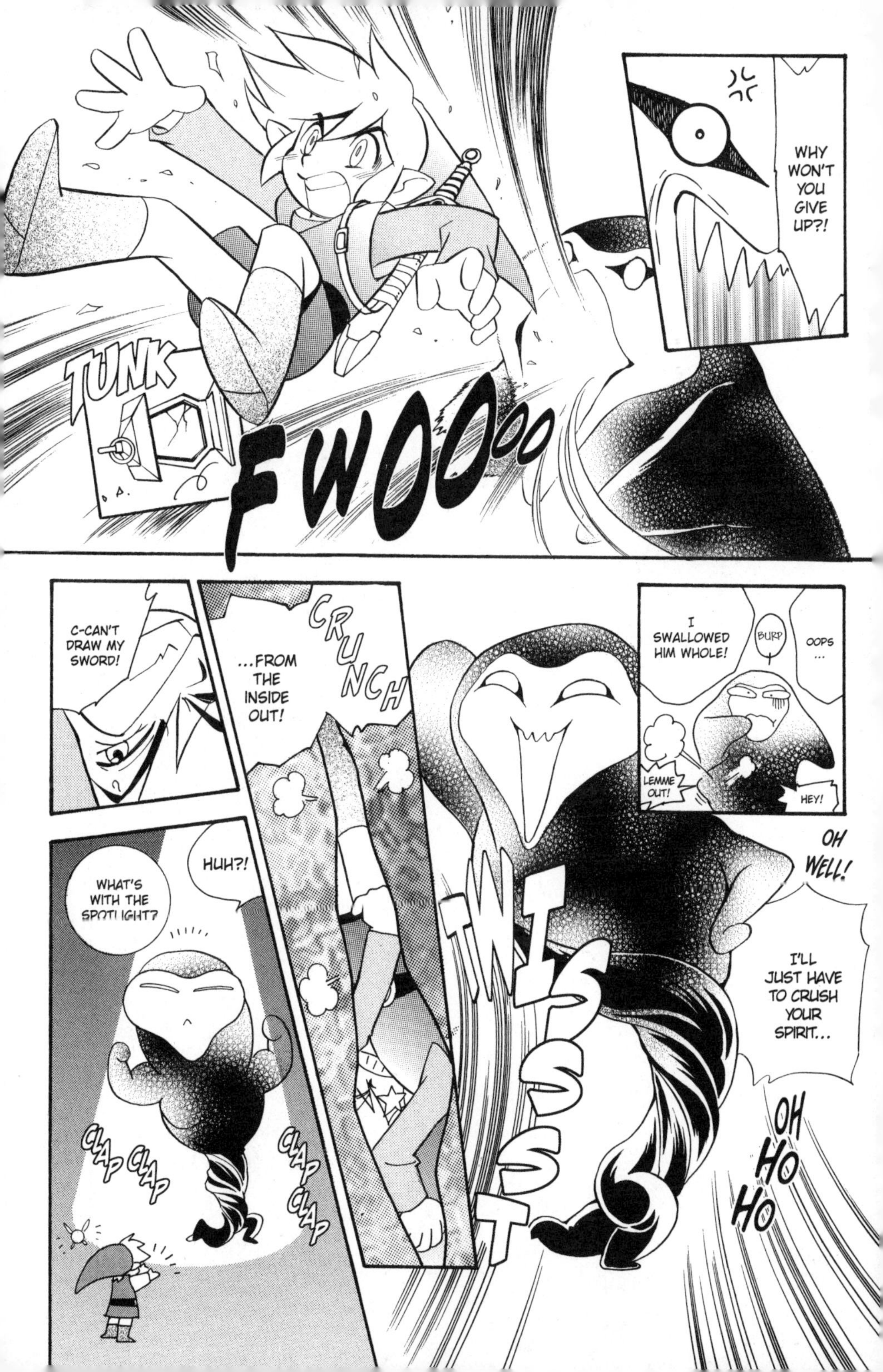
WHY WON'T YOU GIVE UP?!
TUNK
FWOOOOO
I SWALLOWED HIM WHOLE!
BURP
OOPS ...
LEMME OUT!
HEY!
OH WELL!
I'LL JUST HAVE TO CRUSH YOUR SPIRIT...
OH HO HO
TWISSST
CRUNCH
...FROM THE INSIDE OUT!
C-CAN'T DRAW MY SWORD!
HUH?!
WHAT'S WITH THE SPOTLIGHT?
CLAP CLAP
CLAP CLAP

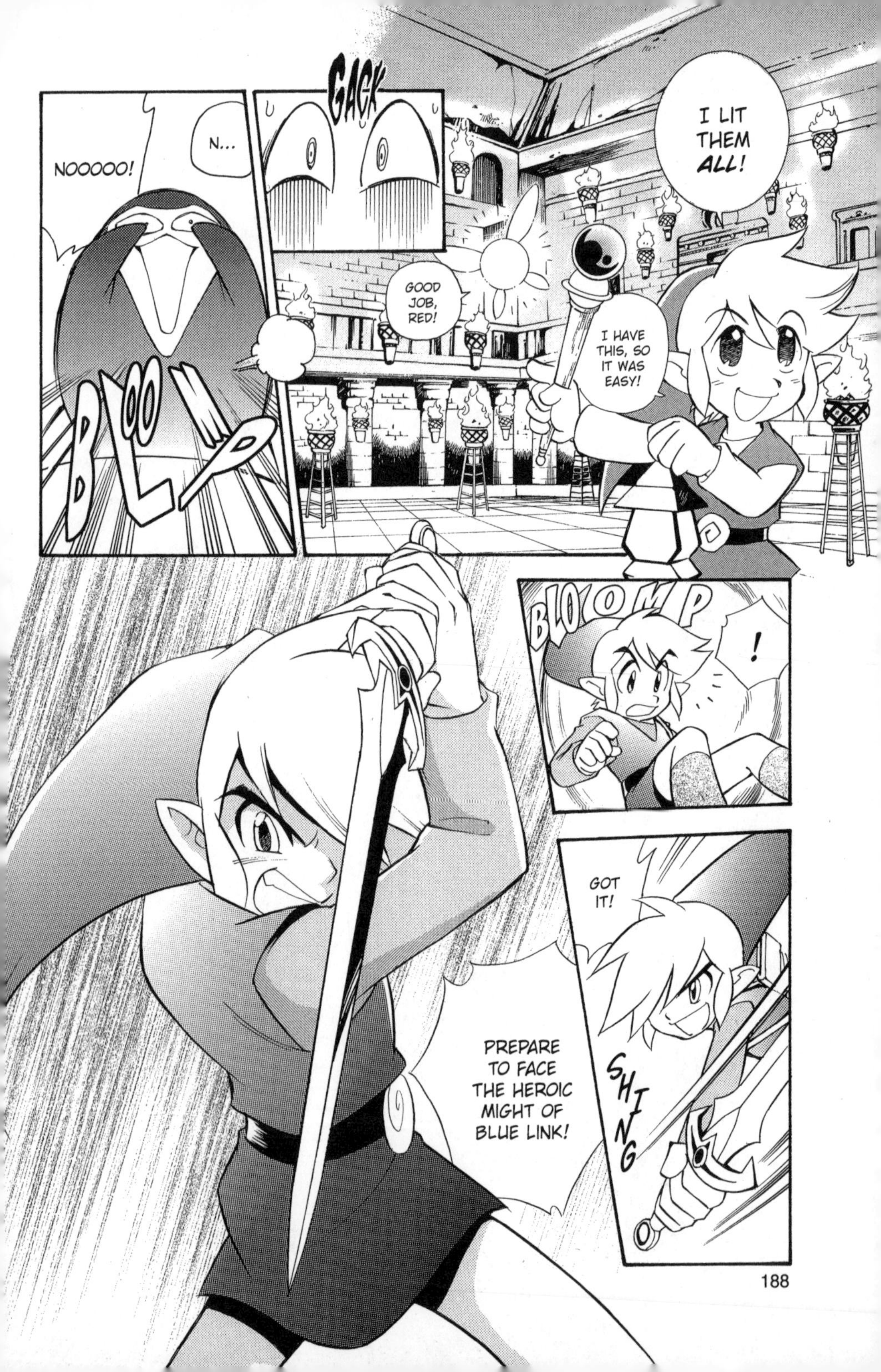
I LIT THEM ALL!
GOOD JOB, RED!
I HAVE THIS, SO IT WAS EASY!
GACK
N...
NOOOOO!
BLOOMP
!
GOT IT!
SHING
PREPARE TO FACE THE HEROIC MIGHT OF BLUE LINK!

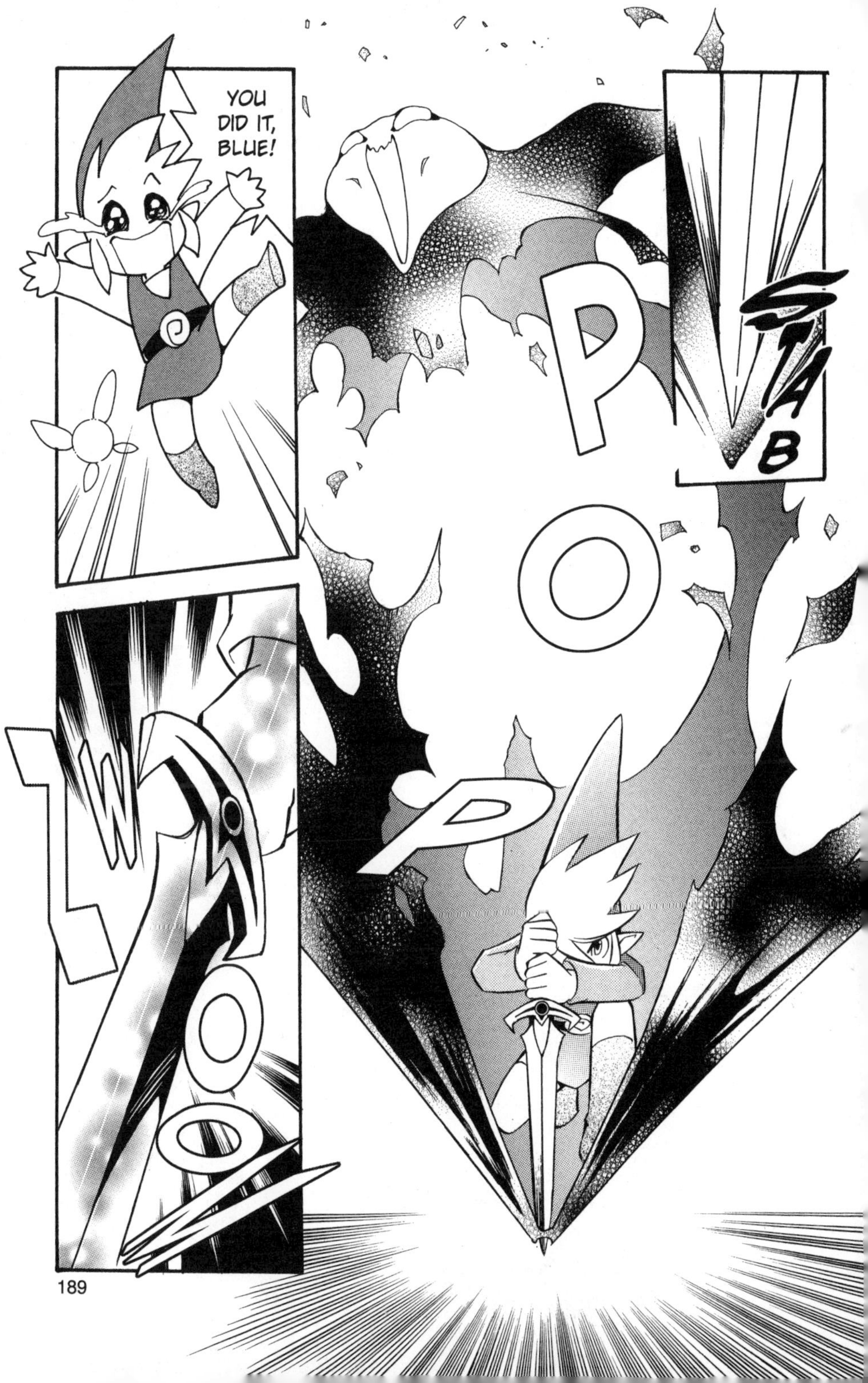
STAB
POP
YOU DID IT, BLUE!
WOO

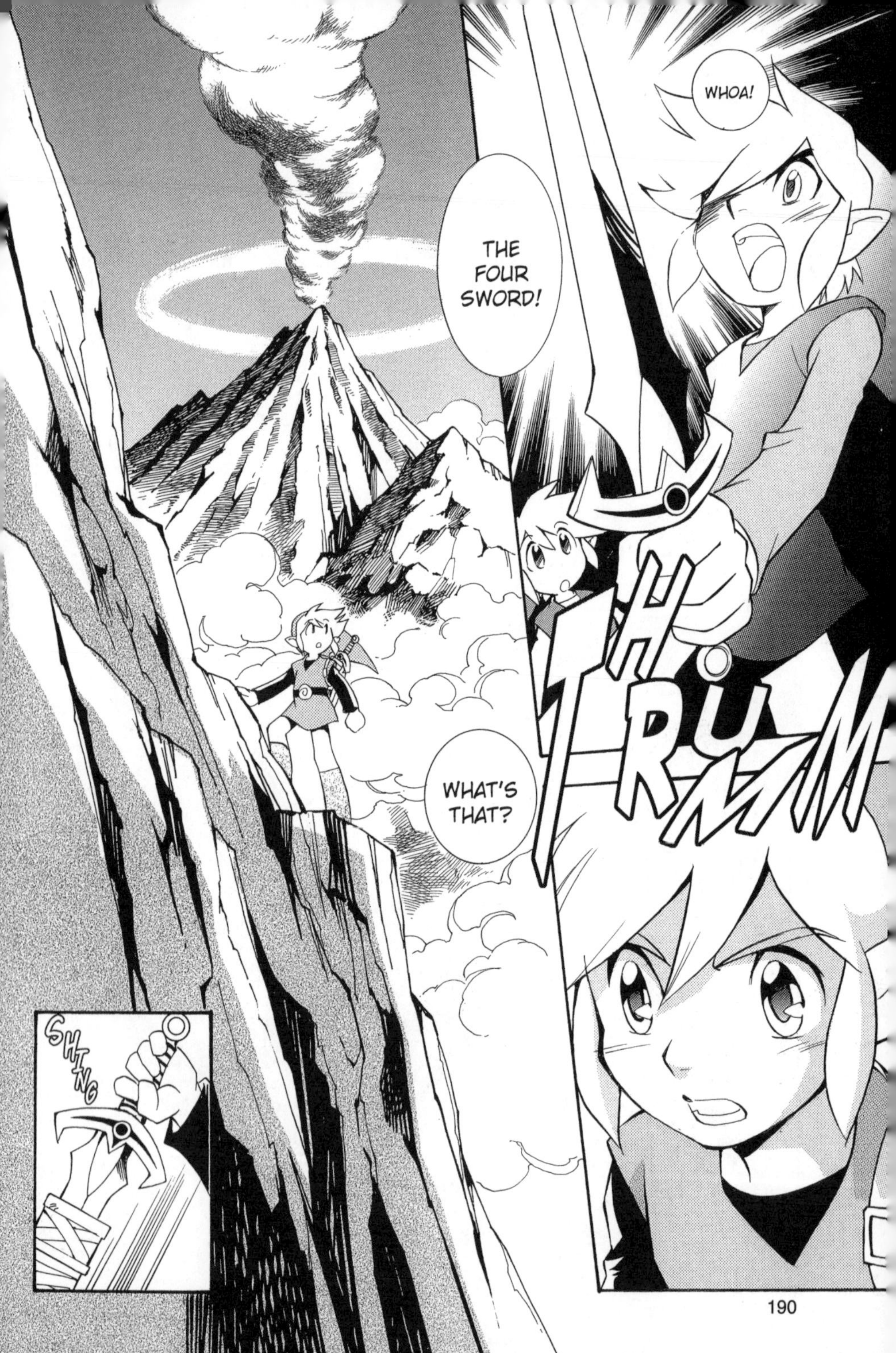
WHOA!
THE FOUR SWORD!
THRUMM
WHAT'S THAT?
SHING

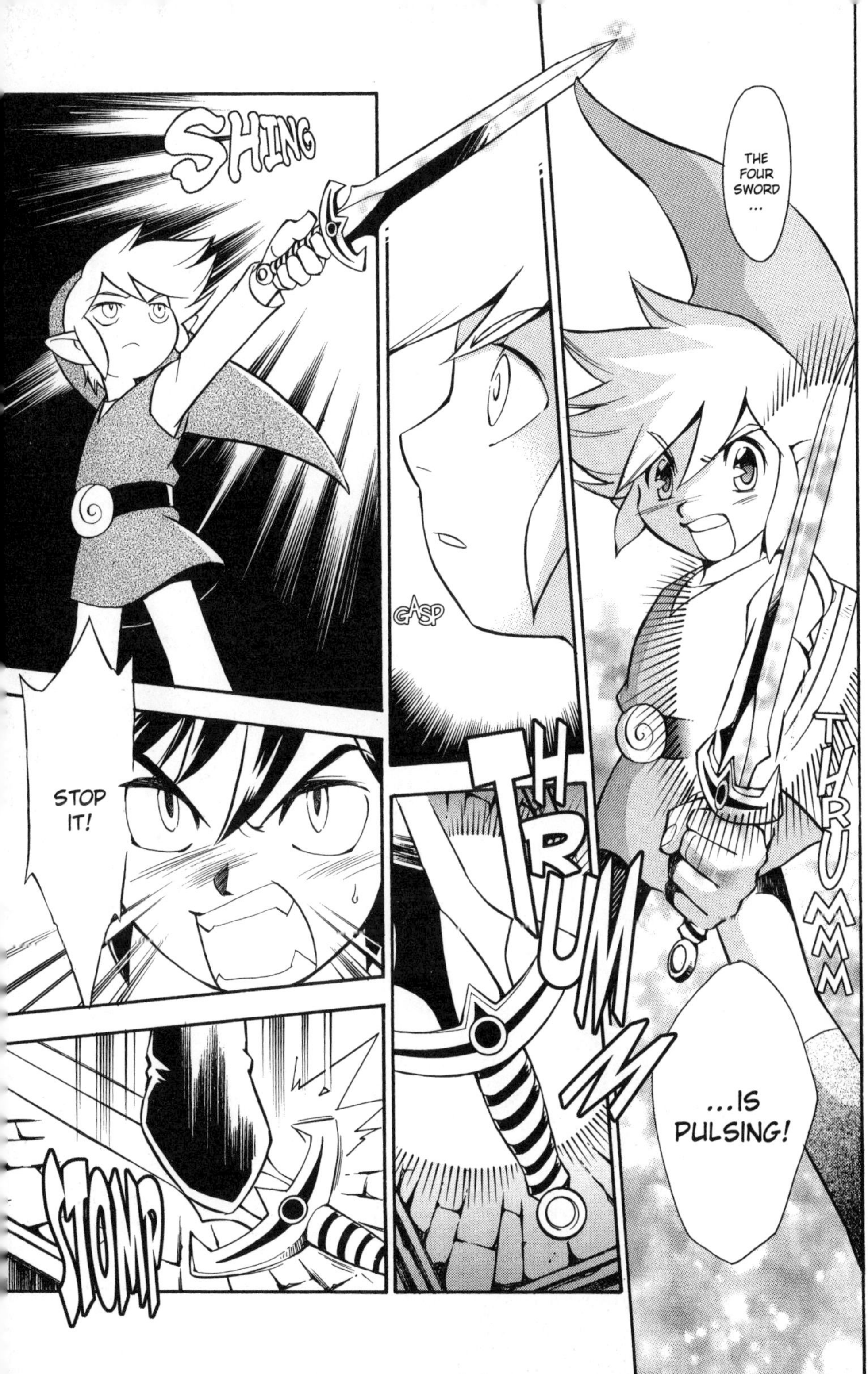
THE FOUR SWORD ...
THRUMMM
...IS PULSING!
GASP
THRUMM
SHING
STOP IT!
STOMP

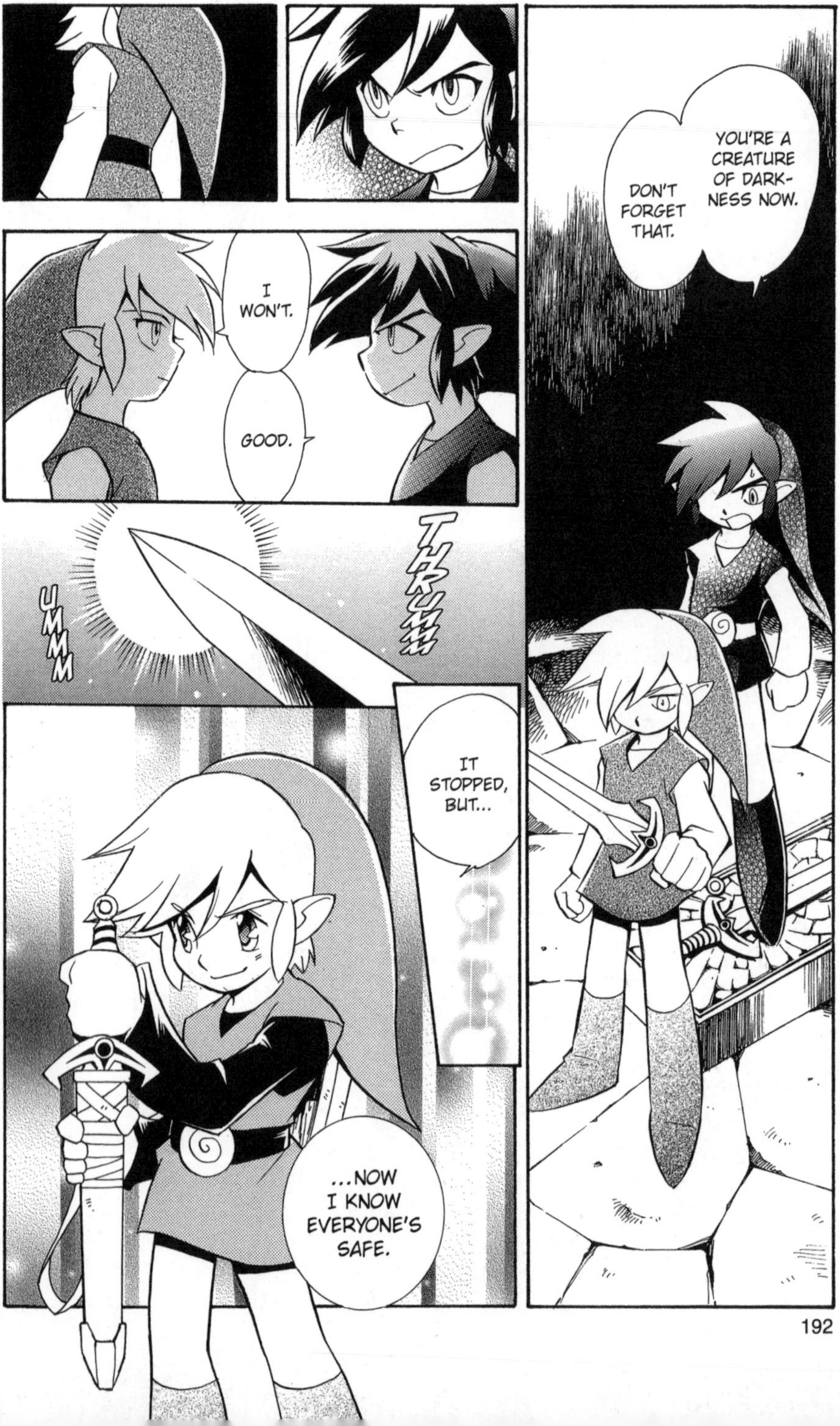

YOU'RE A CREATURE OF DARK-NESS NOW.
DON'T FORGET THAT.
I WON'T.
GOOD.
THRUMM
UMMM
IT STOPPED, BUT...
...NOW I KNOW EVERYONE'S SAFE.

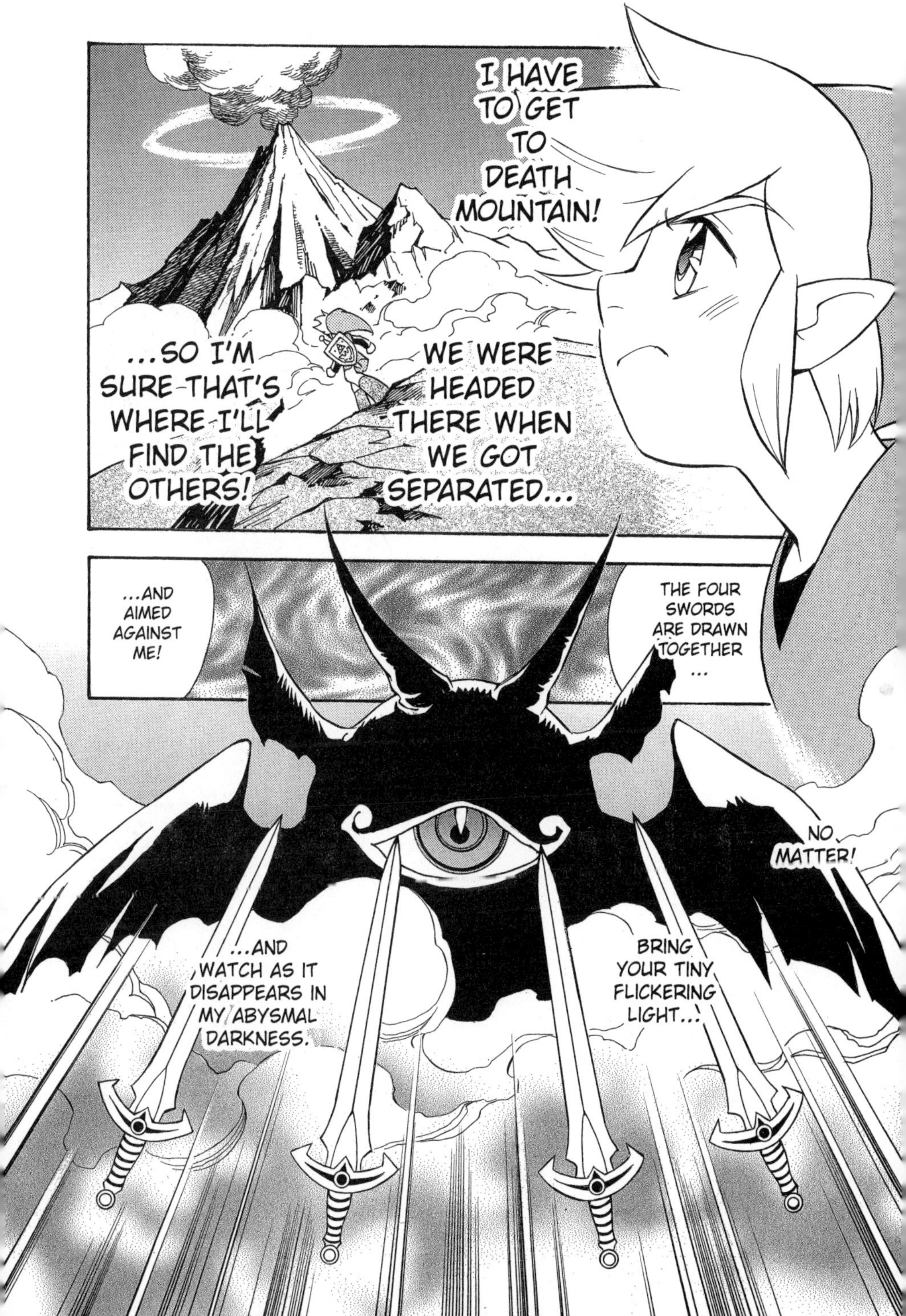
I HAVE TO GET TO DEATH MOUNTAIN!
WE WERE HEADED THERE WHEN WE GOT SEPARATED...
...SO I'M SURE THAT'S WHERE I'LL FIND THE OTHERS!
THE FOUR SWORDS ARE DRAWN TOGETHER ...
...AND AIMED AGAINST ME!
NO MATTER!
BRING YOUR TINY FLICKERING LIGHT...
...AND WATCH AS IT DISAPPEARS IN MY ABYSMAL DARKNESS.

Shadow Link

FOUR SWORDS
ROUGH CHARACTER
ILLUSTRATION 6

CHAPTER 7 Climb Death Mountain!

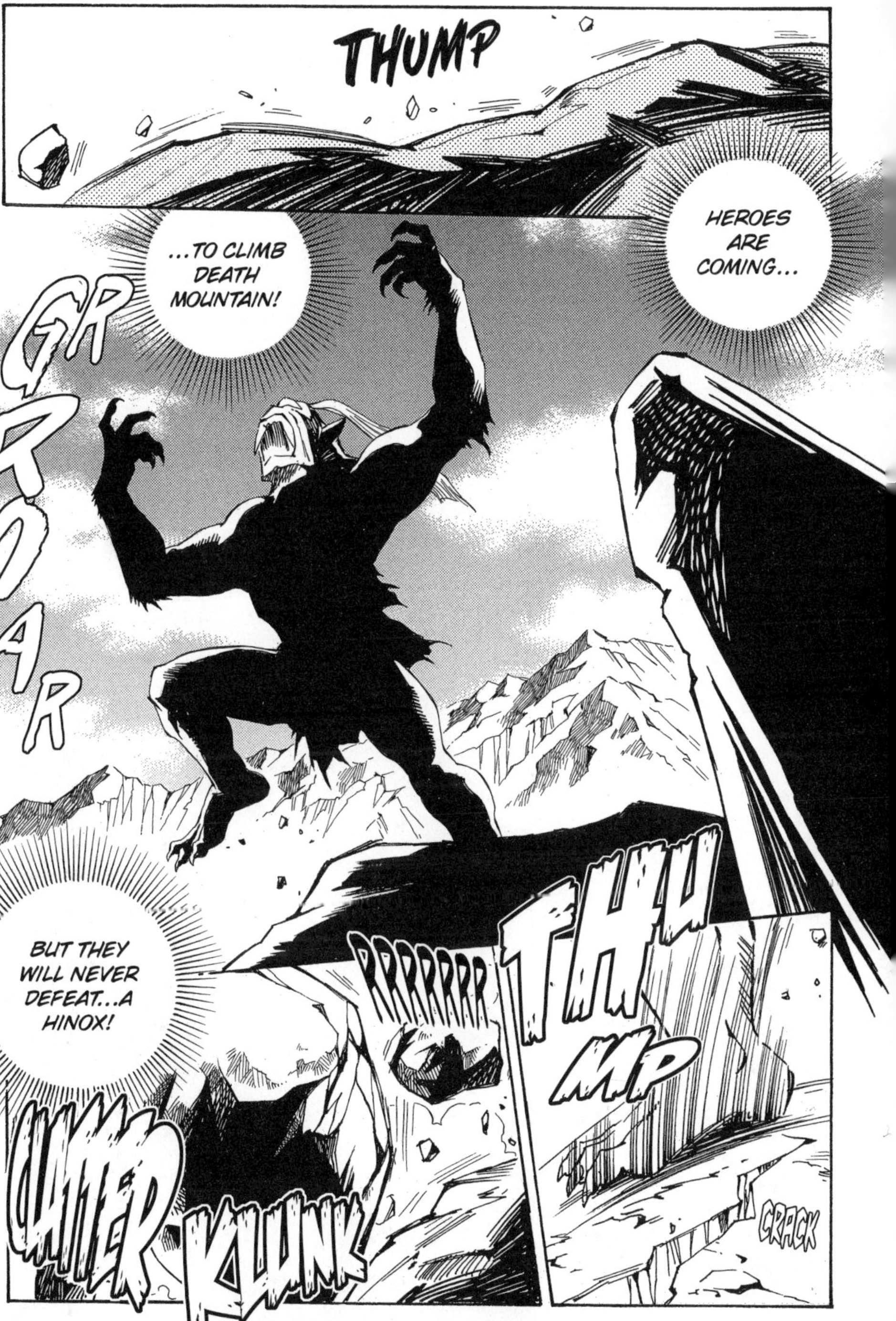
THUMP
HEROES ARE COMING...
...TO CLIMB DEATH MOUNTAIN!
GRROAR
BUT THEY WILL NEVER DEFEAT...A HINOX!
THUMP
CRACK
RRRRRRRR
KLUNK
CLATTER

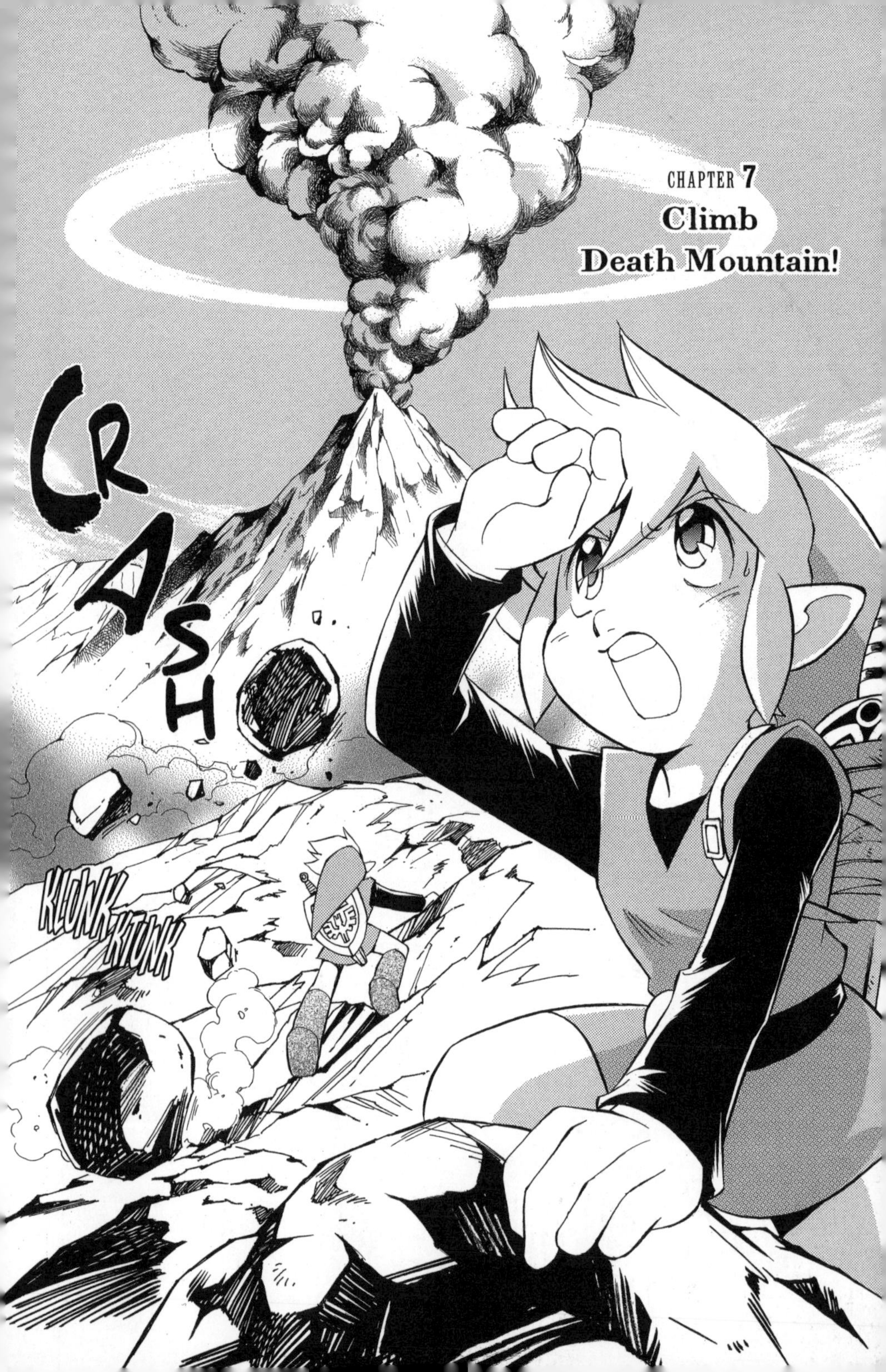
CHAPTER 7
Climb Death Mountain!
CRASH
KLUNK KLUNK

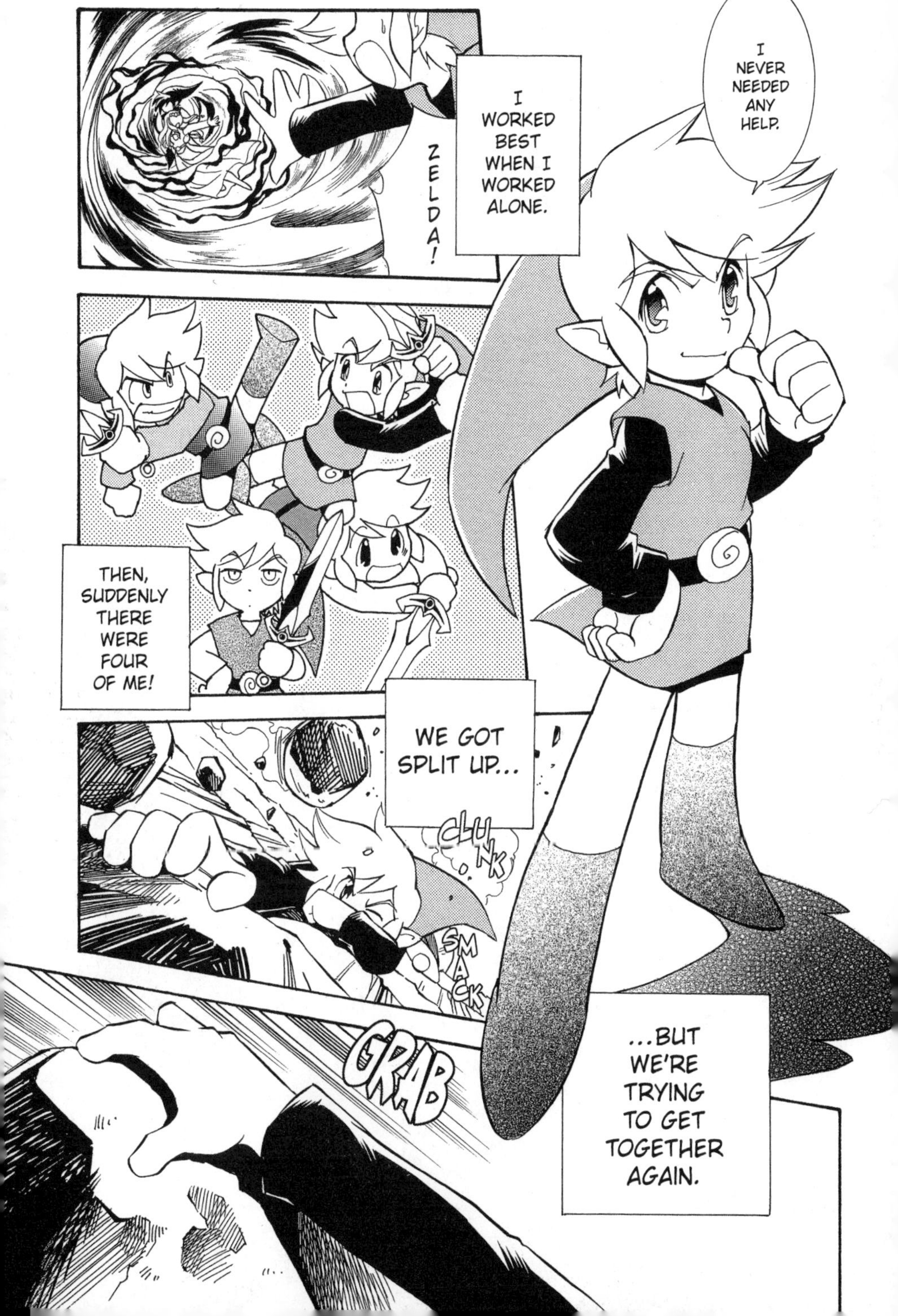

I NEVER NEEDED ANY HELP.
I WORKED BEST WHEN I WORKED ALONE.
ZELDA!
THEN, SUDDENLY THERE WERE FOUR OF ME!
WE GOT SPLIT UP...
CLUNK
SMACK
GRAB
...BUT WE'RE TRYING TO GET TOGETHER AGAIN.

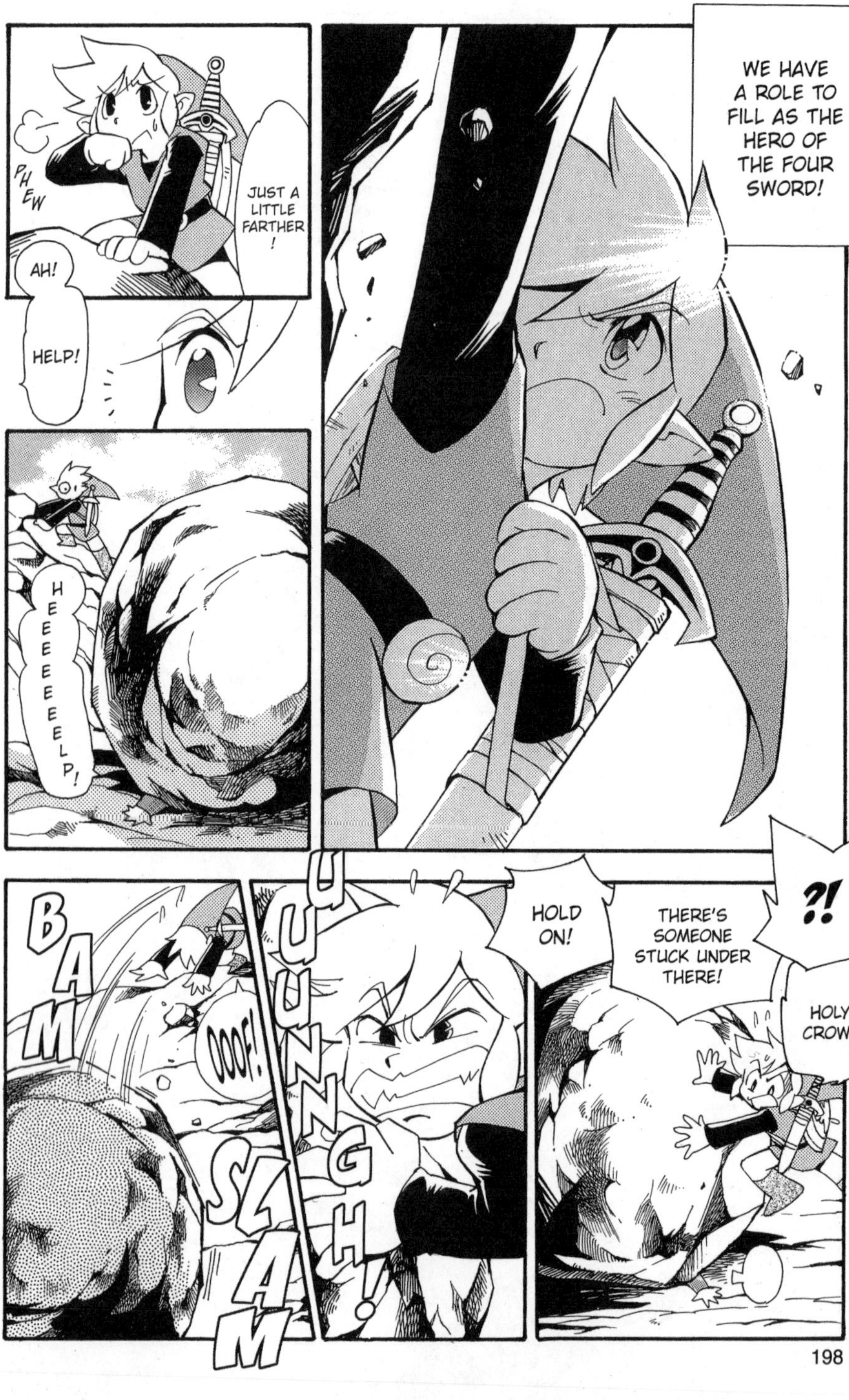
WE HAVE A ROLE TO FILL AS THE HERO OF THE FOUR SWORD!
PHEW
JUST A LITTLE FARTHER!
AH!
HELP!
HEEEEEEEELP!
?!
HOLY CROW!
HOLD ON!
THERE'S SOMEONE STUCK UNDER THERE!
UUUNNNGH!
BAM
OOOF!
SLAM

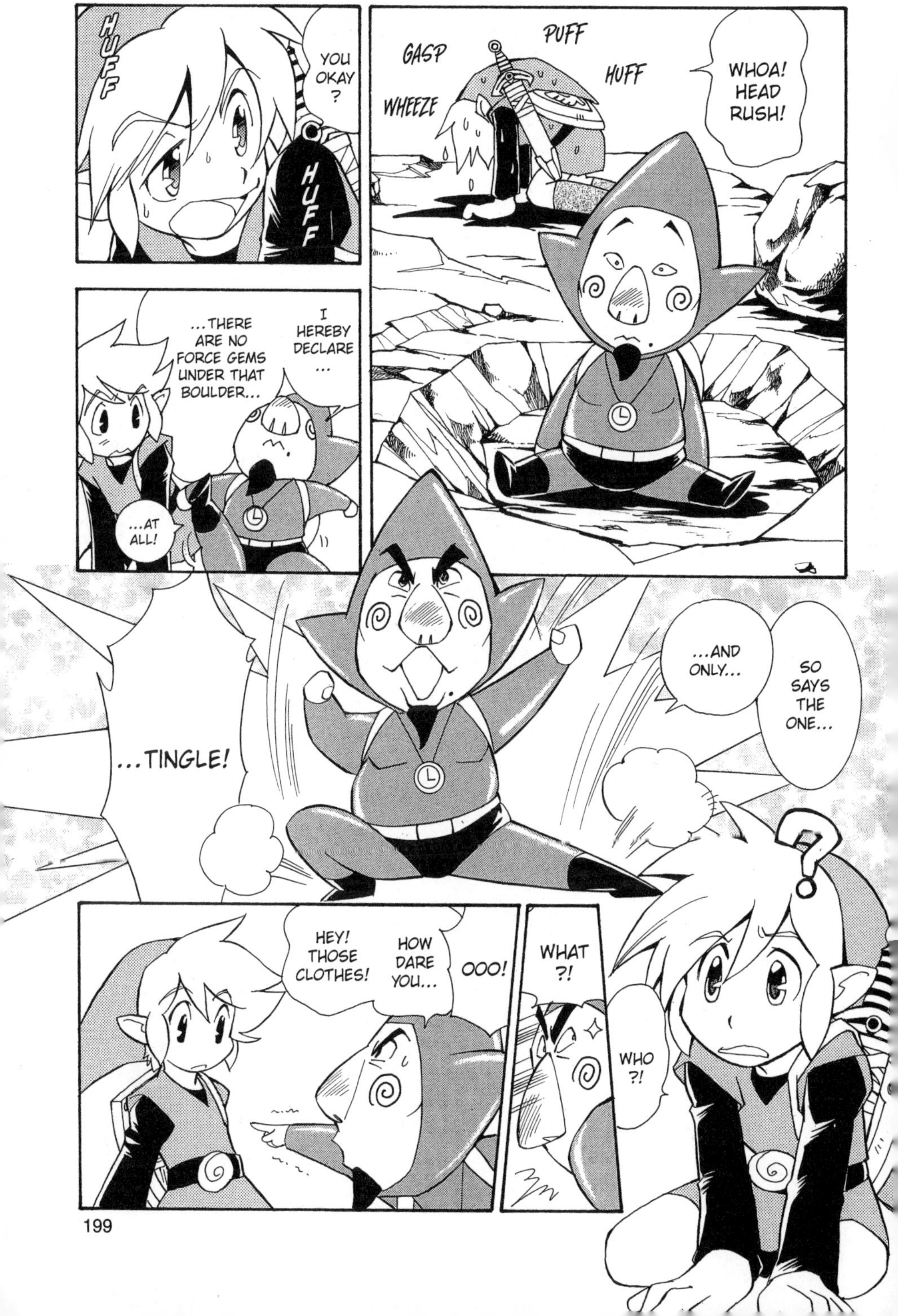
WHOA! HEAD RUSH!
PUFF
HUFF
GASP
WHEEZE
HUFF
YOU OKAY ?
HUFF
HUFF
I HEREBY DECLARE ...
...THERE ARE NO FORCE GEMS UNDER THAT BOULDER...
...AT ALL!
SO SAYS THE ONE...
...AND ONLY...
...TINGLE!
WHAT ?!
WHO ?!
OOO!
HOW DARE YOU...
HEY! THOSE CLOTHES!

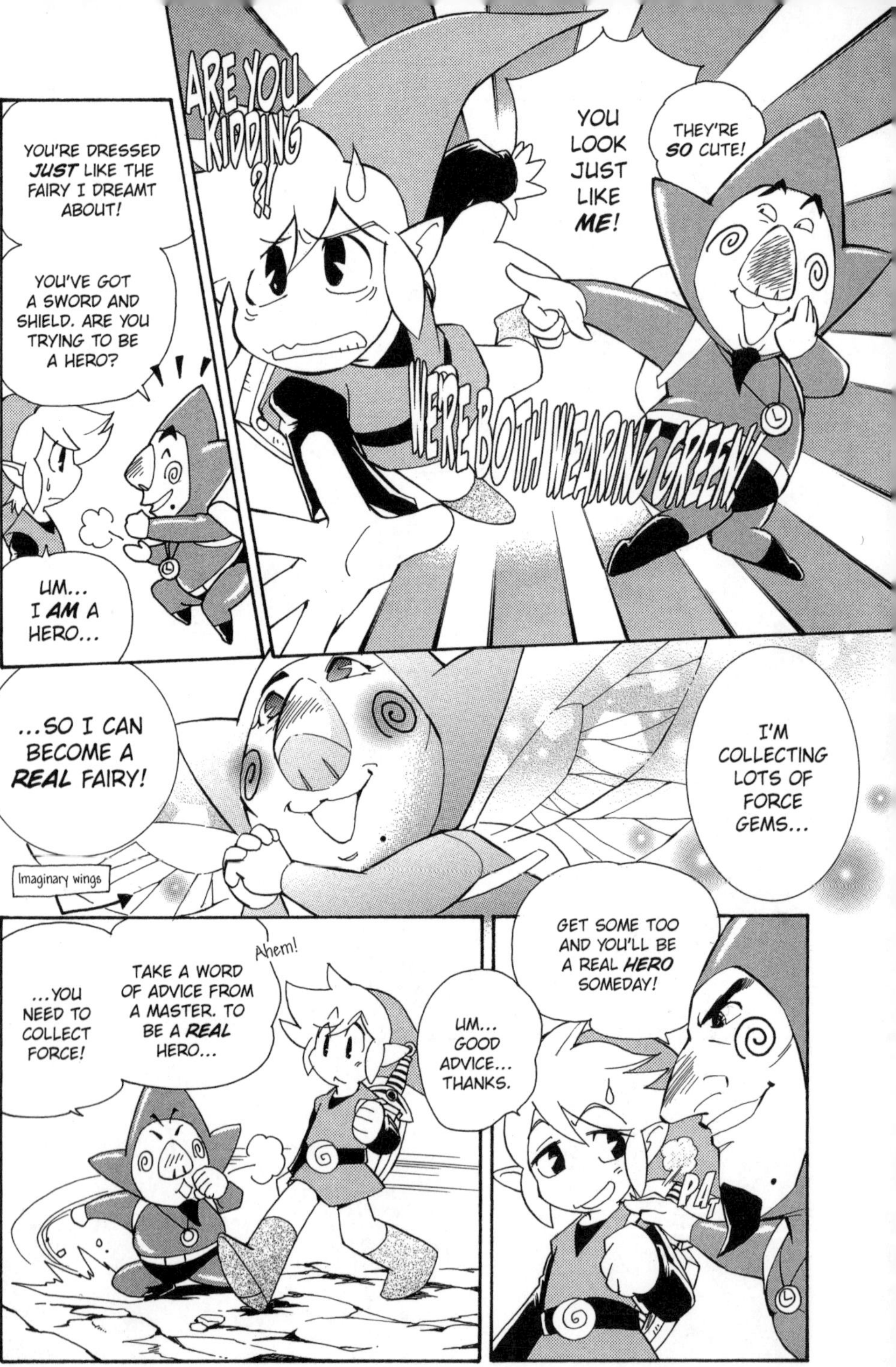
THEY'RE SO CUTE!
YOU LOOK JUST LIKE ME!
ARE YOU KIDDING?!
WE'RE BOTH WEARING GREEN!
YOU'RE DRESSED JUST LIKE THE FAIRY I DREAMT ABOUT!
YOU'VE GOT A SWORD AND SHIELD. ARE YOU TRYING TO BE A HERO?
UM... I AM A HERO...
I'M COLLECTING LOTS OF FORCE GEMS...
...SO I CAN BECOME A REAL FAIRY!
Imaginary wings
GET SOME TOO AND YOU'LL BE A REAL HERO SOMEDAY!
UM... GOOD ADVICE... THANKS.
PAT
Ahem!
TAKE A WORD OF ADVICE FROM A MASTER. TO BE A REAL HERO...
...YOU NEED TO COLLECT FORCE!

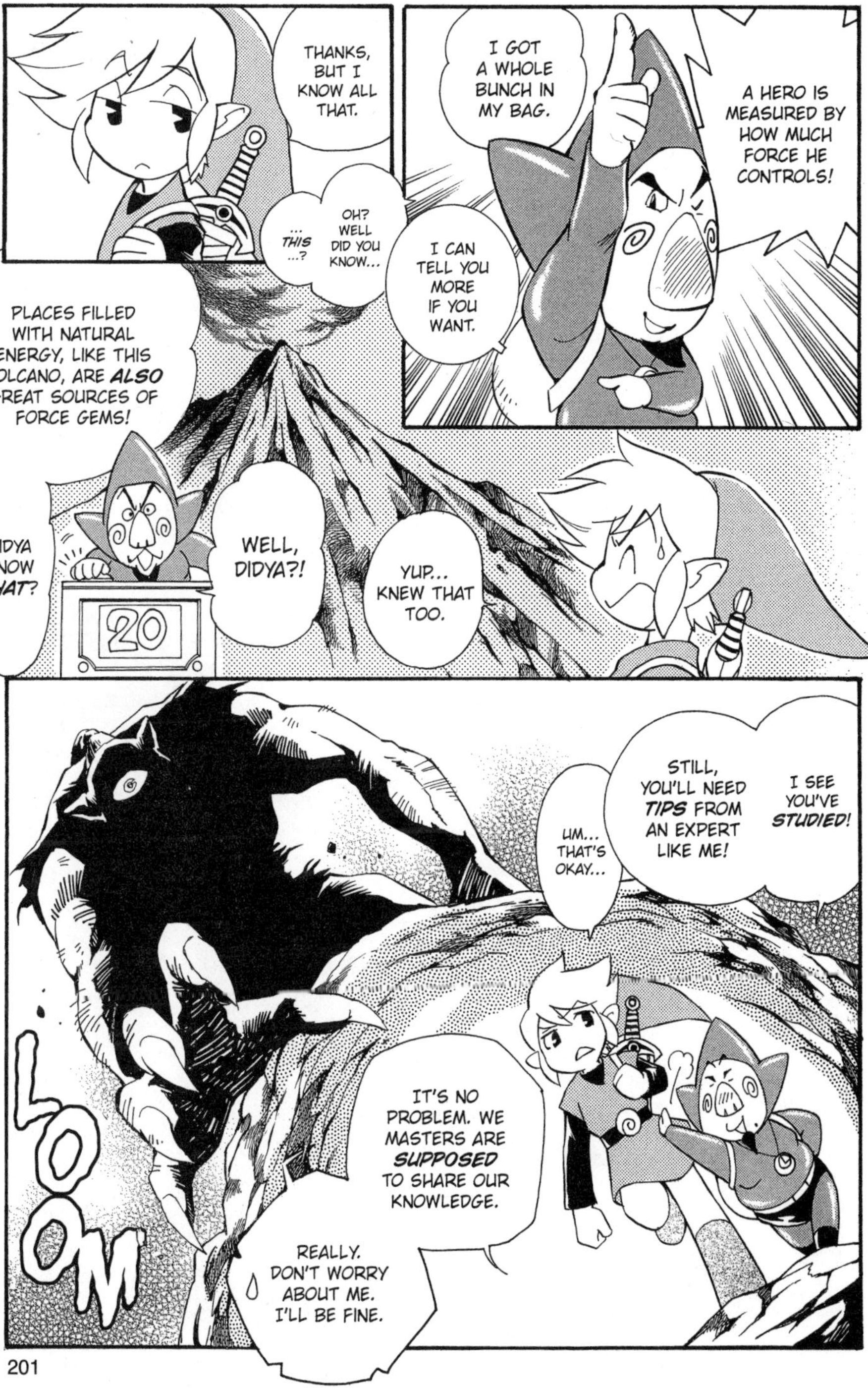
A HERO IS MEASURED BY HOW MUCH FORCE HE CONTROLS!
I GOT A WHOLE BUNCH IN MY BAG.
I CAN TELL YOU MORE IF YOU WANT.
THANKS, BUT I KNOW ALL THAT.
OH? WELL DID YOU KNOW...
...THIS...?
PLACES FILLED WITH NATURAL ENERGY, LIKE THIS VOLCANO, ARE ALSO GREAT SOURCES OF FORCE GEMS!
DIDYA KNOW THAT?
WELL, DIDYA?!
YUP... KNEW THAT TOO.
20
I SEE YOU'VE STUDIED!
STILL, YOU'LL NEED TIPS FROM AN EXPERT LIKE ME!
UM... THAT'S OKAY...
IT'S NO PROBLEM. WE MASTERS ARE SUPPOSED TO SHARE OUR KNOWLEDGE.
REALLY. DON'T WORRY ABOUT ME. I'LL BE FINE.
LOOM

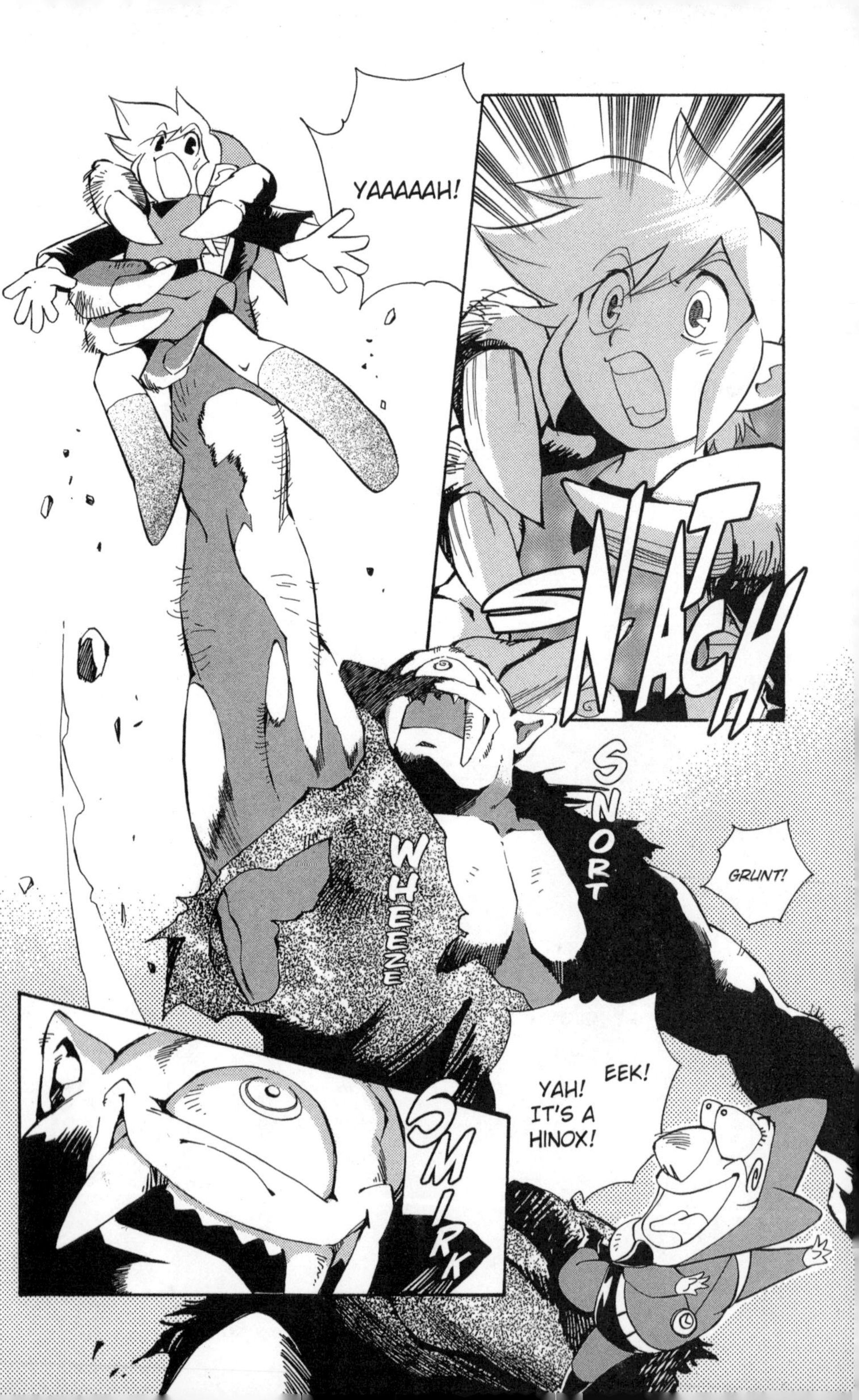
SNATCH
YAAAAAH!
SNORT
WHEEZE
GRUNT!
EEK!
YAH! IT'S A HINOX!
SMIRK

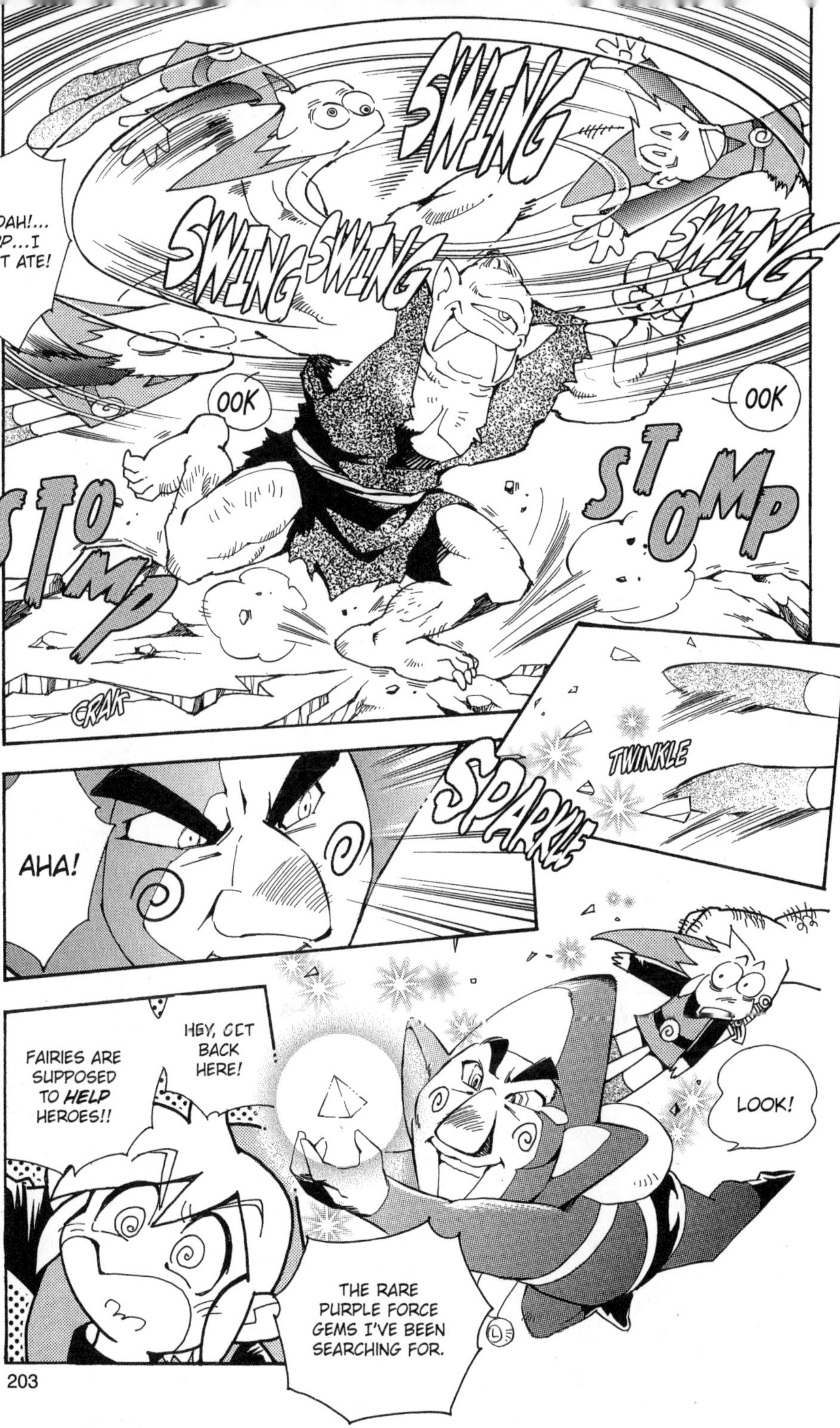
SWING
SWING
OOK
STOMP
SWING
SWING
WHOAH!... URP...I JUST ATE!
OOK
STOMP
CRAK
TWINKLE
SPARKLE
AHA!
LOOK!
HEY, GET BACK HERE!
FAIRIES ARE SUPPOSED TO **HELP** HEROES!!
THE RARE PURPLE FORCE GEMS I'VE BEEN SEARCHING FOR.

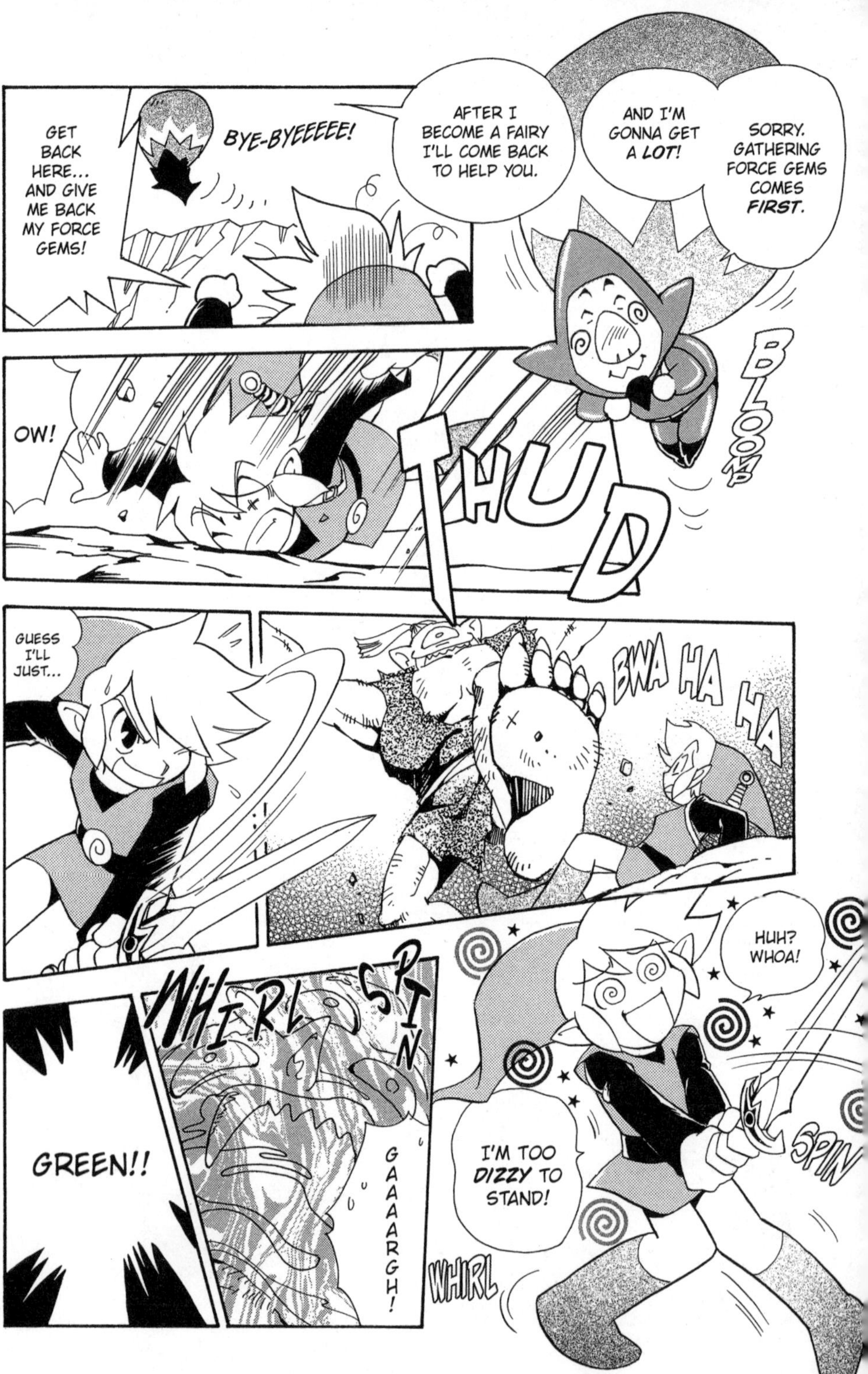
SORRY. GATHERING FORCE GEMS COMES *FIRST*.
AND I'M GONNA GET A *LOT*!
AFTER I BECOME A FAIRY I'LL COME BACK TO HELP YOU.
BYE-BYEEEEE!
GET BACK HERE... AND GIVE ME BACK MY FORCE GEMS!
BLOOMP
THUD
OW!
BWA HA HA HA
GUESS I'LL JUST...
HUH? WHOA!
SPIN
I'M TOO *DIZZY* TO STAND!
WHIRL
WHIRL
SPIN
GAAAAARGH!
GREEN!!

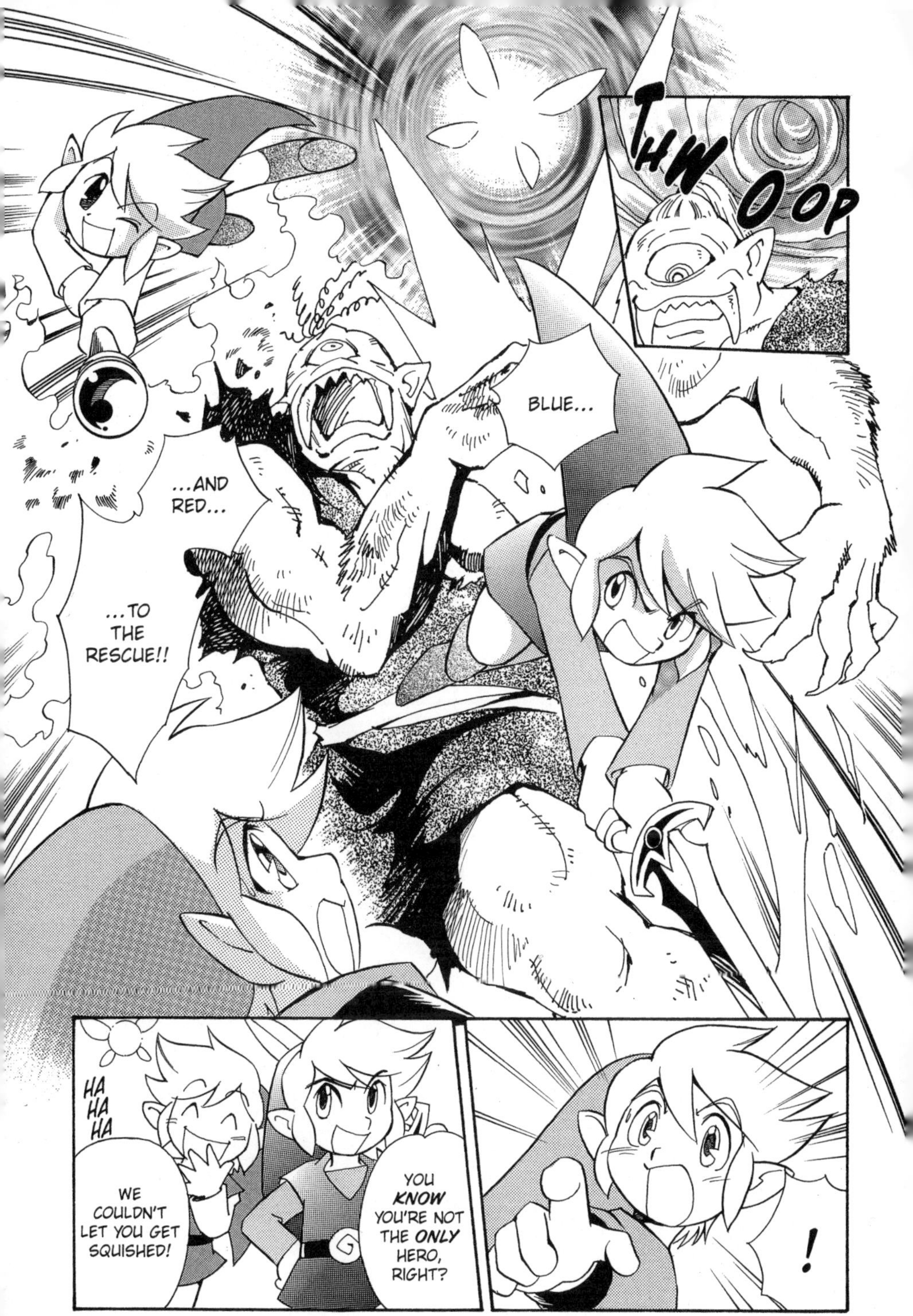
THWOOP
BLUE...
...AND RED...
...TO THE RESCUE!!
!
YOU *KNOW* YOU'RE NOT THE *ONLY* HERO, RIGHT?
HA HA HA
WE COULDN'T LET YOU GET SQUISHED!

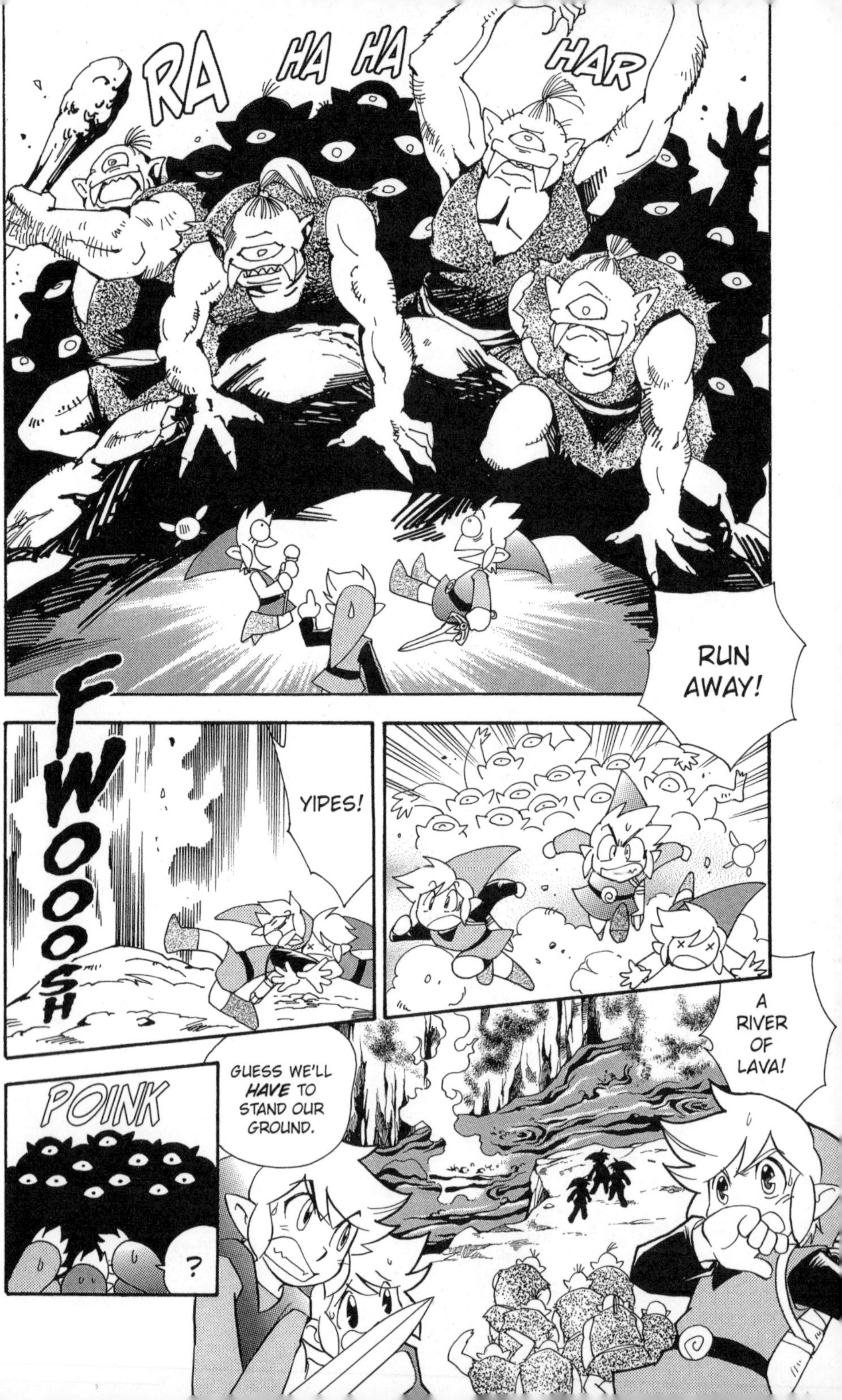
RA HA HA HAR
RUN AWAY!
YIPES!
FWOOOOSH
A RIVER OF LAVA!
GUESS WE'LL *HAVE* TO STAND OUR GROUND.
POINK
?

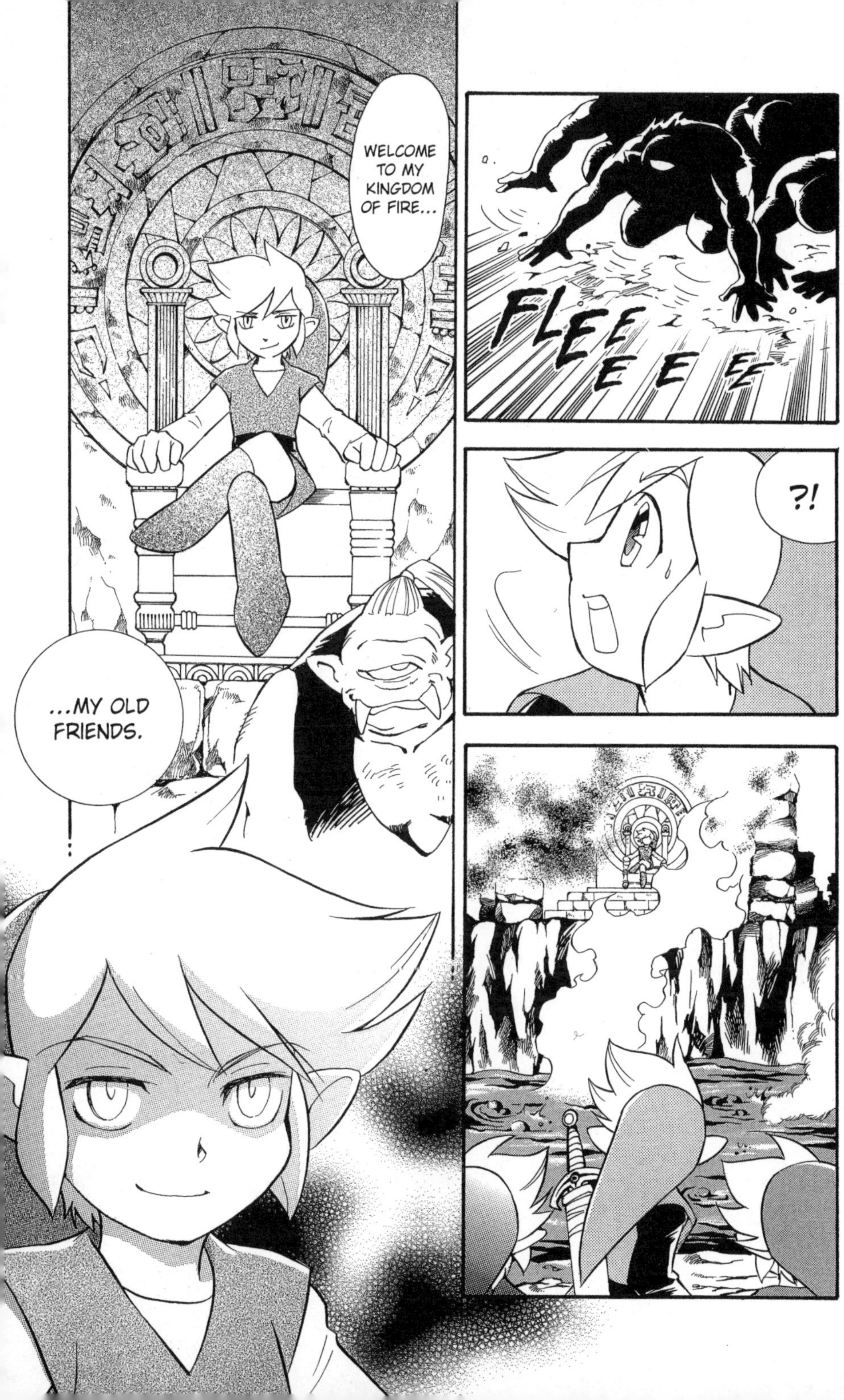
FLEEEEEEE
?!
WELCOME TO MY KINGDOM OF FIRE...
...MY OLD FRIENDS.

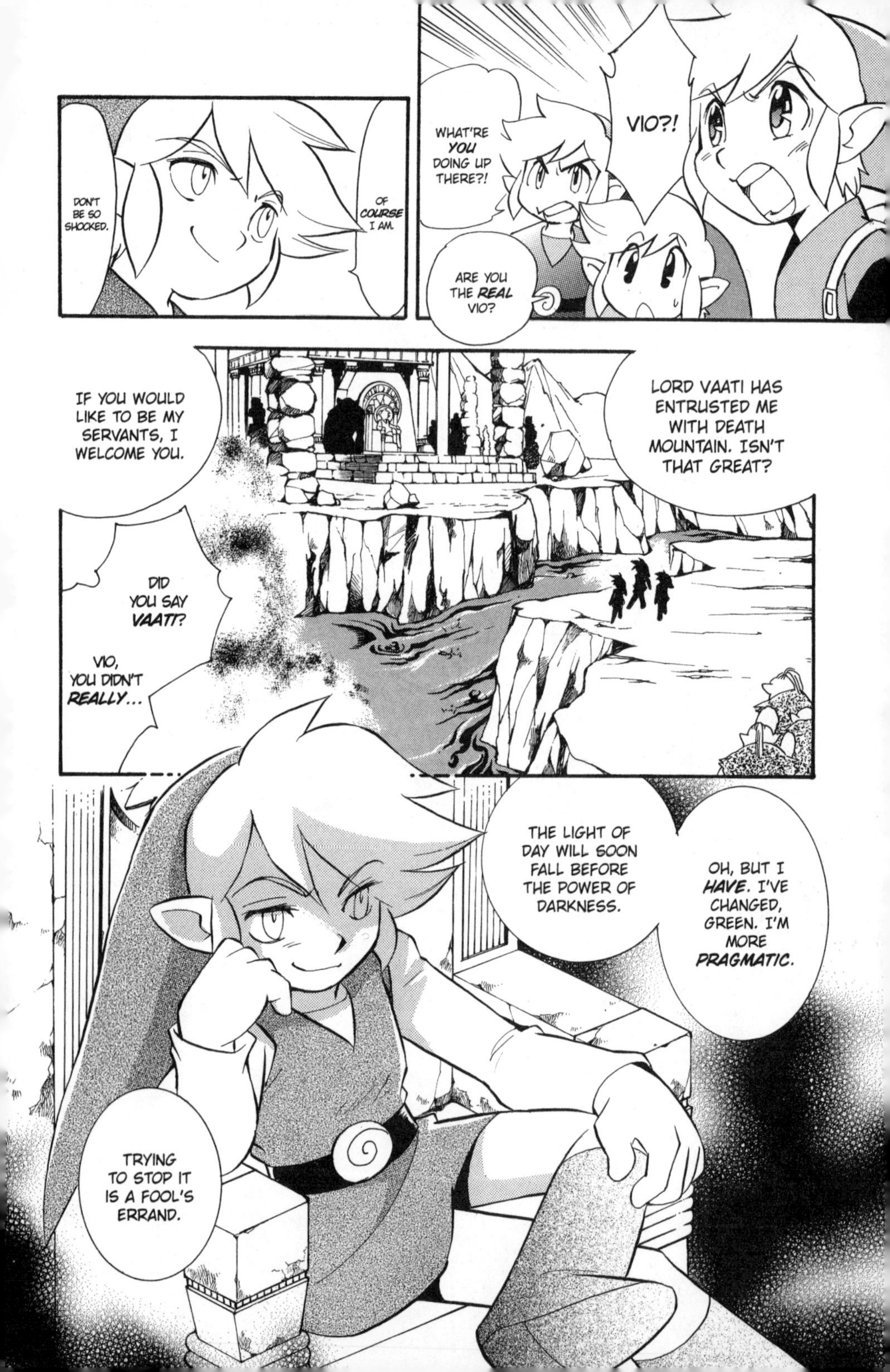
VIO?!
WHAT'RE YOU DOING UP THERE?!
ARE YOU THE REAL VIO?
OF COURSE I AM.
DON'T BE SO SHOCKED.
LORD VAATI HAS ENTRUSTED ME WITH DEATH MOUNTAIN. ISN'T THAT GREAT?
IF YOU WOULD LIKE TO BE MY SERVANTS, I WELCOME YOU.
DID YOU SAY VAATI?
VIO, YOU DIDN'T REALLY...
OH, BUT I HAVE. I'VE CHANGED, GREEN. I'M MORE PRAGMATIC.
THE LIGHT OF DAY WILL SOON FALL BEFORE THE POWER OF DARKNESS.
TRYING TO STOP IT IS A FOOL'S ERRAND.

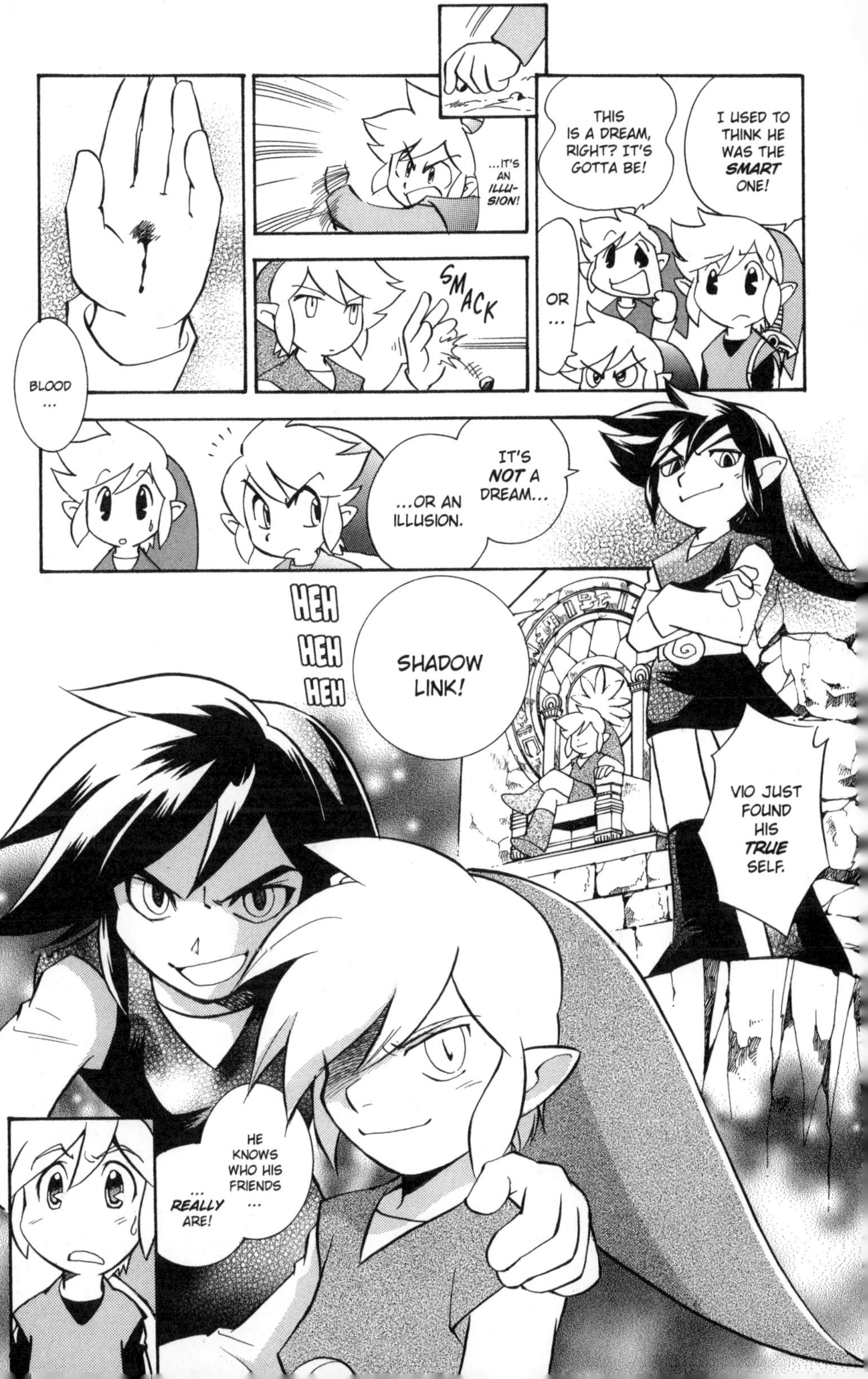
I USED TO THINK HE WAS THE SMART ONE!
THIS IS A DREAM, RIGHT? IT'S GOTTA BE!
OR ...
...IT'S AN ILLUSION!
SMACK
BLOOD ...
IT'S NOT A DREAM...
...OR AN ILLUSION.
SHADOW LINK!
HEH HEH HEH
VIO JUST FOUND HIS TRUE SELF.
HE KNOWS WHO HIS FRIENDS ... REALLY ARE!

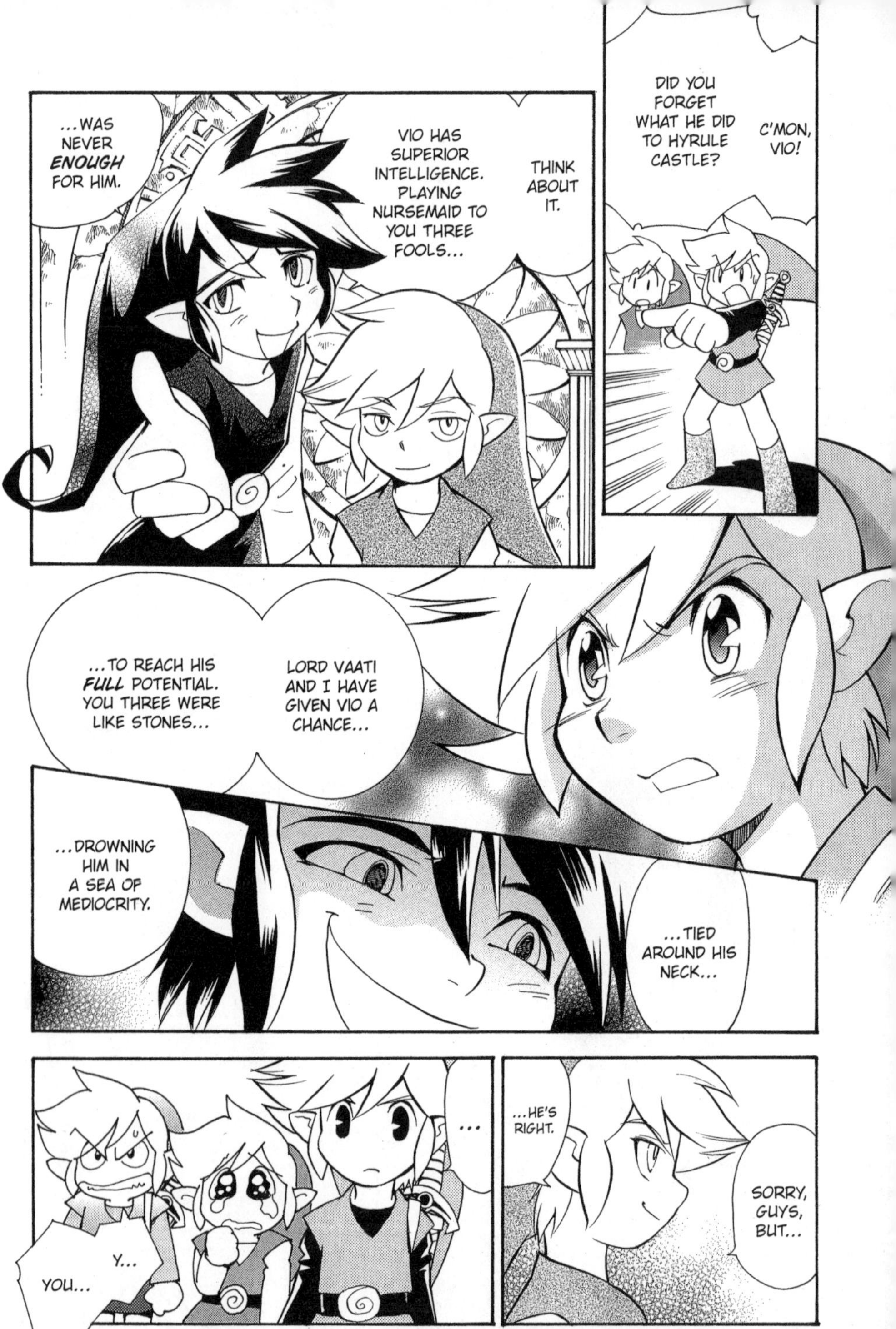
C'MON, VIO!
DID YOU FORGET WHAT HE DID TO HYRULE CASTLE?
THINK ABOUT IT.
VIO HAS SUPERIOR INTELLIGENCE. PLAYING NURSEMAID TO YOU THREE FOOLS...
...WAS NEVER **ENOUGH** FOR HIM.
LORD VAATI AND I HAVE GIVEN VIO A CHANCE...
...TO REACH HIS **FULL** POTENTIAL. YOU THREE WERE LIKE STONES...
...TIED AROUND HIS NECK...
...DROWNING HIM IN A SEA OF MEDIOCRITY.
...HE'S RIGHT.
SORRY, GUYS, BUT...
...
Y... YOU...

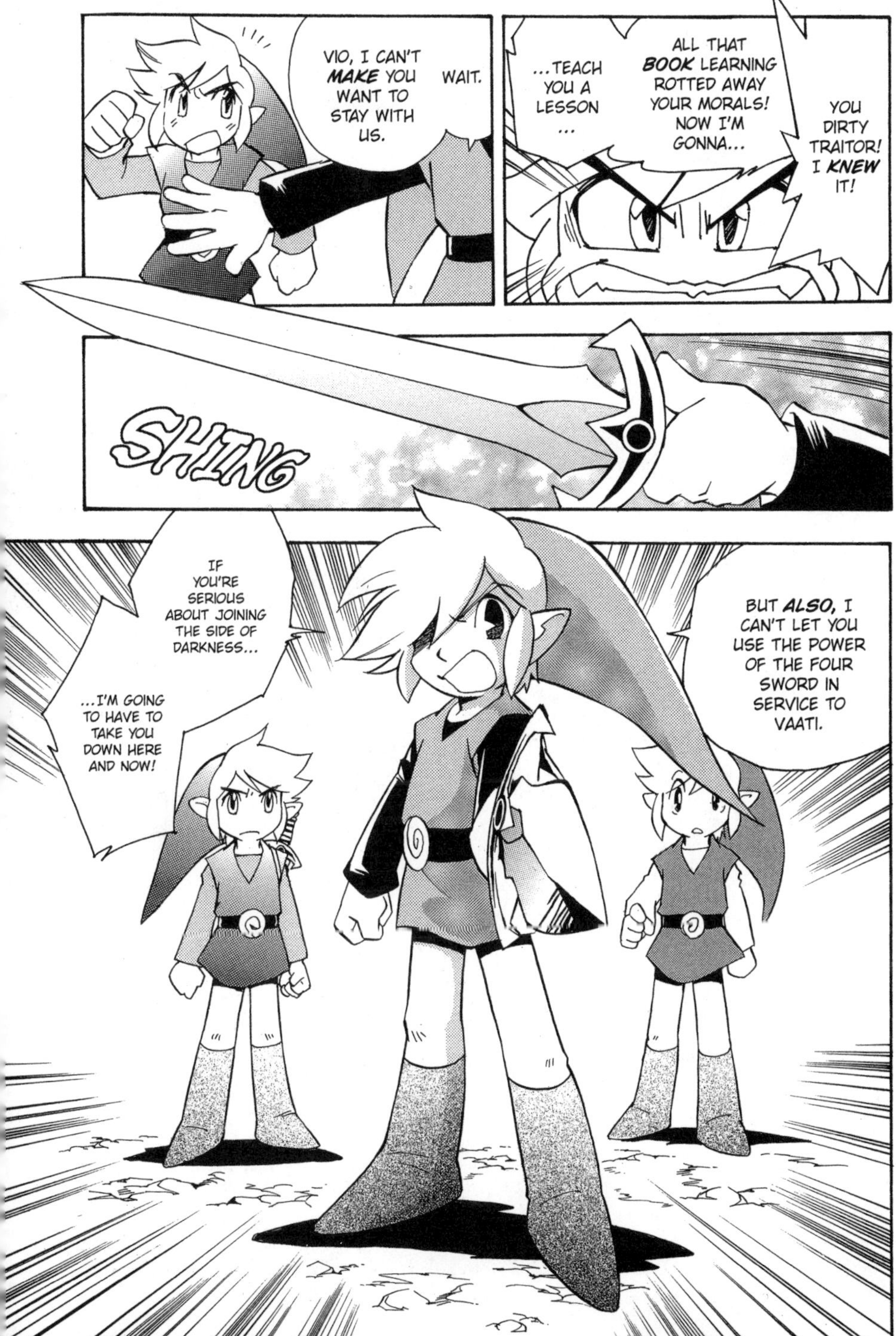
YOU DIRTY TRAITOR! I KNEW IT!
ALL THAT BOOK LEARNING ROTTED AWAY YOUR MORALS! NOW I'M GONNA...
...TEACH YOU A LESSON...
WAIT.
VIO, I CAN'T MAKE YOU WANT TO STAY WITH US.
SHING
BUT ALSO, I CAN'T LET YOU USE THE POWER OF THE FOUR SWORD IN SERVICE TO VAATI.
IF YOU'RE SERIOUS ABOUT JOINING THE SIDE OF DARKNESS...
...I'M GOING TO HAVE TO TAKE YOU DOWN HERE AND NOW!

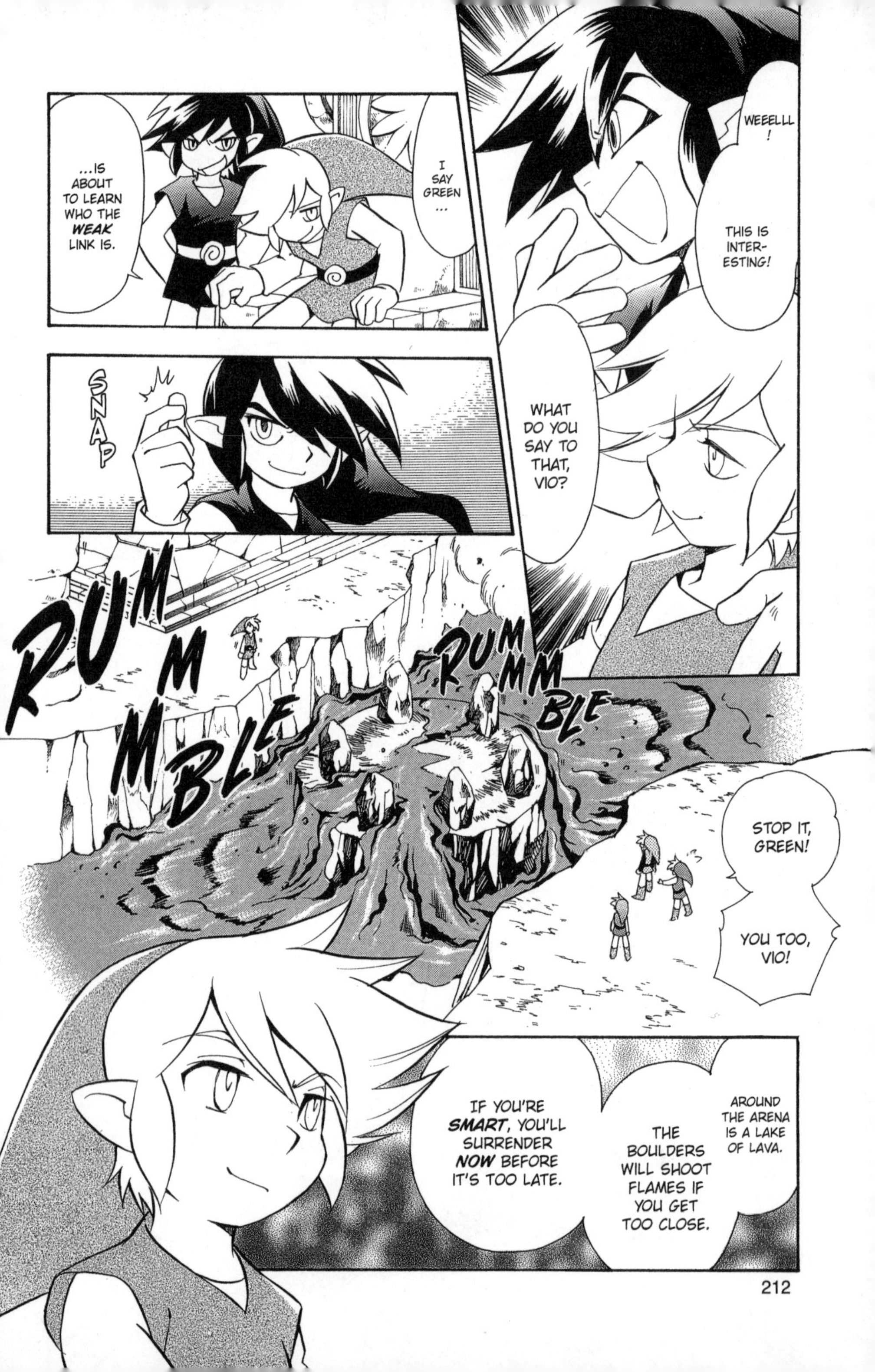
WEEELLL!
THIS IS INTERESTING!
WHAT DO YOU SAY TO THAT, VIO?
I SAY GREEN...
...IS ABOUT TO LEARN WHO THE **WEAK** LINK IS.
SNAP
RUMMMBLE
RUMMMBLE
STOP IT, GREEN!
YOU TOO, VIO!
AROUND THE ARENA IS A LAKE OF LAVA.
THE BOULDERS WILL SHOOT FLAMES IF YOU GET TOO CLOSE.
IF YOU'RE **SMART**, YOU'LL SURRENDER **NOW** BEFORE IT'S TOO LATE.

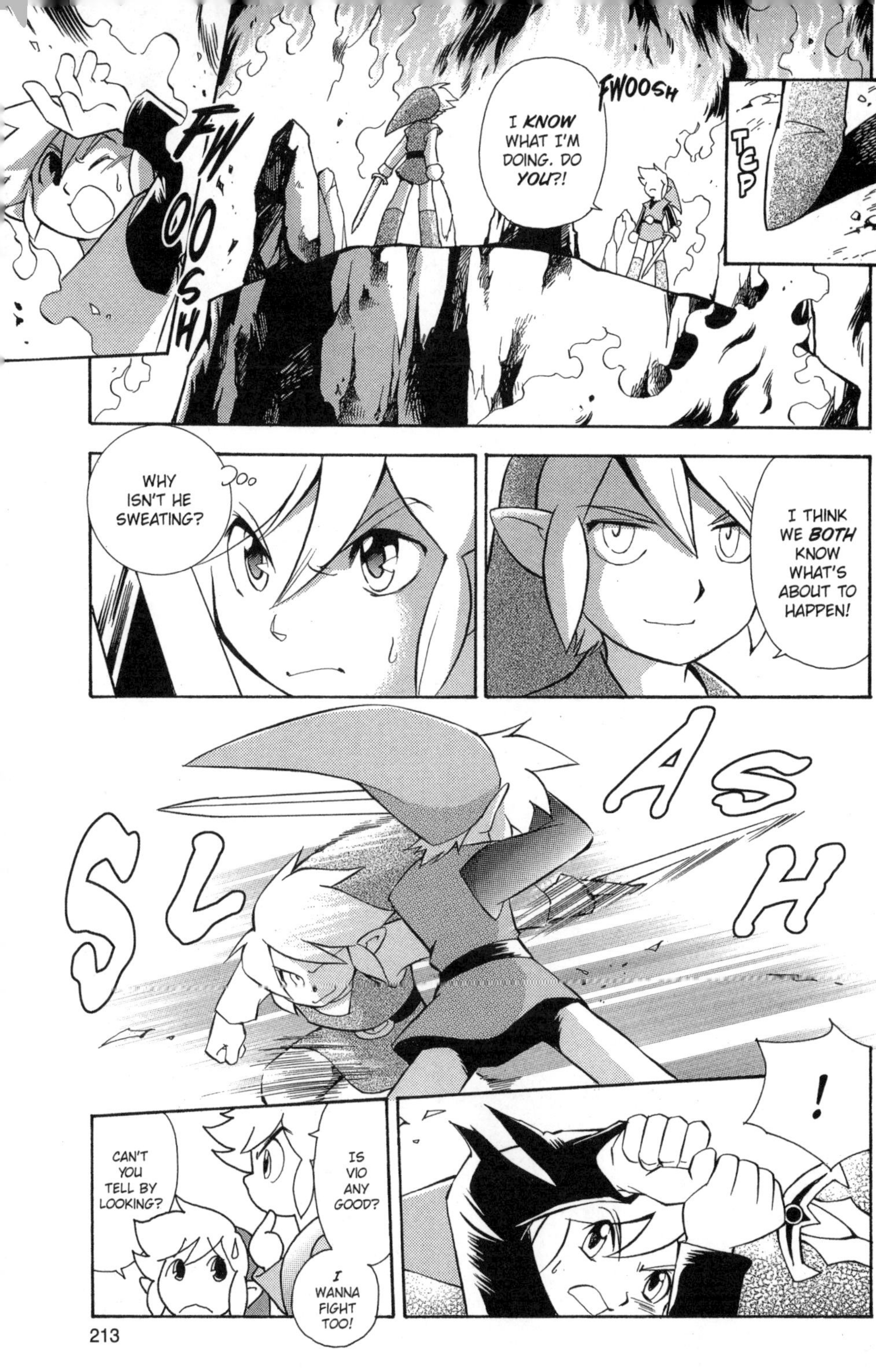
TEP
FWOOSH
I KNOW WHAT I'M DOING. DO YOU?!
FWOOOSH
I THINK WE BOTH KNOW WHAT'S ABOUT TO HAPPEN!
WHY ISN'T HE SWEATING?
SLASH
!
IS VIO ANY GOOD?
CAN'T YOU TELL BY LOOKING?
I WANNA FIGHT TOO!

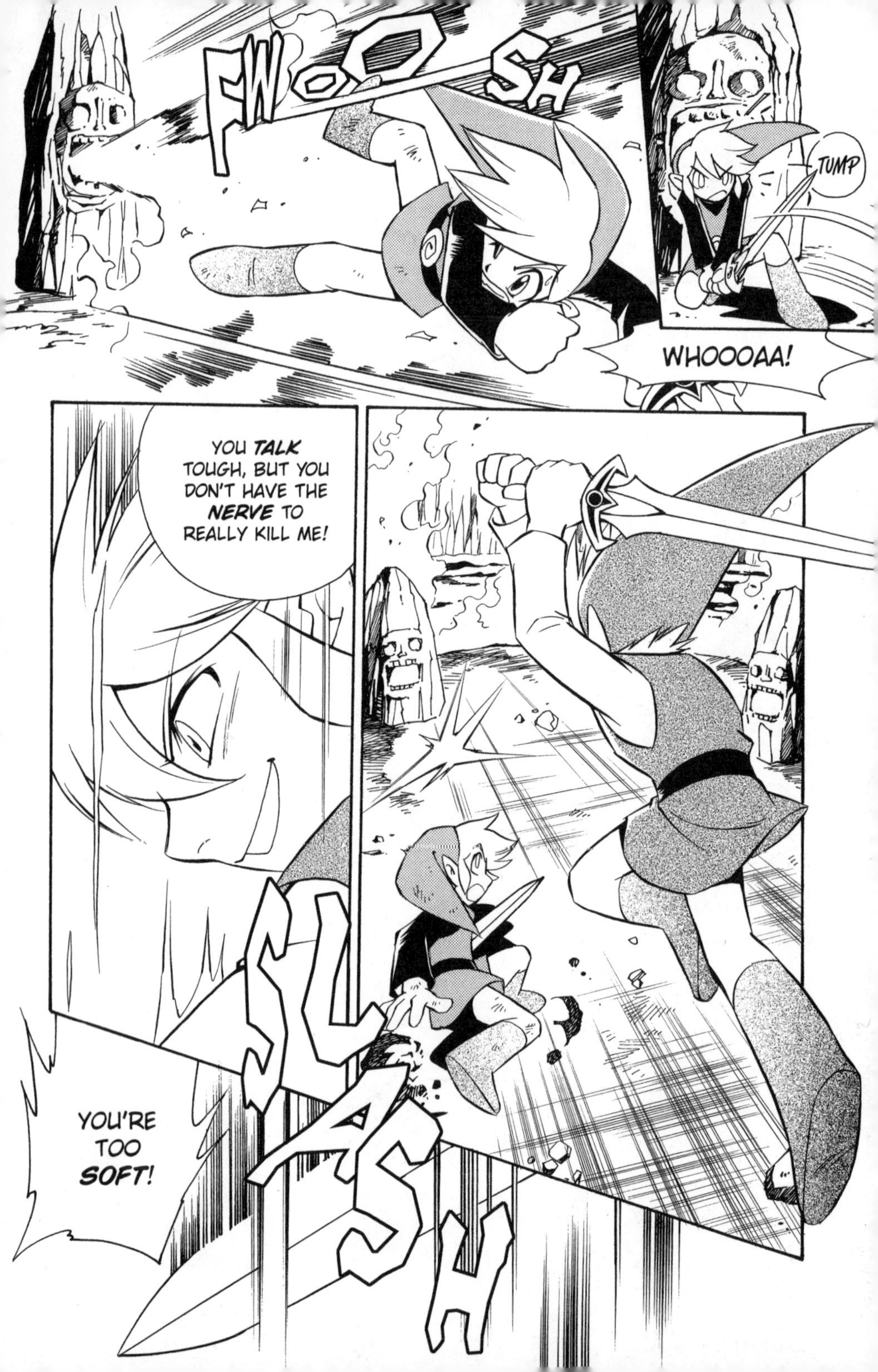
TUMP
WHOOOAA!
FWOOOSH
SLASH
YOU TALK TOUGH, BUT YOU DON'T HAVE THE NERVE TO REALLY KILL ME!
YOU'RE TOO SOFT!

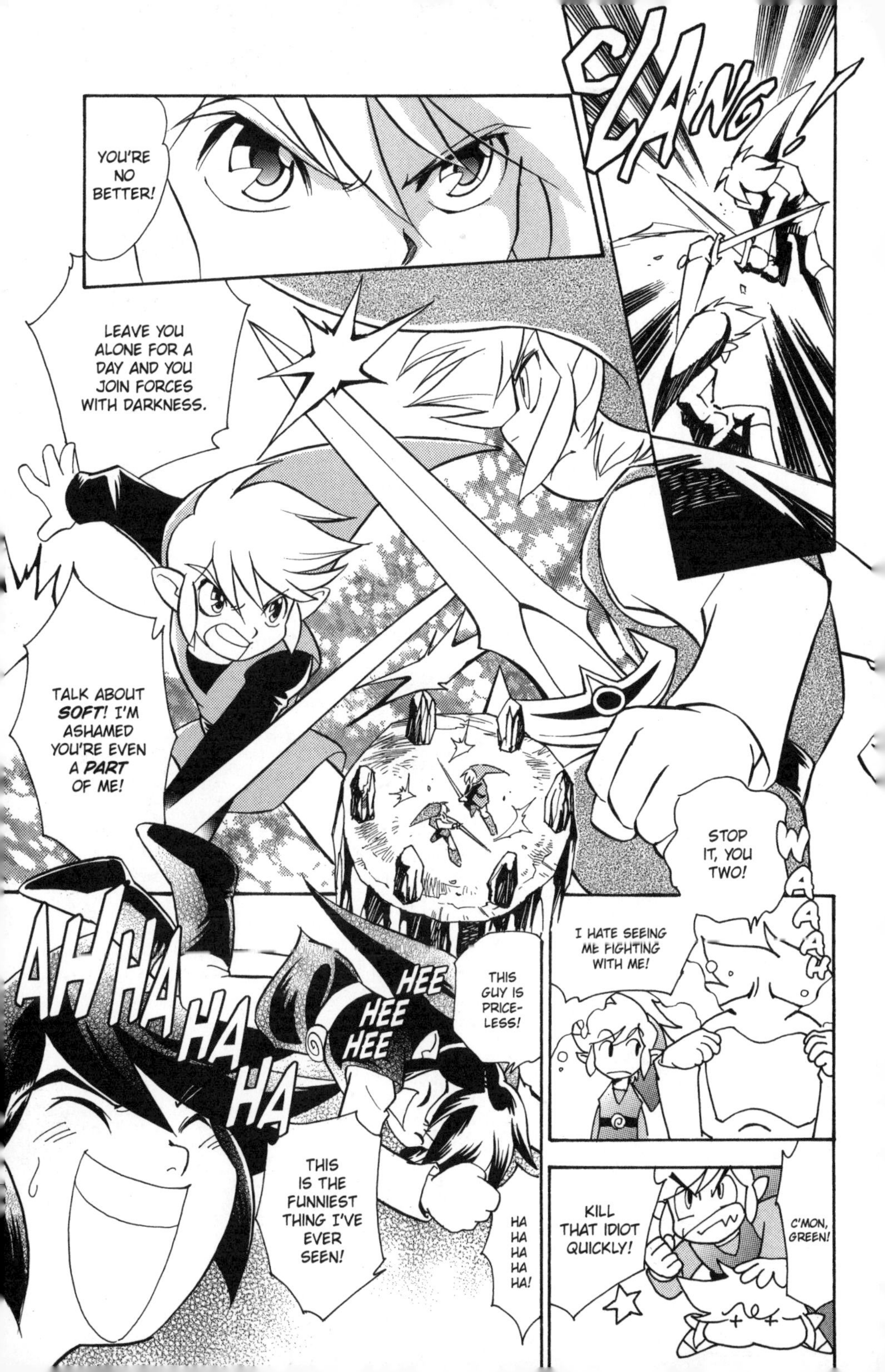
CLANG!!
YOU'RE NO BETTER!
LEAVE YOU ALONE FOR A DAY AND YOU JOIN FORCES WITH DARKNESS.
TALK ABOUT **SOFT**! I'M ASHAMED YOU'RE EVEN A **PART** OF ME!
WAAAH
STOP IT, YOU TWO!
I HATE SEEING ME FIGHTING WITH ME!
C'MON, GREEN!
KILL THAT IDIOT QUICKLY!
THIS GUY IS PRICE-LESS!
HEE HEE HEE
AH HA HA HA HA
THIS IS THE FUNNIEST THING I'VE EVER SEEN!
HA HA HA HA HA!

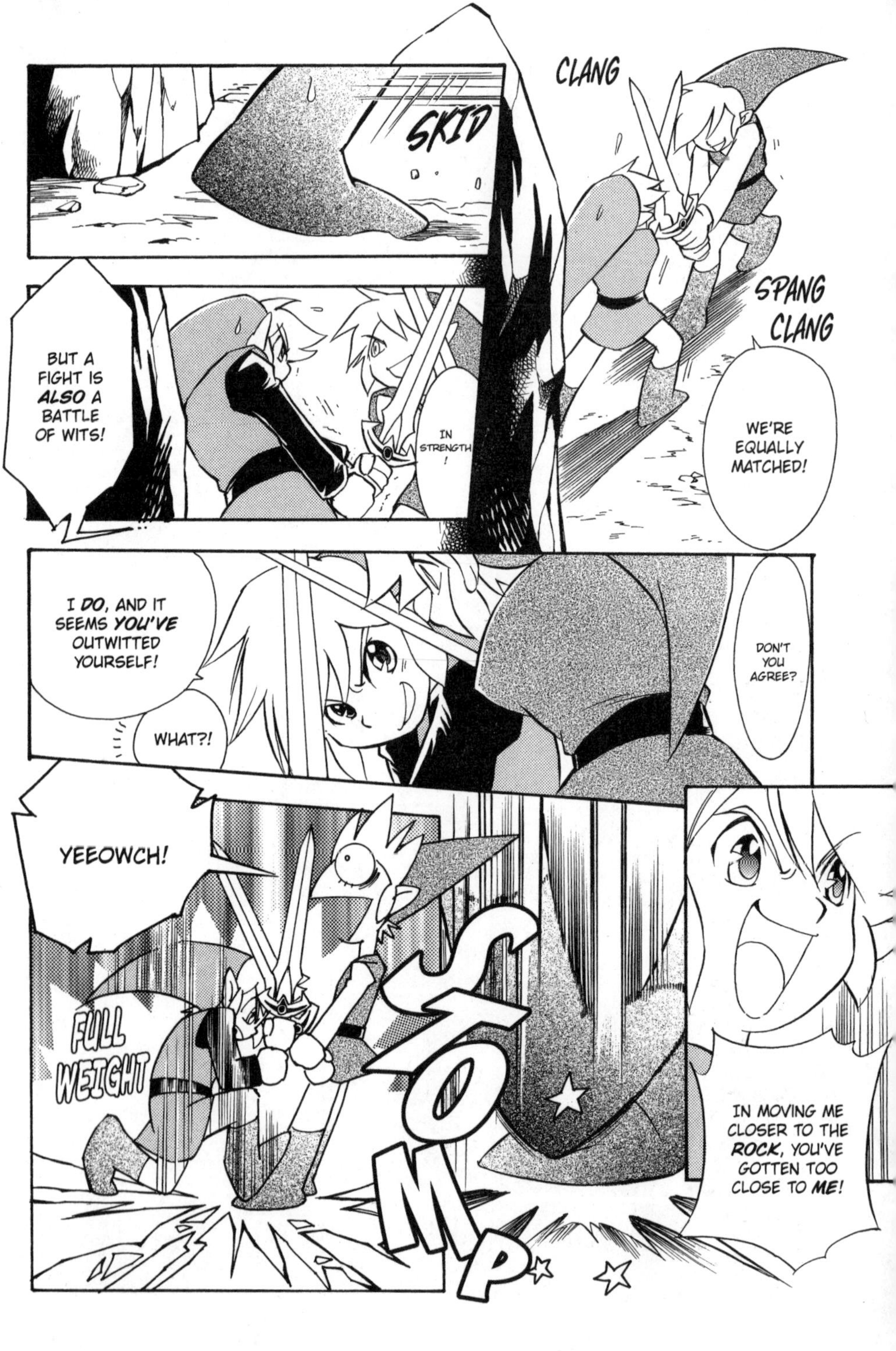
CLANG
SPANG CLANG
WE'RE EQUALLY MATCHED!
SKID
IN STRENGTH!
BUT A FIGHT IS **ALSO** A BATTLE OF WITS!
DON'T YOU AGREE?
I **DO**, AND IT SEEMS **YOU'VE** OUTWITTED YOURSELF!
WHAT?!
IN MOVING ME CLOSER TO THE **ROCK**, YOU'VE GOTTEN TOO CLOSE TO **ME**!
YEEOWCH!
STOMP
FULL WEIGHT

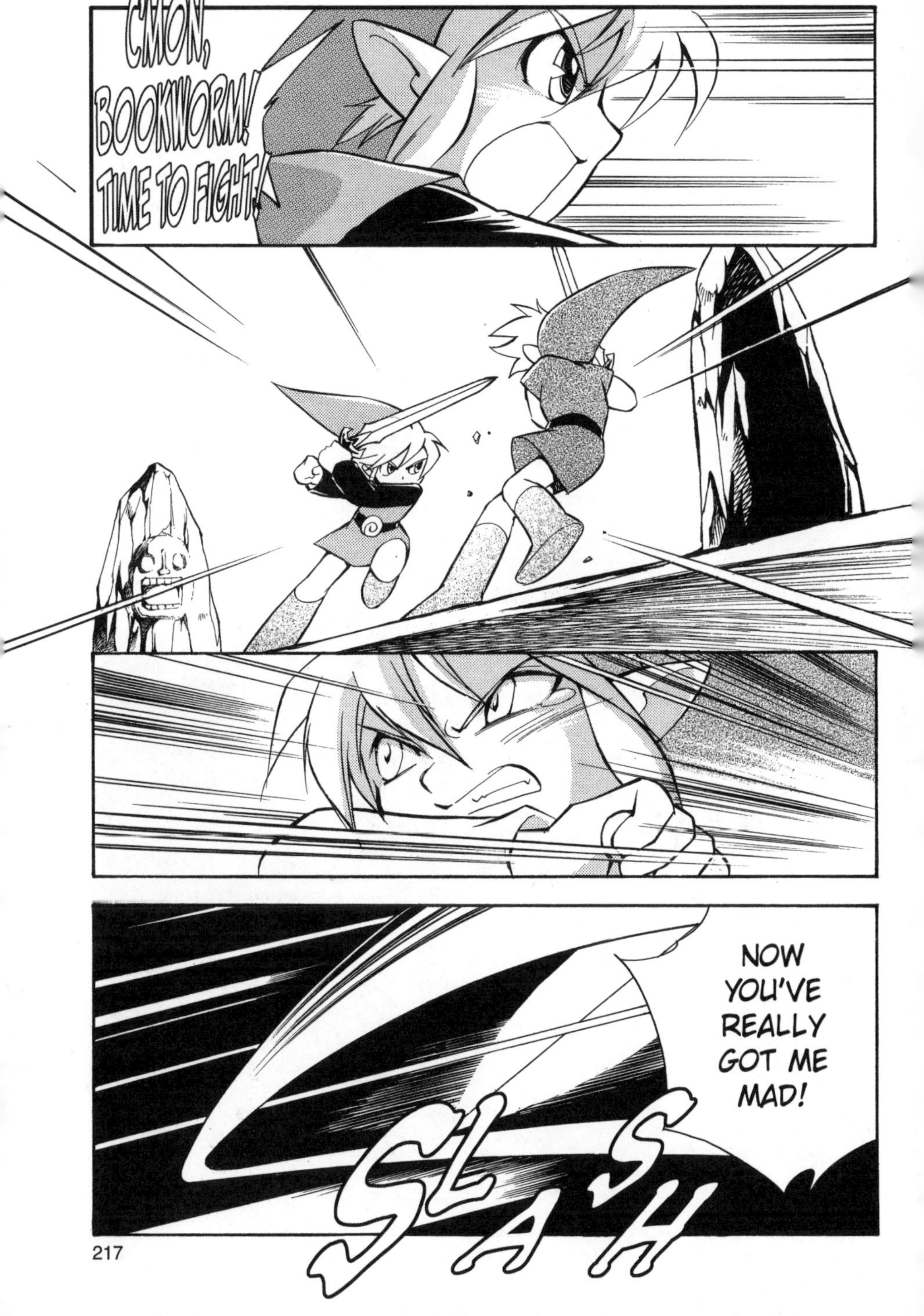
C'MON, BOOKWORM! TIME TO FIGHT!
NOW YOU'VE REALLY GOT ME MAD!
SLASH

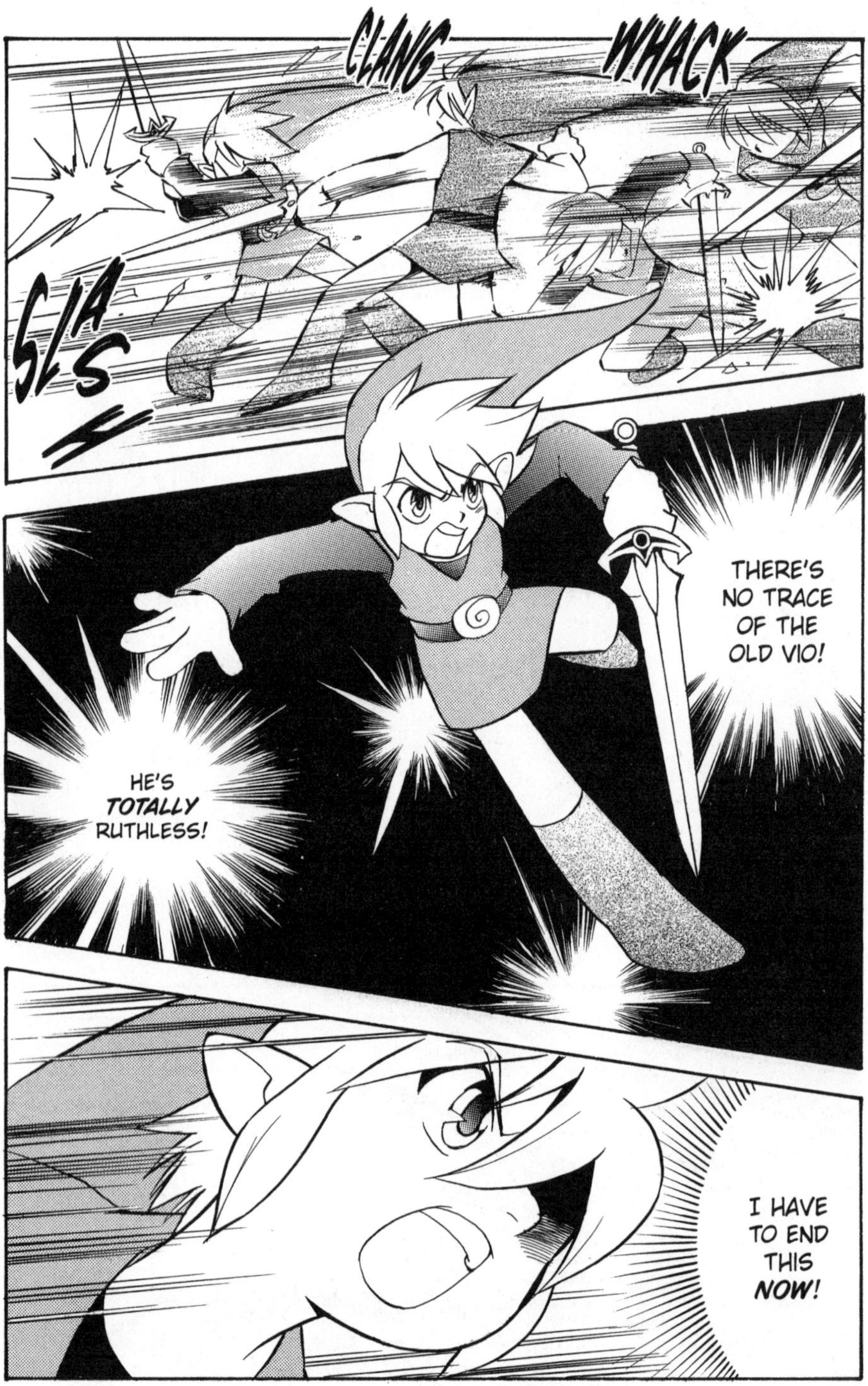
WHACK
CLANG
SLASH
THERE'S NO TRACE OF THE OLD VIO!
HE'S *TOTALLY* RUTHLESS!
I HAVE TO END THIS ***NOW!***

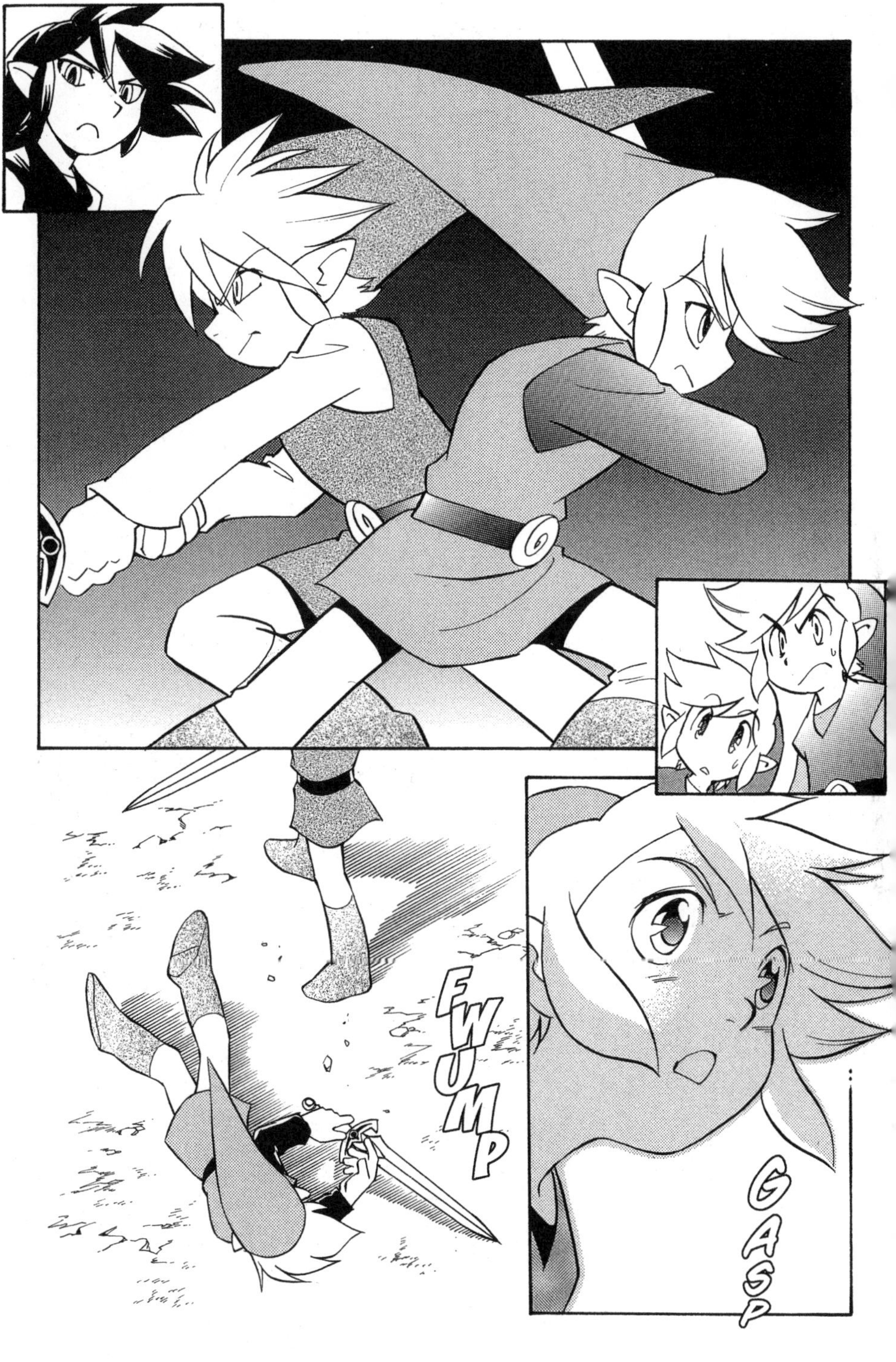
GASP
FWUMP

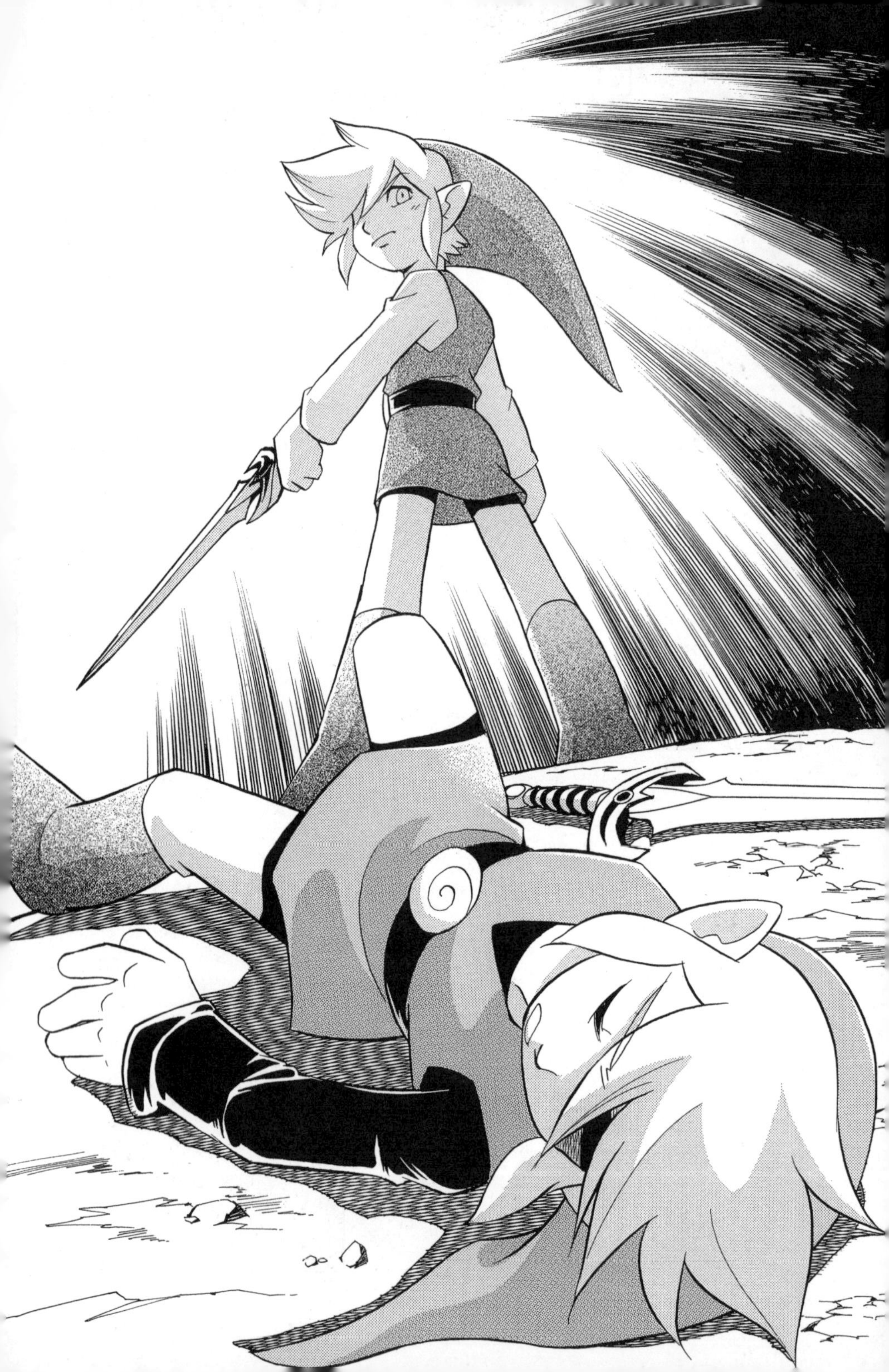

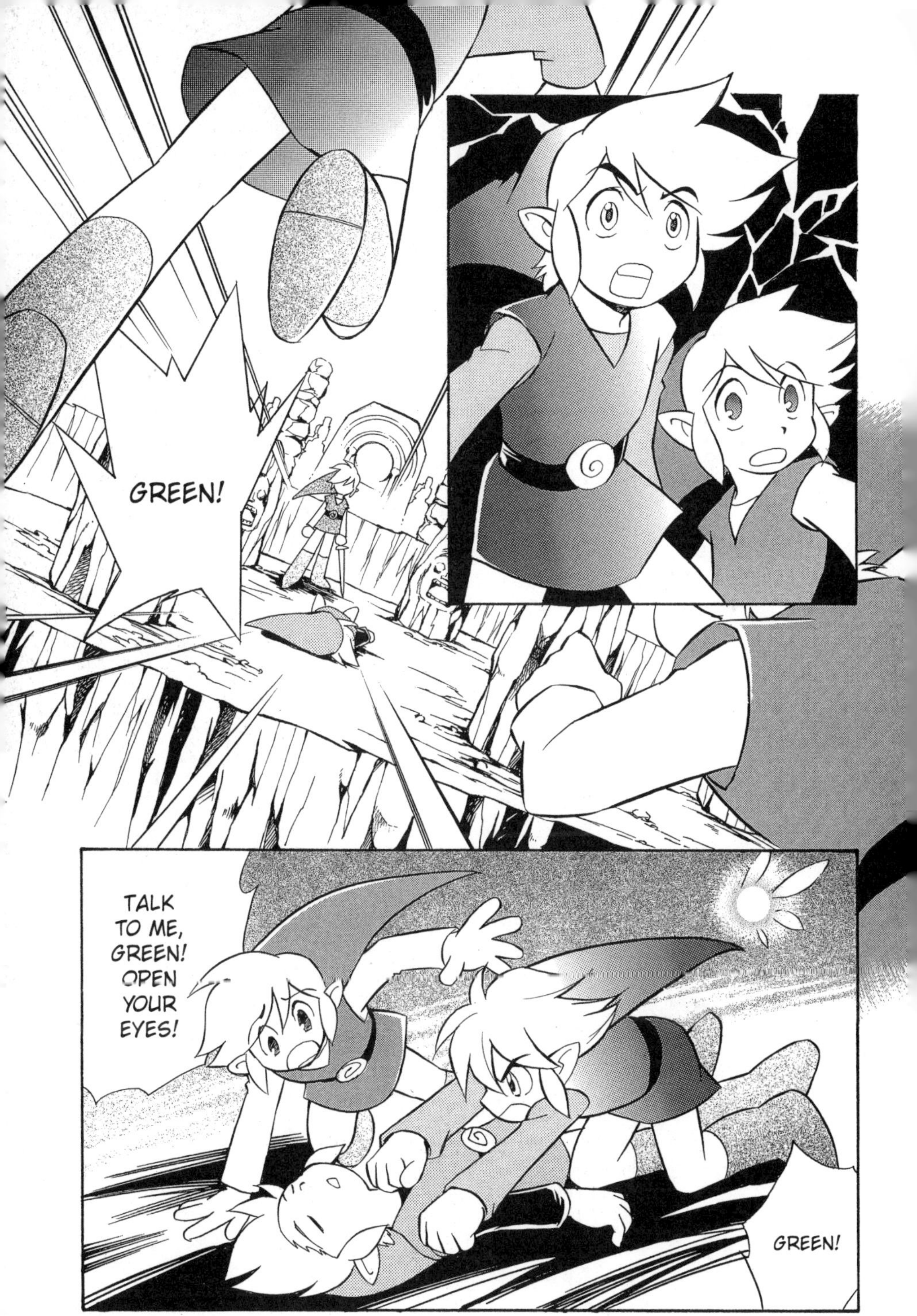
GREEN!
TALK TO ME, GREEN! OPEN YOUR EYES!
GREEN!

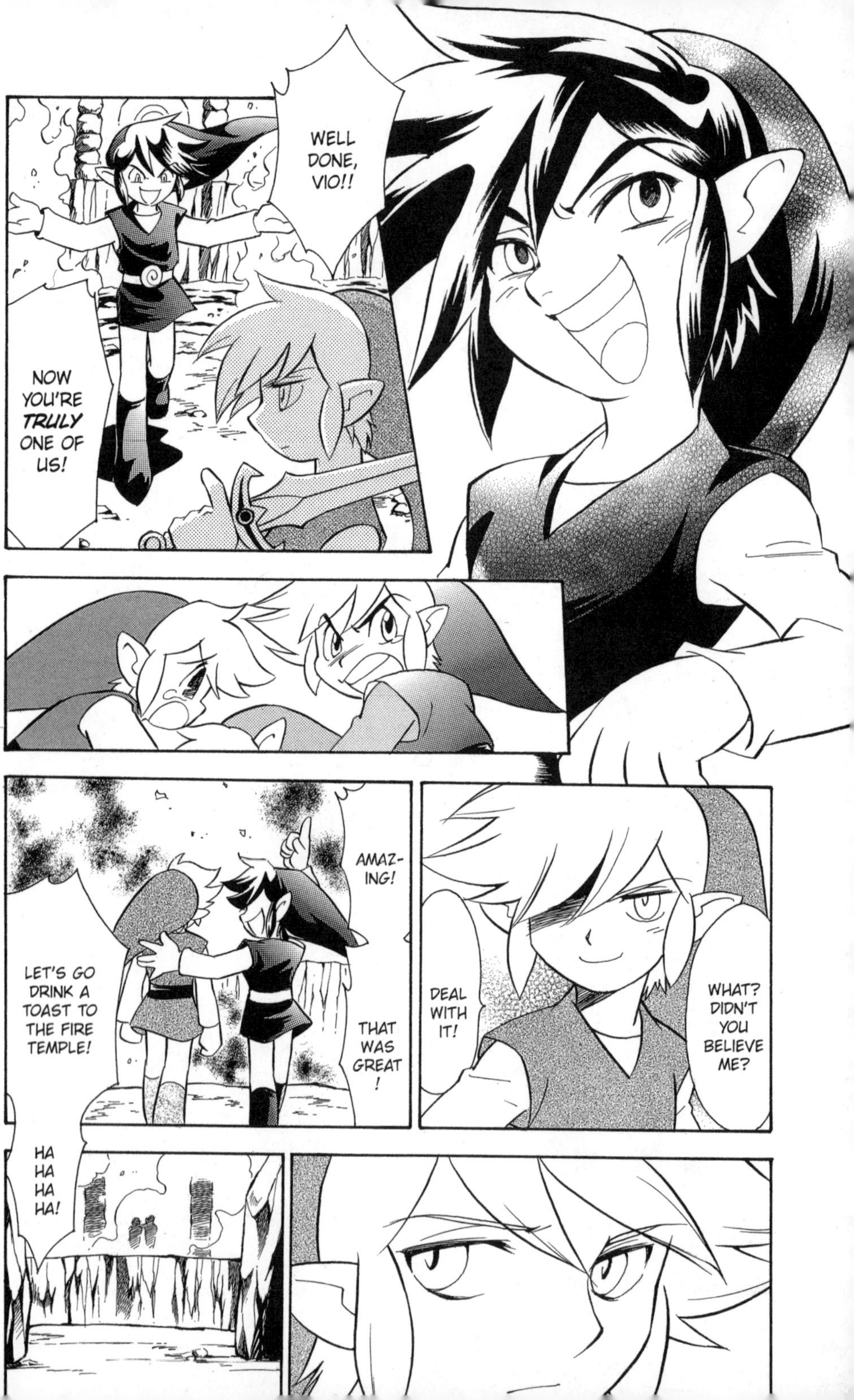
WELL DONE, VIO!!
NOW YOU'RE ***TRULY*** ONE OF US!
WHAT? DIDN'T YOU BELIEVE ME?
DEAL WITH IT!
AMAZ-ING!
THAT WAS GREAT!
LET'S GO DRINK A TOAST TO THE FIRE TEMPLE!
HA HA HA HA!

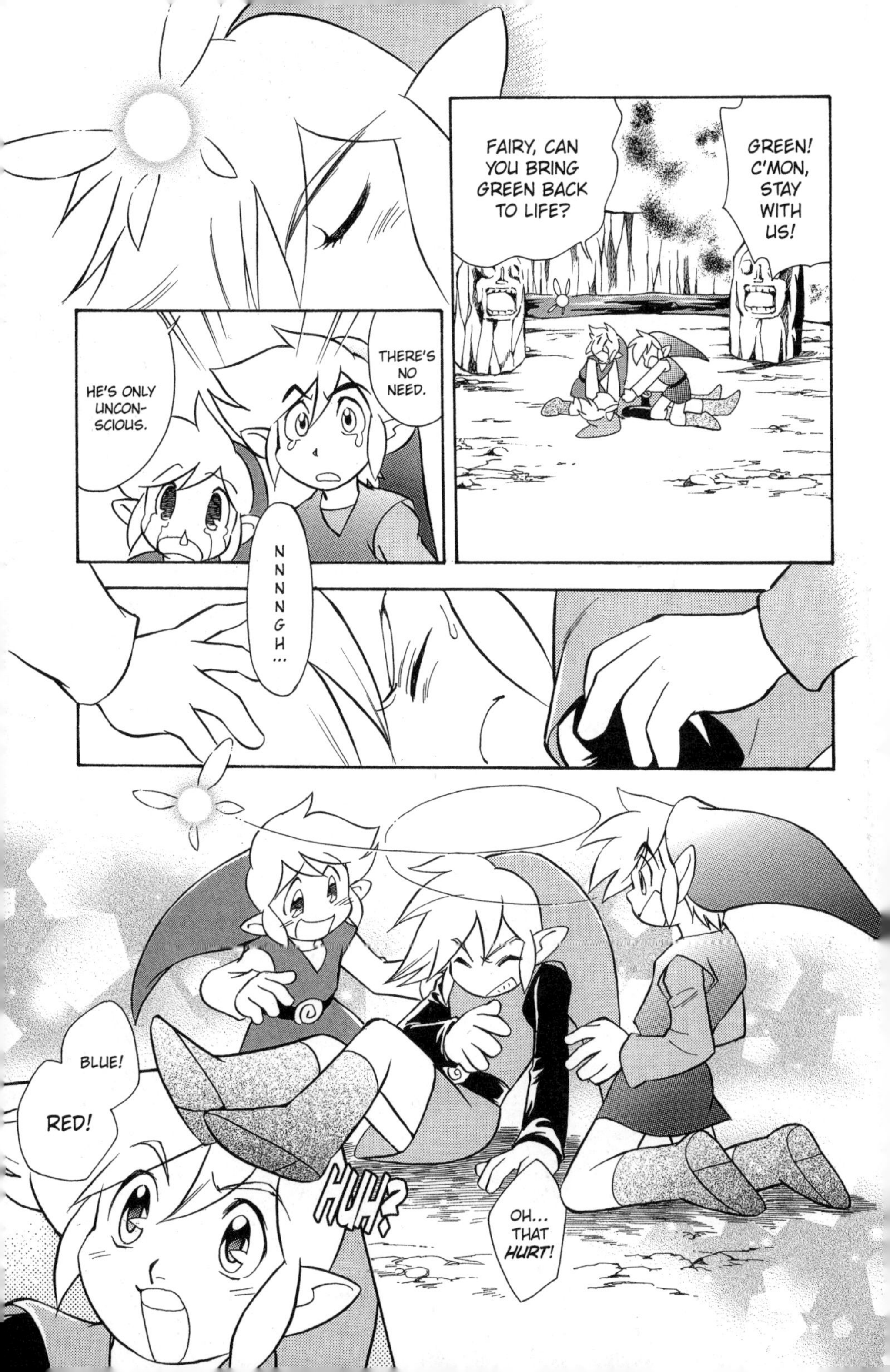
GREEN! C'MON, STAY WITH US!
FAIRY, CAN YOU BRING GREEN BACK TO LIFE?
THERE'S NO NEED.
HE'S ONLY UNCON-SCIOUS.
NNNNGH...
OH... THAT *HURT*!
HUH?
BLUE!
RED!

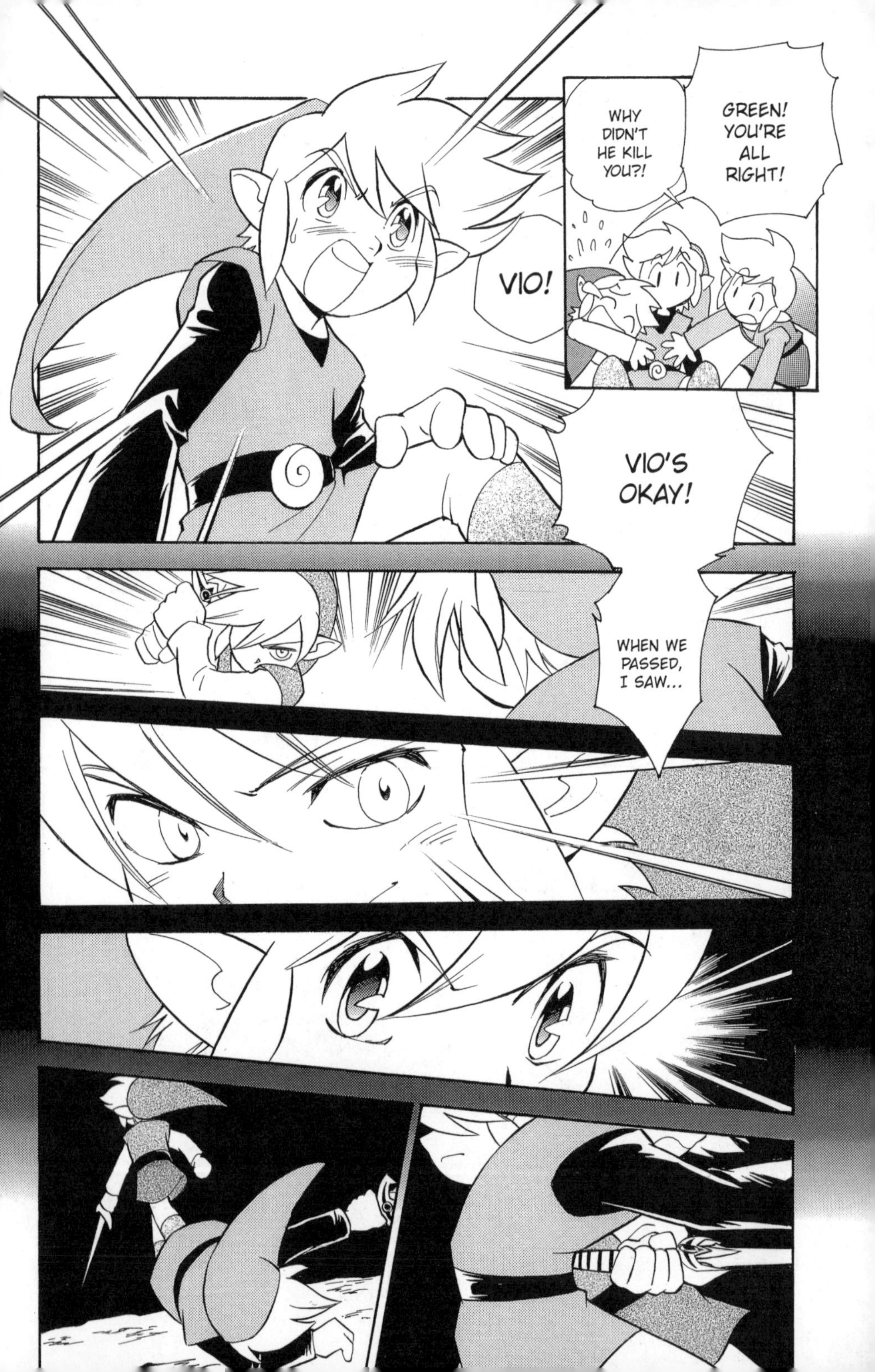
GREEN! YOU'RE ALL RIGHT!
WHY DIDN'T HE KILL YOU?!
VIO!
VIO'S OKAY!
WHEN WE PASSED, I SAW...

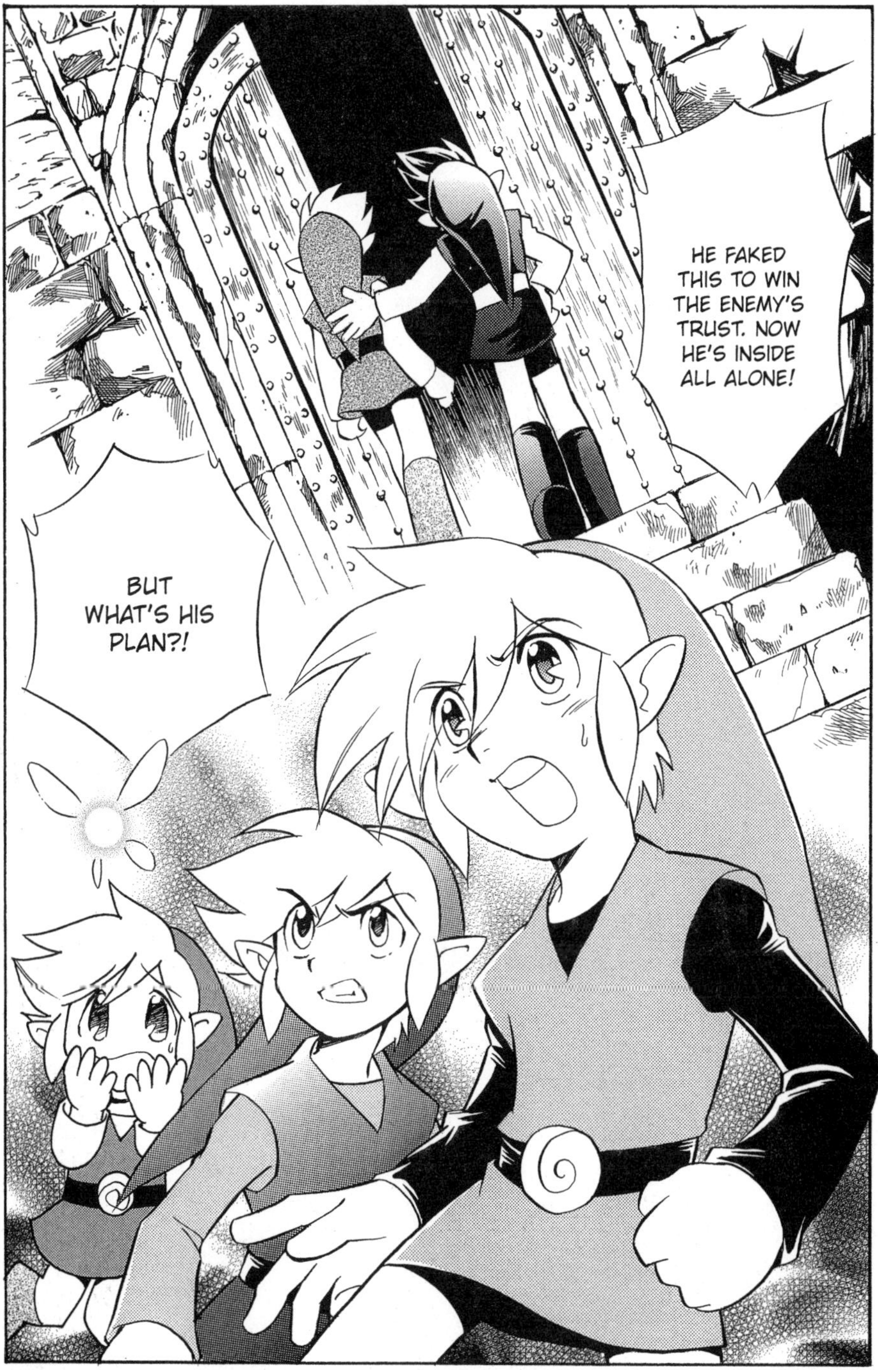
HE FAKED THIS TO WIN THE ENEMY'S TRUST. NOW HE'S INSIDE ALL ALONE!
BUT WHAT'S HIS PLAN?!

CHAPTER 8 Sad Shadow Link

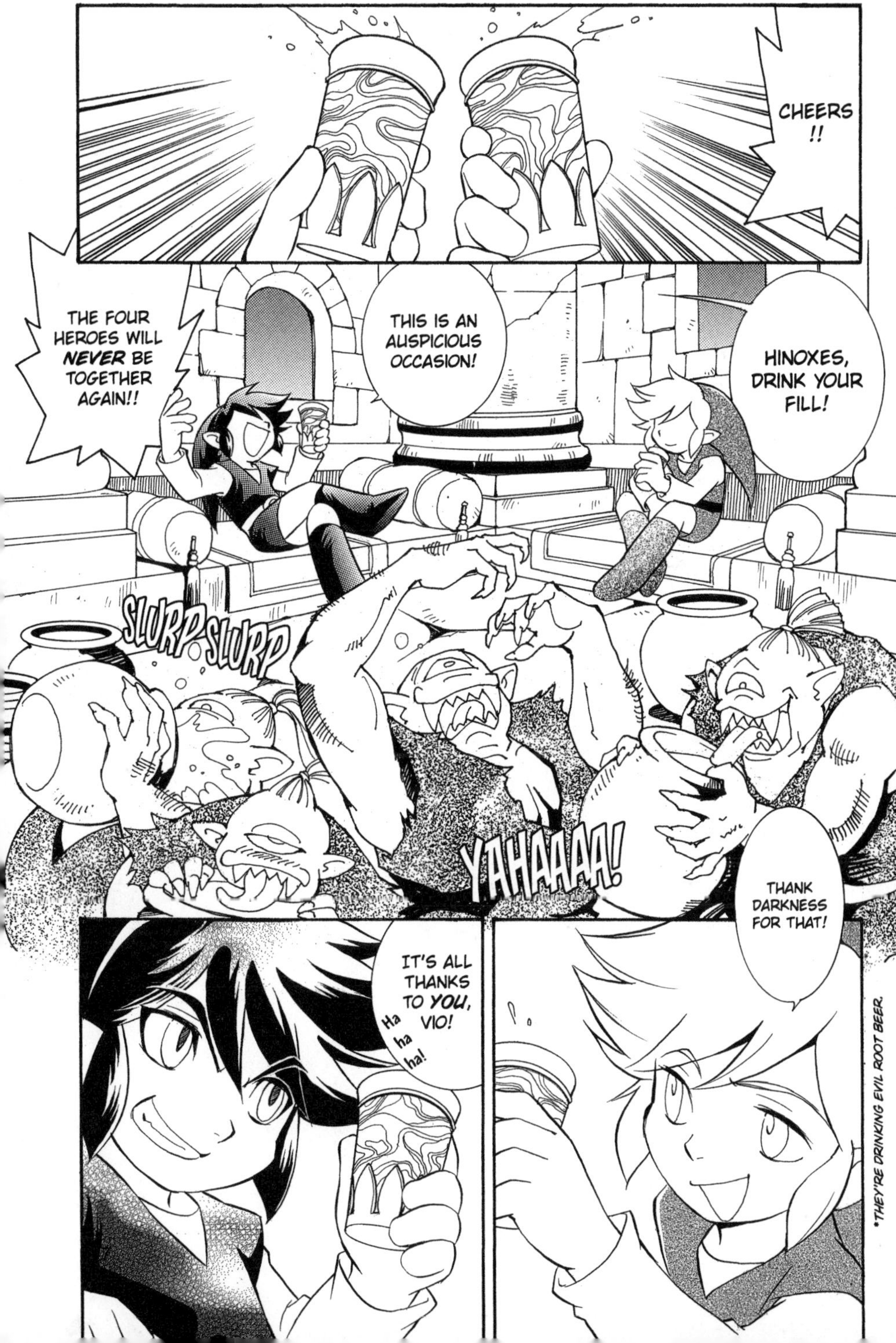
CHEERS!!
HINOXES, DRINK YOUR FILL!
THIS IS AN AUSPICIOUS OCCASION!
THE FOUR HEROES WILL *NEVER* BE TOGETHER AGAIN!!
SLURP SLURP
YAHAAAA!
THANK DARKNESS FOR THAT!
IT'S ALL THANKS TO *YOU*, VIO!
Ha ha ha!

*THEY'RE DRINKING EVIL ROOT BEER.

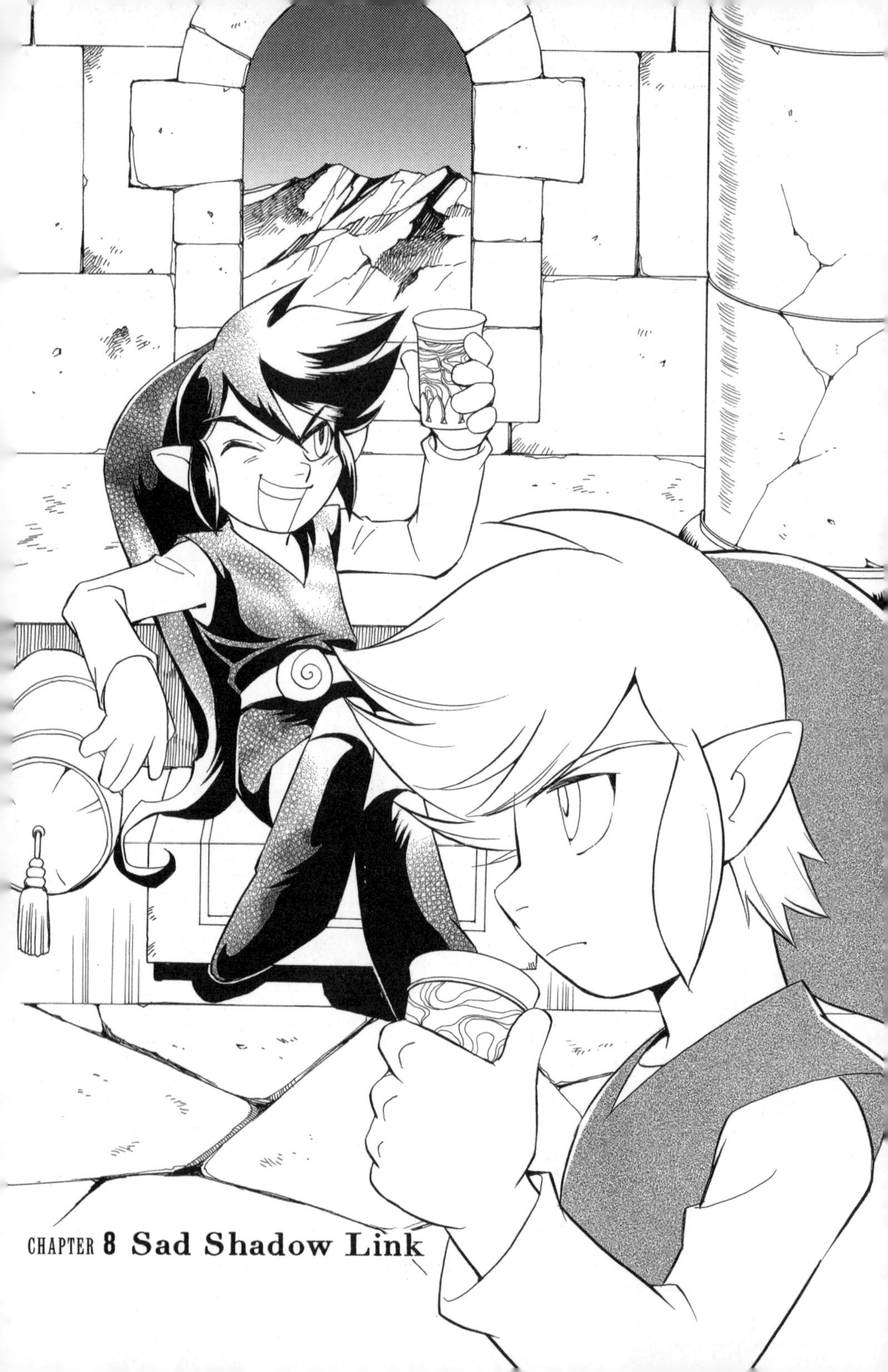

CHAPTER 8 Sad Shadow Link

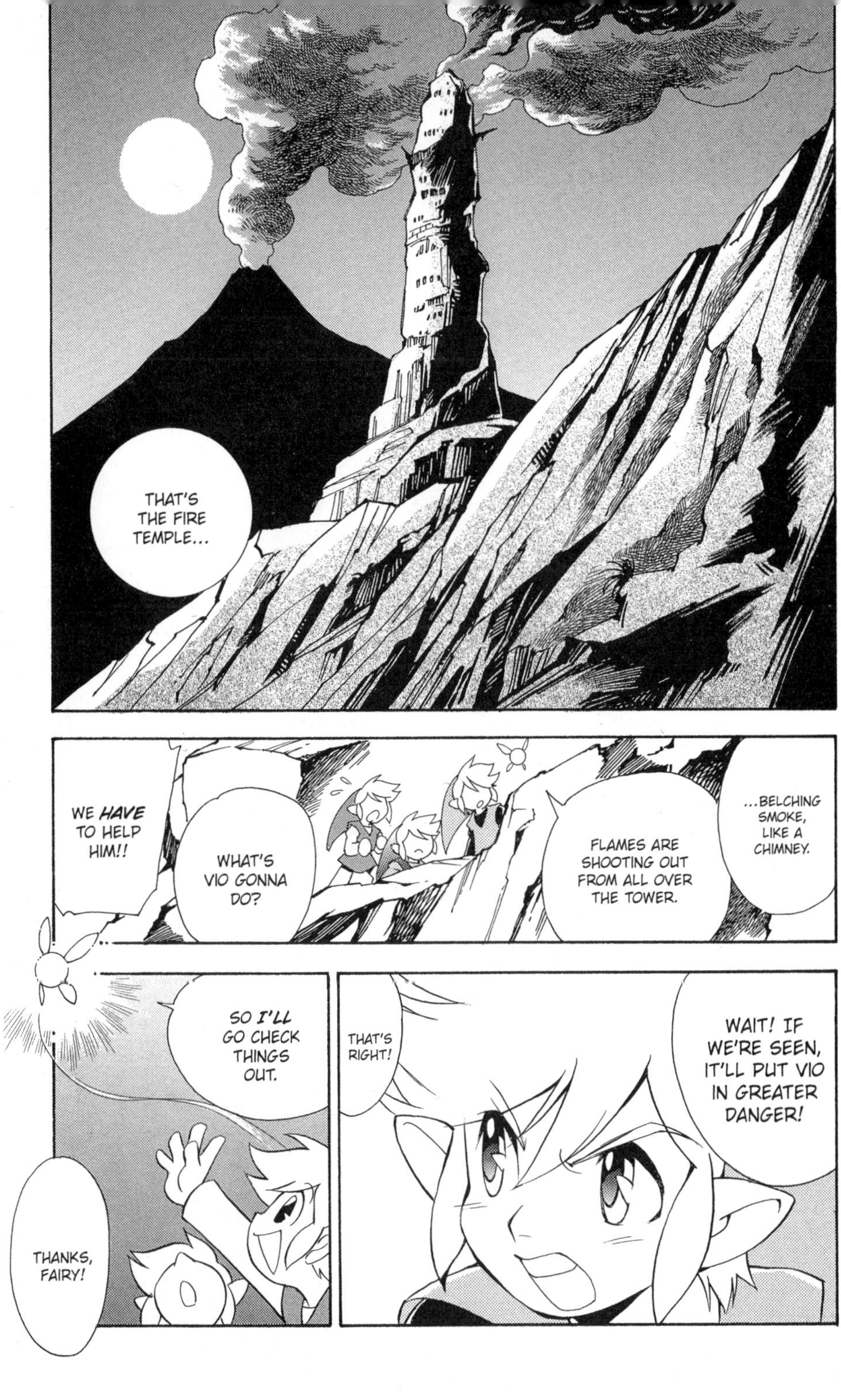
THAT'S THE FIRE TEMPLE...
...BELCHING SMOKE, LIKE A CHIMNEY.
FLAMES ARE SHOOTING OUT FROM ALL OVER THE TOWER.
WHAT'S VIO GONNA DO?
WE *HAVE* TO HELP HIM!!
WAIT! IF WE'RE SEEN, IT'LL PUT VIO IN GREATER DANGER!
THAT'S RIGHT!
SO *I'LL* GO CHECK THINGS OUT.
THANKS, FAIRY!

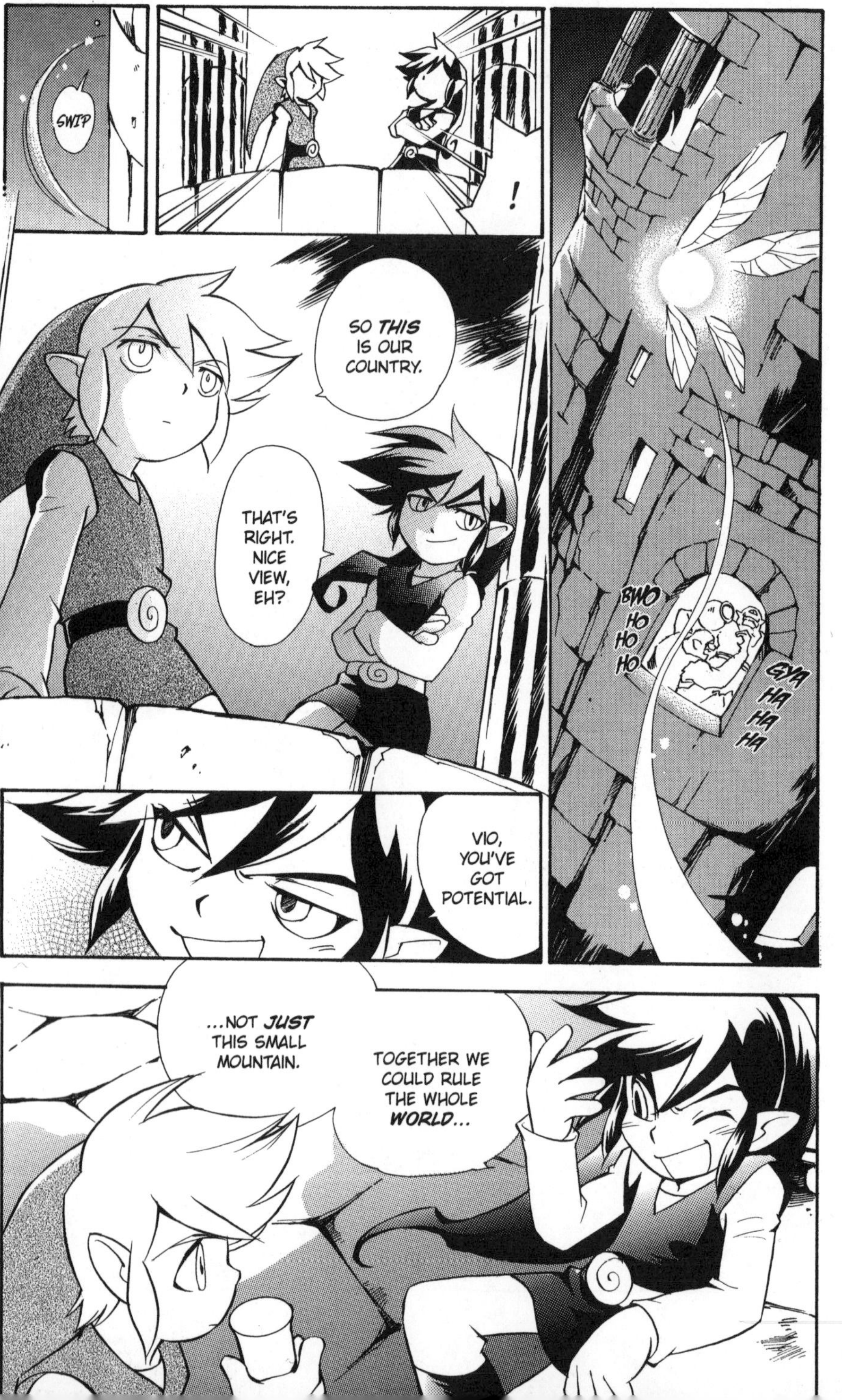
BWO HO HO HO
GYA HA HA HA
!
SWIP
SO *THIS* IS OUR COUNTRY.
THAT'S RIGHT. NICE VIEW, EH?
VIO, YOU'VE GOT POTENTIAL.
...NOT *JUST* THIS SMALL MOUNTAIN.
TOGETHER WE COULD RULE THE WHOLE *WORLD*...

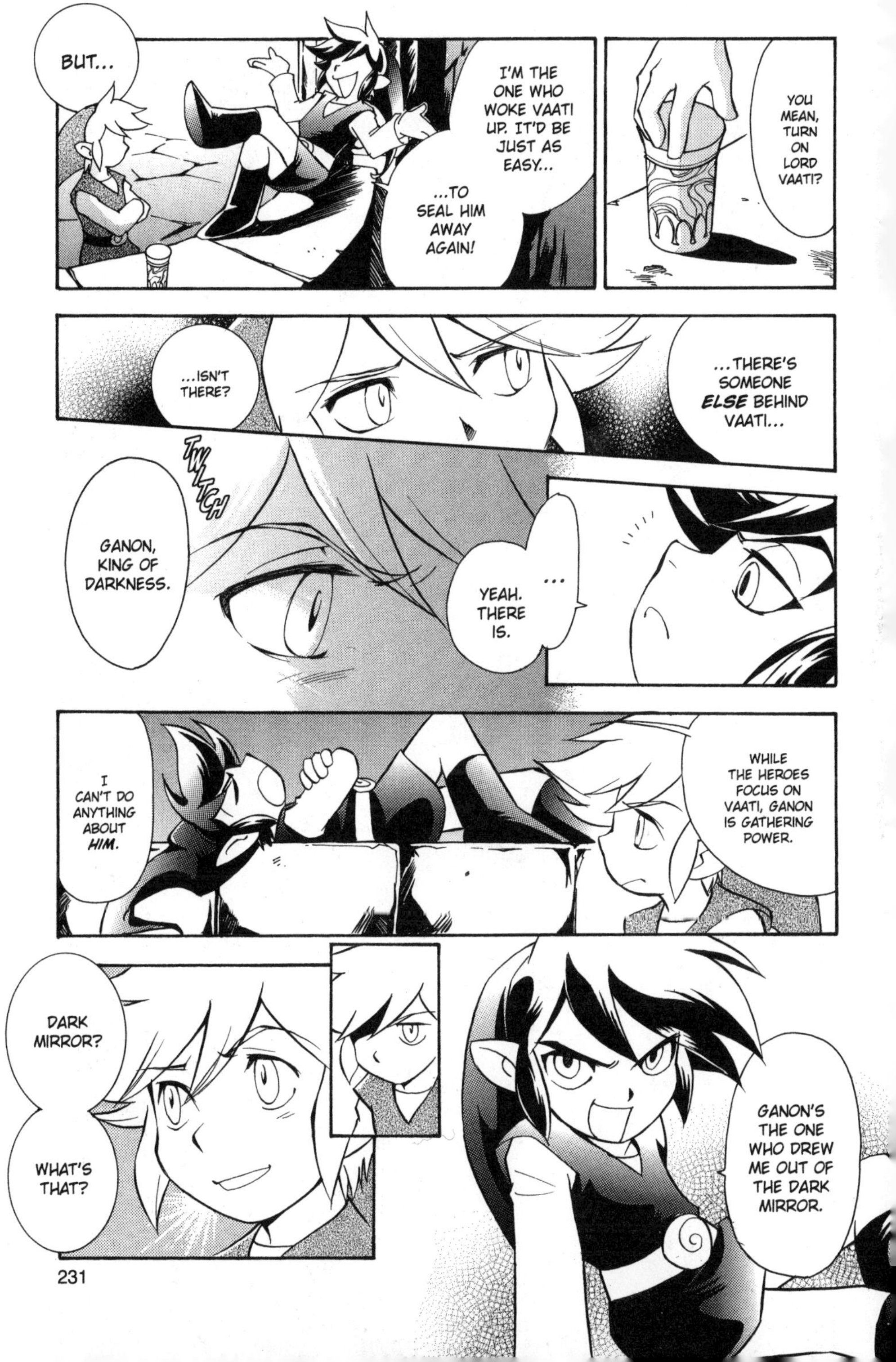
YOU MEAN, TURN ON LORD VAATI?
I'M THE ONE WHO WOKE VAATI UP. IT'D BE JUST AS EASY...
...TO SEAL HIM AWAY AGAIN!
BUT...
...THERE'S SOMEONE ELSE BEHIND VAATI...
...ISN'T THERE?
...
YEAH. THERE IS.
TWITCH
GANON, KING OF DARKNESS.
WHILE THE HEROES FOCUS ON VAATI, GANON IS GATHERING POWER.
I CAN'T DO ANYTHING ABOUT HIM.
GANON'S THE ONE WHO DREW ME OUT OF THE DARK MIRROR.
DARK MIRROR?
WHAT'S THAT?

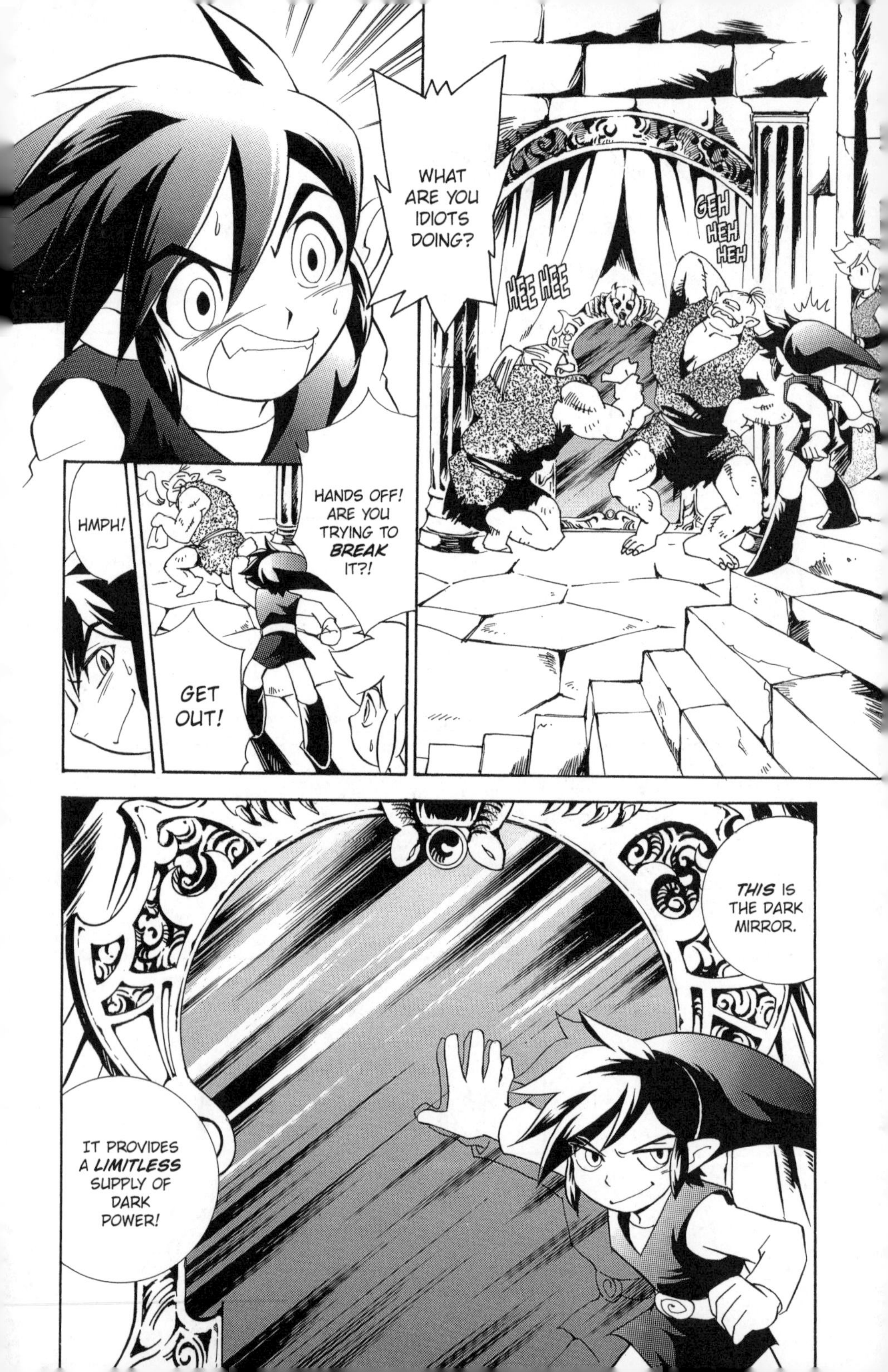
GEH HEH HEH
HEE HEE
WHAT ARE YOU IDIOTS DOING?
HANDS OFF! ARE YOU TRYING TO **BREAK** IT?!
GET OUT!
HMPH!
THIS IS THE DARK MIRROR.
IT PROVIDES A ***LIMITLESS*** SUPPLY OF DARK POWER!

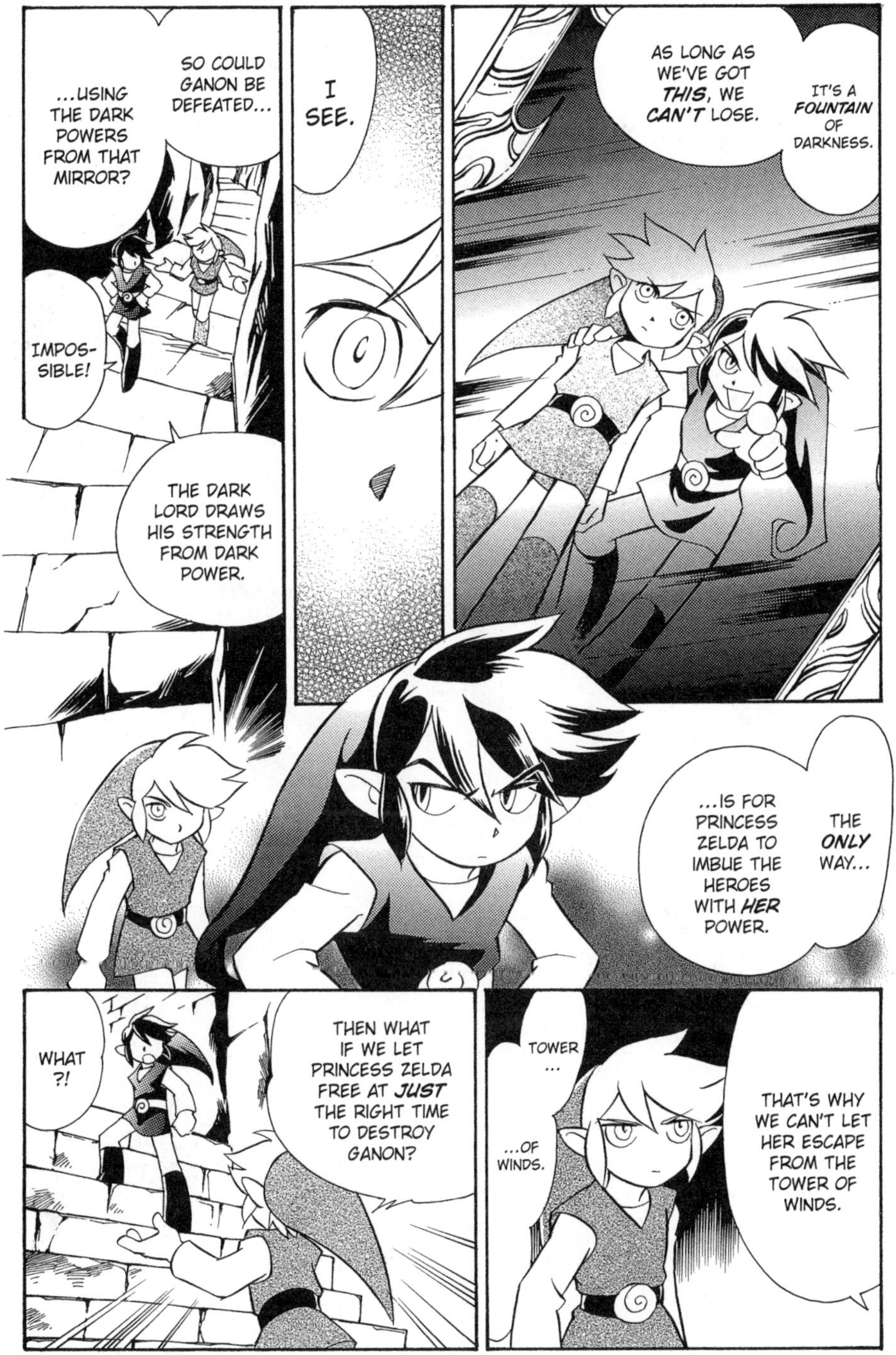
IT'S A *FOUNTAIN* OF DARKNESS.
AS LONG AS WE'VE GOT ***THIS***, WE ***CAN'T*** LOSE.
I SEE.
SO COULD GANON BE DEFEATED...
...USING THE DARK POWERS FROM THAT MIRROR?
IMPOSSIBLE!
THE DARK LORD DRAWS HIS STRENGTH FROM DARK POWER.
THE ***ONLY*** WAY...
...IS FOR PRINCESS ZELDA TO IMBUE THE HEROES WITH ***HER*** POWER.
THAT'S WHY WE CAN'T LET HER ESCAPE FROM THE TOWER OF WINDS.
TOWER ...
...OF WINDS.
THEN WHAT IF WE LET PRINCESS ZELDA FREE AT ***JUST*** THE RIGHT TIME TO DESTROY GANON?
WHAT ?!

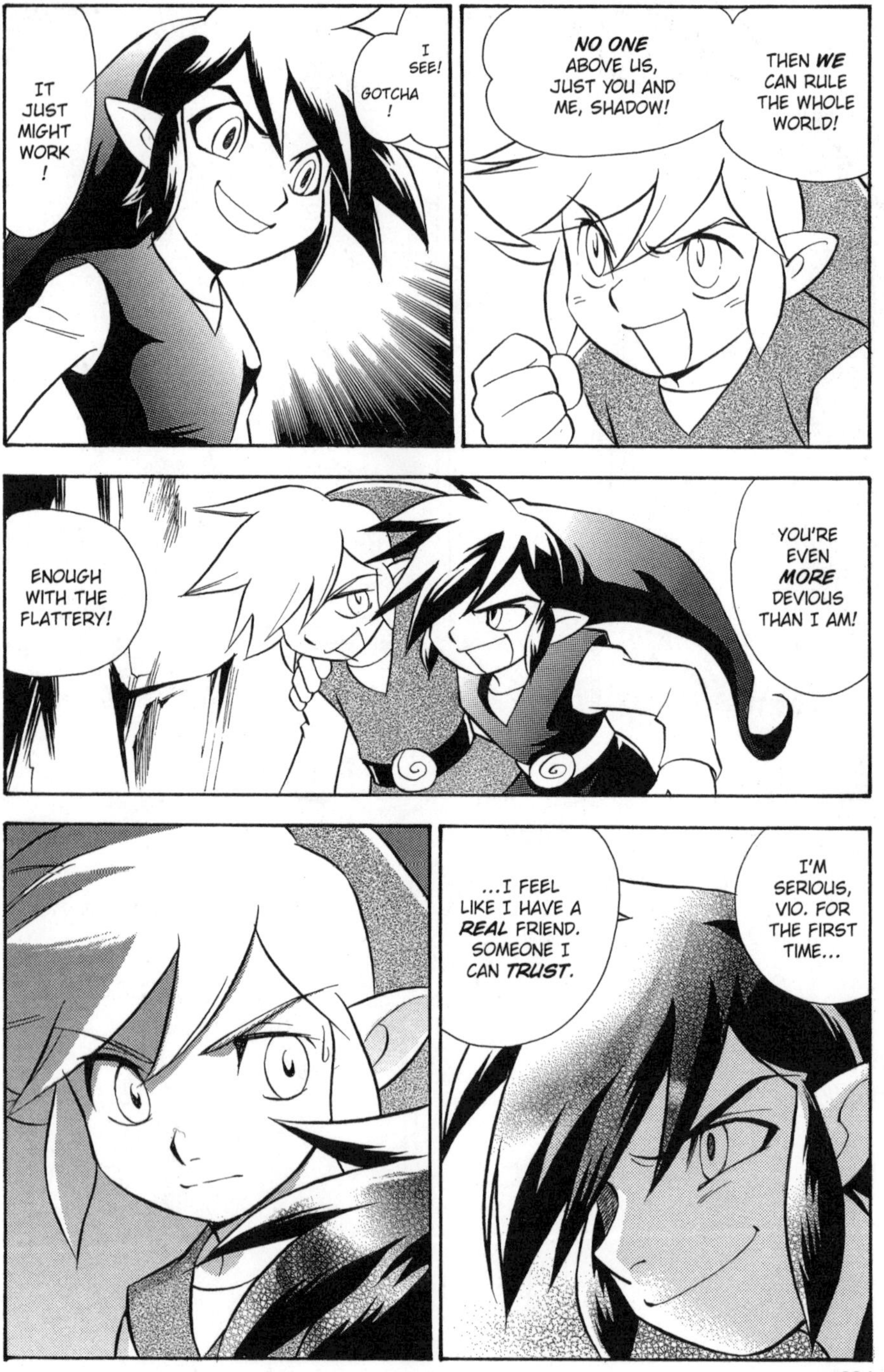
THEN **WE** CAN RULE THE WHOLE WORLD!
NO ONE ABOVE US, JUST YOU AND ME, SHADOW!
I SEE! GOTCHA!
IT JUST MIGHT WORK!
YOU'RE EVEN **MORE** DEVIOUS THAN I AM!
ENOUGH WITH THE FLATTERY!
I'M SERIOUS, VIO. FOR THE FIRST TIME...
...I FEEL LIKE I HAVE A **REAL** FRIEND. SOMEONE I CAN **TRUST**.

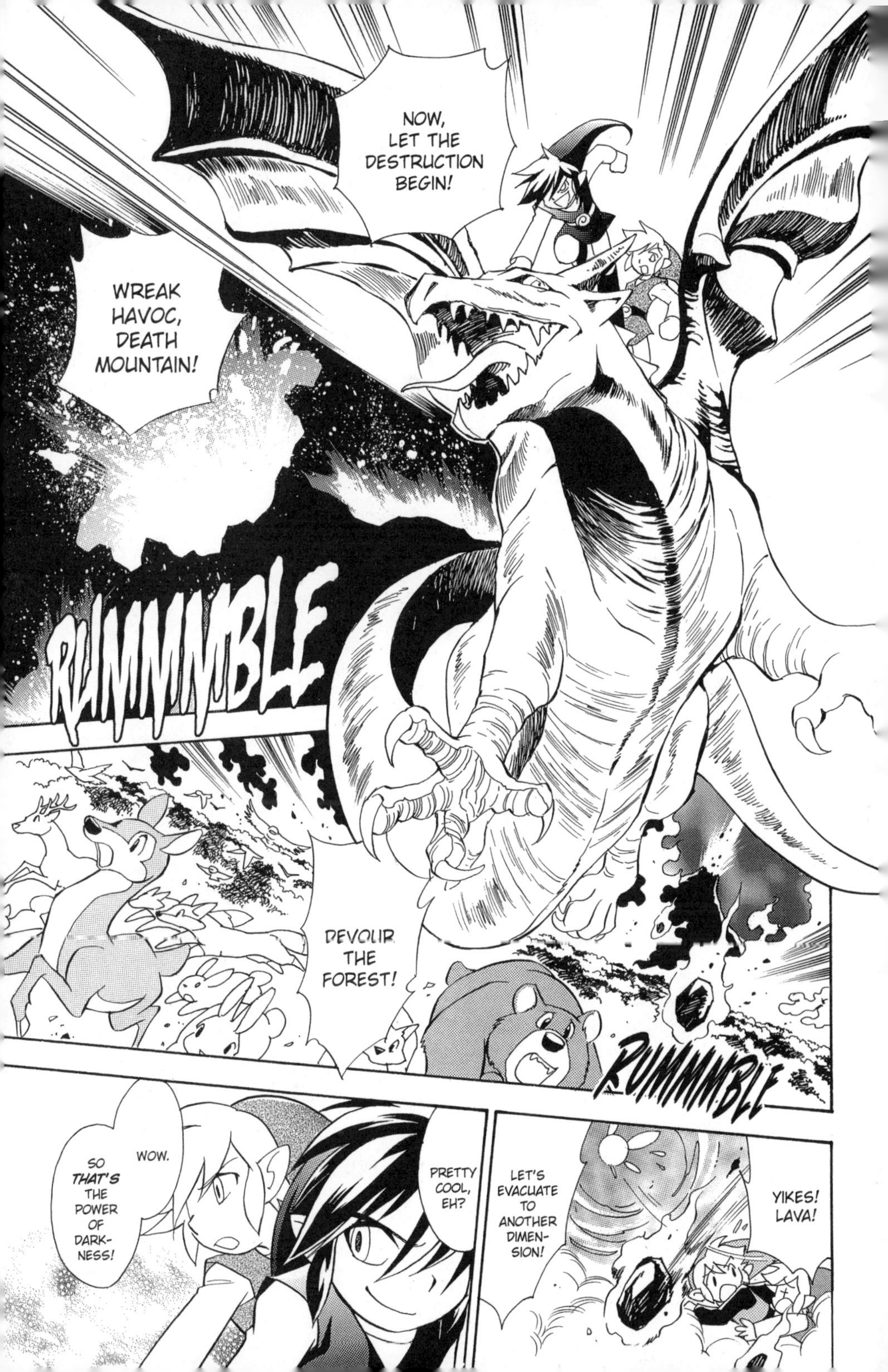
NOW, LET THE DESTRUCTION BEGIN!
WREAK HAVOC, DEATH MOUNTAIN!
RUMMMMBLE
DEVOUR THE FOREST!
RUMMMBLE
YIKES! LAVA!
LET'S EVACUATE TO ANOTHER DIMENSION!
PRETTY COOL, EH?
WOW.
SO ***THAT'S*** THE POWER OF DARKNESS!

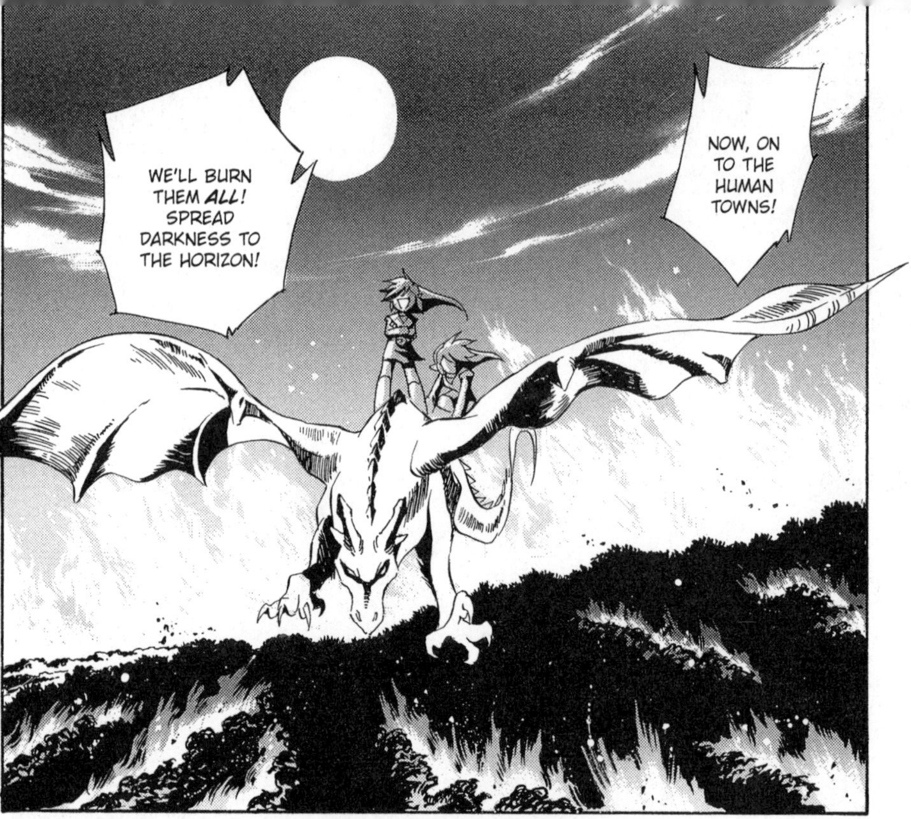
NOW, ON TO THE HUMAN TOWNS!
WE'LL BURN THEM ALL! SPREAD DARKNESS TO THE HORIZON!

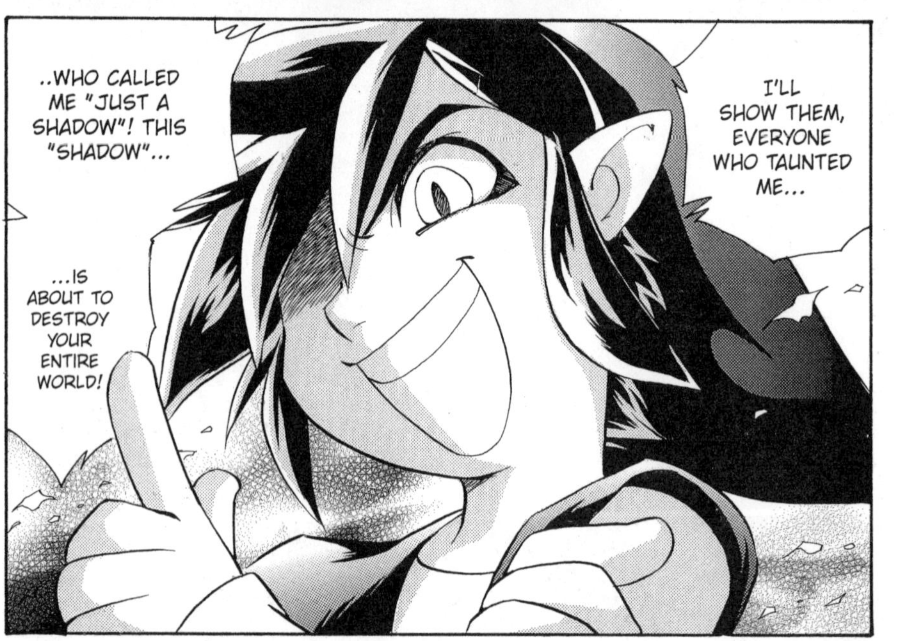
I'LL SHOW THEM, EVERYONE WHO TAUNTED ME...
..WHO CALLED ME "JUST A SHADOW"! THIS "SHADOW"...
...IS ABOUT TO DESTROY YOUR ENTIRE WORLD!

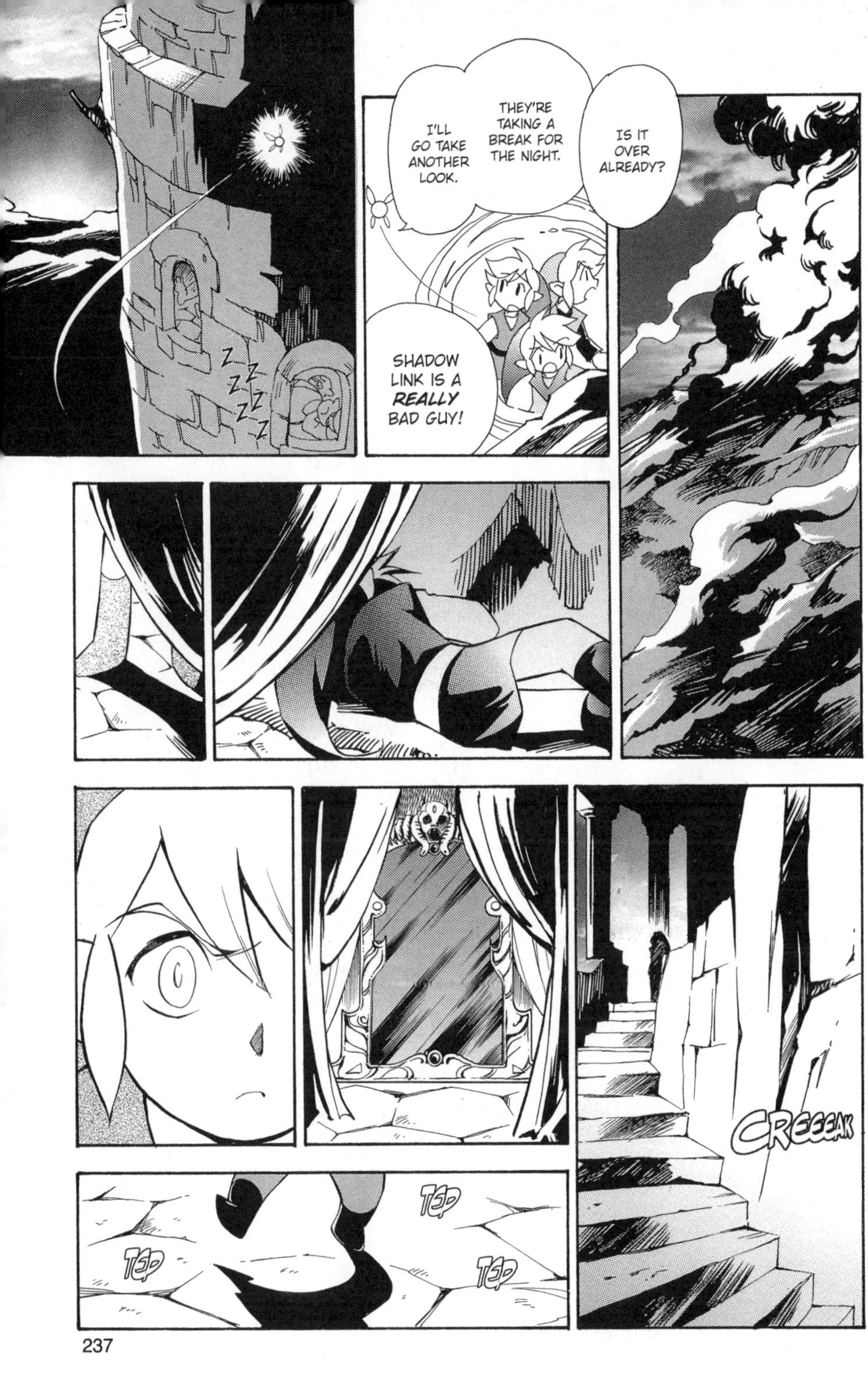
IS IT OVER ALREADY?
THEY'RE TAKING A BREAK FOR THE NIGHT.
I'LL GO TAKE ANOTHER LOOK.
SHADOW LINK IS A **REALLY** BAD GUY!
CREEEAK
TSP
TSP
TSP

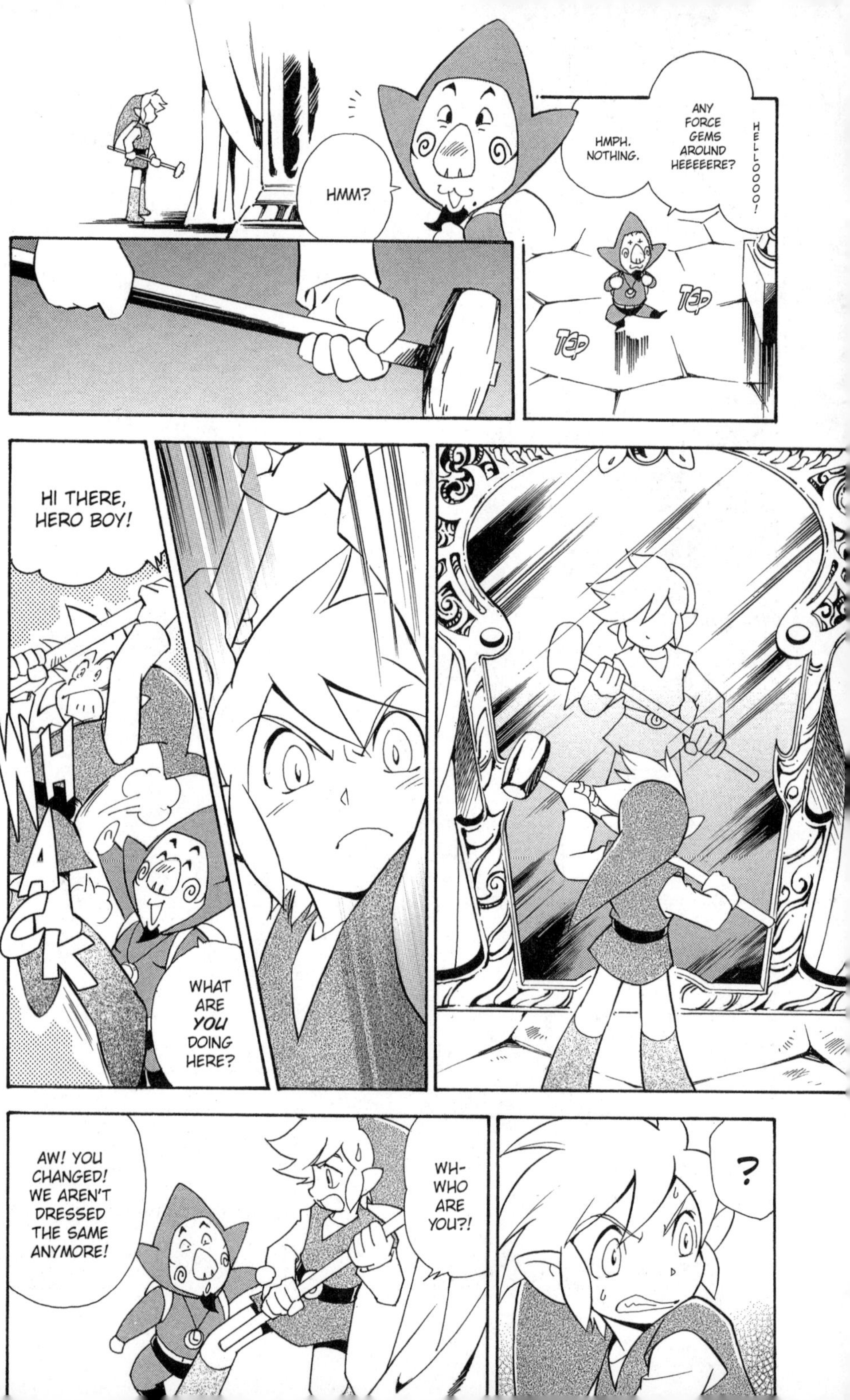
HELLOOOO!
ANY FORCE GEMS AROUND HEEEEERE?
HMPH. NOTHING.
TAP
TAP
HMM?
HI THERE, HERO BOY!
WHACK
WHAT ARE *YOU* DOING HERE?
?
WH- WHO ARE YOU?!
AW! YOU CHANGED! WE AREN'T DRESSED THE SAME ANYMORE!

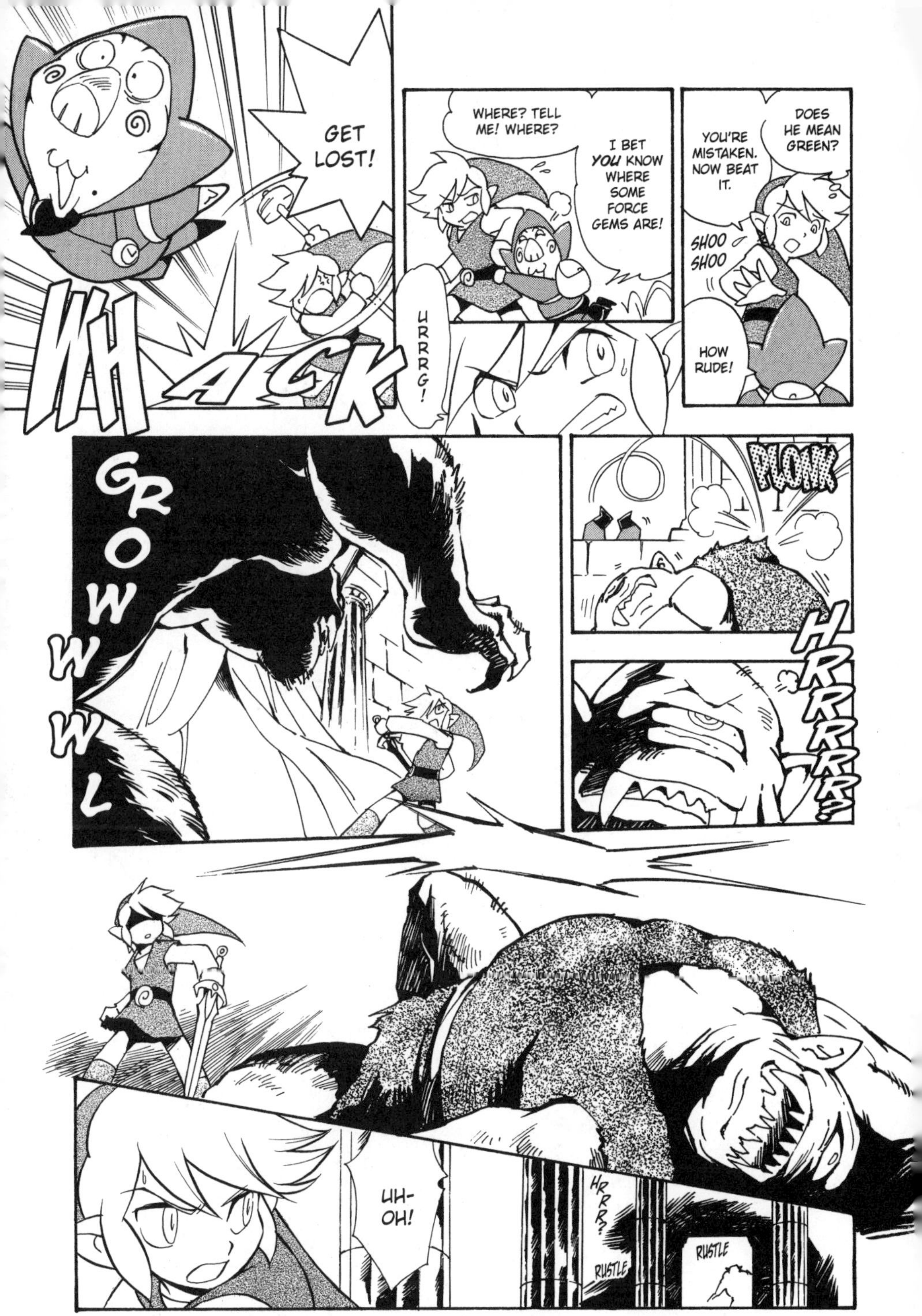
DOES HE MEAN GREEN?
YOU'RE MISTAKEN. NOW BEAT IT.
SHOO SHOO
HOW RUDE!
WHERE? TELL ME! WHERE?
I BET YOU KNOW WHERE SOME FORCE GEMS ARE!
GET LOST!
WHACK
URRRG!
PLONK
HRRRRR?
GROWWWL
HRRR?
RUSTLE
RUSTLE
UH-OH!

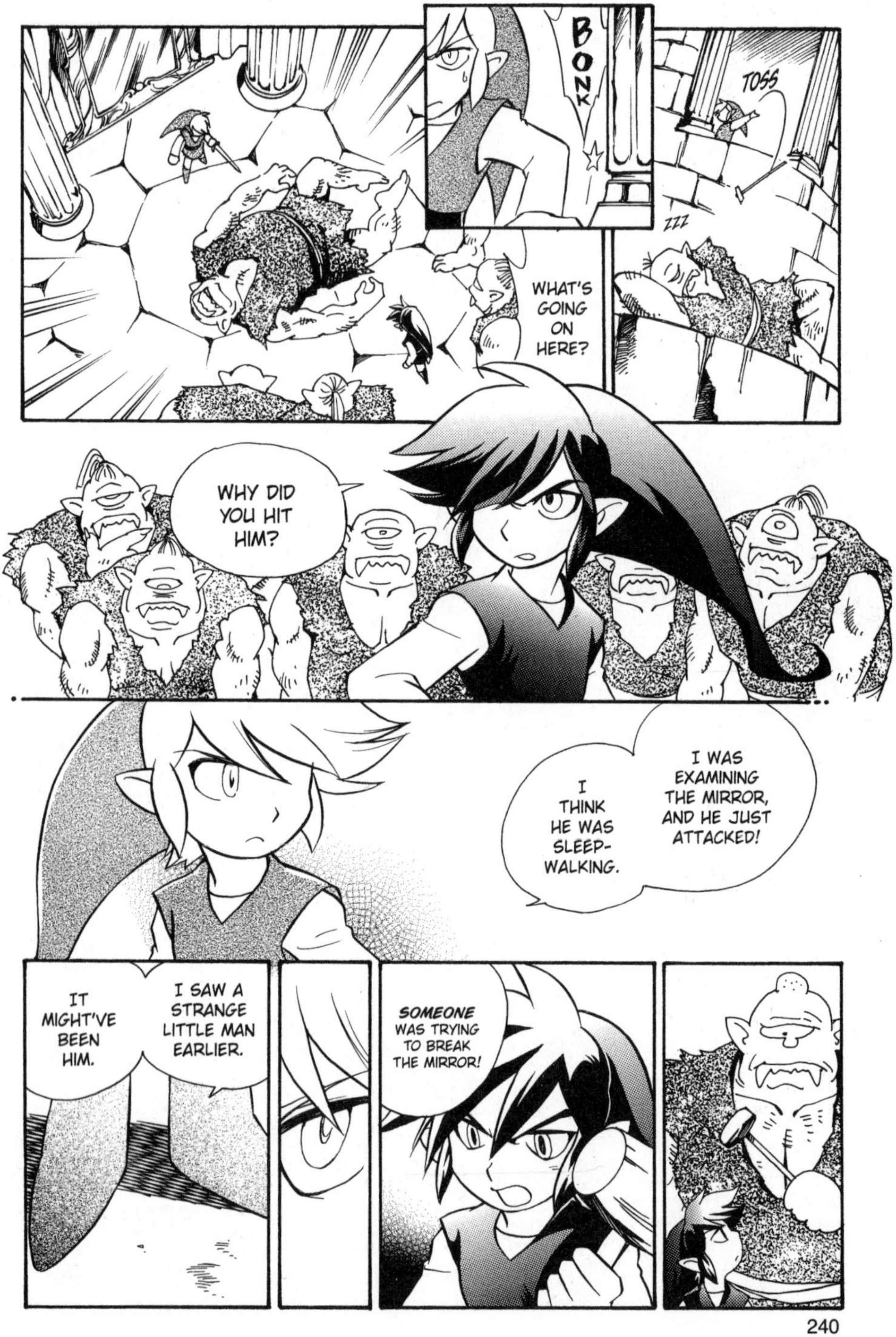
TOSS
ZZZ
BONK
WHAT'S GOING ON HERE?
WHY DID YOU HIT HIM?
I WAS EXAMINING THE MIRROR, AND HE JUST ATTACKED!
I THINK HE WAS SLEEP-WALKING.
SOMEONE WAS TRYING TO BREAK THE MIRROR!
I SAW A STRANGE LITTLE MAN EARLIER.
IT MIGHT'VE BEEN HIM.

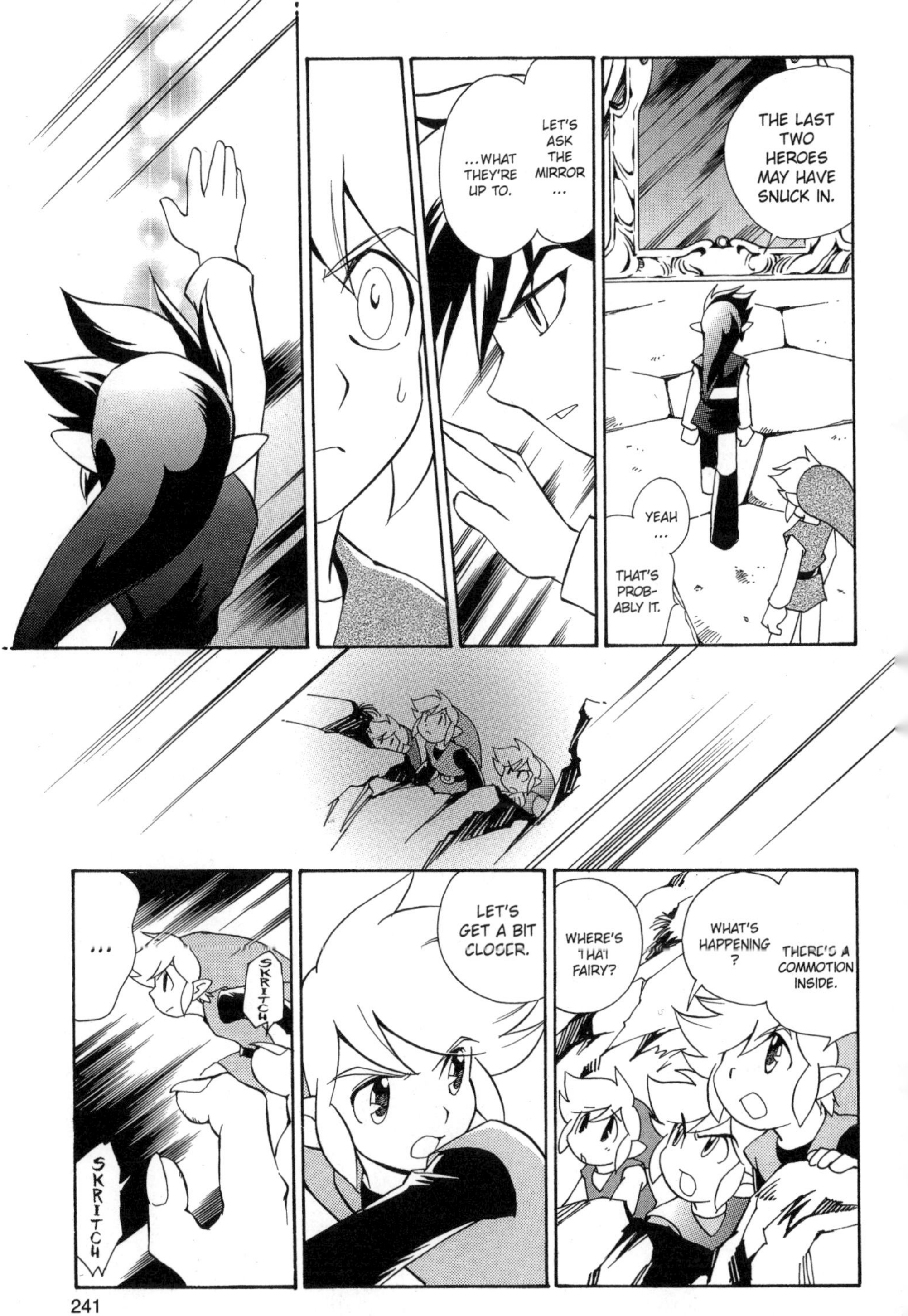
THE LAST TWO HEROES MAY HAVE SNUCK IN.
YEAH... THAT'S PROBABLY IT.
LET'S ASK THE MIRROR...
...WHAT THEY'RE UP TO.
WHAT'S HAPPENING?
THERE'S A COMMOTION INSIDE.
WHERE'S THAT FAIRY?
LET'S GET A BIT CLOSER.
SKRITCH
...
SKRITCH

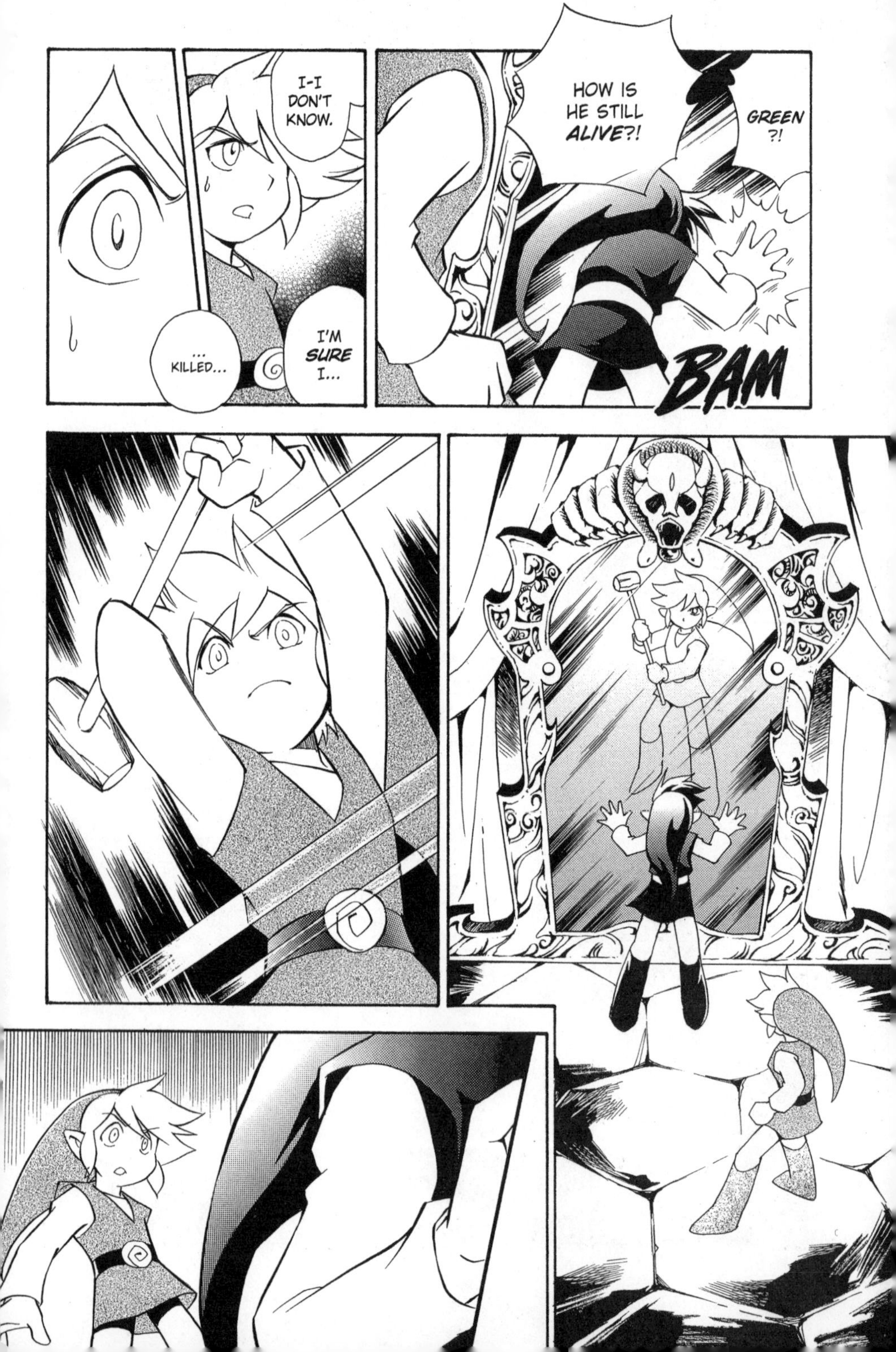
GREEN ?!
HOW IS HE STILL ALIVE?!
BAM
I-I DON'T KNOW.
I'M SURE I...
... KILLED...

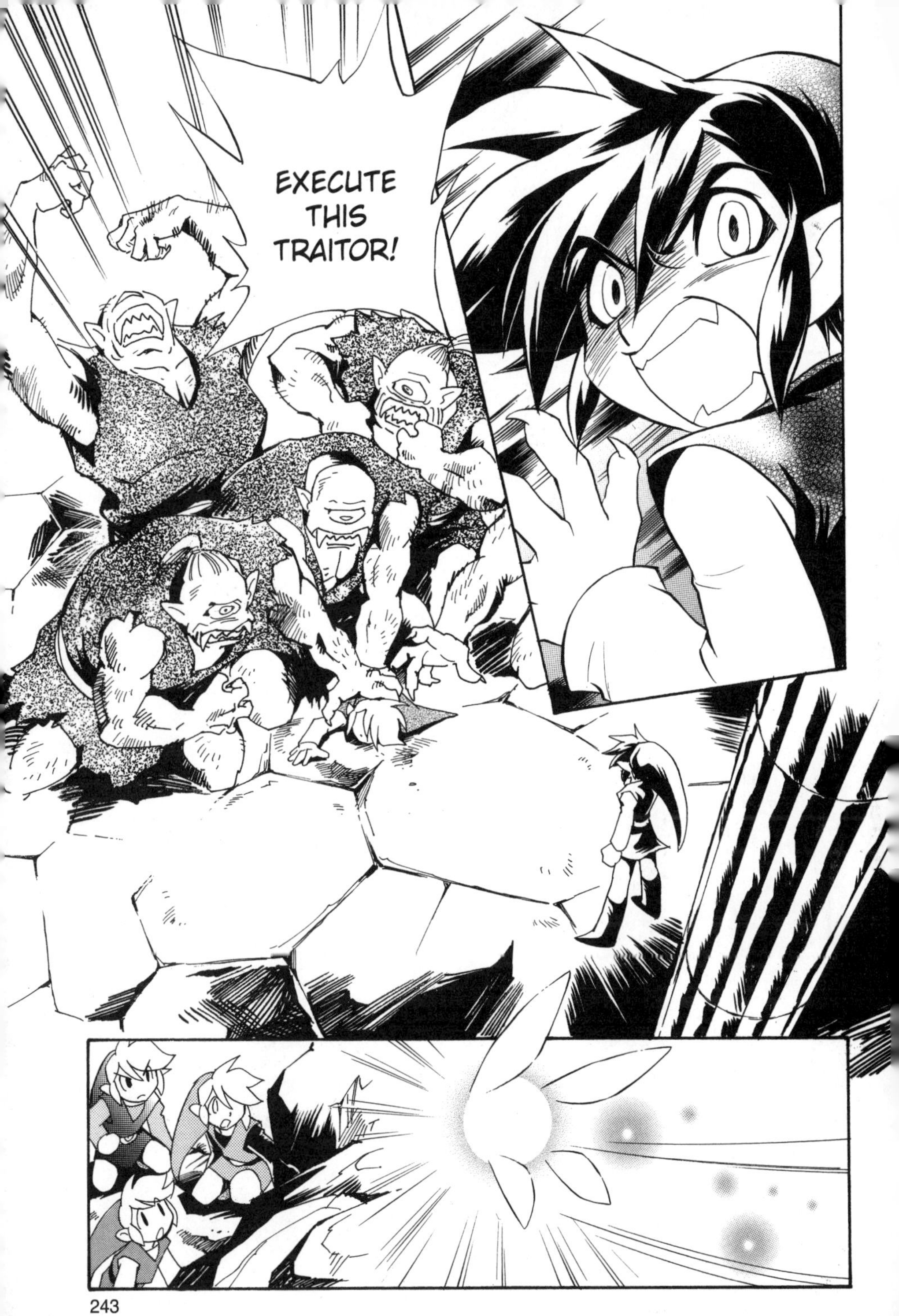
EXECUTE THIS TRAITOR!

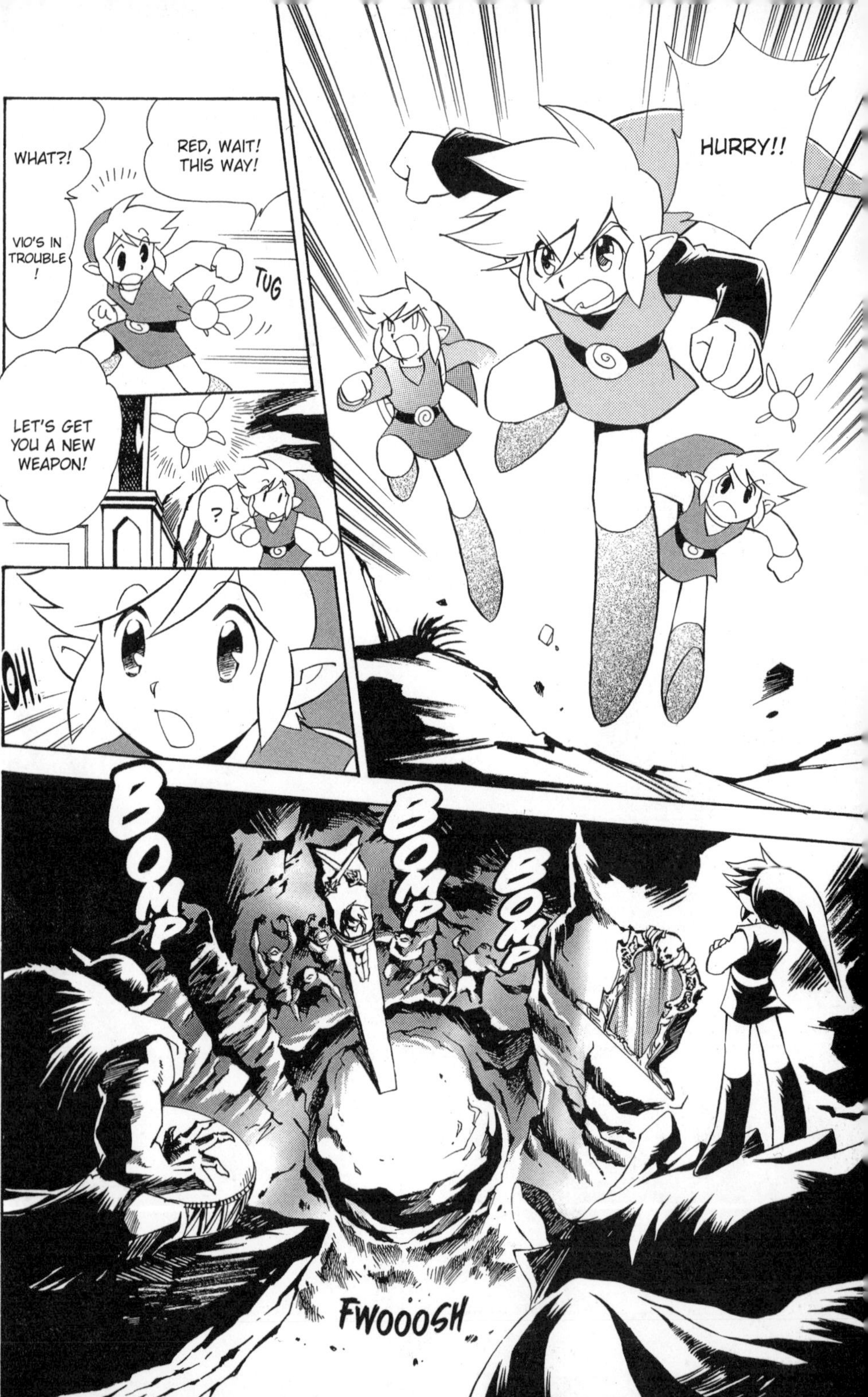
HURRY!!
RED, WAIT! THIS WAY!
WHAT?!
VIO'S IN TROUBLE!
TUG
LET'S GET YOU A NEW WEAPON!
?
OH!
BOMP
BOMP
BOMP
FWOOOSH

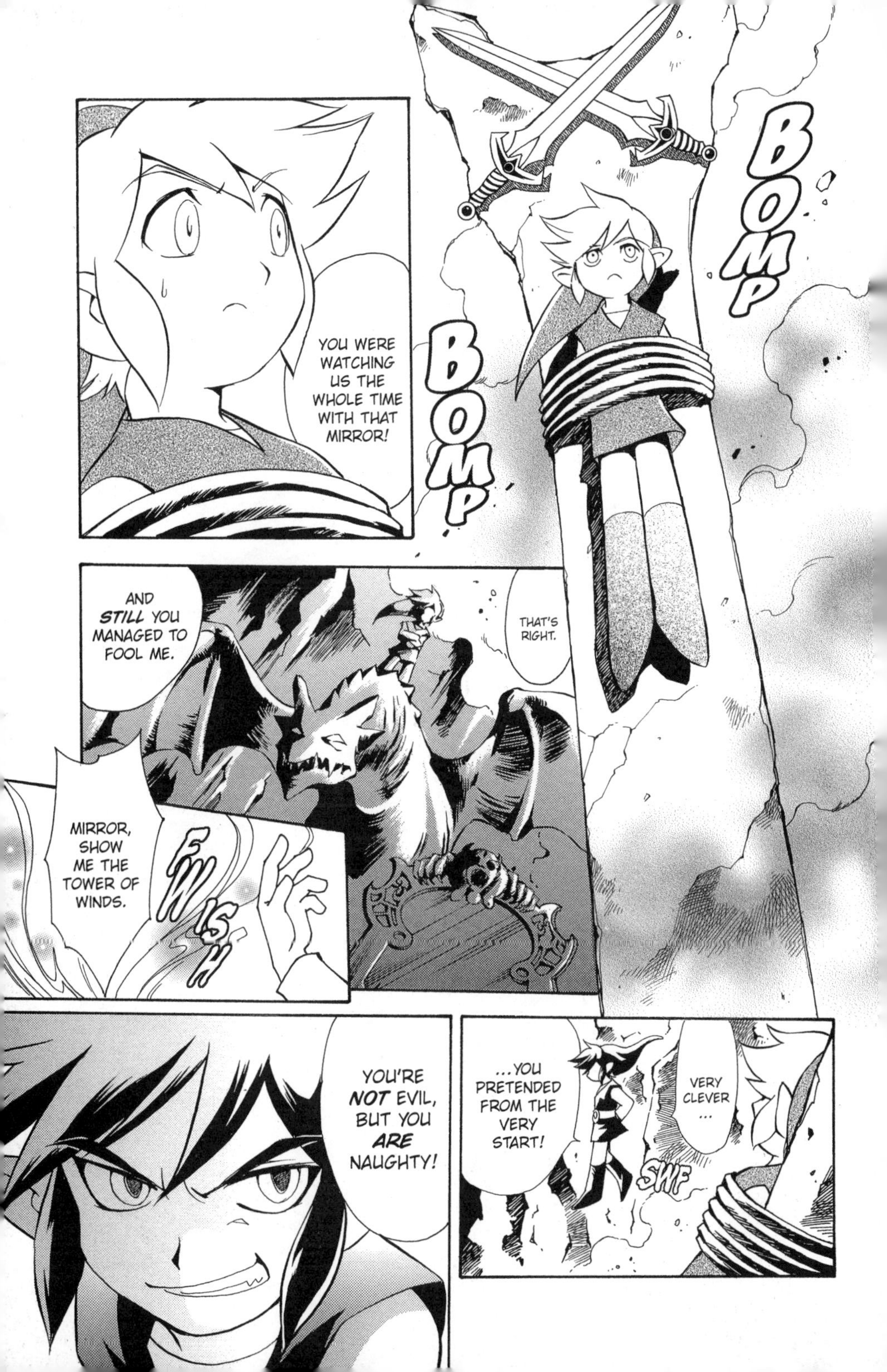
BOMP
BOMP
YOU WERE WATCHING US THE WHOLE TIME WITH THAT MIRROR!
THAT'S RIGHT.
AND STILL YOU MANAGED TO FOOL ME.
MIRROR, SHOW ME THE TOWER OF WINDS.
FWISH
VERY CLEVER ...
...YOU PRETENDED FROM THE VERY START!
SWF
YOU'RE NOT EVIL, BUT YOU ARE NAUGHTY!

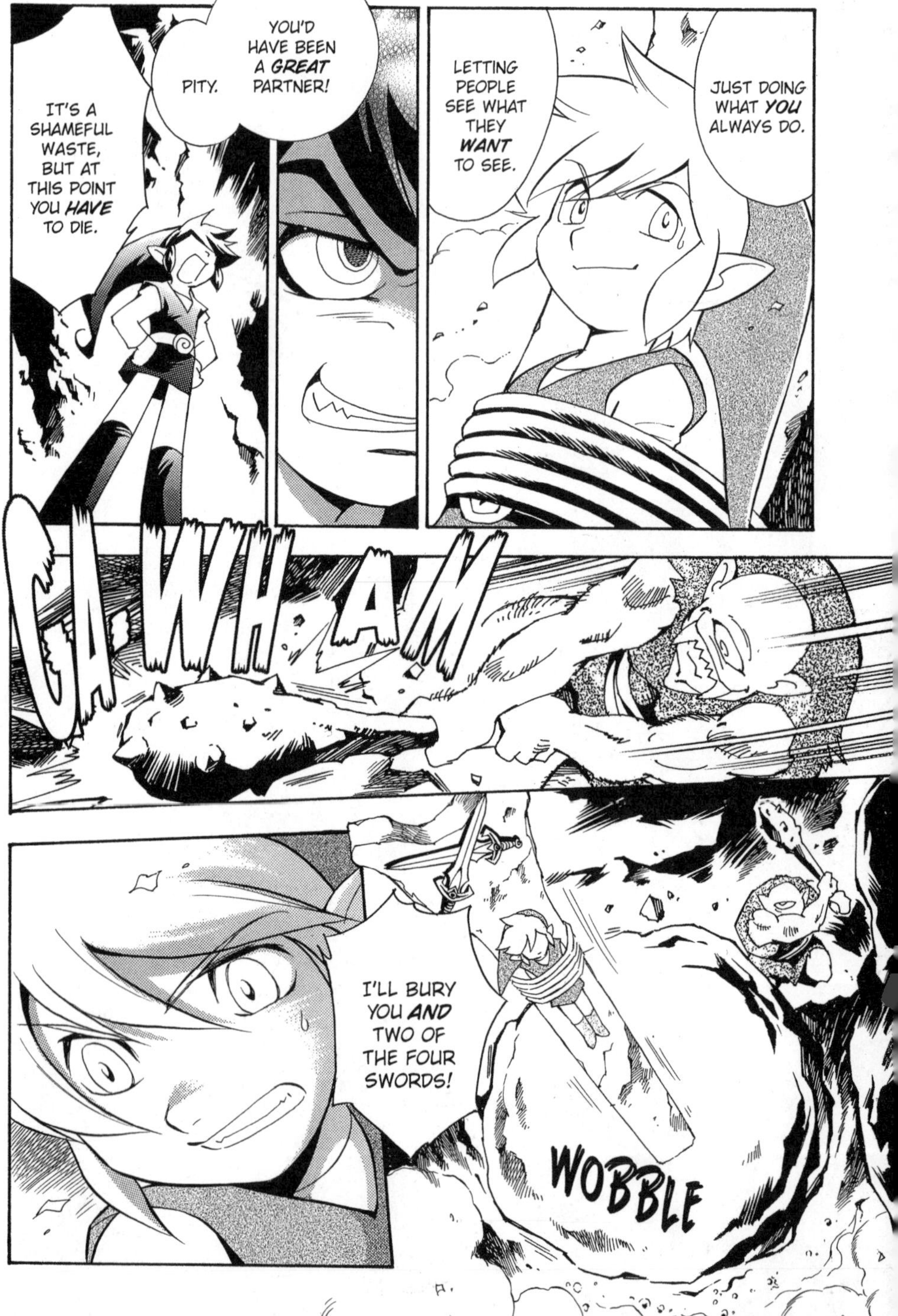
JUST DOING WHAT **YOU** ALWAYS DO.
LETTING PEOPLE SEE WHAT THEY **WANT** TO SEE.
YOU'D HAVE BEEN A **GREAT** PARTNER!
PITY.
IT'S A SHAMEFUL WASTE, BUT AT THIS POINT YOU **HAVE** TO DIE.
GAWHAM
I'LL BURY YOU **AND** TWO OF THE FOUR SWORDS!
WOBBLE

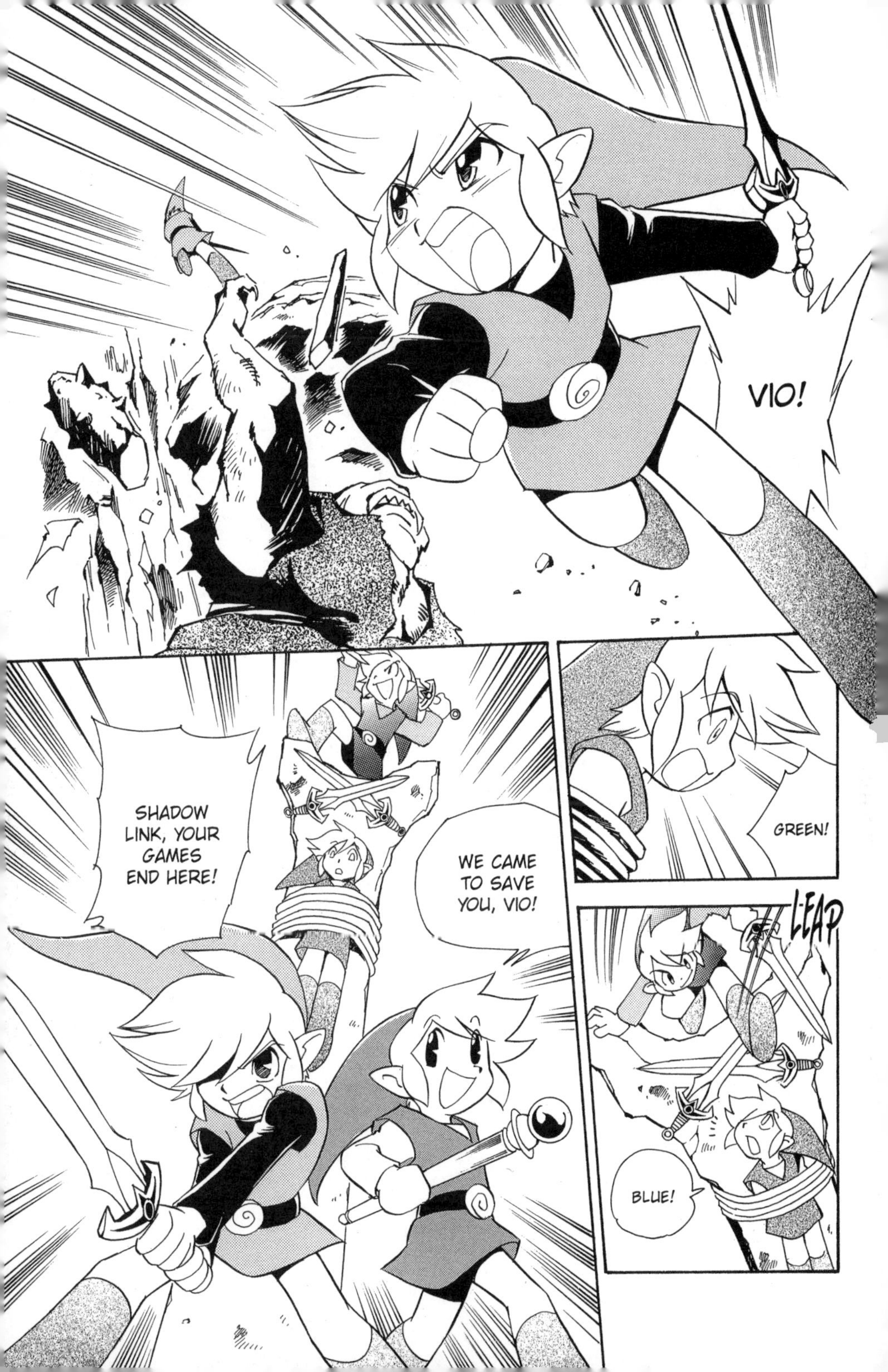
VIO!
GREEN!
LEAP
BLUE!
SHADOW LINK, YOUR GAMES END HERE!
WE CAME TO SAVE YOU, VIO!

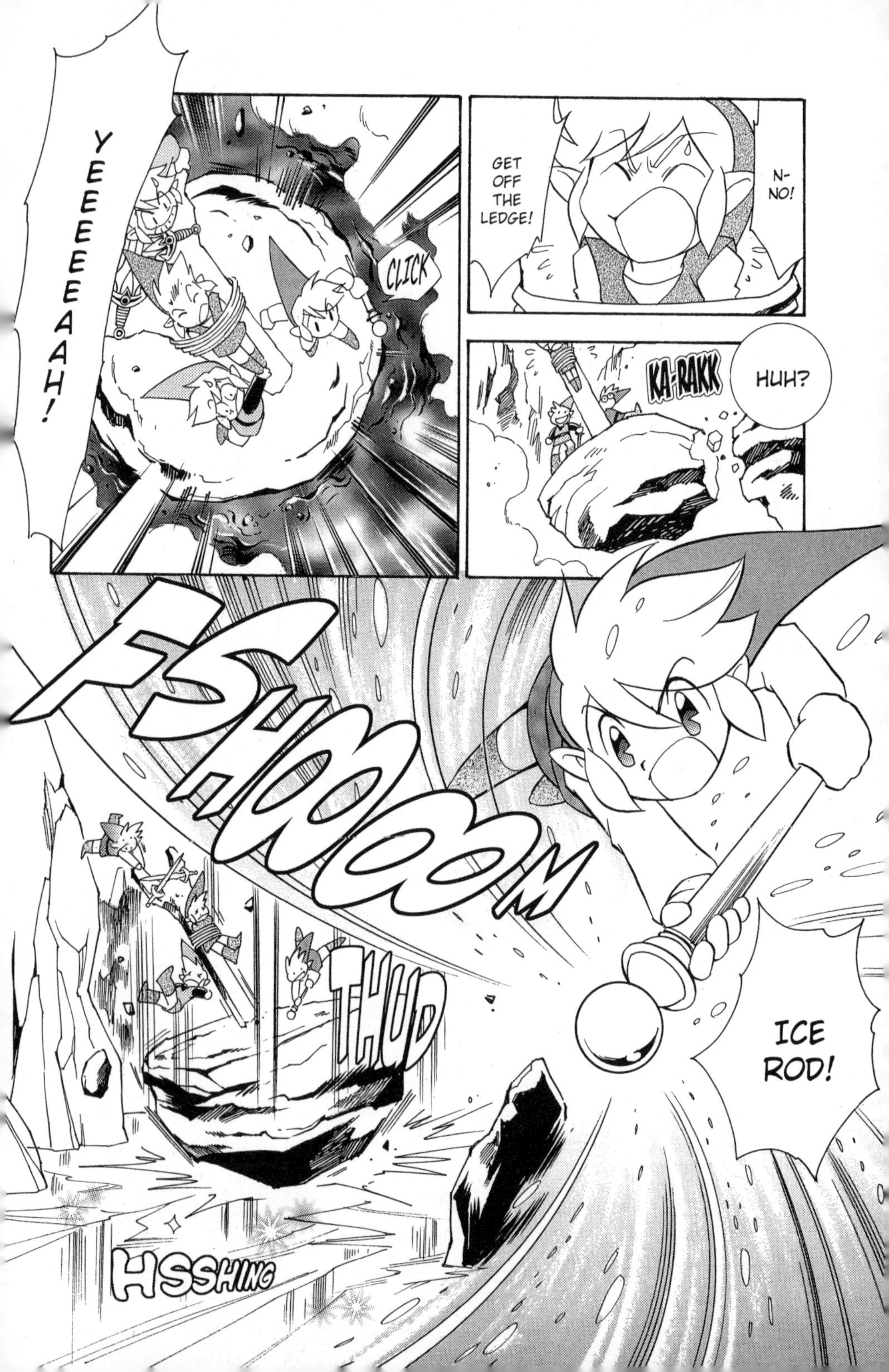
N-NO!
GET OFF THE LEDGE!
KA-RAKK
HUH?
CLICK
YEEEEEEEAAAH!
FSHOOOM
ICE ROD!
THUD
HSSHING

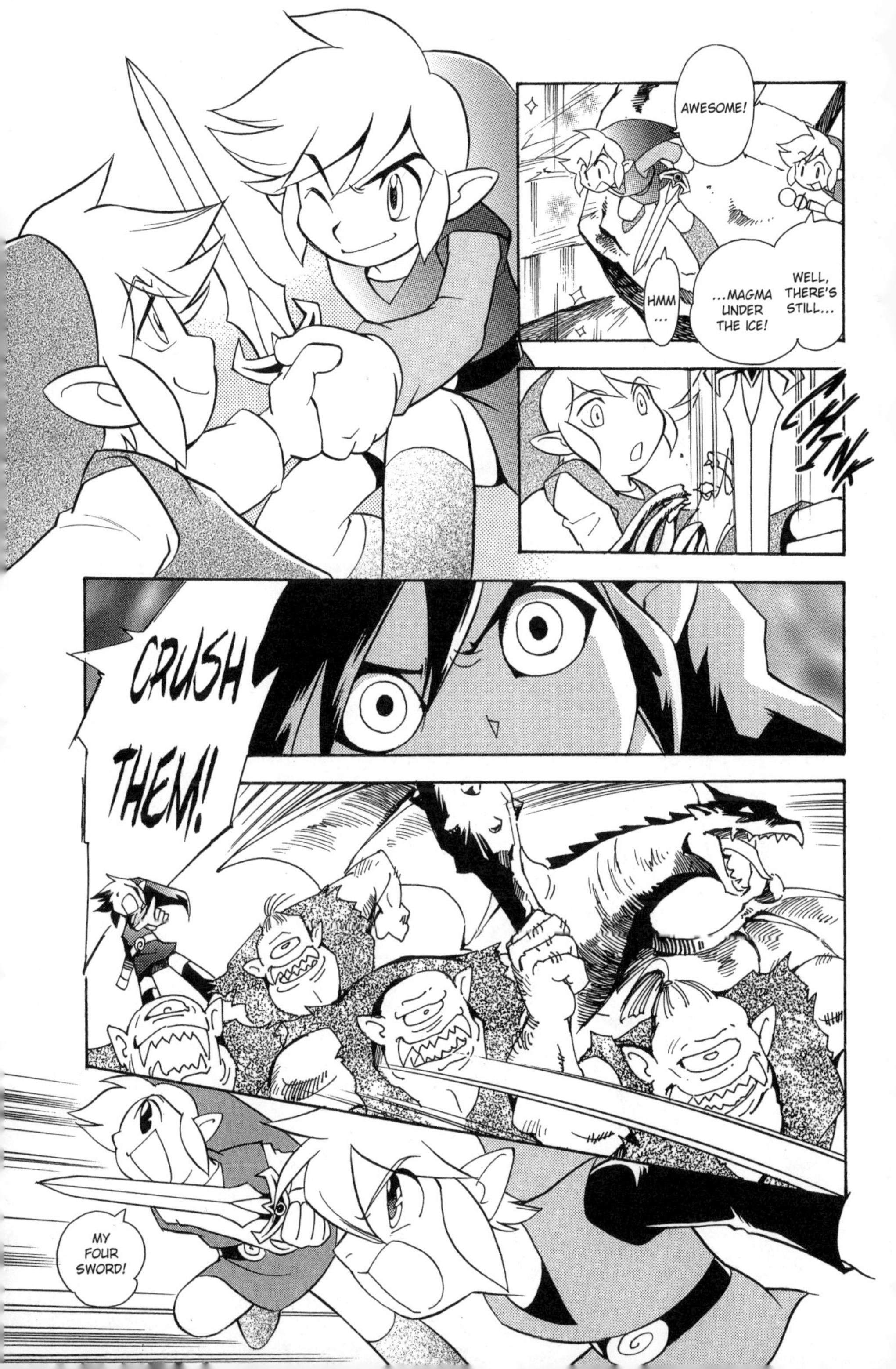
AWESOME!
WELL, THERE'S STILL...
...MAGMA UNDER THE ICE!
HMM...
CHINK
CRUSH THEM!
MY FOUR SWORD!

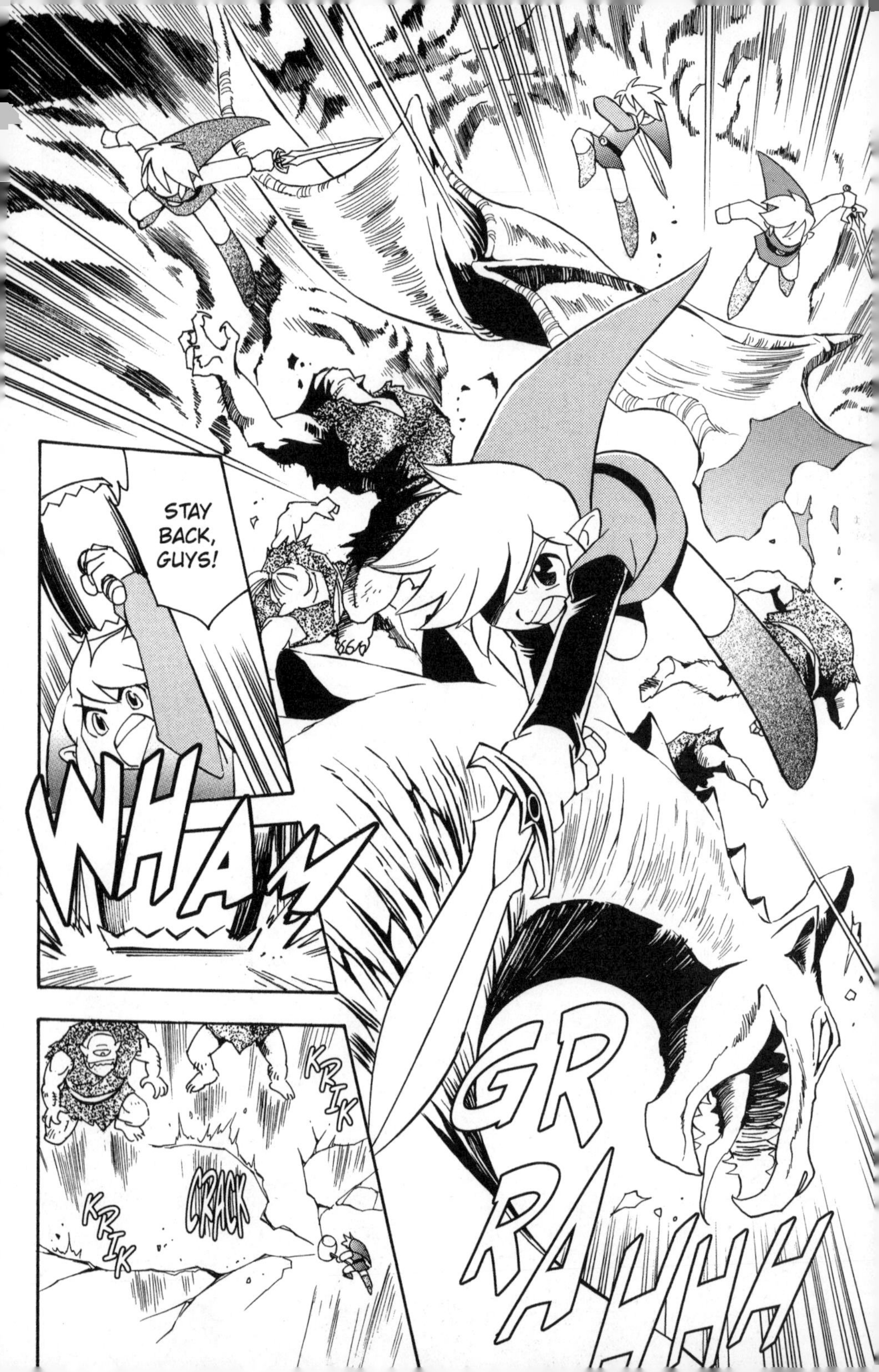
STAY BACK, GUYS!
GR RAHHH
WHAM
KRIK
CRACK
KRIK

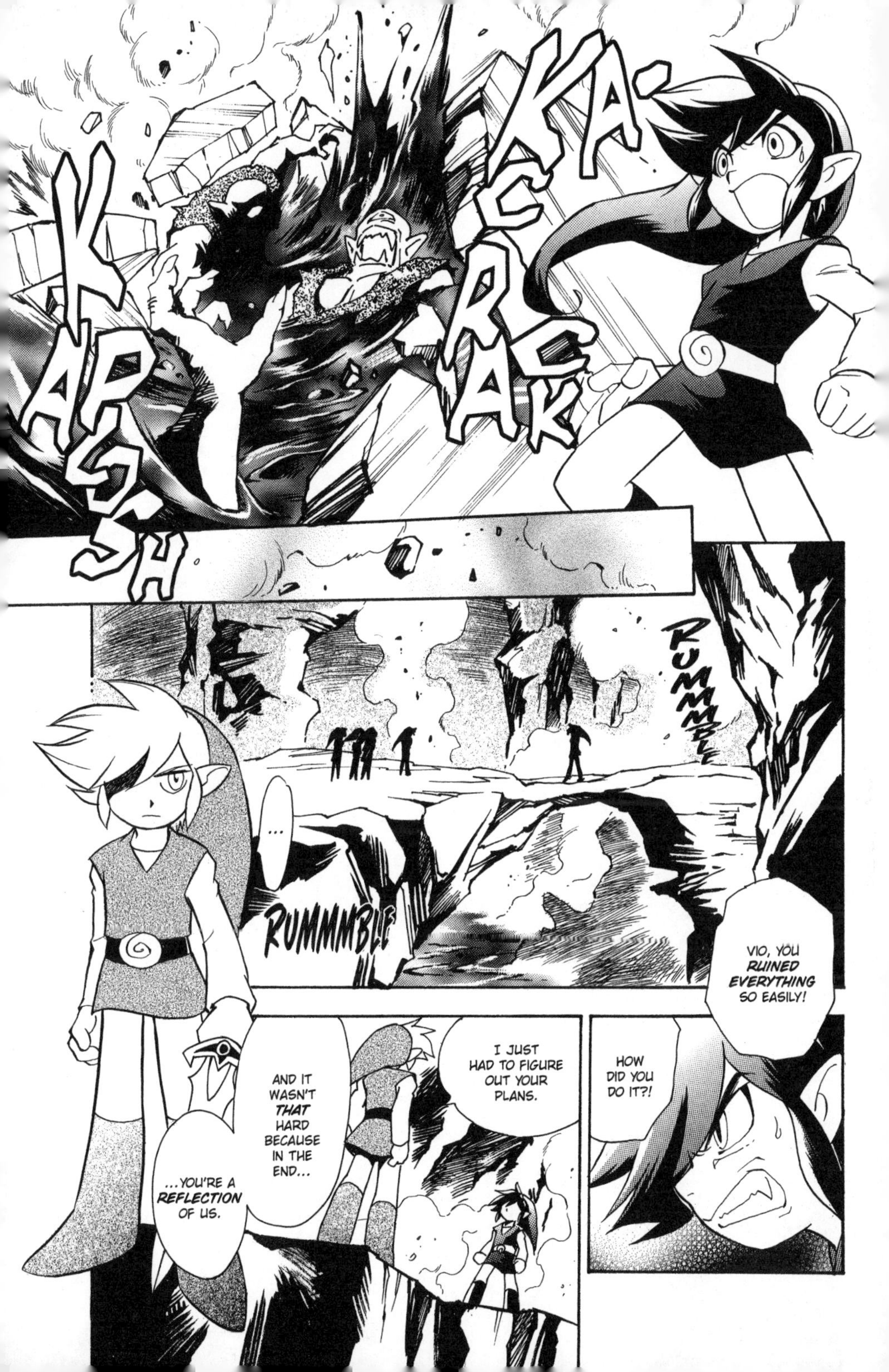
KA-CRACK
KAPOSH
RUMMMBLE
...
VIO, YOU **RUINED EVERYTHING** SO EASILY!
RUMMMBLE
HOW DID YOU DO IT?!
I JUST HAD TO FIGURE OUT YOUR PLANS.
AND IT WASN'T ***THAT*** HARD BECAUSE IN THE END...
...YOU'RE A ***REFLECTION*** OF US.

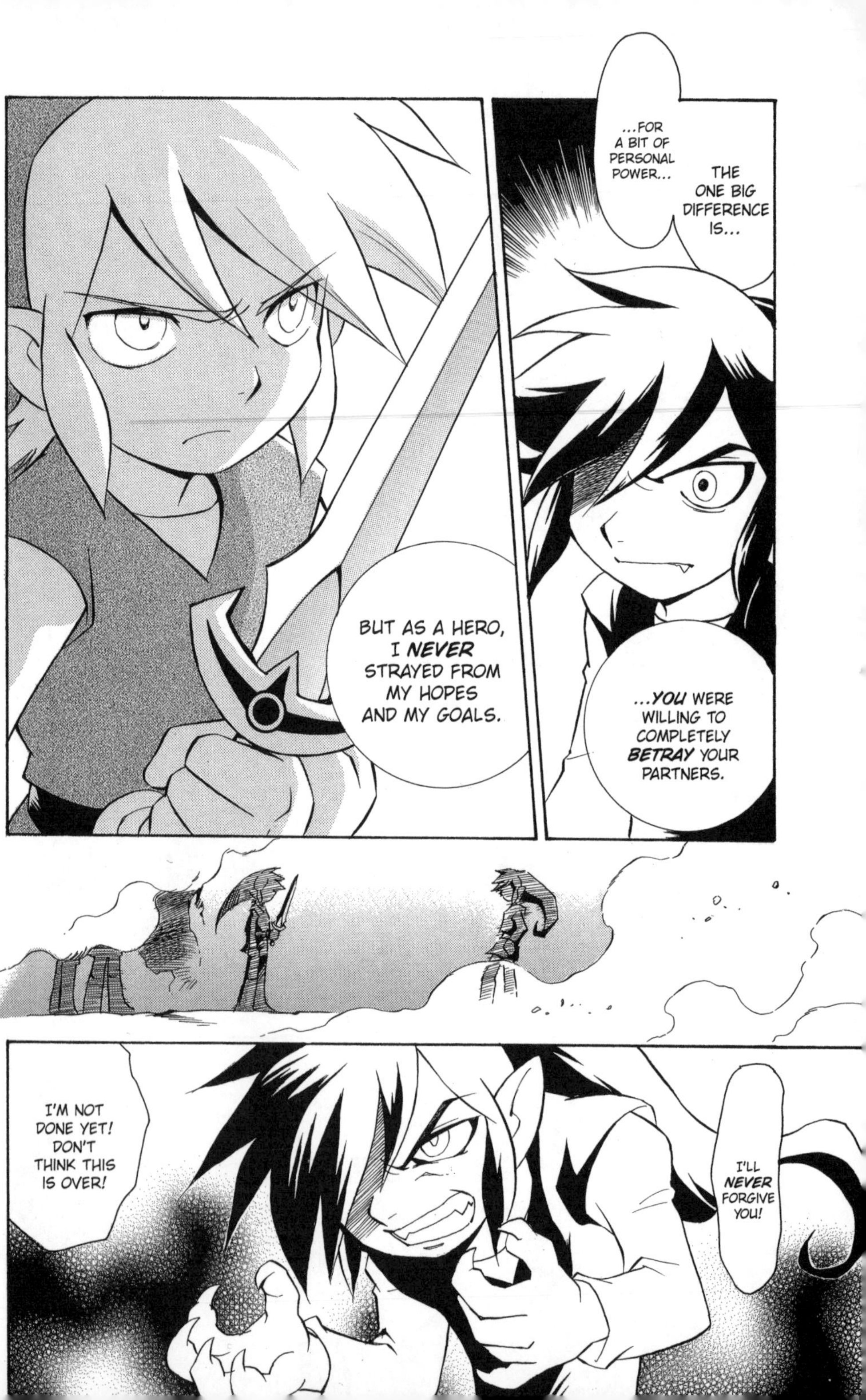
THE ONE BIG DIFFERENCE IS...
...FOR A BIT OF PERSONAL POWER...
...**YOU** WERE WILLING TO COMPLETELY **BETRAY** YOUR PARTNERS.
BUT AS A HERO, I **NEVER** STRAYED FROM MY HOPES AND MY GOALS.
I'LL **NEVER** FORGIVE YOU!
I'M NOT DONE YET! DON'T THINK THIS IS OVER!

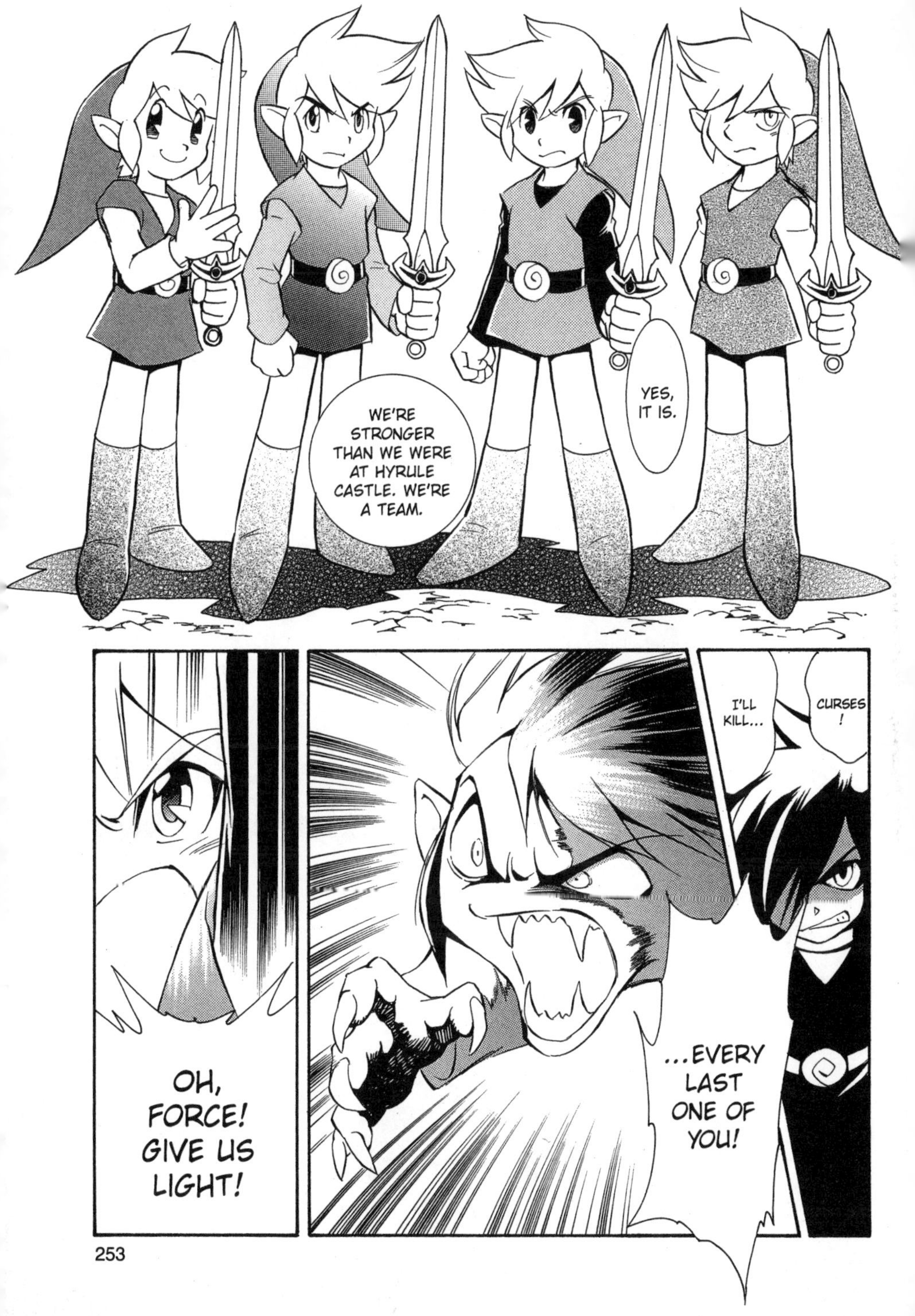
YES, IT IS.
WE'RE STRONGER THAN WE WERE AT HYRULE CASTLE. WE'RE A TEAM.
CURSES!
I'LL KILL...
...EVERY LAST ONE OF YOU!
OH, FORCE! GIVE US LIGHT!

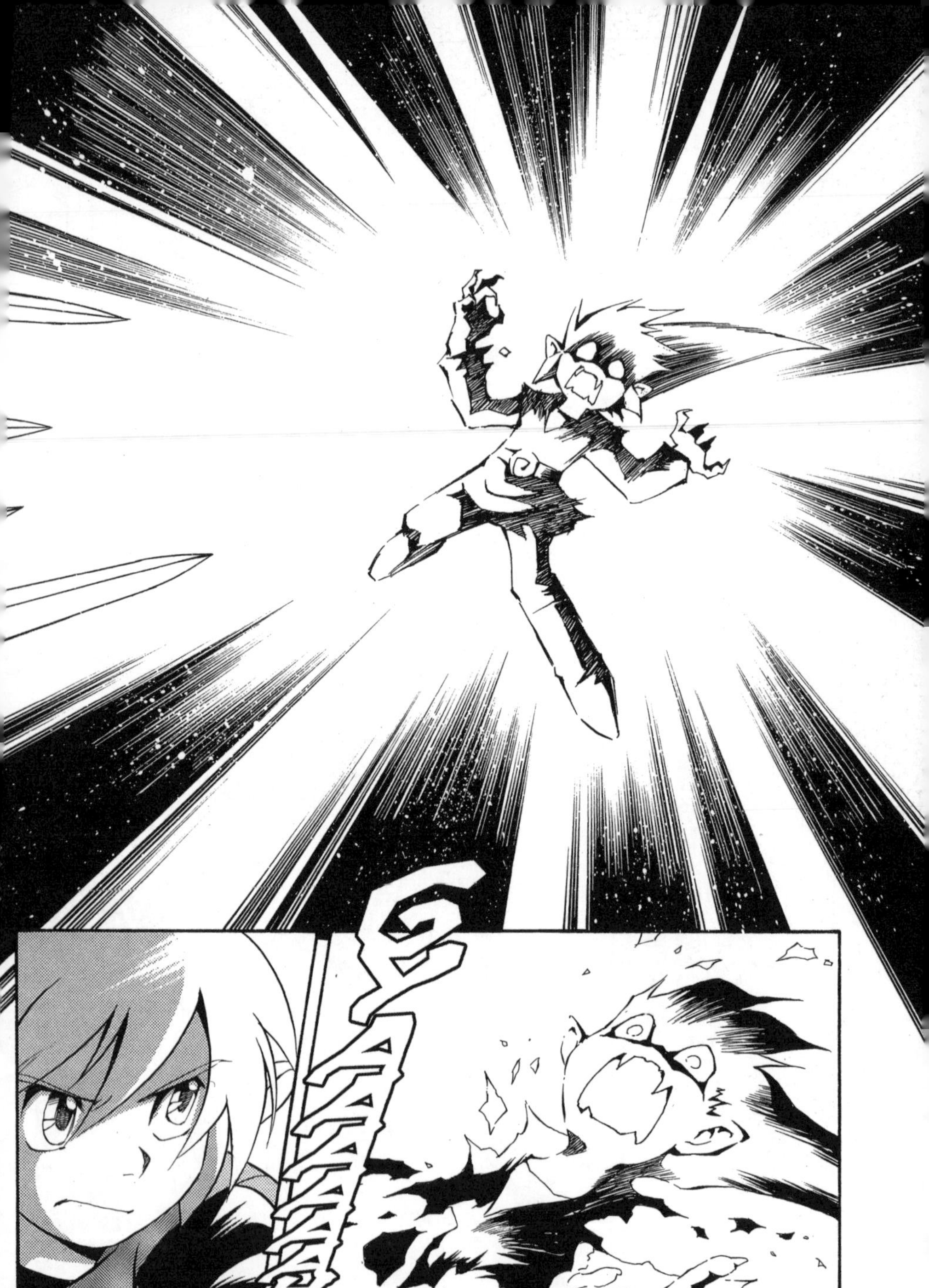

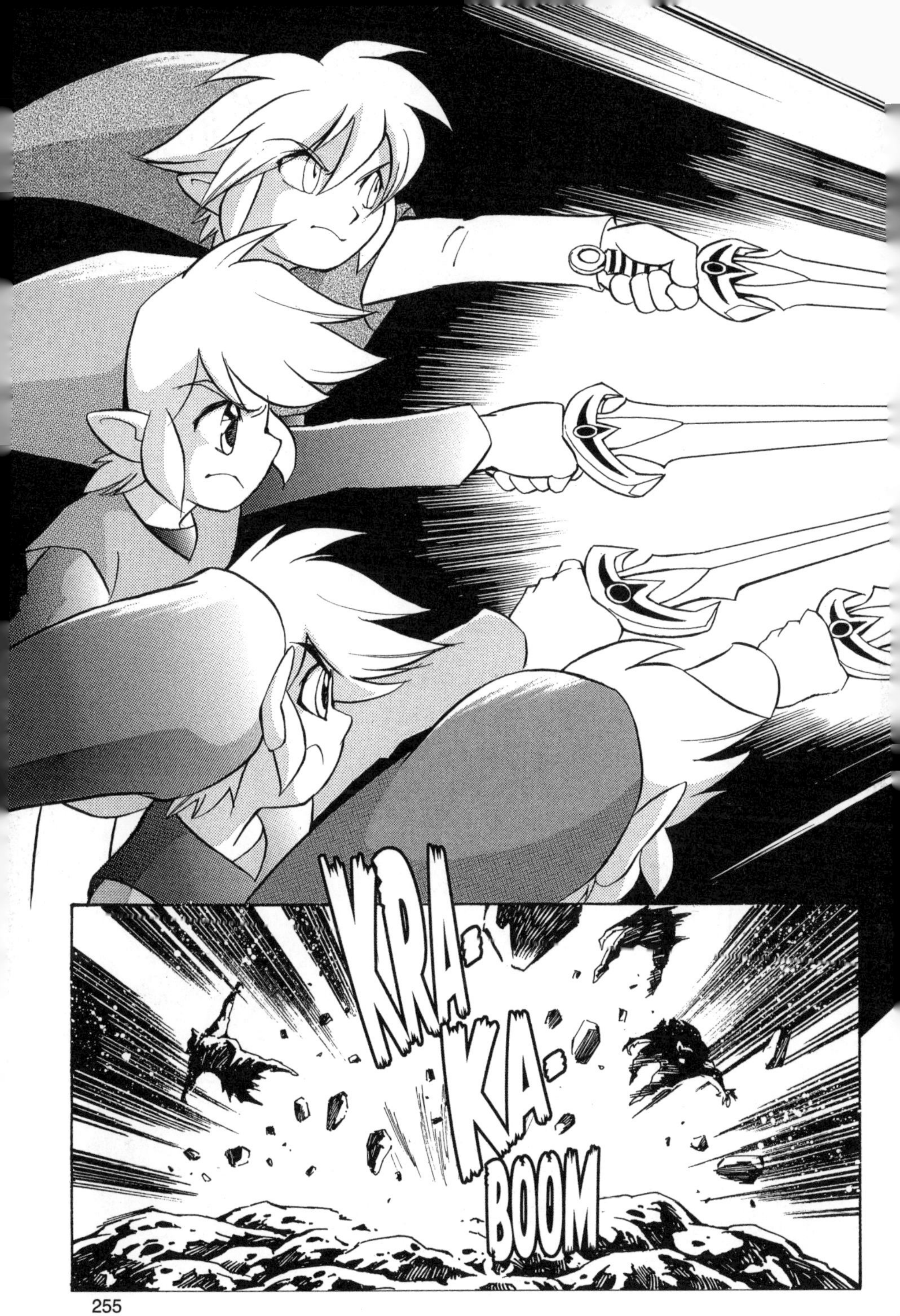
KRA-KA-BOOM

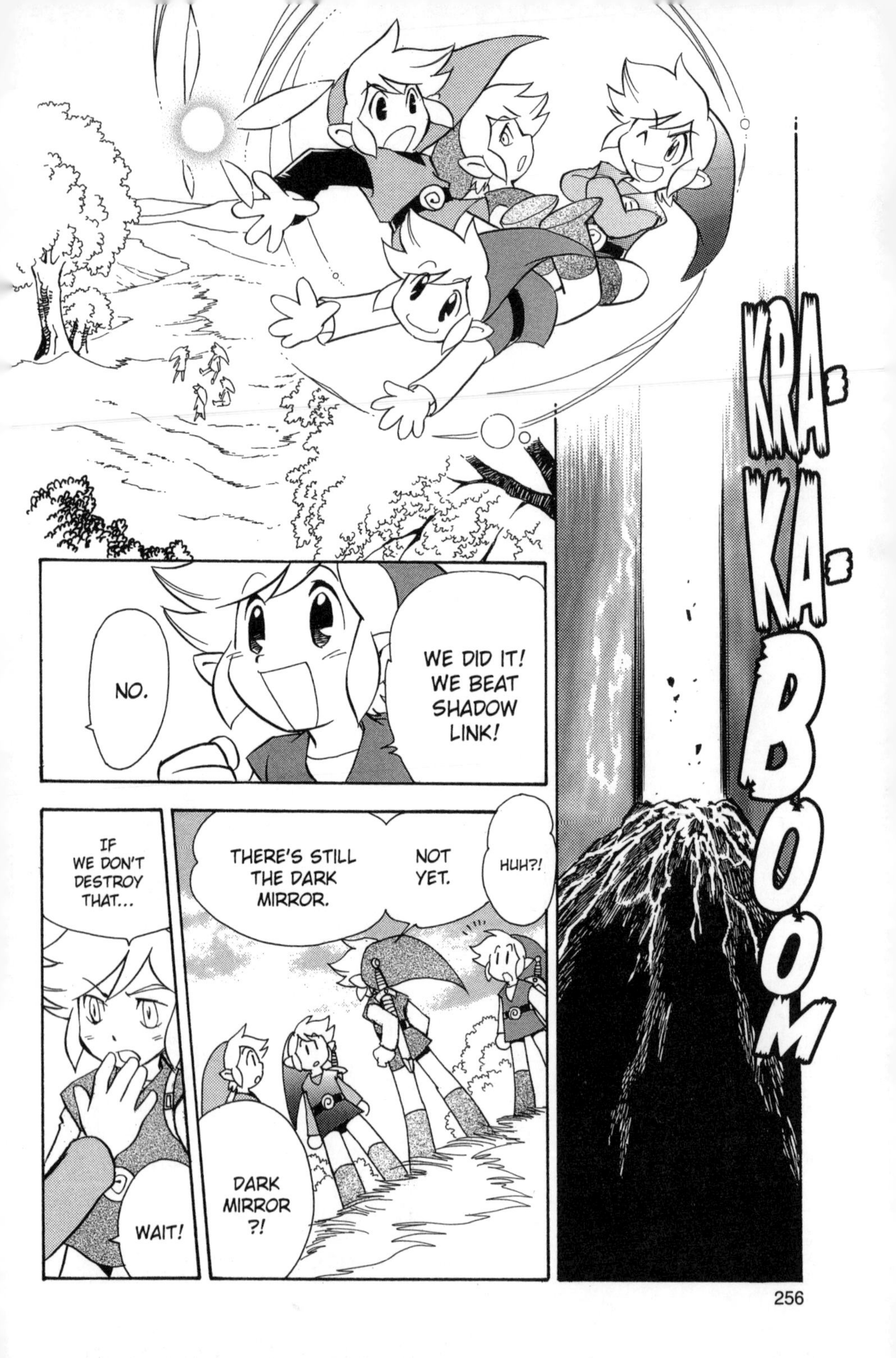
KRA-KA-BOOM
WE DID IT! WE BEAT SHADOW LINK!
NO.
HUH?!
NOT YET.
THERE'S STILL THE DARK MIRROR.
DARK MIRROR ?!
IF WE DON'T DESTROY THAT...
WAIT!

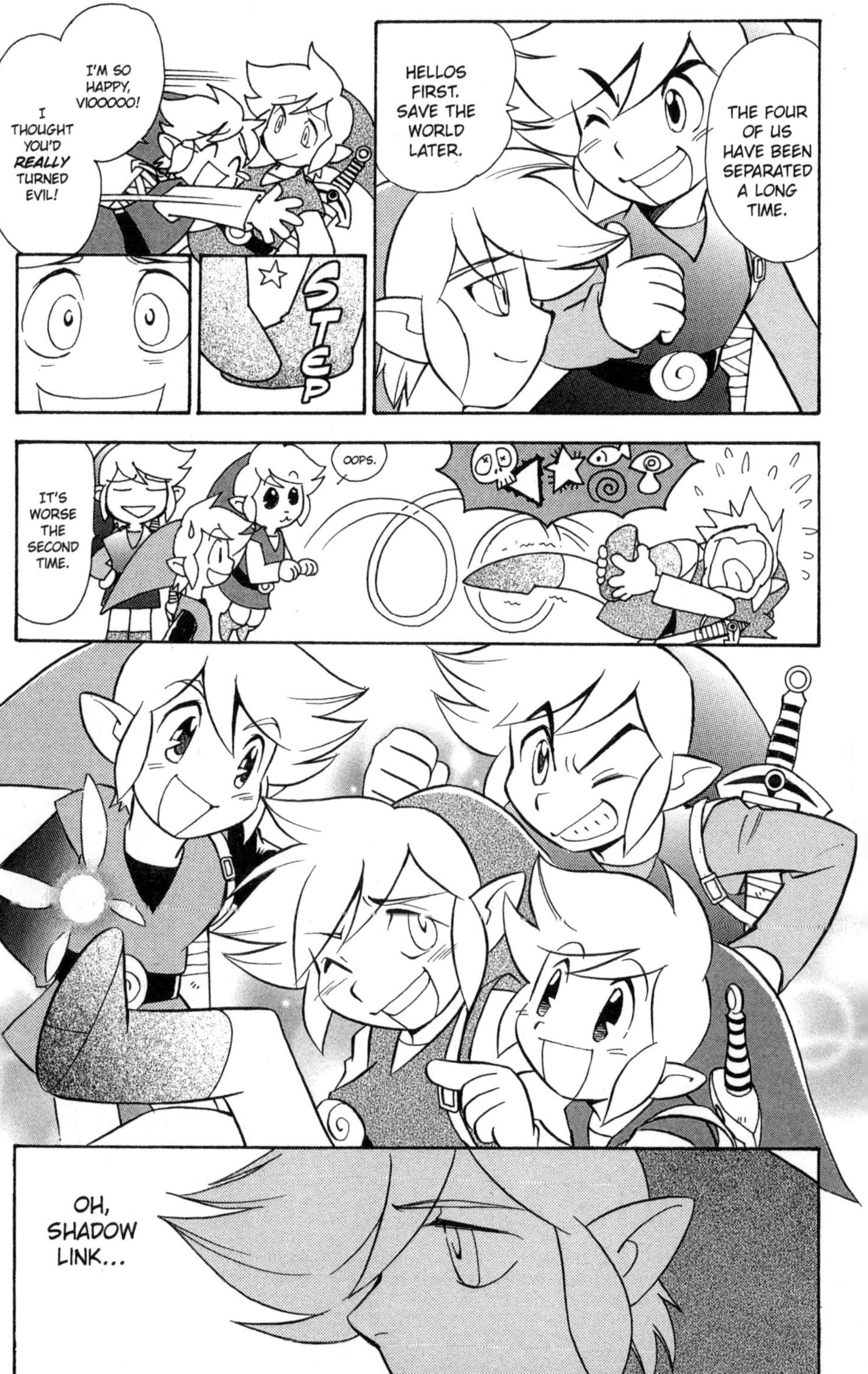
THE FOUR OF US HAVE BEEN SEPARATED A LONG TIME.
HELLOS FIRST. SAVE THE WORLD LATER.
I'M SO HAPPY, VIOOOOO!
I THOUGHT YOU'D **REALLY** TURNED EVIL!
STEP
OOPS.
IT'S WORSE THE SECOND TIME.
OH, SHADOW LINK...

CHAPTER 9 On to the Tower of Winds

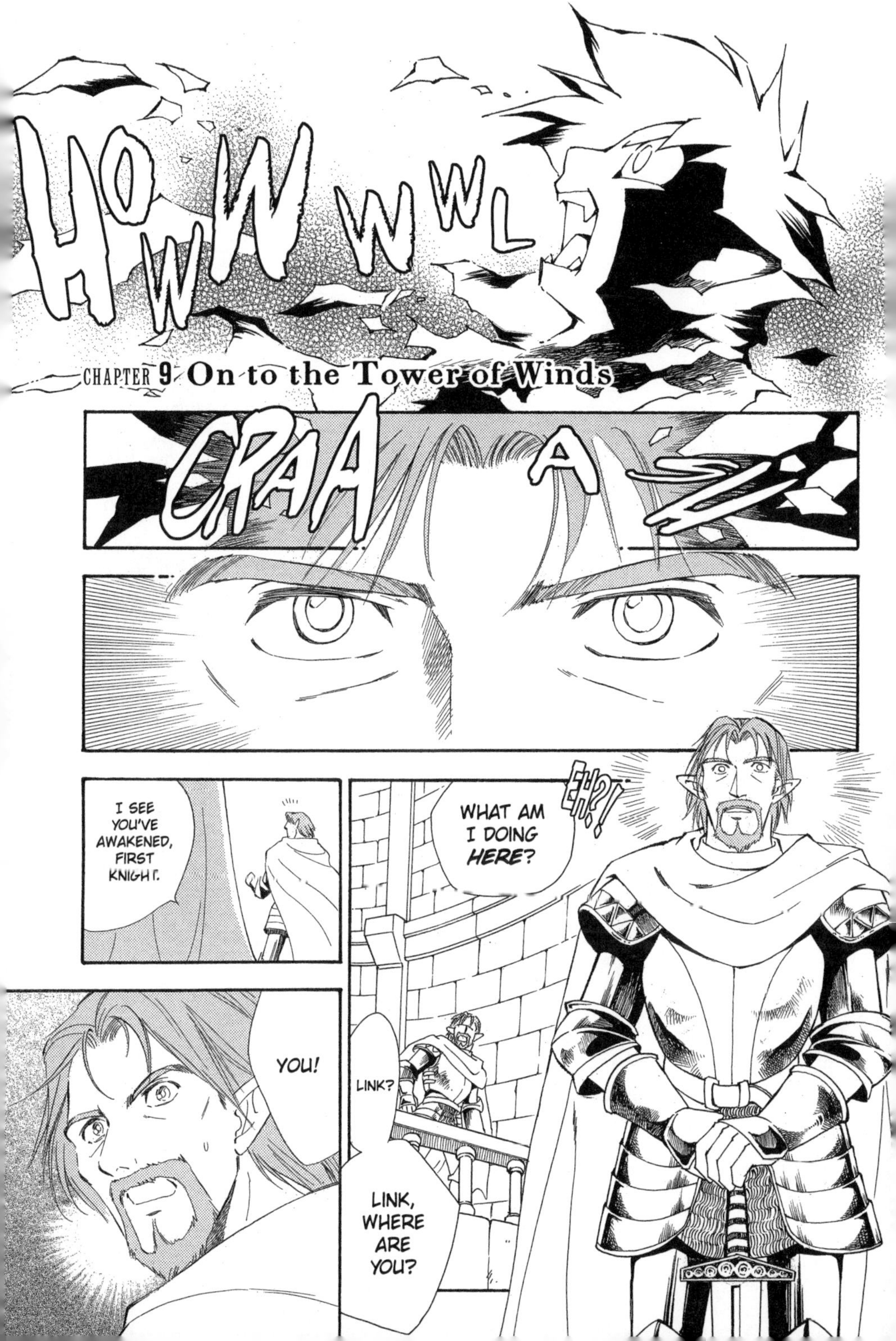

HOWWWWWL
CRAAASH
EH?!
WHAT AM I DOING HERE?
LINK?
LINK, WHERE ARE YOU?
I SEE YOU'VE AWAKENED, FIRST KNIGHT.
YOU!

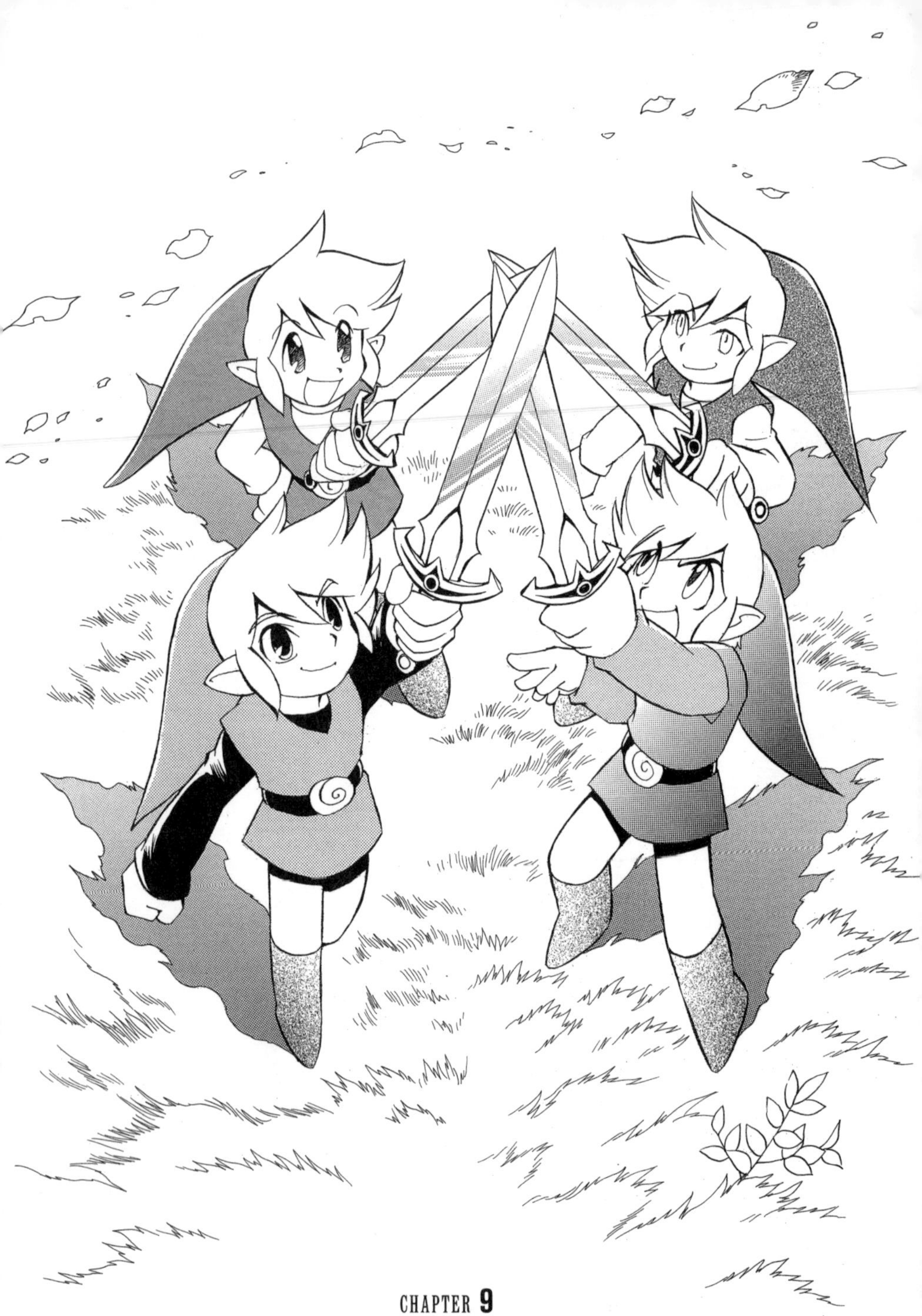

CHAPTER 9

On to the Tower of Winds

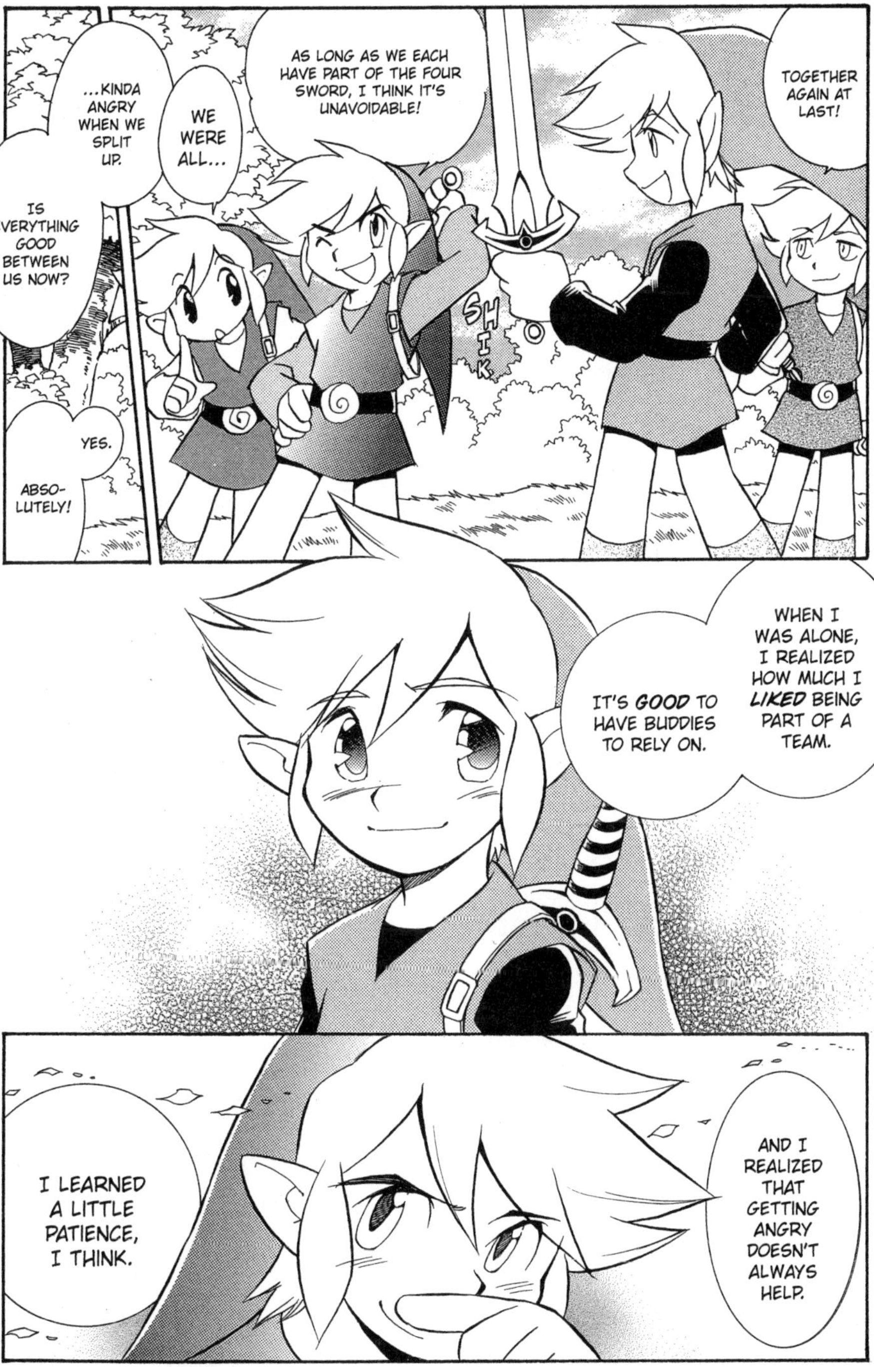
TOGETHER AGAIN AT LAST!
AS LONG AS WE EACH HAVE PART OF THE FOUR SWORD, I THINK IT'S UNAVOIDABLE!
SHIK
WE WERE ALL...
...KINDA ANGRY WHEN WE SPLIT UP.
IS EVERYTHING GOOD BETWEEN US NOW?
YES.
ABSO-LUTELY!
WHEN I WAS ALONE, I REALIZED HOW MUCH I *LIKED* BEING PART OF A TEAM.
IT'S *GOOD* TO HAVE BUDDIES TO RELY ON.
AND I REALIZED THAT GETTING ANGRY DOESN'T ALWAYS HELP.
I LEARNED A LITTLE PATIENCE, I THINK.

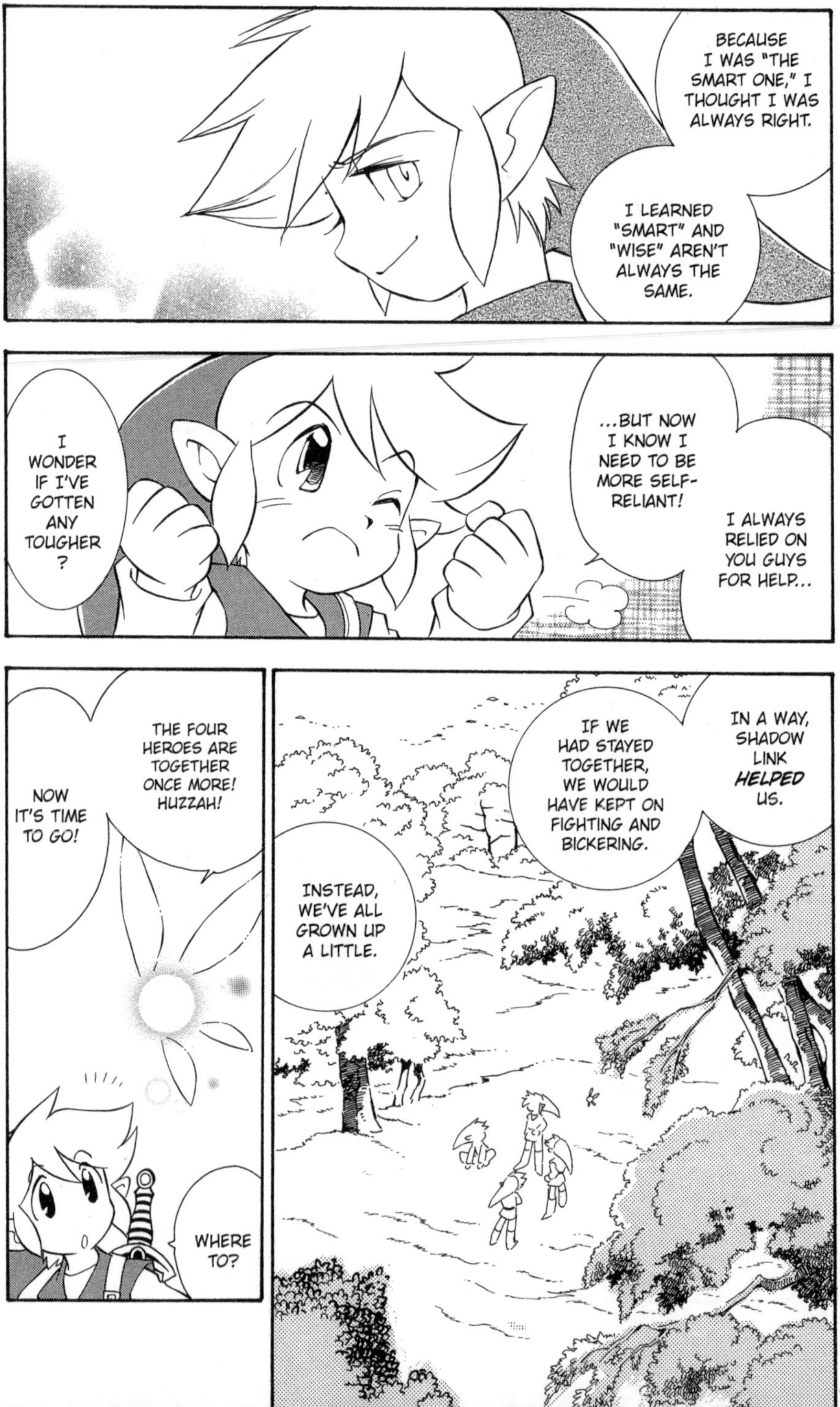

BECAUSE I WAS "THE SMART ONE," I THOUGHT I WAS ALWAYS RIGHT.
I LEARNED "SMART" AND "WISE" AREN'T ALWAYS THE SAME.
I ALWAYS RELIED ON YOU GUYS FOR HELP...
...BUT NOW I KNOW I NEED TO BE MORE SELF-RELIANT!
I WONDER IF I'VE GOTTEN ANY TOUGHER?
IN A WAY, SHADOW LINK ***HELPED*** US.
IF WE HAD STAYED TOGETHER, WE WOULD HAVE KEPT ON FIGHTING AND BICKERING.
INSTEAD, WE'VE ALL GROWN UP A LITTLE.
THE FOUR HEROES ARE TOGETHER ONCE MORE! HUZZAH!
NOW IT'S TIME TO GO!
WHERE TO?

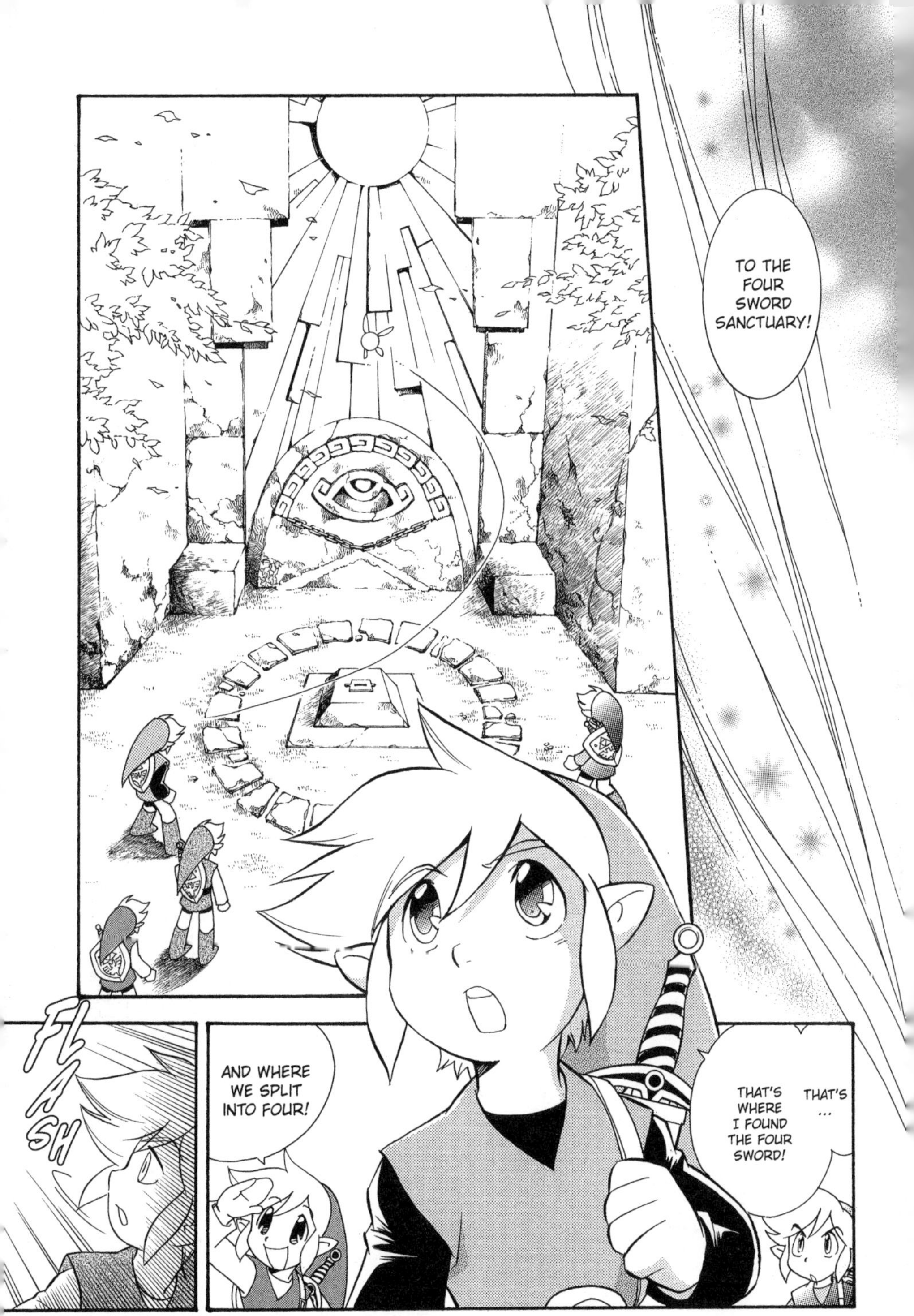
TO THE FOUR SWORD SANCTUARY!
THAT'S ...
THAT'S WHERE I FOUND THE FOUR SWORD!
AND WHERE WE SPLIT INTO FOUR!
FLASH

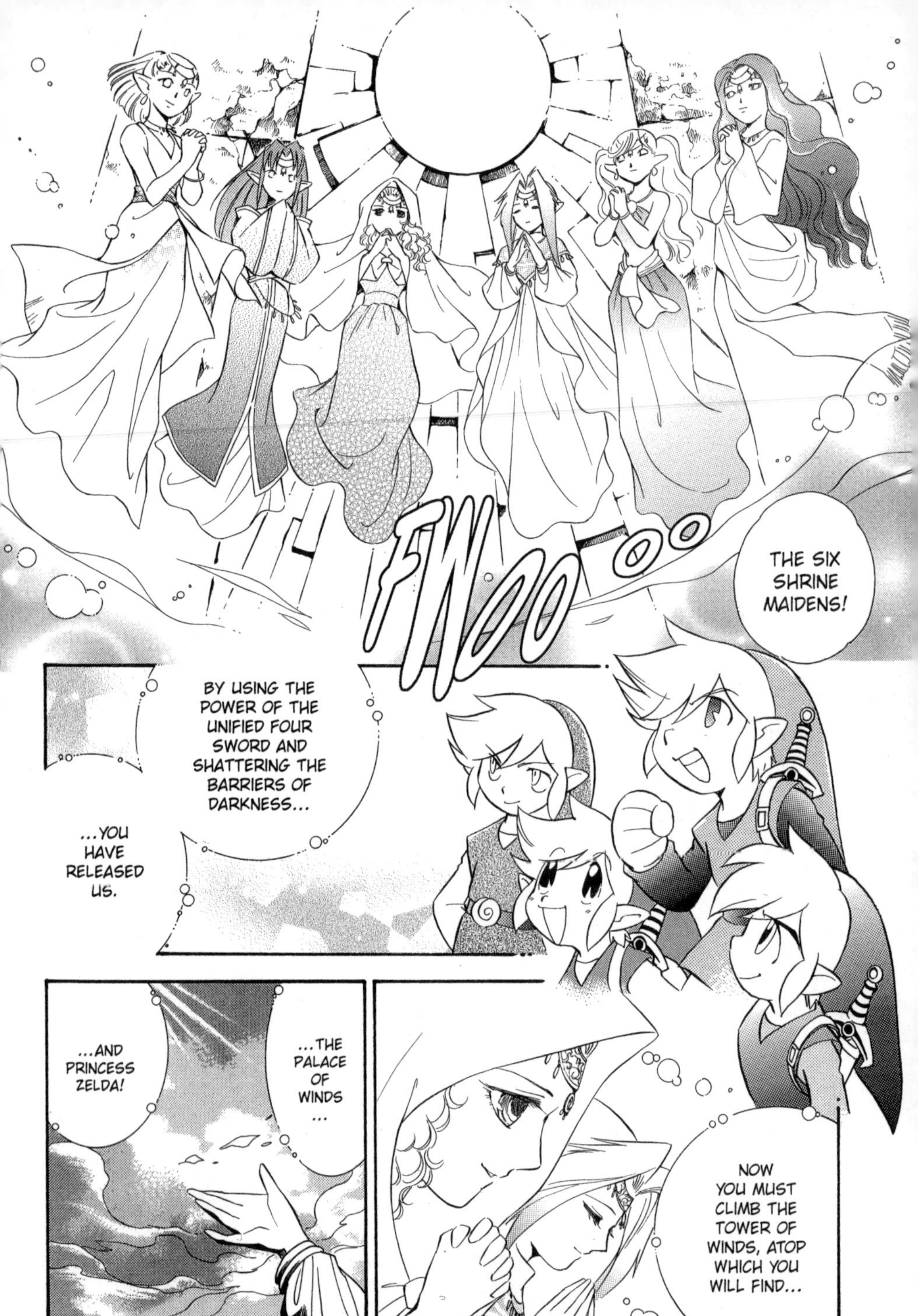
THE SIX SHRINE MAIDENS!
FWOOOO
BY USING THE POWER OF THE UNIFIED FOUR SWORD AND SHATTERING THE BARRIERS OF DARKNESS...
...YOU HAVE RELEASED US.
NOW YOU MUST CLIMB THE TOWER OF WINDS, ATOP WHICH YOU WILL FIND...
...THE PALACE OF WINDS...
...AND PRINCESS ZELDA!

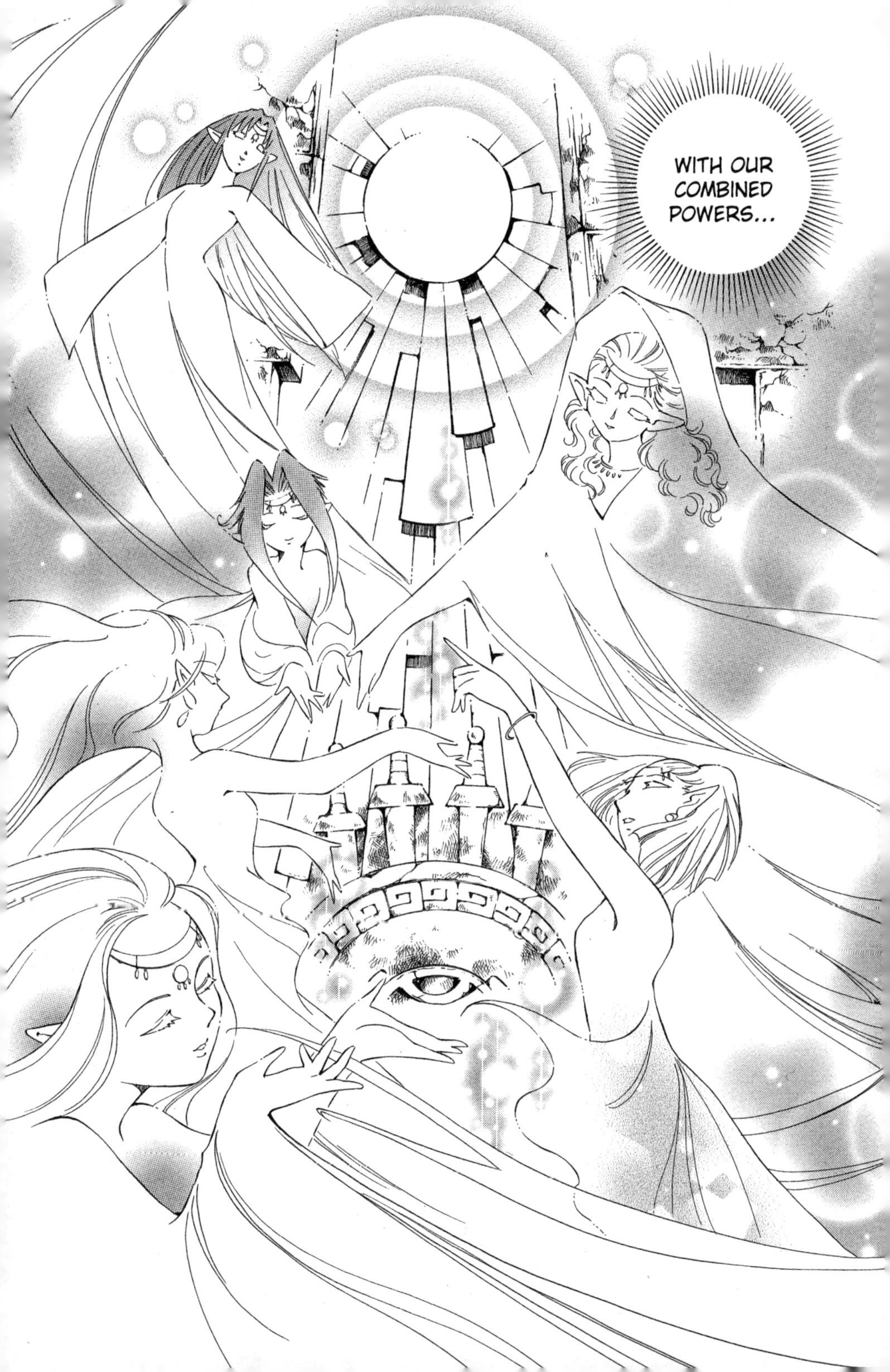
WITH OUR COMBINED POWERS...

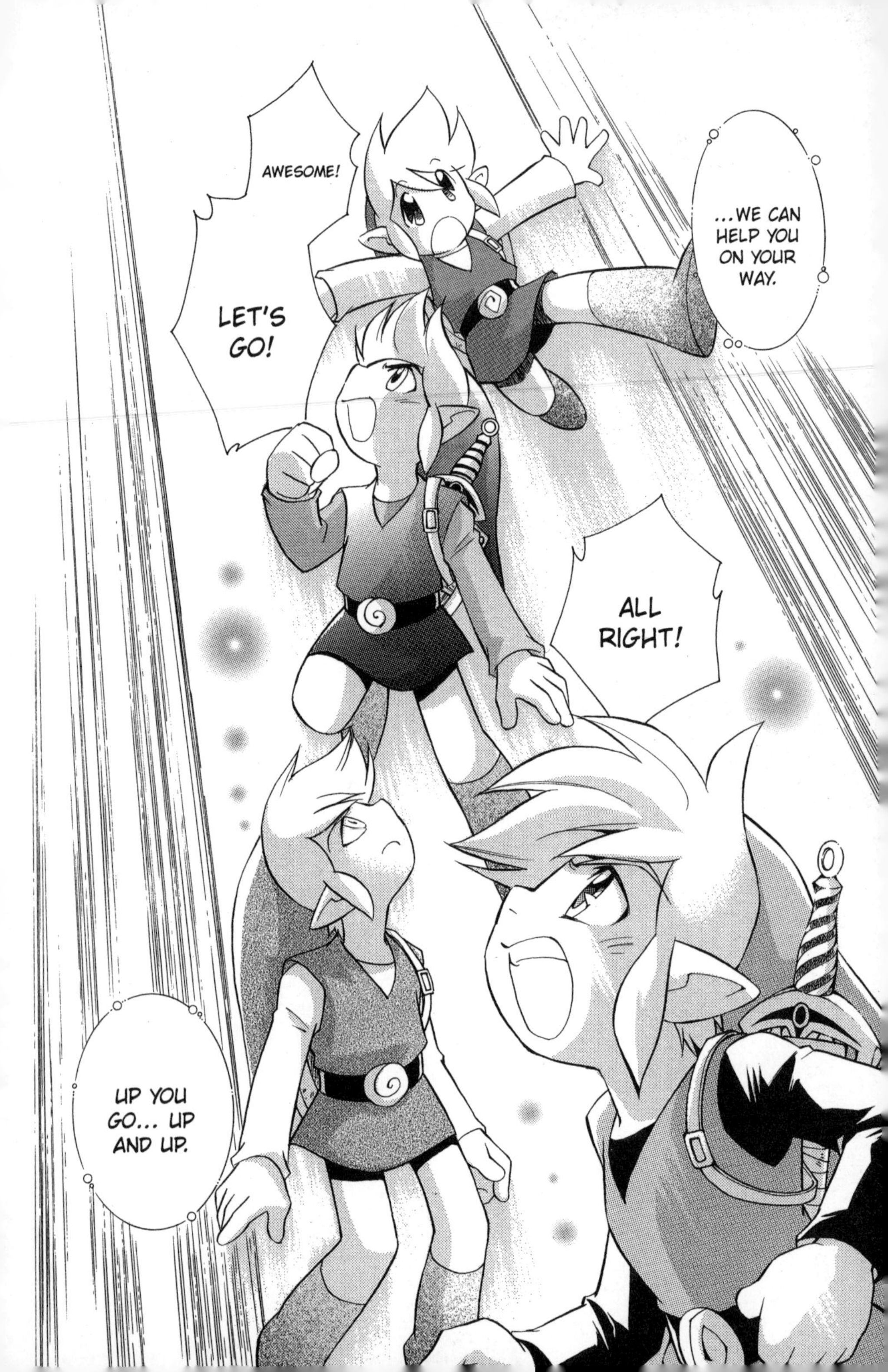
...WE CAN HELP YOU ON YOUR WAY.
AWESOME!
LET'S GO!
ALL RIGHT!
UP YOU GO... UP AND UP.

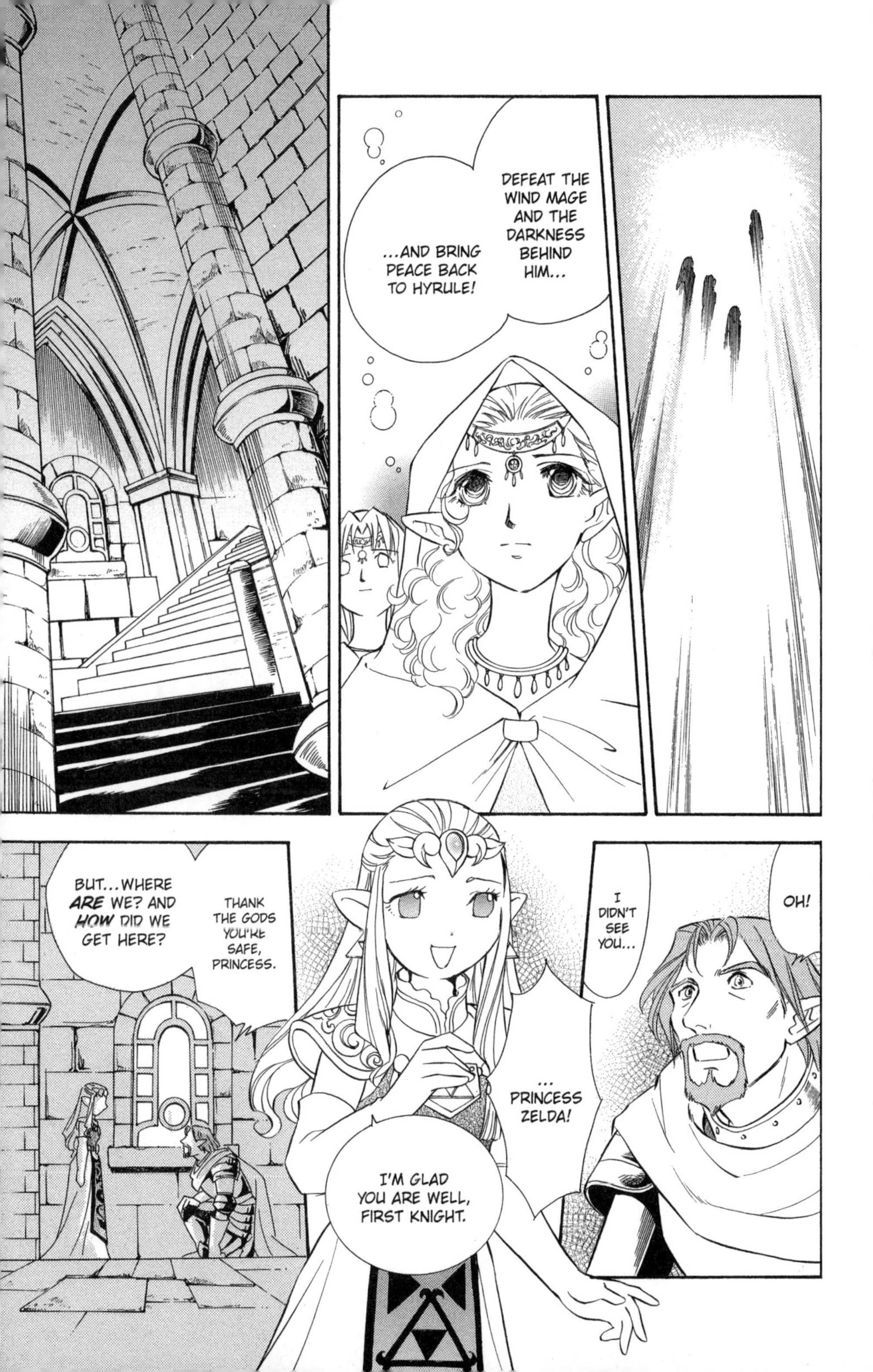
DEFEAT THE WIND MAGE AND THE DARKNESS BEHIND HIM...
...AND BRING PEACE BACK TO HYRULE!
OH!
I DIDN'T SEE YOU...
...PRINCESS ZELDA!
I'M GLAD YOU ARE WELL, FIRST KNIGHT.
THANK THE GODS YOU'RE SAFE, PRINCESS.
BUT...WHERE ARE WE? AND HOW DID WE GET HERE?

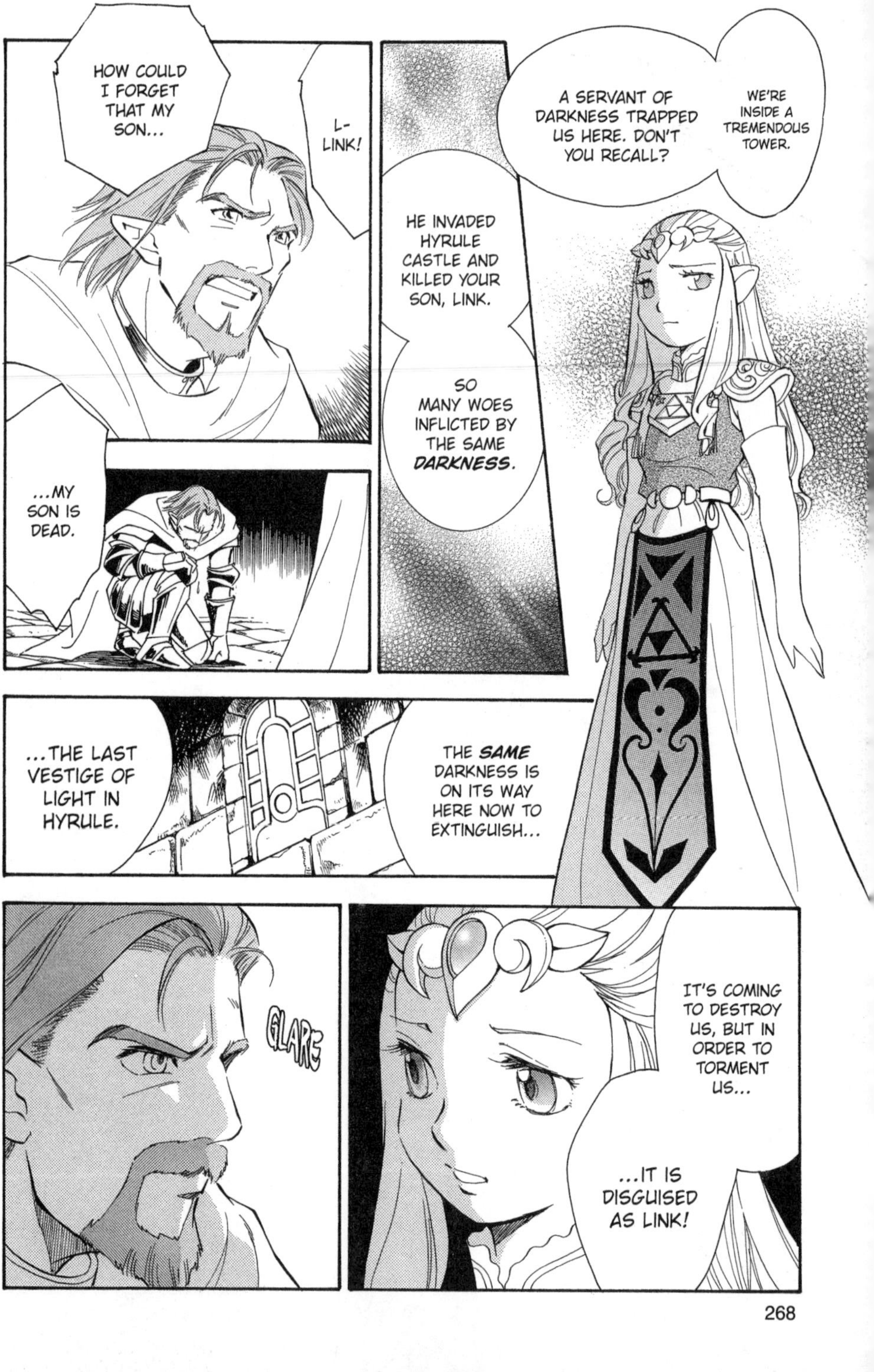
WE'RE INSIDE A TREMENDOUS TOWER.
A SERVANT OF DARKNESS TRAPPED US HERE. DON'T YOU RECALL?
HE INVADED HYRULE CASTLE AND KILLED YOUR SON, LINK.
SO MANY WOES INFLICTED BY THE SAME DARKNESS.
L- LINK!
HOW COULD I FORGET THAT MY SON...
...MY SON IS DEAD.
THE SAME DARKNESS IS ON ITS WAY HERE NOW TO EXTINGUISH...
...THE LAST VESTIGE OF LIGHT IN HYRULE.
IT'S COMING TO DESTROY US, BUT IN ORDER TO TORMENT US...
...IT IS DISGUISED AS LINK!
GLARE

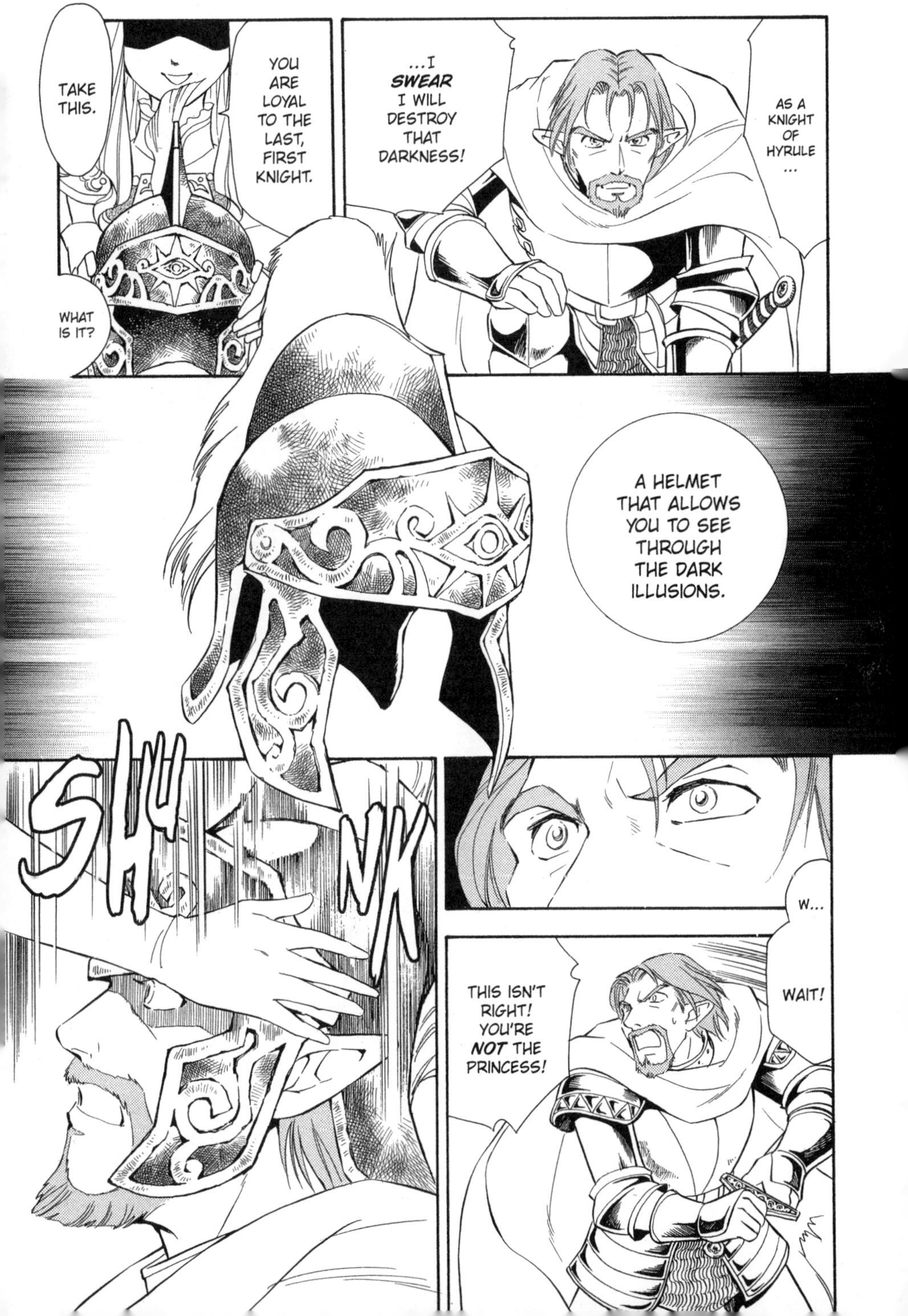
AS A KNIGHT OF HYRULE...
...I **SWEAR** I WILL DESTROY THAT DARKNESS!
YOU ARE LOYAL TO THE LAST, FIRST KNIGHT.
TAKE THIS.
WHAT IS IT?
A HELMET THAT ALLOWS YOU TO SEE THROUGH THE DARK ILLUSIONS.
W...
WAIT!
THIS ISN'T RIGHT! YOU'RE **NOT** THE PRINCESS!
SHUNK

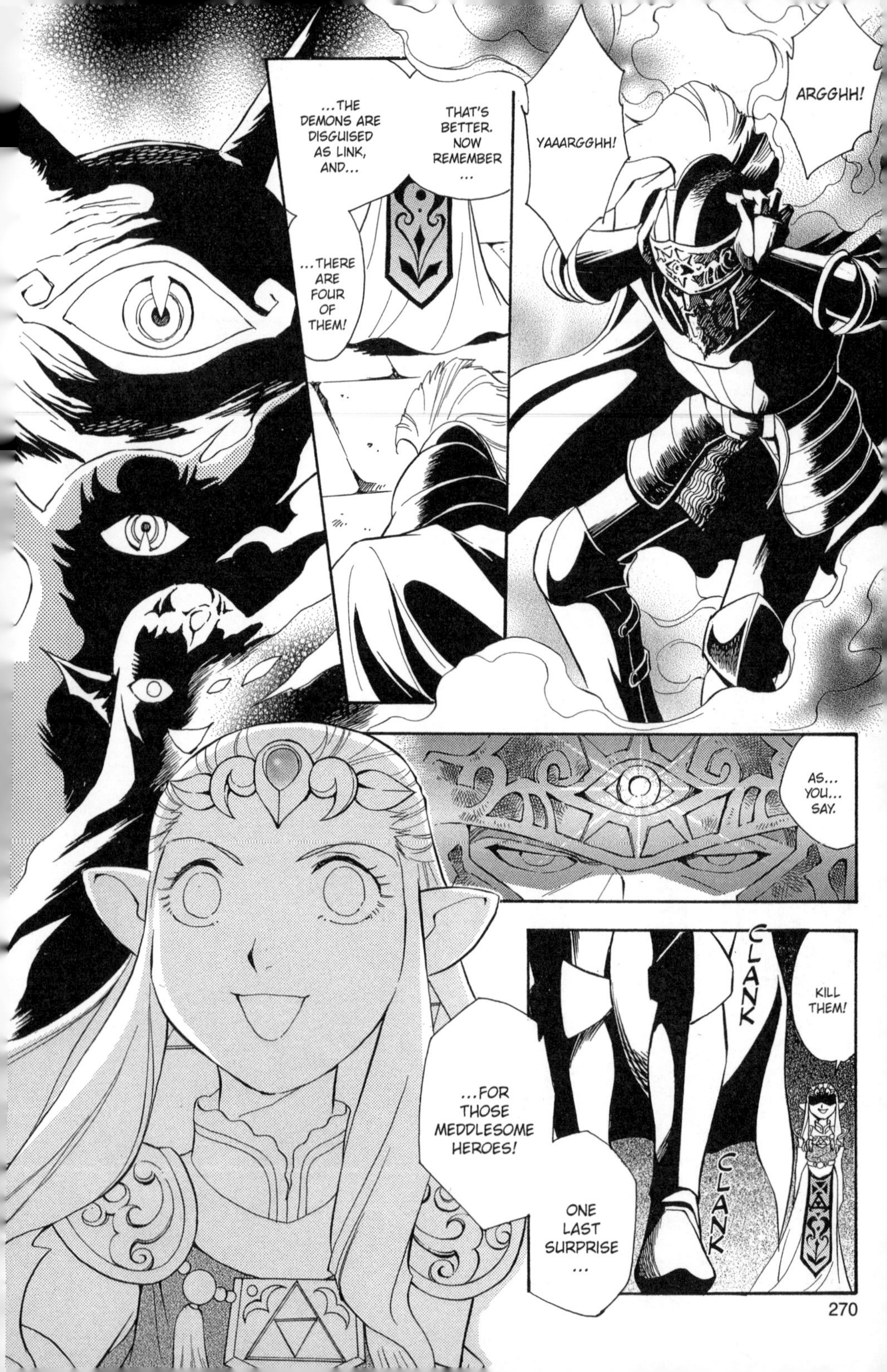
ARGGHH!
YAAARGGHH!
THAT'S BETTER. NOW REMEMBER ...
...THE DEMONS ARE DISGUISED AS LINK, AND...
...THERE ARE FOUR OF THEM!
AS... YOU... SAY.
KILL THEM!
CLANK
CLANK
ONE LAST SURPRISE ...
...FOR THOSE MEDDLESOME HEROES!

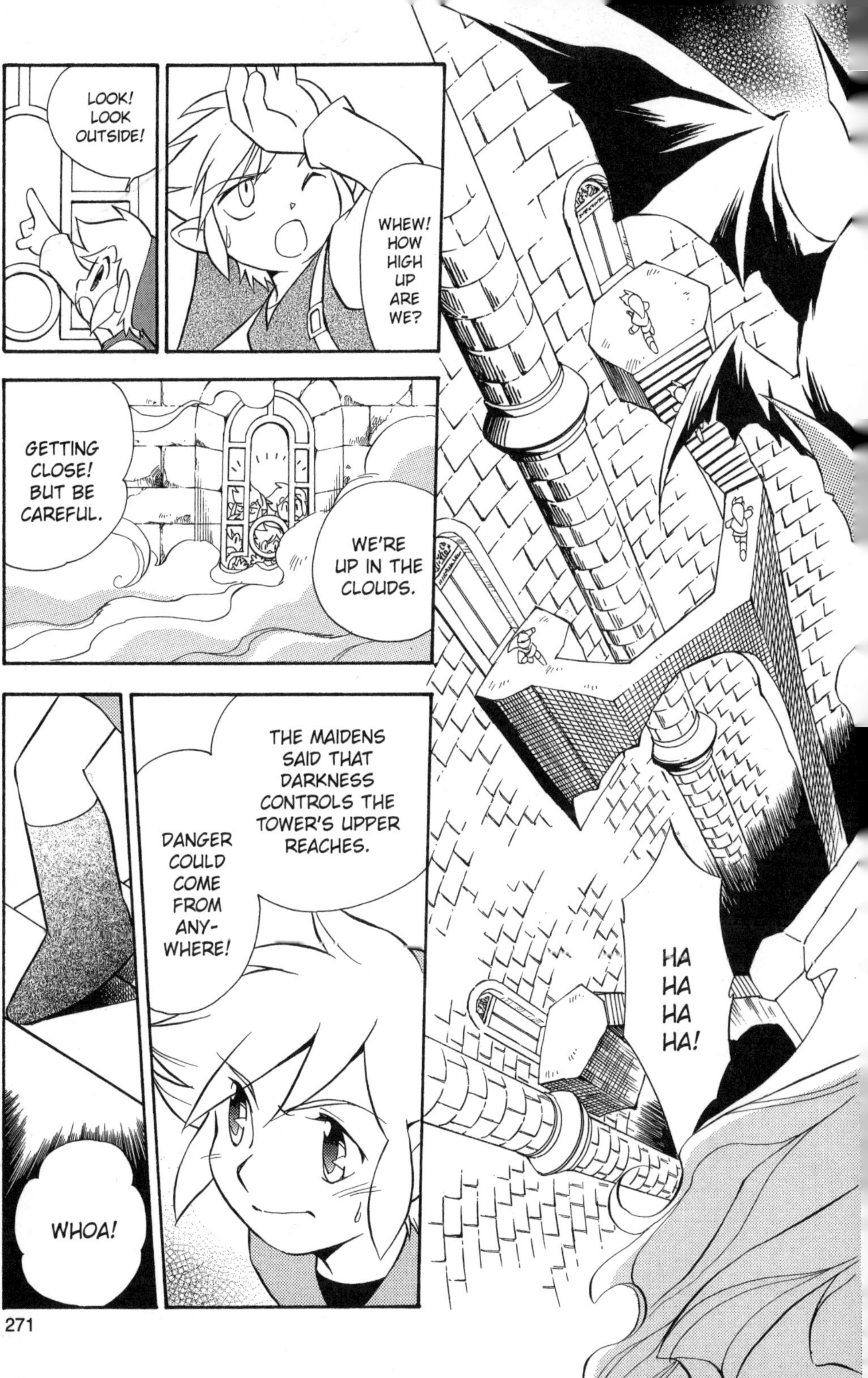
HA HA HA HA!
WHEW! HOW HIGH UP ARE WE?
LOOK! LOOK OUTSIDE!
WE'RE UP IN THE CLOUDS.
GETTING CLOSE! BUT BE CAREFUL.
THE MAIDENS SAID THAT DARKNESS CONTROLS THE TOWER'S UPPER REACHES.
DANGER COULD COME FROM ANY-WHERE!
WHOA!

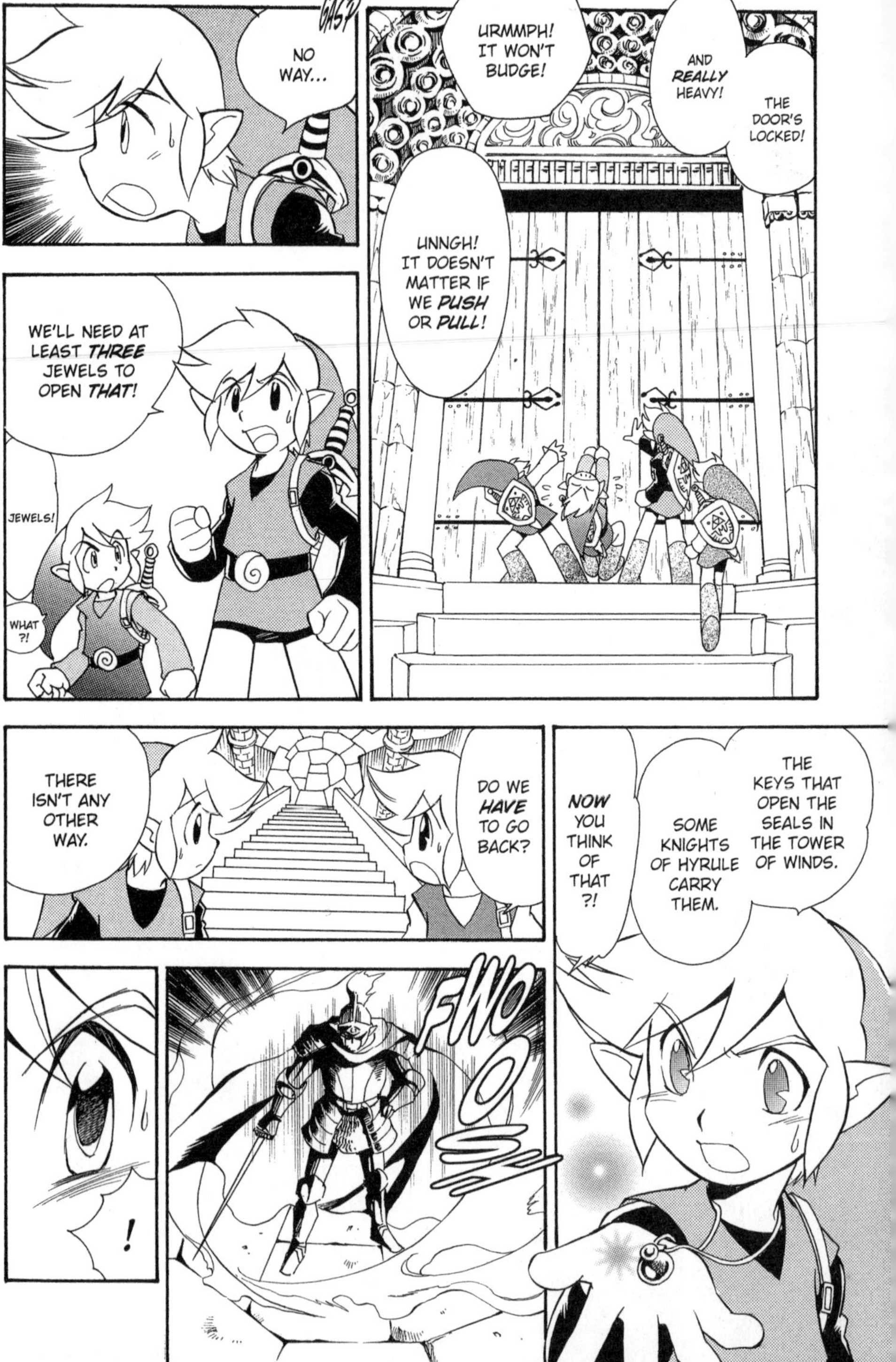
THE DOOR'S LOCKED!
AND REALLY HEAVY!
URMMPH! IT WON'T BUDGE!
UNNGH! IT DOESN'T MATTER IF WE PUSH OR PULL!
GASP
NO WAY...
WE'LL NEED AT LEAST THREE JEWELS TO OPEN THAT!
JEWELS!
WHAT?!
THE KEYS THAT OPEN THE SEALS IN THE TOWER OF WINDS.
SOME KNIGHTS OF HYRULE CARRY THEM.
NOW YOU THINK OF THAT?!
DO WE HAVE TO GO BACK?
THERE ISN'T ANY OTHER WAY.
FWOOOSH
!

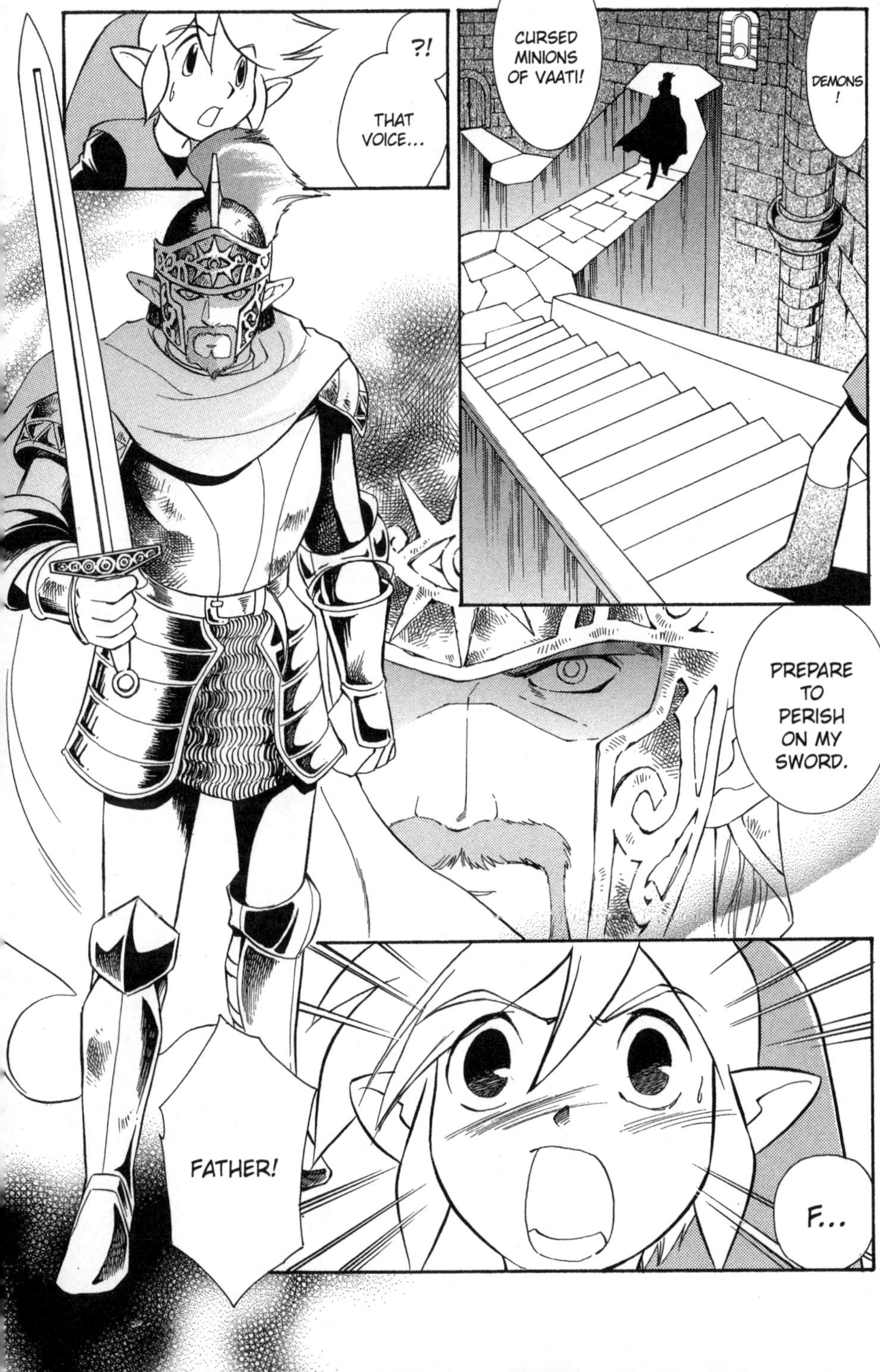
DEMONS!
CURSED MINIONS OF VAATI!
?!
THAT VOICE...
PREPARE TO PERISH ON MY SWORD.
F...
FATHER!

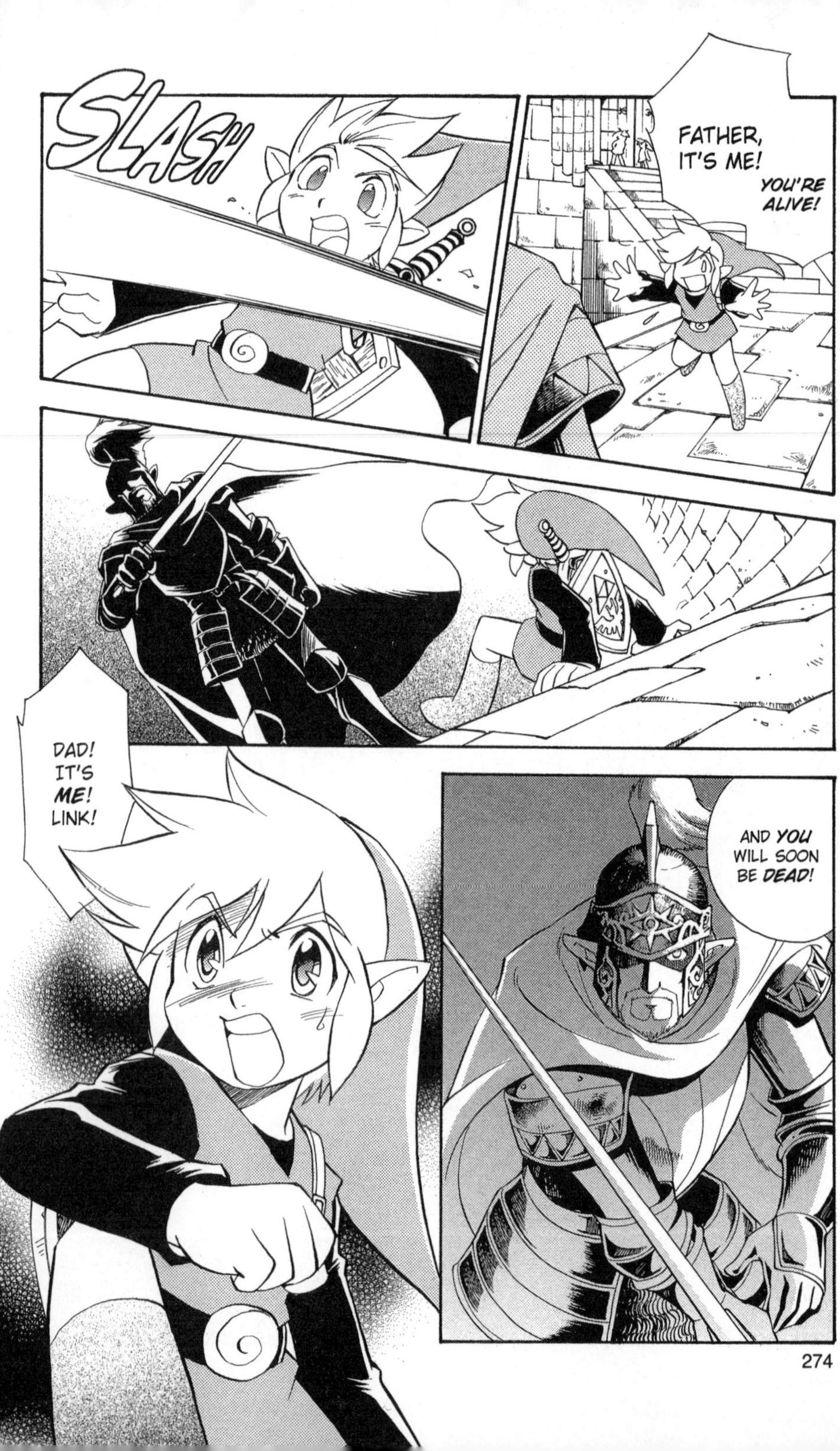
FATHER, IT'S ME!
YOU'RE ALIVE!
SLASH
AND YOU WILL SOON BE DEAD!
DAD! IT'S ME! LINK!

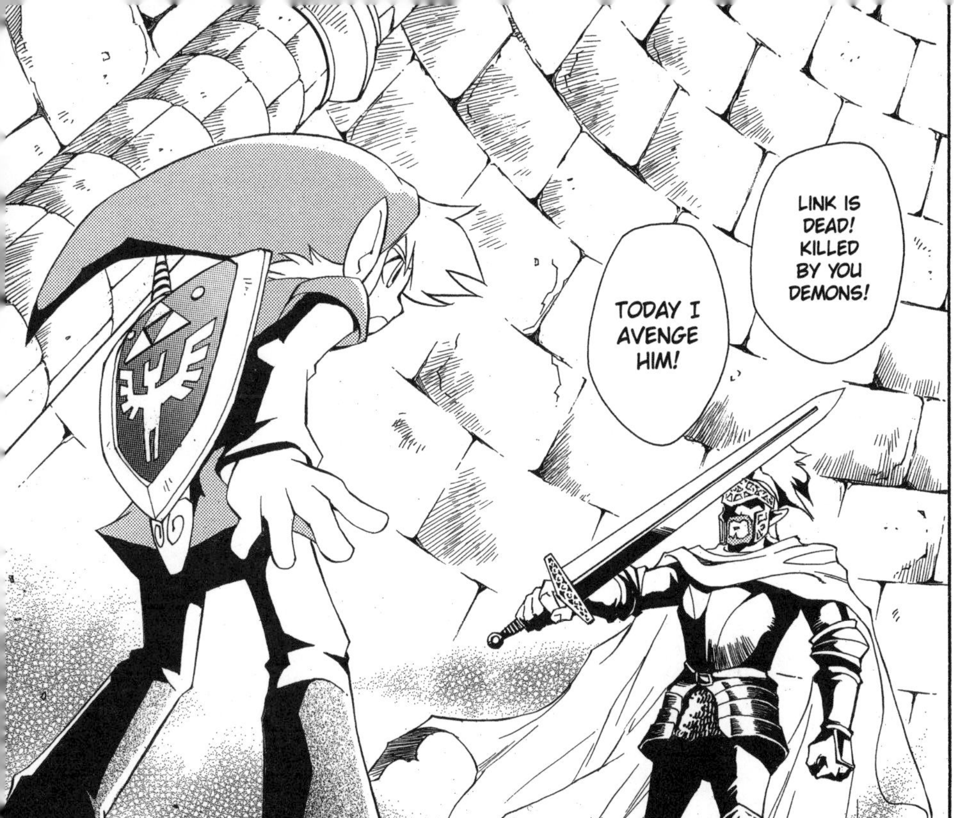
LINK IS DEAD! KILLED BY YOU DEMONS!
TODAY I AVENGE HIM!

CHAPTER 10 A Fight Against Father

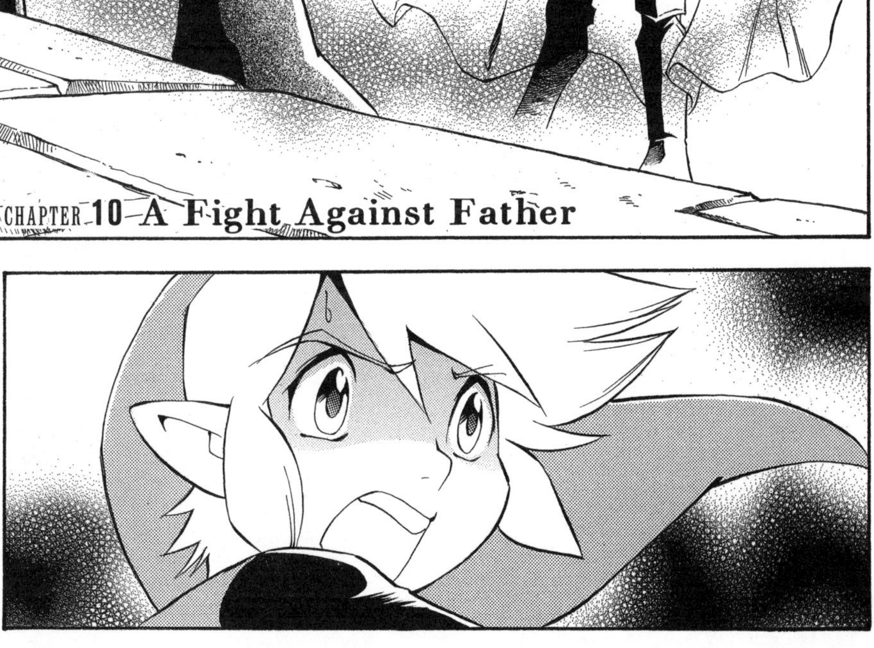

CHAPTER 10 A Fight Against Father

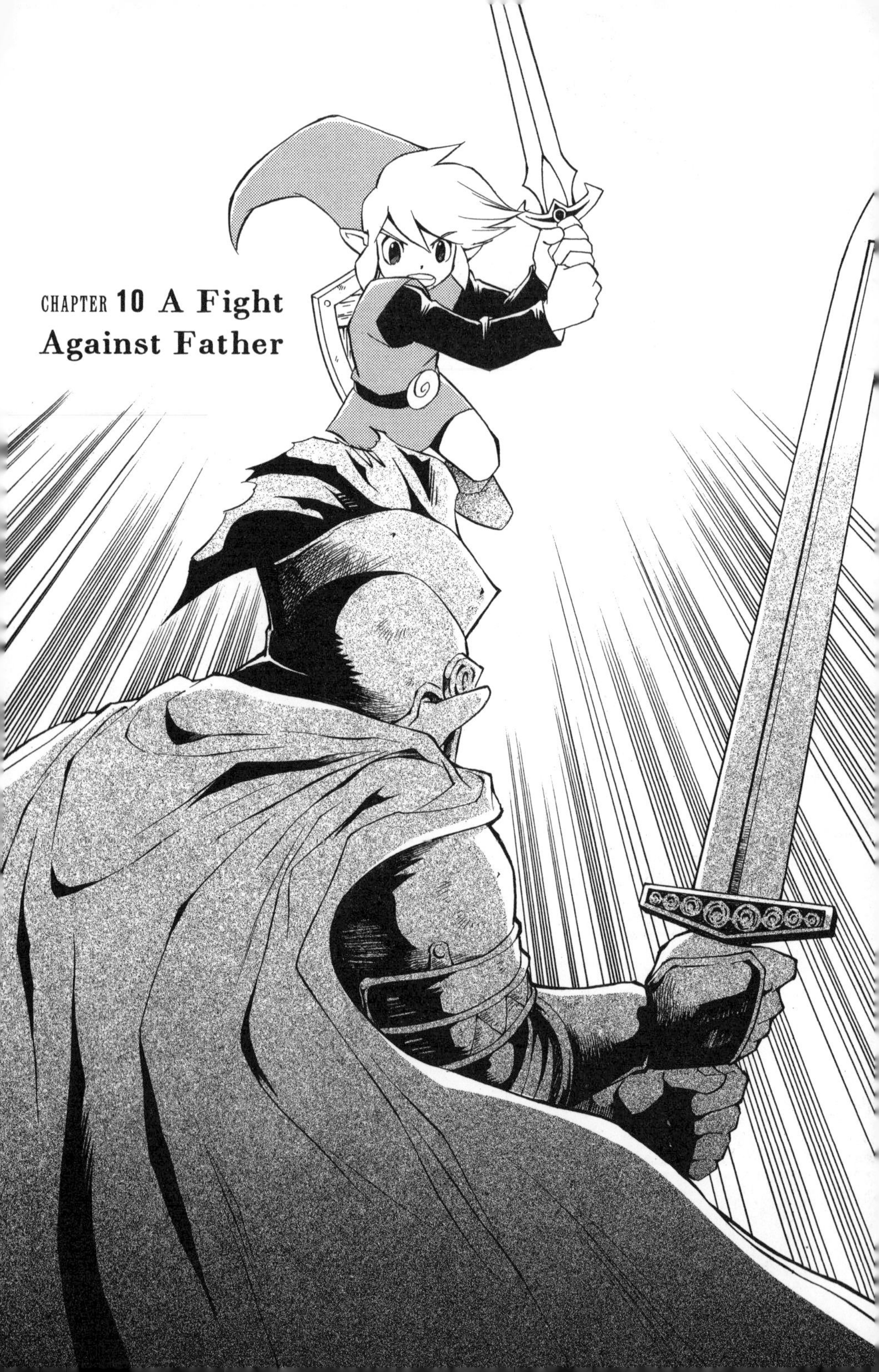

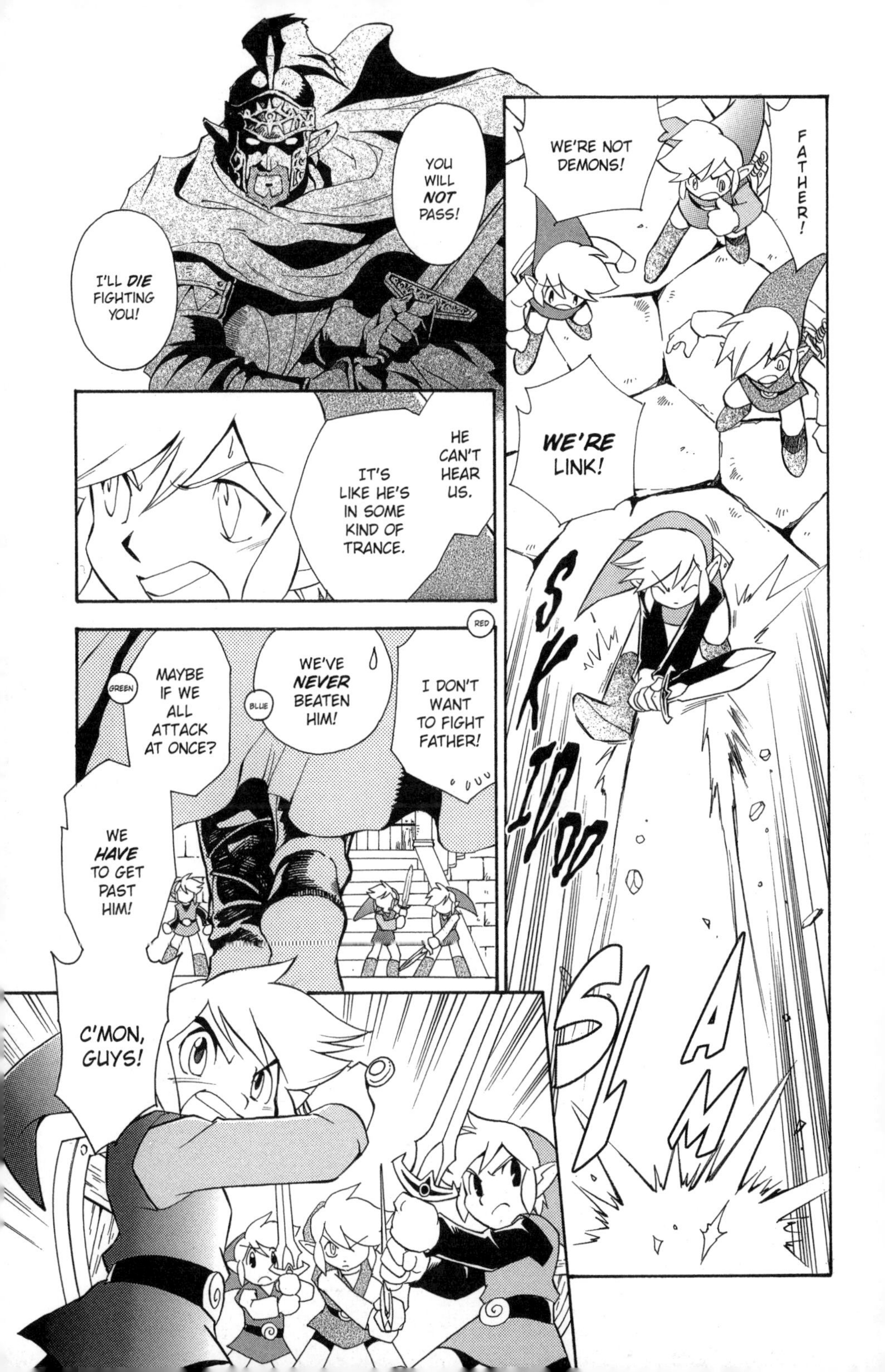
FATHER!
WE'RE NOT DEMONS!
WE'RE LINK!
SKIDDD
SLAM
YOU WILL NOT PASS!
I'LL DIE FIGHTING YOU!
HE CAN'T HEAR US.
IT'S LIKE HE'S IN SOME KIND OF TRANCE.
RED
I DON'T WANT TO FIGHT FATHER!
BLUE
WE'VE NEVER BEATEN HIM!
GREEN
MAYBE IF WE ALL ATTACK AT ONCE?
WE HAVE TO GET PAST HIM!
C'MON, GUYS!

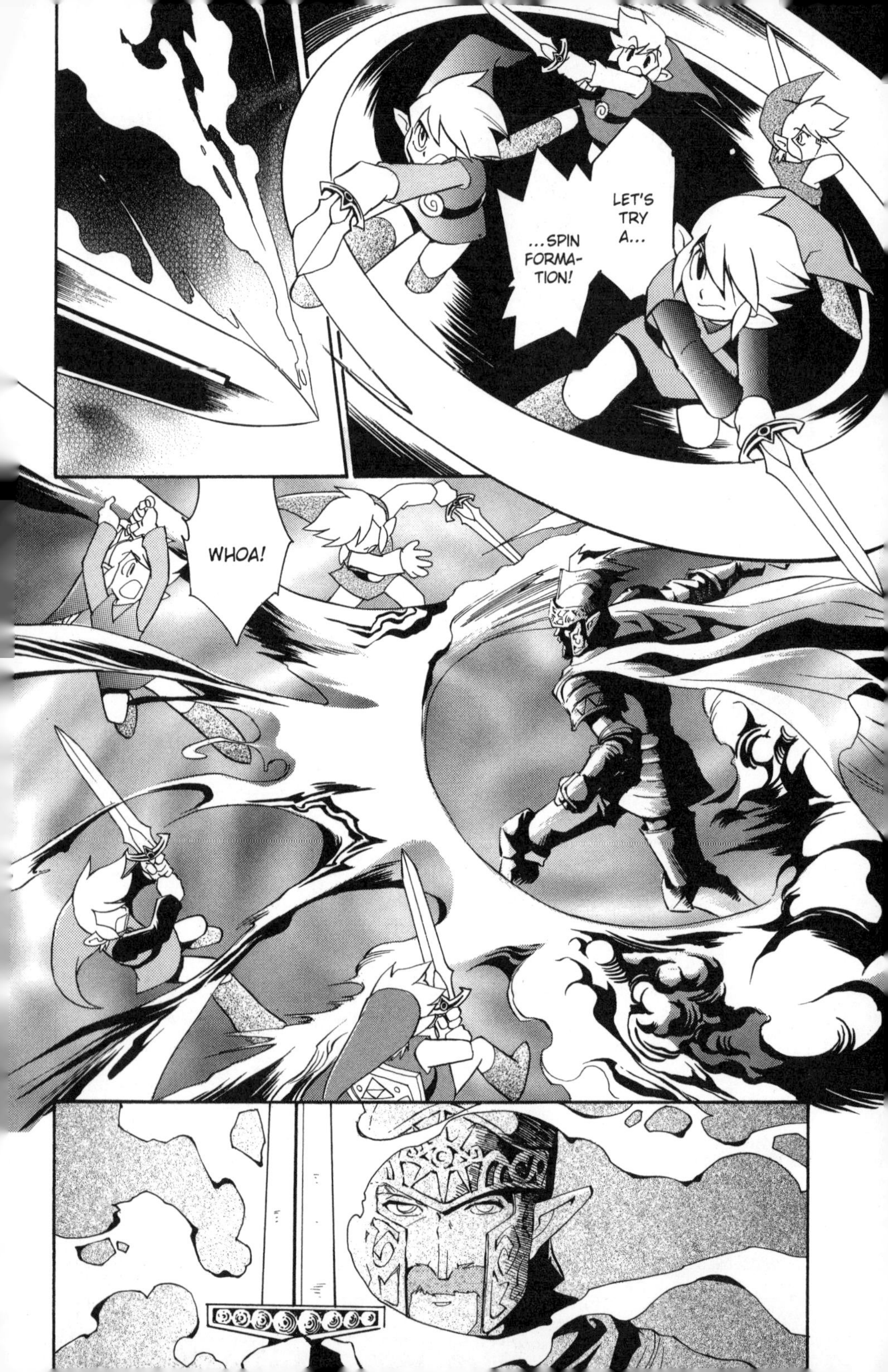
LET'S TRY A...
...SPIN FORMATION!
WHOA!

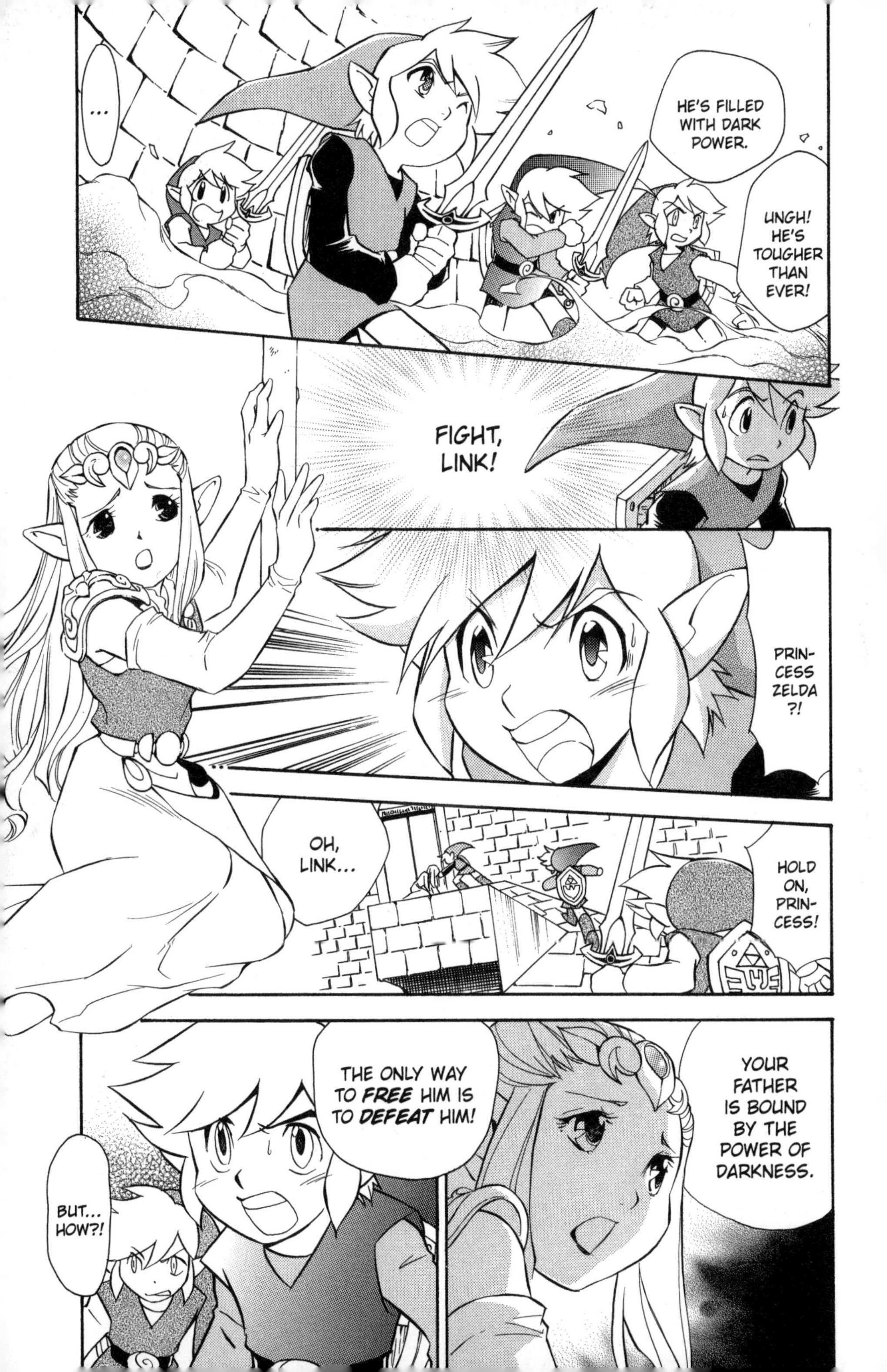
UNGH! HE'S TOUGHER THAN EVER!
HE'S FILLED WITH DARK POWER.
...
FIGHT, LINK!
PRIN-CESS ZELDA?!
HOLD ON, PRIN-CESS!
OH, LINK...
YOUR FATHER IS BOUND BY THE POWER OF DARKNESS.
THE ONLY WAY TO *FREE* HIM IS TO *DEFEAT* HIM!
BUT... HOW?!

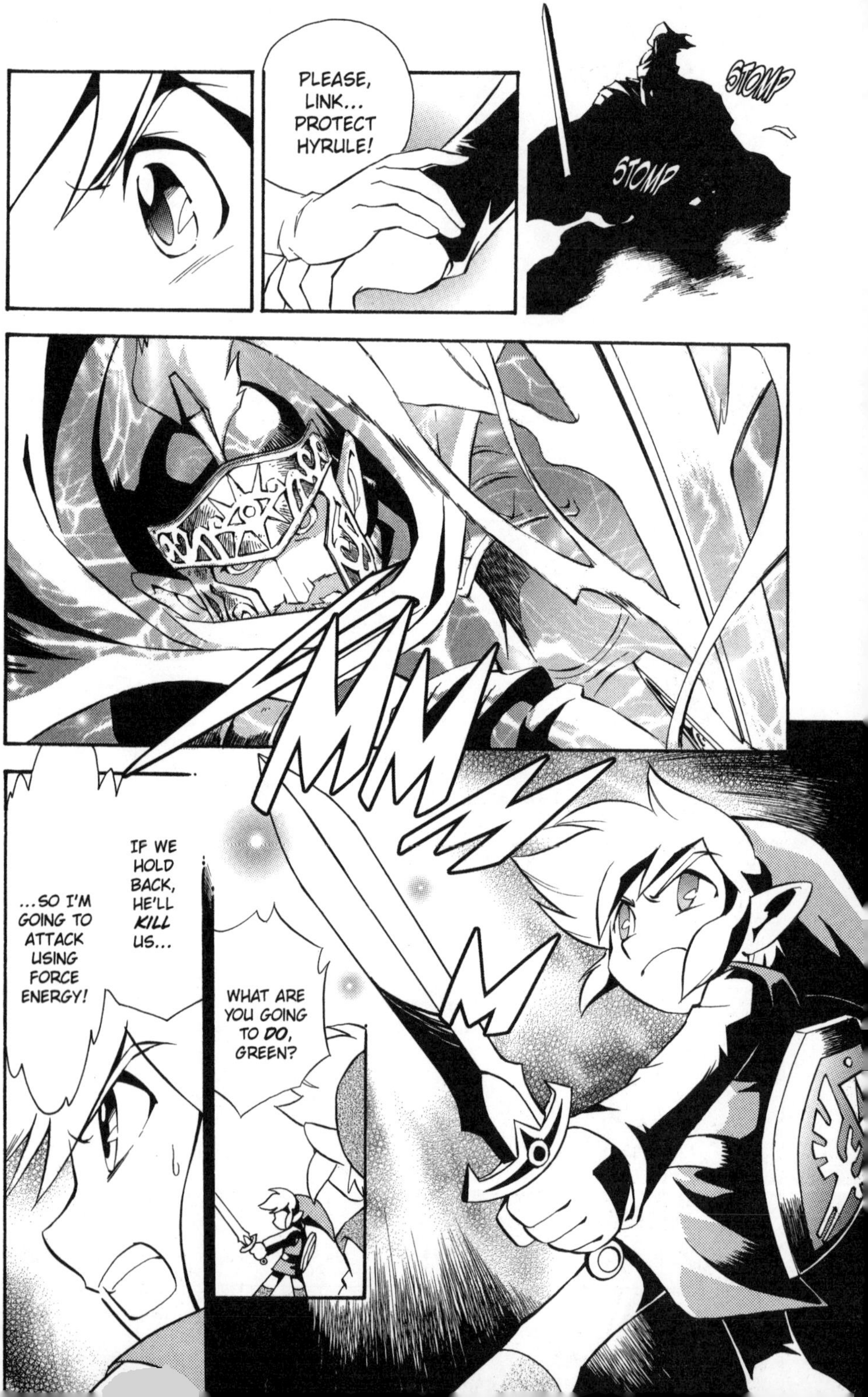
STOMP
STOMP
PLEASE, LINK... PROTECT HYRULE!
WHAT ARE YOU GOING TO DO, GREEN?
IF WE HOLD BACK, HE'LL KILL US...
...SO I'M GOING TO ATTACK USING FORCE ENERGY!

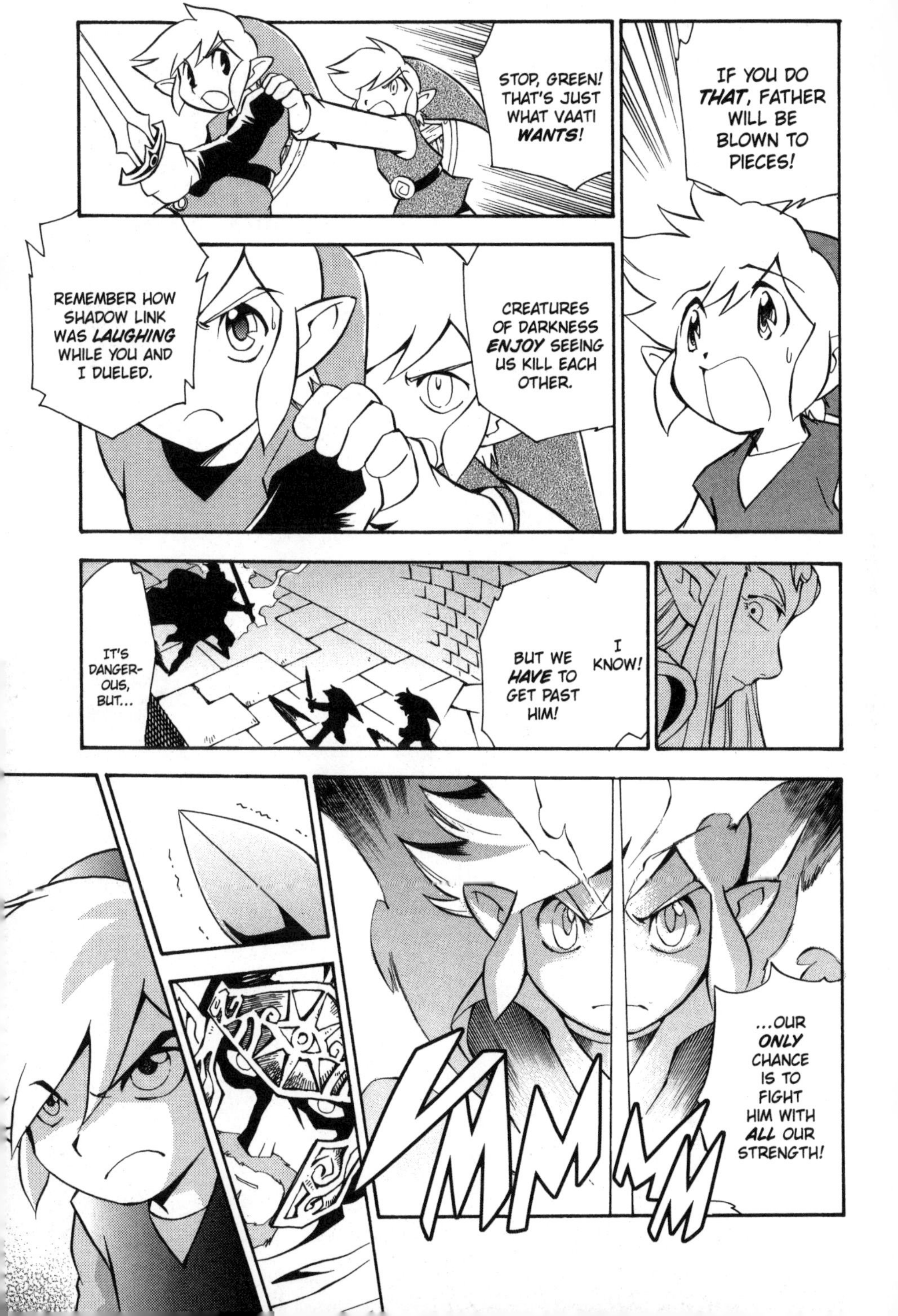
IF YOU DO ***THAT***, FATHER WILL BE BLOWN TO PIECES!
STOP, GREEN! THAT'S JUST WHAT VAATI ***WANTS***!
CREATURES OF DARKNESS ***ENJOY*** SEEING US KILL EACH OTHER.
REMEMBER HOW SHADOW LINK WAS ***LAUGHING*** WHILE YOU AND I DUELED.
I KNOW!
BUT WE ***HAVE*** TO GET PAST HIM!
IT'S DANGER-OUS, BUT...
...OUR ***ONLY*** CHANCE IS TO FIGHT HIM WITH ***ALL*** OUR STRENGTH!

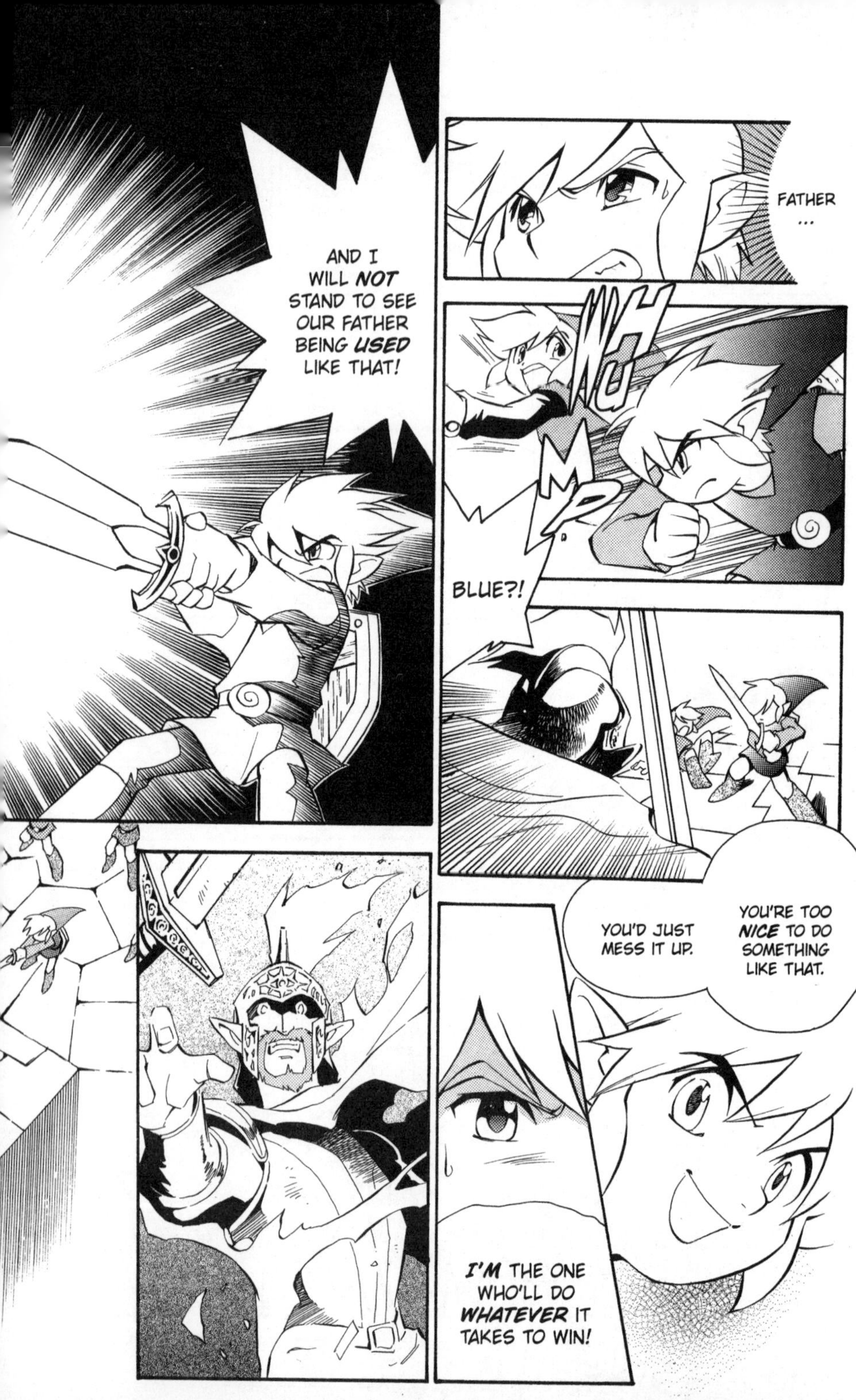
FATHER ...
WHMP
BLUE?!
AND I WILL NOT STAND TO SEE OUR FATHER BEING USED LIKE THAT!
YOU'RE TOO NICE TO DO SOMETHING LIKE THAT.
YOU'D JUST MESS IT UP.
I'M THE ONE WHO'LL DO WHATEVER IT TAKES TO WIN!

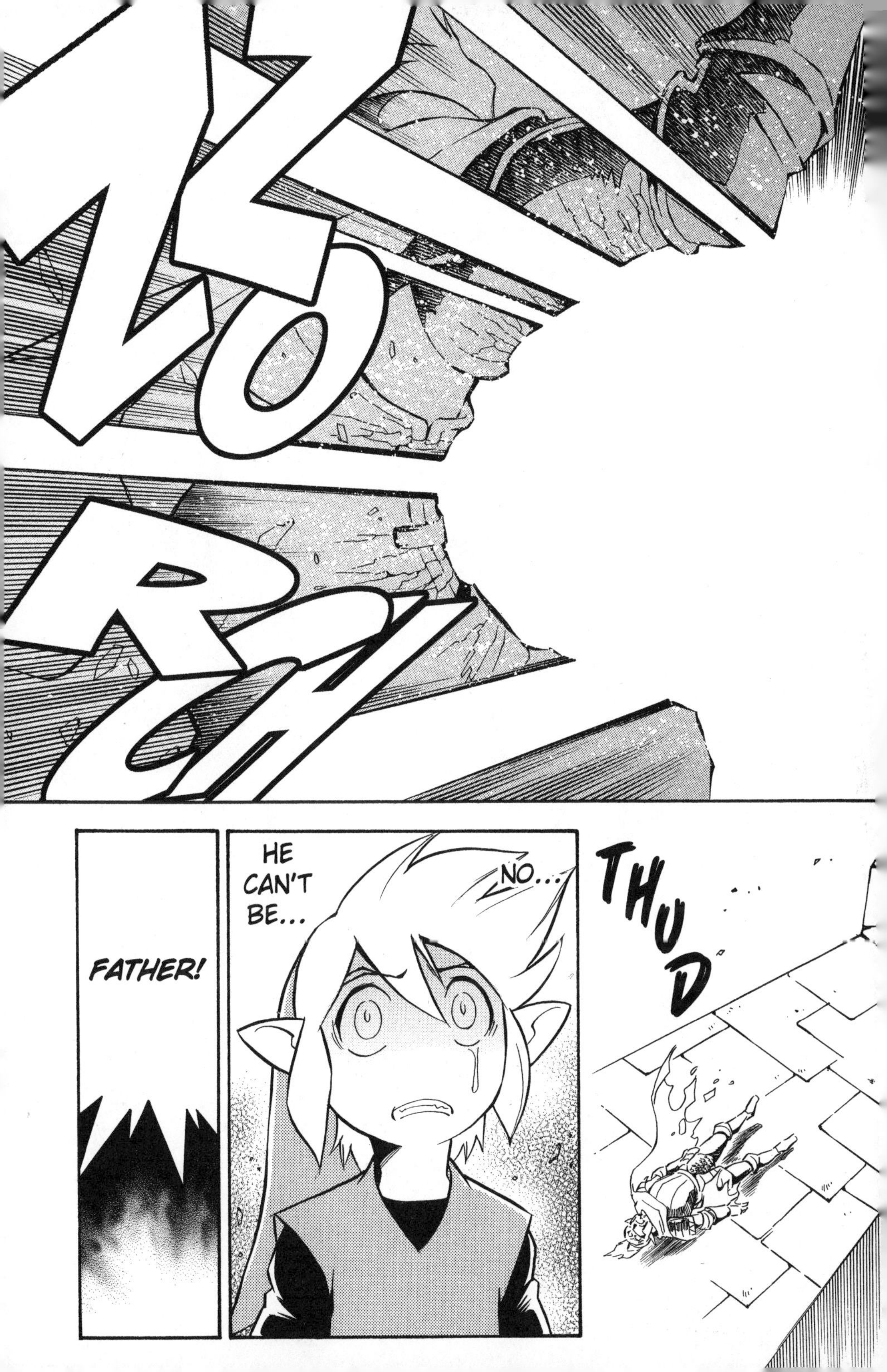
THUD
NO...
HE CAN'T BE...
FATHER!

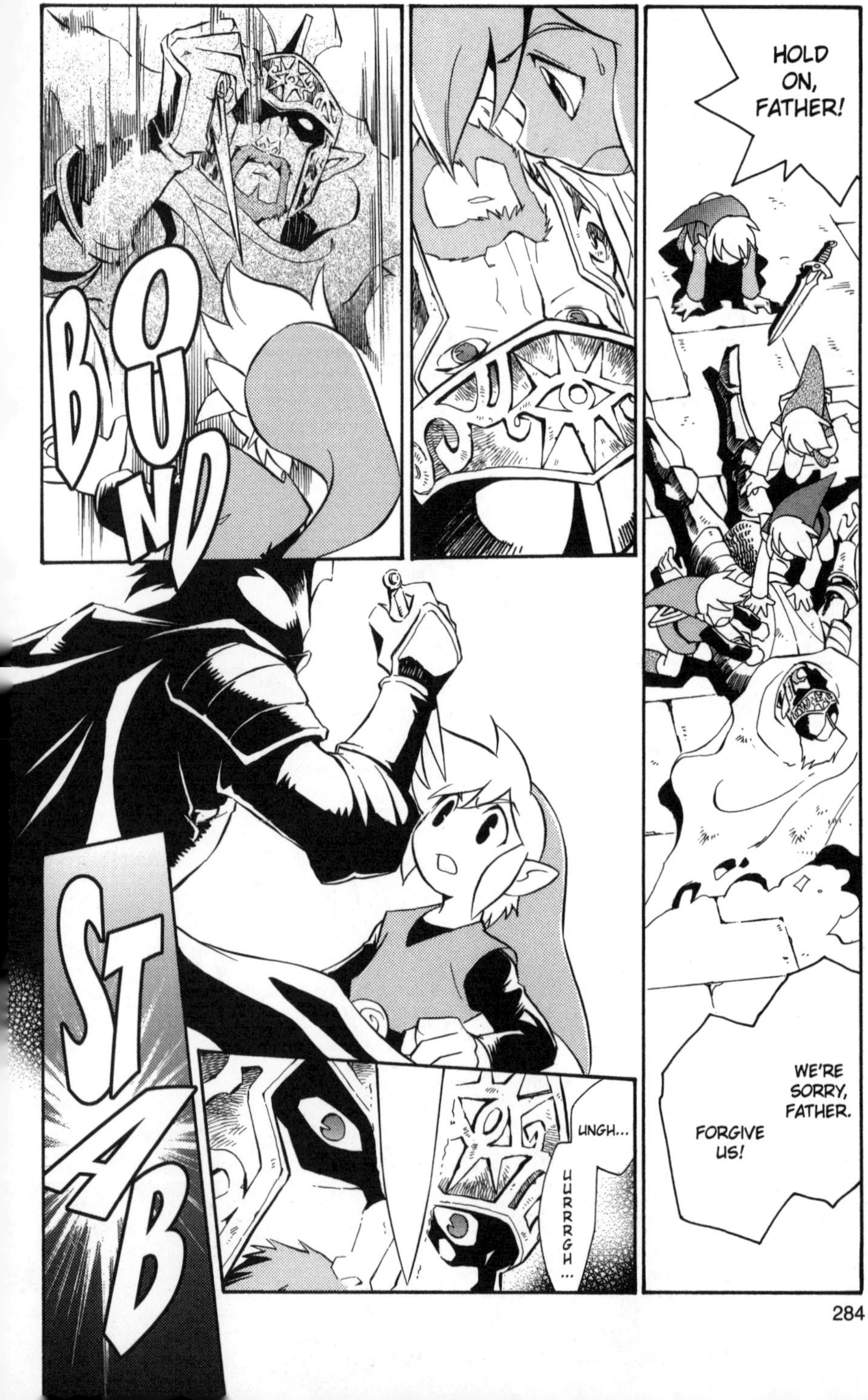
HOLD ON, FATHER!
WE'RE SORRY, FATHER.
FORGIVE US!
BOUND
STAB
UNGH...
HURRRGH...

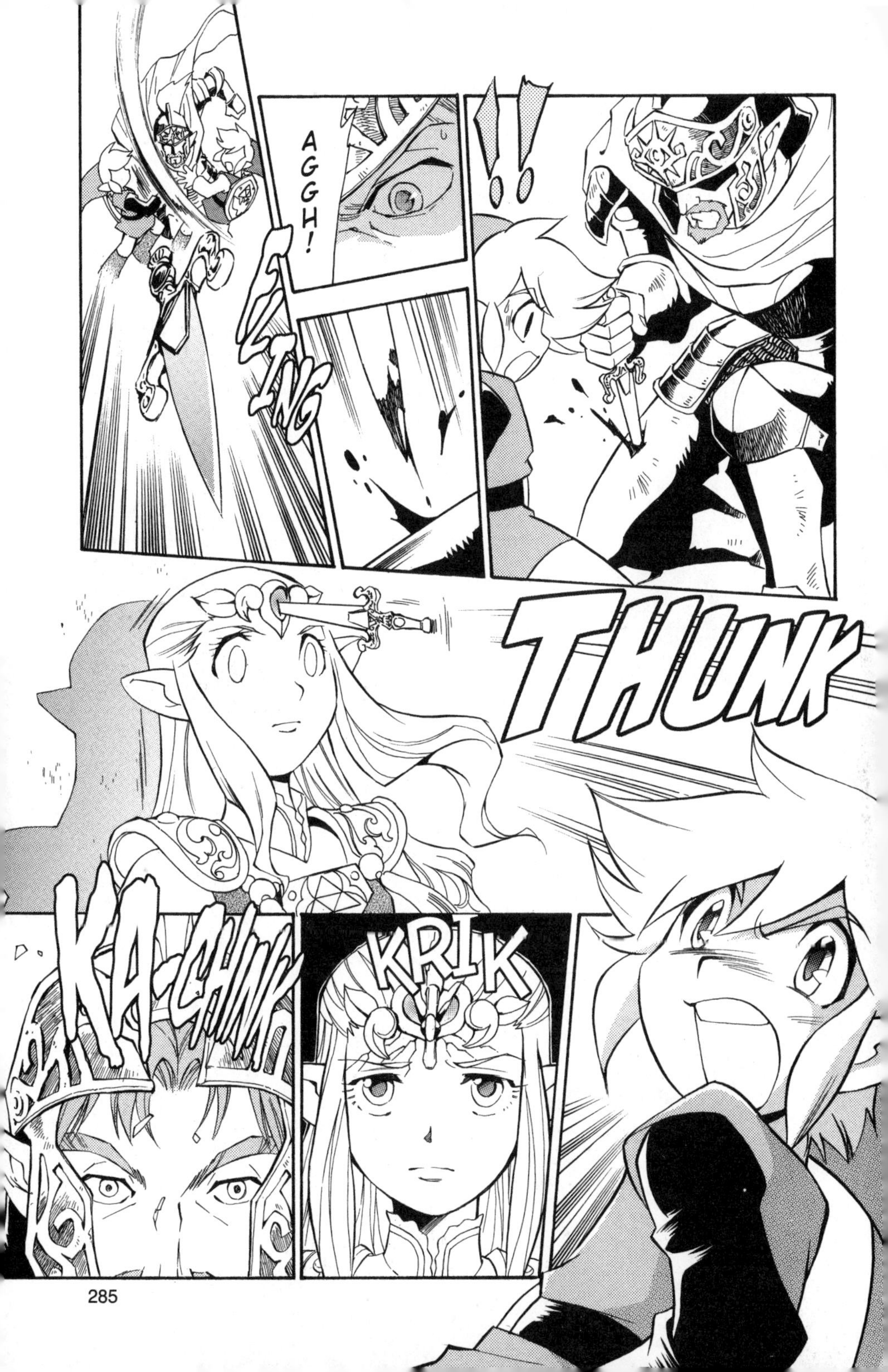
!!
AGGH!
ZING
THUNK
KRIK
KA-CHINK

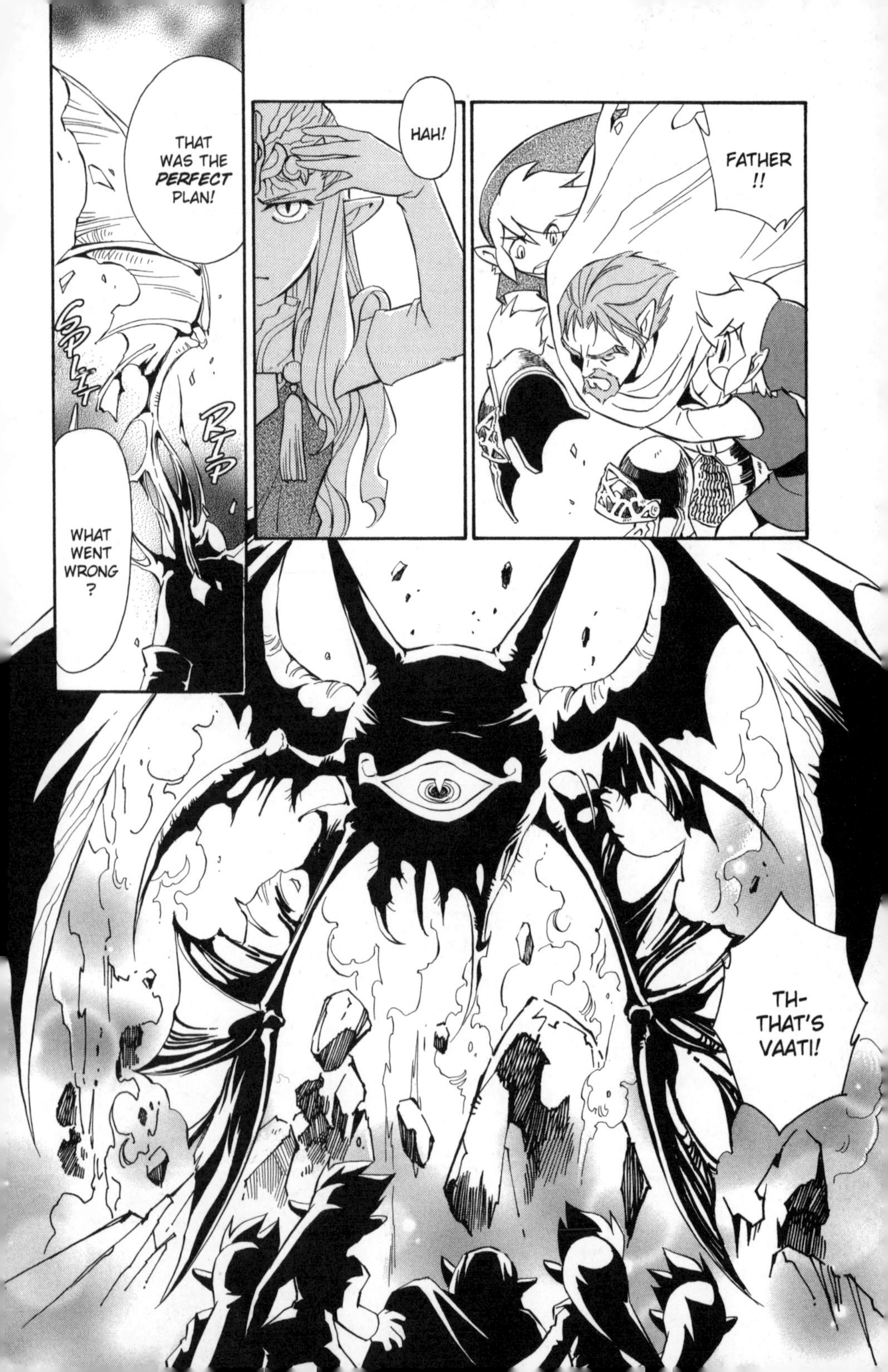
FATHER !!
HAH!
THAT WAS THE *PERFECT* PLAN!
SPLIT
RIP
WHAT WENT WRONG ?
TH-THAT'S VAATI!

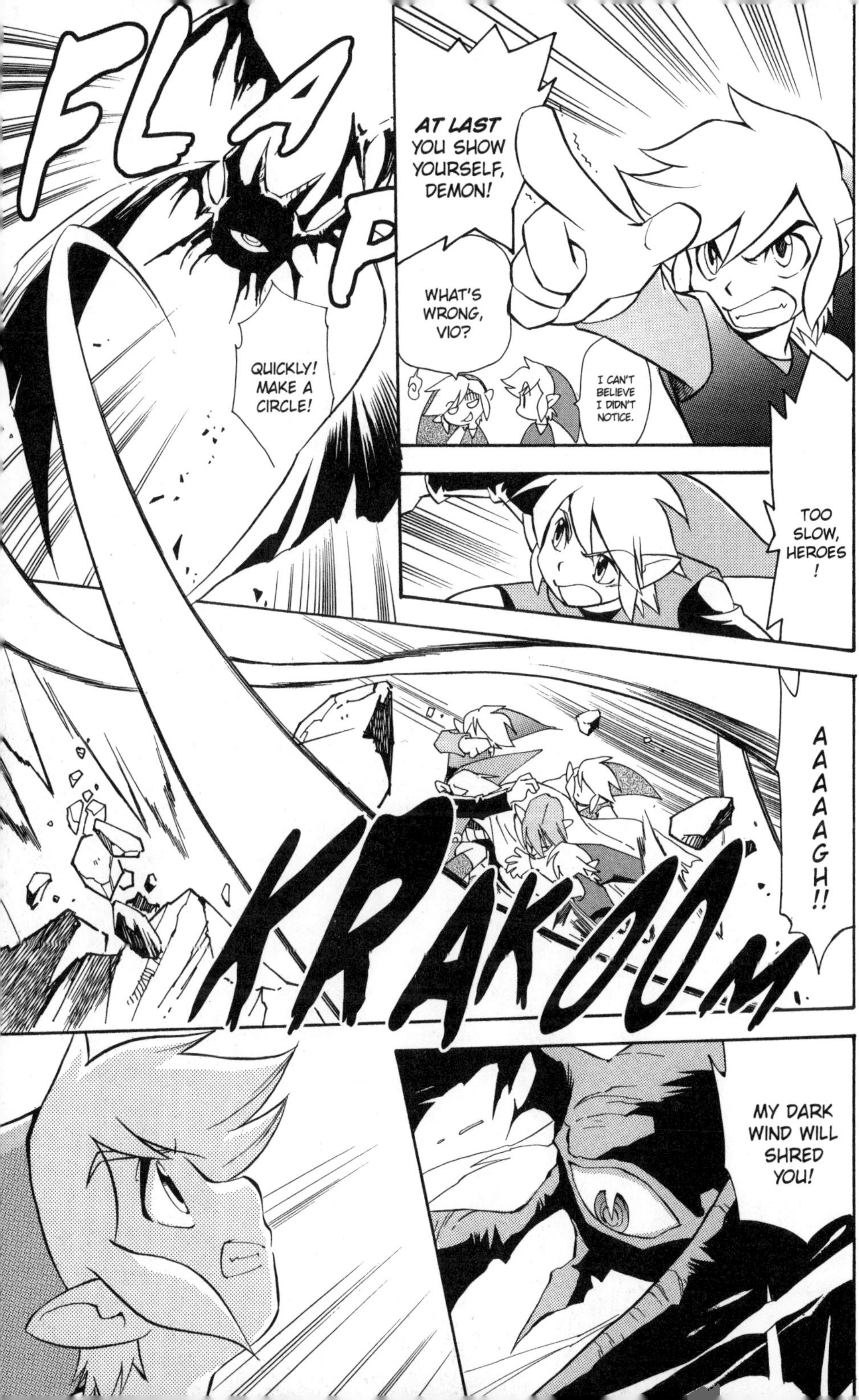
AT LAST YOU SHOW YOURSELF, DEMON!
WHAT'S WRONG, VIO?
I CAN'T BELIEVE I DIDN'T NOTICE.
TOO SLOW, HEROES!
FLAP
QUICKLY! MAKE A CIRCLE!
AAAAAAGH!!
KRAKOOM
MY DARK WIND WILL SHRED YOU!

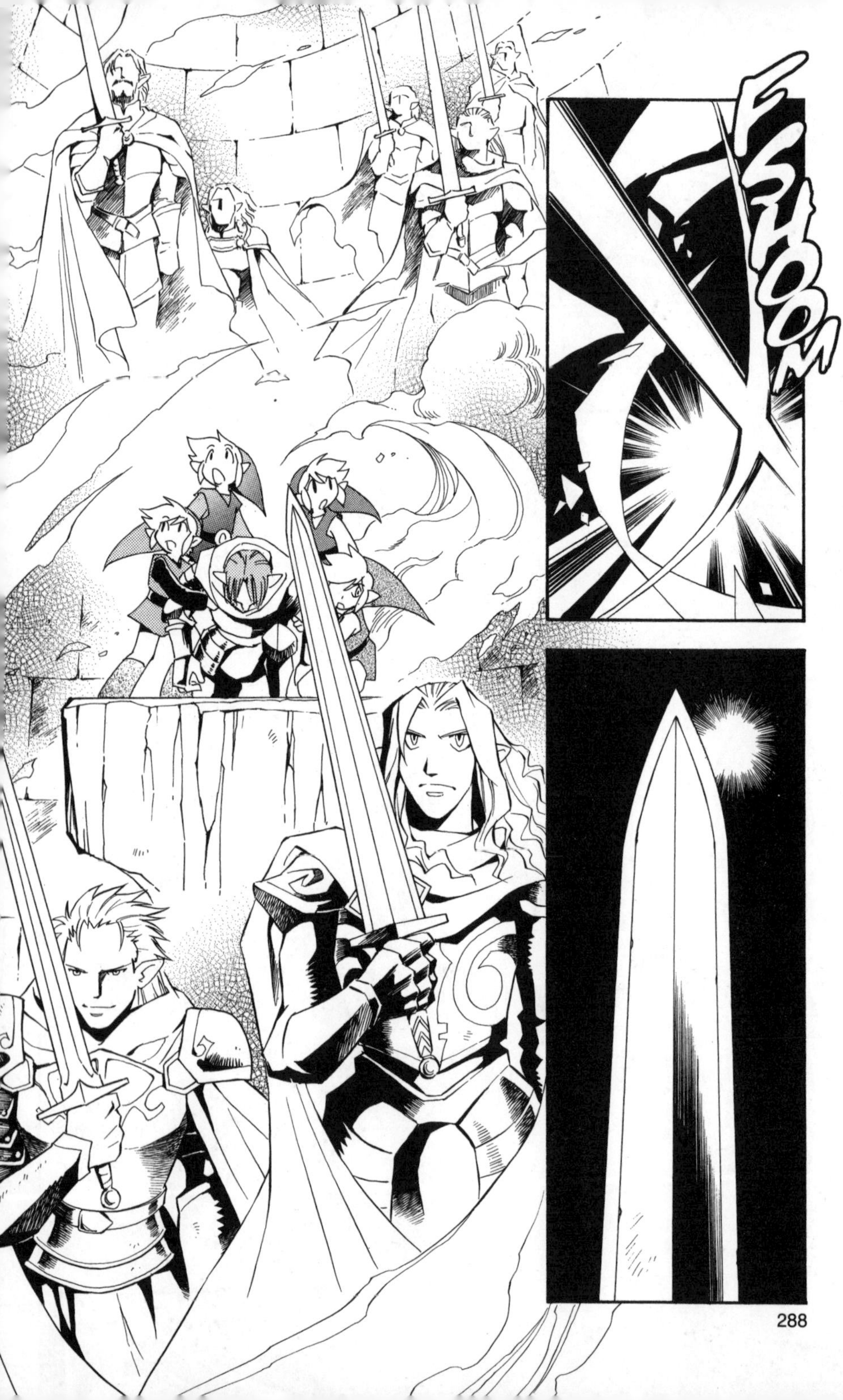
FSHOOM

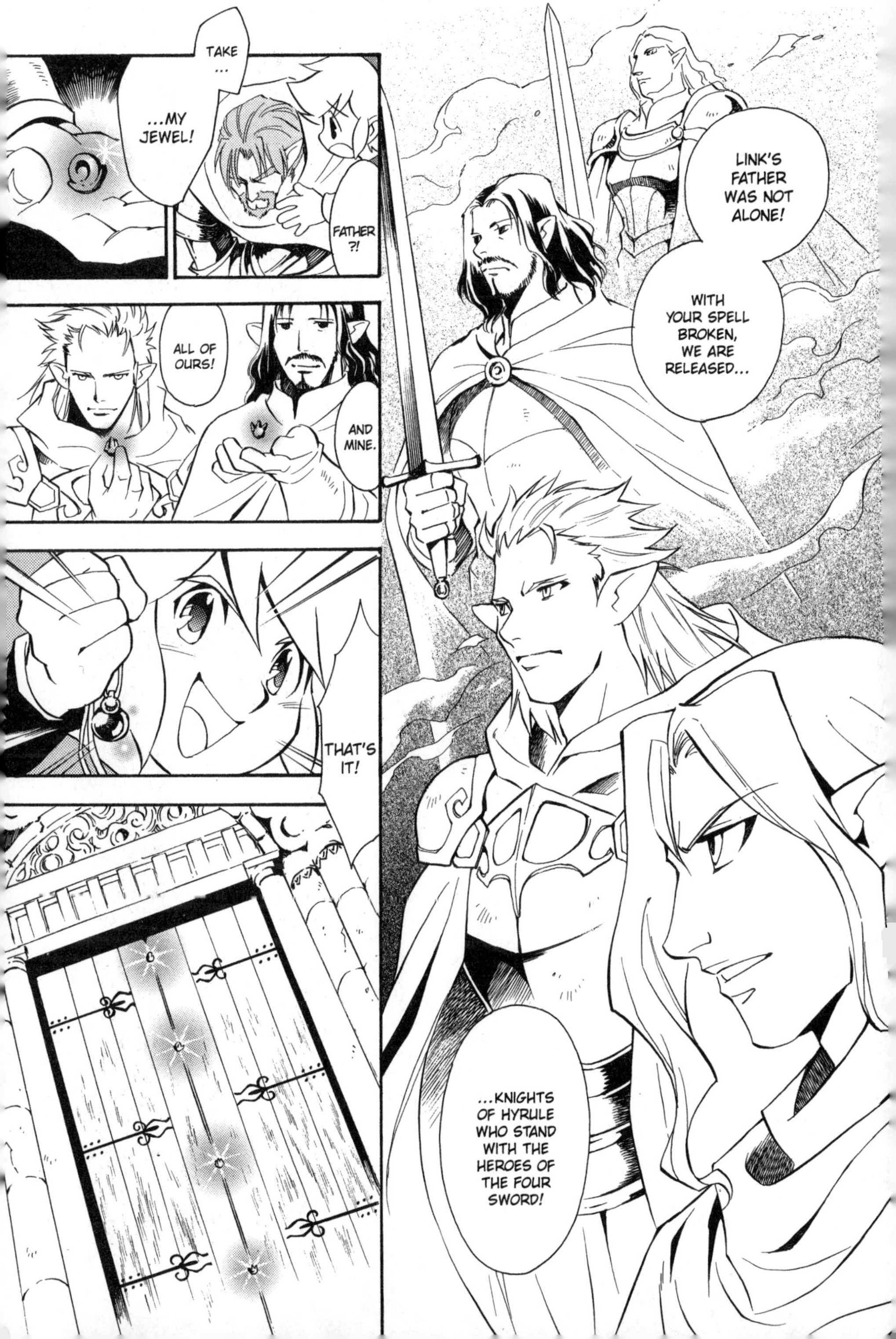
LINK'S FATHER WAS NOT ALONE!
WITH YOUR SPELL BROKEN, WE ARE RELEASED...
...KNIGHTS OF HYRULE WHO STAND WITH THE HEROES OF THE FOUR SWORD!
TAKE ...
...MY JEWEL!
FATHER ?!
AND MINE.
ALL OF OURS!
THAT'S IT!

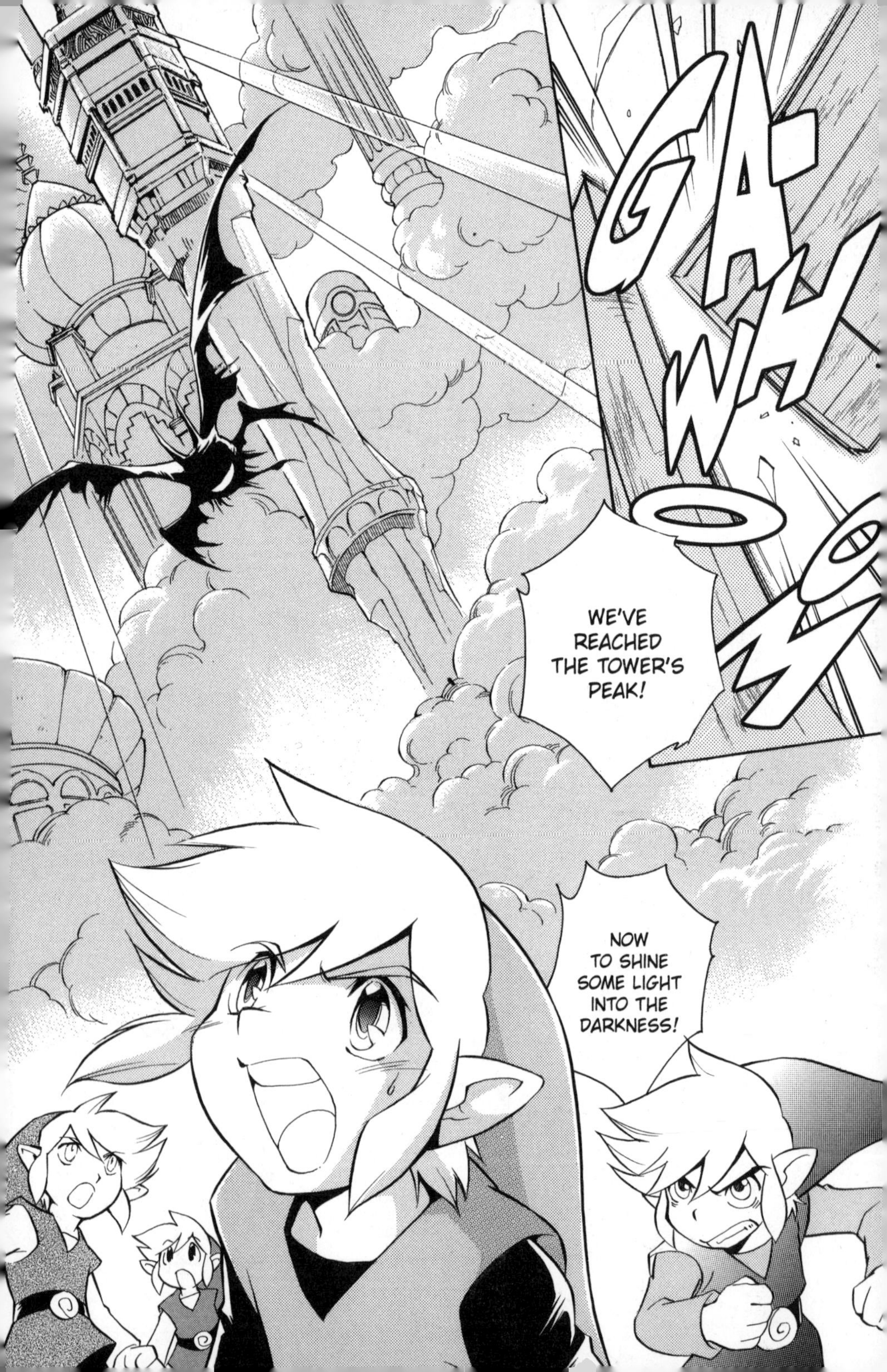
GA-WHOOM
WE'VE REACHED THE TOWER'S PEAK!
NOW TO SHINE SOME LIGHT INTO THE DARKNESS!

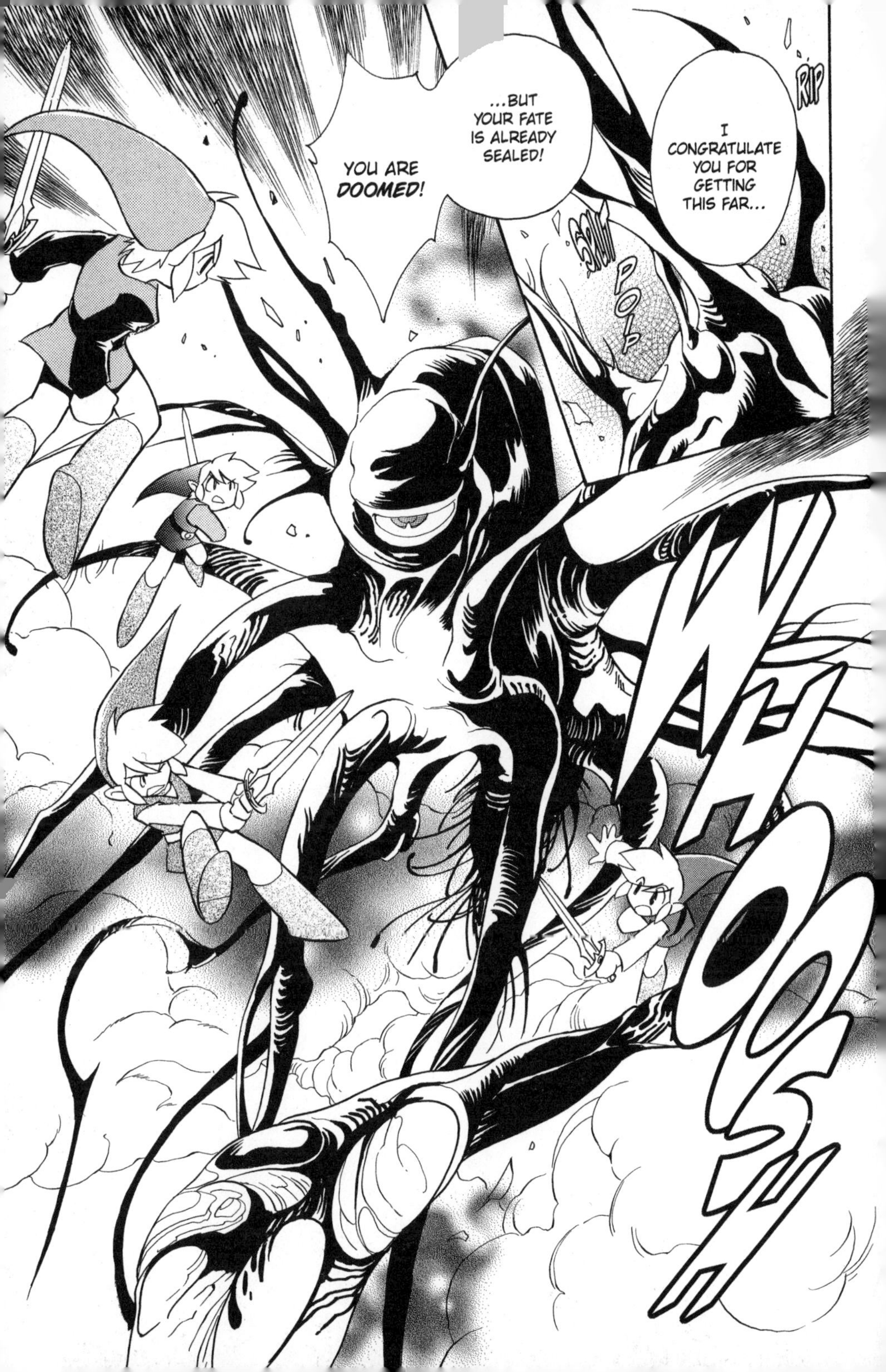
RIP
I CONGRATULATE YOU FOR GETTING THIS FAR...
...BUT YOUR FATE IS ALREADY SEALED!
YOU ARE *DOOMED!*
POP
WHOOSH!

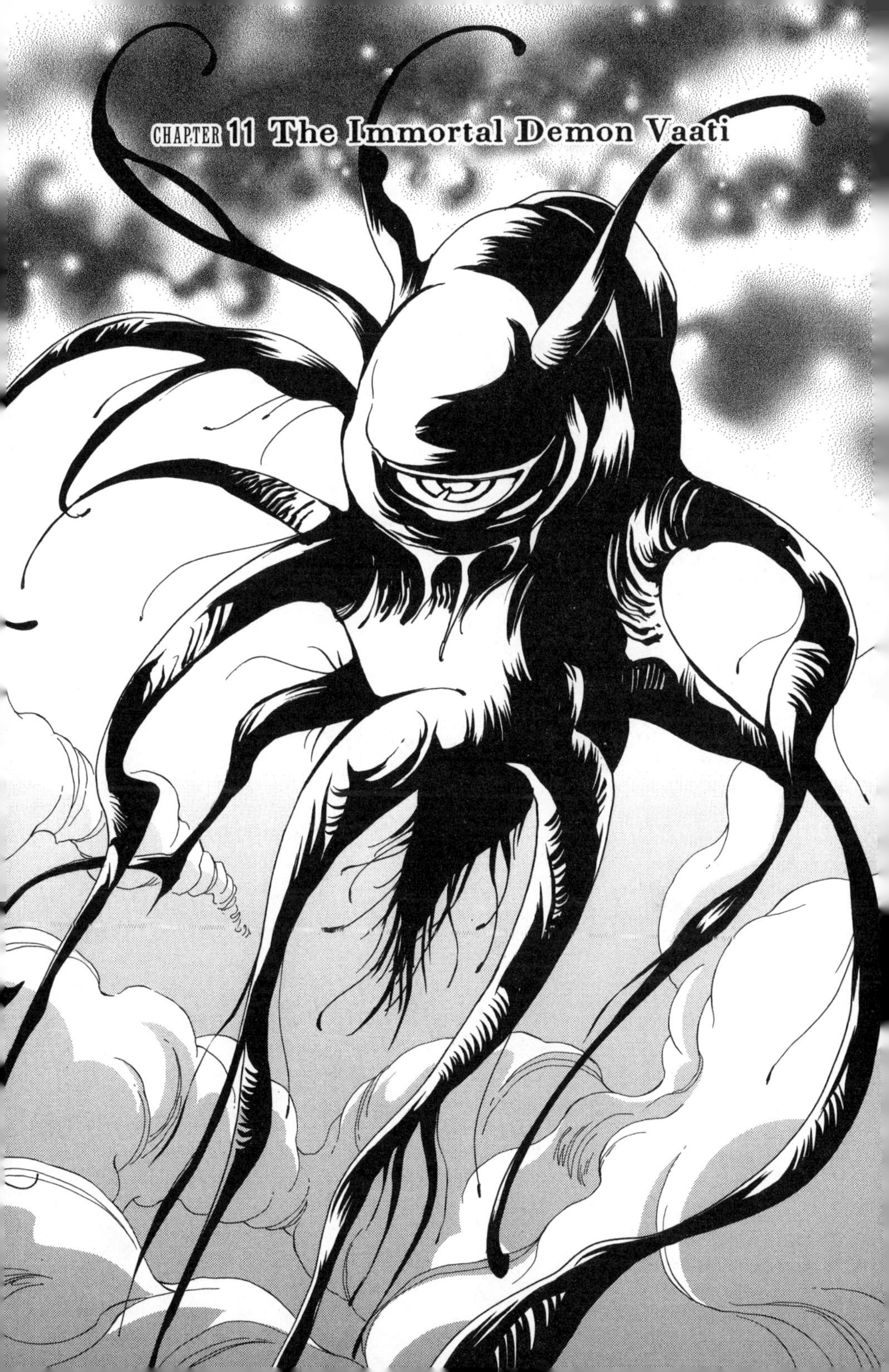
CHAPTER 11 The Immortal Demon Vaati

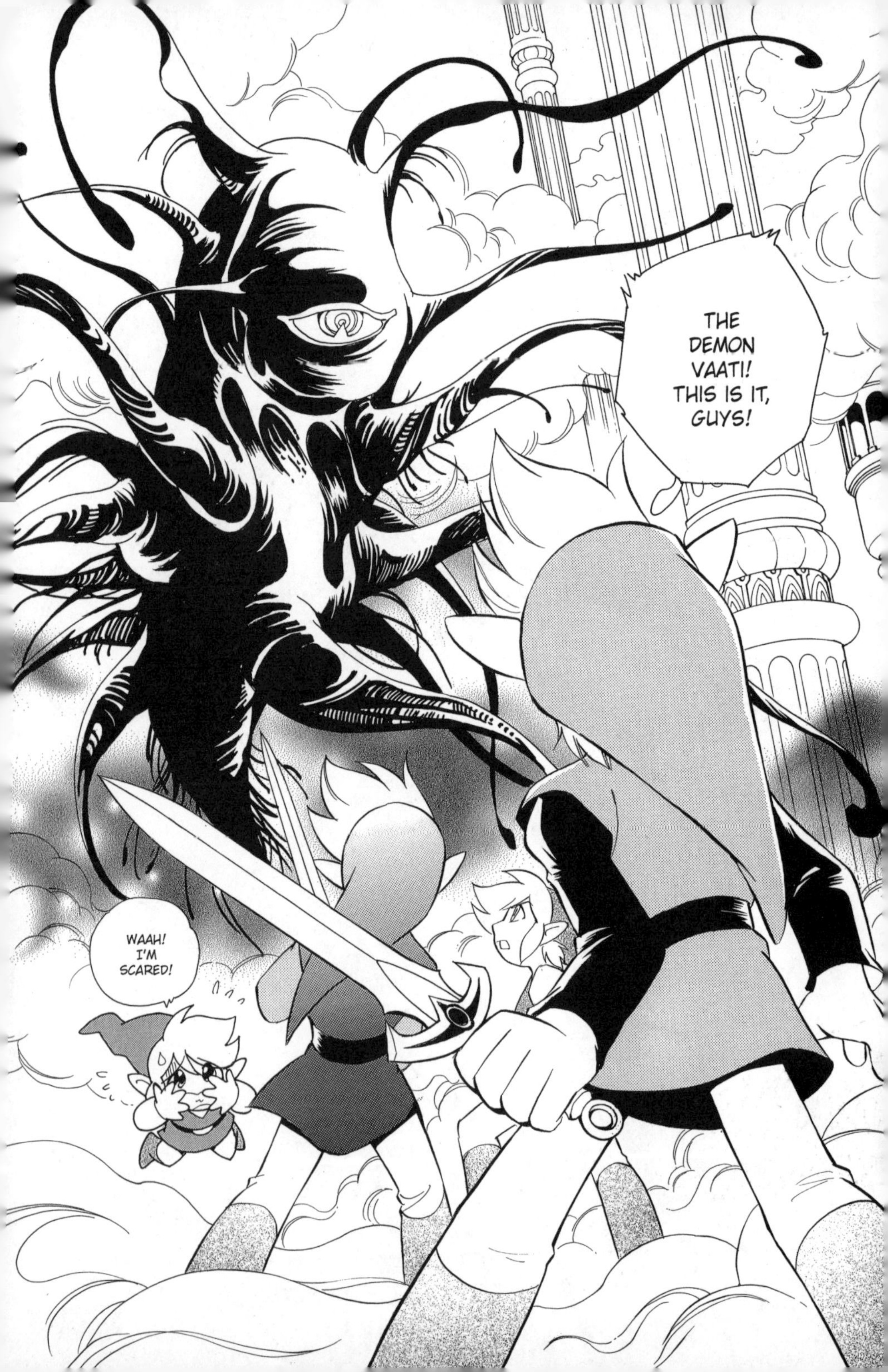
THE DEMON VAATI! THIS IS IT, GUYS!
WAAH! I'M SCARED!

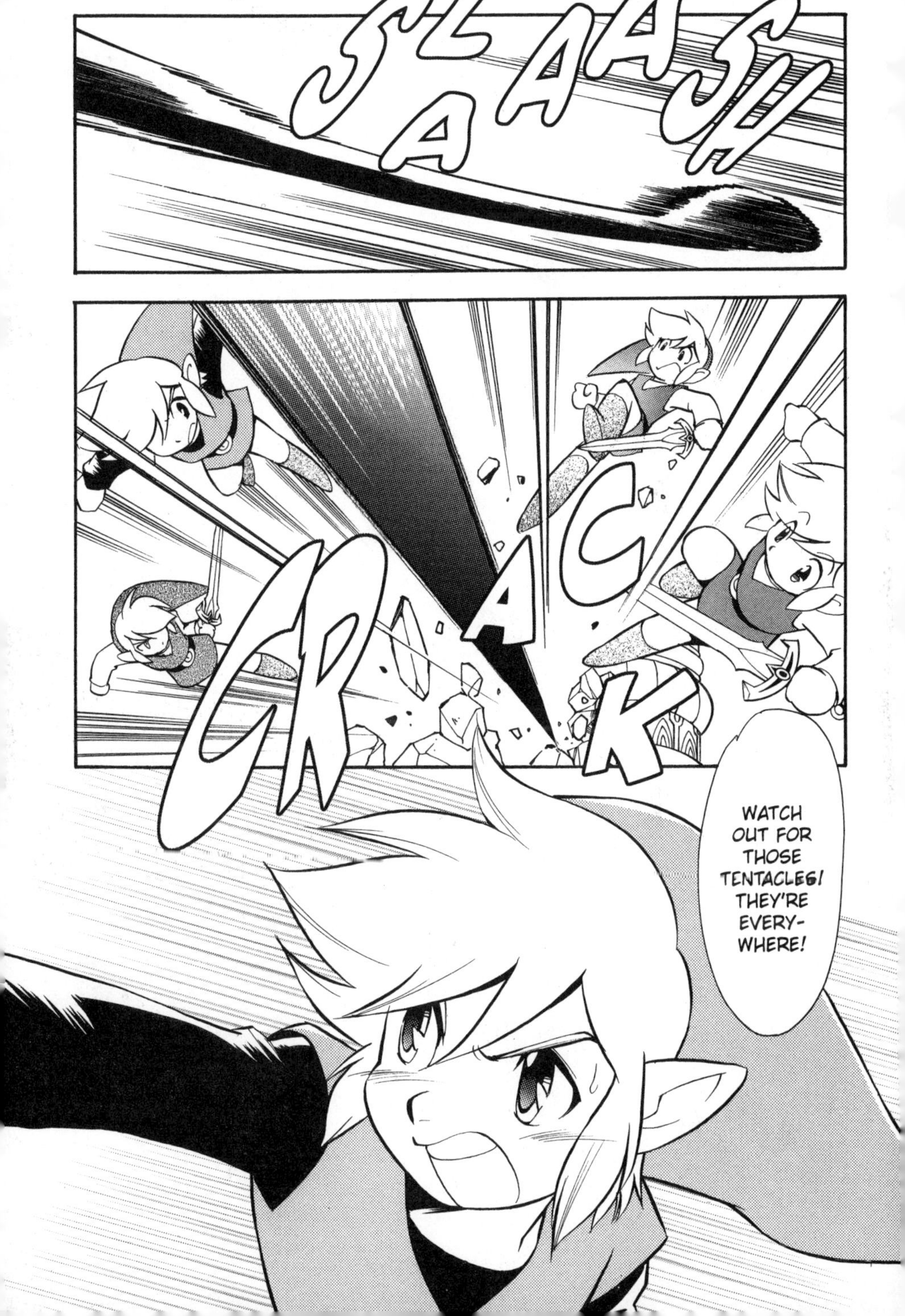
SLAAASH
CRACK
WATCH OUT FOR THOSE TENTACLES! THEY'RE EVERYWHERE!

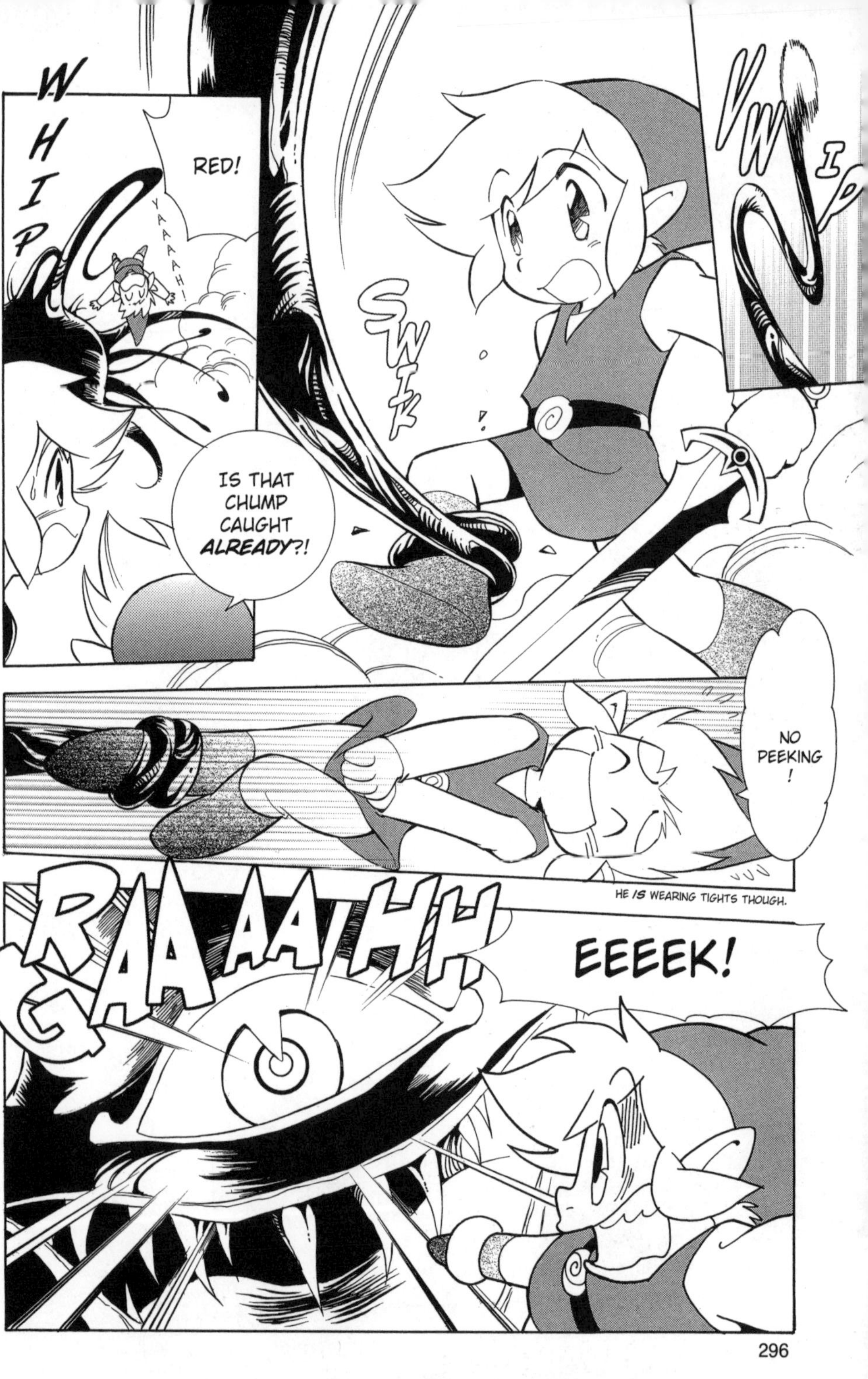
WHIP
SWIK
WHIP
RED!
YAAAAAH!
IS THAT CHUMP CAUGHT ALREADY?!
NO PEEKING!
HE IS WEARING TIGHTS THOUGH.
EEEEK!
GRAAAAHH

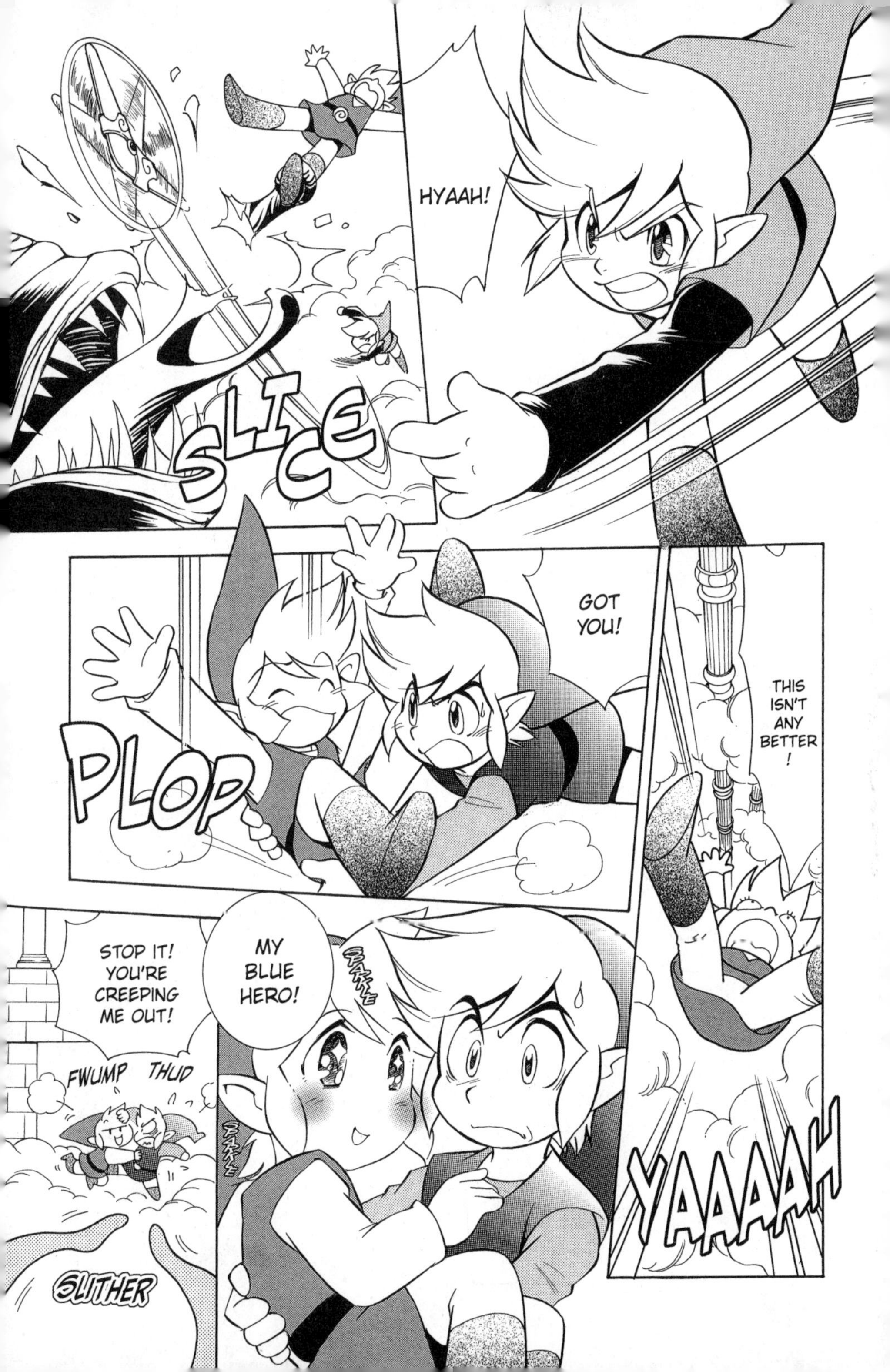
HYAAH!
SLICE
THIS ISN'T ANY BETTER!
YAAAAH
GOT YOU!
PLOP
MY BLUE HERO!
SPARKLE
SPARKLE
STOP IT! YOU'RE CREEPING ME OUT!
FWUMP
THUD
SLITHER

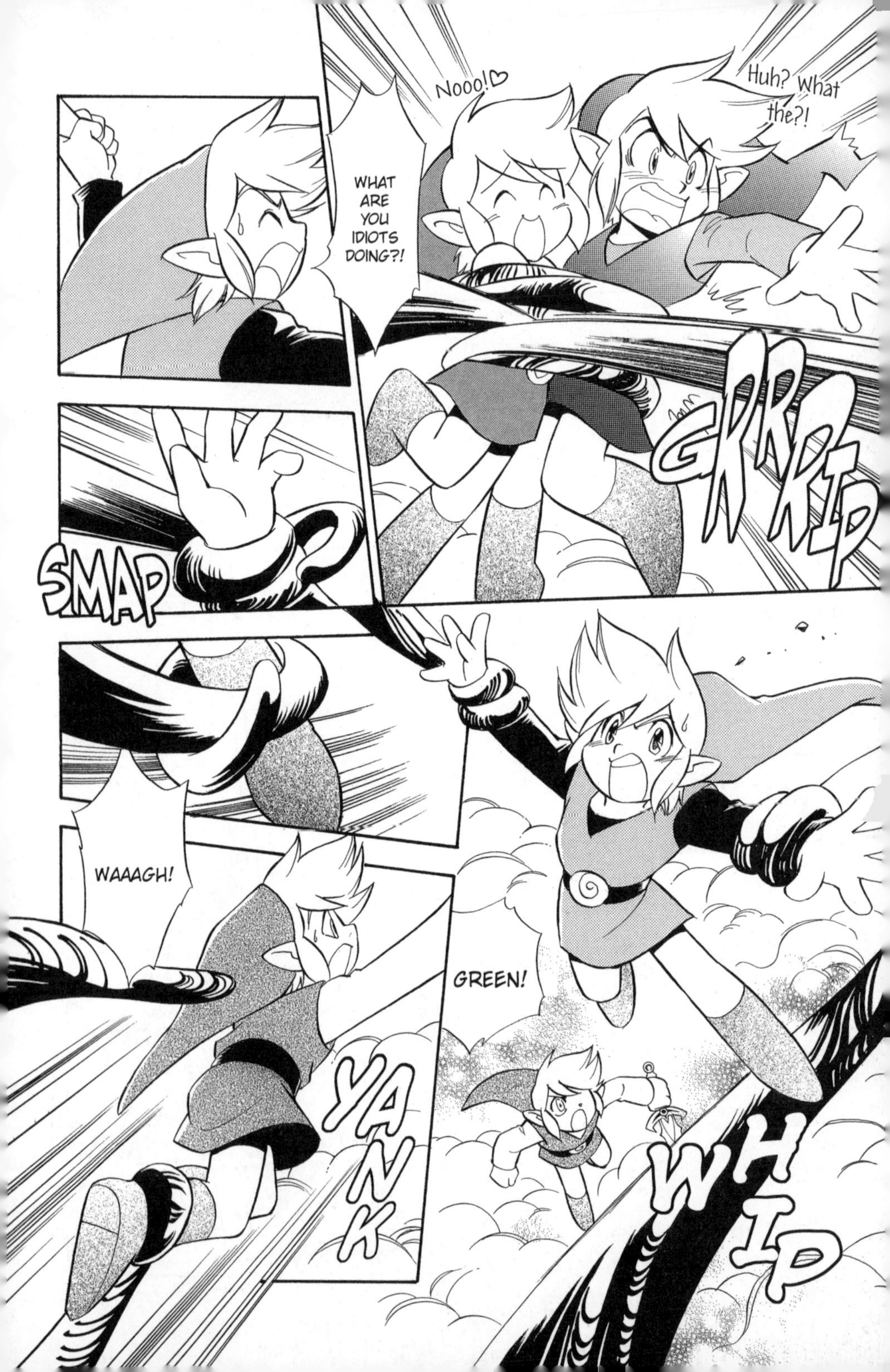
Huh? What the?!
Nooo!♡
WHAT ARE YOU IDIOTS DOING?!
GRRRIP
SMAP
GREEN!
WHIP
WAAAGH!
YANK

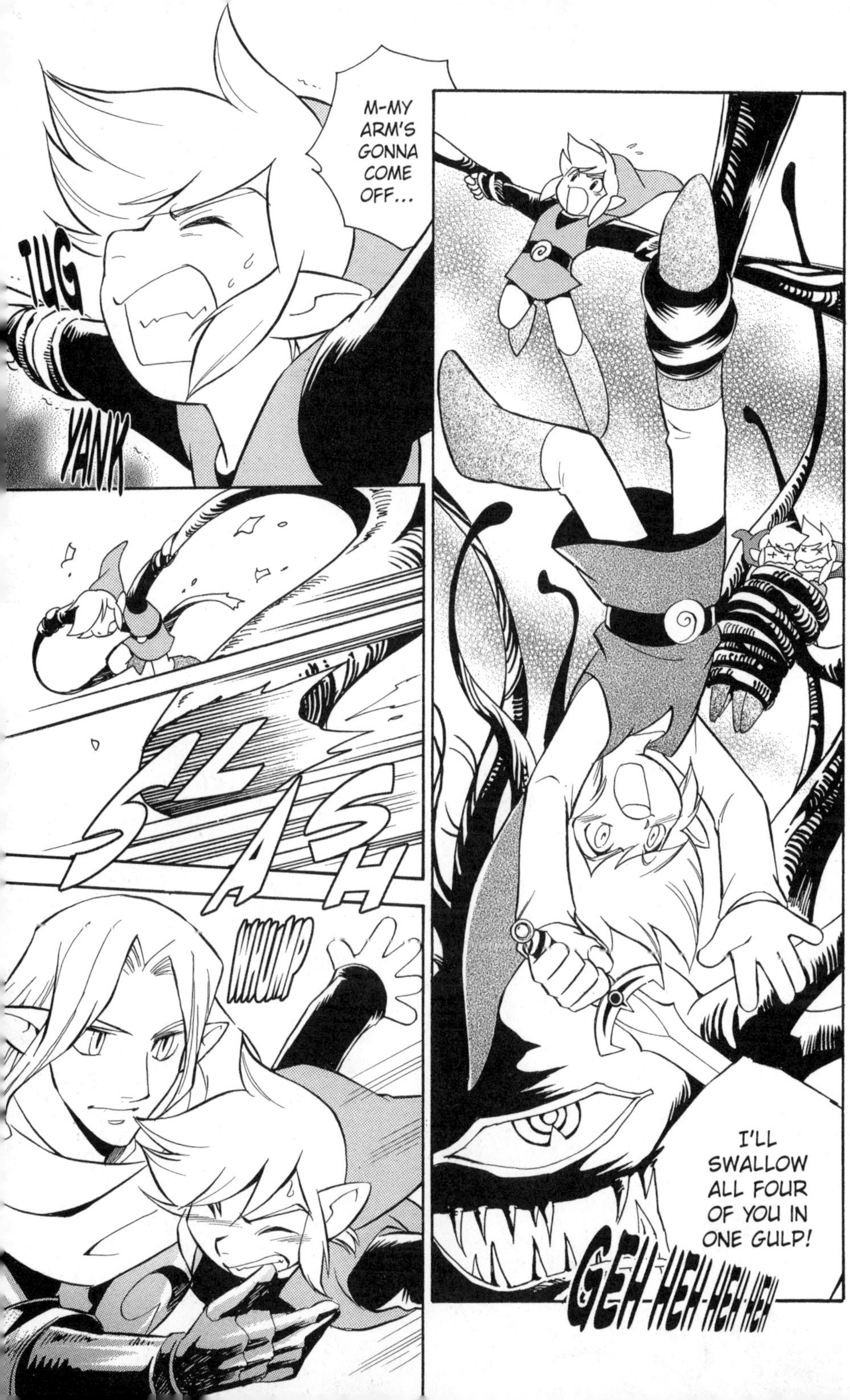
I'LL SWALLOW ALL FOUR OF YOU IN ONE GULP!
GEH-HEH-HEH-HEH
M-MY ARM'S GONNA COME OFF...
TUG
YANK
SLASH
WHUP

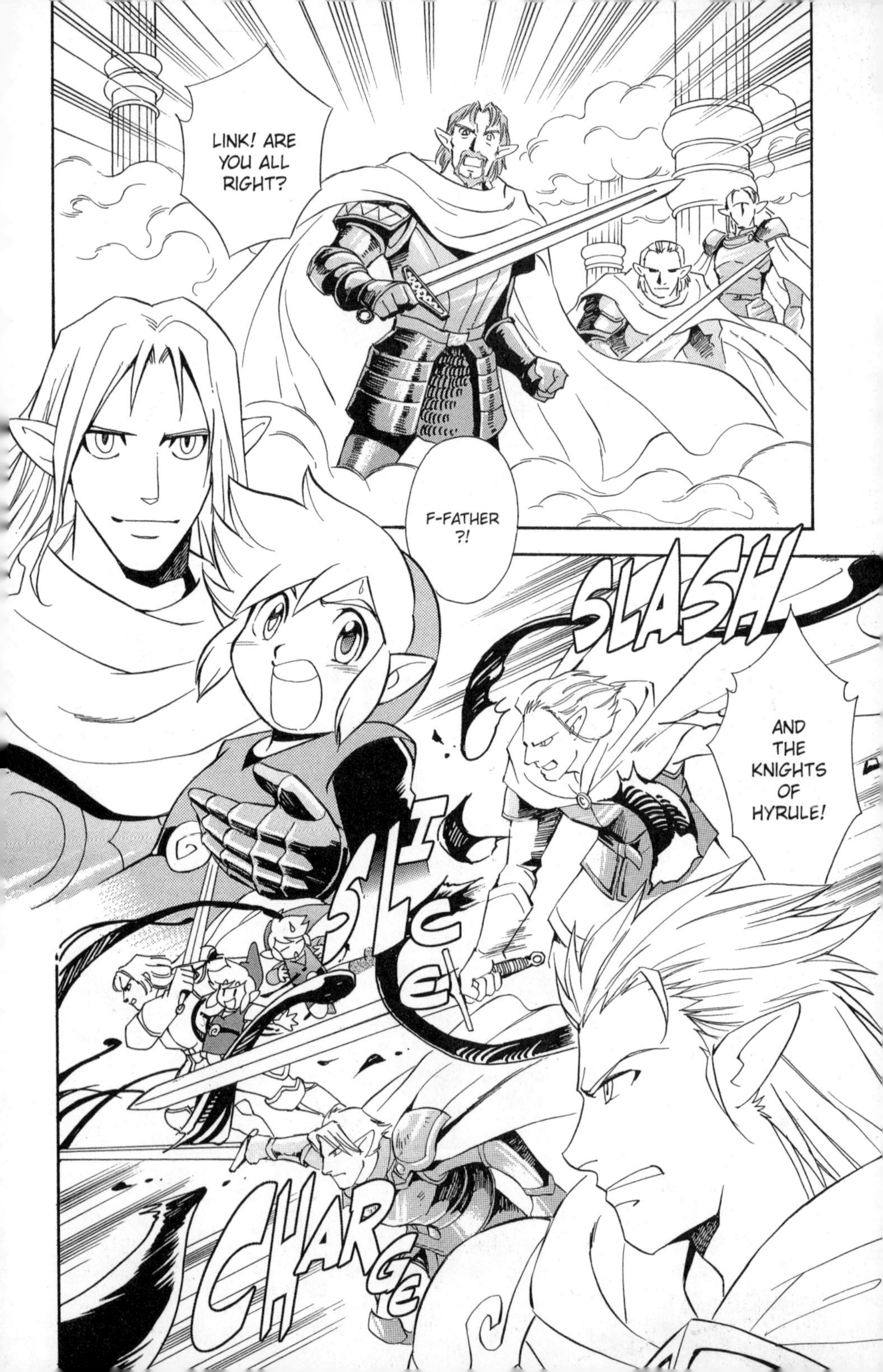

LINK! ARE YOU ALL RIGHT?
F-FATHER ?!
SLASH
AND THE KNIGHTS OF HYRULE!
SLICE
CHARGE

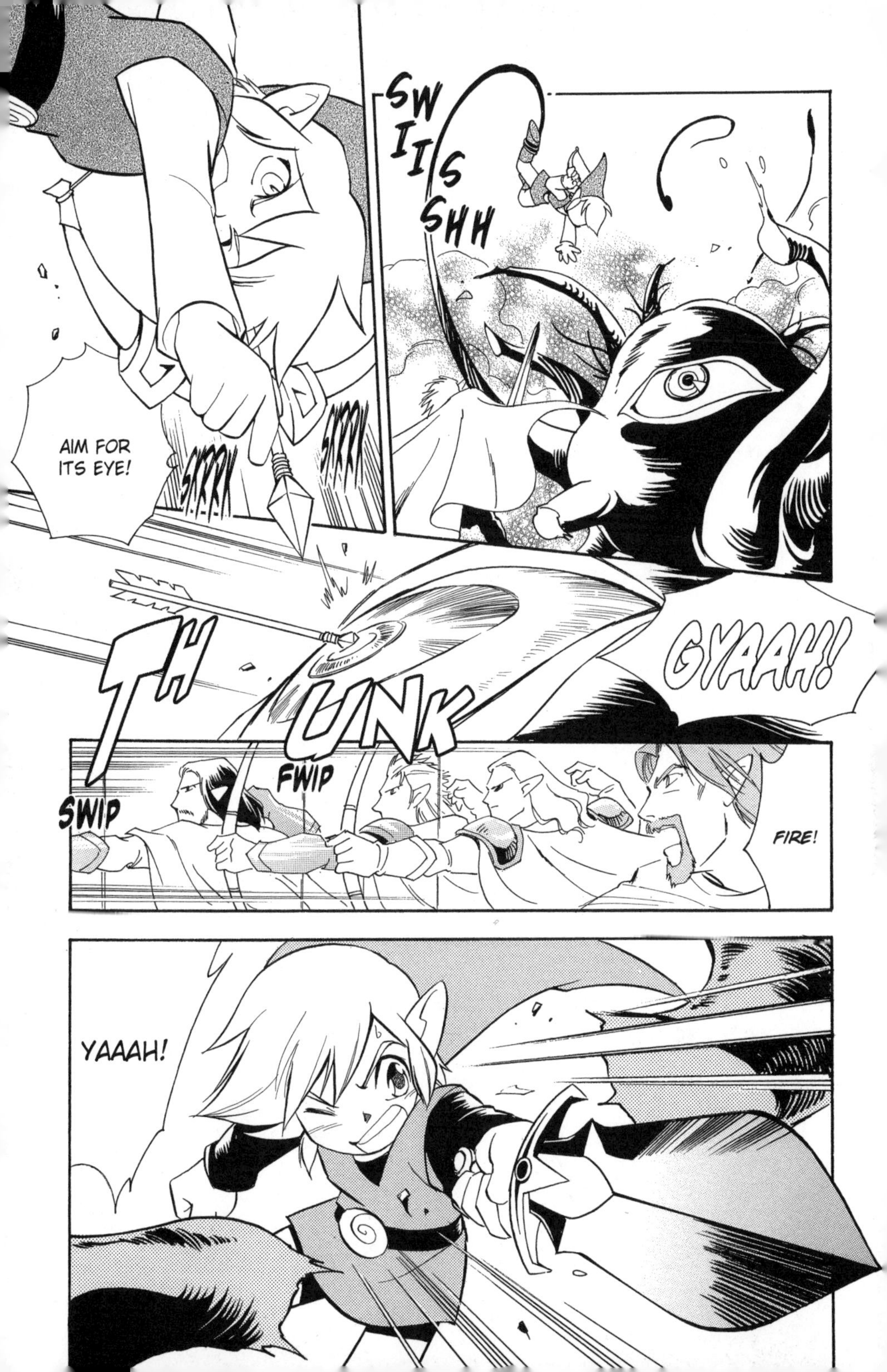
SWIISSHH
AIM FOR ITS EYE!
SKRRK
SKRRK
GYAAH!
THUNK
FIRE!
FWIP
SWIP
YAAAH!

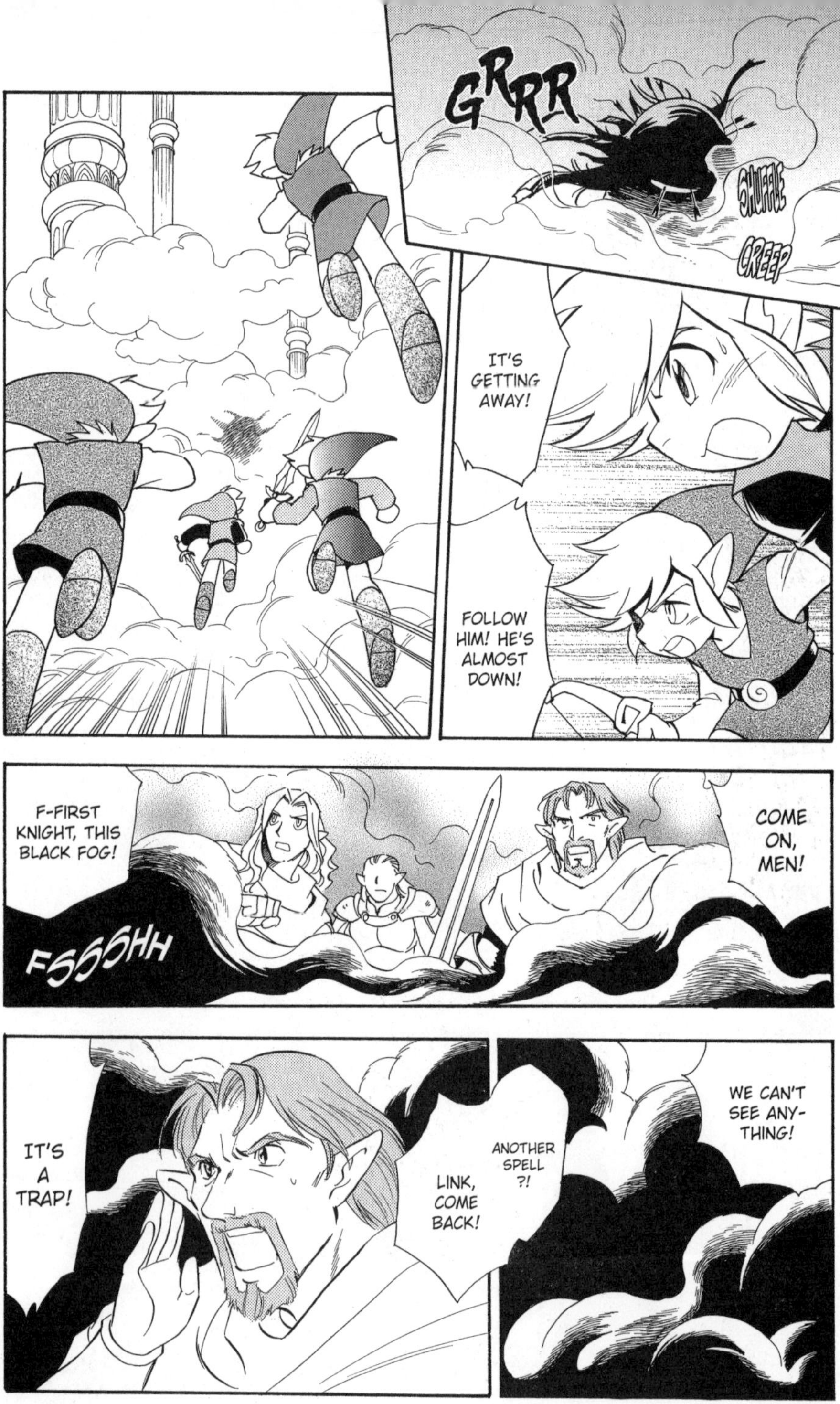
GRRR
SHUFFLE
CREEP
IT'S GETTING AWAY!
FOLLOW HIM! HE'S ALMOST DOWN!
COME ON, MEN!
F-FIRST KNIGHT, THIS BLACK FOG!
FSSSHH
WE CAN'T SEE ANY-THING!
ANOTHER SPELL?!
LINK, COME BACK!
IT'S A TRAP!

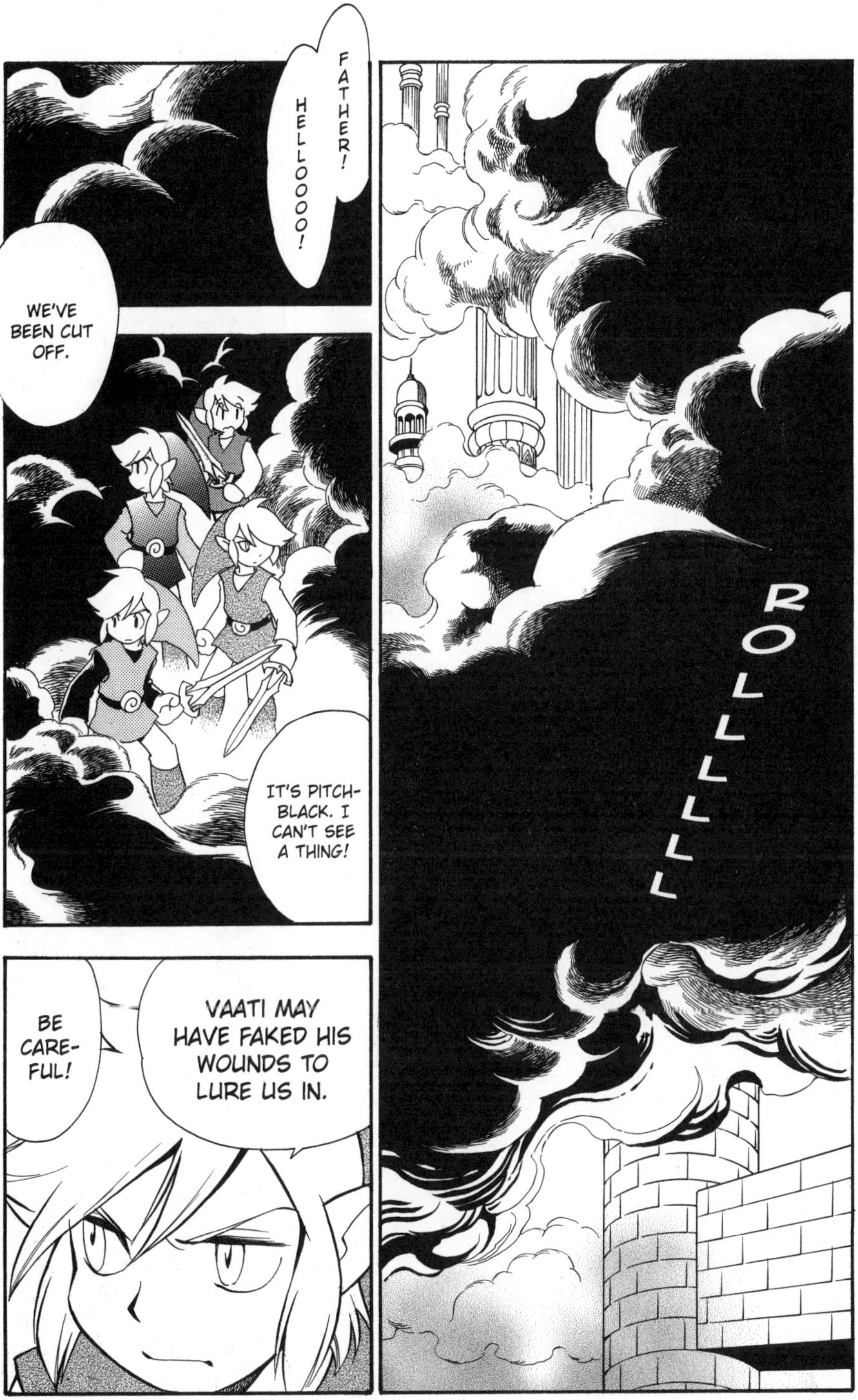
ROLLLLLL
FATHER! HELLOOOO!
WE'VE BEEN CUT OFF.
IT'S PITCH-BLACK. I CAN'T SEE A THING!
VAATI MAY HAVE FAKED HIS WOUNDS TO LURE US IN.
BE CAREFUL!

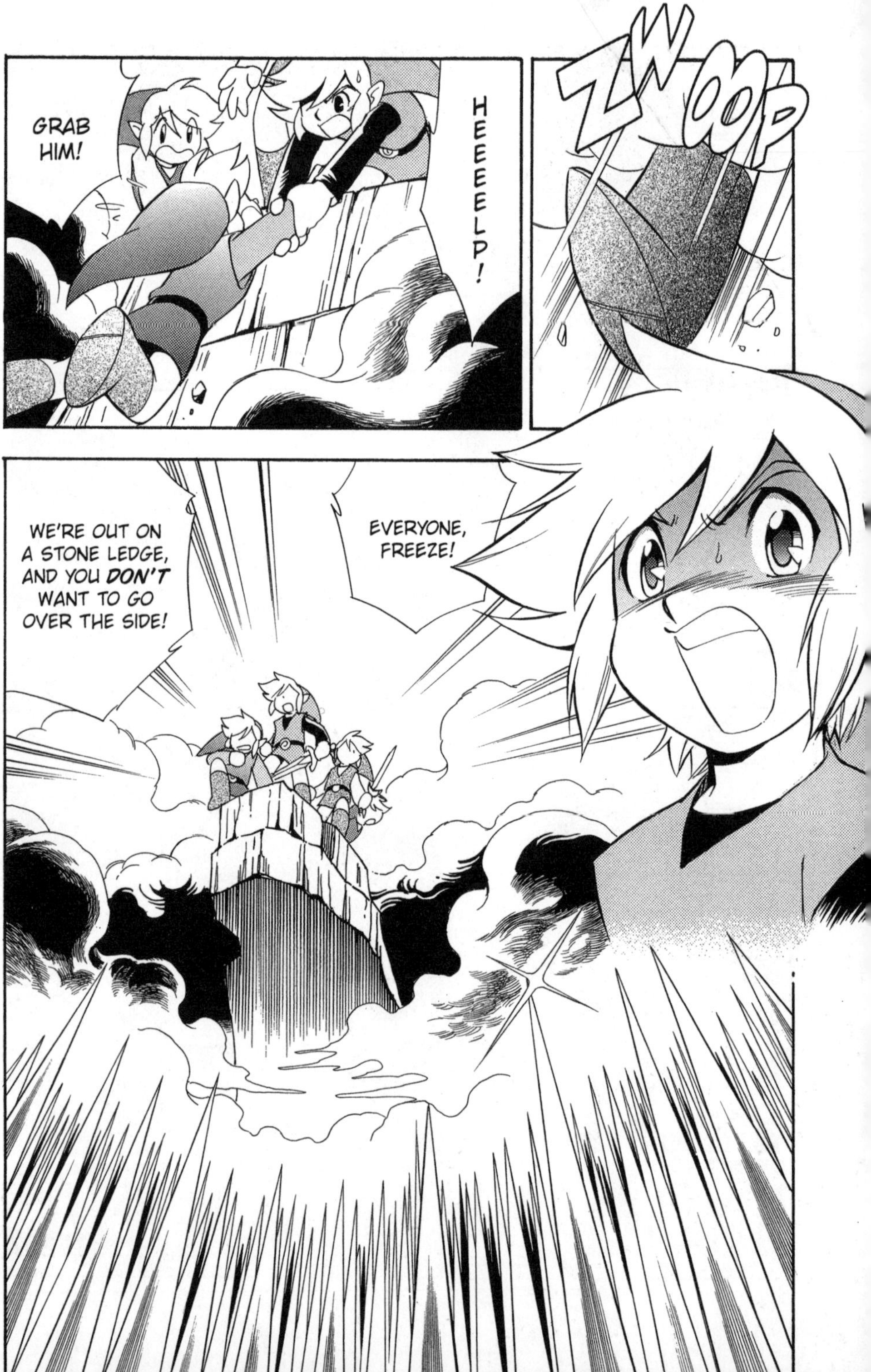
ZWOOOP
HEEEEELP!
GRAB HIM!
EVERYONE, FREEZE!
WE'RE OUT ON A STONE LEDGE, AND YOU **DON'T** WANT TO GO OVER THE SIDE!

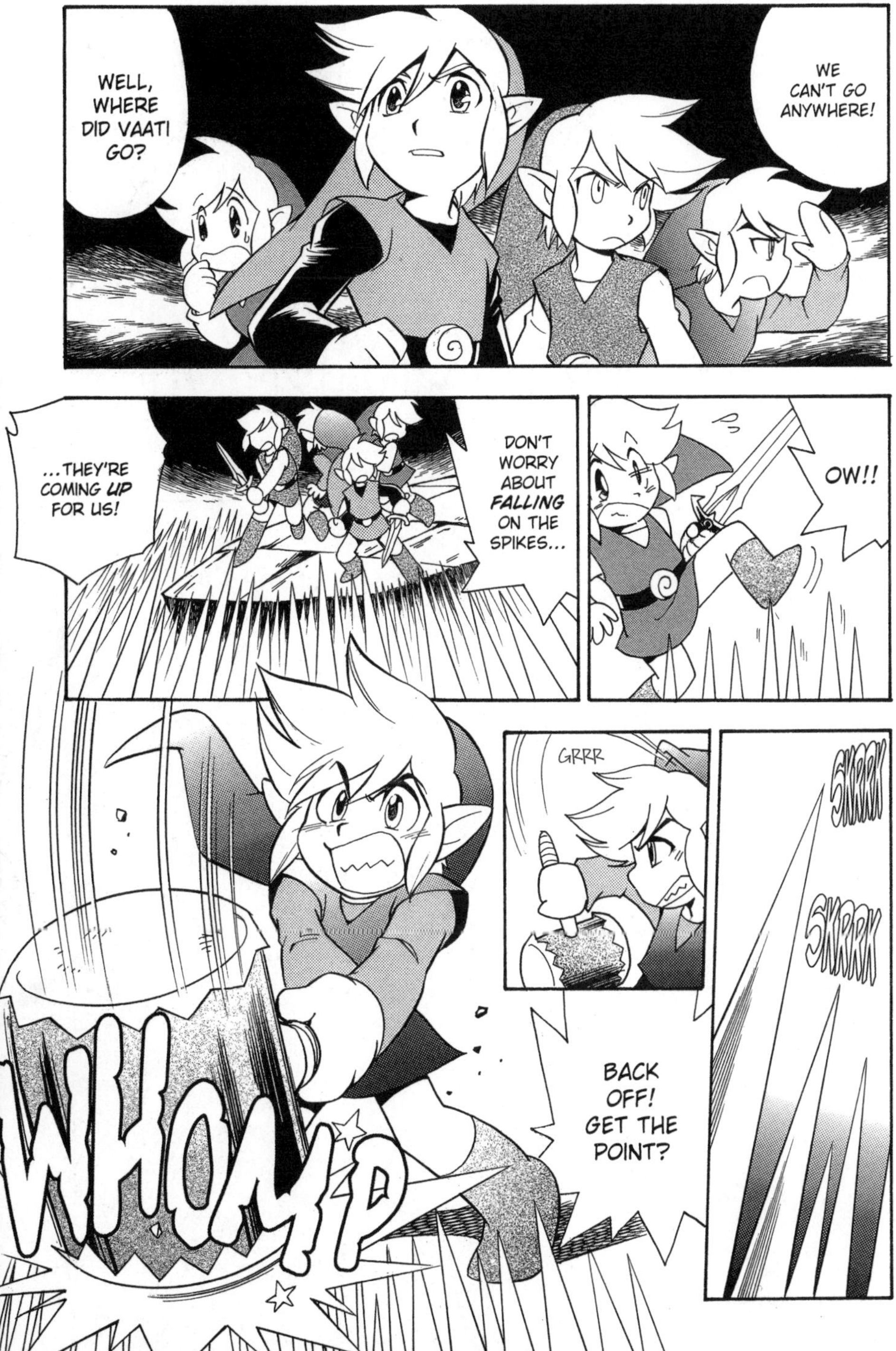

WE CAN'T GO ANYWHERE!
WELL, WHERE DID VAATI GO?
OW!!
DON'T WORRY ABOUT FALLING ON THE SPIKES...
...THEY'RE COMING UP FOR US!
SKRRK
SKRRK
GRRR
BACK OFF! GET THE POINT?
WHOMP

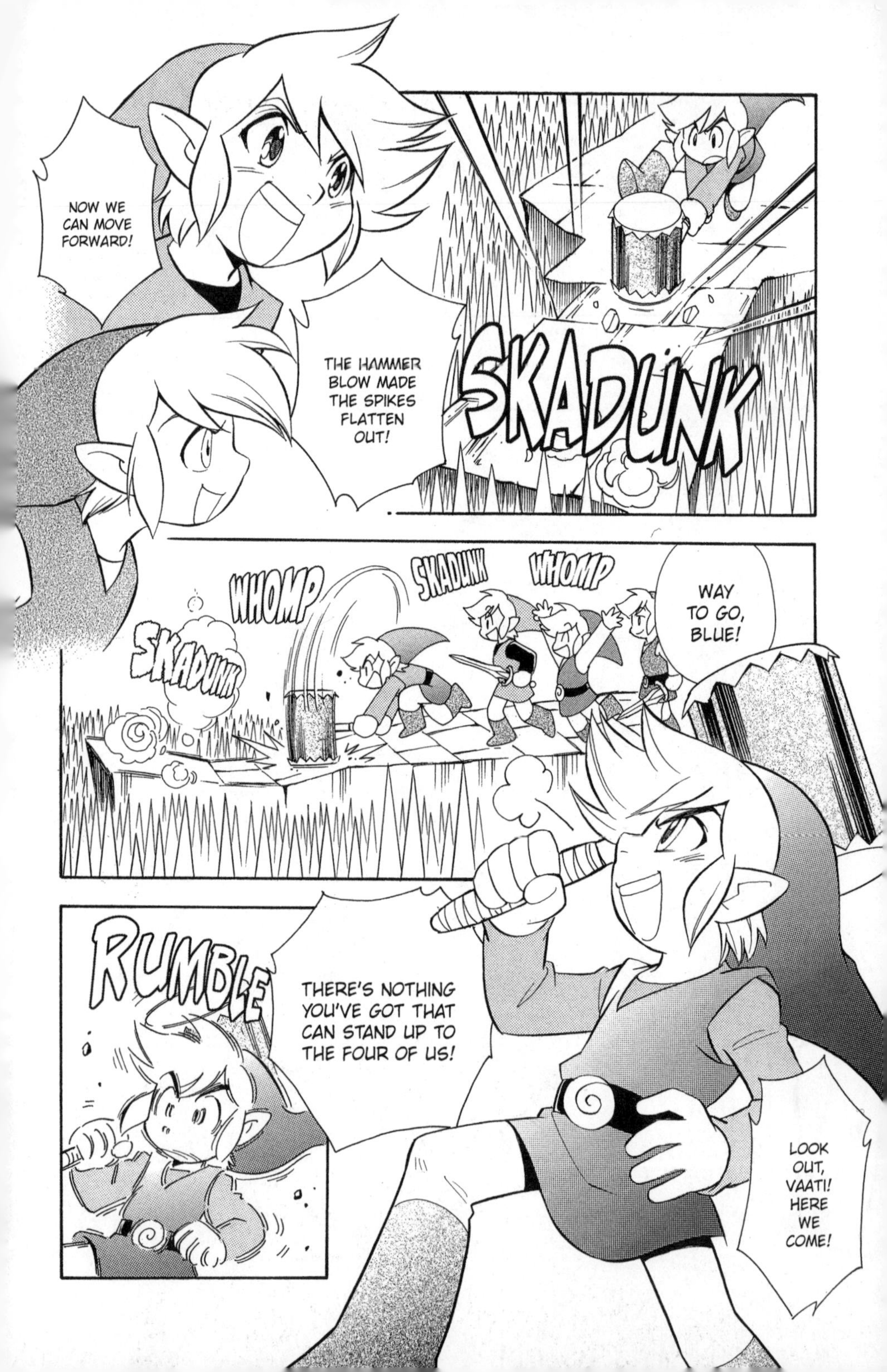
SKADUNK
NOW WE CAN MOVE FORWARD!
THE HAMMER BLOW MADE THE SPIKES FLATTEN OUT!
WAY TO GO, BLUE!
WHOMP
SKADUNK
WHOMP
SKADUNK
THERE'S NOTHING YOU'VE GOT THAT CAN STAND UP TO THE FOUR OF US!
LOOK OUT, VAATI! HERE WE COME!
RUMBLE

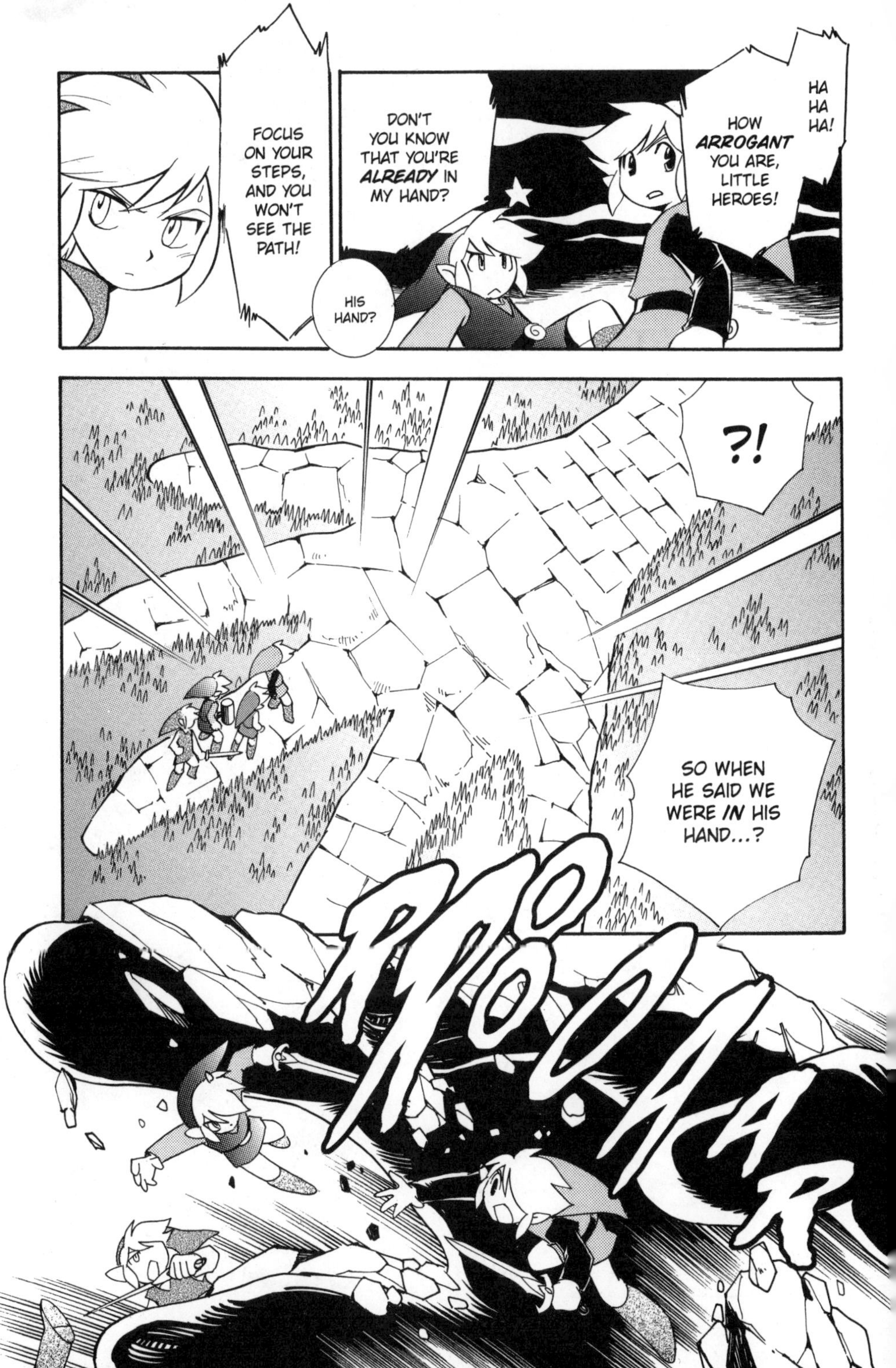
HA HA HA!
HOW ARROGANT YOU ARE, LITTLE HEROES!
DON'T YOU KNOW THAT YOU'RE ALREADY IN MY HAND?
HIS HAND?
FOCUS ON YOUR STEPS, AND YOU WON'T SEE THE PATH!
?!
SO WHEN HE SAID WE WERE IN HIS HAND...?

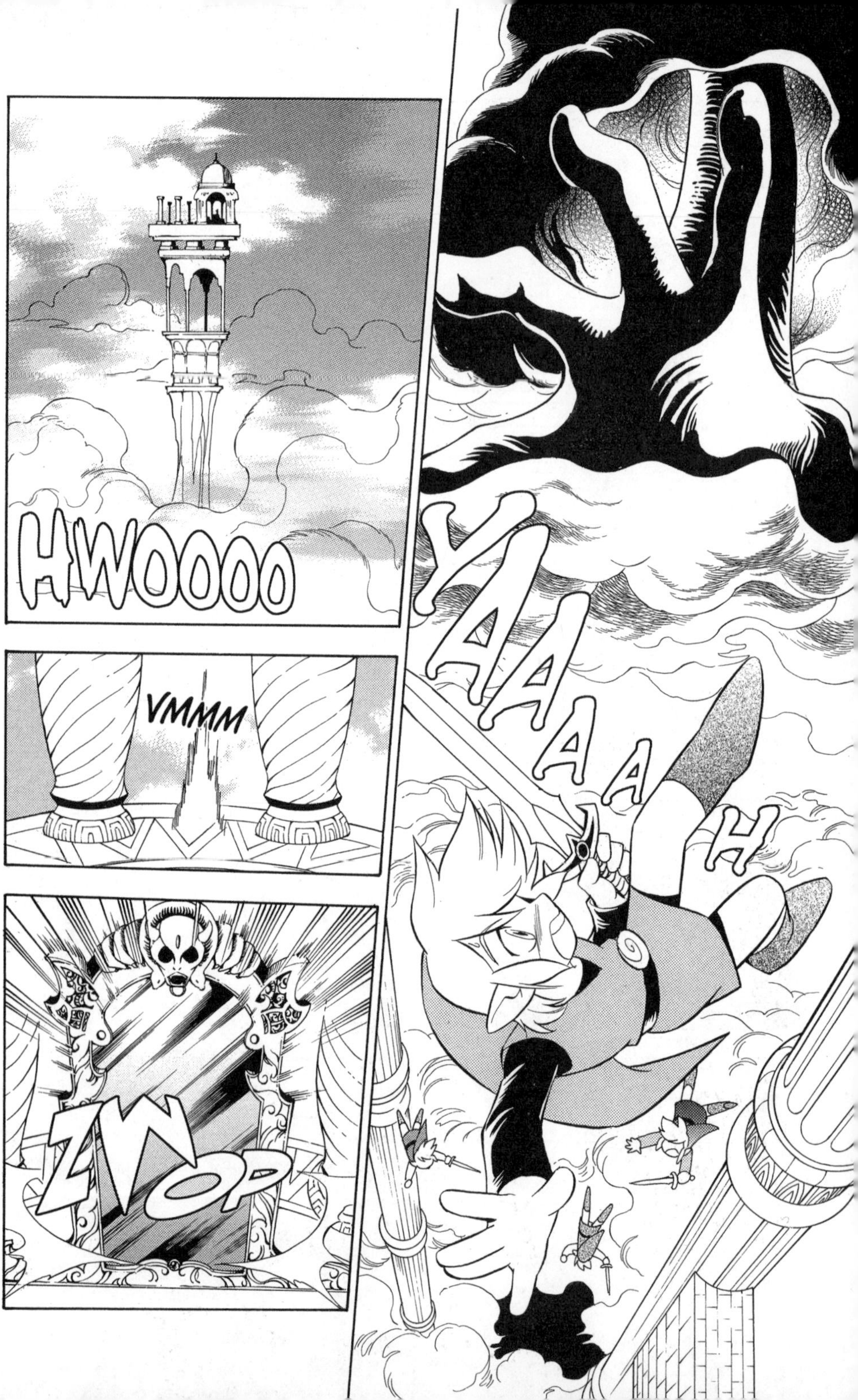
YAAAAAH
HWOOOO
VMMM
ZWOP

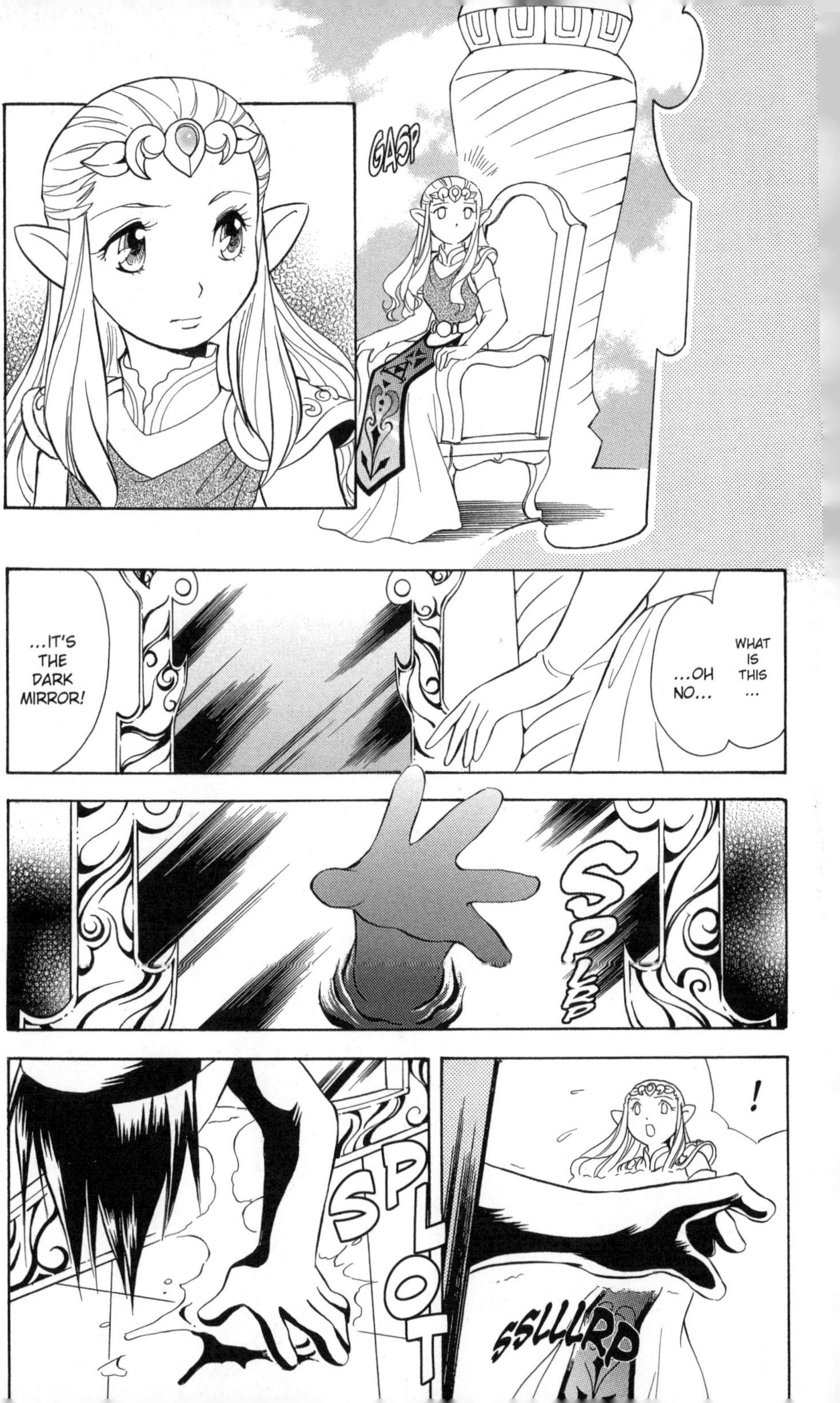
GASP
WHAT IS THIS ...
...OH NO...
...IT'S THE DARK MIRROR!
!
SSLLLRP
SPLOT

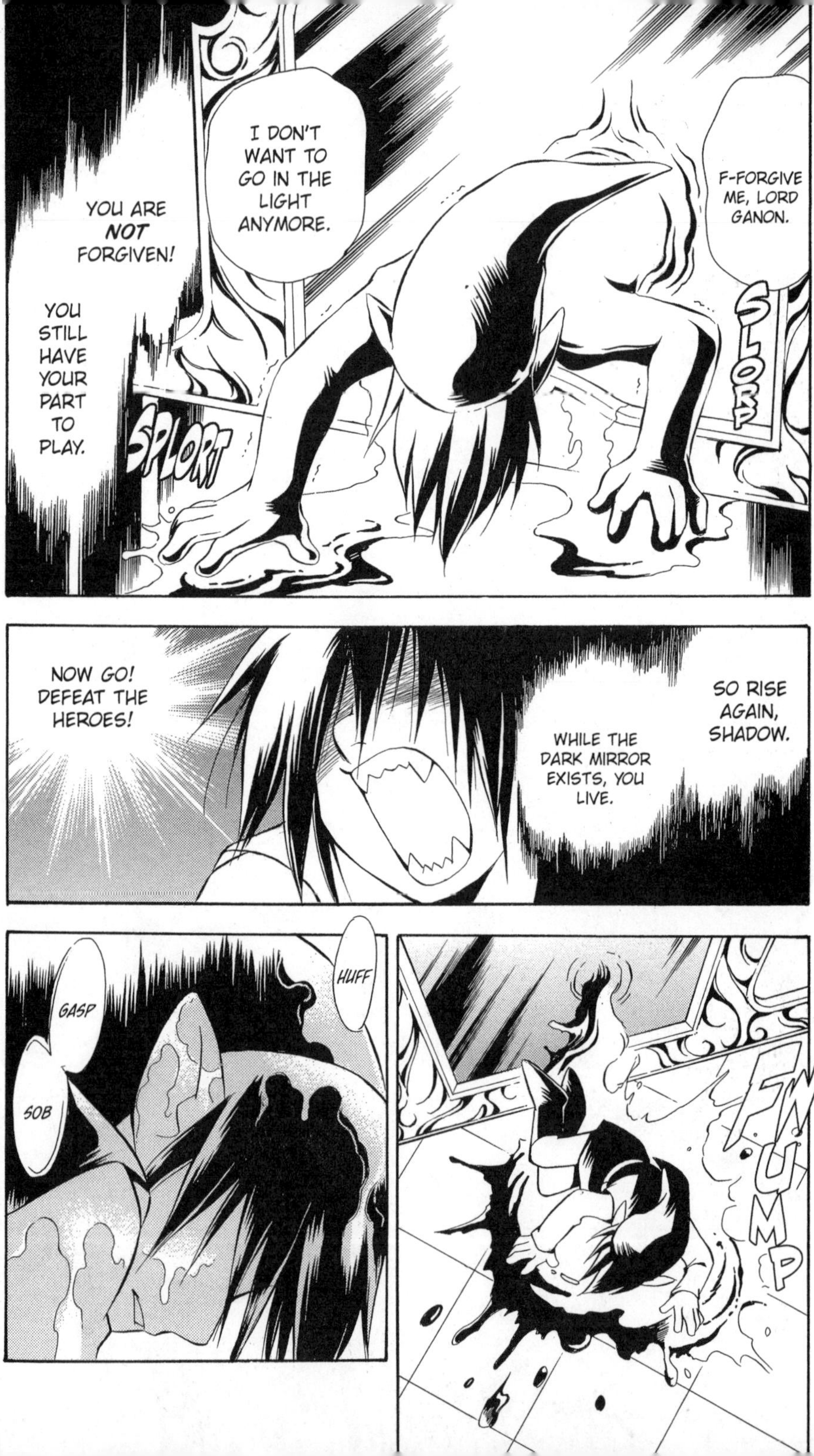
F-FORGIVE ME, LORD GANON.
SLORP
I DON'T WANT TO GO IN THE LIGHT ANYMORE.
YOU ARE **NOT** FORGIVEN!
YOU STILL HAVE YOUR PART TO PLAY.
SPLORT
SO RISE AGAIN, SHADOW.
WHILE THE DARK MIRROR EXISTS, YOU LIVE.
NOW GO! DEFEAT THE HEROES!
FWUMP
HUFF
GASP
SOB

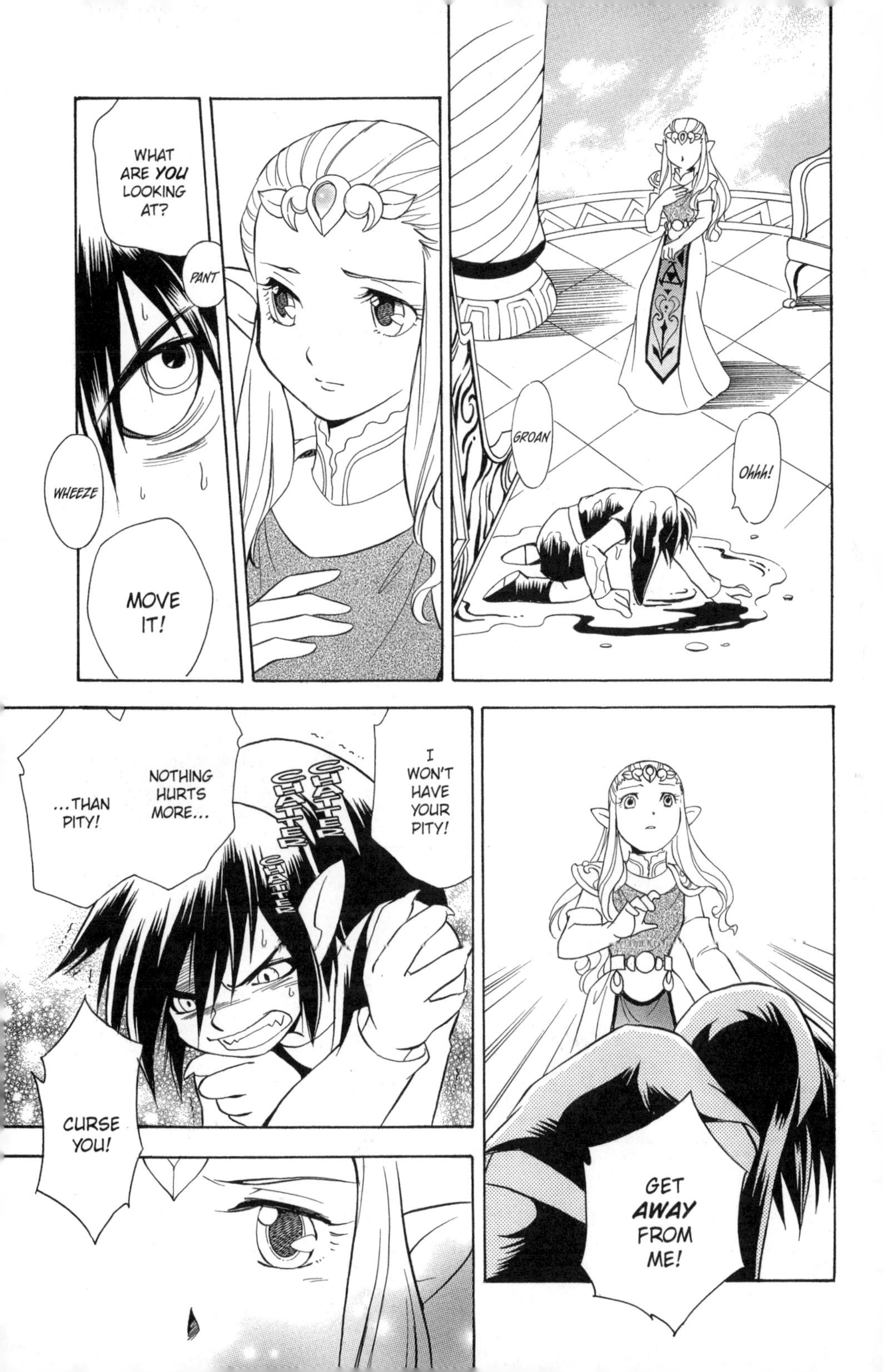
GROAN
Ohhh!
WHAT ARE YOU LOOKING AT?
PANT
WHEEZE
MOVE IT!
GET AWAY FROM ME!
I WON'T HAVE YOUR PITY!
NOTHING HURTS MORE...
...THAN PITY!
CHATTER
CHATTER
CHATTER
CURSE YOU!

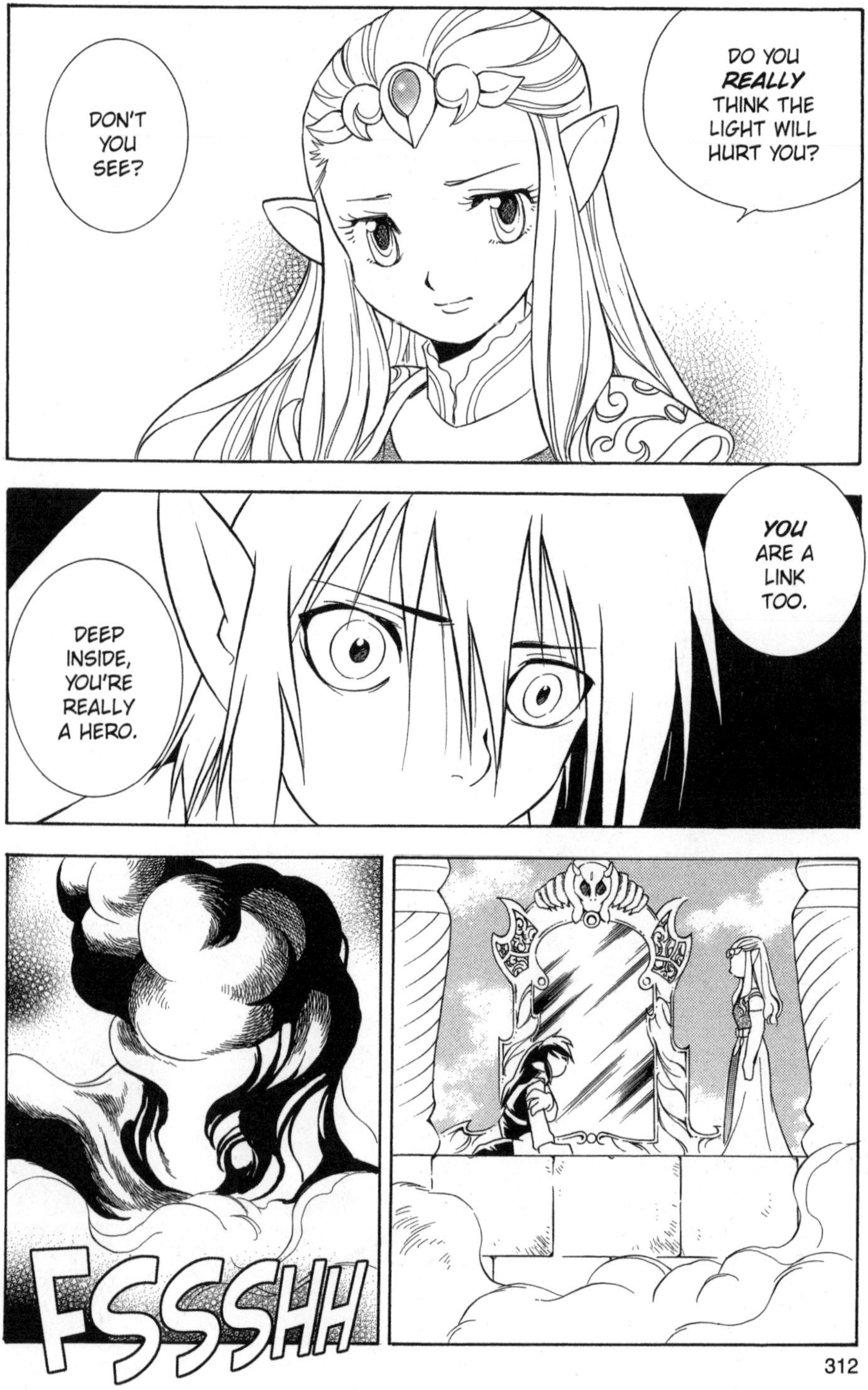
DO YOU **REALLY** THINK THE LIGHT WILL HURT YOU?
DON'T YOU SEE?
YOU ARE A LINK TOO.
DEEP INSIDE, YOU'RE REALLY A HERO.
FSSSHH

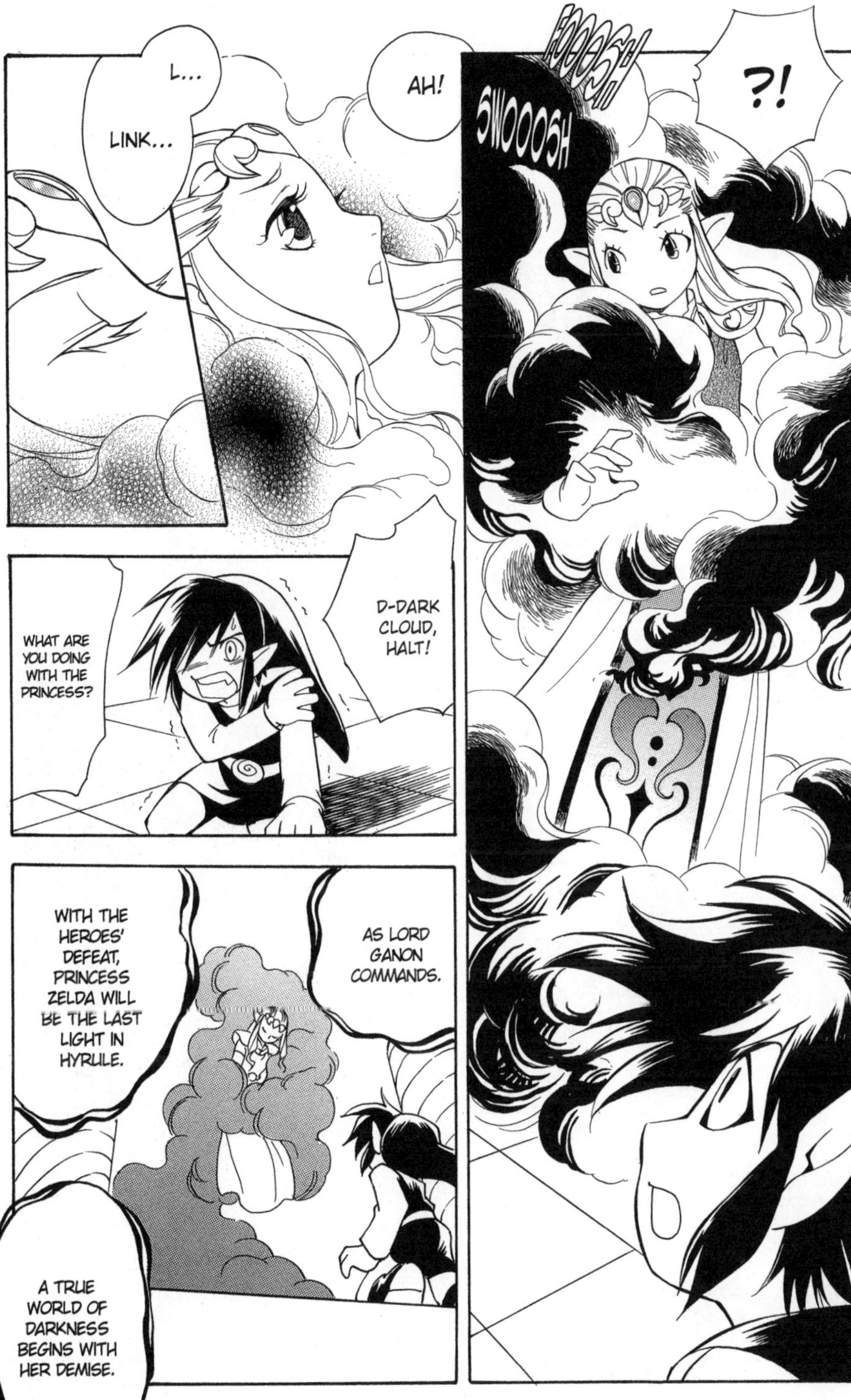
?!
FOOOSH
SWOOOSH
AH!
L...
LINK...
D-DARK CLOUD, HALT!
WHAT ARE YOU DOING WITH THE PRINCESS?
AS LORD GANON COMMANDS.
WITH THE HEROES' DEFEAT, PRINCESS ZELDA WILL BE THE LAST LIGHT IN HYRULE.
A TRUE WORLD OF DARKNESS BEGINS WITH HER DEMISE.

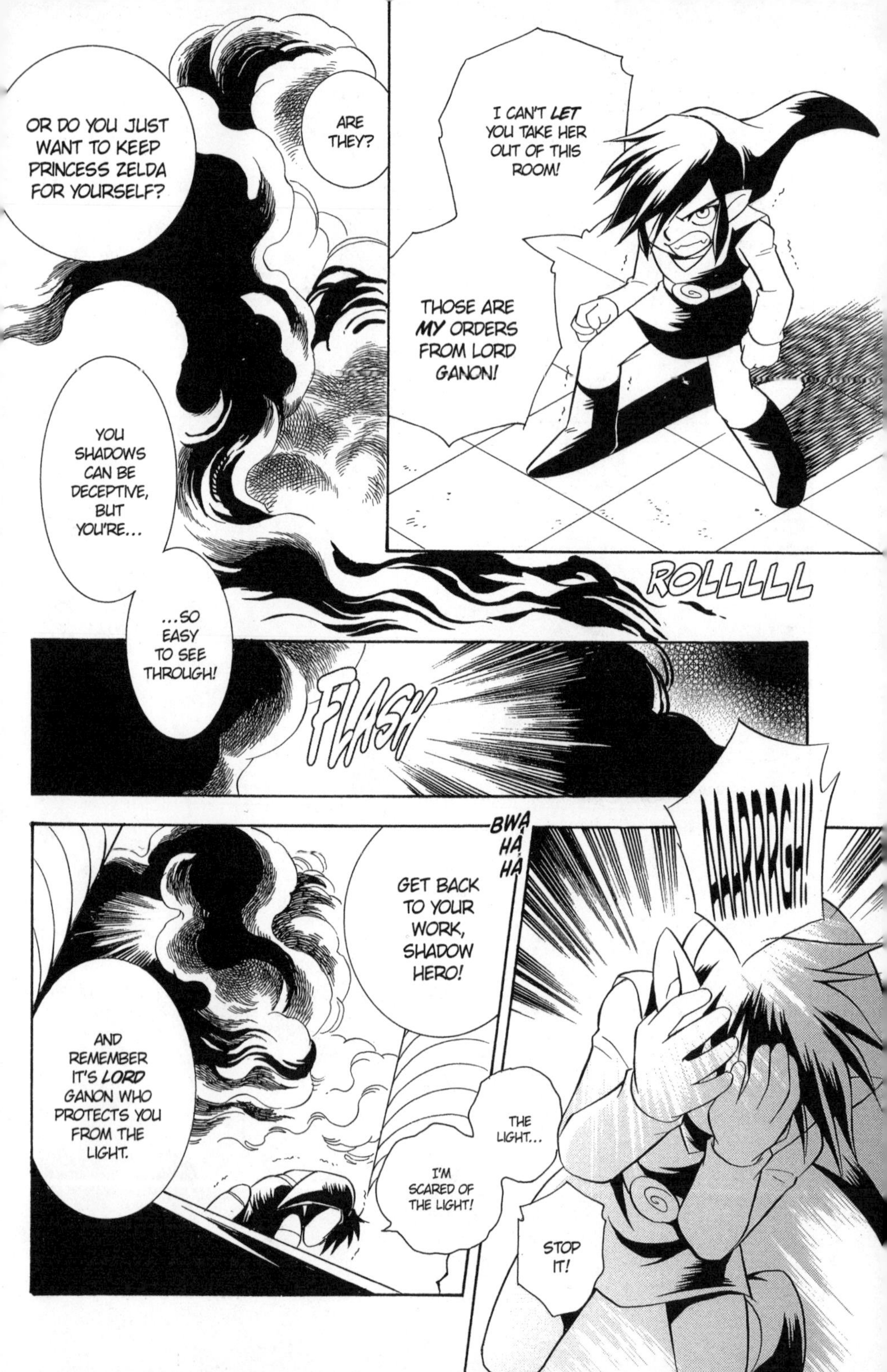
I CAN'T LET YOU TAKE HER OUT OF THIS ROOM!
THOSE ARE MY ORDERS FROM LORD GANON!
ARE THEY?
OR DO YOU JUST WANT TO KEEP PRINCESS ZELDA FOR YOURSELF?
YOU SHADOWS CAN BE DECEPTIVE, BUT YOU'RE...
...SO EASY TO SEE THROUGH!
ROLLLLL
FLASH
AAARRRGH!
THE LIGHT...
I'M SCARED OF THE LIGHT!
STOP IT!
BWA HA HA
GET BACK TO YOUR WORK, SHADOW HERO!
AND REMEMBER IT'S LORD GANON WHO PROTECTS YOU FROM THE LIGHT.

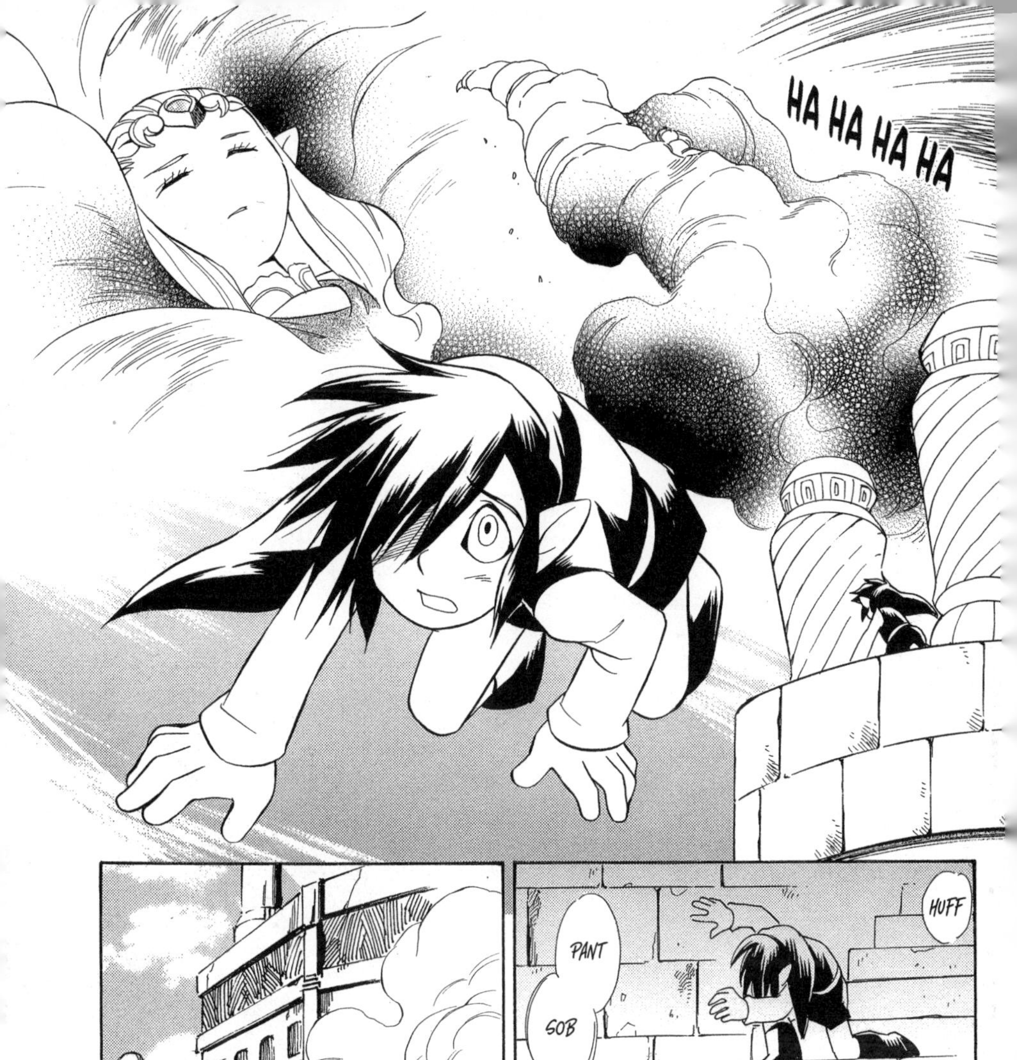
HA HA HA HA

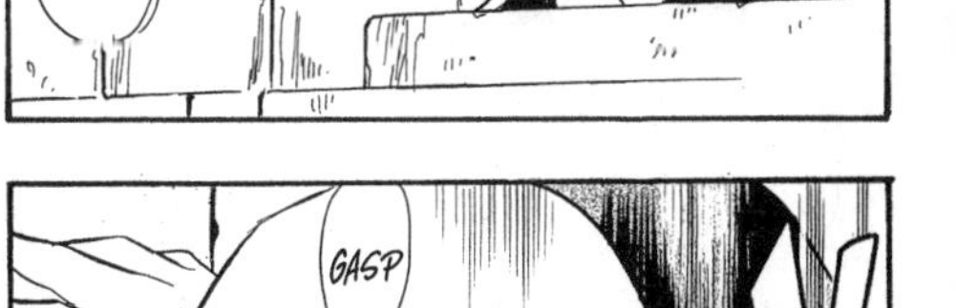
HUFF
PANT
SOB

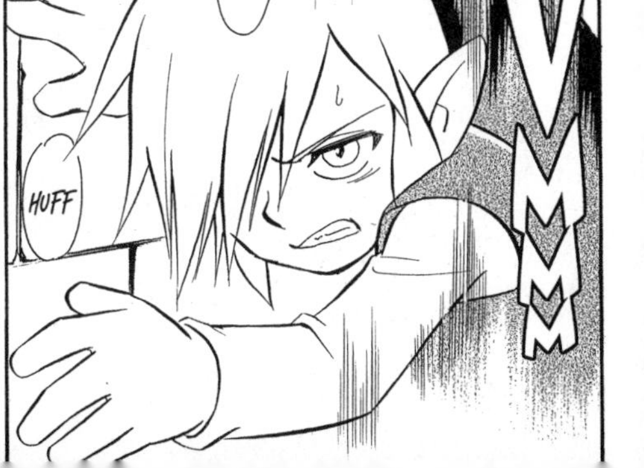
VMMMM
GASP
HUFF

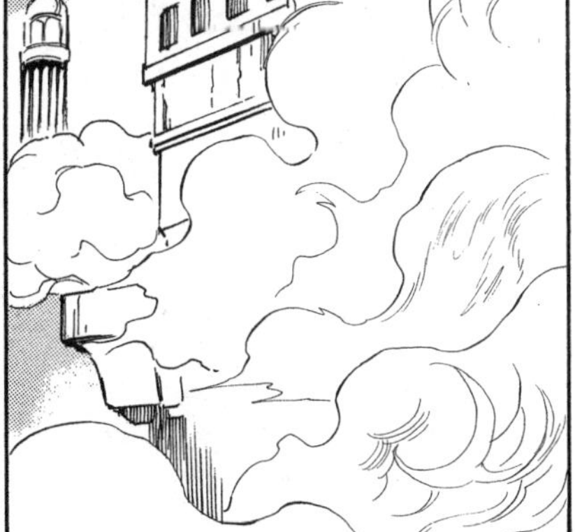

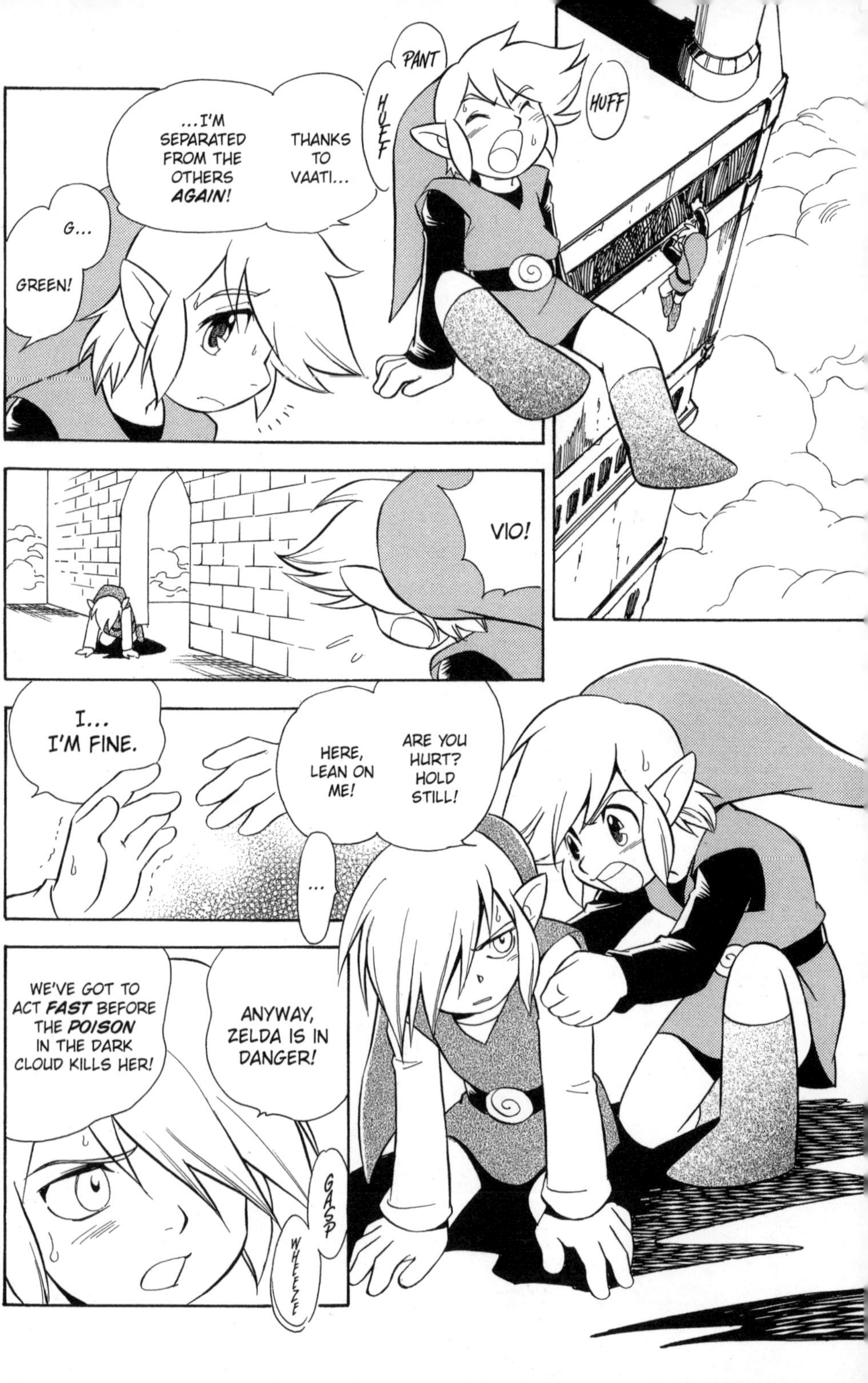
PANT
HUFF
HUFF
THANKS TO VAATI...
...I'M SEPARATED FROM THE OTHERS AGAIN!
G...
GREEN!
VIO!
ARE YOU HURT? HOLD STILL!
HERE, LEAN ON ME!
I... I'M FINE.
...
ANYWAY, ZELDA IS IN DANGER!
WE'VE GOT TO ACT FAST BEFORE THE POISON IN THE DARK CLOUD KILLS HER!
GASP
WHEEZE

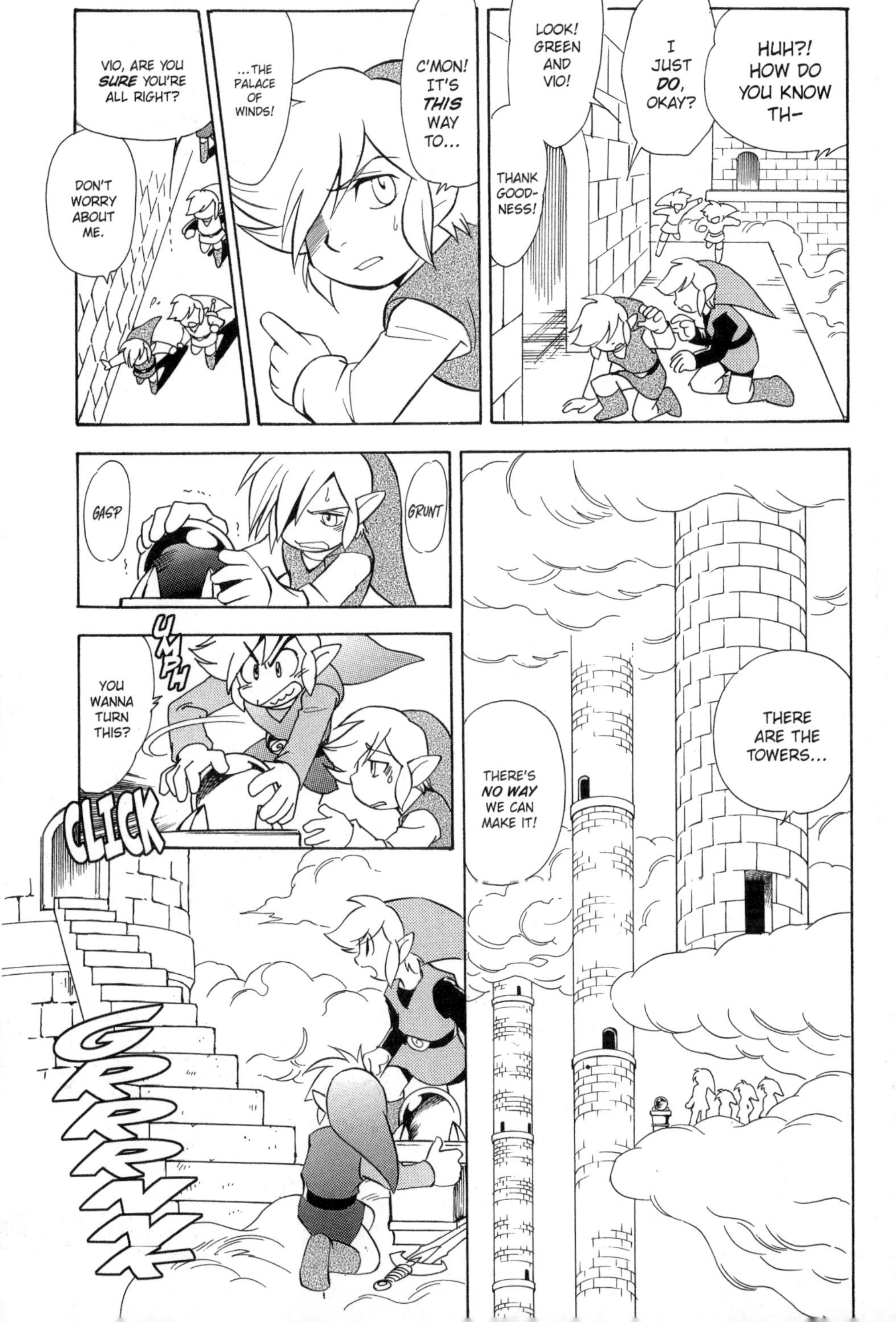
HUH?! HOW DO YOU KNOW TH-
I JUST DO, OKAY?
LOOK! GREEN AND VIO!
THANK GOODNESS!
C'MON! IT'S THIS WAY TO...
...THE PALACE OF WINDS!
VIO, ARE YOU SURE YOU'RE ALL RIGHT?
DON'T WORRY ABOUT ME.
THERE ARE THE TOWERS...
THERE'S NO WAY WE CAN MAKE IT!
GRUNT
GASP
UMPH
YOU WANNA TURN THIS?
CLICK
GRRRNK

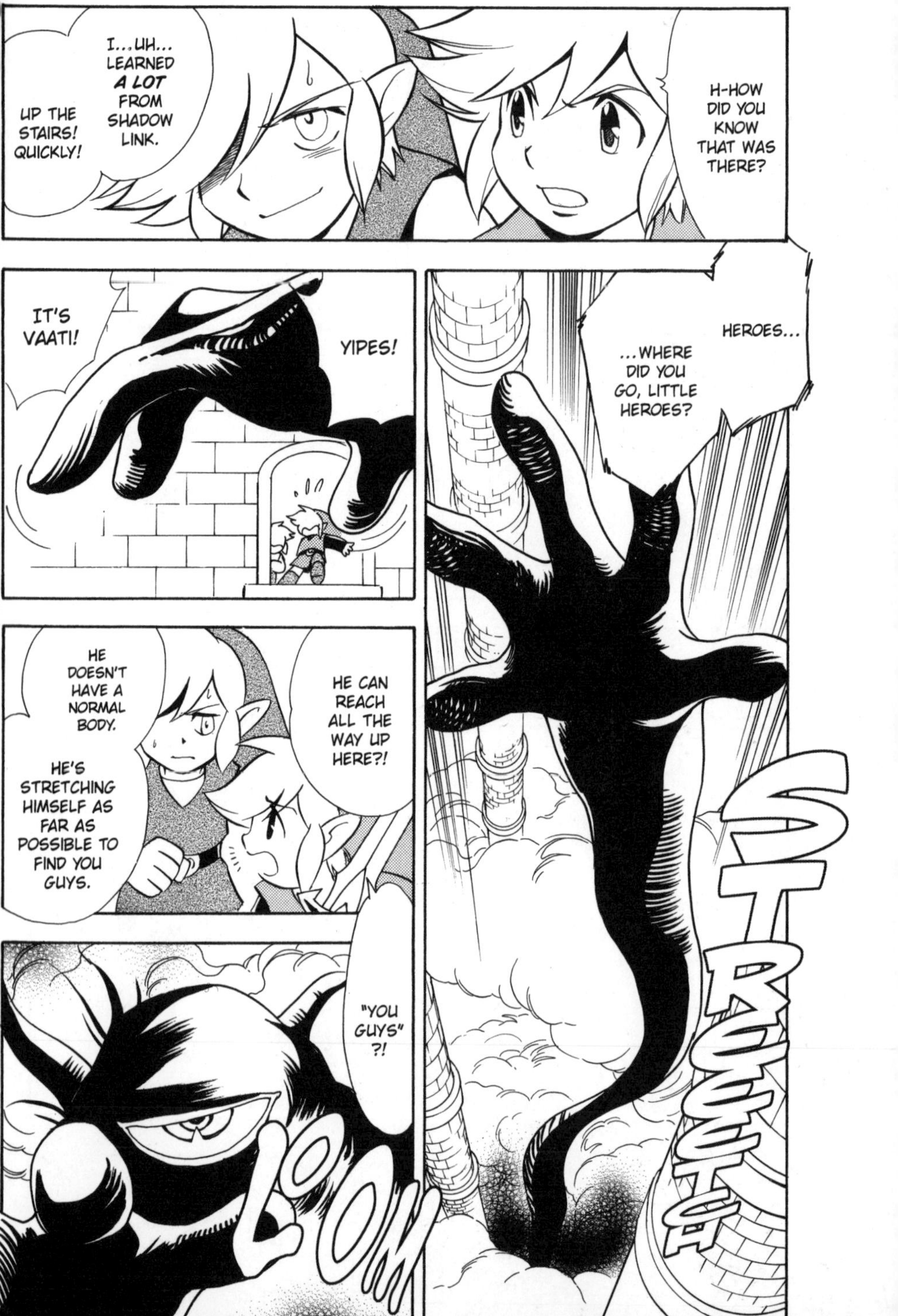
H-HOW DID YOU KNOW THAT WAS THERE?
I...UH... LEARNED **A LOT** FROM SHADOW LINK.
UP THE STAIRS! QUICKLY!
HEROES...
...WHERE DID YOU GO, LITTLE HEROES?
STRETCH
YIPES!
IT'S VAATI!
HE CAN REACH ALL THE WAY UP HERE?!
HE DOESN'T HAVE A NORMAL BODY.
HE'S STRETCHING HIMSELF AS FAR AS POSSIBLE TO FIND YOU GUYS.
"YOU GUYS" ?!
LOOM

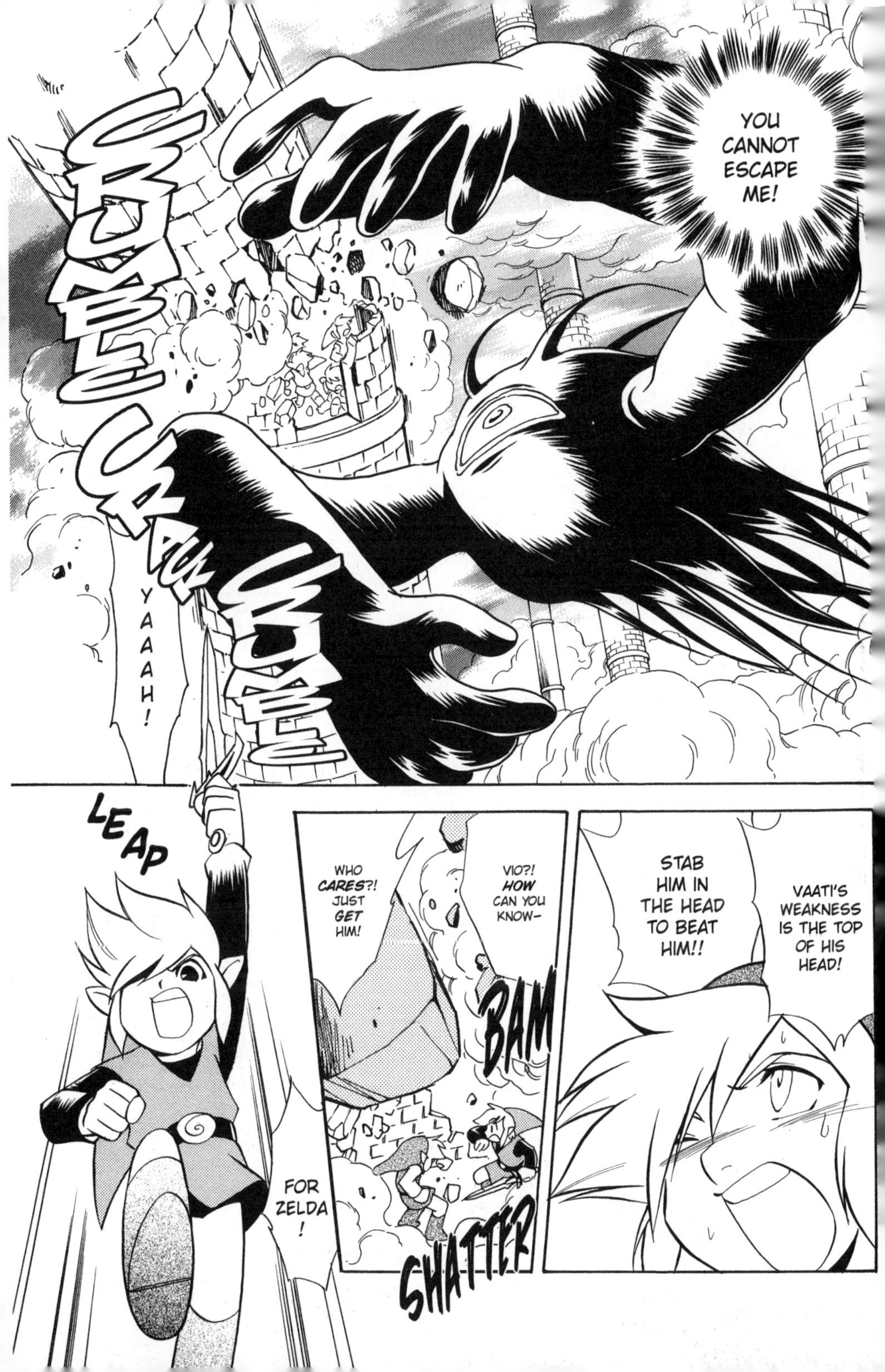
YOU CANNOT ESCAPE ME!
CRUMBLE
CRASH
CRUMBLE
YAAAAH!
VAATI'S WEAKNESS IS THE TOP OF HIS HEAD!
STAB HIM IN THE HEAD TO BEAT HIM!!
VIO?! **HOW** CAN YOU KNOW-
WHO **CARES**?! JUST **GET** HIM!
BAM
SHATTER
LEAP
FOR ZELDA!

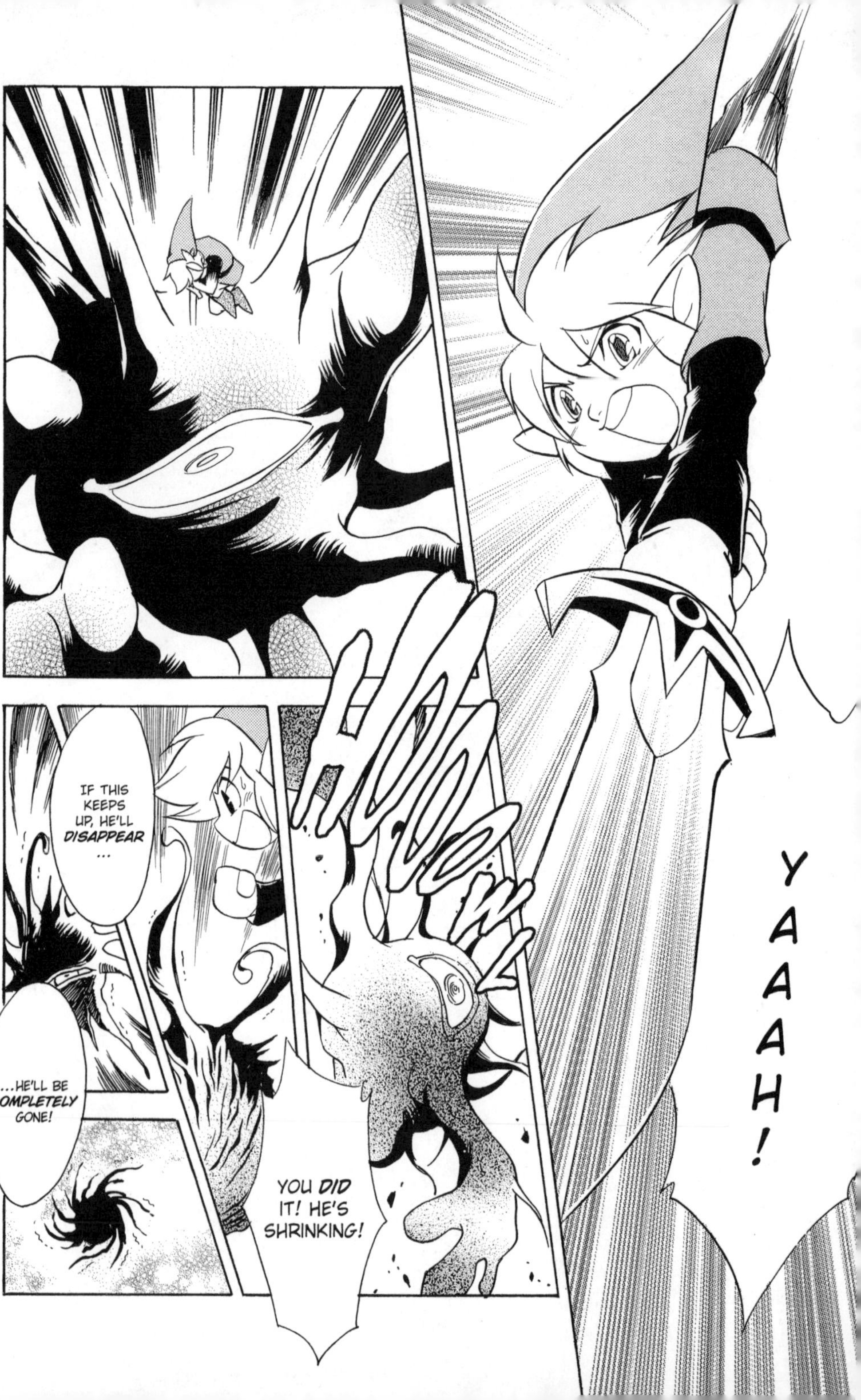
YAAAAH!
YOU DID IT! HE'S SHRINKING!
IF THIS KEEPS UP, HE'LL DISAPPEAR ...
...HE'LL BE COMPLETELY GONE!

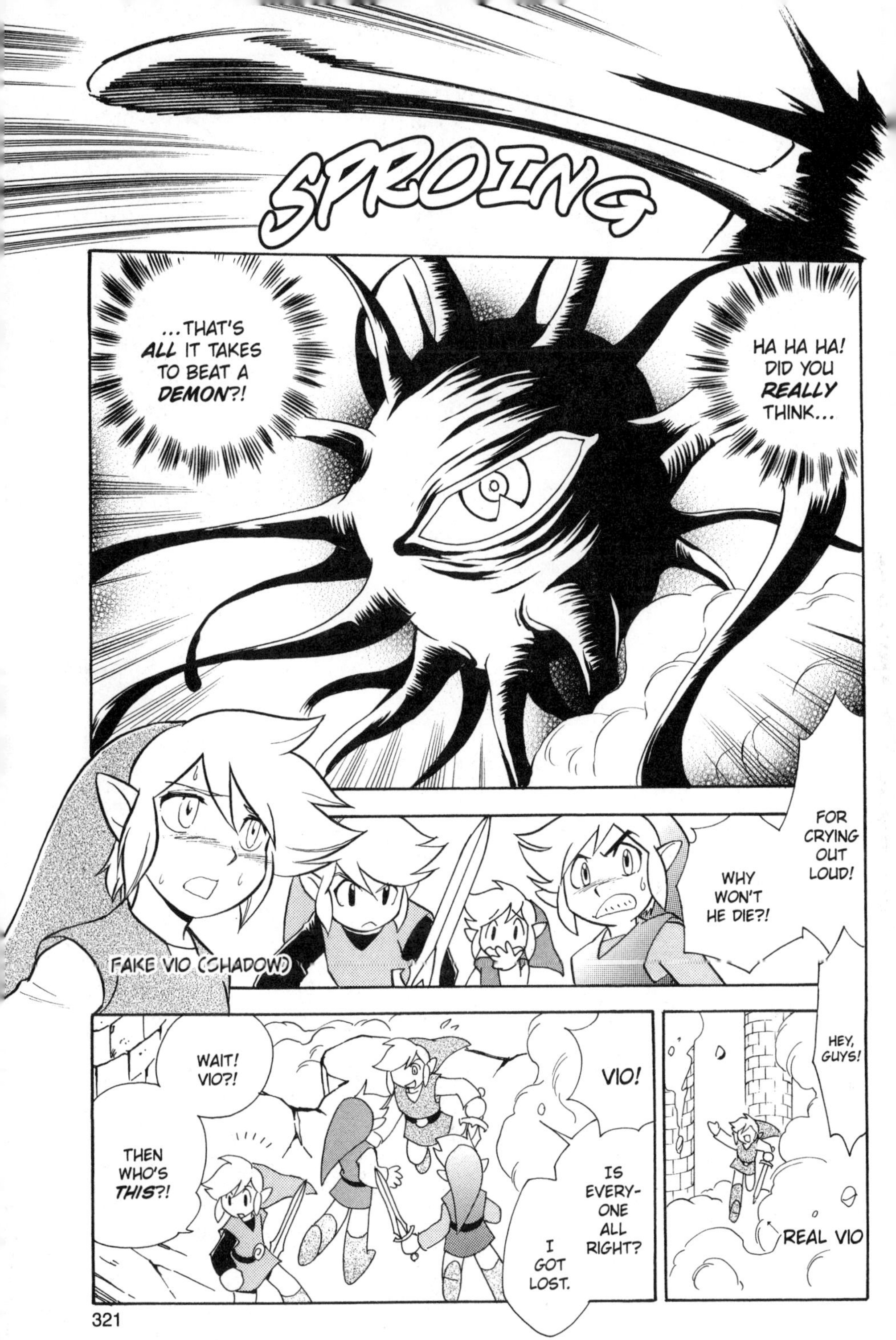
SPROING
HA HA HA! DID YOU REALLY THINK...
...THAT'S ALL IT TAKES TO BEAT A DEMON?!
FOR CRYING OUT LOUD!
WHY WON'T HE DIE?!
FAKE VIO (SHADOW)
HEY, GUYS!
REAL VIO
VIO!
IS EVERY-ONE ALL RIGHT?
I GOT LOST.
WAIT! VIO?!
THEN WHO'S THIS?!

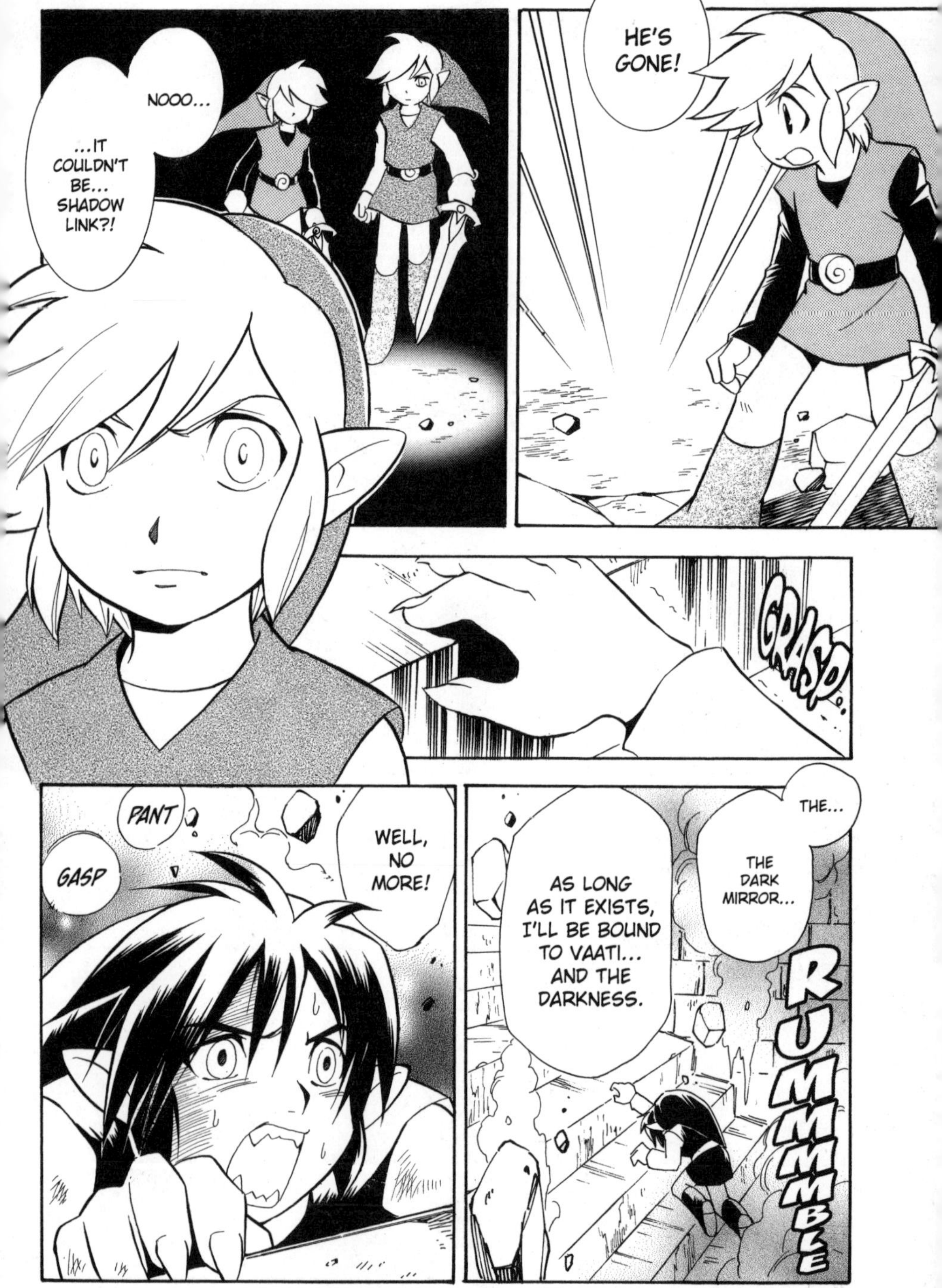
HE'S GONE!
NOOO...
...IT COULDN'T BE... SHADOW LINK?!
GRASP
THE...
THE DARK MIRROR...
AS LONG AS IT EXISTS, I'LL BE BOUND TO VAATI... AND THE DARKNESS.
RUMMMMBLE
WELL, NO MORE!
PANT
GASP

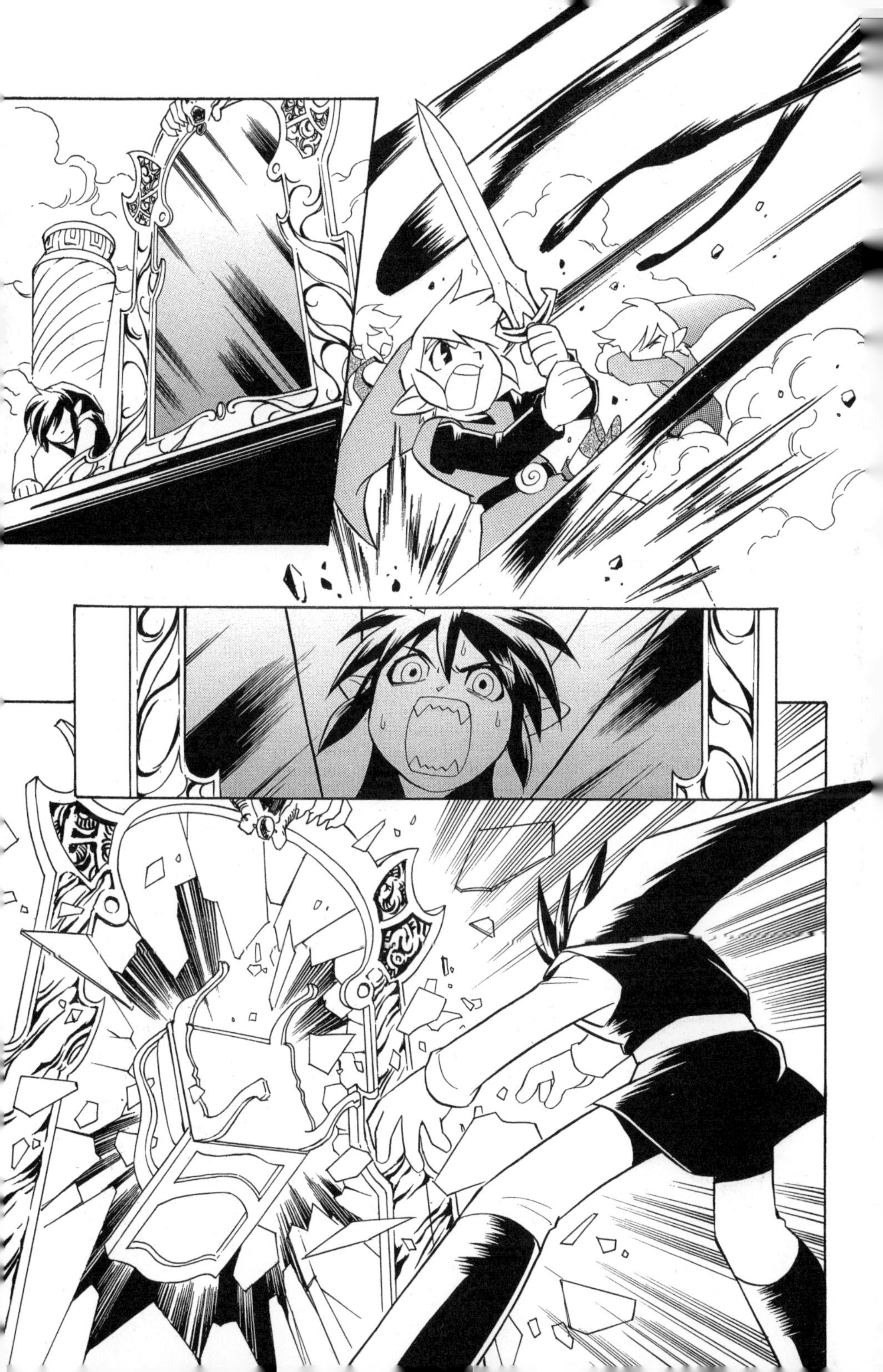

CHAPTER 11 The Four Sword Forever!

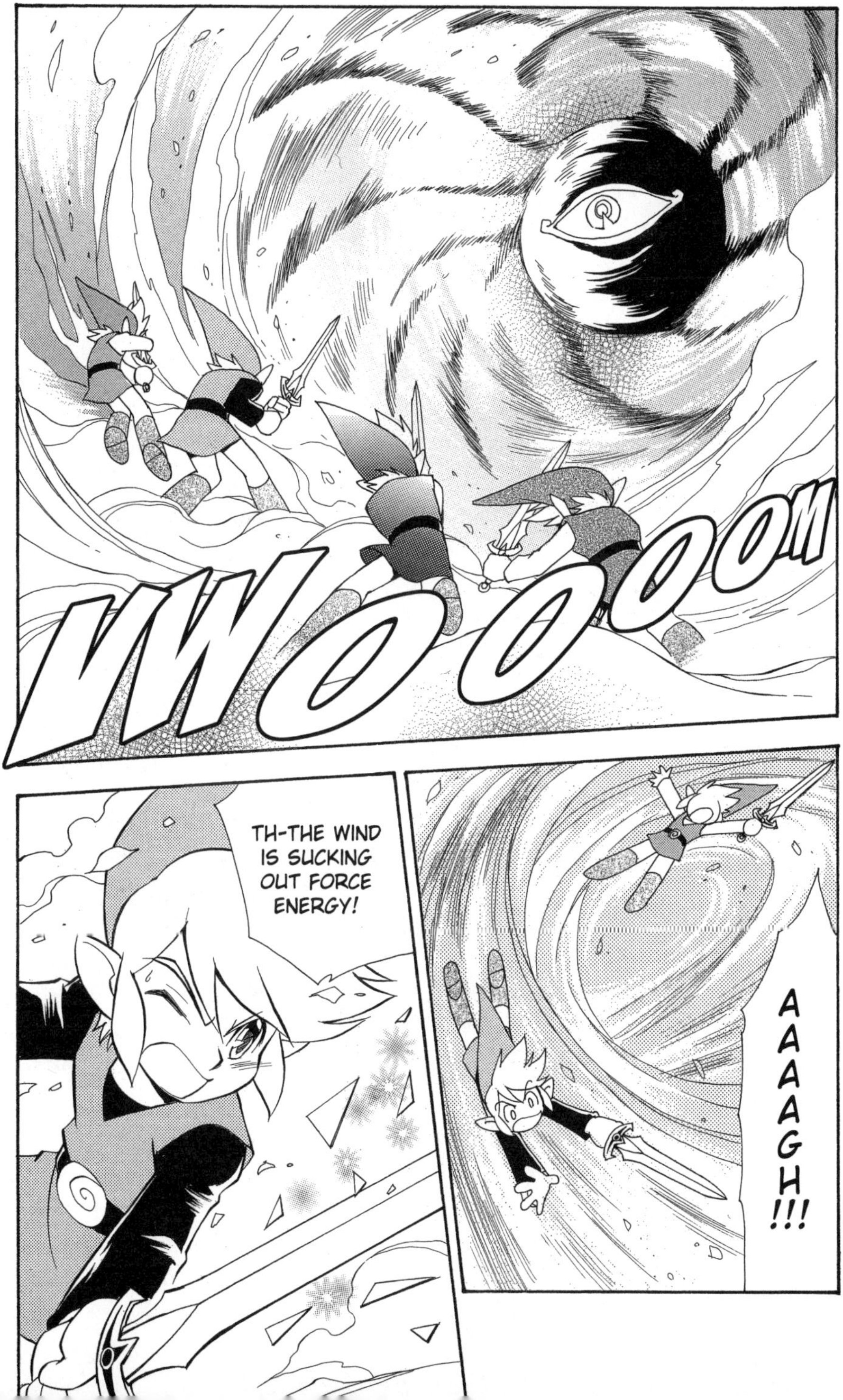
VWOOOOOM
AAAAAGH!!!
TH-THE WIND IS SUCKING OUT FORCE ENERGY!

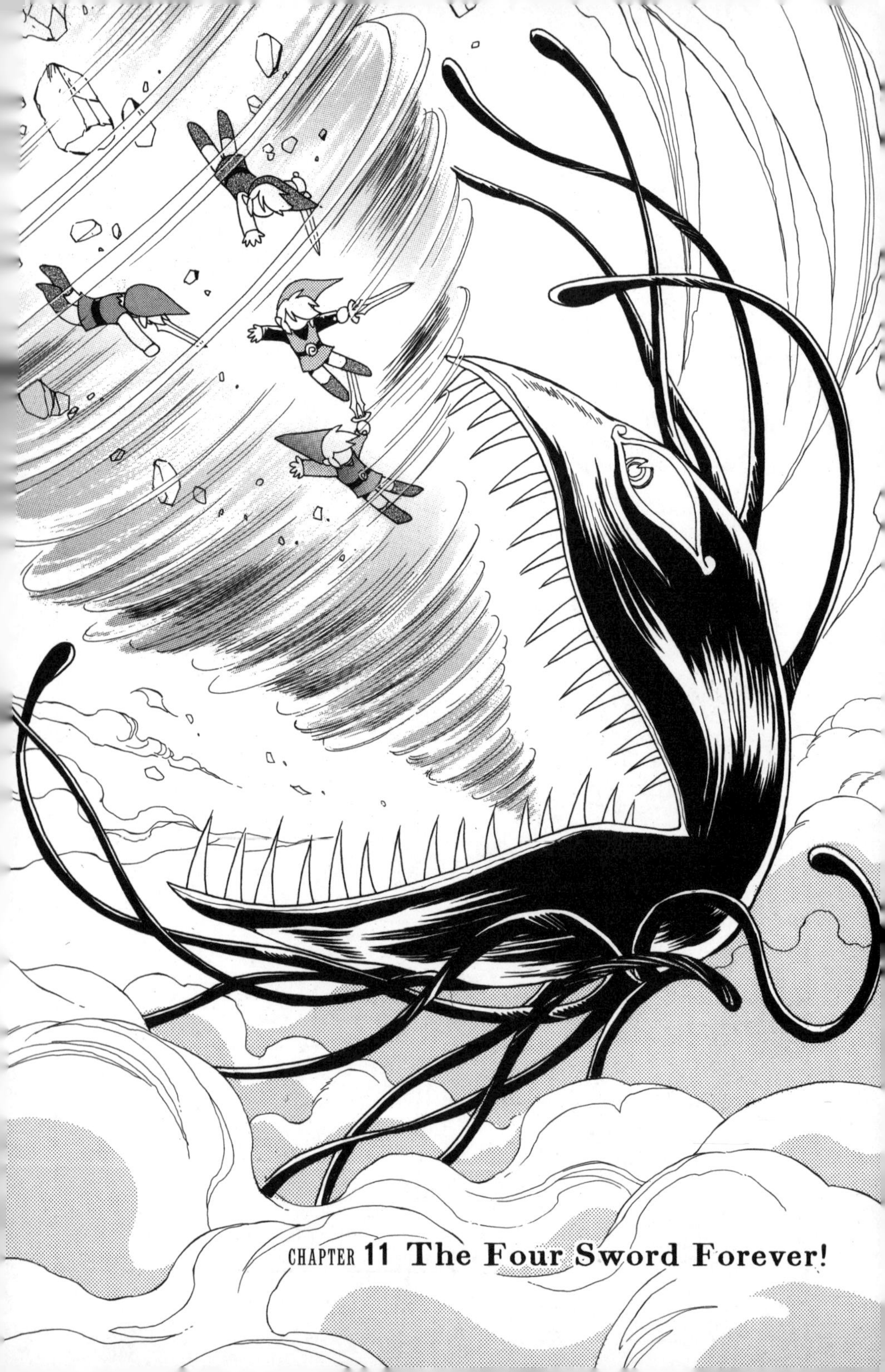

CHAPTER 11 The Four Sword Forever!

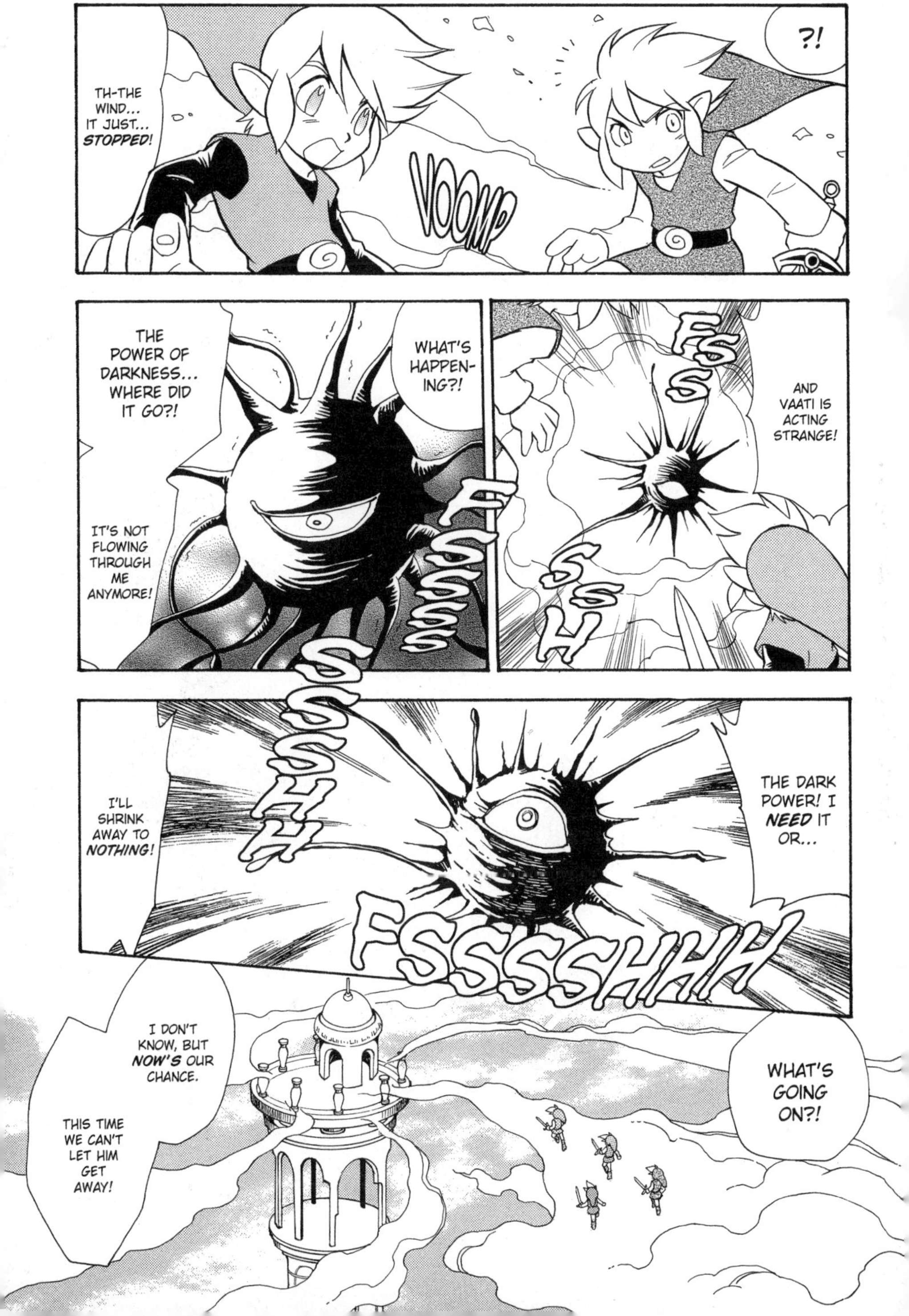
?!
TH-THE WIND... IT JUST... STOPPED!
VOOMP
FSS
AND VAATI IS ACTING STRANGE!
SSH
WHAT'S HAPPEN-ING?!
THE POWER OF DARKNESS... WHERE DID IT GO?!
IT'S NOT FLOWING THROUGH ME ANYMORE!
FSSSSSS
SSSSHH
THE DARK POWER! I NEED IT OR...
I'LL SHRINK AWAY TO NOTHING!
FSSSSHHH
WHAT'S GOING ON?!
I DON'T KNOW, BUT NOW'S OUR CHANCE.
THIS TIME WE CAN'T LET HIM GET AWAY!

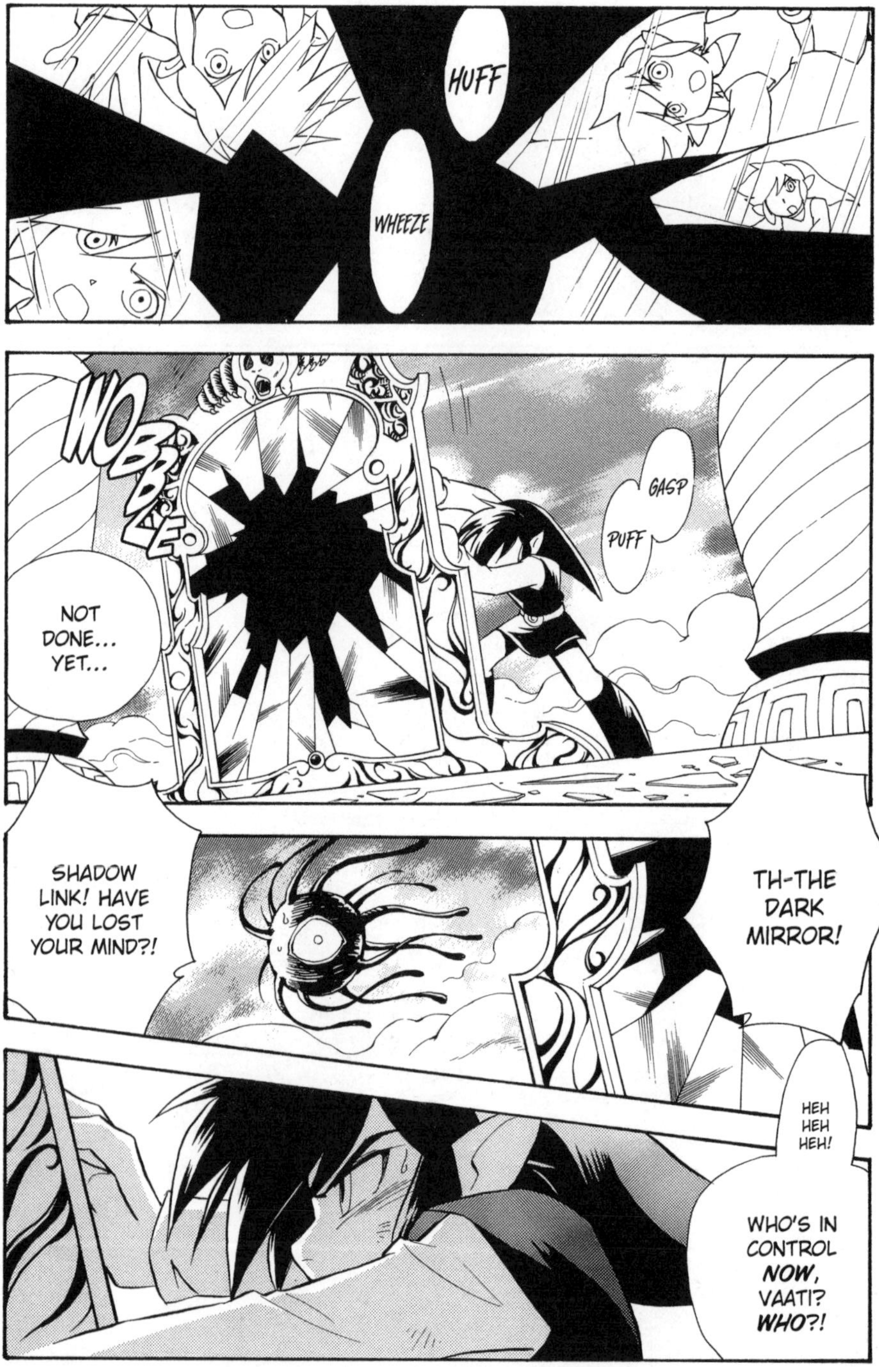
HUFF
WHEEZE
GASP
PUFF
WOBBLE
NOT DONE... YET...
TH-THE DARK MIRROR!
SHADOW LINK! HAVE YOU LOST YOUR MIND?!
HEH HEH HEH!
WHO'S IN CONTROL *NOW*, VAATI? *WHO*?!

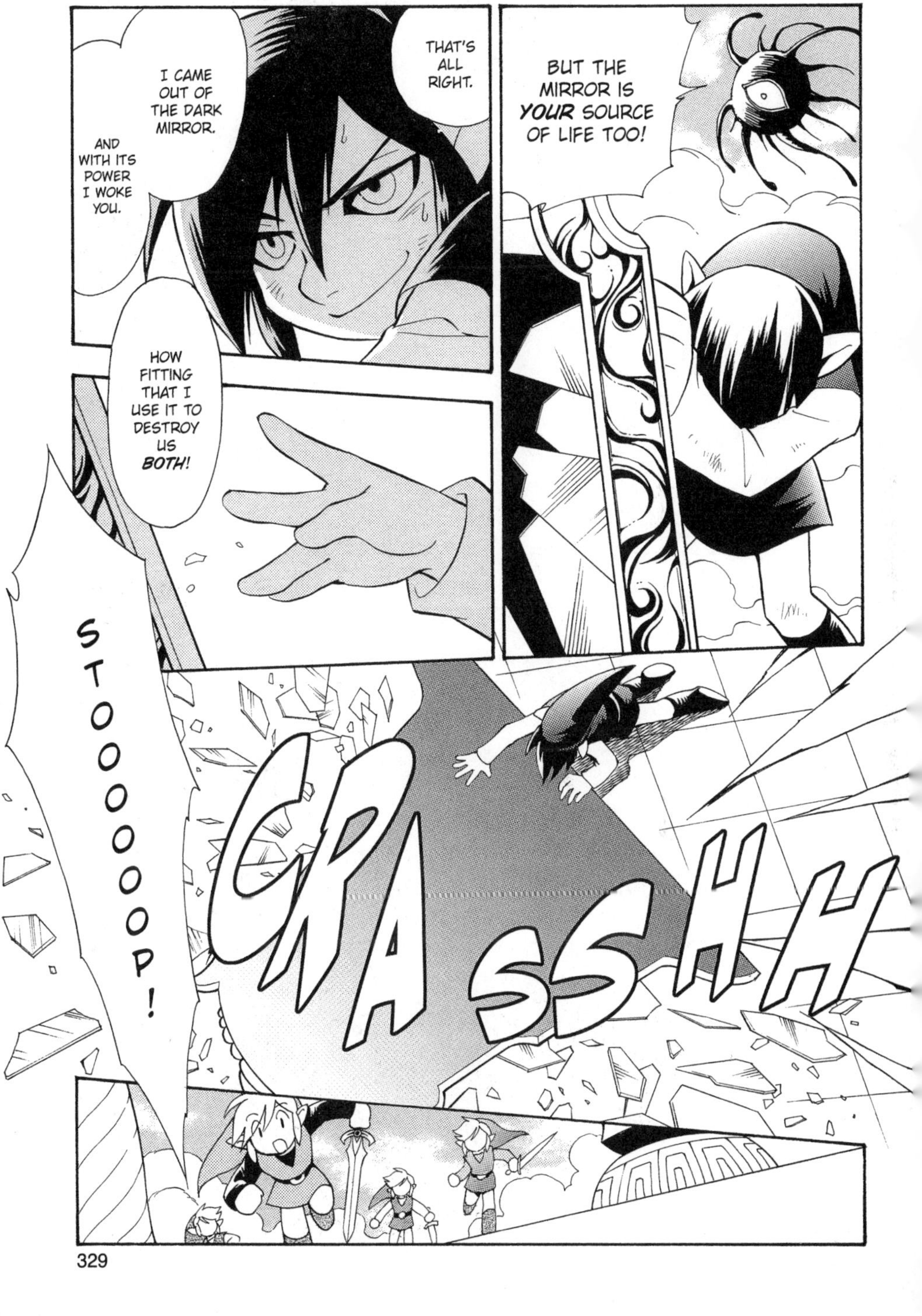
BUT THE MIRROR IS *YOUR* SOURCE OF LIFE TOO!
THAT'S ALL RIGHT.
I CAME OUT OF THE DARK MIRROR.
AND WITH ITS POWER I WOKE YOU.
HOW FITTING THAT I USE IT TO DESTROY US *BOTH*!
CRASSHH
STOOOOOOOP!

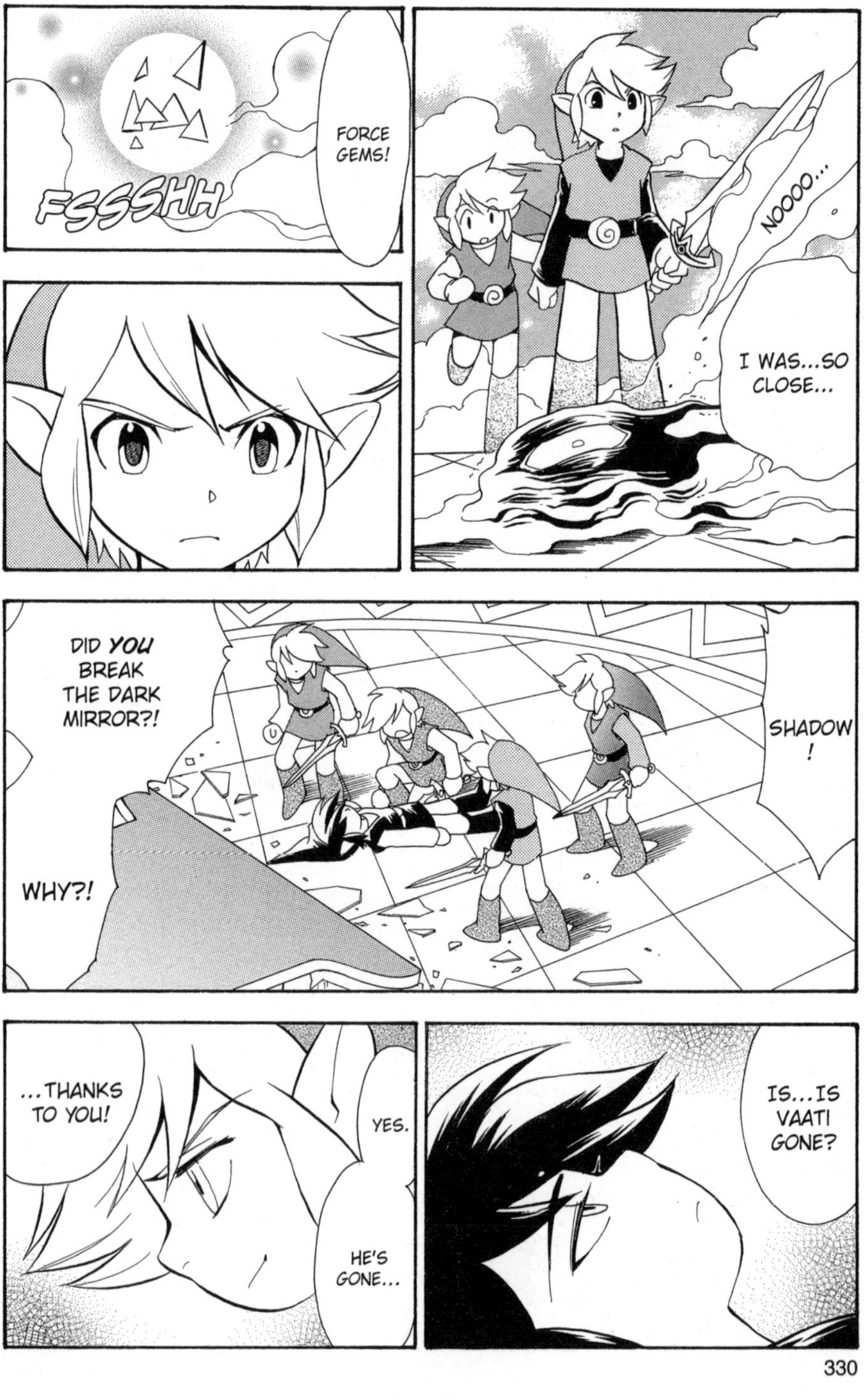
NOOOO...
I WAS...SO CLOSE...
FORCE GEMS!
FSSSHH
SHADOW!
DID *YOU* BREAK THE DARK MIRROR?!
WHY?!
IS...IS VAATI GONE?
YES.
HE'S GONE...
...THANKS TO YOU!

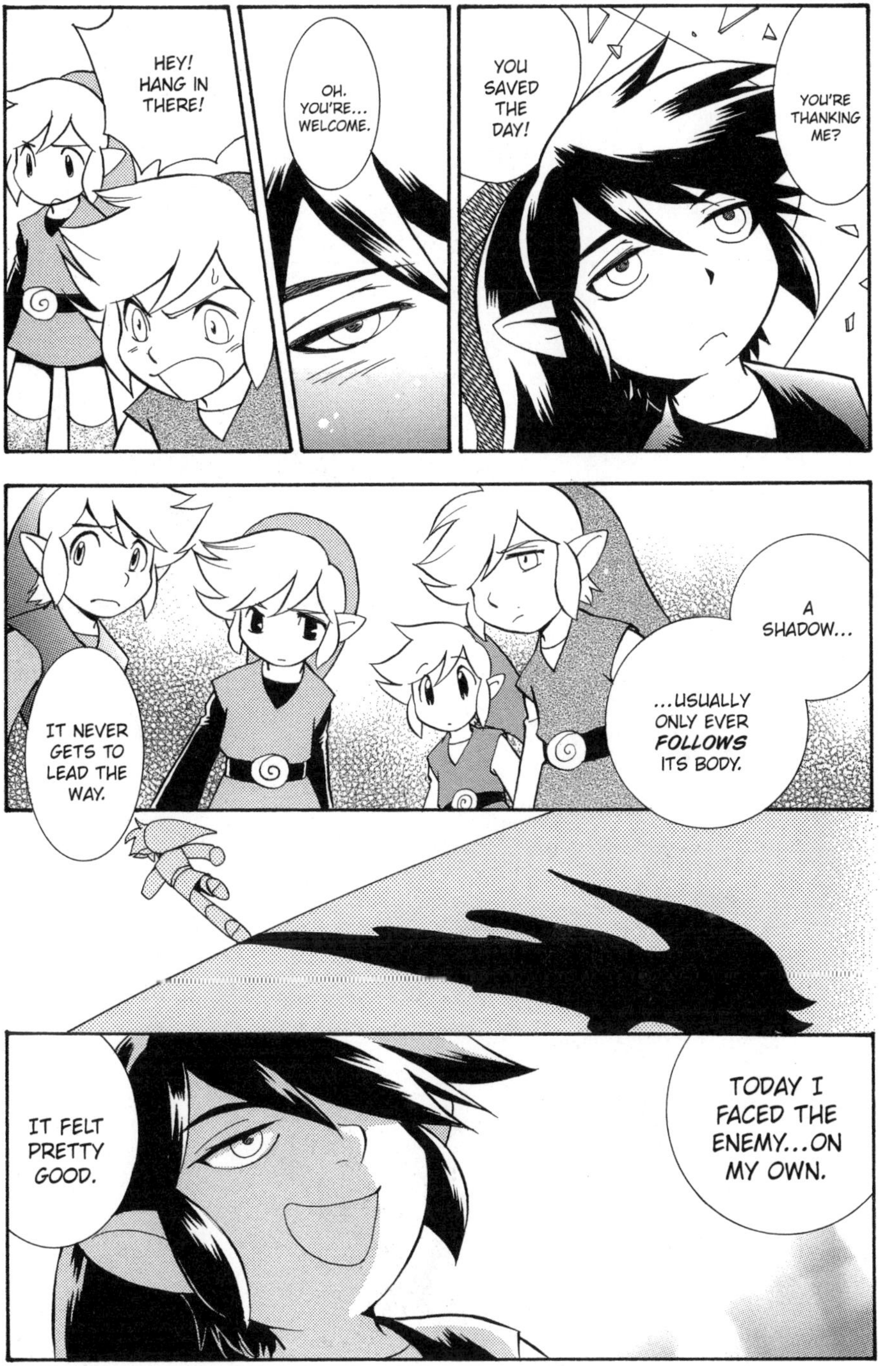
YOU SAVED THE DAY!
YOU'RE THANKING ME?
OH. YOU'RE... WELCOME.
HEY! HANG IN THERE!
A SHADOW...
...USUALLY ONLY EVER **FOLLOWS** ITS BODY.
IT NEVER GETS TO LEAD THE WAY.
TODAY I FACED THE ENEMY...ON MY OWN.
IT FELT PRETTY GOOD.

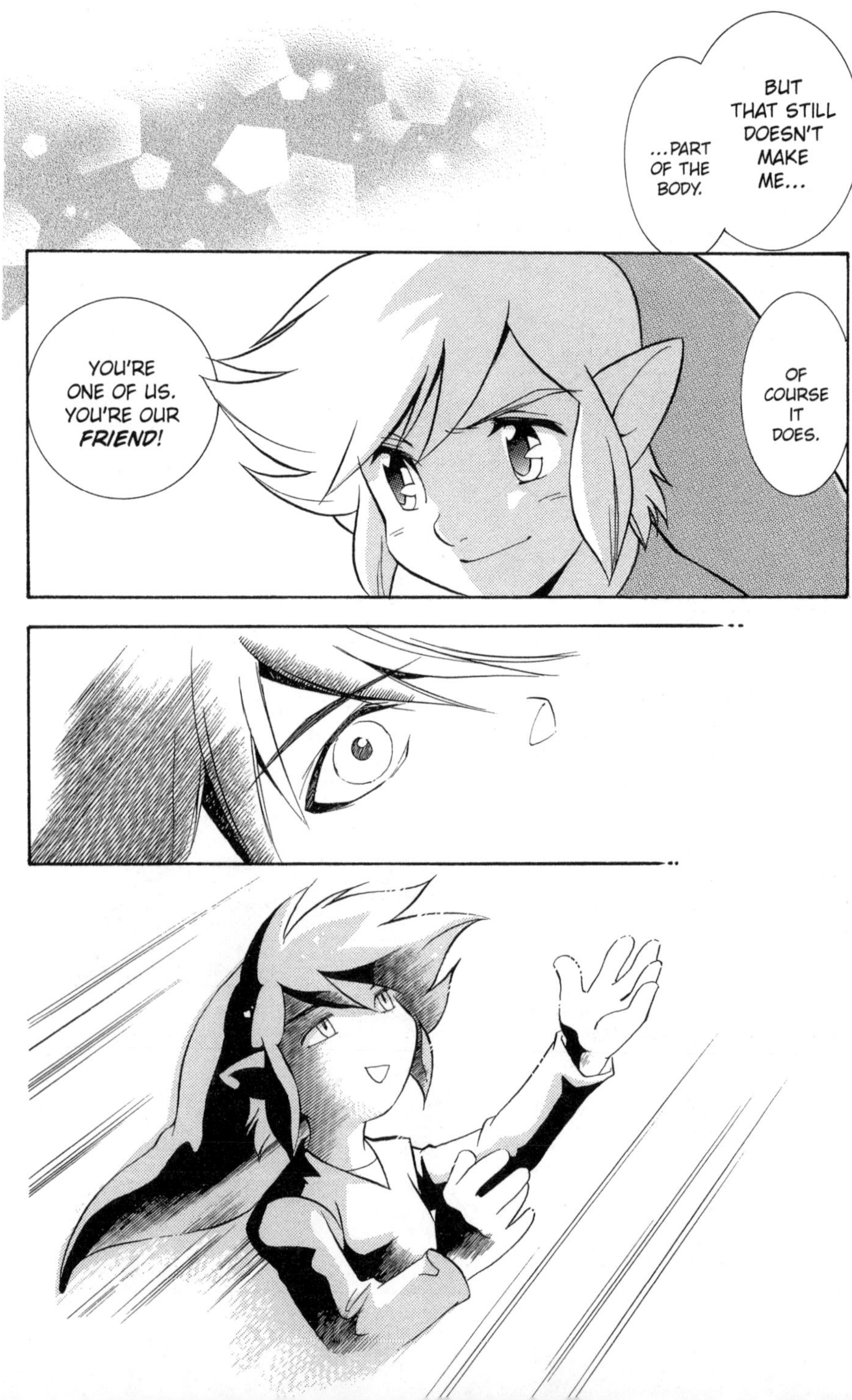
BUT THAT STILL DOESN'T MAKE ME...
...PART OF THE BODY.
OF COURSE IT DOES.
YOU'RE ONE OF US. YOU'RE OUR *FRIEND!*

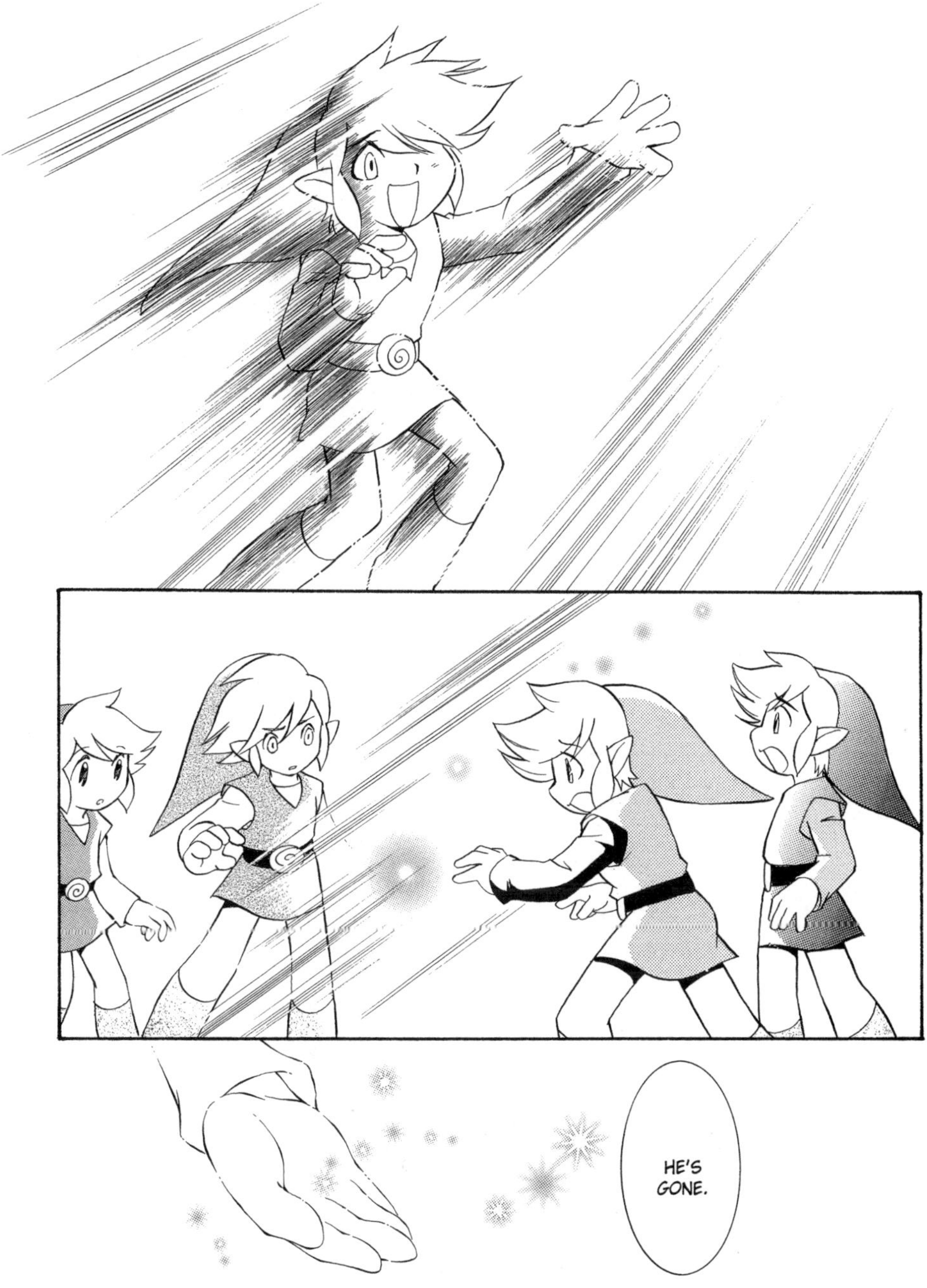
HE'S GONE.

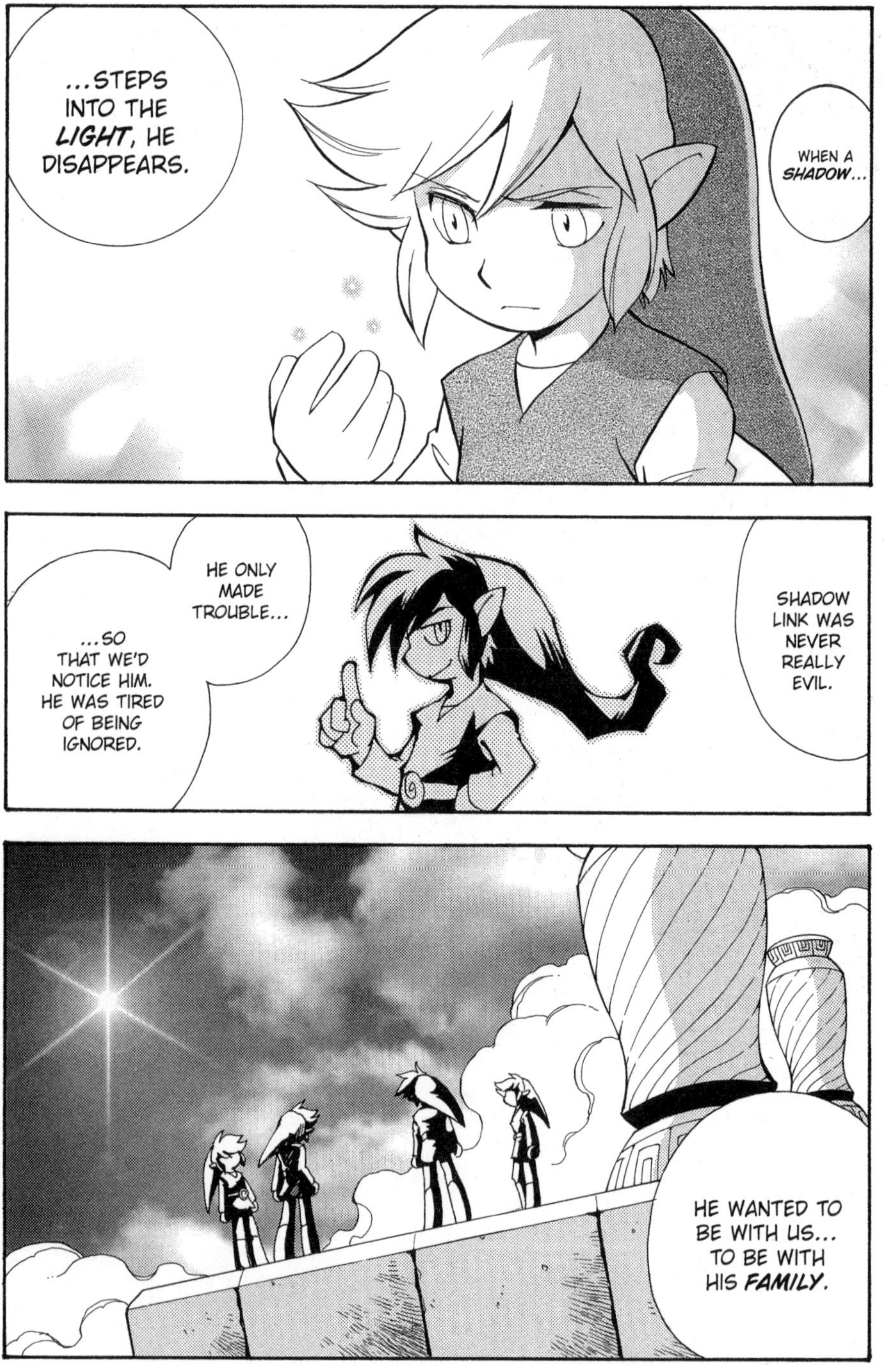
WHEN A *SHADOW*...
...STEPS INTO THE *LIGHT*, HE DISAPPEARS.
SHADOW LINK WAS NEVER REALLY EVIL.
HE ONLY MADE TROUBLE...
...SO THAT WE'D NOTICE HIM. HE WAS TIRED OF BEING IGNORED.
HE WANTED TO BE WITH US... TO BE WITH HIS *FAMILY*.

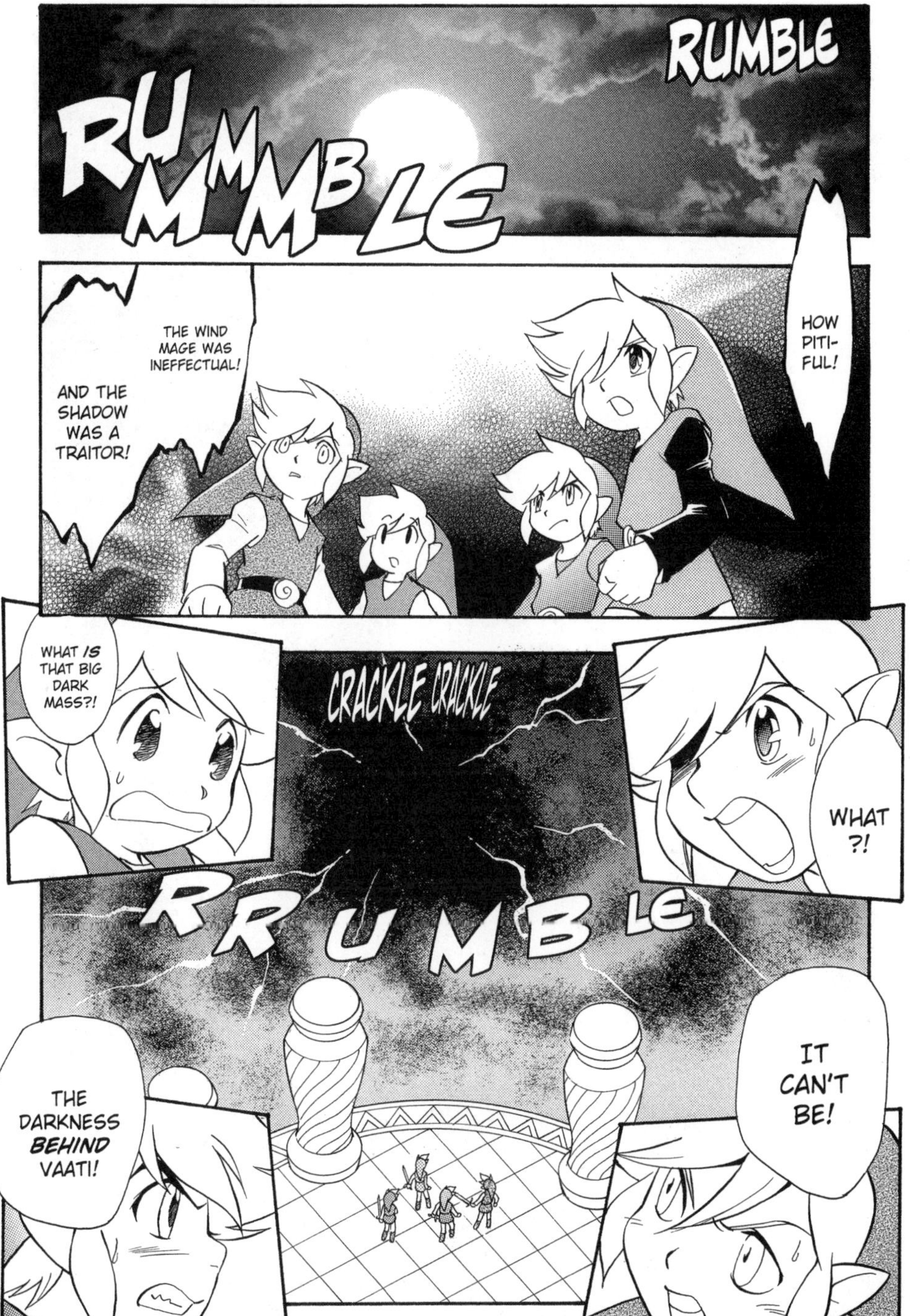

RUMBLE
RUMMMMBLE
HOW PITI-FUL!
THE WIND MAGE WAS INEFFECTUAL!
AND THE SHADOW WAS A TRAITOR!
WHAT ?!
CRACKLE CRACKLE
WHAT *IS* THAT BIG DARK MASS?!
RRUMBLE
IT CAN'T BE!
THE DARKNESS ***BEHIND*** VAATI!

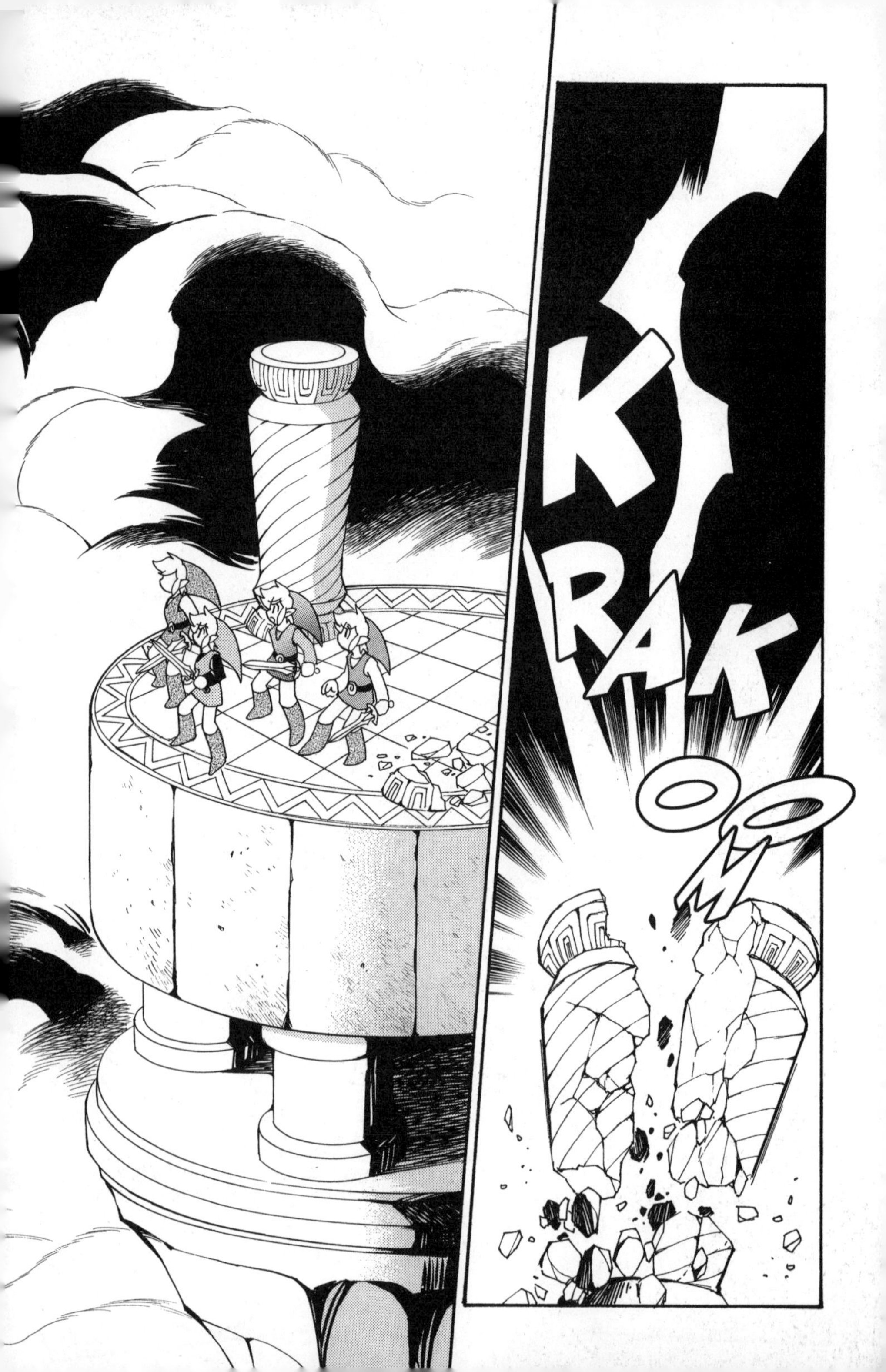
KRAK
OOM

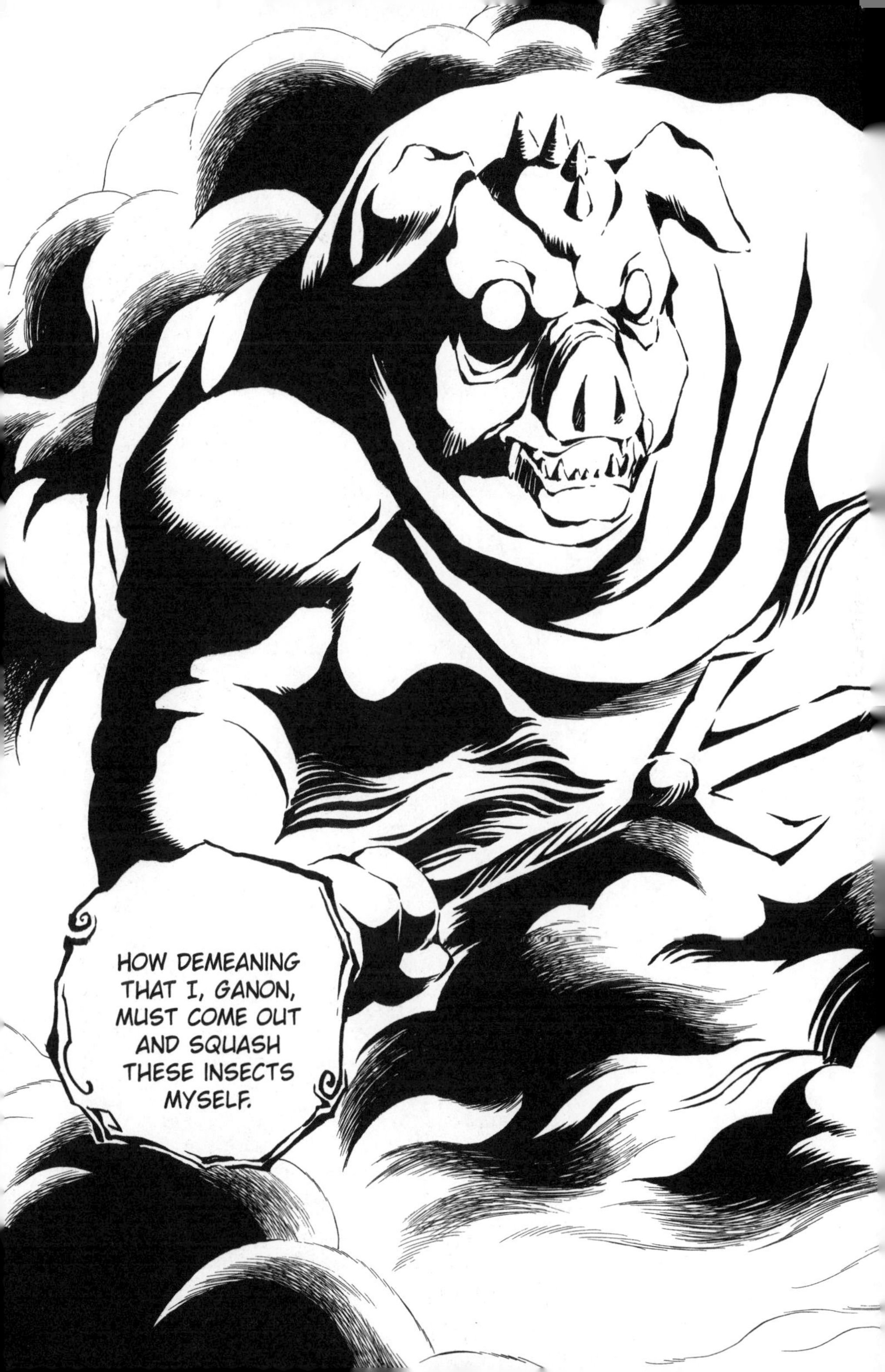
HOW DEMEANING THAT I, GANON, MUST COME OUT AND SQUASH THESE INSECTS MYSELF.

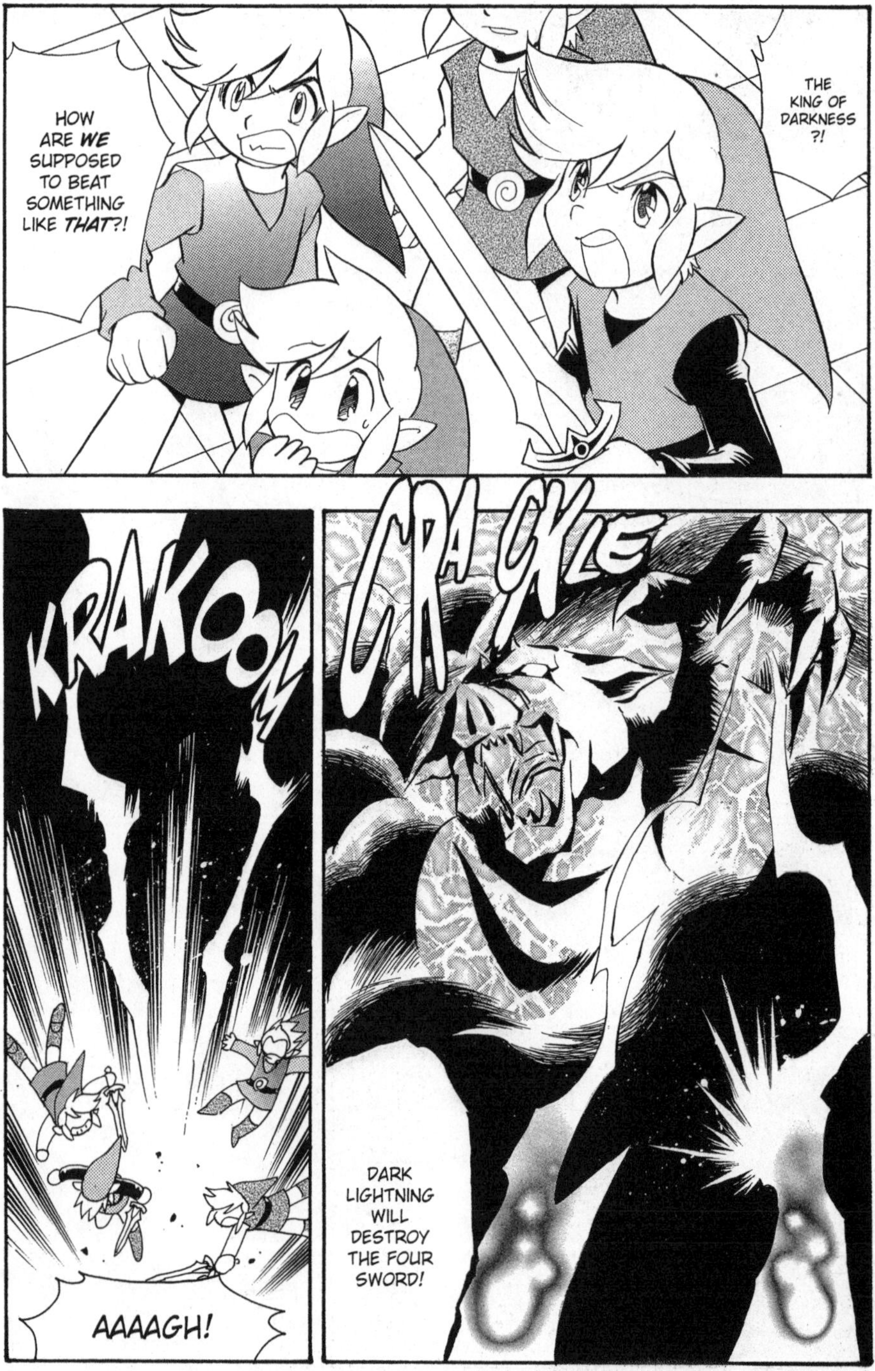
THE KING OF DARKNESS ?!
HOW ARE *WE* SUPPOSED TO BEAT SOMETHING LIKE *THAT*?!
CRACKLE
DARK LIGHTNING WILL DESTROY THE FOUR SWORD!
KRAKOOM
AAAAGH!

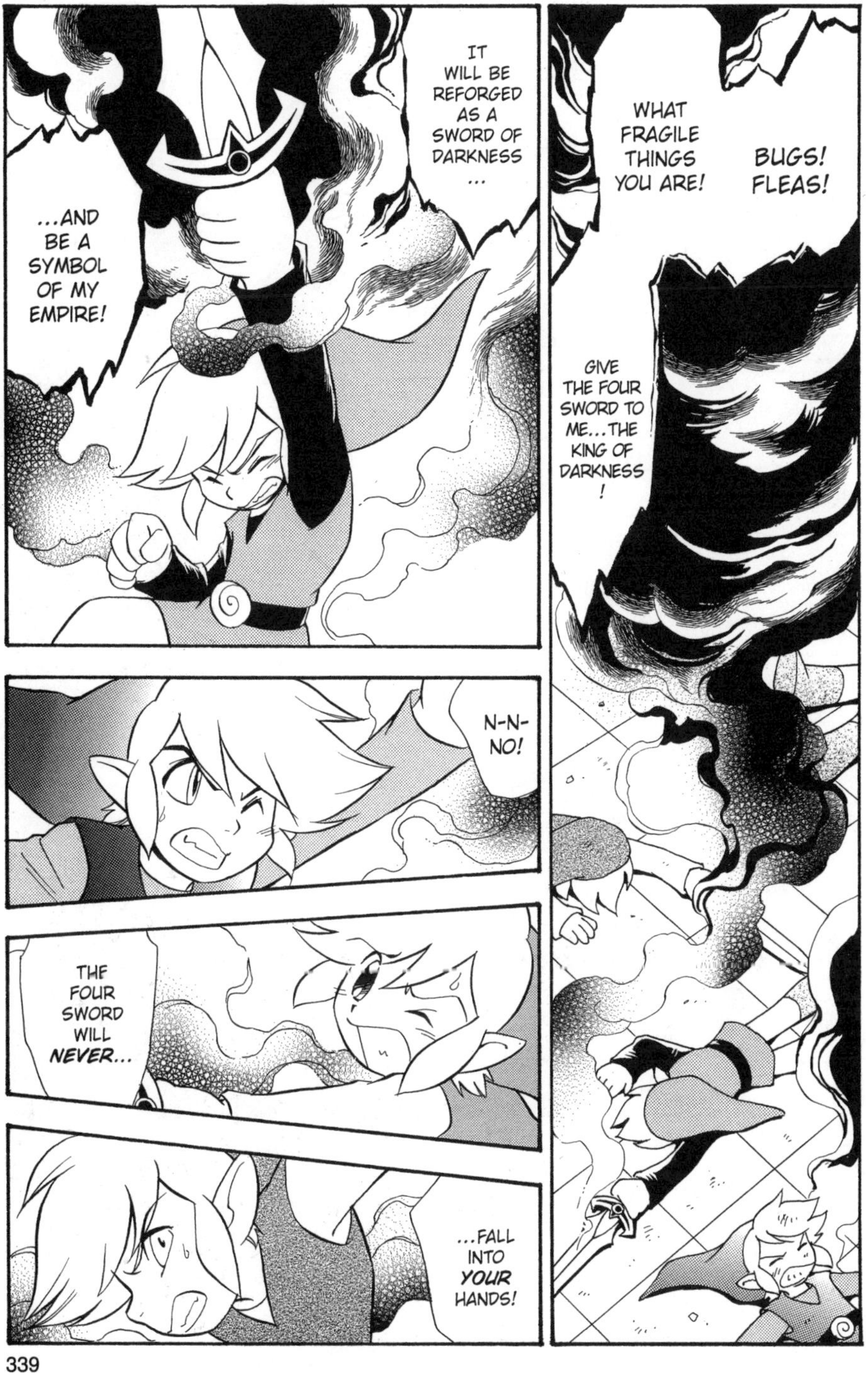

WHAT FRAGILE THINGS YOU ARE!
BUGS! FLEAS!
GIVE THE FOUR SWORD TO ME...THE KING OF DARKNESS!
IT WILL BE REFORGED AS A SWORD OF DARKNESS...
...AND BE A SYMBOL OF MY EMPIRE!
N-N-NO!
THE FOUR SWORD WILL ***NEVER...***
...FALL INTO ***YOUR*** HANDS!

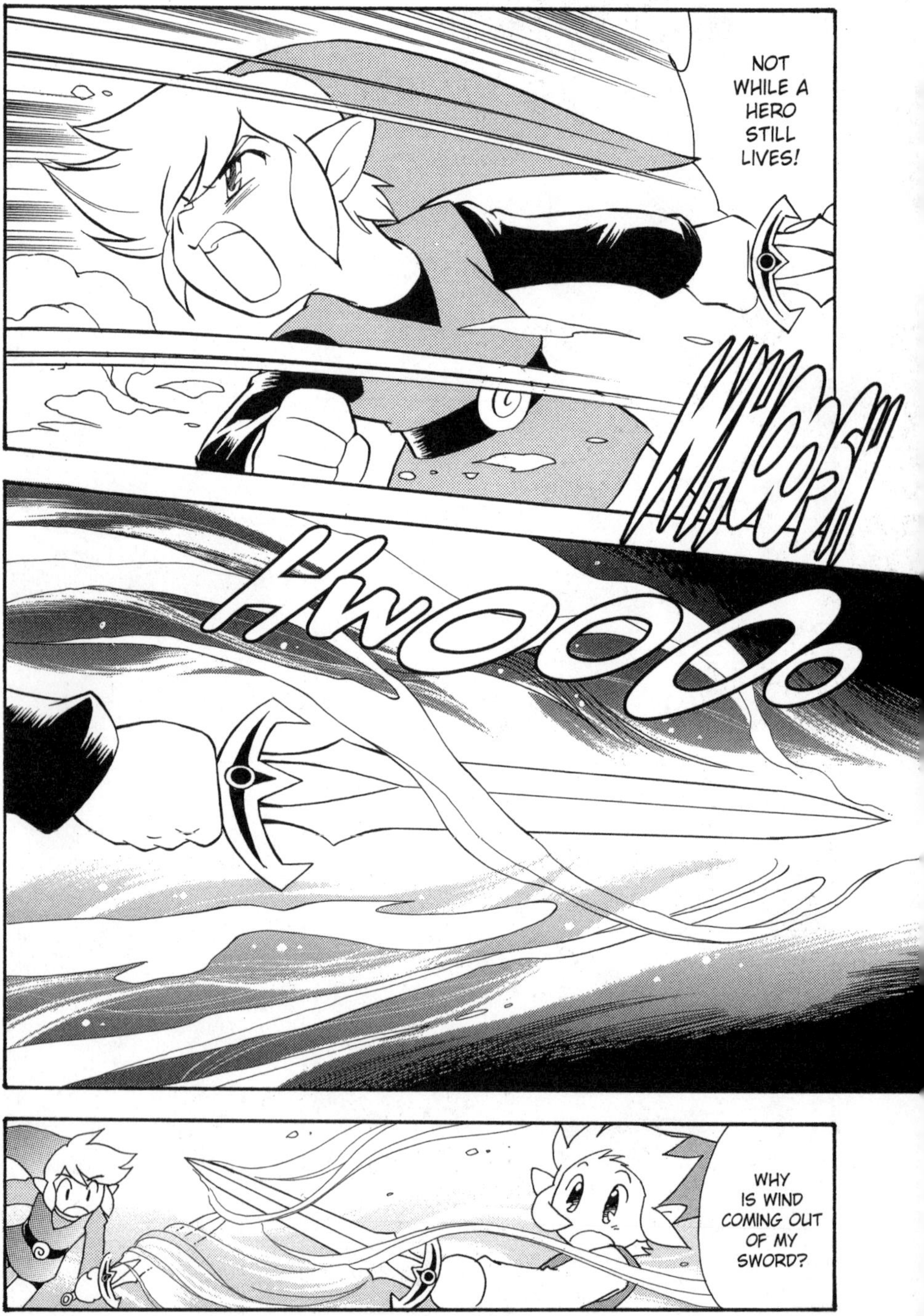
NOT WHILE A HERO STILL LIVES!
HWOOOO
WHY IS WIND COMING OUT OF MY SWORD?

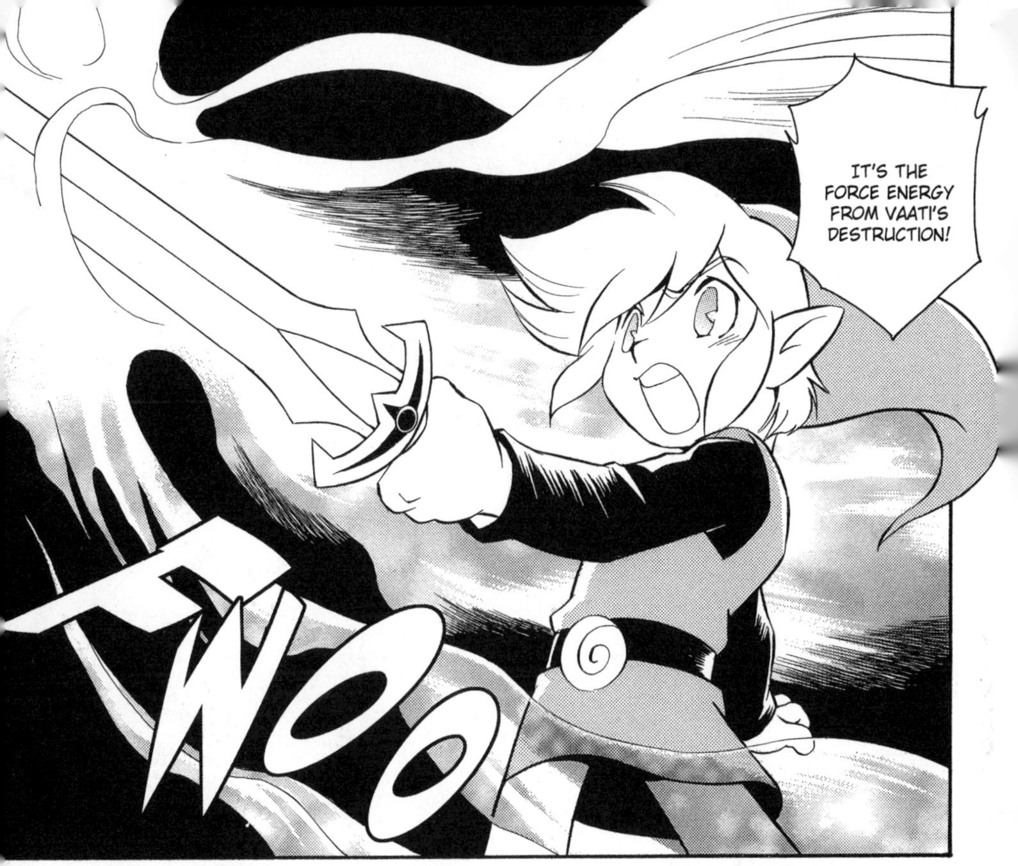
IT'S THE FORCE ENERGY FROM VAATI'S DESTRUCTION!
FWOO

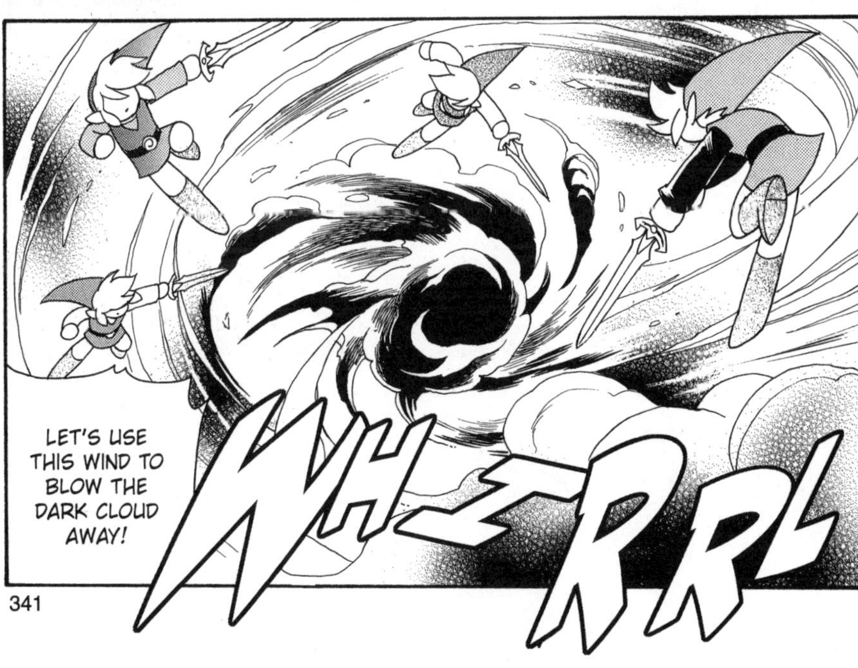
LET'S USE THIS WIND TO BLOW THE DARK CLOUD AWAY!
WHIRRL

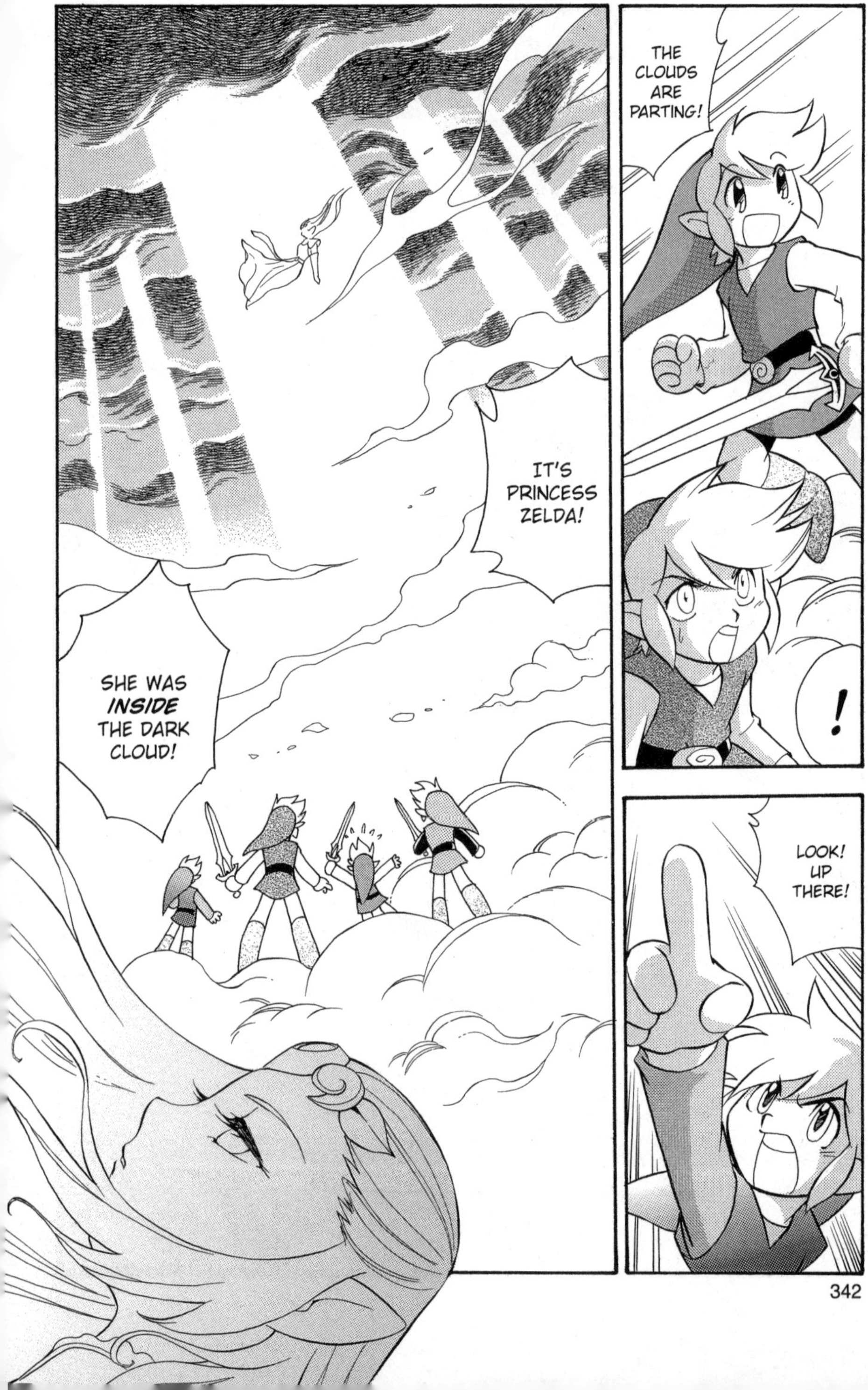
THE CLOUDS ARE PARTING!
!
LOOK! UP THERE!
IT'S PRINCESS ZELDA!
SHE WAS *INSIDE* THE DARK CLOUD!

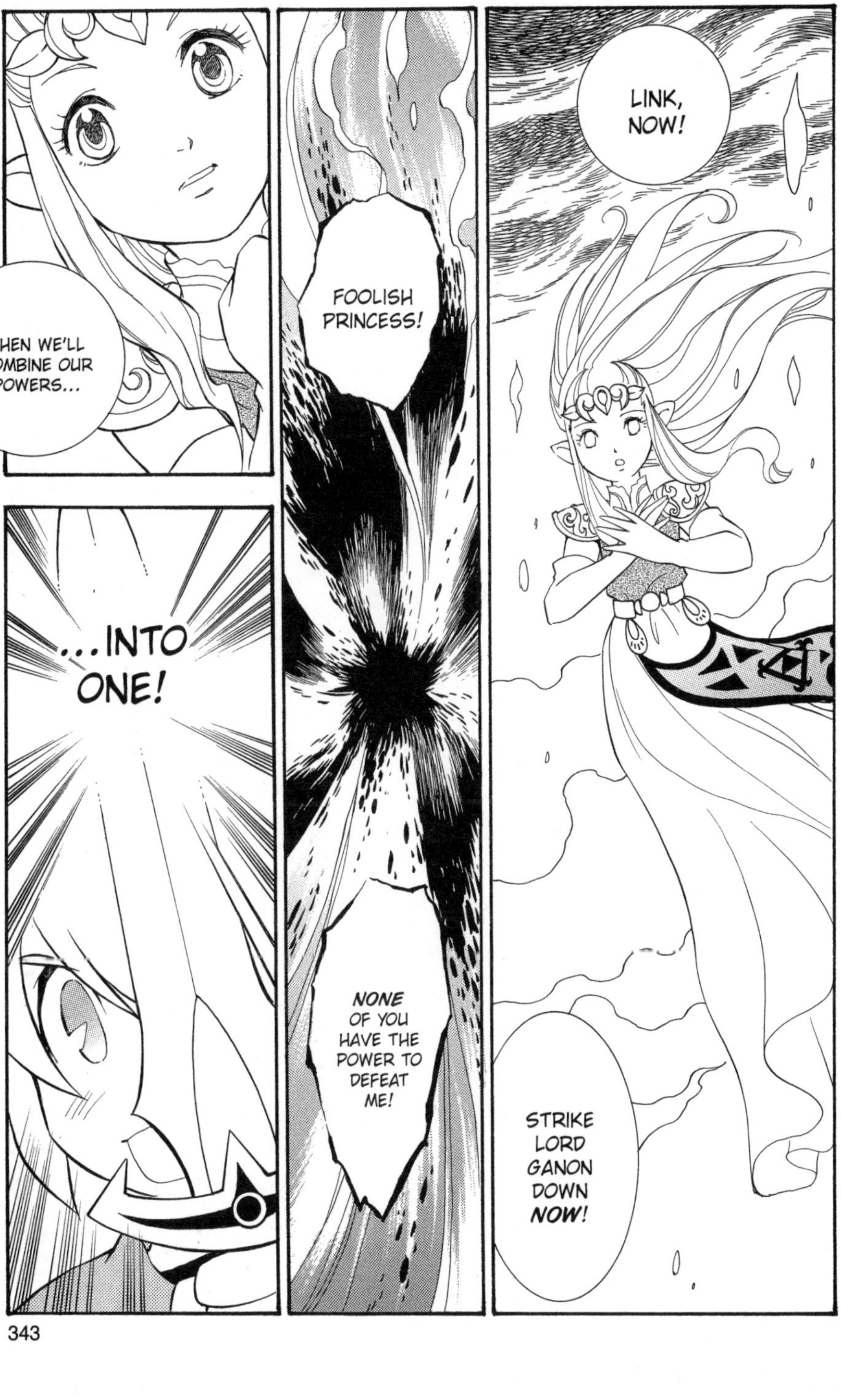
LINK, NOW!
STRIKE LORD GANON DOWN *NOW*!
FOOLISH PRINCESS!
NONE OF YOU HAVE THE POWER TO DEFEAT ME!
THEN WE'LL COMBINE OUR POWERS...
...INTO ONE!

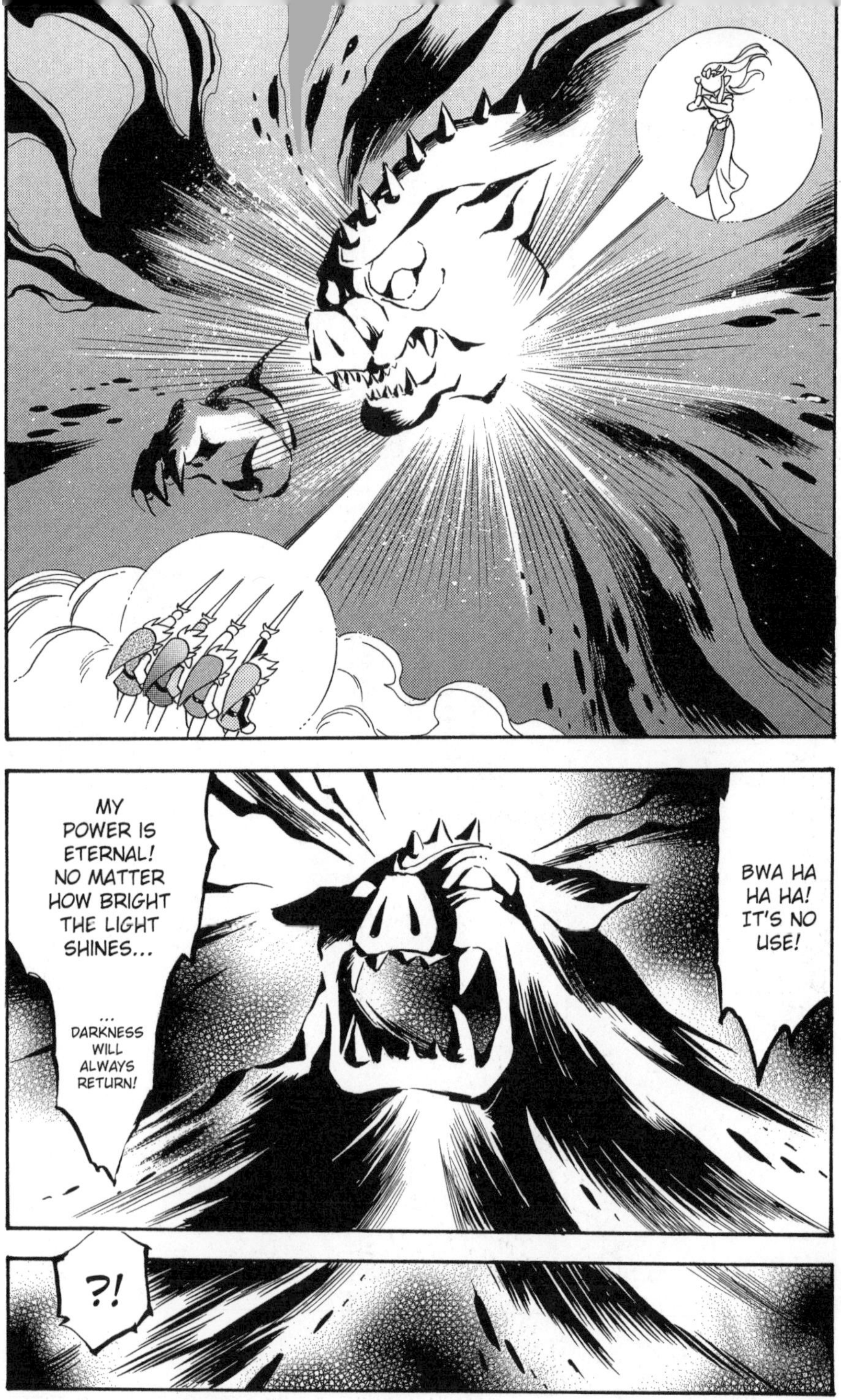
BWA HA HA HA! IT'S NO USE!
MY POWER IS ETERNAL! NO MATTER HOW BRIGHT THE LIGHT SHINES...
...DARKNESS WILL ALWAYS RETURN!
?!

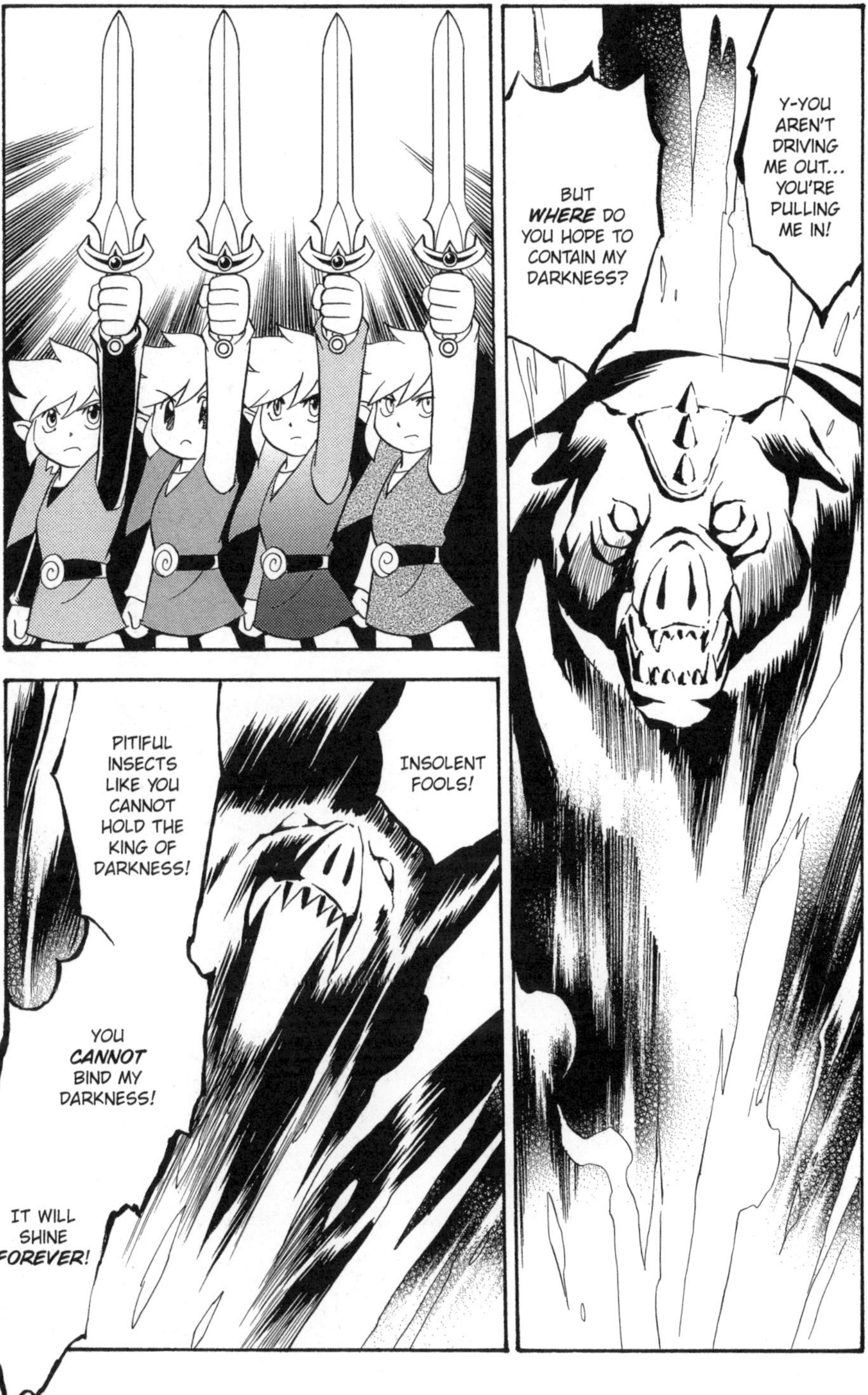
Y-YOU AREN'T DRIVING ME OUT... YOU'RE PULLING ME IN!
BUT **WHERE** DO YOU HOPE TO CONTAIN MY DARKNESS?
INSOLENT FOOLS!
PITIFUL INSECTS LIKE YOU CANNOT HOLD THE KING OF DARKNESS!
YOU **CANNOT** BIND MY DARKNESS!
IT WILL SHINE **FOREVER**!

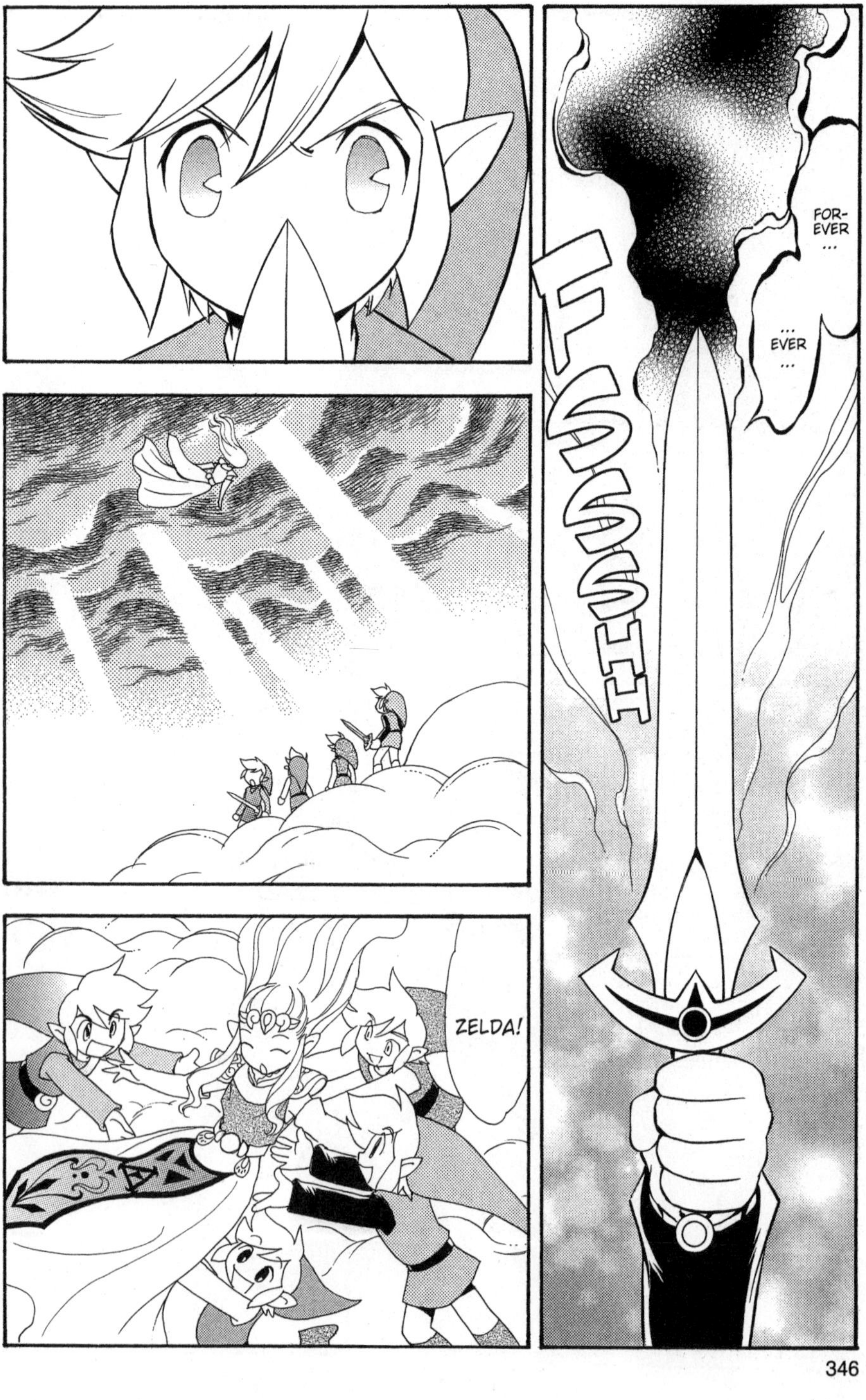
FOR-EVER...
...EVER...
FSSSHH
ZELDA!

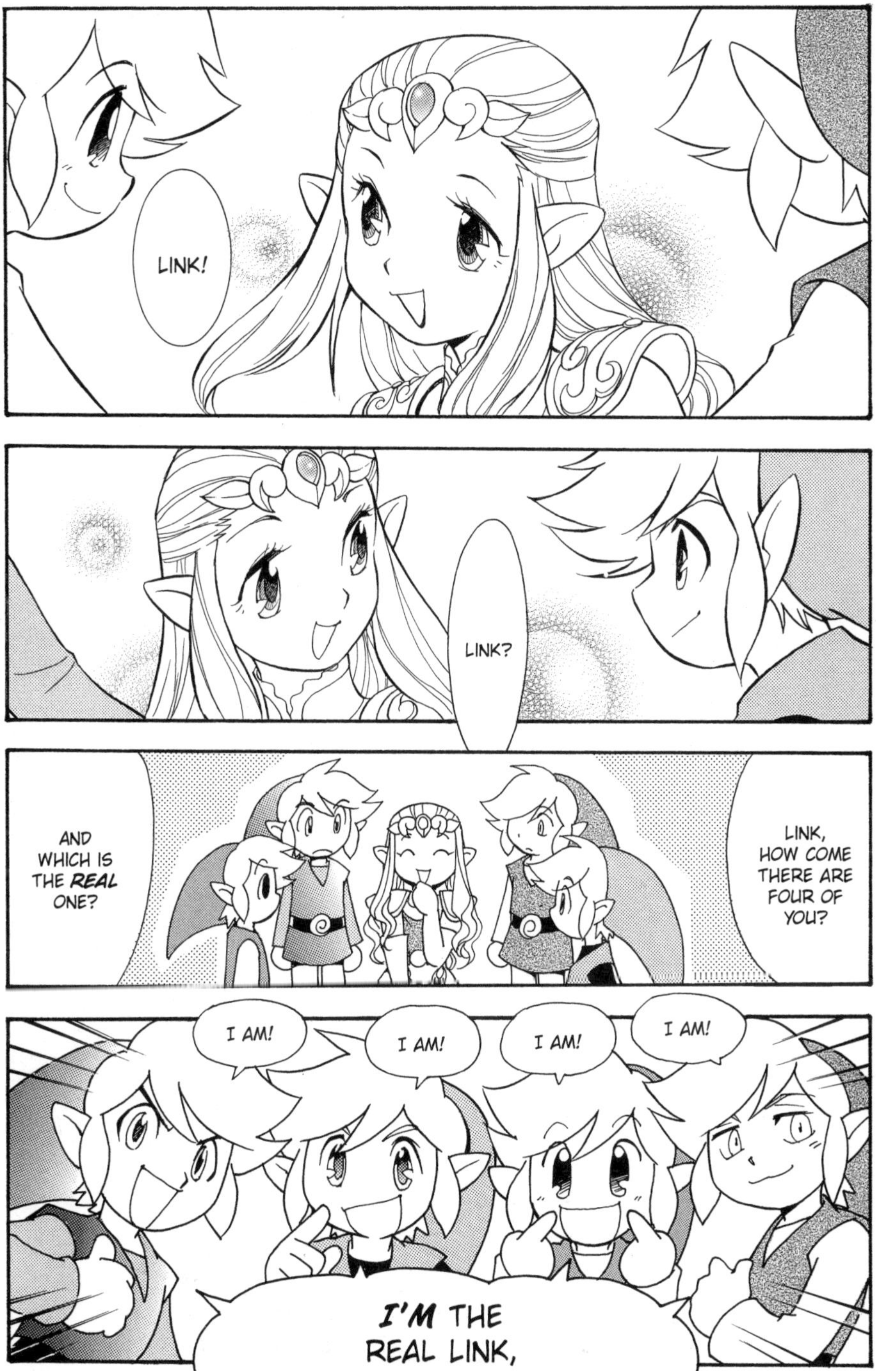
LINK!
LINK?
LINK, HOW COME THERE ARE FOUR OF YOU?
AND WHICH IS THE *REAL* ONE?
I AM!
I AM!
I AM!
I AM!
I'M THE REAL LINK, PRINCESS ZELDA!

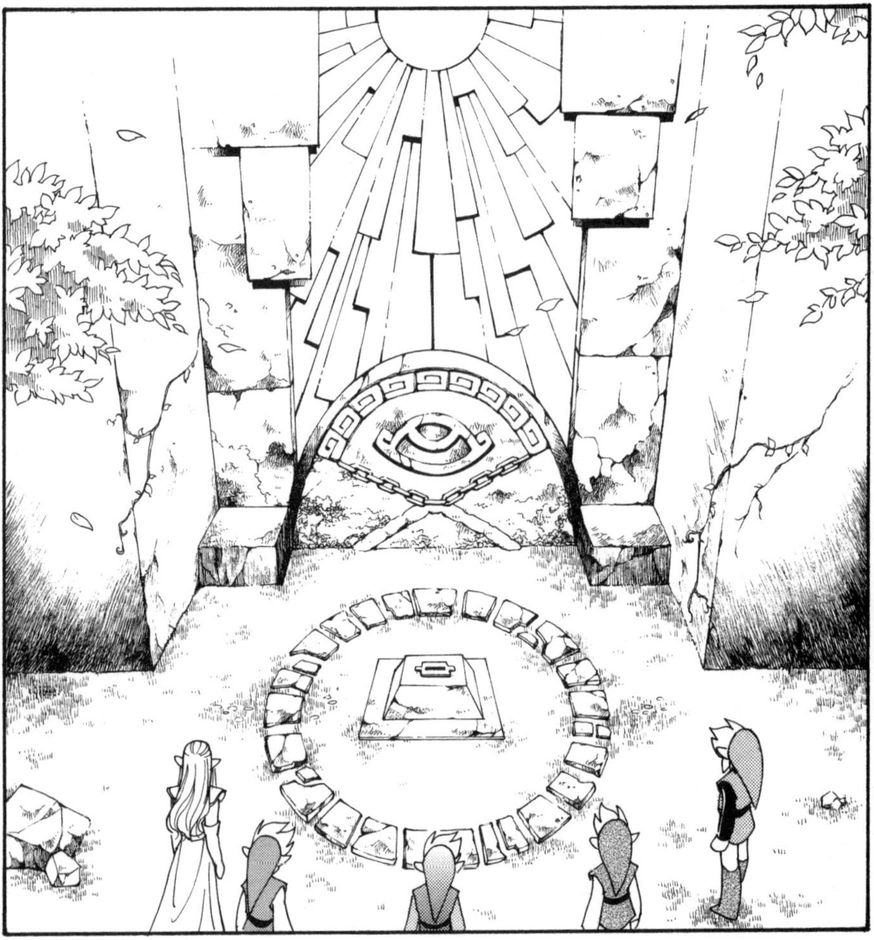

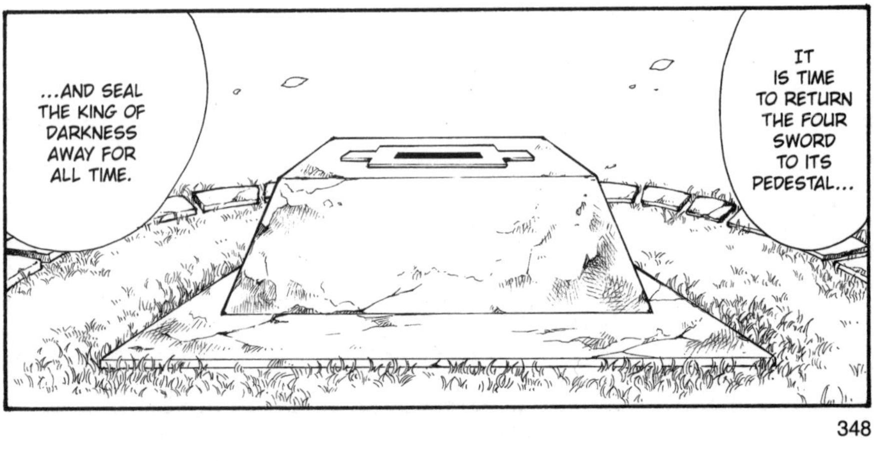
IT IS TIME TO RETURN THE FOUR SWORD TO ITS PEDESTAL...
...AND SEAL THE KING OF DARKNESS AWAY FOR ALL TIME.

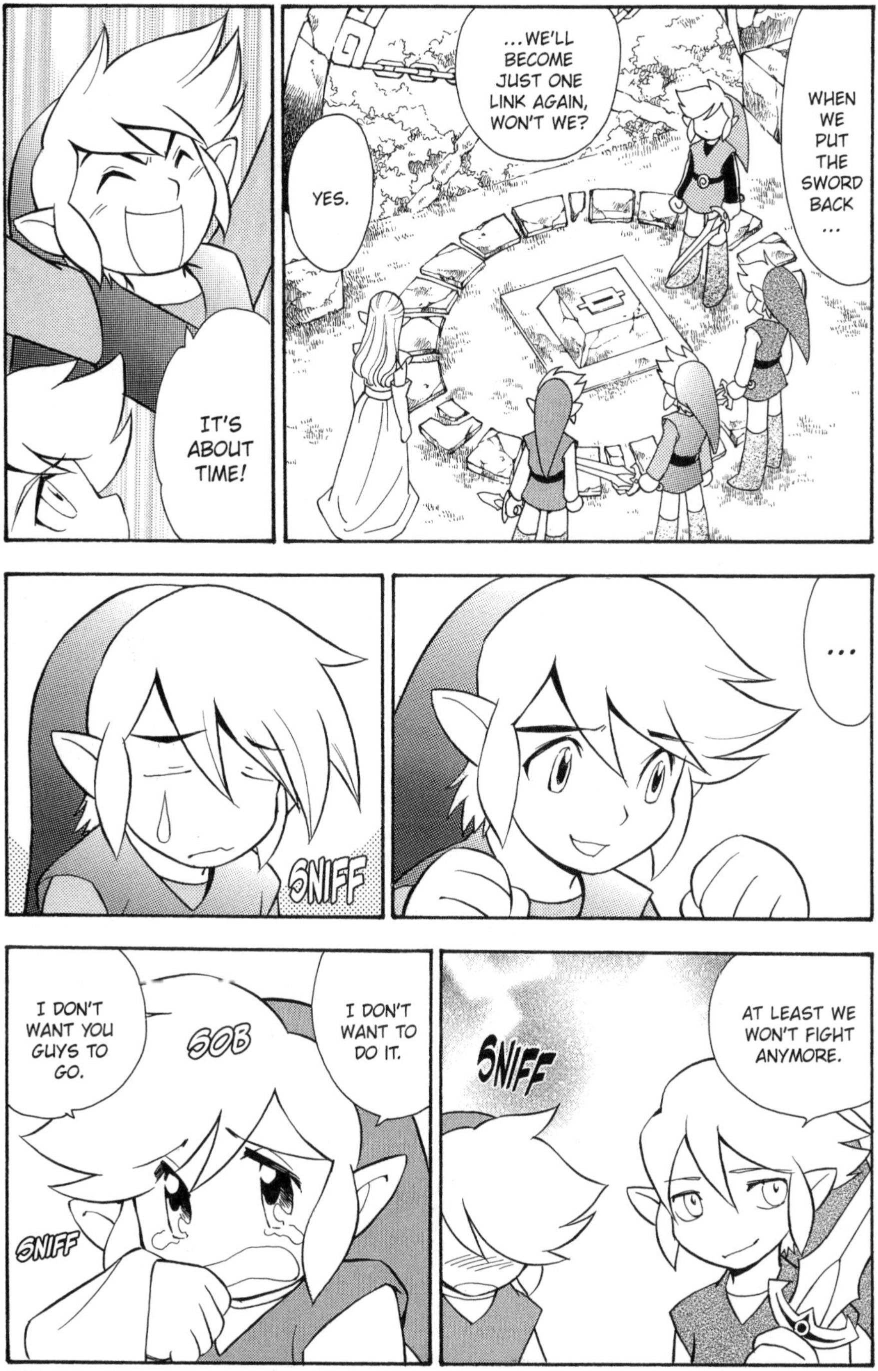
WHEN WE PUT THE SWORD BACK...
...WE'LL BECOME JUST ONE LINK AGAIN, WON'T WE?
YES.
IT'S ABOUT TIME!
...
SNIFF
AT LEAST WE WON'T FIGHT ANYMORE.
SNIFF
I DON'T WANT TO DO IT.
SOB
I DON'T WANT YOU GUYS TO GO.
SNIFF

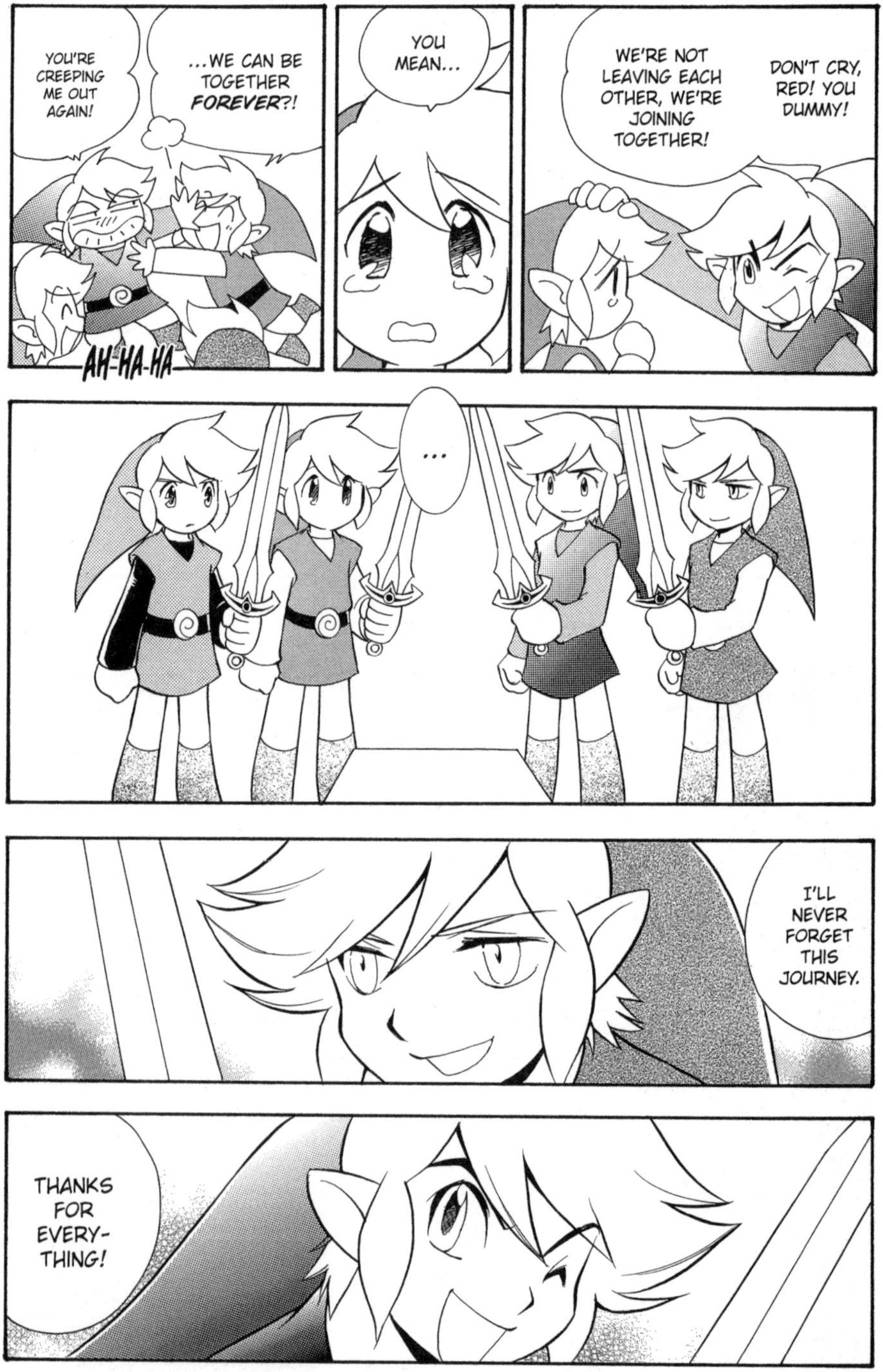
DON'T CRY, RED! YOU DUMMY!
WE'RE NOT LEAVING EACH OTHER, WE'RE JOINING TOGETHER!
YOU MEAN...
...WE CAN BE TOGETHER FOREVER?!
YOU'RE CREEPING ME OUT AGAIN!
AH-HA-HA
...
I'LL NEVER FORGET THIS JOURNEY.
THANKS FOR EVERYTHING!

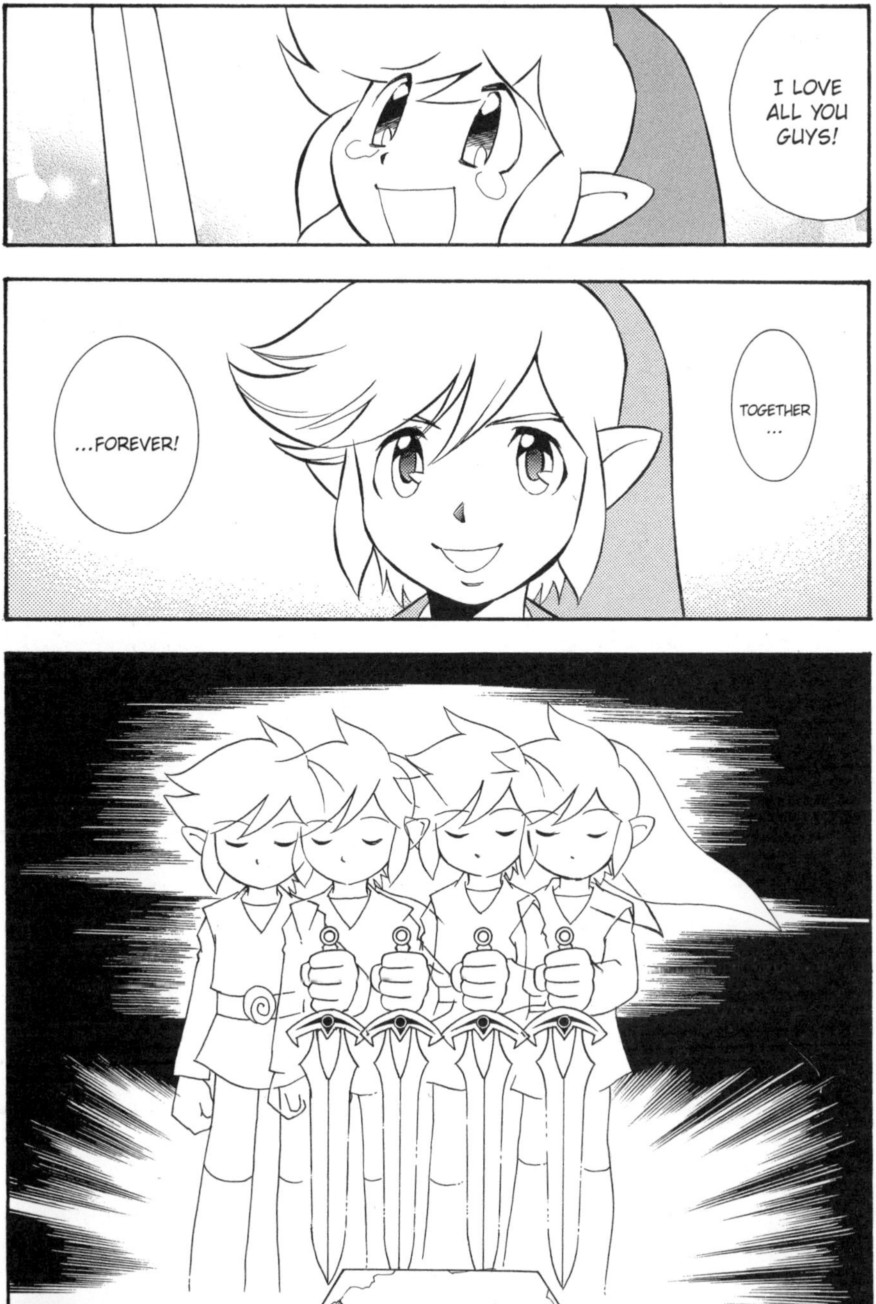
I LOVE ALL YOU GUYS!
TOGETHER...
...FOREVER!

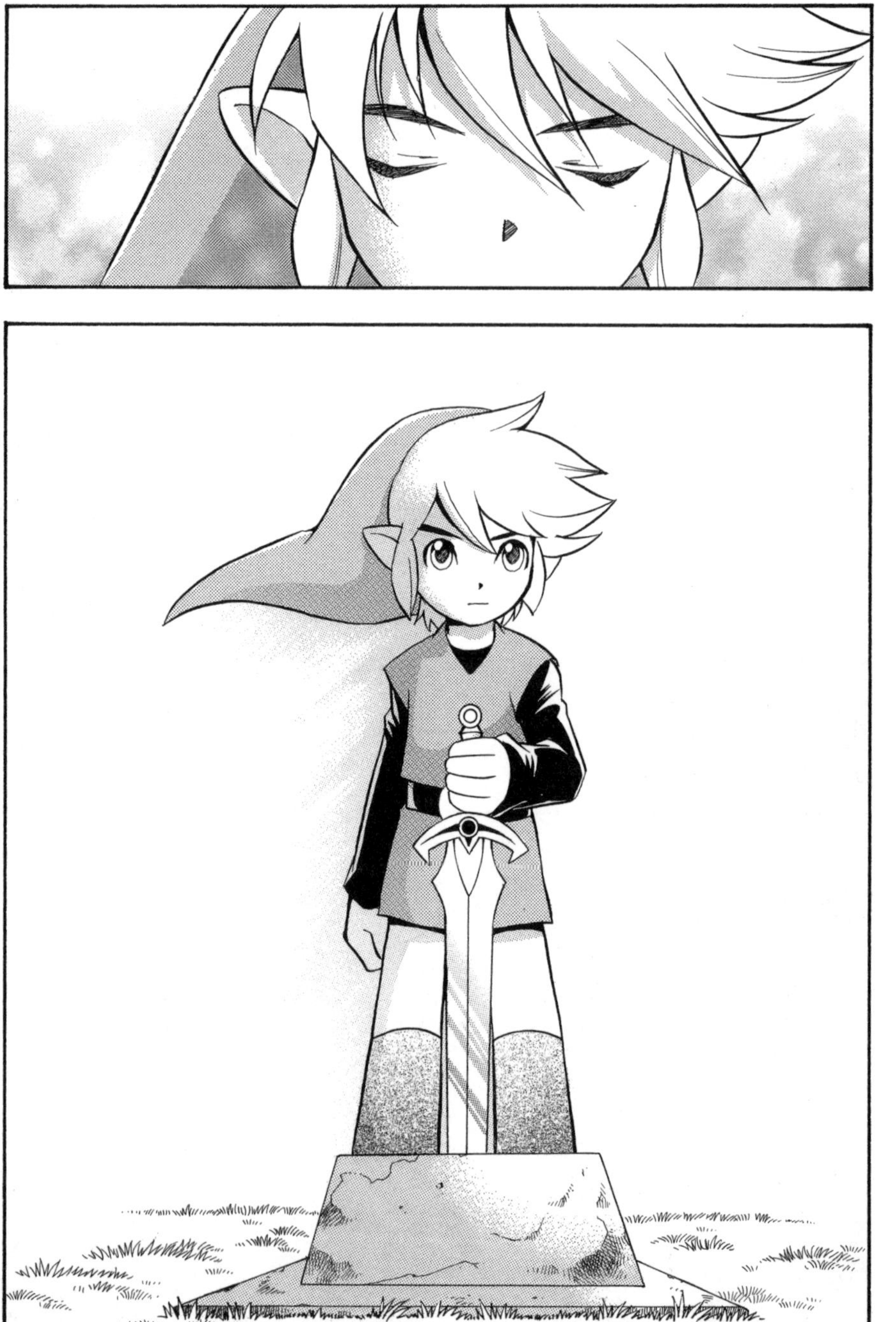

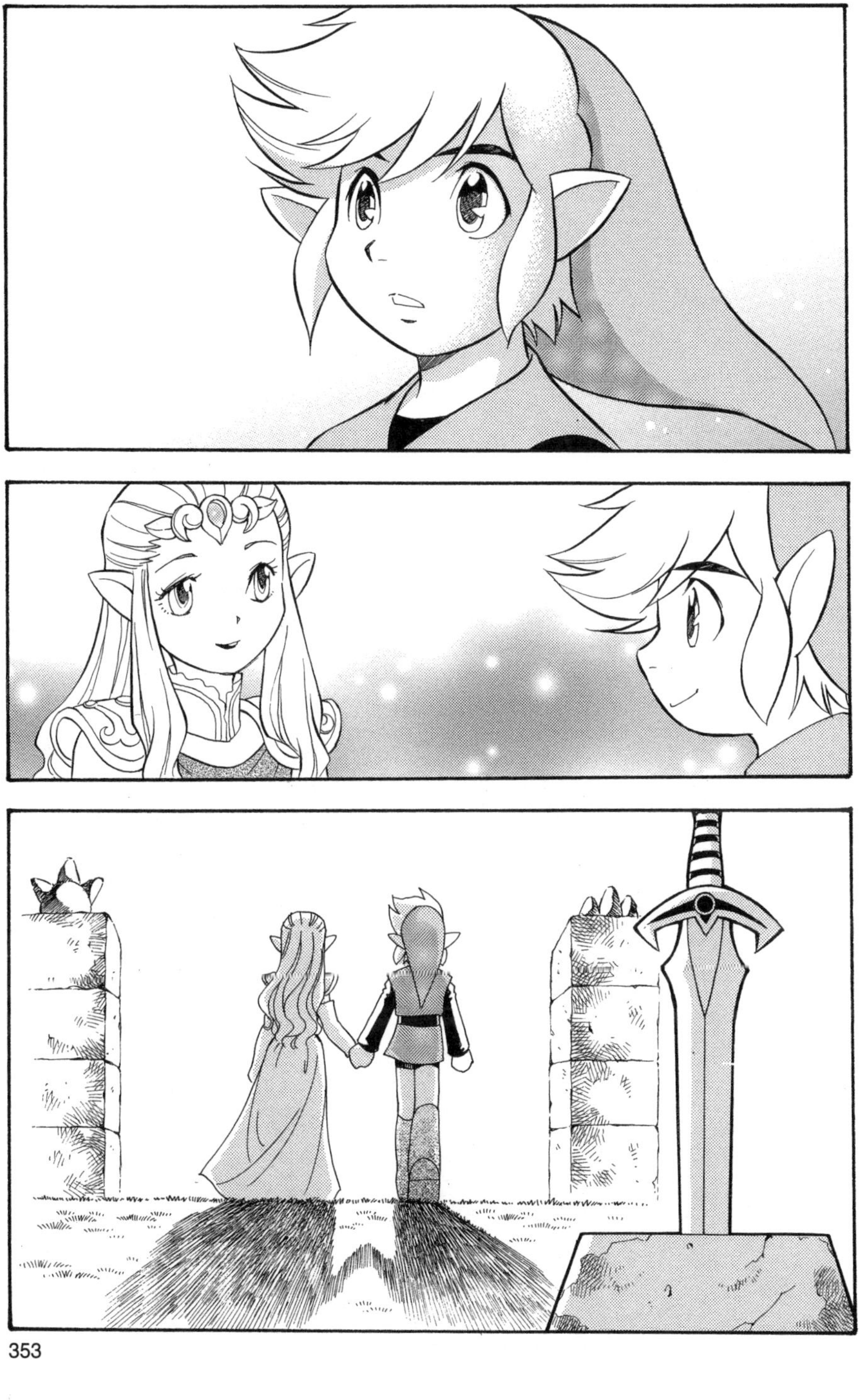

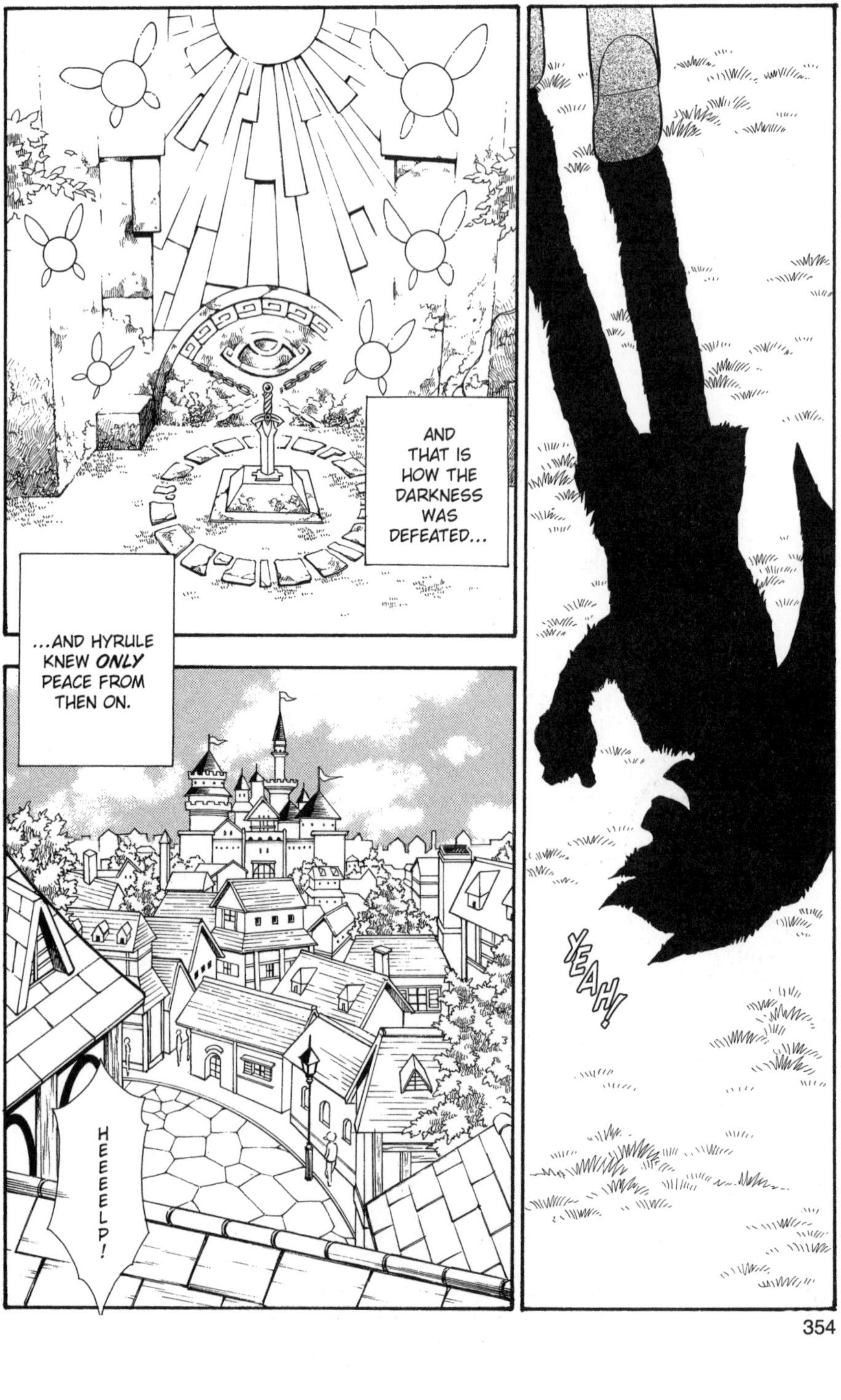
YEAH!
AND THAT IS HOW THE DARKNESS WAS DEFEATED...
...AND HYRULE KNEW *ONLY* PEACE FROM THEN ON.
HEEEELP!

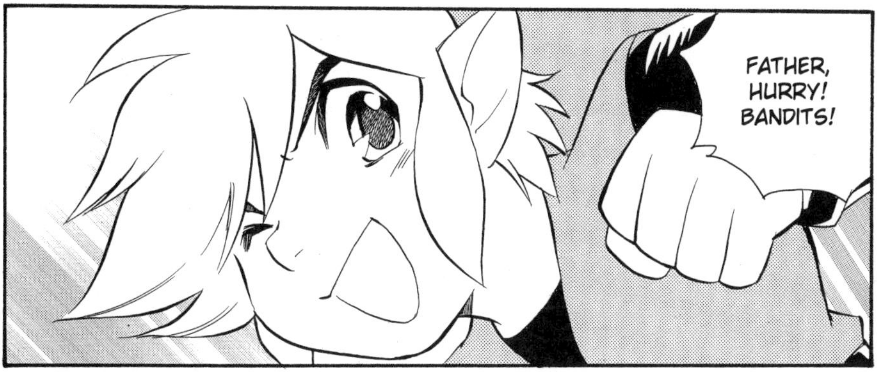
FATHER, HURRY! BANDITS!

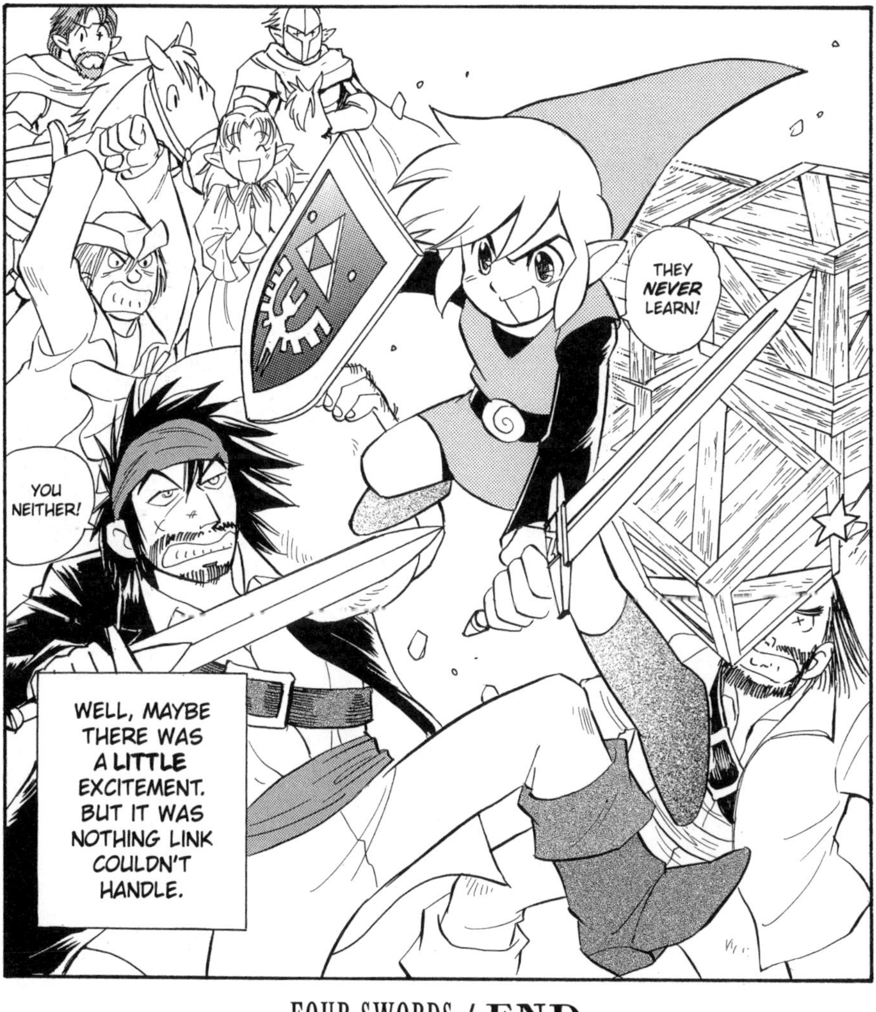
THEY *NEVER* LEARN!
YOU NEITHER!
WELL, MAYBE THERE WAS A **LITTLE** EXCITEMENT. BUT IT WAS NOTHING LINK COULDN'T HANDLE.

FOUR SWORDS / **END**

BONUS MANGA

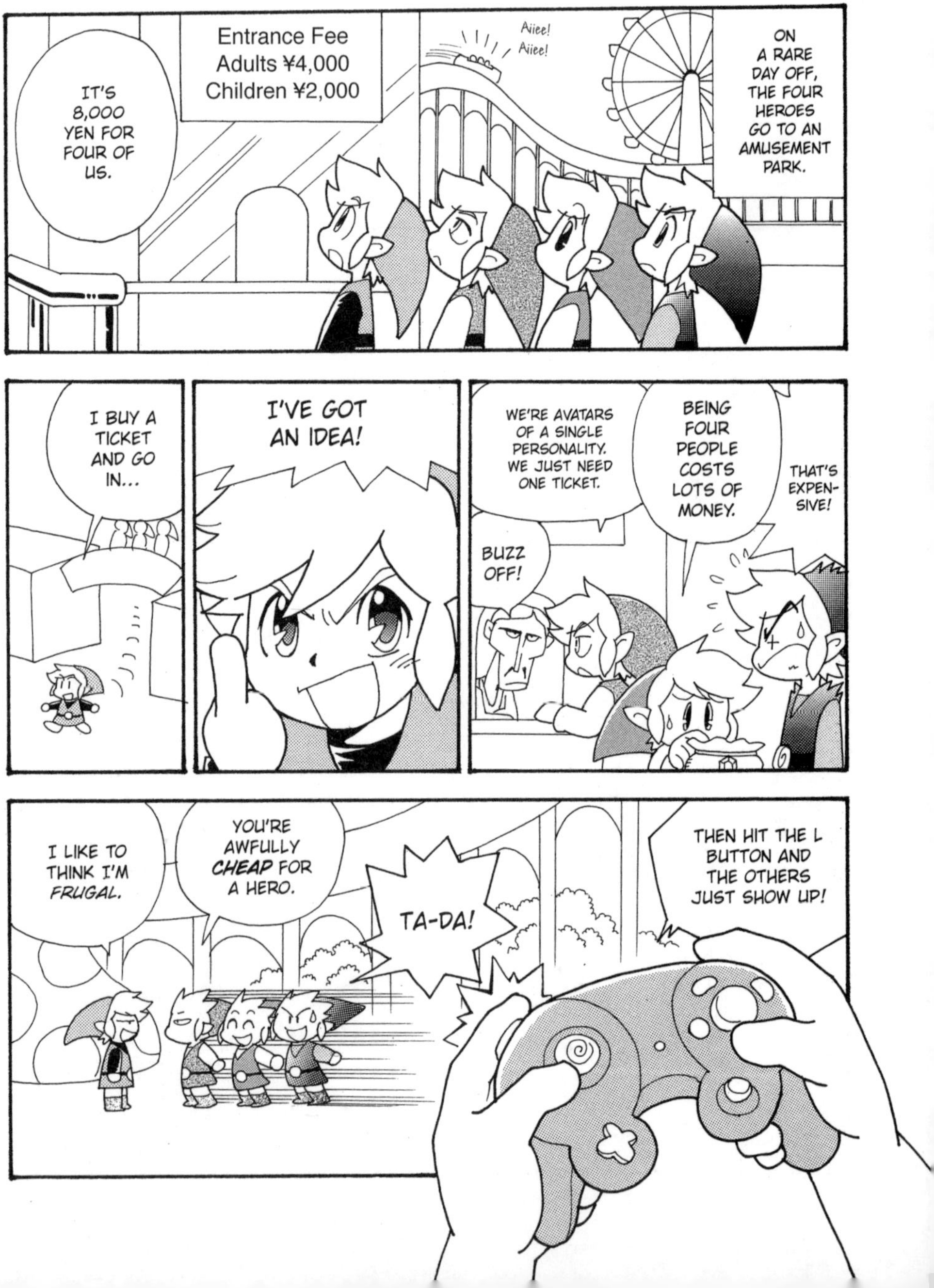

ON A RARE DAY OFF, THE FOUR HEROES GO TO AN AMUSEMENT PARK.
Aiiee! Aiiee!
Entrance Fee
Adults ¥4,000
Children ¥2,000
IT'S 8,000 YEN FOR FOUR OF US.
THAT'S EXPENSIVE!
BEING FOUR PEOPLE COSTS LOTS OF MONEY.
WE'RE AVATARS OF A SINGLE PERSONALITY. WE JUST NEED ONE TICKET.
BUZZ OFF!
I'VE GOT AN IDEA!
I BUY A TICKET AND GO IN...
THEN HIT THE L BUTTON AND THE OTHERS JUST SHOW UP!
TA-DA!
YOU'RE AWFULLY *CHEAP* FOR A HERO.
I LIKE TO THINK I'M *FRUGAL*.

It's a Small Compulsion

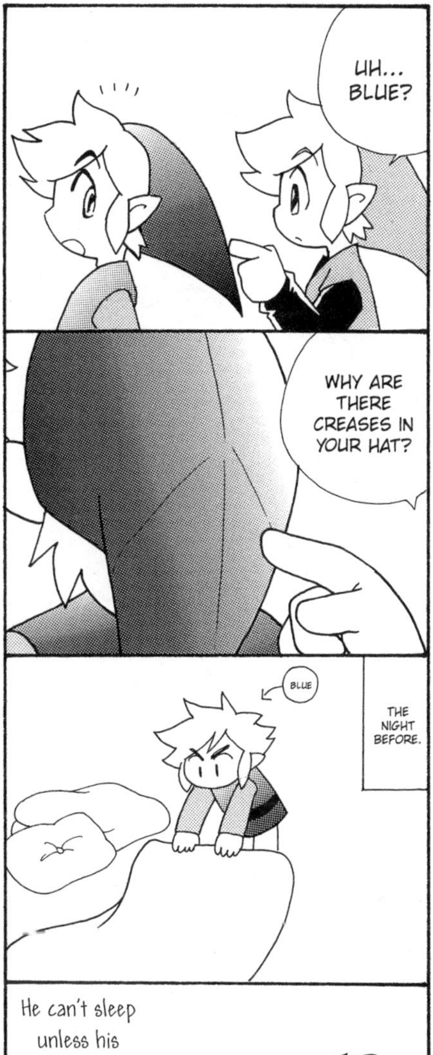
UH... BLUE?
WHY ARE THERE CREASES IN YOUR HAT?
THE NIGHT BEFORE.
BLUE
TIDY
He can't sleep unless his clothes are neatly folded.

Takoyaki*

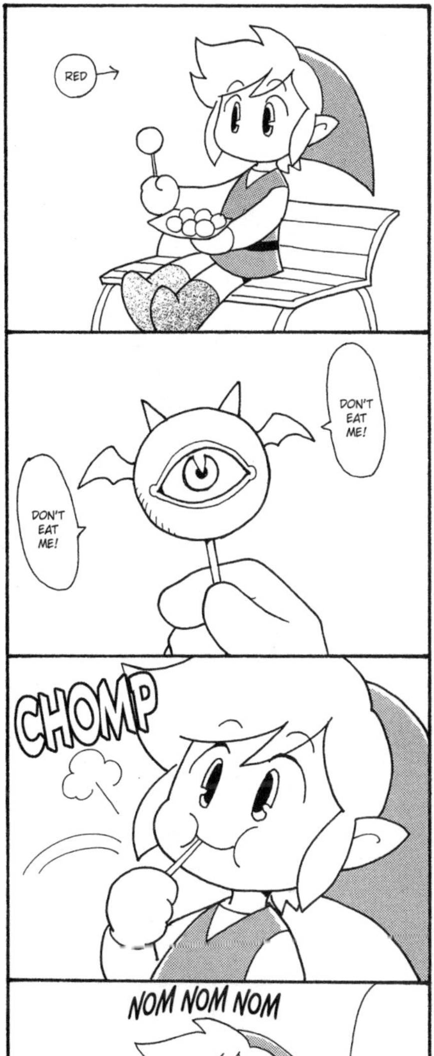
RED
DON'T EAT ME!
DON'T EAT ME!
CHOMP
MMM-MM!
NOM NOM NOM
HELP MEEE!

*TAKOYAKI ARE PIECES OF OCTOPUS, BATTERED AND FRIED.

It's Not Easy Being Purple

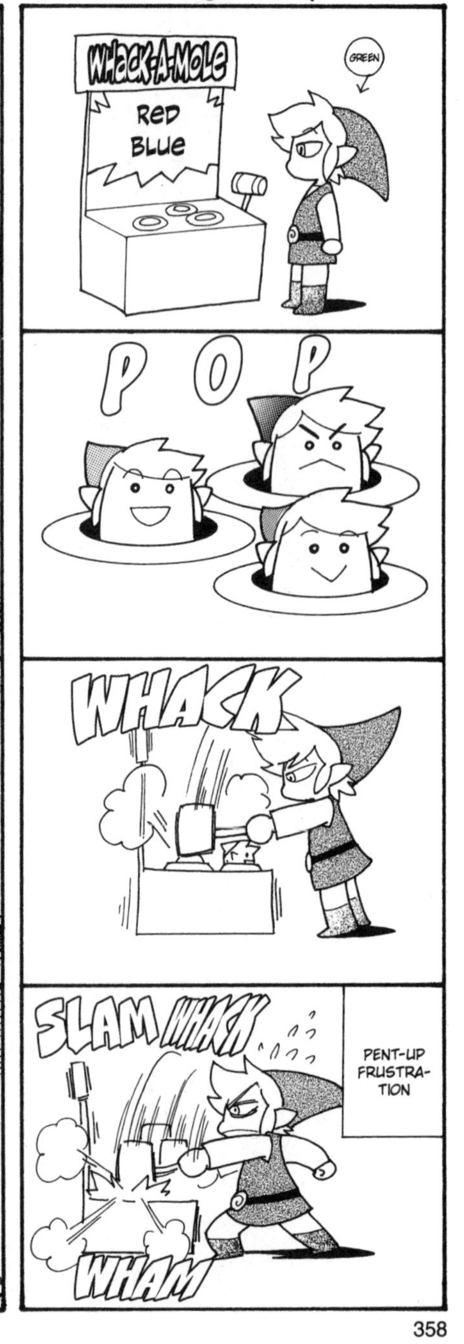
GREEN
WHACK-A-MOLE
RED
BLUE
POP
WHACK
PENT-UP FRUSTRA-TION
SLAM
WHACK
WHAM

About That Time

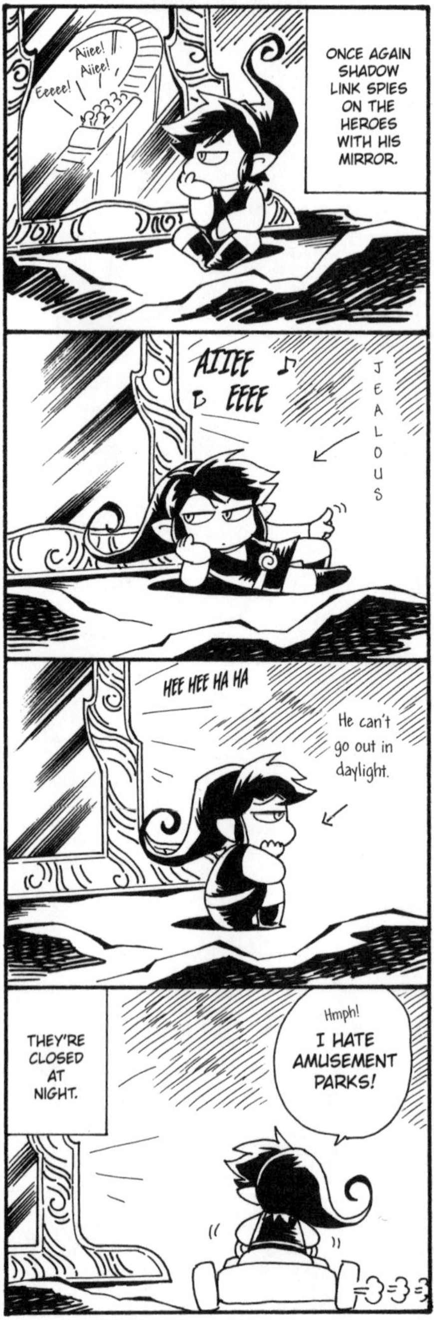
ONCE AGAIN SHADOW LINK SPIES ON THE HEROES WITH HIS MIRROR.
Aiiee! Aiiee!
Eeeee!
JEALOUS
AIIEE EEEE
He can't go out in daylight.
HEE HEE HA HA
Hmph! I HATE AMUSEMENT PARKS!
THEY'RE CLOSED AT NIGHT.

Shadow Link's Blog

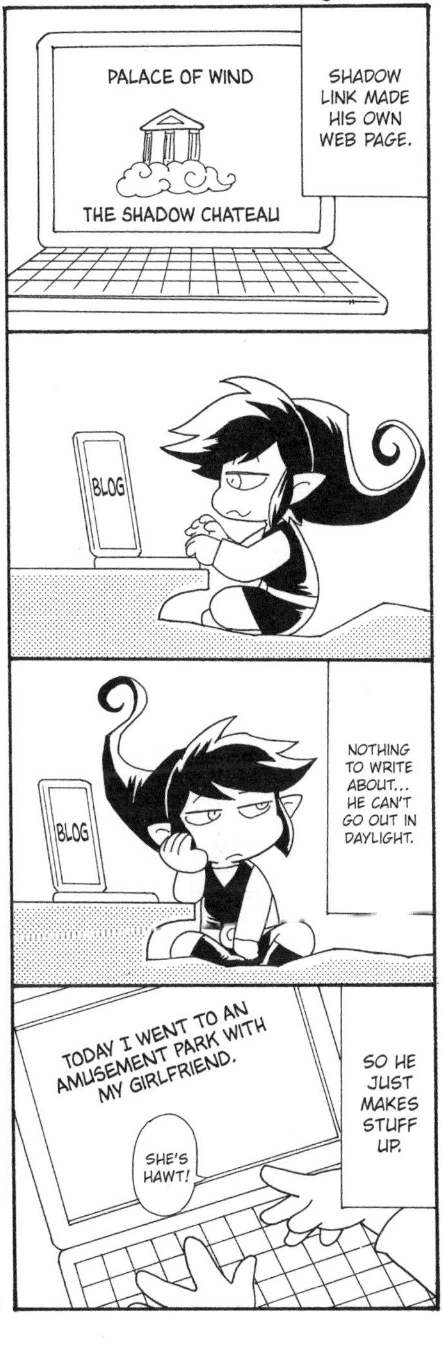
SHADOW LINK MADE HIS OWN WEB PAGE.
PALACE OF WIND
THE SHADOW CHATEAU
BLOG
NOTHING TO WRITE ABOUT... HE CAN'T GO OUT IN DAYLIGHT.
BLOG
SO HE JUST MAKES STUFF UP.
TODAY I WENT TO AN AMUSEMENT PARK WITH MY GIRLFRIEND.
SHE'S HAWT!

Shopping Online

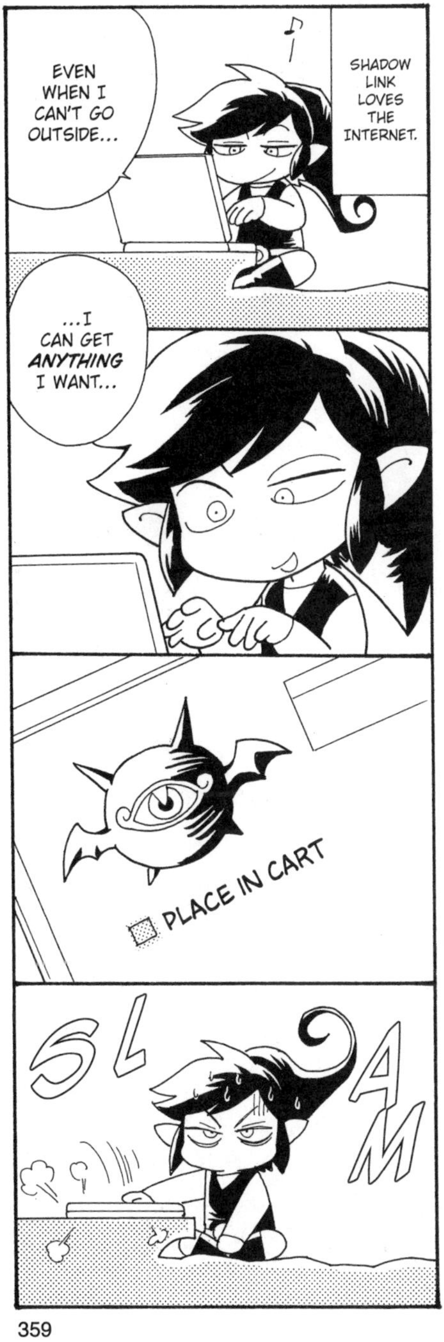
SHADOW LINK LOVES THE INTERNET.
EVEN WHEN I CAN'T GO OUTSIDE...
...I CAN GET *ANYTHING* I WANT...
PLACE IN CART
SLAM

Actually, He Was There

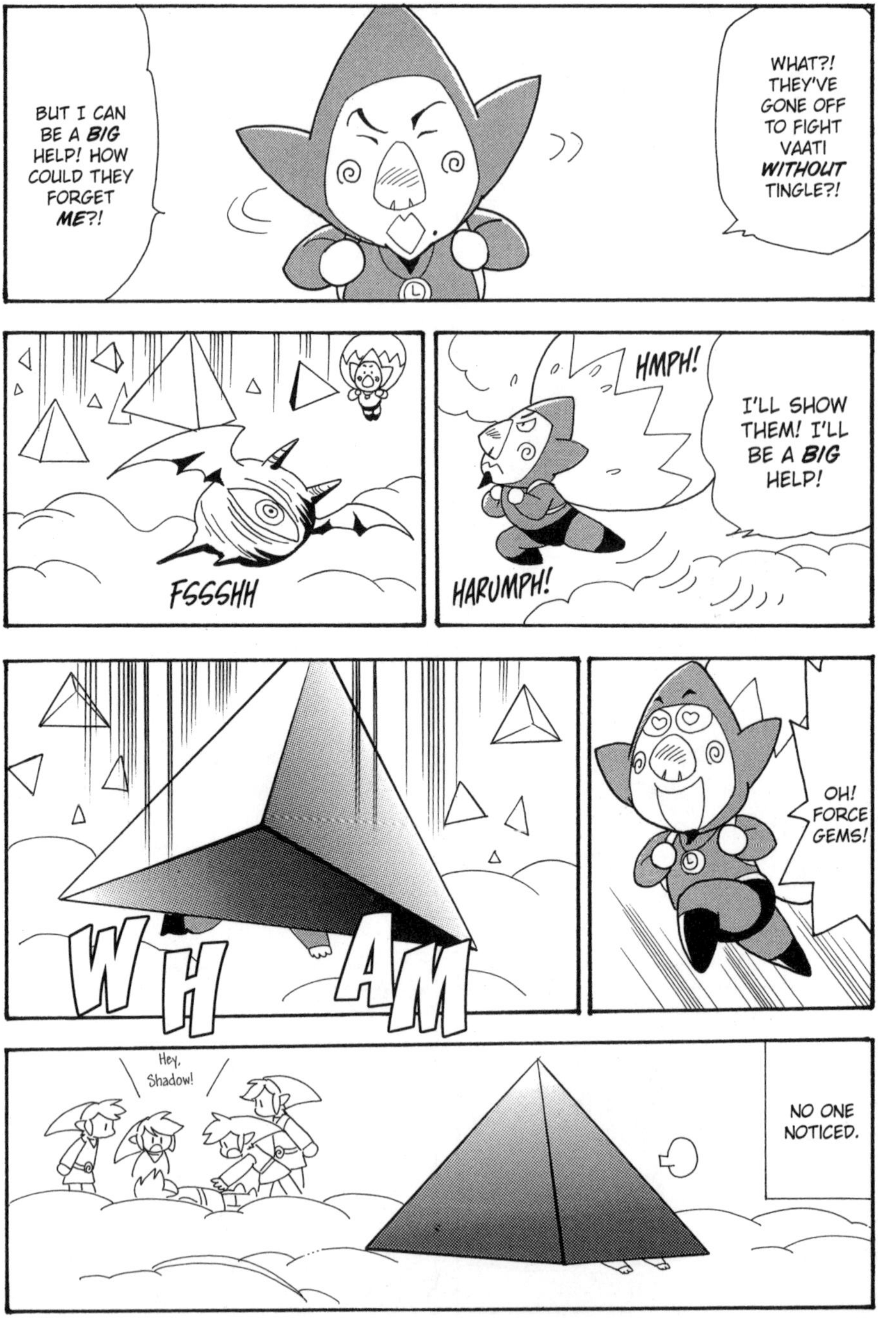
WHAT?! THEY'VE GONE OFF TO FIGHT VAATI **WITHOUT** TINGLE?!
BUT I CAN BE A **BIG** HELP! HOW COULD THEY FORGET **ME**?!
HMPH!
I'LL SHOW THEM! I'LL BE A **BIG** HELP!
HARUMPH!
FSSSHH
OH! FORCE GEMS!
WHAM
NO ONE NOTICED.
Hey, Shadow!

Sukiyaki Day

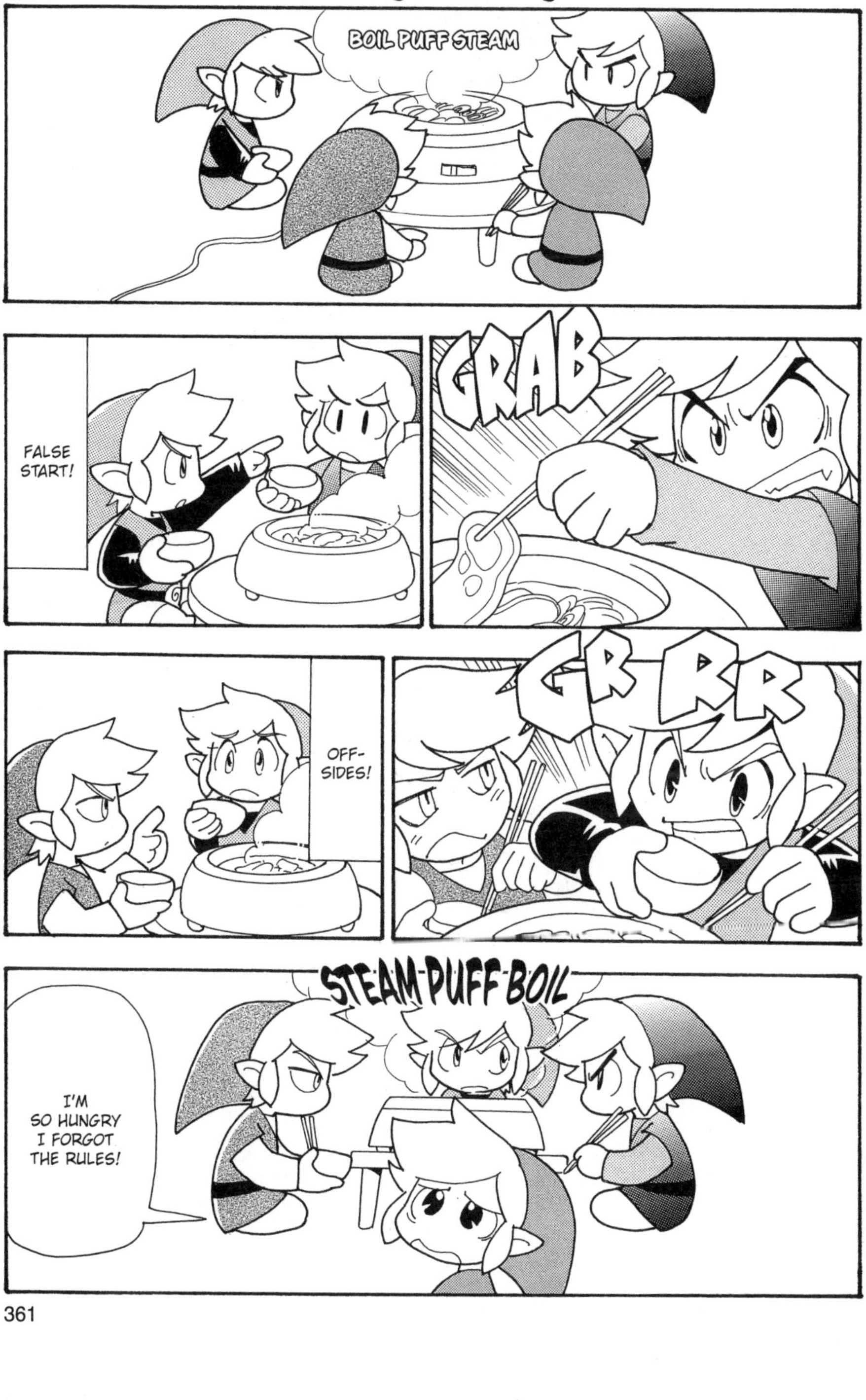
BOIL PUFF STEAM
GRAB
FALSE START!
GRRR
OFF-SIDES!
STEAM PUFF BOIL
I'M SO HUNGRY I FORGOT THE RULES!

Fear Like Never Before

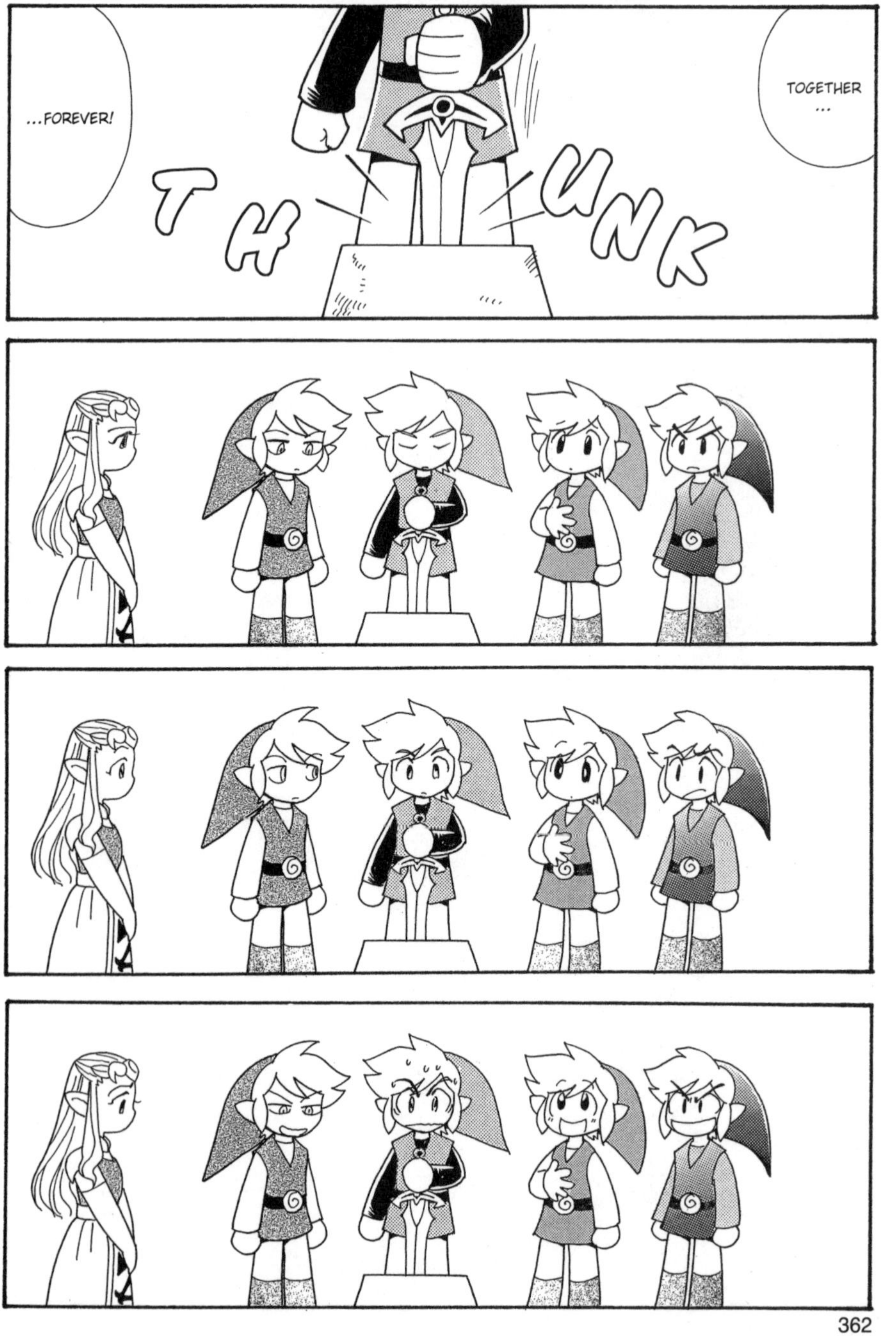
TOGETHER ...
...FOREVER!
THUNK

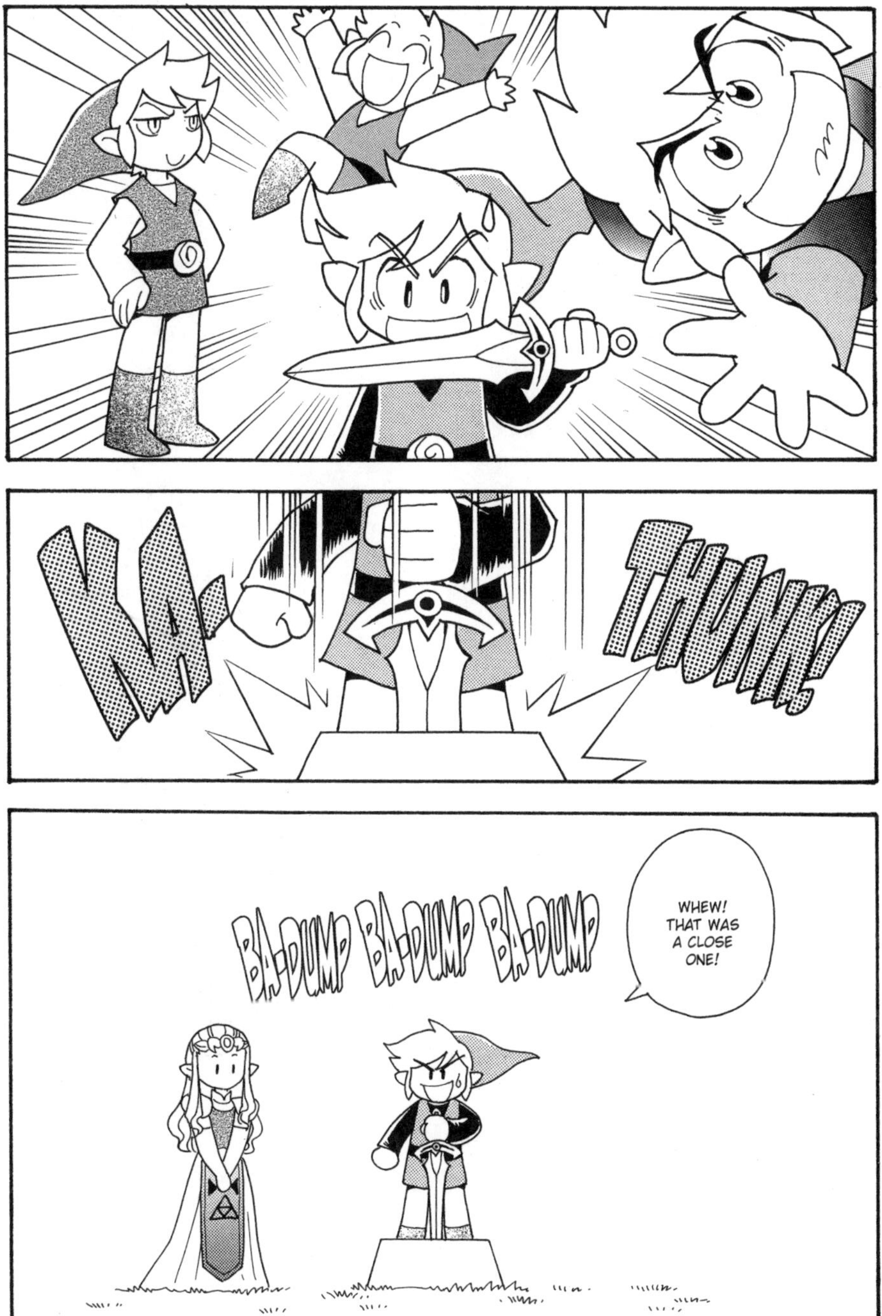
WA-THUNK!
WHEW! THAT WAS A CLOSE ONE!
BA-DUMP BA-DUMP BA-DUMP

THE END

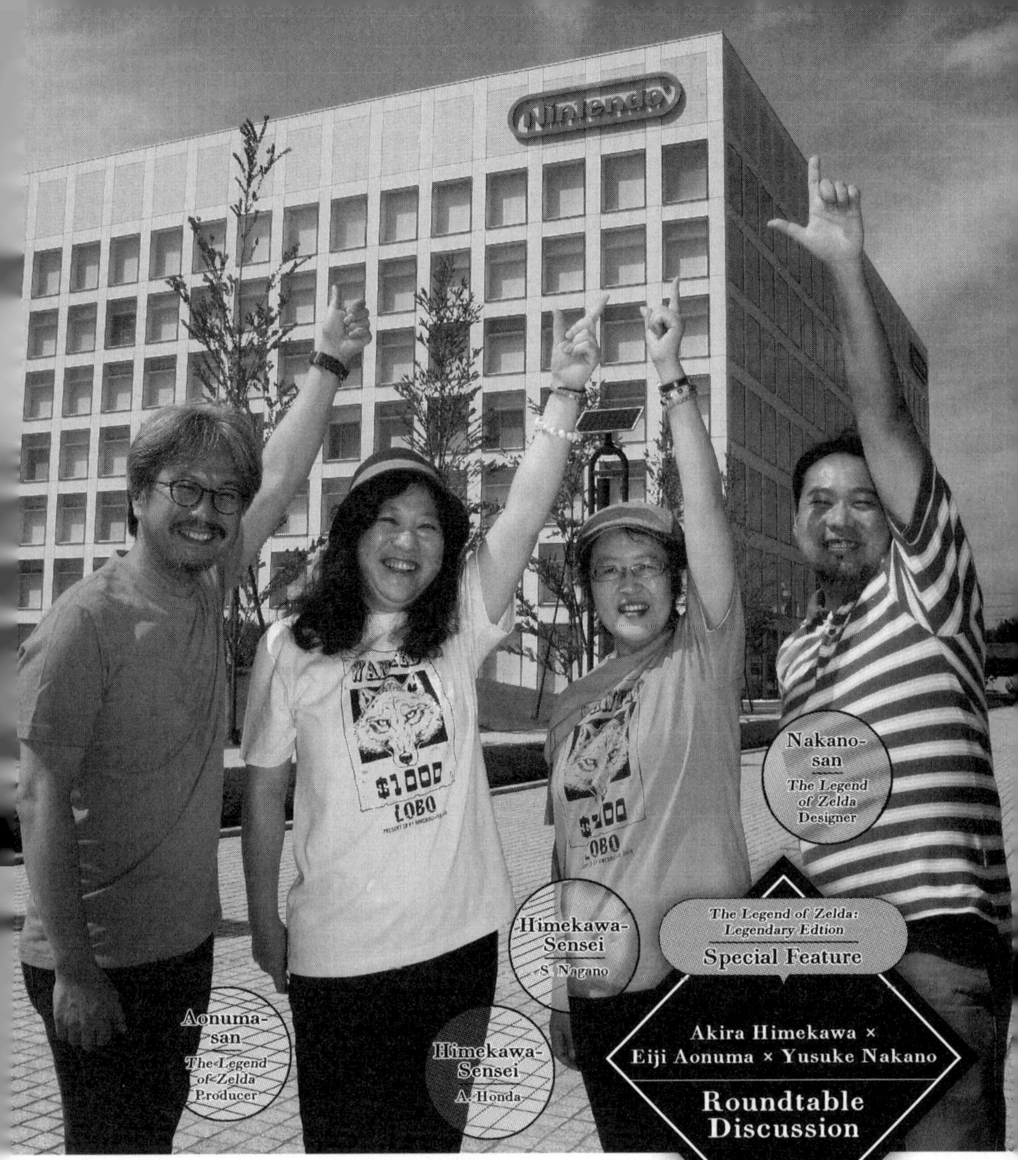
Nintendo
$1000
LOBO
Nakano-san
The Legend of Zelda Designer
Himekawa-Sensei
S. Nagano
Aonuma-san
The Legend of Zelda Producer
Himekawa-Sensei
A. Honda
The Legend of Zelda: Legendary Edtion
Special Feature
Akira Himekawa × Eiji Aonuma × Yusuke Nakano
Roundtable Discussion

Eighteen years creating video games and manga together!!

To commemorate completion of this *Legendary Edition*, video game developers from Nintendo Co., Ltd. and Akira Himekawa discuss the past, present and future of *The Legend of Zelda*!

**This discussion took place on September 30, 2016 at Nintendo Co., Ltd. headquarters. Composition: Kazuya Sakai (Ambit) Photography: Tamaki Okuda*

Roundtable Discussion

Editorial supervision of *The Legend of Zelda: Ocarina of Time* was strict.

Aonuma: Himekawa-Sensei and Nakano, you don't get many opportunities to talk like this.

Honda: Yes. This is only the second time.

Aonuma: Nakano, how did you feel when you heard your visuals were going to be turned into a manga for the time with *The Legend of Zelda: Ocarina of Time*?

Nakano: I was uneasy. I received drafts for review, but I wasn't sure how to comment on them.

Nagano: Do you mean how meticulously you should check it?

Nakano: Yes. The manga was going to fill in content that wasn't in the game, so at first I just checked whether the game was coming to life in the manga. I tried not to force it close to my own artistic style by criticizing it for not resembling my advertising visuals or by focusing too much on the visual style of the game.

Aonuma: And that's still true, right?

Nakano: We've worked together so many times that I think I'm getting better at that. Instead of pushing what I have in my head, I recognize that the authors have their own style with its own characteristics.

Nagano: Yes, you really leave it in our hands now. But you were strict when checking *The Legend of Zelda: Ocarina of Time*. The editor was sending the feedback in mild terms, but it contained some detailed comments.

Honda: We thought, "Nintendo Co., Ltd. is scary!" *(laughs)* The two of us would interpret that feedback, chew it over, and sometimes worry over what it meant.

Nakano: The supervisors on our end were involved in the creation of a manga for the first time, so they didn't have an exact sense for it either. And a lot of people were supervising *The Legend of Zelda: Ocarina of Time*, which led to an even greater degree of comments.

Aonuma: Do you remember what kind of feedback you received?

Nagano: Nintendo Co., Ltd. rejected things that didn't make sense. For example, I had heard in a meeting that when Link takes off his hat, his hair is tied in back. It wasn't in the game, but that was no reason it couldn't be in the manga, so the two of us were excited about it. In Volvagia, we had Link take off his cap and submitted it for review, but Nintendo Co., Ltd. demanded to know the exact reason he had taken off his hat.

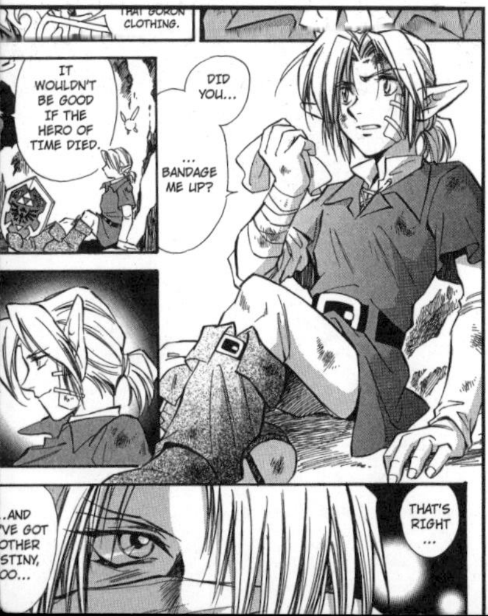
CLOTHING.
DID YOU...
...BANDAGE ME UP?
IT WOULDN'T BE GOOD IF THE HERO OF TIME DIED.
THAT'S RIGHT...

◀ Link with a ponytail in *The Legend of Zelda: Ocarina of Time.*

Honda: We were like, "Huh?! Is a reason necessary?!" *(laughs)*
Nagano: In the end, we said he had hurt his head and got the okay for him to take off his cap, but a lot of feedback was like that and could have led to Nintendo Co., Ltd. refusing permission.
Aonuma: Oh, I see. That's because he never takes off his cap in the game. For us, when something isn't in the game, we wonder if it's all right to do that.
Nakano: Yeah. Back then, we used the game as a standard when reviewing the manga.
Nagano: It was our first time turning a video game into manga. We weren't used to the viewpoint of video game developers, so we were uneasy. When I think about it now, that feedback made sense! *(laughs)*
Honda: That was when we learned that manga and video games are different creations. Manga is about feeling. It's a right-brain sensibility, directly presenting what you see. On the other hand, video games are logical and left-brained, with the art added on. I learned that developers make video games in a rational way and remove anything unnatural.

Aonuma-san admires Himekawa-Sensei's imagination.

Honda: But later, with *The Legend of Zelda: Majora's Mask*, Nintendo Co., Ltd.'s feedback suddenly loosened up. We thought perhaps we had earned approval through having completed *The Legend of Zelda: Ocarina of Time*.
Aonuma: That's right. Another big reason is that—like Nakano mentioned earlier—we had achieved a sense of what to focus on.
Nakano: Yes. We realized we could just leave it to you.
Aonuma: When I read the manga version of *The Legend of Zelda: Ocarina of Time*, what I liked most was Volvagia's side story. It took what was in the game and expanded on it in a way that didn't feel out of place. So when it came time do *The Legend of Zelda: Majora's Mask*, I said it would be fine to include more elements of that nature.
Nagano: That's right. We started with a completely original story about the creation of the mask! *(laughs)*
Aonuma: That was philosophical—and I thought it was great! Even today, I can clearly remember that man (when he made his entrance) and the mysterious creature whose armor became the mask. It's always in a corner of my mind.

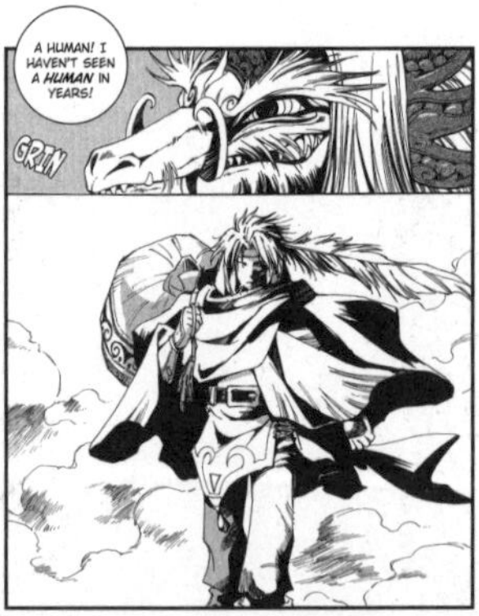
A HUMAN! I HAVEN'T SEEN A *HUMAN* IN YEARS!
GRIN

▲ A side story that accompanied chapter 1 of *The Legend of Zelda: Majora's Mask.*

Roundtable Discussion

Nagano: I'm incredibly happy to hear you say that. The game was still in development at the time, so the only materials you showed us were the cut scenes. The manga was under a deadline, but the game wasn't finished, so we couldn't keep working.

Honda: We had heard that it was a scary game in which the moon falls and destroys everything in just three days, so we expanded upon that and used the blank pages for bonus manga.

Nakano: How could you build a story around such fragmentary information?

Honda: It's like improvisation on the piano in which you hear one phrase and then play a whole song. I love Bali, where there is the Kecak dance and the Barong dance, which portrays the fight between the holy beast Barong and the witch Rangda. I thought such a thrilling folk style matched *The Legend of Zelda: Majora's Mask*. That side story sprang from the realization that we could create *The Legend of Zelda: Majora's Mask* as a union of such Asiatic elements and the mystery and darkness of what we had heard about the plot.

Aonuma: The way you create your original content is amazing. Even when you don't know about the game, you stitch together a world that feels natural. I always think, "This is great!"

Nagano: I remember a reaction like that from you when we did *The Legend of Zelda: A Link to the Past*. You were surprised when you saw the part in the manga where Link turns into a beast and you told me that Link would turn into a wolf in the next *The Legend of Zelda* game.

Aonuma: At the time, we were making *The Legend of Zelda: Twilight Princess* but hadn't announced it yet, so I was amazed at how you seemed to know he would become a wolf! It was like you could see my thoughts, so I was like, "What's with those two?!" *(laughs)*

Yusuke Nakano (Nintendo Co., Ltd.)
From Hokkaido. As a designer involved with artwork and graphic design for various Nintendo Co., Ltd. video games, he has supervised the manga since *The Legend of Zelda: Ocarina of Time*.

Himekawa-Sensei (A. Honda)
From Aichi Prefecture. After being an office worker and animal groomer, among other jobs, she submitted her work to a publisher and debuted as a manga author.

Himekawa-Sensei (S. Nagano)
From Tokyo Prefecture. After debuting as a manga author in *Shonen Big Comic*, she began collaborating with Honda-Sensei as Akira Himekawa.

Eiji Aonuma (Nintendo Co., Ltd.)
Currently, he is a central creator in the development of *The Legend of Zelda* series. He met Himekawa-Sensei when making *The Legend of Zelda: Majora's Mask* and has provided editorial supervision ever since.

Nagano: Link turns into a rabbit in *The Legend of Zelda: A Link to the Past*, and we just expanded on that. We do often overlap what Aonuma-san is thinking.
Aonuma: I wonder if we tend to think alike because we're from the same generation. Of course, we do build upon past motifs when making sequels. This time, because Link had turned into a rabbit, we had him turn into a wolf, but the idea is the same.
Honda: I think your job requires strong manga sensibilities. We have to look at one phrase and imagine where the game will go. If that's off, the result is no good, but I think we've managed to hit close to the mark.
Aonuma: Even including the new material, you aren't far from the game.

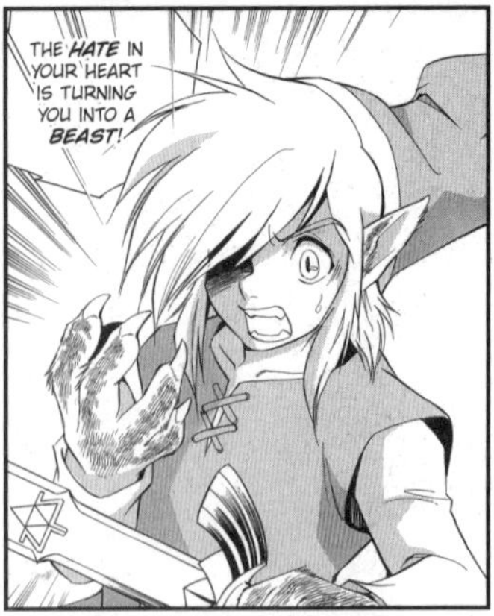
THE HATE IN YOUR HEART IS TURNING YOU INTO A BEAST!
▲ Aonuma-san was surprised to see Link transform into a beast in *The Legend of Zelda: A Link to the Past.*

Honda: That's because we stray from the game on purpose, aside from the main story. If we followed the game exactly, readers would check it and point out what was different. So we guess ahead to the game's destination and chart a path there.
Aonuma: Oh, that's how you figure it out? Then your intuition is incredible. You have a great deal of experience, so you can guess what I'm thinking!
Nagano: No, that's not true! *(laughs)*

The version of Link in *The Legend of Zelda: Hyrule Historia* was for *The Legend of Zelda: Twilight Princess*?!

Honda: We also made the manga version of *The Legend of Zelda: Skyward Sword*—which we did for inclusion in *The Legend of Zelda: Hyrule Historia*—without knowing anything about the game.
Nagano: That publication went on sale about the same time as the game, so we didn't know anything. We really didn't know what to do.
Aonuma: Is that the time we just told you what the game would basically be like?
Nagano: Yes. We fleshed that out and made the manga without ever playing the game.
Honda: It's an epic book that reveals Hyrule's history, and it was going to be hardcover, so we thought the story had to be weighty and decided to portray a time before the events in *The Legend of Zelda: Skyward Sword.*
Nagano: Actually, the version of Link in *The Legend of Zelda: Hyrule Historia* is one that we had prepared for *The Legend of Zelda: Twilight Princess.* We had gone ahead and prepared that because when the game was released in 2006, we had heard that our next series would be *The Legend of Zelda: Twilight Princess.* But that series never happened, so we resurrected that design in 2011 for *The Legend of Zelda: Hyrule Historia.*

Roundtable Discussion

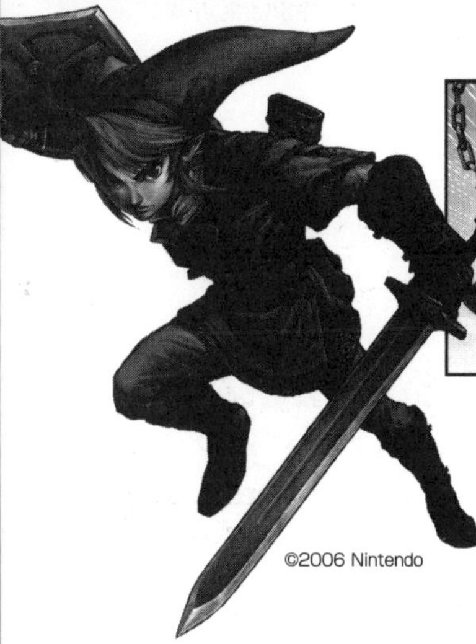

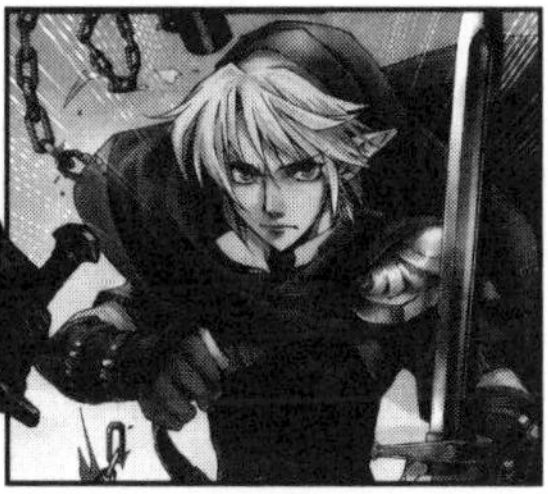

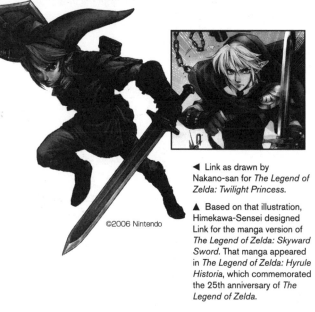

◄ Link as drawn by Nakano-san for *The Legend of Zelda: Twilight Princess.*

▲ Based on that illustration, Himekawa-Sensei designed Link for the manga version of *The Legend of Zelda: Skyward Sword*. That manga appeared in *The Legend of Zelda: Hyrule Historia*, which commemorated the 25th anniversary of *The Legend of Zelda*.

Honda: We came up with that before the release of *The Legend of Zelda: Twilight Princess*.

Nagano: Yes. We based our work on Nakano-san's early illustrations of Link and Princess Zelda in black robes.

Honda: But Nakano-san's art is quite rich, so I remember we worried over the amount of linework to include in the manga, and about whether he was a youth or an adult.

Nagano: At first, we thought he was an adult.

Aonuma: Link did look a lot older early in development of *The Legend of Zelda: Twilight Princess*. So we talked about using mature designs in the game.

Nakano: Yeah. Early on, Link was fairly manly, but when we did a presentation overseas, the response to an older Link wasn't positive *(laughs)*, so we made adjustments and settled on the final image. We wanted him to look rough, but in the end, his features were fairly simple. We didn't give up on that idea, so we made the illustrations fairly detailed to represent that visually.

Aonuma: It was difficult to make the style rough, but Link's wildness shows up in how he turns into a wolf. To me, that wolf is the early, rougher Link.

Nagano: That early impression may be why Link looks a bit sturdier in *The Legend of Zelda: Hyrule Historia*. At first, I thought Link in *The Legend of Zelda: Twilight Princess* wasn't cute, that he scowled and never smiled.

Aonuma: Yes, Link in the manga is similar to the manlier Link.

Nagano: At the time, I thought that was why Link would say lines like he never had before, like when negotiating with Princess Zelda. But Link in *The Legend of Zelda: Hyrule Historia* wouldn't work well for the current series. When we played the game, that image we had of him disappeared.

Honda: We still value that inspiration from before we played the game, but Link in the current series for *The Legend of Zelda: Twilight Princess* is a version of the character that we came up with after seeing the game. So he isn't completely an adult. We include negative aspects of him, so he feels like the more immature version.

Nakano: That comes across as I read it.

Honda: Since the serialization period is longer than in a student magazine restricted to one year, I hope that by the end of the story he will have grown into the Link of *The Legend of Zelda: Hyrule Historia*.

Turning the detailed art of *The Legend of Zelda: Twilight Princess* into manga is hard!

Aonuma: Until then, Nakano did his illustrations based on the models in the games, but for *The Legend of Zelda: Twilight Princess*, we changed to basing the game model on an illustration by Nakano.

Nakano: Which means that character design for *The Legend of Zelda: Twilight Princess* was in my hands from the start.

Nagano: The incredible degree of detail in Nakano-san's work for *The Legend of Zelda: Twilight Princess* is a reflection of his enthusiasm.

Nakano: Yes. I can't help it, because I care about it.

Honda: But thanks to that detail, drawing the manga for *The Legend of Zelda: Twilight Princess* is really hard. The patterns and so forth are so detailed that drawing it takes three times longer than a regular manga! *(laughs)*

Nagano: As artists, we feel like we have to make it like the original. For a video game, you make one model and move it around, but in manga you have to draw everything from a new angle for each panel. Sometimes we even spend a whole day on one panel.

Honda: But for *The Legend of Zelda: Four Swords*, we did 30 pages in three days.

Nakano: That's because the amount of detail in *The Legend of Zelda: Four Swords* is completely different. When I heard there would be a series, I thought it would be all right to omit whatever you could omit! *(laughs)*

Honda: But that's no good. If we leave things out, *The Legend of Zelda* fans will point out how it's different.

Nakano: I wouldn't like that either, so when I check the draft, I compare it to my design sketches and game screens for a close look at the designs, but the degree of detail is so incredible that I've come to think it might be all right if readers complain! *(laughs)* I'm trying not to be too demanding unless the differences are big.

Nagano: When your feedback for the back cover of the first graphic novel for *The Legend of Zelda: Twilight Princess* said that the pattern on Zant wasn't a spiral, I thought, "Now that's picky!"

Aonuma: So you actually do point out small differences!

Nakano: Sorry, but I really love Zant. From now on, I'll let things slide for everyone but him! *(laughs)*

Roundtable Discussion

In-Depth Scenes Only Possible in Manga

Nakano: However, I never expected you to delve into Ooku that much.

Honda: You know how monkeys mirror human society? I wanted to show that.

Nagano: Link transforms into a wolf this time, so I wanted to show a world that we hadn't done before as seen through animal eyes.

Aonuma: When he becomes a wolf in the game, I wanted to do more with how he can understand animals, so when I see your manga, I'm jealous!

Honda: Does the manga sometimes show what you had in mind?

Aonuma: It's incredible! It's much like your ability to expand upon the original content, which we discussed earlier. *The Legend of Zelda: Twilight Princess* and the other books show a lot that I wanted to do if there had been more time.

Honda: Oh! *(laughs)*

Aonuma: What pleased me the most this time was how the story starts with Midna in her true form. That was something I wanted to show earlier in the game, but it wasn't ready until the end of development, so it was too late.

Honda: Until the end of the game, you don't know her true form, but you know from the beginning in the manga, so I could plan what to show and when to show it.

Aonuma: If I had seen that design from the start, I would have said we should show it from the beginning! *(laughs)*

Honda: Then the game would have been more flowery from the start. A big reason we can do that in the manga is that so much time has passed since the release of *The Legend of Zelda: Twilight Princess.*

Aonuma: Yes, that's right. It's something you can't show without the game. *(laughs)*

Nagano: Readers know what Midna really looks like, but Link doesn't. We still haven't decided whether he'll see Midna's true form sometime before the end. I hope readers will enjoy seeing how that turns out.

Nakano: The timing for revealing Midna's true form to Link is tricky.

Thirty Years of *The Legend of Zelda* and 25 years of the manga life

Honda: As of 2016, I've been a manga author for 25 years, and I've spent most of my manga life working on *The Legend of Zelda*.

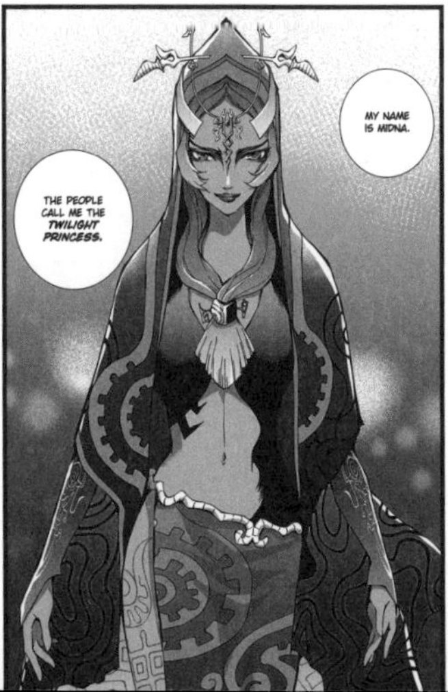
MY NAME IS MIDNA.
THE PEOPLE CALL ME THE TWILIGHT PRINCESS.

◀ Midna's true form when she appears in the first chapter. *The Legend of Zelda: Twilight Princess* is currently appearing in MangaONE.

Roundtable Discussion

Nagano: Practically all our work since *The Legend of Zelda: Ocarina of Time* in 1998 has been for *The Legend of Zelda*.

Aonuma: In 2016, *The Legend of Zelda* turns 30, so we've worked together for quite some time. I'm glad that you can also do *The Legend of Zelda: Twilight Princess*.

Nagano: There were twists and turns on the road to serialization.

Aonuma: Yes. We've worked together for a long time, so we've spent a lot of time hashing things out. We know you pour your souls into this single franchise, so we can't casually ask if you'll tackle the next series too. And you can't easily say you will.

Nagano: When it came to beginning serialization of *The Legend of Zelda: Twilight Princess*, we needed to steel ourselves because we knew that it would be hard work once we started. But ever since we finished *The Legend of Zelda: Phantom Hourglass*, we have received a lot of invitations to events in Japan and especially abroad, so we hear praise from fans and witness directly the immense popularity of *The Legend of Zelda*.

Honda: We borrowed *The Legend of Zelda* and created something that we think is cool, and people overseas welcomed that, which has increased our confidence.

Nagano: Because of that, when it came to starting a series, we actually wanted to do *The Legend of Zelda: Breath of the Wild*. Thus, we didn't intend to revive *The Legend of Zelda: Twilight Princess*. But when we thought about the voices of players in Japan and overseas, we thought they would all want to see this.

Honda: We had to finish this before we could move on.

Nagano: We became aware of the players around the world in 2010, when nothing was in serialization. We're conscious of them as we tackle *The Legend of Zelda: Twilight Princess*, so we know we can't ease up when it comes to the art.

Aonuma: As a reader, I'm looking forward to what happens next.

Honda: Ever since the start, you've told us you think it's interesting.

Aonuma: Uh-huh!

Nakano: I read with my editor's eyes, so I point out things that you could delve into in order to make it more fun. *(laughs)* I've always loved manga, and long ago I even wanted to become a manga author.

Aonuma: Huh? So did I!

Nakano: For that reason, part of me wonders along with you about how to make the next part interesting. That may be why I sometimes offer rude feedback.

Honda: No, compared to before, it's totally fine! *(laughs)*

Aonuma: I can't wait for the next installment of *The Legend of Zelda: Twilight Princess*! Let's keep working hard!

Himekawa: *(both together)* Yes, let's!

COVER GALLERY

OCARINA *of* TIME

ORACLE *of* SEASONS
ORACLE *of* AGES

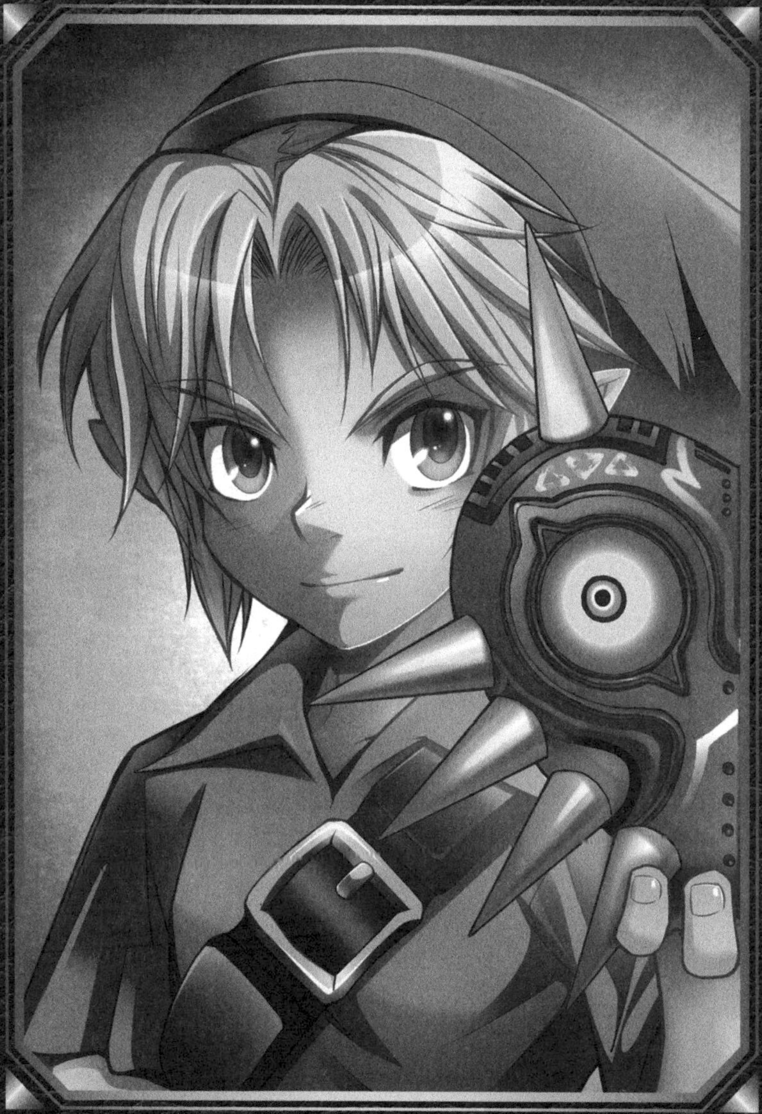

THE MINISH CAP
PHANTOM HOURGLASS

FOUR SWORDS

A MESSAGE FROM THE AUTHOR
FOR THE LEGENDARY EDITION

Up to four players can play *The Legend of Zelda: Four Swords Adventures*, controlling four Links wearing different colors: green, blue, red, purple. So we wanted to create a character-based manga in which they would look the same but have different personalities. The previous three *The Legend of Zelda* works that we had done were more classical fantasy than typical entertainment, with a feeling you get when you watch movies and children's literature. This time, however, we wanted something that felt much more like a typical manga, so we aimed to show teamwork, with readers liking all four Links plus Shadow Link. There was an especially strong fan response in Japan and overseas to the friendship between Purple Link and Shadow Link. As manga authors, we feel blessed that the characters' feelings came across so clearly. Enjoy the banter between the five!!

AKIRA HIMEKAWA

THE LEGEND OF
ZELDA™
FOUR SWORDS
LEGENDARY EDITION

TRANSLATION John Werry, Honyaku Center, Inc.
ENGLISH ADAPTATION Steven "Stan!" Brown
LETTERING John Hunt
ORIGINAL SERIES DESIGN Sean Lee
ORIGINAL SERIES EDITOR Mike Montesa
LEGENDARY EDITION DESIGN Shawn Carrico
LEGENDARY EDITION EDITOR Joel Enos

THE LEGEND OF ZELDA: FOUR SWORDS
- LEGENDARY EDITION -
VIZ MEDIA EDITION

STORY AND ART BY **AKIRA HIMEKAWA**

The Legend of Zelda: Four Swords
- Legendary Edition -
TM & © 2017 Nintendo. All Rights Reserved.

ZELDA NO DENSETSU
4TSU NO TSURUGI PLUS [KANZENBAN]
by Akira HIMEKAWA
© 2016 Akira HIMEKAWA
All rights reserved.
Original Japanese edition published by SHOGAKUKAN.
English translation rights in the United States of America,
Canada, the United Kingdom, Ireland, Australia
and New Zealand arranged with SHOGAKUKAN.

ORIGINAL DESIGN Kazutada YOKOYAMA

Printed in the U.S.A.

Published by VIZ Media, LLC
P.O. Box 77010
San Francisco, CA 94107

10 9 8 7 6 5 4 3 2 1
First printing, July 2017

www.viz.com